REPRINTS OF ECONOMIC CLASSICS

FACTS AND FACTORS
IN ECONOMIC HISTORY

EDWIN FRANCIS GAY

Facts and Factors in Economic History

Articles by former Students

OF

EDWIN FRANCIS GAY

REPRINTS OF ECONOMIC CLASSICS

AUGUSTUS M. KELLEY · PUBLISHERS
NEW YORK · 1967

First Edition 1932

(Cambridge: Harvard University Press, 1932)

Reprinted 1967 by
AUGUSTUS M. KELLEY · PUBLISHERS

LIBRARY OF CONGRESS CATALOGUE CARD NUMBER

67 - 27546

PRINTED IN THE UNITED STATES OF AMERICA
by SENTRY PRESS, NEW YORK, N. Y. 10019

PREFACE

PROFESSOR EDWIN FRANCIS GAY has devoted full twenty-five years of his life to the furtherance of the study of economic history at Harvard University. His labors have been characterized largely by his search, alone or with the collaboration of others, for greater light on the facts and factors in his chosen field. The foundation for his work was laid during the period of his own student days in Europe. Perhaps the chief conviction that Professor Gay brought back from Europe, particularly from Germany, was the need for research in economic history. Contribution to the satisfaction of this need has seemed possible either by personal research or by training others to do scientific work. In fact, Professor Gay has chosen to follow both courses, although his time and energy have been given with exceptional lavishness to his students, particularly to candidates for the higher degrees.

Professor Gay's lectures have always been stimulating, not merely by reason of the shafts of light which illumine his treatment of causation or his elaboration of conclusions, but also by the steady barrage of fact after fact with which his instruction has been conveyed. His conferences with students have sometimes been yet more provocative because more direct. His frequent challenges, his manifold suggestions, and his gentle chiding, always interspersed with timely encouragement, have meant much to the contributors of this volume. Nor can any of his students fail to recall his many courtesies outside the class or conference room, or the richness and inspiration of a friendship given fully and without thought of time or trouble to all who asked it and even to those who showed the need without asking. So great a gift can only be acknowledged with the grateful realization that it is a germinating force that will never cease to bear fruit in all who have received it.

Men who have come under the stimulating power of Professor Gay's instruction have gone out to many walks of life — to teaching, business, law, and public service. Something of the breadth of his indirect influence may be gathered from the diversity of position represented in the present contributing group, while something of the permanency of his inspiration is suggested by the fact that, wherever located, his students have had the eagerness and capacity to prepare essays for this volume. Divers of his students whose names are not found on this roll would gladly have added to this tribute, had not unyielding commitments stood in their way, or had not the interests of later years drawn them into other fields of learning or activity remote from economic history.

It is fitting that the present enterprise should have been carried on with the co-operation of the Graduate School of Business Administration, Harvard University, by reason of the constructive service which Professor Gay rendered during his deanship. Acknowledgment of assistance, generously given by many students and business associates, must remain quite inadequate. We are specially indebted to Miss Elva C. Tooker, under whose careful scrutiny the volume has been prepared for publication, and to Mrs. Helen W. Parsons and Miss Arita Kelley for aid at every stage. The officials of the Harvard University Press have facilitated the publication of this volume as a tribute to a distinguished Harvard professor and to a former syndic of the Press.

Arthur H. Cole
A. L. Dunham
N. S. B. Gras
Committee in Charge

CONTENTS

FACTS AND FACTORS
IN ECONOMIC HISTORY

THE IMPORTANCE OF
ECONOMIC HISTORY

W. T. JACKMAN

HISTORY as a subject of study has long occupied an important place in the university curriculum, and, with advancing time and a larger arena of events to be considered, its importance becomes greater and greater. The history which has heretofore bulked so large has been to a great extent political and military — the story of monarchs, laws, treaties, wars, revolutions, and the like. For this study there was abundant material provided in books of statutes, decrees of parliaments and kings, expenditures for wars, the development of armies and navies, and so forth.

But it was not until about the middle of the last century that economic history came into prominence. The study of the development of industry, of commerce, of finance, of taxation, of transportation, and of agriculture was undertaken, apparently, largely to introduce elements of reality into what was previously the theoretical study of economic principles. The disciplinary value of philosophy had been an important part of economic theory, but, for many, the purely abstract reasoning had not enough connection with the world of reality to be of the most vital interest. It was this desire to save political economy from a career of unprofitable abstraction that led to the activities of the historical economists.

The historical school had its origin in Germany and there is no mystery concerning its rise. In the same way that the classical political economy was molded by English utilitarianism, so the German historical economics was an outgrowth of German philosophy. In each case economics was building upon the current metaphysics of the home country. Each was a distinctive national product, and, although the historical movement has won adherents in other countries, it still retains a peculiarly German character. This is not due so much to the reading of the works of the great German historical economists like Hildebrandt, Knies, and Schmoller and their disciples as to the spirit of these great leaders conveyed to those who studied under them and by the latter imparted in its richness to those who in turn have been under their guidance. It has been the communication of that spirit indirectly that has aroused a deep and far-reaching response in this field of economic research. One does not need to talk long with any of the older historical economists of the present day to understand how much they have been influenced by personal and professional contact with such men as Gustav Schmoller and his professional associates and followers.

Before the work of the historical economists was begun, the tendency was to discuss economic principles as applicable under conditions which were more or less static. But with the historical economists came the view of the economic order as a stage of development. The present could only be understood in the light of the past. Society was conceived of as an organism with a life-history similar to that of organic nature; and just as the organism must be studied with reference to its environment and the stage it occupies in the scale of life, so must the economic and social mechanism be studied as a stage in the onward progression. The works of Darwin and Spencer, treating of the evolution of society through natural law, were sufficient to give potent impetus to the historical study of economic facts and conditions. In the realm of natural science everything was altered by the evolutionary processes; and, since society itself was likewise an entity subject to evolutionary changes, the most vital method of studying its economic and social structure and nature was by the careful historical study of the facts, past and present. To trace the present economic system through the changing fabric of earlier centuries was to understand it in a way not possible to those who had not this background.

It is not difficult to trace the effect of this upon the present methods of teaching and of analyzing economic problems. In many of our business schools the use of the "case system" has been recognized as one of the latest and best developments. Under this system specific examples are taken from the experience of business men. The conditions leading up to the particular problem are carefully detailed, so as to give the background and the environment essential to the complete understanding of the issue.[1] As nearly as possible, in the study of these cases, the instructor endeavors to present to the student what the future outcome would be of particular decisions of that problem and what the natural reactions of these decisions would be upon the other business elements in that environment. Letting his class see the flow of cause and effect from the past, through the present, to the future, in the case in hand, the instructor then leads his students to form their own conclusions as to what should be done under these particular circumstances. The conclusions will vary, sometimes widely, and in many cases it is impossible to say that a certain decision is right or wrong. The thing to be sought through such studies is, not the accumulation of a series of precedents to guide future action under similar conditions, but the ability to think through the problem with a balance and sanity of judgment which arise from taking into account basic principles as they have operated through the

[1] See, for instance, C. E. Fraser, *Problems in Finance* (1927).

recent past and are likely to operate in the immediate future.

But, if this method of studying a business problem, through relating it with the past, with the present combination of circumstances, and with the probable future result, tends to produce clear thinking and judicious action, the study of the more remote past and its evolution down to the present, giving the accumulated experience of different peoples in meeting broad economic and social problems, contributes to still greater poise of mind through having a broader basis for making discriminating judgments. It is true that this may have little effect in the day-to-day decisions of a business office, but in the broader organization of commercial affairs it is of paramount significance. A comprehensive knowledge of the economic history of European nations, for example, would show us that trade between nations, like mercy, is not "strained" — it is not developed by force or pressure, but may be advanced by encouragement and helpful relations; that trade treaties, intended to foster dealings between nations, are of little avail unless there be established between these nations a sympathetic contact; and that in the pursuit of commerce the effects of personal contact and moral integrity are much more potent than the outward support of political or governmental agencies.

Another phase of this study of the historical economic development pertains to the organization of industry. There are not a few today who regard the present system of division of labor and mass production as the product of the ingenuity and inventiveness of human genius on the part of present-day industrialists. But the fact is that the existing system is the outgrowth of a long line of previous advances. Under the early household economy, when each family was dependent upon the labor and skill of its own members, we find occasional evidences of some small measure of specialization among the members of the family group. It was because of this that there was ushered in the later stage of the handicraft or gild system under which some men, because of the skill which they had attained, were able to set up as masters in particular lines of service, such as the cordwainers, the weavers, the carpenters, the glovers, the goldsmiths, the bakers, and the barber-chirurgeons and peruke-makers. Even at this early stage, then, we have the same system of division of occupations which is such a prominent part of the industrial structure of the present time.

But out of the gild or handicraft system there grew the later domestic system, under which the capitalist merchant, who organized the market for the sale of the products produced in the homes, was able to put pressure upon the producers by requiring their products to be up to a certain standard of quality before he would accept them. This made it necessary for those home producers who desired to be employed continuously to produce high-class goods; and, in order to do this, specialization on the part of some member or members of the family was essential. In those homes where mediocrity of product was the general rule there was much in the way of unemployment or at least intermittent employment. At this stage of industry, agriculture was also carried on as a by-employment; but those families which found ready sale for their manufactured products had to show expert skill in manufacture, and most of them had to carry on their agriculture by junior members of the family, with the assistance of outsiders where required.

In the transition from the domestic to the factory system, it was just those who, like the Pitts, had carried on skilled work on a large scale, who were ready to take advantage of the use of machinery in the factory. When, as in the best adaptation of the domestic system, high-grade production was carried on through specialized skill, workers had to confine themselves to one class of work. For example, the worker in a particular grade of woolens had to confine his attention to that alone in order to keep his hands in such condition that he could know the quality of his materials. As soon as one kind of work had reached that stage of specialization, it was ready to be taken over by a machine; and, in consequence, specialization of labor in the factory—or division of labor, as it is called—came to be simultaneous and collective rather than consecutive and individual. Then, when the market for the product had been organized on a wider basis, mass production in the factory was possible.

Now, there are some people in public life who seem to have and to give the impression that the people of one country are far ahead of all other countries in economic development and that this is due to "the distinctive power of the modern business executives to grapple with new problems with courage and poised minds and without dependence on the guides of precedent and tradition." But a wider knowledge of the way in which our present life has grown out of the progressive advances of the past, and of the methods by which issues akin to those of the present have been settled in earlier days, would put a very distinct quietus upon the tendency to display any national self-satisfaction with present-day accomplishments. The national and international benefits which we have today are the outcome of the labors, struggles, wisdom, discernment, and judicious action of the nations and their leaders in earlier ages; and the material progress of any one nation is much more closely related to the general progress of all countries than to any inherent virtues of that one nation.

Not only in trade and in industry but in nearly all other lines of economic life we are debtors to the past, and the more fully we know the economic history of our own and other countries, east as well as west, the more qualified we are to make decisions along the basic lines of economic welfare. One of the most vital of these subjects is railway transportation. In most of the countries of the world there is government ownership of railways, and the results of that policy have been very varied. There are strong theoretical arguments in favor of the government owning and operating railways and using them for the public good; but there are other strong arguments from a practical point of view which show the defects of that system. The conclusiveness of these arguments rests upon the way in which this system has worked out; but in determining this issue consideration must be given to the different attitudes of different peoples toward governmental control. In the case of Italy, for example, nearly every known system has been tried, namely, private ownership and state operation, state ownership and private operation, state ownership and state operation, and private ownership and private operation; but after a comprehensive study of railroad systems in other countries and of the most appropriate system for Italy, it was decided that for the immediate future the railroads should be leased to two private companies. On the other hand, the German railways were taken over for ownership and operation by the state and so continued till after the War. But a militaristic state has entirely different conditions from those of democratic countries, and the system which was an appropriate part of a war machine under one supreme over-lord would be singularly unsuited to a country which has a popularly elected and representative government. Similarly, a socialistic state, such as some of the Australian States, is very likely to have political influences so prominent that a government of this kind fails to make its railways prosperous and progressive.[1] The point which we wish to impress is that when people are confronted with such problems as have far-reaching importance, the verdict of the past, as drawn from the replete facts of economic history, furnishes a valuable guide in the determination of present issues.

However, the best results are not obtained by the purely inductive method of economic history nor by the deductive method of pure theory but by a combination of both. It is highly desirable to know what the past has to teach us, as revealed by the facts brought out by the economic historian, and the realities revealed by the latter have been very useful in correcting some of the abstract deductions of the theoretical economist. But behind all the facts revealed by the research of the historical economists there are causes at work to produce such results, and it is here that the work of the economist enters to vitalize the observations of the historian. The human mind is not content merely with facts but seeks an explanation of these facts; and in seeking causes or explanations it must judge from a knowledge of basic human motives, psychical qualities, environmental tendencies, and fundamental economic principles which are generally accepted. It is only by merging into an organized whole the facts adduced by economic history and the economic reasons for these facts that we can get the development of a synthesis which will constitute a real science.

Perhaps we cannot do better than quote the words of one who made for himself a great place in the realm of pure theory, but who recognized the importance of both

[1] For a short summary of the experience of many countries with railways, see the statement of W. M. Acworth in the *Hearings before the Joint Subcommittee on Interstate and Foreign Commerce*, 65th Cong., 1st sess., pt. 12 (1917).

the inductive and the deductive method when he said that
the integration of these two

recognizes the utility — for technical reasons — of tracing causal connections, not only from special to general, but also, for the sake of
experiment, from general to special. It thereby often discovers links in
the chain of causes which were, of course, present in the complex, empirical facts, but which were there so deeply inwrapt that they would
hardly, if ever, have been discovered by a purely inductive method.[1]

Some vital social results have also emerged as the outcome of historical economic studies. While abstract economics is largely concerned with the material forces in the
production of wealth and the basic principles in its distribution, economic history takes us back into all the environmental factors which have attended economic life and
shows us the intimate and mutual reactions of social and
economic conditions. Under the household economy members of the family had a personal interest in one another;
they worked and lived together and had all interests in
common. Under the gild system, the apprentices and
journeymen lived with the master and his family and
shared sympathetically in the family fortunes, but the master and his family had economic interests in the results of
the sale of the product which were not shared by the apprentices or journeymen. In other words, the cleavage
between employer and employee was beginning to be
seen. In the domestic system the capitalist employer had
no connection with the homes of his workers, except to
give out and take back work; there was no bond of common interest between employer and employee except the
dependence of the employee upon the capitalist for materials to work up and for a market for the finished product. Finally, under the factory system, the employer was

[1] Böhm-Bawerk, "Method in Political Economy," in *Annals of the American
Academy of Political and Social Science*, vol. i (1890–91), p. 263.

largely dissociated from his workers, and the only contact there was between them, under typical conditions, was that of a "captain of iron amid his troops."

This subjection (*Niedergang*) of the worker to the will of the employer shows a continuously increasing severance of intimate personal relations between the two classes, and the social conditions of the working classes were deplorable. In 1799, one of the centers of the Lancashire cotton industry was described in these words:

Rochdale is another crowded manufacturing place. It was really wonderful to see the swarms of children crawling in and out of the houses. The poorer class of people here were all clad in blue flannel — the produce of their own labour. Few either of the women or children wore shoes or stockings. Indeed the latter seem to be articles which may very well be dispensed with even in situations where one would at first imagine them a much greater convenience, & at a season of the year when an universal covering would appear to be almost necessary. If the legs of a London beau be protected sufficiently by so thin a vestment as silk, surely the hardier skin of a sturdy labourer may endure one degree (if it can amount to a degree) of cold greater for the sake of economy.[1]

The reports of commissions in the 1830's present infinitely worse conditions concerning men, women, and children in the factories.

What was the response of the economists of that time? Adam Smith's doctrine of laissez faire and his opposition to anything like control of the industrial mechanism were generally accepted, and factory owners salved their consciences with the view that this was a régime when everybody should look out for himself and when there should be no interference from authority. Coming down a little later, McCulloch and Ricardo, and still later Mill, paid practically no heed to the amelioration of the lot of the workers but devoted their thought to the organization of the ma-

---

[1] British Museum, Additional Mss., 32,442, p. 13.

terial agencies (including labor) for economic purposes. It is true that Malthus wrote his "Essay on Population" about the time that the evil effects of the Industrial Revolution were being seen in their true light; but he, too, was more interested in the questions of the relation of population to the means of subsistence and the methods of checking the increase of population than in considering the improvement of the condition of the working classes. In his day the government and the employing classes seemed to be more concerned with having a large population to provide cheap labor for the factories than with bringing about better social conditions for the laborers and their families.

Historical studies of economic and social conditions from earlier to later times have shown that under earlier systems of industry there were some distinct benefits in the way of home life and social environment. For example, the gild regulations were framed with the object of providing equality of opportunity by placing restrictions upon individual initiative; in other words, production was checked in order to have a more equal distribution of wealth. These studies of former conditions have served to throw into clearer light the defects attendant upon the factory system; and the workers have been drawn more firmly together into unions, and even into communist organizations, in order that the worker may receive a larger share of the product of his labor and that the rich may not become richer while the poor become poorer. It is evident that such studies in economic history have served to create a social conscience, and among present writers and thinkers upon economic subjects the interaction of social and economic forces is shown very prominently.

One has only to consult the textbooks on economic principles which have been written in the last forty years to realize how intimately the social are mingled with the economic factors as influences upon human conduct in the pursuit of wealth. In the words of Francis A. Walker, "Nothing that importantly influences the production and distribution of wealth can be neglected by the economist. All human history becomes his domain. The other sciences, alike the physical and the moral, become tributary to the science he cultivates."[1] The late Professor Alfred Marshall emphasized the intimate relation of social, economic, and religious influences in many of his statements, as when he said:

Poverty is a great and almost unmixed evil . . . and when sickness comes, the suffering caused by poverty increases tenfold. [Or again,] Now at last we are setting ourselves seriously to inquire whether it is necessary that there should be any so-called "lower classes" at all: that is, whether there need be large numbers of people doomed from their birth to hard work in order to provide for others the requisites of a refined and cultured life. . . . The hope that poverty and ignorance may gradually be extinguished derives indeed much support from the steady progress of the working classes during the [nineteenth] century.

Then he gives a concise picture of the fundamental differences between the earlier ages and the modern times.[2] How strongly he was influenced by a broad knowledge of the facts of economic history becomes clear in a study of the earlier chapters of his work,[3] in which he "emphasized the notion that economics is a science of life, and is akin to biology rather than to mechanics" — in other words, it is a progressive unfolding of the forces at work among men in the ordinary business of life for the attainment and use of the material requisites of well-being. Speaking of the German school of historical economists, he says:

[1] Walker, *Political Economy* (New York, 1887).
[2] Marshall, *Principles of Economics* (London and New York, 1898), Introduction, pp. 2–8.
[3] *Ibid.*, chaps. ii–iv.

It would be difficult to over-rate the value of the work which they and their fellow workers in other countries have done in tracing and explaining the history of economic habits and institutions. It is one of the great achievements of our age; and . . . has done more than almost anything else to broaden our ideas, to increase our knowledge of ourselves, and to help us to understand the central plan, as it were, of the Divine government of the world.[1]

As we have in biology the possibility of tracing life from lower to higher forms, from the lowest form of life, the single-celled amoeba, to the most complicated cell structure of man, so we have in economic history the opportunity of seeing some elements of the essential nature of economic progress. What constitutes economic progress? At a time when an international disruption, such as that of the World War of 1914–18, causes the unloosing of all the forces of evil, including human and material destruction, and this is followed by a world-wide outbreak of influenza which takes the lives of millions of people, we ask ourselves: "Is the world getting better?" But when these conditions are followed by the economic depression of 1920–21, and, after a few years, by the greatest worldwide depression known in modern times, following the business collapse of 1929, we are compelled to ask with continuous insistence: "What constitutes economic advance, if there is such a thing?" We shall not get any answer to this persistent question by merely surveying the world of the present time, with all its dislocation of industry and its unemployment, its erection of international trade barriers in the form of high tariffs, and its attempts at the promotion of self-sufficiency and national wealth on the part of most of the world's great commercial nations. Nor shall we obtain an answer in the crashing of great business organizations, which were built up in years of prosperity and were supposed to be invulnerable.

[1] *Ibid.*, pp. 70–71.

Economic history shows us great nations which formerly wielded enormous power, such as Assyria, Greece, Rome, and Spain, which have since been destroyed or reduced to an infinitesimal fraction of their past greatness, and other nations which, though small at first, and circumscribed in area and physical resources, have come to wield world-wide influence. Each nation which has made substantial progress seems to have done so by a succession of advances and retrogressions; the movement upward has been repeatedly checked by slipping backward, and, when these declines have been halted, the nation, building upon its new and additional experience, has then advanced a little further than before. But when we look at the world as a whole, those nations which have exercised the most influence upon its progress have done so, not because of their material wealth, but because of the permeation of their progressive ideas and thoughts; and the economic progress of the world consists in the application of those material and immaterial forces which make for an increasingly higher status of human life. How much of this advance is due to material conditions, such as labor-saving improvements, better homes, and more wholesome food, and how much is due to immaterial conditions, such as the spread of education, more wholesome social environment, higher moral tone, and a higher estimate of the value of life, it is not possible now to determine. It is sufficient to say that among the various contributory elements which have brought about the desire for effecting better and better living conditions in the world as a whole, the study of economic history has been one of the most productive for leadership. To see the outreaching of man toward higher things, from the earlier days to the present, is to have a faith in the outcome which produces activity toward that end. This applies not only to the white race but also to the colored races, and the welfare of the one is bound up vitally with that of the others.

In the subject of economic history — as, indeed, in many other subjects — the greatest benefit is that which is realized by the individual whose mind becomes steeped in it. As in philosophy, psychology, biology, or astronomy, the accomplished thinker and research inquirer sees realms of reality and suggestions of truth far beyond anything which he can express, so is it in the case of economic history. The man whose mind can range thoughtfully, and be at home, in the vast fields of human endeavors and relations in the past will inevitably feel the tide of life and progress carrying him on to his best service; more than that, his mind will grasp realities beyond the most distant past and still more significant than those which are distinctively economic. Economic history is not mere historical material; it is life, and living men make it according to the ways they think and act.

THE ECONOMICS OF POPULATION IN ANCIENT GREECE

A. B. WOLFE

THE eddy of Indo-European migration which, long before the dawn of recorded history, brought the primitive Greeks, still in the bronze stage of culture, from their original home in the Balkan peninsula into the land that was to be Hellas, had spent its force by the middle of the tenth century B.C. At the close of this movement, which covered several centuries if not a millennium or two, Greece was the settled pastoral and agricultural land of the Homeric epics. All this early colonization, called by the historians of ancient Greece "the Great Migrations," but great only relatively to the limited geographical stage on which it took place, was primarily agricultural in nature, wherein it differed significantly from the colonization of the Phoenicians. While trade interests, starting with the piracy which the simple Greeks learned from the Phoenicians, were not entirely lacking, they played a subordinate rôle. This fact, among others, is warrant for believing that the great migrations were induced by population pressure.[1] When we approach the dawn of the historical period and find these grass-land and mountain peoples, hitherto strangers to the sea and to navigation, pushing out from the mainland and from island to island, conquering and settling as they go, we may be confident that land hunger and subsistence needs were driving them on. If plunder had been their

[1] F. J. Teggart in *The Processes of History* (1928), p. 66, holds that peoples do not migrate unless they have to. General negatives of this sort are of course dangerous.

only motive, they would have filled their ships and sailed back home. Instead of that, their marauding expeditions were followed up by steady streams of settlers.

After the great migrations, a period of two centuries or so witnessed no striking geographical shifts of Greek population. By the end of the eighth century, however, great changes were in process. Migratory impulses, induced by unsettled political conditions and redundant agricultural population, were instituting a new series of movements. Colonization on a large scale, with forethought and public organization and support, was for two centuries or more a central feature of Greek economic and political policy. This famous movement, which planted flourishing colonies from the eastern end of the Euxine, a thousand miles distant, to the coasts of Corsica and Spain, equally far away in the opposite direction, and rimmed the Mediterranean with Greek settlements wherever land could be found and the original inhabitants driven out, reached its height in the seventh century B.C. In the sixth century it dwindled, when colonial expansion was brought to a standstill by the Persians on the east, the consolidation of the Punic settlements in the west, and abrupt climatic limitations north and south.

Unfortunately there are no data for even a remote numerical estimate of Greek population during these centuries. We can only infer, from the magnitude of the colonization movement itself, and from the economic and political maladjustments which played so important a rôle in its long continuance, that the population of Greece proper reached a density persistently in excess of the agricultural resources of the country. There is some sociological ground, also, for inferring overpopulation, in the practise of infanticide, abortion, and homosexualism. Hesiod, about 700 B.C., was already recommending restriction of

the size of the family, and Aristotle states that homosexualism was legalized in Crete to discourage a too rapid increase
of population.[1]

At the beginning of the seventh century there was an
acute agrarian problem and widespread rural unrest. We
need not take the lamentations of Hesiod too seriously, for
he was a poet and doubtless also something of a propa-
gandist. There is other evidence that the lot of the coun-
tryman was one of extreme poverty and insecurity, and
that this was not a mere transitory condition.[2] Before the
time of Solon, Greece had taken on the aspect of an old
country, as indeed it was. Swamps were drained, hillsides
terraced, and agriculture was encroaching on grazing land,
so that cattle had become scarce and a significant change in
diet had taken place. Cereals and pickled fish became the
common food of the masses. Grain production failed to
keep pace with population, and already in the seventh century Athens was probably importing wheat. In Solon's
time export of wheat was prohibited, and in later times the
grain trade was subjected to stringent regulation because a
regular supply of corn was a matter of life and death to the
Athenians.[3] In general, Greece never was a land suited to
grain culture, since the soil had no great fertility and the
country, outside of Thessaly, was everywhere cut up by
mountains. Not more than a fifth of the land in Attica was
devoted to grain, and the yield was low, for Greek agriculture was always primitive in its methods. As late as the
fifth century B.C. the ploughshare of Homeric times was
still in use, with no change save the addition of a metal
point, and there was no rotation of crops.[4] It is therefore

[1] *Politics*, II, 10.
[2] Cf. G. Glotz, *Ancient Greece at Work* (1926), pp. 80, 81, 98, 99; P. Giraud,
La propriété foncière en Grèce (1893), pp. 81ff.
[3] Glotz, *op. cit.*, pp. 297, 298.
[4] J. Beloch, *Griechische Geschichte* (2nd ed.), vol. ii, pt. i, p. 87.

not unlikely that soil exhaustion made its influence felt, and that the hard condition of the cultivator, so gloomily depicted by Hesiod, was due to physical as well as to political causes.

Whenever overpopulation appears, difference of opinion is sure to exist as to whether it is to be attributed to natural causes or to institutional maladjustment. Malthus, relying on Plato and Aristotle, found in the operation of positive checks in Greece merely an early instance of natural law governing the relation of population to productive resources. There is an element of truth in this view, but it is by no means the whole story. The redundancy of population was without doubt in part due to institutional factors — to changes in land ownership and tenure and to exploitation by absentee landlords. More broadly speaking, it was due also to the fact that the Greeks could never bring themselves to a national, as opposed to a city-state, political organization, and thus pool their resources in the interest of productive and trade efficiency. In the repeated class conflicts which fill the checkered pages of Greek history, there is ample evidence of repeated political maladjustments and chronic economic waste. The Greeks, like many other peoples, were far from making the most of their meager natural resources, even with the productive technique at their disposal. Still, the natural causes remained, and it is not unlikely that even in the absence of political strife Greek population would early have exceeded the power of Greek soil to provide its subsistence.[1]

To whatever causes, physical or political, we may attribute it, the pressure of population must be looked upon as the main motivating force back of the emigration move-

---

[1] For a different view, see J. Toutain, *The Economic Life of the Ancient World* (1930), p. 25; P. Giraud, *op. cit.*; A. Jardé, *The Formation of the Greek People* (1926).

ment in this second period of colonization. Between the
pressure which produced the migrations of the primitive
Greeks and that which led to the development of the far-
flung Greek colonial empire there was this difference: the
great migrations were set in motion by external pressure;
the colonization of the eighth to the sixth century was the
result of internal pressure. Not all the Greek colonists, it is
true, sought land. Trade interests also were involved. As
the internal rural-urban movement swelled, as the cities
grew apace, as slaves began to be imported in large numbers, and as an urban proletariat was added to that of the
rural districts, population continued to exceed the domestic food supply, and the cities were virtually under compulsion to develop external trade.

Under such conditions, it is not surprising that governments were not without conscious incentive to promote
emigration and colonization. Chronic unemployment was
as great a danger to the established order then as now; wise
precaution motivated attempts to drain off the surplus
population. Emigration has always been a favorite device
of governments to relieve such tensions, but it has rarely
proved to be more than a temporary palliative. In Greece,
the surplus population remained and continued to increase,
notwithstanding the thousands who departed to the colonies. The imperative necessity for providing for this continued surplus could be met only by the import of grain.
The only way to pay for the imported food and raw materials was to export olive oil and manufactured goods, for
which happily the colonies themselves offered increasing
demand — although the tribute which Athens levied on
the other members of the Delian League in the fifth century helped her for a time to balance her external trade
account. It is estimated that Athens was dependent upon
the import of foreign grain to about the same extent that

England is today.[1] Greek colonization and the Athenian policy of regulating foreign trade in the interest of food supply constitute perhaps the first definite historical example of the augmentation in a planned and orderly manner of national food supply by means other than direct agricultural production or war and piracy.

If not a result of colonization, a significant accompaniment of it was thus the development of town industries, and in their train a new urban proletariat, which eventually found itself driven to the wall by the enormous increase of slave labor. As colonization and trade developed Greek industry, industrial enterprise, forcing wages down to a starvation level through the cut-throat competition of slave labor, was creating a new problem of urban unemployment. In the presence of the new urban proletariat, which was rarely diffident in making known its sentiments, it is not surprising that the Athenian government redoubled its efforts to develop and protect its external corn trade, and to organize it to the end of assuring regularity in the inflow of foodstuffs.[2] That in spite of this care the supply was not always assured is shown, at a later date, by the famous corner in Egyptian wheat by Cleomenes in 330 B.C., when there was a general famine in Greece.

For the student of the relation between population movements and institutional changes, causes and results are the important center of interest. Natural and social causes co-operated to bring about the marvelous expansion of the Greeks around the rim of the Mediterranean, but it is difficult to avoid the conclusion that the social

---

[1] E. Meyer, *Die wirtschaftliche Entwicklung des Altertums* (1895), p. 39. Cf. Beloch, *op. cit.*, vol. i, pt. i, pp. 264–269; P. Mombert, *Bevölkerungslehre* (1929), p. 31; Wilamowitz-Mollendorf, "Staat und Gesellschaft der Griechen," in *Die Kultur der Gegenwart* (1910), p. 400.

[2] On the extreme solicitude of the Athenians for the foreign grain supply, see Glotz, *op. cit.*, pp. 297, 298, and Bury, *History of Greece* (1900), p. 354.

were in large measure derived from the physical causes, and that the fundamental factor in Greek expansion was lack of natural balance between population and resources. Land scarcity and limited agricultural productivity, as Plato makes Socrates point out, are fruitful incentives to aggressive warfare; and to this the Greeks were by no means averse. Finding room for expansion, seizing land wherever they could, and founding flourishing agricultural colonies, the people of Greek extraction increased to numbers which would have been entirely impossible had the Greeks been confined to their own narrow valleys and stony hillsides. At its height in the fifth century, the colonial population was at least equal to that of Greece proper.[1]

Greek colonizing enterprise constituted one of the most remarkable in all history, if the limited resources of the Greek cities, the undeveloped state of navigation, and the great distances covered are considered. But, like similar movements in modern times, it brought on new problems, and, like these later enterprises, it also developed into an economic imperialism which was regarded as essential to national self-preservation, but was also motivated by the urge of private interests to power and profit. Developing from simple beginnings, in which the mother cities exchanged their oil and manufactures for colonial foodstuffs and raw materials, into an extensive network of commercial enterprise, it nevertheless only shifted the population problem from the country to the city and solved it only temporarily and partially. Perhaps it was the "manifest destiny" of the Athenians to drift into economic imperialism; perhaps that destiny was only a by-product of the activities of traders and promoters who had ends of their own to subserve; perhaps the government entered

[1] Beloch, *op. cit.*, vol. ii, pt. i, p. 86.

upon it in the naïve faith that it would relieve social tensions and solve the problem of population and food supply once for all; but its net results were to increase the seriousness and magnitude of that problem, through the growth of slavery, the increase of the urban proletariat, and the vital dependence on foreign trade, and finally to plunge Athens into the futile fratricidal strife of the Peloponnesian War.

It is well known that there are no reliable and accurate numerical data on the size and movement of population in ancient times. The famed censuses of Rome covered, until the time of Augustus, only adult male citizens. The one census said to have been made in Athens, by Demetrios of Phalerum (c. 317 B.C.), did not include women and children. It is therefore impossible to trace with any confidence, and in other than general terms, the growth and decline of Greek population. Fortunately, however, there are bases for rough estimates in the official lists of citizens, which were practically military registers. These lists were of such importance to the state that from the fourth century B.C. they were engraved on stone, and a great number have accordingly been preserved. These catalogues, with other indirect data, have been subjected to elaborate critical analysis by Beloch and other historians. Despite all the erudite labor expended, however, our knowledge of the size and movement of Greek population, even in Athens, for which the data are less inadequate than for the rest of Greece, remains very uncertain.

From the fact that Athens took no considerable part in the colonization movement of the eighth century it is inferred that she felt no serious overpopulation at that time. By the fifth and fourth centuries, however, the extreme solicitude of the Athenians for their grain trade indicates that the population problem had become serious. Busolt estimates that Attica could never support more than

130,000 people from its own fields.[1] It was no accident, therefore, which led Plato and Aristotle to see in the pressure of population one of the fundamental problems of city-state politics, for in their time Attica was doubtless one of the most densely peopled portions of the western world.[2] At the time of the Persian Wars, 492–479 B.C., the citizen-class population of Attica is thought to have been between 75,000 and 90,000, and the total population (inclusive of metics and slaves) about 150,000.[3] Cavaignac[4] ventures the figure of 1,000,000 for the population of the Greek peninsula at this time.

In the half-century between the repulse of Persia and the Peloponnesian War, the Athenian population increased materially, although in the meantime Athens sent out 10,000 colonists, with their families, and fought over thirty wars, which cost her probably around 40,000 men.[5] These losses were more than made good by the natural increase which was made possible by the development of commerce and industry, and by the import of slaves.[6]

The date 431 B.C. is pivotal in Greek history because it marked the outbreak of the disastrous Peloponnesian War

[1] *Griechische Staatskunde* (3rd ed., 1926), pt. ii, p. 759.

[2] Beloch puts its density in 431 B.C., at the outbreak of the Peloponnesian War, at over 200 per square mile (*op. cit.*, vol. ii, pt. i, p. 85).

[3] Beloch, *Die Bevölkerung der Griechisch-Römischen Welt* (1886) [hereafter referred to as *Bevölkerung*], p. 99. For Beloch's long analysis of the sources, including military levies and losses, grain consumption, and estimated number of slaves, see *ibid.*, pp. 57–99. Beloch reckons the total population in ancient times at four times the number of male citizens of military age (18 to 60). Even if the basic data as to the number of adult male citizens were full and accurate, it is obvious that the choice of a factor by which to calculate the total population, derived from comparison with the age and sex composition of modern populations as it must be, involves an element of serious uncertainty. (Cf. his *Griechische Geschichte*, vol. iii, pt. i, p. 270.)

[4] *Population et capital dans le monde Méditerranéen antique* (1925), p. 65.

[5] O. Seeck, *Geschichte des Untergangs der antiken Welt* (4th ed.), vol. i, p. 338.

[6] Beloch, *Griechische Geschichte*, vol. ii, pt. i, pp. 79–84; vol. iii, pt. i, p. 264; A. Andréadès, "La population de l'Attique aux Vᵉ et IVᵉ siècles," *Metron*, vol. vii, no. 3 (1928), p. 114.

and the beginning of the end of Athenian greatness. Much interest has therefore attached to the question of the size of the Athenian population at this time. The numerous estimates which have been made have all rested upon the famous passage in Thucydides in which Pericles spurs the citizens to war and recounts the resources which Athens can command.

They had thirteen thousand hoplites, besides the sixteen thousand who occupied the fortresses or who manned the walls of the city. For this was the number engaged on garrison duty at the beginning of the war, whenever the enemy invaded Attica: they were made up of the older and younger men, and of such metics as bore heavy arms. The Athenian cavalry, so Pericles pointed out, numbered twelve hundred, including mounted archers; the foot-archers, sixteen hundred; of triremes fit for service the city had three hundred. The forces of various kinds which Athens possessed at the commencement of the war, when the first Peloponnesian invasion was impending, cannot be estimated at less.[1]

It is possible that Pericles, under the stresses of the moment, did not bear in mind the need of meticulous clarity for the benefit of future historical statisticians; it is possible, also, that Thucydides did not remember accurately what Pericles actually said. In any event, a vast amount of laborious logic and conjecture has been expended by historians, mainly German, in attempts to determine the meaning of the figures. A survey of the results of these attempts affords an instructive illustration of the uncertainties of population estimates based upon fragmentary and obscure data.

Taken at their face value, Thucydides' figures total 31,800 citizens (including an indeterminate number of metics) available for military duty. Assuming that the citizens of military age (18 to 60) constituted one-fourth of the total citizen-class population, that population would be put at 127,000. The matter is not so simple as this,

[1] Thucydides, II, 13, Jowett's translation (2nd ed., 1900), vol. i, pp. 112, 113.

however. In the first place, the slaves and probably most of the metics are not included, and secondly, it is uncertain whether the figures were meant to include all the citizens of military age or only the land troops. Moreover, it is not clear whether all citizens liable to service, or only those fit for duty, were included. If the figures apply only to the land troops, the men necessary for the manning of the fleet must be added. Delbrück thinks that besides metics and slaves, at least 15,000 and possibly 25,000 citizens were required for the fleet, and concludes, from consideration of other passages in Thucydides, that the figures were meant to cover all citizens of military age. He amends them, however, on the ground that the field army numbered only 15,800 (13,000 hoplites plus 1,600 archers and 1,200 horsemen) and that the number of reserves (men below 20 and above 45 or 50 years of age) must have been smaller than the number of men of active military age. In this way he arrives at a total of 36,000 citizens. He adds 6,000 to 8,000 metics — presumably adult males — but does not attempt a figure for the slaves.[1] Meyer arrives at a much more liberal estimate, 55,500 citizens and about 14,000 metics, corresponding to a citizen-class population of 170,000, 42,000 of the metic class, and a total free population of 212,000.[2]

Beloch argued in his earlier work that the text of Thucydides is corrupt and that the figure of 16,000 reserves is an error for 6,000.[3] Later, he retracted this emendation, having concluded that the 16,000 included *all* the hoplites. Assuming that the heavy-armed metics numbered 3,000,

---

[1] *Geschichte der Kriegskunst* (1908), vol. i, pp. 20, 24. Some of Delbrück's reasoning, especially his inclusion of the cleruchs, is criticized by E. Meyer, *Forschungen zur alten Geschichte*, vol. ii, pp. 151, 152.

[2] *Ibid.*, p. 179.

[3] *Bevölkerung*, pp. 60–66. Numerical errors of this kind were more likely to occur when Roman numerals were in use.

he now held that there were 13,000 citizen hoplites, and that Thucydides simply made the mistake of counting 13,000 hoplites twice.[1]

With estimates of the citizens ranging from 30,000 to 60,000, it is evident that calculations of the total Athenian population, in view of the still greater uncertainty as to the number of metics, and the unknown number of slaves, are extremely uncertain, though based on better data than are available for other parts of Greece or other periods of Greek history. Putting the free population at 135,000, and adding 100,000 slaves for good measure, Beloch, in 1886, estimated the Attic population, 431 B.C., at over a quarter of a million.[2] In his later work he reduced this to 200,000.[3] Kahrstedt, calculating five persons to each citizen of military age (instead of four, as in Beloch's calculations), and, like Beloch, putting the slaves arbitrarily at 100,000, figures the total population at 250,000, or at most 300,000.[4] We are safe in concluding that the total population of

[1] "Grieschische Aufgebote I," *Klio*, vol. v (1905), p. 371.

How widely estimates based on Thucydides vary is indicated in the following summary:[a]

	Citizens
Von Wilamowitz (*Aristotles*, vol. ii, p. 210)	60,000
P. Oestbye (*Die Zahl der Burger von Athen*, 1894), "at least"	40,000
E. Meyer (*Forschungen*, vol. ii, p. 149)	55,000
H. Francotte (*L'industrie*, vol. i, p. 161)	30,000
H. Delbrück (*Kriegskunst*, vol. i, p. 24), including the cleruchs	36,000
E. Cavaignac (*Études sur l'histoire financière d'Athènes*, p. 161), including the cleruchs	45–50,000
Beloch (*Bevölkerung*, p. 99)	35,000
Beloch (*Griechische Geschichte*, vol. ii, pt. i, p. 80)	40,000

[a] Cf. Busolt, *Griechische Staatskunde*, pt. ii, p. 764.

[2] *Bevölkerung*, p. 99.

[3] *Griechische Geschichte*, vol. ii, pt. i, p. 80; vol. iii, pt. i, p. 273; vol. iii, pt. ii, p. 393.

[4] "Die Bevölkerung des Altertums," *Handwörterbuch der Staatswissenschaften* (4th ed.), vol. ii, p. 661. Cf. W. S. Ferguson, *Greek Imperialism* (1913), p. 42; Andréadès, *op. cit.*, pp. 116–118.

Attica in the golden age of Pericles did not exceed the latter figure.

For several decades after the Peloponnesian War, Athens could raise only 7,000 hoplites, about half the pre-war number. There were comparable reductions in the numbers of *thetes*, metics, and slaves. The total population was reduced to not much over half the size it had attained at the time of the first Persian War.[1] It took a century to restore the numbers of 431 B.C. From an exhaustive analysis of the available sources, Beloch arrives at the following estimate of the movement of Attic population.[2] The figures can be taken only as distant approximations.

Year (B.C.)	Citizens	Metics	Slaves	Total
431	120,000	30,000	80,000	230,000
425	90,000	22,500	60,000	170,000
403	80,000	22,500	35,000	140,000
355	90,000	30,000	65,000	185,000
338	93,000	37,500	85,000	215,000
313	80,000	37,500	90,000	210,000

For the population of the whole of Greece proper, the estimates are exceedingly problematic, although Beloch devotes several hundred pages to the task.[3] In his earlier work, he put the population, including that of Epirus and Macedonia, in 431 B.C., at 3,000,000 "at least"; in his later work, at 4,000,000 "at most."[4] For the beginning of the fourth century B.C., he estimates a total of 3,500,000 for Greece proper, and 7,000,000 for Greece proper, the Aegean islands, Crete, Cyprus, Cyrene, and the Greek portions of

---

[1] Beloch, *Bevölkerung*, p. 57; *Griechische Geschichte*, vol. iii, pt. i, p. 273; Andréadès, *op. cit.*, p. 115.

[2] *Griechische Geschichte*, vol. iii, pt. ii, pp. 386–418. Cf. Cavaignac, *op. cit.*, p. 61.

[3] *Bevölkerung*, pp. 109–305; *Griechische Geschichte*, vol. iii, pt. i, chap. viii.

[4] *Bevölkerung*, pp. 494, 506; *Griechische Geschichte*, vol. ii, pt. i, p. 86.

Italy and Sicily. For the Greek-speaking world at large, including the cities of the west and south coasts of Asia Minor, the south coast of Thrace, and the Hellespont and Pontus, he rounds off with a grand total of 8,000,000.[1]

It would be instructive to outline the movement of Greek population outside of Greece proper, in view of the importance of the colonies and of the profound changes during the Alexandrian period, but sources are hopelessly lacking. Even the estimates of a specialist like Beloch can be accepted as little more than well-considered guesses. We know that the colonies drew off some surplus population and gave some relief for a time to agrarian difficulties; but this population movement also stimulated the growth of the Greek cities and the development of economic imperialism and dependence on import of foodstuffs and raw materials. While there is little or no evidence of decline of population in Greece proper before the second century B.C., the population of the colonies, as above noted, increased until, at the beginning of the fourth century B.C., it equaled that of the Mother Country.

In the long drawn out and senseless struggle of the Peloponnesian Wars, lasting to 404 B.C., one city-state after another, Athens, Sparta, Corinth, Thebes, went down to defeat, and the material civilization of Greece did not recover till the time of Alexander. The Age of Pericles gave way to a long period of stagnation. Athens, which under Pericles was the intellectual, artistic, political, and economic center of the eastern Mediterranean, never fully recovered from the shock. Of the eighty-five years between the beginning of the Peloponnesian Wars and the entrance of Philip into Delhi, not less than fifty-three were years of major Hellenic wars. Every one of these wars inflicted a deep wound on the national welfare. When an army in-

[1] *Ibid.*, vol. iii, pt. i, p. 297.

vaded enemy territory it destroyed the harvests, uprooted the vineyards, cut down the fruit trees, and burned the villages — devastation which a generation could hardly repair. Scarcely any part of Greece escaped one or more such calamities in these eighty-five years. To the physical devastation was added the heavy taxation and the economic depression inseparable from long wars.[1]

Such squandering of men and resources, in internecine conflict between petty states, any one of which was hardly larger than an average county in New York or Ohio, reflects the fact that the Greeks, despite the culture of the intellectuals and the heritage of art, literature, and philosophy which the Age of Pericles was bequeathing to posterity, were yet cursed with a fatal ineptitude for government on a national, let alone an imperial, scale, and with a temperament and sentiments by which they came legitimately from their recent barbarian past. In spite of, or because of, their political philosophy, the Greeks never really emerged from the influence of the tribal ideal. The Greek might be "a citizen of no mean city," but he never, like the Roman, learned loyalty in the grand manner or conquest and exploitation on a truly imperialistic scale.

While the Peloponnesian War set the seal on Athenian decline, and, with the plague, caused a decrease in population which it took a century to make good, all accounts agree that the decline in Greece at large was less serious. After a temporary setback, Greek population apparently continued to increase until, in the Alexandrian period, the great exodus to the newly conquered countries of Asia and Africa made its influence felt. That there was still nothing in the nature of depopulation is indicated by the complaint, everywhere except in Athens and Sparta, of overpopula-

---

[1] *Ibid.*, p. 314. For the later ravages of the Roman armies in Greece, see Rostovtzeff, *Social and Economic History of the Roman Empire.*

tion, and by the ease with which great levies of troops were raised.

In 346 B.C., Isocrates advised Philip of Macedon to attack the Persians, on the ground that it was necessary either to overthrow the Persian monarchy or take enough territory from it to provide for the establishment of new Greek colonies to be settled with the dangerous masses of idle vagrants who were roaming about Greece.[1] Taking account of the probable population pressure in the fourth century and the attendant economic conditions in Greece proper, it is not hard to see that the radical population doctrines advanced by Plato and Aristotle were not drawn out of such thin air as is sometimes supposed. Twelve years after he expressed it, the desire of Isocrates was realized, through Alexander, and the ideas of Plato and Aristotle, in the face of the widened world of opportunity for Greek enterprise, lost much of their force.

The period between Alexander's conquests and the time when the Romans began to overrun Greece was the high point in Greek prosperity as well as in the geographical spread of Greek culture. The Greek people must have had a rather remarkable vitality at this time, for in spite of the thousands who emigrated after Alexander had opened up the East, the population of Greece appears to have held its own until the middle of the second century B.C.[2] To attribute, with Polybius, the stationary character of the population during two centuries to deliberate childlessness is to be content with too superficial an explanation, and to

[1] W. Wilcken, "Alexander der Grosse und die hellenistische Wirtschaft," Schmoller's *Jahrbuch* (1921), 45 Jahrgang, p. 351.

[2] J. L. Myers ("The Causes of Rise and Fall in the Population of the Ancient World," *Eugenics Review*, vol. vii, April, 1915, p. 38), by somewhat dubious inference, estimates the population of the Greek peninsula, exclusive of Sparta and Epirus, at about four million in 337 B.C. With a somewhat excessive allowance for Macedonia, he puts the total population in 168 B.C. at 4,370,000 (*ibid.*, p. 41).

ignore both the significantly large numbers drained away to the East and the economic conditions which made small families popular among the city bourgeoisie. Ferguson, indeed, argues that the practises censured by Polybius fell into disuse in Athens during an eighty-year period of prosperity beginning 166 B.C., that "large families — families of three or four sons and the usual complement of daughters — were normal among the rich and fashionable people of Athens at this time," and that an increase of the citizen-class population resulted.[1] This view may be correct, although it does not seem to be shared by other historians, but eventually Athens, like the rest of Greece, sank into relative insignificance, both demographically and economically.

During the time of the Alexandrian Empire the Greeks constituted the strongest ethnic element in the population of the eastern Mediterranean region.[2] Considering the immense field opened abroad to Greek enterprise, it is not surprising that Greece proper sank into secondary importance in this later Hellenic world, and that its population ceased to increase. At its height, this broader Greek world contained probably not less than nine million Greek-speaking people, by no means all of Greek race, however. Kahrstedt likens the change in the demographic composition of the Hellenized Asiatic and African countries to that of North America after the coming of Europeans. The comparison is somewhat strained, however, since North America had only a thin population of scattered Indian tribes, while Africa and Asia were old countries with advanced civilizations and relatively dense populations. While their population had doubtless declined since the

---

[1] W. S. Ferguson, *Hellenistic Athens* (1911), p. 374.

[2] Polybius, XXXVI, 17, 5; Beloch, *Griechische Geschichte*, vol. iii, pt. i, p. 267; Kahrstedt, *op. cit.*, p. 662.

great days of Assyrian, Babylonian, and Persian power,
that which remained in the fourth and third centuries B.C.
was probably an asset, rather than an obstacle, to the de-
velopmental activities of the invading Greeks. New Greek
cities sprang up like mushrooms, and both old and new
cities grew rapidly. Alexandria, Antioch, Ephesus, Sardis,
and Miletus had their boom period and became more populous than Athens or Syracuse had ever been. Kahrstedt
believes that western Asia, from the Hellespont to the Eu-
phrates and the Dead Sea, had in Pompey's time a population of twenty million, notwithstanding the slave-raiding
of the Romans.[1] Without committing ourselves to hypothetical figures, we can hardly doubt that the Hellenic
world had a population which cast in the shade any that
had hitherto existed on an equal area in the West.

While the decline of the population of Greece proper was
accelerated after the Roman conquest, 146 B.C., the beginning of the decline cannot be attributed to Roman rule,
because it appeared at a time when the whole Greek
peninsular was free of foreign domination. Some diminution of prosperity, with an accompanying decrease in
population, was to be expected with the tremendous expansion into the East in post-Alexandrian times. It is
probable that the Greek emigrants were drawn from the
most vigorous and enterprising part of the population and
that Greece therefore suffered from the "reversed selection" which has so frequently been regarded as one of the
by-products of strong migratory movements.[2]

Glotz, apparently afflicted with the "dépopulation" obsession so common among French writers, attributes the
decline of population to the extreme individualism of the
Greeks. By the end of the fourth century B.C., he alleges,

---

[1] *Ibid.*, p. 663; Beloch, *Bevölkerung*, pp. 499, 500.
[2] Cf. Toutain, *op. cit.*, p. 93.

the towns were experiencing a "marriage crisis" and the "reign of the courtesans." He admits that *hetairai* were always prominent in Greece and that Greek husbands were never notable for fidelity, but now illicit unions no longer shocked anybody.[1] To this change in morals, and to laws prescribing equal inheritance of property, he ascribes the reluctance to marry and to rear more than one or two children. He also finds significance in the fact that abortion was punishable only under certain circumstances and that exposure of infants was common. There is no proof, however, that the Greeks had changed their attitude toward these practises since earlier times.

Glotz merely echoes Polybius, who wrote his history in the second century, after the establishment of Roman rule, and whose famous lament sounds like a modern screed on race suicide:

> We see in our time throughout the whole of Greece such a shrinking of the birth rate and, in a word, such depopulation, that the towns are deserted and the fields lie waste, although there are neither continual wars nor epidemics. . . . The cause of the evil is manifest. . . . From vanity, from avarice or from cowardice men are unwilling either to marry or to bring up children without marrying; at the most they will have only one or two in order that they may leave them a fortune and ensure them a luxurious existence: thus the plague has rapidly assumed dangerous proportions. If once war or sickness comes to claim its tribute in these families . . . the line inevitably dies out and, just as with swarms of bees, the cities, becoming depopulated, quickly lose their power.[2]

Polybius is obviously describing sentiments and attitudes characteristic of the capitalistic urban bourgeoisie of the time. Whether similar attitudes were prevalent among the miserable country folk may be doubted. To establish the existence of family limitation stringent and widespread

[1] *The Greek City and its Institutions* (1929), pp. 295-298.
[2] Polybius, XXXVI, 17.

enough to be regarded as a major factor in the decline of population at this time needs more evidence than the citation of a few famous liaisons in the upper classes, quotations from the comedies, or appeal to authorities who, from association, are likely to overlook real causes. To point to family limitation — which is as much a symptom as a cause — as the basic cause of the decrease in population, as Glotz and Seeck [1] do, is to distort perspective. In the anarchy of the Roman civil wars, fought out as they were on Greek soil, the Greek population was bound to suffer a pronounced decline. Seeck's reference to the decline of population in Euboea,[2] an agricultural region removed from the main theater of conflict, is not convincing, since, as Beloch [3] points out, the inscriptions indicate a thriving urban life in many parts of Greece. The rural population in relatively peaceful regions like Euboea was kept sparse by continual drift to the cities.

There was doubtless family limitation, but it is unnecessary to regard it as evidence of moral degeneracy, or as the fundamental cause of depopulation, when economic depression and political disturbance, due to continual warfare, were patently the underlying causes.[4] The Roman wars, however, were but the culmination of internal and external forces, which, from the fourth century, had been preparing for the decline of Greece.

Internally, the primary cause of the steady decline of economic life in Greece proper was, as Rostovtzeff flatly states, "the constant, almost uninterrupted, succession of wars in which the cities were involved in the fourth and

---

[1] *Op. cit.*, vol. i, pp. 348 ff.

[2] *Ibid.*, pp. 348, 349.

[3] *Bevölkerung*, p. 499.

[4] For conditions in Greece at the time of the Roman civil wars, see V. Chapot, *The Roman World* (1928), pp. 172–175; Beloch, "Die Bevölkerung im Altertum," *Zeitschrift für Socialwissenschaft*, vol. ii (1899), p. 510.

third centuries B.C."[1] The work of destruction carried on by the Greeks themselves was accelerated, after 146 B.C., by Roman misrule and exploitation, and completed by the Mithridatic and Roman civil wars. Rome made some feeble efforts to rehabilitate the population, but without success. At the end of the civil wars, not only Greece proper but the entire Hellenic East "lay ruined and prostrate beneath the feet of Roman capitalists and profiteers,"[2] and the decline of the Greek population continued into Empire times, when the land, in the hands of a few large landholders, was abandoned to brush and pasture.

Externally, the cause of the decline was the shifting of the economic center of gravity to the Hellenic East and Egypt in the fourth century, and to Italy and Rome in the third. As a result of this change, the prosperity and population of Greece would have declined even had internal wars, and probably, also, the growth of slavery, not been important contributing factors. Athenian prosperity was based on commercial and industrial capitalism, which was to suffer irreparably from the rise of new centers — Alexandria, Antioch, Seleucia — and the development of new trade routes between the East and the rising Roman state in the west. The commanding position of Athens was undermined by structural changes in Mediterranean trade which left Greece to one side of the main current of the world's affairs. In this respect Athenian decline was comparable to that of Venice and Genoa in the sixteenth century, when Portuguese and Dutch enterprise opened the sea route to India[3] — comparable, also, to declines on vastly greater scale which from similar causes the future probably holds in store for the prosperity and population

---

[1] *Op. cit.*, p. 1. Cf. Paul-Louis, *Ancient Rome at Work* (1927), p. 271.

[2] Rostovtzeff, *op. cit.*, p. 9.

[3] Cf. Mombert, *op. cit.*, p. 40.

of certain nations existing at the present time. Neither reason nor history affords warrant for supposing that human populations can remain static, demographically, geographically, or economically; and the main ground for regret, if regret has a place in a survey of the rise and fall of a civilization and a people, is not the Alexandrian expansion of the Greeks, to the ultimate damage of the Mother Country, but the inability of the Greeks themselves to rise above a barbarous particularism, and the final insensitiveness and brutal destructiveness of Roman imperialism.

THE INFLUENCE OF ECONOMIC ENVIRONMENT ON THE DEVELOPMENT OF PUBLIC REVENUES IN ENGLAND

CHARLES PHILLIPS HUSE

THE student of public finance who seeks an explanation for the changes which have taken place in the ways in which governments get a living will find it largely in economic, political, and social conditions. While there are many forces that may determine the particular direction which a revenue system may take, none is of more importance than economic environment. A system which is not adapted to the prevailing economic conditions cannot long endure. Where economic conditions are primitive, the public revenues will be obtained in the simplest ways; where more advanced, a corresponding development in the sources of public income will eventually take place. We shall follow the development of economic life in England from earliest times to the present, in order to trace over a long period this relation between private and public methods of getting a living.

The inhabitants of Britain in historic times were of Celtic origin. By the time of Caesar's expedition in 55 B.C., and probably for two or three centuries before this event, the Britons got their living chiefly from grazing and agriculture. The southern part of the island, fertile and more accessible to trade, was further advanced than the northern, having developed some industry and commerce.

Probably as early as 200 B.C. the Britons were making coins of gold copied in a rough manner from the gold staters of Philip of Macedon. Ornaments were fashioned from bronze, iron, and gold. Tin, mined in Cornwall, found its way throughout the Mediterranean basin.

There is almost nothing to show how public revenues were raised in the Celtic period. It is probable, however, that the revenue systems of the various independent tribes were not unlike that of the Germans described by Tacitus. The maintenance of the chief's household and the conduct of war would be the main expenditures. In a period when there was but little division of labor, the upkeep of the royal household would be met by the products of the king's own lands, supplemented by gifts from his subjects and the booty of war. Military service, from which the Druid priests were exempt, provided for the most important branch of public expenditures.

In the century following Caesar's visits to Britain, the southern part of the island came more and more under Roman influences. Trade with Romanized Gaul increased, stimulating British industry. Just before the conquest, Britain was sending to Rome tin, grain, cattle, gold, silver, iron, slaves, and hunting dogs. Her advance in wealth at this time was aided by the long reign of Cymbeline, who put an end to tribal warfare and cultivated the friendship of the Romans.

The succeeding period of Roman control in Britian extended from A.D. 43 to A.D. 410. During these years Britain continued the economic development begun under the Celts. Roman civilization brought to the island the means of improving and extending agriculture, manufactures, and commerce. Roman roads, cities, technical knowledge, and credit increased the wealth of the country, though they brought greater inequality in possessions. While agriculture became the dominant industry, grazing still remained important. Both domestic and foreign commerce increased.

This higher economic order of the Romans required more public services than were required by the tribal economy of the Celts. Consequently, taxation, which means compulsory contributions for public purposes, became necessary. By the time of the Empire, Romans had become accustomed to paying taxes, and they extended to the people of the conquered provinces the same opportunity. In doing so, they showed good judgment in employing in each province the particular system which seemed best adapted to its economic environment. The chief taxes imposed upon the Britons were the poll tax, the cattle tax, at so much a head, and a tax payable in kind from the produce of agricultural land, usually a tenth.[1] All these were primitive taxes, adapted to a country where agriculture and grazing were the chief industries. Though money would be used in the trading centers, its use in the country districts would not be general. The taxes in kind would often have to be delivered at a distant warehouse, making cartage almost as burdensome as the tax itself.

In the latter half of the fourth century Britain began to suffer from the disasters which were threatening the Empire. The disturbances in Gaul and Italy cut down her exports. The withdrawal of Roman capital, technical experts, and, finally, the legions left the Britons unable to withstand the assaults of the Celts from the north and later of the Teutons from the east. It was these Teutons — the Angles, Saxons, and Jutes — who in the fifth and sixth centuries gradually extended their conquests over a large part of Roman Britain.

[1] S. Dowell, *A History of Taxation and Taxes in England* (1884), vol. i, pp. 5–6.

It was to be expected that in the process of subjugating the island, the more advanced economic order, which had been developed under the Romans, would disappear. Roman roads fell into decay and Roman cities, with their industries, gave place to small agricultural villages. The Anglo-Saxons brought methods of getting a living even simpler than those followed by the Celts at the beginning of the Roman occupation. At the end of the first century A.D., when Tacitus wrote his *Germania*, these Teutons were apparently an agricultural people, supplementing their husbandry by grazing and hunting. They had some industry but probably very little commerce. The first three centuries of life in England appear to have made but little change in the economic order of the Anglo-Saxons, though a little domestic trade and the export of slaves to the Franks had developed. Economic self-sufficiency in the early Anglo-Saxon period was furthered by continual intertribal conflicts.

The public-revenue system of the early Anglo-Saxons was in keeping with their rude agricultural economy. When the various tribes conquered land, they divided it between king, eorls, and ceorls, to be held subject to the threefold obligation of sending warriors to the host, repairing fortresses, and working on bridges, and other burdens such as entertaining the king. This folkland, held by folkright, could not be alienated from the family. In time, however, the king and his council, by granting charters to churches and very great men,[1] in some cases converted folkland into bookland, thereby making it alienable. Bookland was often relieved from the customary obligations except the *trinoda necessitas*, mentioned above.[2] From these claims on the holders of the land and the prod-

---

[1] F. W. Maitland, *Domesday Book and Beyond* (1921), p. 257.
[2] T. P. Taswell-Langmead, *English Constitutional History* (9th ed., 1929), p. 12.

uce of his own domain, the king was able to meet the few public needs. Fines in the king's courts contributed something even in the early centuries of Anglo-Saxon occupation. Payments in this period would be made in services or in kind, for money was little used. In primitive finance, where so many public wants are met directly by services, revenues and expenditures are largely identical.

The last three centuries of Anglo-Saxon rule saw a distinct advance in economic organization, though it is doubtful if England regained the position reached under the Romans. Among the factors contributing to the development of industrial and commercial life were the Christian missionaries, who brought England into closer contact with the life of the Continent, the process of political consolidation, the coming of the Danes, who combined trading with piracy, and, finally, Norman influence. The early part of the ninth century saw both the union of all England south of the Forth under Egbert, king of Wessex, and the first serious ravages of the Danes. Later in the century these Northmen began to conquer and settle different parts of the country, founding towns which became centers of trade and industry. Finally, when Cnut became king of England in 1016 Danish influence was at its height.

Along the new trade routes established by the Danes, Chester, Lincoln, Leicester, and York arose on the sites of old Roman cities. Many of the Anglo-Saxon boroughs, built in the period of Danish invasion for military purposes, gave way in importance to these new centers located with reference to commercial routes. By 1066 there were about one hundred towns, but most of these were overgrown villages largely dependent on agriculture. First among the trading towns was London, visited at the end of the tenth century by merchants from Normandy, Aquitaine, Germany, and Flanders. England's chief exports were slaves, tin, and wool.[1] The growth of trade brought more precious metals into circulation, probably mined largely in England. Money payments by tenants are found as early as 900.

This economic progress was reflected in a corresponding development of public finance. We find Alfred spending the royal revenues not only for the army, public works, and the maintenance of officials but also for a navy, education, poor relief, the endowment of monasteries, and the encouragement of industry. From various causes, such as the pressure of the Danes, individual misfortune, and possibly the economy of collecting taxes through a lord, a manorial system had by the end of the Anglo-Saxon period been superimposed upon many of the formerly free village communities. Moreover, the lords of these manors in many instances held from the king on a basis much like that of Norman feudalism.

The proceeds of the royal domain, the duties connected with the holding of land, and fines in the royal courts continued to be the mainstay of the king's revenue until well after the Norman conquest. In the latter part of the Anglo-Saxon period the kings, however, found it necessary to meet the increase in public needs by resorting, on special occasions, to taxation. War, so often responsible for the introduction of new taxes, was in this case the immediate cause. The taxes were known as the Danegeld and the shipgeld.

In 991 Aethelred the Unready adopted the plan of buying off the Danes by the payment of 10,000 pounds of silver. The amount of the tribute had to be increased to 16,000 pounds in 994, 24,000 in 1002, and 30,000 in 1007. In 1014 it was 21,000.[2] The raising of such large quantities

[1] W. E. Lunt, *History of England* (1928), pp. 67–68.
[2] Maitland, *op. cit.*, p. 3.

of silver was made possible by the increase in the precious metal, which growing trade and industry had distributed throughout England. This tax, known as the Danegeld, was imposed at a rate varying at different times from one to four shillings on each hide. A hide seems to have been originally a family allotment, and later a measure of area, ordinarily consisting of 120 acres.[1] For purposes of taxation, however, it also came to be used as a measure of value. This fiscal hide was based on the productive capacity of an estate as determined not only by its arable land but also by other factors, especially its plough-teams.[2] The Danegeld of Domesday, and probably of Anglo-Saxon times as well, was levied in accordance with fiscal hides. Originally raised as a tribute, the tax continued to be levied occasionally as a source of royal revenue until 1162. In 1018 Cnut raised 72,000 pounds by the Danegeld, besides a special contribution of 11,000 pounds from London.[3] This was used to pay off his Scandinavian army, a policy in contrast with the usual method of paying one's followers in the land of the conquered country. Cnut coined great quantities of silver pennies.

When danger threatened, every shire was required to contribute ships and their equipment in proportion to the number of hundreds it contained. In raising the shipgeld of 1008, every three hundreds was called on to provide a ship, every ten hides a small boat, and every eight a helm and coat of mail.[4]

In addition to taxation by civil authorities, the Church, beginning in 787, levied a tithe, and from early in the tenth century a penny on every hearth,[5] sometimes called

[1] *Ibid.*, pp. 387–389.
[2] P. Vinogradoff, *English Society in the Eleventh Century* (1908), pp. 144–176.
[3] Maitland, *op. cit.*, p. 3.
[4] C. Oman, *England before the Norman Conquest* (1910), p. 569.
[5] W. Stubbs, *The Constitutional History of England* (1874), pp. 228–230.

fumage. Fumage was not paid by the poor. The Anglo-Saxon taxes, based largely on land, were adapted to an agricultural stage and so conformed roughly to the principle of equality of sacrifice which struggles to assert itself in the history of taxation.

Upon the basis of the already developed manorial system and its partly formed superstructure, William the Conqueror imposed Norman feudalism. The lords of the manor were to hold their land from the king on the basis of military or other honorable tenure. The character of the services required from these vassals, which had not been clearly defined in the Saxon period, was now definitely established. The peasants in turn, whether free or unfree, held, as previously, from the lord of the manor in return for payments in services, goods, or money. To prevent the decentralizing tendency of subinfeudation, William made every vassal swear fealty first of all to the king.

The progress in industry and trade which began in the latter part of the Anglo-Saxon period continued after the Norman conquest. Naturally, England came more under the influence of continental industry, which at this time and for centuries to come surpassed that of the English. French artisans came to England to practice their crafts and alien merchants brought their wares to English fairs. While for many centuries the mass of the people were still to get their living from agriculture, yet the importance of the trading and manufacturing class in the towns was growing.

Though the urban population probably did not increase much before the thirteenth century, the character of town life was changing.[1] Instead of remaining overgrown villages where agriculture was supplemented by a little

[1] A. P. Usher, *An Introduction to the Industrial History of England* (1920), pp. 161–162.

manufacturing and trading, especially in cattle and corn, the towns were becoming the abodes of artisans and merchants. The formation of the gild merchant as early as the beginning of the twelfth century and of the craft gild a little later points to this change. In the thirteenth century grain from the lord's demesne was being sold on a large scale in the market. Likewise the peasants, instead of merely disposing of their surplus corn in the towns, were gradually commuting their services into money payments and producing primarily for a market. A marked rise in the price of grain in the thirteenth century, probably due to the growth of the town population and the opening of foreign markets for English grain, hastened this process. The raising of corn for the market and the payment of rents with the money received was destined eventually to break down the self-sufficing manorial economy.[1] This economic change also contributed to the weakening of the feudal superstructure. The increase of industry and trade created stocks of manufactured goods in little shops and added more household furnishings to manor house and cottage.

When we turn to the public-revenue system in the two centuries following the conquest, we find it closely related to the economic environment of the period. The king still received a large revenue from his domain. Domesday shows that the Conqueror held 1,422 of the 9,250 manors in England. The king's manors were scattered in about thirty shires.[2] In the Anglo-Saxon period and for a time after the conquest the limited use of money and the difficulty of carting provisions caused the king and his retinue to travel from one royal manor to another, in order to consume the income from the domain.

[1] N. S. B. Gras, *The Evolution of the English Corn Market* (1915), pp. 11-31.
[2] *Ibid.*, pp. 3-4.

The feudal payments were another important source of revenue. These took care of the chief military and certain other public needs. The holder of a knight's fee, of which there were about five thousand at the time of the Conqueror, was required to furnish in case of need, for a period of forty days in a year, a knight with full equipment. Sometimes the vassal held from the king in return for administrative services. The maintenance of a road or a bridge was in certain cases taken care of under this system of feudal tenure. The three customary aids and the incidents, such as relief, wardship, and escheat, brought revenue. Moreover, the king could tallage his tenants, demanding contributions from them on occasions of unusual expense. This right parliament apparently forced him to give up in 1332.[1]

The revenue from the domain and from feudal payments came to the king by virtue of his position as head of the feudal order. In addition there were certain revenues that grew out of his political power, inherited from Anglo-Saxon kings. He could call out the militia, the old Anglo-Saxon fyrd. In some districts, he could require guard duty or work on bridges and walls,[2] survivals, probably, of Anglo-Saxon obligations. He could take certain cases into the royal courts and derive fines and fees therefrom. On the royal progress he could exercise the right of purveyance, taking horses, carts, provisions, and personal services at his own prices. He could obtain revenue from the Jews, who were regarded as his chattels. In the course of time, revenue came from the sale of charters to towns and gilds. Finally, the king had the rather indefinite power to levy taxes. Unlike the feudal payments, due to a suzerain in

---

[1] F. W. Maitland, *Constitutional History of England* (1909), p. 179.

[2] N. Neilson, *Customary Rents*, Oxford Studies in Social and Legal History, vol. ii (1910), pp. 133–142.

return for the privilege of holding land, taxes were compulsory contributions paid to the king for public purposes. Public purposes, it is true, generally meant for several centuries the king's purposes. Although taxes in the early feudal period, when not levied arbitrarily, were granted by the Great Council in accordance with the feudal theory of personal consent, the development of a representative parliament later caused them gradually to lose this feudal aspect.

The Danegeld of Saxon times was continued under the Normans. Though this tax was levied for the last time in 1162, there are traces of it in many districts for the next two centuries under the name of hidage.[1] Danegeld was also succeeded for a short time by carucage, a tax on ploughed land.

The reign of Henry II saw a distinct advance in the public-revenue system. Henry I had already commuted the military service of his ecclesiastical vassals into a money payment. This payment, known as scutage or "shield money,"Henry II extended to his lay vassals early in his reign. Both Henry and his vassals found the substitution of money payments and the consequent hiring of mercenaries for foreign wars more convenient than direct contributions of services. The privilege of paying scutage, however, in lieu of service, required in each individual case the consent of the king.[2] Scutage was paid for the last time in the fourteenth century. It was a feudal payment rather than a tax.

Henry II also introduced a tax on personal property. This tax owes its origin to the efforts of the Church to secure aid for the crusaders. At the time of the first crusade

---

[1] *Ibid.*, pp. 115-120.
[2] S. K. Mitchell, *Studies in Taxation under John and Henry III* (1914), pp. 17-18, 312.

voluntary contributions were obtained. In 1166, however, when the Moslem threat against Jerusalem was becoming serious, England joined with France in levying a compulsory contribution upon property. Henry's tax of 1166, imposing a light rate on both rents and movables, served as a model for the Saladin tithe of 1188, which demanded one-tenth of rents and personal property. In the latter tax, however, a jury of his neighbors was used to pass on the oath of the contributor. Henceforth the jury method was to hold an important place in English taxation.

The tax on movables, used first in England for religious purposes, was not employed for lay purposes until the country was forced in 1193 to contribute toward the ransom for Richard. Its returns at that time were unsatisfactory.[1] During the century and a half following the Saladin tithe, personalty was taxed occasionally, sometimes the levy covering both rent and movables, sometimes only movables, and sometimes particular kinds of personal property. Moreover, the tax was seldom imposed on the whole of England at the same time, a practice in keeping with the revenue policy of this early period, when the king was accustomed to ask the different sections or classes in turn for aid. The assessment lists for the borough of Colchester in 1295 reveal but little household furniture, valuables, or even stock in trade. In 1301 the assessors found somewhat more household goods by visiting every room in the house. Grain and cattle made up the greater part of the movables taxed in Colchester.[2] It is doubtful whether the amount of personal property in England of the twelfth century warranted the introduction of a tax on movables at that time. Gradually, however, in the thirteenth and fourteenth cen-

[1] H. W. C. Davis, *England under the Normans and Angevins* (1905), pp. 271, 319–320.
[2] Dowell, *op. cit.*, vol. i, pp. 251–258.

turies the importance of personal property grew, furnishing a real basis for such a tax.

By the time, however, that movables were available in satisfactory amount, the development of this tax took a turn which is very common in the history of taxation. While at first the different estates and later parliament granted the king varying fractions of rents and movables, the fraction came in time to be fixed at one-tenth in the cities, boroughs, and ancient demesne lands, and one-fifteenth in the rest of the country. The assessors would then be required to assess at the legal rate all taxable property they could find. There were, however, so many complaints because of the severity of the assessment of 1332 that at the next levy in 1334 the royal commissioners were directed to take a fixed sum from the various communities in commutation. The sums fixed in 1334 continued thereafter to be the amounts which the respective communities were required to raise and deliver to the king. The rated tax had become an apportioned tax. One-fifteenth and one-tenth meant for the whole realm about thirty-nine thousand pounds, a sum reduced only as decadent towns persuaded parliament to allow a reduction. The grant of one or more fifteenths and tenths would automatically make known to each community how much it must contribute.[1]

Each community would then proceed to collect the tax on rents and movables, in other words, on property. Soon the well-known weakness of a property tax showed itself. Since lands would remain and movables disappear from the assessors' list with the death or removal of the owner, the tendency was, in spite of the growth of personal property, for the quotas to be collected more and more from real estate. Custom, especially strong in the Middle

[1] *Ibid.*, vol. i, pp. 95–98.

Ages, caused the assessors to follow old lists rather than make new ones. While the law made the rate one-tenth in the cities, boroughs, and lands of the ancient demesne and one-fifteenth elsewhere, this meant in practice one-tenth on the selling value of movables and one-fifteenth on the income from real estate. Since land in feudal days was seldom sold, rents would be the logical measure of the tax on real estate. Personal property, on the other hand, would be sold rather than rented. Consequently, movables would naturally be assessed on their selling value. Professor Seligman points out that the heavier rate on movables was probably due to the greater power of the peers, whose wealth was largely in land, to the fact that movables often represented surpluses, and, especially, to the tendency of personalty to escape taxation.[1] Such necessary articles as clothing and seed corn were often exempted. Because of the difficulty of reaching personal property and of protests when the law was strictly enforced, this discrimination was greatly modified in practice. Thorold Rogers found evidence that movables were valued by the assessors much below their true selling value.[2]

The increasing use of money in private dealings from the twelfth century onward is reflected in the character of the royal revenues. These came to be payable in money, chiefly silver coins. The coins were taken at the exchequer by weight rather than by tale, a wise practice in those days of worn and clipped coins.

The advance in commerce and industry, which became marked in the thirteenth century, continued in the fourteenth and fifteenth, apparently little checked by the Hundred Years' War and the Wars of the Roses. The

[1] E. R. A. Seligman, *Essays in Taxation* (10th ed., 1925), pp. 41–43.
[2] J. E. T. Rogers, *The Economic Interpretation of History* (1888), p. 127.

population of England increased and town life developed further. While some industries suffered from the wars, the demand for wool brought wealth to capitalist farmers, and the spread of the woolen industry developed a rich class of manufacturers. Many of the old chartered towns, however, with their gild restrictions, found it hard in the fifteenth century to compete with the less regulated domestic system rapidly growing in the country districts. By the end of the fifteenth century .the self-sufficing manorial economy had broken down and personal villeinage had practically come to an end, though England still remained predominantly agricultural. Foreign as well as internal trade grew.

This increase in foreign commerce brought into prominence the customs, a method of taxation little used by the king before the latter part of the thirteenth century. As long as England did not have much trade, indirect taxes could be used but little. There did exist, however, even in the later Anglo-Saxon times, a system of town customs. In this period, when both economic and political life were little centralized and few goods came from abroad, tolls were charged by individual towns on commodities entering or leaving their gates. These charges fell on goods of British as well as of foreign origin. After the conquest the rapid increase in the number of exemptions, combined with the extension of the royal power, brought about a decline in the importance of the town customs, though a few have survived to the present century. In their earlier years they served as models for the national customs, which we find in existence soon after the conquest, originating in the right of the king to control trade.[1]

The king's customs previous to 1275, with few exceptions, are designated by Professor Gras as semi-national.

[1] N. S. B. Gras, *The Early English Customs System* (1918), pp. 13–27.

In their political origin and in the fact that they were levied on goods entering or leaving the realm they resembled national customs; but in their exemptions, their local variations in rates, and their frequent assignment to individuals or towns they partook of the local system. This was but natural when markets were local. These semi-national customs were lastage, a general duty on goods exported, scavage, a general duty on goods imported, the wine custom, and the wine prise. Both the towns and the king often collected their tolls in goods, though generally in money. These semi-national customs gradually gave place in the thirteenth and fourteenth centuries to national ones which were better suited to the widening area of trade.[1]

The grant of 1275 on exports of wool, woolfells, and hides, with no exemptions allowed, marks the beginning of the customs as an important branch of the national revenue.[2] Foreign wars created the occasion and expanding trade provided the economic basis for the development of the customs. Among the exported articles which contributed to the customs revenue in the fourteenth and fifteenth centuries, wool and woolen cloth stand first. The growth of the cloth trade in Flanders and elsewhere created an increasing demand for wool, which England, not so densely populated as the neighboring continental countries, was able to supply. Consequently, when the growth of the corn market caused the villeins to seek to commute their services into money payments, the lords, in many cases, reluctant to hire laborers for agricultural purposes, turned their home farms into sheep pastures and, in Tudor times, even enclosed the common fields for this purpose. Because of her strong position as a wool-producing country, England was able to place a heavy tax upon wool with-

[1] *Ibid.*, pp. 27-48.   [2] *Ibid.*, p. 63.

out injuring the foreign market.[1] The customs records indicate the existence as early as 1303 of a woolen industry, producing for export as well as for home consumption. They also show the importation of raw materials as well as manufactured goods.[2]

In 1303 a complete system of duties on goods exported and imported by aliens was established. Each tun of wine imported was to pay 2s. Among other provisions there appears an ad valorem or poundage rate on the market price of all merchandise exported or imported, not covered by specific rates. Both these customs served as prototypes of the later parliamentary grants, known as the subsidy of tunnage and poundage. The continuance of this practice of valuing goods in terms of money indicates that by the fourteenth century a complete money economy prevailed in the seaports.[3]

Under the Tudors, England developed her resources more rapidly. Soon English merchants, in larger numbers, banded together for overseas trade. The decline of feudalism, the alienation of part of the royal domain, and the growth of public expenditures had made taxes an important source of revenue. For two centuries, parliament had asserted, with varying success, its exclusive right to control taxation. The problem of the politic Tudor monarchs was to secure sufficient parliamentary grants to meet increasing public needs without losing control over the way in which the money was to be spent. What the Tudors succeeded in doing either by tact or economy, Charles I was later unable to do.

Toward the middle of the sixteenth century there began a rise in the general level of prices which continued for over

---

[1] Rogers, *op. cit.*, p. 130.
[2] Gras, *The Early English Customs System*, pp. 106–117.
[3] *Ibid.*, pp. 66–67, 122.

a century. The rise was due primarily to the influx of gold and silver from the new world, though at first debasement of the coinage was also a factor. This advance in commodity prices, while fees, rents, and taxes tended as always to lag behind, made the financial problems of even the thrifty Elizabeth difficult. It was an economic force which drove her less able successors to resort to arbitrary fiscal measures, thereby contributing to the factors which brought England to civil war.

To meet the increasing public burdens, the Tudors tried especially to reach the class of moneyed capitalists which had grown up in the towns. Two closely related methods used for this purpose were the benevolence and the forced loan. As used by the popular Edward IV, the benevolence was, to some extent, a freewill offering, but, as developed by his successors, it was practically a compulsory contribution. The forced loan was not always repaid. Both methods, in spite of parliamentary protests, were used occasionally to the time of Charles I.

Henry VIII developed, however, in the subsidy a parliamentary tax on personal as well as real property. This at the outset was, like the original fifteenth and tenth, a rated tax with a heavier rate on movable than on landed property. Persons paying on lands would not pay on goods, and vice versa. The assessment and collection of the tax was placed in the hands of the central government and provision was made for revaluation. The subsidy, however, followed the course of the fifteenth and tenth: it became apportioned and fixed, and tended to fall chiefly on realty.[1] A subsidy came to mean in the later years of Elizabeth's reign the sum of approximately £80,000. This inelasticity was especially vexatious in the face of rising expenditures. The fifteenth and tenth continued side by

[1] Dowell, *op. cit.*, vol. i, pp. 193–200.

side with the subsidy into the Stuart period, the usual practice being to grant two fifteenths and tenths with every subsidy. The former tax was used for the last time in 1624; the latter, in 1663.

The Tudors took advantage of the expansion in foreign trade to secure larger revenues from the customs. The valuations of dutiable articles, which in the years just after 1303 had not deviated much from market prices, came in time to be fixed for longer periods. By the time of the Tudors, these official valuations covering most taxable goods were issued as "books of rates." The first national book of rates was probably issued by Henry VIII. There was no general revision until 1558, but from then on the rise in prices compelled more frequent changes.[1]

Not only did the later Tudor monarchs raise the valuations, in order to increase the customs revenue, but they also levied duties without parliamentary sanction. In doing so, they made more extensive use of an old royal prerogative, the right to levy an imposition, known in the thirteenth century as the maltolt.[2] Employed still more widely by James I and Charles I, these impositions aroused the hostility of the rapidly growing trading element, so closely identified with the Puritans.

The growth of this trading class was the most significant economic factor in the development of the English revenue system in the seventeenth century. At this time England began to draw nearer to Holland in the race for commercial and financial supremacy. The small size of Holland and its early development of manufacturing, commerce, and finance had made possible the extensive use of the excise in that country. The Long Parliament of the Puritans, hard pressed for revenue, forced this excise system upon the

[1] Gras, *The Early English Customs System*, pp. 122–129.
[2] *Ibid.*, pp. 89–94.

unwilling English. Though condemned by the Cavaliers, the new tax was soon adopted by them in the territories under their control. It was, however, a better revenue producer for the parliamentary army, which dominated the great metropolitan market area. The excise could not have produced a substantial revenue during the period of Puritan ascendancy, or have been retained afterward as an increasingly important branch of English revenue, if, by the seventeenth century, England had not developed an important trading element. In fact, economic conditions might have permitted the adoption of the excise under Elizabeth. They did, indeed, bring in her day its forerunner, the patent of monopoly. Professor Price has pointed out that political and economic integration had reached a point under Elizabeth where she was able to guarantee monopoly over a wide industrial area.[1] While the Queen received little money revenue from the patents, she was able in this way to keep down the royal payroll. Where a Norman king in a strictly agricultural order would have rewarded favorites with lands, this Tudor monarch was able to grant lucrative trade privileges. Charles I, who got much more revenue from these monopolies, really prepared the way for the parliamentary excise.

The Long Parliament also raised substantial sums by taxing property under the system of monthly assessments. After using the subsidy for the last time in 1663, the government of the Restoration resorted occasionally to the monthly assessment. With the accession of William and Mary property taxation in the well-known land tax of 1692 once more assumed an important place in the revenue system. At first a rated tax on both personal and real property, it soon followed the course of the fifteenths and

[1] W. H. Price, *The English Patents of Monopoly* (1913), pp. 4-7.

tenths and the subsidies, becoming apportioned, fixed, and resting largely on realty. In 1755 the land tax produced £1,000,000, as against £1,780,000 from the customs and £3,660,000 from the excise.[1]

Another change in the revenue system, dating from the end of the seventeenth century, was the use of the voluntary public loan as a dependable source of revenue. This establishment of public credit on a sound basis was made possible by a political event, the complete victory of parliament over the king, and by an economic development, the rise of commercial banking in England.

In the latter part of the eighteenth century England entered upon a period of very rapid economic change. Internal peace, combined with increasing prestige abroad, gave favorable political conditions. The development of banking, the increase of the merchant marine, the breaking down of local restrictions, and the growth of both national and foreign markets had provided an auspicious economic environment. Then came the inventions, not new to England, but more significant and in greater numbers. Agriculture, which had held first place for centuries, gave way in the nineteenth century to industry and commerce. Division of labor increased to a large degree.

This economic change could not fail to affect the public-revenue system. With the coming of the industrial era the amount of taxpaying ability, not adequately reached by the existing taxes, was much increased. This was especially true of income from personal earnings. England, the first country to experience the industrial change, was logically the first country to adapt to modern conditions a tax which up to the present time seems the best suited, at least as a national tax, to the new order. It was in the struggle with France that Pitt in 1799 secured from parliament the en-

[1] Dowell, *op. cit.*, vol. ii, p. 130.

actment of his plan for an income tax. From this beginning has grown a tax which now provides England with a large part of her national revenue and has also been adopted by many other countries. The success of the personal income tax is due not only to its adaptability to present economic conditions but also to its appeal to modern democratic ideals. Property taxes cannot adequately take into account the individual's ability to pay. An income tax can, however, include income from personal earnings as well as from property. It can determine the individual's net income by making allowance for such items as interest paid out and losses. It allows the exemption of the smaller incomes. It also permits the levying of a lower rate on incomes from personal earnings and the use of higher rates in the case of large incomes.

The new economic environment was also responsible for a radical change in the character of England's indirect taxes. The more numerous representatives of the manufacturing and commercial element in parliament secured relief from the many burdensome excise taxes. They also helped to do away with a tariff which, protective for over a century, restricted importations of raw materials and foodstuffs, and, consequently, narrowed the market for British manufactures. In the middle of the nineteenth century the excise system was reduced practically to a tax on alcoholic liquors and the tariff was restricted to only a few well-chosen articles, taxed strictly for revenue purposes.

This brief survey of the development of the public revenues in England has shown the dependence of the revenue system on economic conditions. The practical application of this fact in economic history is that, while a country must consider many factors in framing its fiscal system, it must by all means keep in mind the economic environment.

THE CONSENT OF THE ENGLISH LOWER CLERGY TO TAXATION, 1166-1216

W. E. LUNT

THE lower clergy of England developed such right of consent to taxation as they obtained in association chiefly with royal or papal taxes imposed upon their chattels and incomes. Before taxes of this type began to be levied, the papacy had placed no general taxes upon the English clergy. The earlier royal taxes were collected from those members of the clergy who possessed the kinds of property upon which they were assessed, but none of them fell upon the generality of the lower clergy,[1] with the possible but improbable exception of Danegeld and the analogous hidage.[2] Whatever may have been the truth with regard to the universality of the application of these two taxes to the lower clergy, they had no part in the development of a clerical right of consent. Whenever we have information

[1] That few of the lower clergy held lands by the feudal tenures upon which scutage and some of the royal customary aids were paid appears from an inspection of the pipe rolls. The aids, *dona*, and tallages paid by boroughs or tenants of the royal demesne did not affect the lower clergy who lived outside these areas. The *dona* taken from the clergy were paid only by prelates and communities of religious.

[2] The lands of many priests and churches were assessed to geld in *Domesday-Book* (2 vols., 1783), e. g., vol. i, pp. 4, 13, 16, 27, 65, 76, 203, 272–279, 344; vol. ii, pp. 27, 195, 331, 342. Land held by frank almoin is also assessed there (vol. i, p. 65). But only a portion of the lands of all the parish churches in England is listed in the survey (A. Ballard, *The Domesday Inquest*, London, 1906, pp. 181–196, 248, 249). The remainder may have been exempt, or it may have been included without specific mention under the names of the lords of estates who were responsible to the royal officials for the render of the geld.

that the king sought approval for their levy, we find that he consulted only the barons or the great council.[1]

Possibly some measure of precedent for the consent of the lower clergy to royal or papal taxes was supplied by the practice with regard to episcopal aids. In 1159 Henry, bishop of Winchester, made a gift of 500 marks to the king for the expedition to Toulouse. Subsequently he convoked the priests of his diocese and asked them to grant an aid for his reimbursement. They consented willingly. On at least one other occasion he obtained from his clergy the voluntary concession of a pecuniary aid in a similar manner, though he did not collect the tax.[2] These incidents, taken in conjunction with the contemporary theory of the voluntary character of gracious feudal aids,[3] establish some degree of probability that English custom gave to the lower clergy the right to consent to the grant of aids desired by their bishops.[4] Twenty years later the third council of the Lateran incorporated this principle in the universal law of the Church. "We also forbid," reads its decree, "bishops to presume to burden their subjects with tallages and exactions. We maintain, however, that they

[1] Possibly the Danegeld was levied sometimes at the sole initiative of the king (W. A. Morris, *Constitutional History of England*, New York, 1930, pp. 216–218, 306; W. Stubbs, *The Constitutional History of England*, 6th ed., Oxford, 1897, vol. i, pp. 618–620). We hear occasionally of the barons or the great council being consulted (F. Liebermann, *Die Gesetze der Angelsachsen*, 3 vols., Halle, 1898–1916, vol. i, p. 636; below, p. 78).

[2] Giraldus Cambrensis, *Opera*, J. S. Brewer, J. F. Dimock, and G. F. Warner, eds., Rolls Series (8 vols., London, 1861–91), vol. iii, pp. 357, 358.

[3] Glanvill, bk. ix, chap. viii, *apud* W. Stubbs, *Select Charters and other Illustrations of English Constitutional History* (8th ed., Oxford, 1895), p. 163. See also the exposition of the theory and the references given by G. B. Adams, *Origins of the English Constitution* (New Haven, 1912), pp. 253–255.

[4] Giraldus relates several instances of aids levied by two bishops of St. Davids. Though he describes them as tyrannical, he mentions the consent of the clergy in every case except one, in which he does not say whether it was given or not. Apparently the two bishops were Peter and Geoffrey, who held office from 1176 to 1215 (*op. cit.*, vol. iii, pp. 140–143, 351).

may ask from their subjects a moderate aid *cum caritate* for the many exigencies which sometimes arise, if the cause is manifest and reasonable."[1] Neither the custom nor the law had any application to kings or popes, but they provided a background of tradition from which the lower clergy may possibly have evolved an opinion that their consent ought to be essential for the imposition upon them of extraordinary taxes. I have not been able, however, to establish any definite historical connection between the theory of episcopal aids and the practice of royal or papal taxation of the lower clergy.

The first known tax imposed by king or pope on the movables or income of the English lower clergy was established by Henry II in 1166. During the lenten season of that year the English king crossed to France,[2] where he had an interview with Louis VII. The French king, who had recently imposed a tax on his subjects for the aid of the Holy Land, urged his powerful vassal to do likewise.[3] On May 3, at Le Mans, Henry consulted with the archbishop of Rouen, three Norman bishops, the bishop of Le Mans, and some of his barons. A week later he met a much larger assembly of archbishops, bishops, and barons from Normandy, Maine, Anjou, Touraine, Brittany, and Gascony.[4] "With the counsel and consent of all" he ordered

---

[1] *Corpus Iuris Canonici*, Decretal. Gregor. IX, lib. iii, tit. xxxix, c. vi, A. Friedberg, ed. (2 vols., 2nd Leipzig ed., 1922), vol. ii, p. 623. See also the comment of Bernardus Papiensis on this canon (*Summa Decretalium*, E. A. T. Laspeyres, ed., Ratisbon, 1860, p. 124).

[2] Ralph of Diceto, *Opera Historica*, W. Stubbs, ed., Rolls Series (2 vols., London, 1876), vol. i, p. 318.

[3] Robert of Torigni, "Chronica," in *Chronicles of the Reigns of Stephen, Henry II, and Richard I*, R. Howlett, ed., Rolls Series (4 vols., London, 1884–89), vol. iv, pp. 226, 227; Gervase of Canterbury, *Historical Works*, W. Stubbs, ed. (2 vols., London, 1879–80), vol. i, p. 198.

[4] The decree is preserved by Gervase (vol. i, pp. 198, 199). Another statement in the document makes it appear that earls and vavasors as well as barons were present.

in each of his lands the payment by clerks and laymen[1] of twopence in the pound from their movables and revenues[2] in 1166, and one penny a year for the four following years. A man who did not have a pound was required to give a penny if he possessed a house or an office. The proceeds were to be used for the aid of "the oriental land and church." The exceptionally specific enumeration of those who confirmed this enactment creates a presumption that the lower clergy were not consulted.

Since none from England is mentioned among the groups which approved the ordinance, presumably it applied only to Henry's French dominions. Nevertheless the tax was levied in England. Ralph of Diceto tells of a collection for Jerusalem concluded in this year, in which an oath was taken and chests in each church were used for the receipts.[3] Assessment under oath by the contributor and the deposit of the resulting sum in a locked chest kept in his parish church were characteristics of the levy in the Angevin fiefs in France.[4] The rate was also the same, sixpence in the pound,[5] though the tax in England was paid in one year instead of being extended over five. Ralph's account receives confirmation from the pipe roll for the fiscal year 1166–67. Although the receipts are not entered there, the expenditure of £7 10s. for the ship "which crossed with the alms for the oriental church" is recorded.[6] By whose authority the tax was levied in England does not appear. Since Henry II remained in France for the rest of the year,[7] the chroniclers have little to say about affairs in

---

[1] "Hoc faciant archiepiscopi, episcopi, abbates qui regale habent, et clerici, comites, barones, vavasores, milites, cives, burgensi, rustici."

[2] "De omni mobili . . . et de redditibus similiter."

[3] *Op. cit.*, vol. i, p. 329.

[4] W. E. Lunt, *Valuation of Norwich* (Oxford, 1926), pp. 2, 3.

[5] Fourpence in the mark, according to Ralph.

[6] *Publications of the Pipe Roll Society* (London, 1884–), vol. xi, p. 194.

[7] Robert of Torigni, *op. cit.*, vol. iv, pp. 226–229.

England. Under these circumstances their silence about consideration of the tax by any English assembly has no significance.[1] But in view of the manner in which the legislation was enacted for Henry's French lands, it may be doubted if the English lower clergy were given any opportunity to grant or to refuse the tax.

Before the lower clergy were again taxed by the king, legislation was passed by the third council of the Lateran in 1179 to protect them against taxation by laymen. The conciliar constitution, after reciting how "consules civitatum et rectores, nec non et alii, qui potestatem habere videntur," impose charges on churches, forbids the practice for the future under penalty of anathema, "unless *episcopus et clerus* should have seen such necessity or utility, that, without any exaction, they should think subsidies ought to be given by the churches for alleviating the common utilities or necessities, where the resources of laymen do not suffice."[2]

The interpretation of this legislation is difficult. That it applied only to spiritualities and not to temporalities is clear enough.[3] Of two other aspects of the law important in the present problem I have found no authoritative explanation.[4] Who were the clergy whose consent was neces-

---

[1] The only assembly of which I have found mention was one of bishops and abbots convened at London by Richard de Lucy, the justiciar. The only business recorded by the chroniclers was a decision to appeal to the pope against Becket (Gervase of Canterbury, *op. cit.*, vol. i, p. 200; William of Canterbury, "Vita S. Thomae," in *Materials for the History of Thomas Becket, Archbishop of Canterbury*, J. C. Robertson, ed., Rolls Series, 7 vols., London, 1875–85, vol. i, p. 56; Roger of Hoveden, *Chronica*, W. Stubbs, ed., Rolls Series, 4 vols., London, 1868–71, vol. i, p. 266).

[2] *Corpus Iuris Canonici*, Decretal. Gregor. ix, lib. iii, tit. xlix, c. iv.

[3] On the distinction between spiritualities and temporalities, see Lunt, *op. cit.*, pp. 69–78.

[4] I have looked in the *Apparatus super Libros Decretalium* of Innocent iv [Venice, 1481] and in the *Summa* of Hostiensis (Lyons, 1568). Since it is difficult to locate a specific subject in either work, I may have missed some pertinent comment.

sary along with that of the bishop? Possibly the consent of the other prelates in the diocese was sufficient. The logical implication would seem to be that the clergy who would be taxed should be consulted. Since the chief purpose of taxing spiritualities was to reach the lower clergy, who possessed little temporal property, the statute would seem to lack point if *clerus* did not designate the diocesan clergy generally. Did the statute make it necessary for kings to obtain the consent of the bishop and clergy in order to tax their spiritualities? The legislators evidently had their attention directed primarily toward local authorities and particularly toward Italian communities where consuls and rectors were common. "The others who are seen to have power" may have included kings,[1] but it seems probable that others of like kind with consuls and rectors were meant.[2] This supposition is supported by the use of *episcopus* in the singular. The contemplated taxation was expected to be confined to the limits of one diocese.[3] If royal taxation was intended to be brought within the scope of the act, the plural of *episcopus* would seem to have been the natural expression. A study of English practice previous to 1272 casts only a dim light on the import of the canon. In 1269 the lower clergy invoked it, as it had been amended in 1215,[4] for protection against imposition by the king of a tax on their spiritual revenues without their consent.

---

[1] So interpreted, for example, by F. M. Powicke, *Stephen Langton* (Oxford, 1928), p. 91; A. Cartellieri, *Philipp II August König von Frankreich* [hereafter referred to as *Philipp II*] (4 vols., Leipzig, 1899–1921), vol. ii, p. 18; G. Phillips, *Kirchenrecht* (8 vols., Regensburg, 1855–89), vol. iii, p. 247.

[2] E. Mack, *Die kirchliche Steuerfreiheit in Deutschland seit der Dekretalensetzgebung* (Stuttgart, 1916), pp. 18, 19; G. le Bras, *L'Immunité réelle* (Rennes, 1920), pp. 58–63, 77. C. J. von Hefele implies that the law applied to kings but was not enforced against them (*Conciliengeschichte*, 2nd ed. by A. Knöpfler, 9 vols., Freiburg im B., 1873–90, vol. vi, pp. 292, 293).

[3] A. Gottlob, *Die päpstliche Kreuzzugs-Steuern des 13 Jahrhunderts* (Heiligenstadt, 1892), pp. 13, 14.

[4] Below, pp. 85–86.

Since they finally granted the tax, the incident indicates merely that the lower clergy in 1269 thought of the law as applicable to royal taxation.[1] The interpretation is of too late a date to be carried back with confidence to the period before 1216.[2]

The conciliar decree produced no apparent effect upon the attitude of Henry II. In 1185 he imposed a tax which probably fell upon the lower clergy. Once more the purpose was to aid the Holy Land. Its needs were brought to Henry's attention by Heraclius, the patriarch of Jerusalem, who set out in 1184 to seek the help of European princes for the distressed kingdom. After some months in Italy, Heraclius came to England,[3] bearing a papal letter which urged the English king to comply with the patriarch's request.[4] What he desired was the royal promise to lead a crusade. Henry gave his answer at a council held at London in March of 1185. With the advice of his bishops, abbots, earls, and barons,[5] he declined the proffered honor, but promised Heraclius a large sum of

---

[1] *Persecution and Liberty: Essays in Honor of George Lincoln Burr* (New York, 1931), pp. 160, 161.

[2] The same is true of an incident of still later date. In 1330 the clergy of the province of Canterbury in convocation declined to grant a subsidy to the king. They put forward as one of four reasons that the council of the Lateran prevented them from burdening the Church when, as was then the case, laymen had conceded a subsidy sufficient to meet the necessity alleged by the king as the cause for the desired clerical grant ("Annales Paulini," in *Chronicles of the Reigns of Edward I and Edward II*, W. Stubbs, ed., Rolls Series, 2 vols., London, 1882–83, vol. i, p. 348).

[3] Cartellieri, *op. cit.*, vol. ii, pp. 18–21.

[4] Given by Roger of Hoveden, *op. cit.*, vol. ii, p. 300; Giraldus Cambrensis, *op. cit.*, vol. viii, p. 204; William of Newburgh, "Historia Rerum Anglicarum," in *Chronicles of the Reigns of Stephen, Henry II, and Richard I*, vol. i, p. 245.

[5] *Gesta Regis Henrici Secundi Benedicti Abbatis* [hereafter referred to as *Gesta Regis*], W. Stubbs, ed., Rolls Series (2 vols., London, 1867), vol. i, p. 336. Ralph of Diceto says, "Cantuariensis electus et Cantuariensis ecclesiae suffraganei, Dunelmensis episcopus, abbates conventualium locorum praelati, comites et barones" (*op. cit.*, vol. ii, p. 33). "Totius Angliae primoribus," Gervase of Canterbury, *op. cit.*, vol. i, p. 325.

money.[1] In April both patriarch and king went to France, where discussion with Philip Augustus did not alter Henry's decision.[2]

In order to recoup himself for his gift, Henry turned to his subjects. Sometime after May 19, Archbishop Baldwin addressed a letter to his suffragans.[3] After dwelling upon the woes of Jerusalem and telling how Heraclius had come to Henry, he concludes: "For he [i. e. Henry], seeing lamentable peril to threaten the holy city, put a magnificent and munificent hand into his own treasures, and, with the common counsel of the bishops, earls and barons of the land, instituted an impost,[4] which do you diligently and effectively cause to be observed throughout each of the parishes of your dioceses,[5] according to the form which is written below."[6] The unfortunate loss of the form leaves the nature of the tax unknown. It is tempting to assume with Luchaire[7] that "the Ordinance concerning a Con-

[1] *Ibid.*; William of Newburgh, *op. cit.*, vol. i, p. 247; Giraldus Cambrensis, *op. cit.*, vol. viii, pp. 203–208.

[2] The *Gesta Regis* implies that the council of London postponed the answer in order to consult with Philip, and that Henry and Philip together later promised to aid with men and money (vol. i, pp. 336–338). Roger of Hoveden follows the *Gesta Regis* (*op. cit.*, vol. ii, pp. 302–304). The others state that the refusal of the leadership and the offer of money were made at London, though Giraldus and William of Newburgh indicate that the subject was further discussed in France. Ralph of Diceto does not mention the money. He speaks of a conference between Henry and Philip, but is silent about the subject of discussion (*op. cit.*, vol. ii, pp. 33, 34).

[3] The letter is undated. I place it after May 19, because Baldwin does not style himself archbishop-elect. He received his pallium and was installed on that date (Gervase of Canterbury, *op. cit.*, vol. i, p. 326).

[4] *Collectam.*

[5] *Episcopatus vestri.*

[6] J. P. Migne, *Patrologiae Cursus completus* (216 vols., Paris, 1844–90), vol. ccvii, pp. 306–308. This tax seems to have been unknown to modern historians of the reign.

[7] "L'Ordonnance de Philippe-Auguste sur la Dîme de Croisade de 1185," *Revue historique*, vol. lxxii (1900), pp. 334–338. See also the reply of Cartellieri and a further statement of Luchaire in the same periodical (vol. lxxiii, pp. 61–64; vol. lxxvi, pp. 329, 330).

tribution to be made in Aid of the Holy Land" should be dated 1185 instead of 1184,[1] but I am too sceptical of the authenticity of the ordinance [2] to conjecture that it is the form mentioned by Baldwin. There is, moreover, a difference in the mode of administration. The tax described in the ordinance was to be collected in each diocese by a Templar and a Hospitaller. Baldwin's tax was in charge of the bishop in each diocese. Without much doubt the tax of 1185 was similar to that of 1166. The parish was the unit for the collection of both, and the administration of both was under the general supervision of each bishop in his diocese. It seems to be a reasonable assumption that the lower clergy were included among the taxpayers in 1185 as they had been in 1166. If so, they were not consulted about the tax. Baldwin's official communication mentions the counsel of only earls and barons. If the tax was voted in the council of London held in March of 1185, as seems probable, the chroniclers amply verify the statement of the archbishop.

The Saladin tithe of 1188 was established in France by the joint action of Philip Augustus and Henry II. On January 21, in the presence of a large number of archbishops, bishops, and barons from the Capetian and Angevin lands, both sovereigns took the cross. With the "common counsel" of those assembled they ordered their lay and clerical subjects to pay a tenth of their incomes [3] and movables for a year.[4] A few days later Henry held an assembly at Le Mans, attended by two archbishops and

---

[1] I have edited the text in *English Historical Review*, vol. xxxvii (1922), pp. 336–342.

[2] I have stated my reasons in the *Valuation of Norwich*, pp. 4–6.

[3] *Redditibus.*

[4] Joint decree (William of Newburgh, *op. cit.*, vol. i, p. 273). On the kinds of property exempted from the tax and on its administration, see Lunt, *Valuation of Norwich*, pp. 6–8; Cartellieri, *Philipp II*, vol. ii, pp. 52–74.

five bishops from Normandy, Anjou, Maine, and Touraine, the archbishop of Canterbury, the bishop of Lichfield,[1] Henry's son Richard, and barons from Anjou, Maine, and Touraine. In their presence he published a decree laying down detailed regulations for the collection of the tithe in his French provinces.[2]

Directly after these events the active king returned to England. On February 11 he convoked at Geddington a *magnum concilium*,[3] where the ordinance recently enacted at Le Mans was made applicable to England.[4] Concerning the membership of this council contemporaries differ significantly. Three chroniclers employ the conventional terms to describe its composition. The *Gesta* designates the archbishops, bishops, earls, and barons as summoned;[5] Gervase of Canterbury names those in attendance as *praesules et principes*;[6] and William of Newburgh calls them *praesules et proceres*.[7] Roger of Hoveden, who copied the *Gesta*, adds to the list of those who were convened abbots and many other clerks and laymen.[8] Still more significant is the statement made by the monks of Canterbury in a contemporary letter. They say: "Habuit autem in proximo dominus rex apud Norhamtun [9] colloquium cum episcopis totius Angliae et Walliae et principibus et procuratoribus terrae."[10] Since the proctors commonly em-

---

[1] The prelates are named in the *Gesta Regis*, vol. ii, p. 30.

[2] Decree given in *Gesta Regis*, vol. ii, p. 30; Roger of Hoveden, *op. cit.*, vol. ii, p. 335.

[3] *Ibid.*, p. 338.

[4] Gervase of Canterbury, *op. cit.*, vol. i, p. 409; William of Newburgh, *op. cit.*, vol. i, pp. 274, 275.

[5] Vol. ii, p. 33.

[6] *Op. cit.*, vol. i, p. 409.

[7] *Op. cit.*, vol. i, p. 275.

[8] *Op. cit.*, vol. ii, p. 338.

[9] Northampton is a few miles from Geddington.

[10] *Chronicles and Memorials of the Reign of Richard I*, W. Stubbs, ed., Rolls Series (2 vols., 1864–65), vol. ii, p. 167.

ployed in ecclesiastical affairs represented their principals and possessed legal powers to commit their principals,[1] the use by monks of the phrase "proctors of the land" connotes the presence of a representative element in the council. If representatives were present, however, it does not necessarily follow that they took part in all the business transacted at the council. Gervase and William state that the king treated of the Holy Land with the magnates, and mention no others as present. The popular element may have attended merely to take part in the public session, where the cross was preached and the privileges of the crusaders were read aloud,[2] though it is not readily apparent why representatives should have been summoned for this purpose alone. When all of this evidence has been taken into consideration, the use of the technical term *procuratores* by ecclesiastics seems to leave a balance of probability that a representative element attended this council. The mention by Roger of clergy as present in addition to bishops and abbots establishes a possibility that the lower clergy were among those represented. Possibly representatives of the lower clergy took part in the grant of the Saladin tithe.

The Saladin tithe produced an outburst of complaint such as was occasioned by no other tax of the reign of Henry II. The levy of 1166 received only the barest mention by one chronicler, and that of 1185 appears to have been overlooked entirely by contemporary historians. In 1188 Peter of Blois protested vigorously against the taxation of the Church by the state; but he was writing of the tenth raised in the domains of Philip Augustus.[3] The criti-

---

[1] A contemporary canonist says of the procuratory power: "Effectus procurationis est, ut ratum sit quod geritur cum procuratore, ac si cum domino gestum esset" (Bernardus Papiensis, *op. cit.*, p. 24).

[2] *Gesta Regis*, vol. ii, p. 33.

[3] Migne, *op. cit.*, vol. ccvii, pp. 71–75, 335–340, 354–356.

cisms in England were directed chiefly against the severity of the processes used to compel payment and against the weight of the taxation.[1] Opponents, says the author of the *Gesta*, were imprisoned and held in chains "until they had paid the last farthing."[2] Gervase of Canterbury has "each and all grieve over so great a burden,"[3] and many are the kindred expressions of opinion. Among the English complaints, however, no trace of dissatisfaction with the authority by which the tax had been imposed is expressed.

To raise the money for Richard's ransom a series of taxes was imposed in 1193 and 1194. An explanation of their nature is necessary in order to determine which of them were paid by the lower clergy. The first, which was called indiscriminately an aid or a tallage,[4] was a quarter of income (*redditus*). It did not extend to chattels,[5] and it was probably confined to revenues from land.[6] Among the

---

[1] *Gesta Regis*, vol. ii, p. 59; William of Newburgh, *op. cit.*, vol. i, p. 282; Giraldus Cambrensis, *op. cit.*, vol. viii, p. 253; Ralph of Coggeshall, *Chronicon Anglicanum*, J. Stevenson, ed., Rolls Series (London, 1895), pp. 24, 25; Ralph of Diceto, *op. cit.*, vol. ii, p. 73; Roger of Wendover, *Chronica, sive Flores Historiarum*, H. O. Coxe, ed., Eng. Hist. Soc. (London, 1841–44), vol. iii, p. 16.

[2] Vol. ii, p. 33.

[3] *Op. cit.*, vol. i, p. 422.

[4] *Three Rolls of the King's Court in the Reign of King Richard the First, A.D. 1194–95* [hereafter referred to as *Three Rolls*], F. W. Maitland, ed., Pubs. of Pipe Roll Soc., vol. xiv (London, 1891), pp. 78, 80, 107, 108, 113; *Pubs. of Pipe Roll Soc.*, n. s., vol. vi, pp. 261, 262.

[5] The official records cited in the preceding note establish that it was a quarter. That it was a quarter of revenues rests upon the statements of chroniclers. All contemporary chroniclers agree in this definition except Roger of Hoveden. He says: "mater regis et justiciarii Angliae statuerunt quod universi, tam clerici quam laici, quartam partem redditus sui de hoc anno darent ad redemptionem domini regis, et tantum superadderent de mobilibus suis." In a later passage, however, he describes the aid simply as "quartam partem . . . reddituum" (*op. cit.*, vol. iii, pp. 210, 225). Gervase of Canterbury, *op. cit.*, vol. i, p. 519; Ralph of Coggeshall, *op. cit.*, p. 60; Ralph of Diceto, *op. cit.*, vol. ii, p. 110; Roger of Wendover, *op. cit.*, vol. iii, p. 73. In Normandy it was a "quartam partem redditus" (*Magni Rotuli Scaccarii Normanniae sub Regibus Angliae*, T. Stapleton, ed., Soc. of Antiquaries, 2 vols., London, 1840–44, vol. i, p. 270).

[6] I infer this from the names of the payers occasionally preserved in the scant official records we have. They consist of the returns made by local juries in the

clergy only prelates were responsible for the quarter.[1] The laymen who paid it appear to have been landlords or free tenants.[2] The Cistercians and the religious of the order of Sempringham, whose income was derived more largely from their flocks than from the cultivation of the soil, contributed their crop of wool for the year 1193.[3] The lower clergy paid a tenth of their revenues.[4] It was collected not by those who assembled the quarter in each hundred, but by the bishops.[5] The government also took from the clergy the chalices and other treasures of gold and silver found in

county of Wilts to an inquiry of the itinerant justices in 1194 and a receipt roll of the exchequer for Easter term 1195 (*Three Rolls*, pp. 78–115; *Pubs. of Pipe Roll Soc.*, n. s., vol. vi, p. 262). Sir James H. Ramsay also holds that *redditus* were rents (*A History of the Revenues of the Kings of England*, 2 vols., Oxford, 1925, vol. i, p. 212).

[1] All of the chroniclers cited above, p. 73, n. 5, agree on this except Ralph of Coggeshall and Roger of Hoveden in the passage quoted. In his second statement Roger says that only part of the clergy paid the fourth, but he does not specify what part. Yet secondary historians almost universally ascribe payment of the fourth to all the clergy.

[2] *Three Rolls*, pp. 78–115; *Pubs. of Pipe Roll Soc.*, n. s., vol. vi, p. 262. Ralph of Diceto, *op. cit.*, vol. ii, p. 110, and Ralph of Coggeshall, *op. cit.*, p. 60, mention among laymen who paid it only earls and barons. Gervase of Canterbury, *op. cit.*, vol. i, p. 519, and Roger of Hoveden, *op. cit.*, vol. iii, pp. 210, 225, say all laymen. Roger states, however, that Richard addressed his original letter of request for an aid to earls, barons, and free tenants, *op. cit.*, vol. iii, p. 208. The entries on the roll indicate that others than tenants-in-chief paid the fourth. It was paid in boroughs and cities as well as in manors and hundreds (*Three Rolls*, pp. 83, 95, 99).

[3] "Annales Monasterii de Waverleia," in *Annales Monastici*, H. R. Luard, ed., Rolls Series (5 vols., London, 1864–69), vol. ii, p. 248; Ralph of Diceto, *op. cit.*, vol. ii, p. 110; Roger of Hoveden, *op. cit.*, vol. iii, p. 210; *Pubs. of Pipe Roll Soc.*, n. s., vol. iii, p. 69.

[4] Ralph of Diceto, *op. cit.*, vol. ii, p. 110; *Pubs. of Pipe Roll Soc.*, n. s., vol. vi, p. 263. See also Roger of Hoveden, *op. cit.*, vol. ii, p. 225; "Ann. Mon. de Waverleia," in *op. cit.*, vol. ii, p. 248.

[5] Compare *Three Rolls*, pp. 78–115, with *Pubs. of Pipe Roll Soc.*, n. s., vol. vi, p. 263. The tenth was paid by the bishop of Winchester *de auxilio ecclesiarum eiusdem episcopatus*. The bishops themselves paid the quarter. Cf. *Pubs. of Pipe Roll Soc.*, n. s., vol. vi, p. xvii. See also Roger of Hoveden, *op. cit.*, vol. iii, p. 225. The tenth seems to have been levied also from the clergy of Normandy (*Rot. Scacc. Normanniae*, vol. i, pp. 220, 221).

cathedral, monastic, and parish churches.[1] These precious objects were taken as a loan with pledge that they would be returned.[2]

Because the first aid proved to be inadequate, a second aid or tallage was exacted before Michaelmas of 1193.[3] Its nature is problematical. It is called in the official entries the aid of "ten shillings and more." [4] Maitland suggested that it was a tax on those who owned chattels worth ten shillings or land worth ten shillings a year.[5] Which it may have been, if either, is left unsettled by any evidence that has come to my attention.[6] If it was a quarter of personal property assessed on those possessing ten shillings and more, color would be given to Roger of Hoveden's *et tantum superadderent de mobilibus suis*.[7] The second aid was paid by laymen,[8] and probably by the higher clergy.[9] It does not appear to have been due from the lower clergy, who seem on this second occasion to have contributed a twentieth of their incomes.[10] Like the quarter and the tenth, the aid of "ten shillings and more" and the twentieth were levied by different sets of collectors.[11]

[1] Roger of Hoveden, *op. cit.*, vol. iii, p. 210; Ralph of Diceto, *op. cit.*, vol. ii, p. 110; Ralph of Coggeshall, *op. cit.*, p. 60; Jocelin de Brakelonde, "Cronica," in *Memorials of St. Edmund's Abbey*, T. Arnold, ed., Rolls Series (3 vols., London, 1890–96), vol. i, p. 251; *Pubs. of Pipe Roll Soc.*, n. s., vol. vi, p. 263.

[2] Royal letter (Roger of Hoveden, *op. cit.*, vol. iii, p. 209).

[3] *Pubs. of Pipe Roll Soc.*, n. s., vol. iii, p. 73; William of Newburgh, *op. cit.*, vol. i, p. 400.

[4] *Pubs. of Pipe Roll Soc.*, n. s., vol. vi, p. 261; *Three Rolls*, pp. 86, 91, 95.

[5] Introduction to *Three Rolls*, pp. xxiii, xxiv.

[6] The sums paid in each hundred for the second aid are generally much less than those paid for the first and considerably less than those paid for the hidage, though there are exceptions. Maitland notes that the lack of a constant relation eliminates the possibility that the second aid was assessed on the hide.

[7] Above, p. 73, n. 5. Secondary historians are nearly unanimous in the assumption that a quarter of both revenues and movables was paid, but they seem to rely solely on the statement of Roger of Hoveden.

[8] *Three Rolls*, pp. 87, 88, 90, 108; *Pubs. of Pipe Roll Soc.*, n. s., vol. vi, pp. 261, 262.

[9] *Ibid.*, p. 261.　　　　　　　　　　[10] *Ibid.*, pp. 262, 263.

[11] Compare *ibid.* with *Three Rolls*, pp. 78–115.

After the proceeds of the second aid had been gathered, the government found itself still short of the desired sum. On April 1, 1194 a third aid or tallage was imposed.[1] This was a hidage or carucage of two shillings on the hide assessed like the old Danegeld.[2] It was paid by those who held any of the lands subject to the levy. Some of the lower clergy paid it,[3] though presumably the number was not large.[4] In addition to these imposts a scutage of a pound on the knight's fee[5] and a tallage of the cities, boroughs, and royal demesne were collected in 1194.[6]

It seems impossible to determine beyond doubt whether these taxes were raised with the expressed consent of the various classes who paid them, or whether "the national consent was taken for granted."[7] The evidence tending to support the first view may be marshalled first. Roger of Hoveden records that Richard sent to England messengers bearing "to all archbishops and bishops and abbots and earls and barons and clerks and free tenants letters, in which the king asked humbly that all, both clerical and lay, would render to him such an aid for his ransom that he might feel grateful to them."[8] This has the appearance of a request which could be refused.[9] Ralph of Diceto, in-

---

[1] Roger of Hoveden, *op. cit.*, vol. iii, p. 242; *Pubs. of Pipe Roll Soc.*, n. s., vol. v, pp. xxiv, 126.

[2] Maitland, Introduction to *Three Rolls*, pp. xxiv, xxv.

[3] *Three Rolls*, p. 98.

[4] Above, p. 62.

[5] *Pubs. of Pipe Roll Soc.*, n. s., vol. v, p. xxiv; index under *scutagium ad redemptionem*.

[6] Roger of Hoveden, *op. cit.*, vol. iii, p. 264; *Pubs. of Pipe Roll Soc.*, n. s., vol. vi, p. xxiv. That the tallage was levied for the ransom is shown by the heading in the roll at p. 249.

[7] Stubbs, *The Constitutional History of England*, vol. i, p. 540.

[8] "Per quos rex humiliter postulavit ut universi, tam clerici quam laici, tale auxilium facerent ei ad redimendum eum, unde ipse sciret eis grates" (*op. cit.*, vol. iii, p. 208).

[9] *Grates* might appear to give some ground for the assumption that the levy was of the nature of a gracious aid, but it is placed in the wrong clause. Richard did not ask the freemen of England to pay an aid *de mera gratia sua*, but to pay

deed, says the payment of the fourth, the wool, and the tenth was decreed "by common assent."[1] Since the phrase occurs in a passage setting forth the devotion displayed by the king's lieges in raising the ransom, possibly it means no more than that public sentiment approved the taxation.[2] More significant is the story told by Roger of Hoveden about Geoffrey, archbishop of York. Like other bishops,[3] he acted as a collector of the fourth from the prelates of his diocese. When he asked the canons of York to pay the quarter, they refused, alleging that by this demand he was overthrowing the liberties of the Church.[4] Since this was only one of many causes of friction between the canons and the tempestuous archbishop,[5] the personal feeling between the two may have been the principal reason for the denial. Nevertheless, one group of prospective taxpayers thought they had a right of assent. Unfortunately there is no sequel to inform us whether their claim was made good.[6]

an aid that would evoke his *grates*. A letter issued by King John demonstrates that this *grates* formula has no implication of a gracious aid. It reads, "Rex etc. militibus, burgensibus de Constant' et Carentiis etc. Mandamus vobis quod bonum auxilium et efficax faciatis ad firmandum castrum nostrum de Moreton' unde vobis grates scire debeamus" (*Rotuli Litterarum Patentium in Turri Londinensis asservati*, T. D. Hardy, ed., Record Commission, vol. i, 1835, p. 28). Possibly the letters described by Roger were of the type addressed to the prior and convent of Canterbury on March 30. If so, the aid Richard asked in them was a loan (*Chronicles and Memorials of the Reign of Richard I*, vol. ii, p. 361).

[1] *Statutum est assensu communi persolvere* (*op. cit.*, vol. ii, p. 110).

[2] Gervase of Canterbury makes a statement which might possibly be construed to mean that more or less popular assemblies had a voice in establishing some of the taxes. He says, "Convocati sunt iterum et iterum apud Lundoniam tam ecclesiasticae quam seculares personae, ut subtilius requirerent si quid esset residuum ad solvendum" (*op. cit.*, vol. i, p. 519). I deem the object of these more minute inquiries to have been arrears; but a possible construction might make the purpose to discover remaining objects on which taxes could be levied.

[3] Roger of Hoveden, *op. cit.*, vol. iii, p. 225.

[4] *Ibid.*, p. 222.

[5] The canons eventually appealed to the pope. Their grievances are listed in the commission of the delegates appointed to hold inquiry. Financial exactions are among them, but not this particular incident (*ibid.*, pp. 279–281).

[6] Note should be made of the instruction issued to the itinerant justices ordering them to inquire concerning the aids *quis quantum promiserit, et quan-*

The evidence which points in the other direction begins with a letter addressed by Richard to his mother, the justices, and his lieges. Therein he adjures them, by the fealty which binds them to him, to be solicitous in the acquisition of the funds needed for his ransom.[1] Possibly this adjuration was so strong as to have had the practical force of a command, but it was not in the technical form of a mandate.[2] Beyond suggesting loans, the king in this letter did not instruct his ministers how they were to obtain the money. "On the authority of these letters," says Roger of Hoveden, "the mother of the king and the justices of England decreed" that the fourth, the scutage, the wool, and the gold and silver of churches be given, "as the king in his mandate had commanded."[3] Ralph of Coggeshall likewise says: "The edict was issued by the justices of the king."[4] William of Newburgh assigns the institution of the second and third aids also to the ministers,[5] but the third, which was the hidage, was decreed by the king in a session of his great council.[6] Several chroniclers describe those taxes of which they speak as paid compulsorily.[7]

Without the light of further evidence I see no way to reconcile all of these statements. The compulsory char-

---

tum reddiderit et quantum a retro sit (ibid., p. 263). The right to promise may imply a right not to promise, or the right to promise what amount one chooses. Probably it means simply how much each was answerable for. In the pipe roll of the next year, *promissa* sometimes means no more than debt (*Pubs. of Pipe Roll Soc.,* n. s., vol. vi, p. 248, and index under *promissa*).

[1] April 19, 1193 (Roger of Hoveden, *op. cit.,* vol. iii, pp. 208–210).

[2] Roger calls it a mandate (*ibid.,* p. 211). William of Newburgh says, "Rex ... procuratores regni Angliae cunctosque fideles et devotos suos ... frequentibus comonebat mandatis uti redemptionis suae pretium modis omnibus praeparentis, liberationem suam maturarent" (*op. cit.,* vol. i, p. 399).

[3] *Op. cit.,* vol. iii, pp. 210, 211.

[4] *Op. cit.,* p. 60.

[5] *Op. cit.,* vol. i, p. 400.

[6] Roger of Hoveden, *op. cit.,* vol. iii, p. 242.

[7] Ralph of Coggeshall, *op. cit.,* p. 60; William of Newburgh, *op. cit.,* vol. i, p. 399.

acter of the payments does not necessarily conflict with a popular grant of the taxes, for it was the custom that a lord could distrain for payment of a gracious aid, once it had been conceded.[1] If the consent of the several classes affected was obtained before the ministers issued their decree, several apparently conflicting statements would harmonize. This hypothesis, however, runs counter to Roger of Hoveden's assertion that the ministerial order was issued on the authority of the royal letter. Moreover, it lacks sufficient evidential support. Richard's letters of appeal addressed to his subjects were not necessarily followed by conferences in which his subjects could express their will; Ralph of Diceto's *assensu communi* is too vague a phrase to permit postulation upon it of a popular assembly or series of assemblies;[2] and the refusal of the canons of York probably took place after the issue of the ministerial ordinance.[3] The most that seems reasonably certain is that the third aid was imposed by the great council, and that a group of canons claimed the right not to pay the first aid.

About the sanction for the levy of the tenth and the twentieth from the lower clergy we know least of all. Ralph of Diceto brings the tenth under his *assensu communi*. He says naught of the twentieth, and I find no other chronicler who mentions specifically the authority for the levy of either. Perhaps it is significant that Stephen Langton, who was formulating his *Quaestiones* nearly contemporaneously, in a discussion of the taxation of the clergy mentions the ransom of Richard as an example of

---

[1] Glanvill, bk. ix, chap. viii, in *op. cit.*

[2] Stubbs interprets the phrase similarly (Introduction to Roger of Hoveden, *op. cit.*, vol. iv, pp. lxxxiii, lxxxiv). See also his *Histoire constitutionelle de l'Angleterre*, C. Petit-Dutaillis, ed., vol. i (Paris, 1907), p. 605, n. 1.

[3] It did, if, as seems probable, Gervase of Canterbury refers to the same incident as Roger of Hoveden (*op. cit.*, vol. i, p. 520).

an occasion when assistance might properly be given to a lay ruler from the goods of the Church.[1]

In view of these various contemporary descriptions, the designation of the taxes collectively as the customary aid for the ransom of the lord seems unwarranted.[2] The extension of the taxation to other forms of property than knights' fees does not necessarily indicate that the taxes were not regarded by contemporaries as a customary aid.[3] The aid levied by Henry I for the marriage of his daughter took the form of a hidage,[4] and such a tax fell upon tenants who did not hold by knight's service.[5] The chief difficulty with the assumption that the taxation constituted a customary aid is the possibility that it may have been a gracious aid. The "humble" request which Roger of Hoveden has Richard address to his subjects is remarkably like the formula used a few years later by King John in asking for a gracious aid.[6] As long as we are in the dark about the compulsory or voluntary manner of the establishment of the taxation, the question of customary or gracious aid must be left unanswered.

When King John first sought financial help from the lower clergy,[7] he asked for a gracious aid. On September 8,

[1] Powicke, op. cit., pp. 91–93.

[2] Stubbs so classifies the taxation (Introduction to Roger of Hoveden, op. cit., vol. iv, p. lxxxiv).

[3] Ramsay implies that customary aids were exigible only from knights' fees (Angevin Empire, p. 330).

[4] Henry of Huntingdon, Historia Anglorum, T. Arnold, ed., Rolls Series (London, 1879), p. 237.

[5] Above, pp. 62, 76; Ballard, op. cit., pp. 249, 250; P. Vinogradoff, English Society in the Eleventh Century (Oxford, 1908), p. 452; F. W. Maitland, Domesday Book and Beyond (Cambridge, 1907), pp. 120–122.

[6] T. Rymer and R. Sanderson, Foedera, A. Clarke and F. Holbrooke, eds., Record Commission, vol. i (London, 1816), p. 87.

[7] The fortieth of revenues levied for the Holy Land in 1201, at John's request, on the lands of the English magnates affected only those of the clergy who held lay fees (Roger of Hoveden, op. cit., vol. iv, pp. 185–189; H. F. Delaborde, "A propos d'une Rature dans un Registre de Philippe-Auguste," Bibliothèque de l'École des Chartres, vol. lxiv, 1903, p. 310; Rot. Lit. Pat., vol. i, p. 5).

1202 he "humbly" petitioned the archbishop and the clergy of the province of Canterbury to confer upon him an aid to promote the purposes of an alliance which he had concluded with King Otto of Germany to his and their advantage. Archbishop Hubert and Geoffrey Fitz Peter, the justiciar, were named to them as the recipients of the gifts which each of them should make.[1] The aid was supplementary to other taxes which were being demanded of other classes. In December the abbots of the Cistercian order were requested to give a *gratuitum subsidium* for the war against Philip Augustus.[2] In 1203 various groups of the king's subjects paid scutage, tallages, and gifts,[3] while the earls and barons contributed a seventh,[4] which, according to Roger of Wendover, was assessed on chattels,[5] and, according to the annalist of Bury St. Edmunds, was *septima pars reddituum*.[6] The clergy appear to have answered the king favorably, for in 1204 John acknowledged receipt from the archbishop of Canterbury of £2,000 for the work of his nephew Otto.[7] About the grant or the nature of the aid I have discovered nothing.[8] The inclusion of the clergy

[1] *Ibid.*, p. 18.

[2] Rymer, *Foedera*, vol. i, p. 87. There was also a systematic canvass of the king's subjects for loans (*Rot. Lit. Pat.*, vol. i, pp. 12, 14).

[3] S. K. Mitchell, *Studies in Taxation under John and Henry III* (New Haven, 1914), pp. 53–63.

[4] *Ibid.*, pp. 62, 63; *Rotuli de Liberate ac de Missis et Praestitis regnante Johanne*, T. D. Hardy, ed., Record Commission (London, 1844), pp. 43, 47.

[5] *Op. cit.*, vol. iii, p. 173. Roger puts the imposition of the seventh after John's return to England in December, 1203, but the documents cited in the preceding note are dated in June and July, 1203.

[6] "Cont. Florence of Worcester," B. Thorpe, ed., Eng. Hist. Soc. (London, 1849), vol. ii, p. 165; "Annales S. Edmundi," *Ungedruckte anglo-normannische Geschichtsquellen*, F. Liebermann, ed. (Strassburg, 1879), p. 142.

[7] December 5 (*Rot. Lit. Pat.*, vol. i, p. 48).

[8] Mitchell implies that the seventh was extended to the clergy (*op. cit.*, p. 62). So also does K. Norgate, *John Lackland* (London, 1902), p. 101. Since the statement of Roger of Wendover that the seventh was paid by earls and barons is supported by the little documentary evidence discovered (*Rot. de Liberate*, pp. 43, 47; Mitchell, *op. cit.*, pp. 62, 63, nn. 251, 253), and the annalists of Bury St. Edmunds say it was paid by barons and conventual monasteries

generally in the address of the royal letter of request creates a presumption that the lower clergy were consulted. When John again asked the clergy for a gracious aid, the lower clergy received an opportunity to express their opinion. The tax desired was a complement to the gracious aid of a thirteenth of revenues and chattels[1] imposed on every layman of England of whosesoever fee he might be.[2] The thirteenth was granted in a great council which held its last session at Oxford on February 10, 1207,[3] by the common counsel of archbishops, bishops, abbots, priors, and magnates.[4] Unless the royal letters specifying the grantors of the aid are silent about some classes which attended the great council at Oxford, the lay and spiritual magnates committed all laymen to the payment of an aid. The prelates did not so treat the lower clergy. The thirteenth was paid by the lay tenants of bishops, chapters, religious communities, and parochial churches, and by religious communities on their demesnes.[5] Whether the bishops were taxed on their demesnes is a moot question.[6] Aside from the loose state-

("Cont. Florence of Worcester," vol. ii, p. 165; "Ann. S. Edmundi," p. 142), presumably only the clergy who had lay fees paid it. There is no reason to suppose that the aid given by the clergy of the province of Canterbury was a seventh.

[1] On this tax see Mitchell, op. cit., chap. iii.

[2] Writ of February 17 (Rot. Lit. Pat., vol. i, p. 72); Gervase of Canterbury, op. cit., vol. ii, Introduction, p. lviii.

[3] Ibid.; itinerary in Rot. Lit. Pat., vol. i, Introduction.

[4] Royal letter of May 26 (Rot. Lit. Pat., vol. i, p. 72).

[5] Rotuli Litterarum Clausarum in Turri Londinensi asservati, T. D. Hardy, ed., Record Commission, vol. i (1833), pp. 79–85; "Annales Prioratus de Dunstaplia," in Annales Monastici, vol. iii, p. 29. Apparently the thirteenth extended to lay fees as well as to laymen.

[6] Their demesnes were not specified as taxable in the writ, but neither were the demesnes of the monks, which were undoubtedly taxed. An exemption of the bishop of Bath and Wells and his tenants from the aid implies that the bishop and his tenants were responsible for the payment unless exempted (Rot. Lit. Claus., vol. i, p. 79). A statement of the total receipts from the thirteenth says that they came "tam de comuni quam de finibus religiosorum et de donis episcoporum" (Rotuli de Oblatis et Finibus in Turri Londinensi asservati Tempore Regis Johannis, T. D. Hardy, ed., Record Commission, 1835, p. 459).

ments of chroniclers,[1] however, there is no indication that the lower clergy were bound by the action of the council of Oxford to pay an aid from their own revenues and chattels. Indeed, there is evidence to the contrary. According to the Annalist of Waverley,[2] John held a council at London on January 8, which was attended by bishops, abbots, priors, earls, and barons.[3] He asked the prelates to permit *personas et beneficiatos ecclesiarum* to give him a portion of their revenues. The prelates would not consent. At the council of Oxford, held on February 10, all of the prelates present from the provinces of Canterbury and York denied another request for the same thing.[4] Thereafter the king appealed directly to the lower clergy. In a letter of April 30, addressed to the archdeacon, the official, and all the clergy of Canterbury,[5] he states that

---

[1] "Pontifices vero et viri religiosi cujuscunque professionis essent, omnes indiscrete cum rege et suis pro se et hominibus suis pacem fecerunt ut melius potuerunt" ("Ann. de Margan," in *Annales Monastici*, vol. i, p. 28); "Johannes . . . extorsit omnem tertiam decimam partem . . . de episcopis, abbatibus, prioribus, canonicis, clericis, laicis, divitibus, et de omni populo simul" (Cont. William of Newburgh, *op. cit.*, vol. ii, p. 509); "tam de clericis religiosis et saecularibus quam de laicis" (Thomas Wykes, in *Annales Monastici*, vol. iv, p. 52); "tam a domibus religiosis quam a laicis" ("Ann. Monasterii de Bermundeseia," in *Annales Monastici*, vol. iii, p. 450), and "Annals of Winchester and Waverley," F. Liebermann, ed., *Ungedruckte anglo-normannische Geschichtsquellen*, p. 184; "Rex fecit tallagium per Angliam de tertia decima; episcopos nec ecclesias cathedrales nec eorum feoda talliavit" ("Ann. Prioratus de Wigornia," in *Annales Monastici*, vol. iv, p. 395); *a clericis et laicis* ("Ann. Monasterii de Wintonia," in *Annales Monastici*, vol. ii, p. 79); *tam clerici quam populi* (*Hist. et Cart. Monasterii S. Petri Gloucestriae*, vol. i, p. 23); "tam de laicis quam viris ecclesiasticis et praelatis" (Roger of Wendover, *op. cit.*, vol. iii, p. 210).

[2] *Annales Monastici*, vol. ii, p. 258.

[3] John came to England late in November or early in December, 1206 (*Rot. Lit. Pat.*, vol. i, p. 68). He celebrated Christmas with his magnates at Winchester (Roger of Wendover, *op. cit.*, vol. iii, p. 209). On January 12, 1207 he announced an ordinance established by the counsel of his barons (*Rot. Lit. Pat.*, vol. i, p. 68).

[4] "Ann. Mon. de Waverleia," in *op. cit.*, p. 258.

[5] "Rex H. archidiacono et Magistro T. officiali et toti clero archiepiscopatus Cantuariensis salutem." The archdeacon and the official were addressed because the archbishopric was for practical purposes vacant.

he has previously asked them for an aid for the defense of the liberty of the Church and for the defense and recovery of his lands, "to which," he says, "you answered that at three weeks after the Easter now past [1] you would provide the form and mode of giving that aid to us and that you would then give us a certain answer." He therefore asks them to provide an effective aid and to make their reply known at that time without delay.[2] On May 26 another royal letter was sent to the same addressees, requesting them to give such an aid that rectors of neighboring churches might the more readily be invited to render an aid.[3] This letter does not mention the preceding correspondence. The letters leave it doubtful whether the lower clergy granted an aid or not.[4] They leave little doubt that the levy of an aid from the lower clergy on this occasion had been rendered dependent upon the consent of the lower clergy by the action of the prelates taken at the councils of London and Oxford. The intention of the king to consult the rectors of the diocese or province of Canterbury[5] and the rectors of the neighboring dioceses or province seems to be placed beyond peradventure by the second royal letter.

Though John did not subsequently tax the income or chattels of the lower clergy,[6] before the close of his reign

---

[1] Namely, May 13.

[2] *Rot. Lit. Pat.*, vol. i, p. 71.　　　　[3] *Ibid.*, p. 72.

[4] The first letter seems to imply that only the form and mode of an aid are left to be settled, but the implication is far from certain. The second is merely a request for an aid, as if nothing were settled.

[5] Whether *archiepiscopatus* should here be translated "diocese" or "province" seems doubtful.

[6] John's arbitrary and compulsory levy of 1210 seems to have been confined to the regular clergy (Ralph of Coggeshall, *op. cit.*, p. 163; Cont. William of Newburgh, vol. ii, pp. 510–512; Roger of Wendover, *op. cit.*, vol. iii, pp. 234, 235; Gervase of Canterbury, *op. cit.*, vol. ii, p. 105; "Ann. de Margan," in *op. cit.*, pp. 29, 30; "Ann. Mon. de Wintonia," in *op. cit.*, p. 81; "Ann. Prioratus de Dunstaplia," in *op. cit.*, p. 32). Three chroniclers use *clerus* in a vague manner that might include the secular clergy ("Ann. de Theokesberia," in *Annales Monastici*,

one further event of possible significance in the development of a right of consent to royal taxation by the lower clergy took place. In 1215 the decree of 1179 protecting the clergy against the imposition by laymen of taxes on their spiritualities [1] was revised.[2] An addition which specifies that one who has incurred ecclesiastical censure for placing a tax on the clergy without their consent does not obtain release from the censure when his term of office ends indicates that the new legislation, like the old, was directed primarily against Italian communes. It contemplates offices held for shorter terms than life.[3] The principal amendment was to the effect that the pope should be consulted before the bishop with his clergy should give voluntary aid to consuls and rectors of cities or to others, even if they should see the necessity or the utility of such a grant.

The revised canon not only preserves the obscurities of the original, but it also creates new ones. It leaves in doubt whether the bishop and clergy must or merely ought to consult the pope.[4] If consultation was imperative, it is still questionable whether the pope could command or merely advise what was to be done.[5] English practice

vol. i, p. 59; "Ann. Mon. de Waverleia," in *op. cit.*, pp. 264, 265; *Hist. et Cart. S. Petri Gloucestriae*, vol. i, p. 24). The property of some churches was confiscated as the result of conditions growing out of the interdict and excommunication.

[1] Above, p. 66.

[2] *Corpus Iuris Canonici*, Decretal. Gregor. ix, lib. iii, tit. xlix, c. vii.

[3] Powicke, however, interprets the amendment to mean that "ecclesiastical penalties and disabilities arising out of excommunication and other action endured beyond the lifetime of the offending princes, unless their successors repudiated their action within a month of succession" (*op. cit.*, p. 91).

[4] The subjunctive in the sentence, *Romanus Pontifex prius consulatur*, may be translated either way.

[5] For a variety of interpretations of the points raised above, see Gottlob, *op. cit.*, pp. 41, 42; Mack, *op. cit.*, pp. 21, 30–32; Le Bras, *op. cit.*, pp. 64–72; von Hefele, *op. cit.*, vol. v, p. 894; Powicke, *op. cit.*, p. 91; Thomassin, *L'ancienne et nouvelle Discipline de l'Eglise*, M. André, ed., vol. vi (Bar-le-Duc, 1866), p. 266; L. Tosti, *Storia di Bonifazio VIII e de' suoi Tempi* (2 vols., Milan, 1848), vol. i, pp. 248, 249; J. Haller, *Papsttum und Kirchenreform*, vol. i (Berlin, 1903), p. 41.

during the reign of Henry III indicates either that consultation was not compulsory in the case of royal taxes, or that the requirement was disregarded.[1]

The story of the taxes imposed upon the lower clergy by papal authority may be told more briefly. Lucius III was the first pope who may have called upon the lower clergy of England to contribute to the needs of the papal camera. In 1184 he requested an *auxilium* both from Henry II and *ab clericatu Angliae* for the defense of the patrimony of St. Peter against the Romans. The king, who received the petition, sent a messenger to England to consult the bishops. They met in the presence of Ralph Glanvill, the justiciar, and "by their common counsel notified the lord king that it could be turned into a custom to the detriment of the kingdom, if he should permit the nuncios of the lord pope to come into England to make a collection." They advised him to give an aid to the pope, saying "that it would be more tolerable and would please them better, that the lord king, if he should wish, should receive from them recompense for the aid which he should give to the lord pope."[2] The king accepted their advice,[3] and gave a large sum to the pope.[4] Roger of Hoveden, who borrows the main portion of his narrative from the *Gesta*, makes one important alteration. He says that *episcopi et clerus* were consulted and gave the advice.[5] The loose usage of *clericatus* and *clerus* by contemporary chroniclers renders obscure the two points of fundamental importance to the present inquiry.[6] Was the aid to be paid by the lower

[1] *Persecution and Liberty: Essays in Honor of George Lincoln Burr*, pp. 160, 161, 166.
[2] *Gesta Regis*, vol. i, p. 311.
[3] *Ibid.*
[4] Roger of Hoveden, *op. cit.*, vol. ii, p. 283.
[5] *Ibid.*
[6] For examples, see above, p. 73, n. 5, p. 74, n. 1, p. 83, n. 1.

clergy as well as the prelates, or only by the bishops and other prelates? Was the advice given by the bishops alone, by the bishops and other prelates, or by the bishops in consultation with other prelates and the lower clergy? The phraseology of the chroniclers provides no certain guidance among these possible interpretations. On the other hand, the account establishes a strong probability that it was customary to obtain the consent of some of the clergy who were to be taxed before a papal aid was levied.

Indeed, the papacy does not appear yet to have burdened the clergy with any taxes except voluntary subsidies.[1] The earliest of these which has come to my attention was the work of Urban II. In 1093 he asked the prelates of southern France to supply him with gifts to aid in the restoration of the liberty of the apostolic see, which was threatened by an antipope.[2] Alexander III (1159–81), as a result of his exile from Rome, experienced a chronic shortage of funds.[3] He consequently made it a common practice to request gifts from the clergy of various parts of Europe for the use of the church laboring under a schism.[4] As a rule he addressed only the prelates, though on one occasion he petitioned an archbishop to raise a specified sum from the churches of his diocese.[5] The only demand of the kind made upon the English clergy previous to 1184,

---

[1] The census paid by monasteries receiving the protection of St. Peter was compulsory once it was established, but it was due from comparatively few monasteries (W. E. Lunt, "Financial System of the Mediaeval Papacy in the Light of recent Literature," *Quarterly Journal of Economics*, vol. xxiii, 1909, pp. 275, 276).

[2] Migne, *op. cit.*, vol. cli, pp. 368, 369.

[3] Lunt, "Financial System of the Mediaeval Papacy in the Light of recent Literature," in *op. cit.*, p. 261.

[4] Migne, *op. cit.*, vol. cc, pp. 109, 405; vol. ccvii, p. 468; P. Jaffé, *Regesta Pontificum Romanorum* (2nd ed., 2 vols., Leipzig, 1885–88), no. 11814; Draco Normannicus, in *Chronicles of the Reigns of Stephen, Henry II and Richard*, vol. ii, p. 740.

[5] Migne, *op. cit.*, vol. cc, pp. 405, 406.

so far as I have discovered, occurred in 1173. It was confined to prelates and did not affect the lower clergy.[1] All of these subsidies were analogous to the gracious aids of feudal lords. Exceptional financial needs were alleged by the pope, and his letters took the exhortatory and not the mandatory form.

This tradition of the voluntary character of papal aids was broken by Clement III. On February 10, 1188 he ordered the archbishop of Canterbury and his suffragans to employ the papal and episcopal authority to force the clerks under their jurisdiction to aid the Holy Land from their goods.[2] He further instructed each bishop to appoint a committee of clerks to collect and disburse the money. Since no rate or amount of taxation was specified, the contribution partook more of the nature of compulsory alms than of a tax. The use of the mandatory power to compel monetary payments from the clergy was, however, an innovation of fundamental importance.

The extension of the principle to taxation pure and simple was the work of Innocent III. On December 27, 1199 he issued an encyclical mandate commanding prelates and their subject clergy to pay to the bishops a fortieth *omnium ecclesiasticorum reddituum et proventuum suorum* in aid of the Holy Land.[3] The mandate was given force by the threat of divine judgment for disobedience

---

[1] Ralph of Diceto, who is our only informant, says that a papal nuncio collected much money from prelates, but he does not specify the nature of the levy. Since the proceeds were "to be converted to the use of the church laboring in a schism," it is a reasonably safe assumption that the aid was of the same voluntary character as the others raised for that purpose (vol. i, pp. 378, 379). F. Makower calls it a voluntary subsidy, without explanation of his reasons (*The Constitutional History and the Constitution of the Church of England*, London, 1895, p. 27, n. 58).

[2] Giraldus Cambrensis, *op. cit.*, vol. viii, pp. 236–239. The same bull was addressed to the episcopate of other provinces (J. von Pflugk-Harttung, *Acta Pontificum Romanorum inedita*, 3 vols., Tübingen, 1881–86, vol. iii, p. 417).

[3] Several orders were allowed to pay a fiftieth instead of a fortieth.

and the relaxation of a quarter of enjoined penance for its honest fulfilment.[1] If the strength of this first mandate was somewhat impaired by the lack of mundane penalties for its violation,[2] the deficiency was easily remedied. In 1215, with the approval of the fourth council of the Lateran, Innocent III decreed "that all clerks, subjects as well as prelates, should give in aid of the Holy Land a twentieth part of ecclesiastical revenues for three years" under penalty of excommunication.[3] The compulsory character of the papal taxation of the clergy was thus rendered complete.

The period from 1166 to 1216 marked decisive turning-points with regard to consent to taxation by the lower clergy of England. Taxes imposed by the papacy ceased to be voluntary and became mandatory. After 1216 the lower clergy rarely received an opportunity to voice assent or dissent to papal taxes.[4] Taxes levied by royal authority followed another course. Henry II, unless he took action of which we have no record, consulted only the prelates in attendance at the great council about the imposition of the early taxes which he collected from the income and chattels of the lower clergy. He may have asked the consent of the lower clergy to the Saladin tithe. Richard, when he taxed the spiritualities of the lower clergy for his ransom, may have done likewise. John sought the consent of the lower clergy probably in 1202 and certainly in 1207. During the reign of Henry III the practice followed by John was maintained.[5]

---

[1] Copies of the letter (Roger of Hoveden, *op. cit.*, vol. iv, pp. 108–112; Ralph of Coggeshall, *op. cit.*, pp. 113–116; Migne, *op. cit.*, vol. ccxiv, pp. 828–832).

[2] Lunt, *Valuation of Norwich*, pp. 10–12.

[3] Hardouin, *Acta Conciliorum*, vol. vi (Paris, 1714), pp. 71–78. The collection did not begin until 1217 (Lunt, *Valuation of Norwich*, pp. 13–18).

[4] *Persecution and Liberty: Essays in Honor of George Lincoln Burr*, pp. 117–169.   [5] *Ibid.*

THE FIRST BENEVOLENCE

H. L. GRAY

"THE First Benyvolence" is the marginal caption of the brief account given by perhaps the best contemporary London chronicle, Vitellius A XVI, of the mayoralty year November 1, 1474–November 1, 1475. The text runs as follows:

In this yere the kyng called before hym the Mayr and severally the Aldermen and by fair meanes cawsid theym to gyve hym a certayn money toward his viage in to Fraunce; and the Mayr gave hym xxx^{ti} li and some of thaldermen xx markes and the least x li. And so in like wyse he sent for all the thryfty Comoners of the Cite, whiche for the most party graunted the wages of half a man for a yere after vi d. by the day, which is iiii li. xi s. iii d. And after this he went and sent abowte all the land, whereby he Raysed moche good; and this was called a Benyvolence. And this yere, the iiiith day of July, the kyng Rood thrugh the Cite toward the See side and so to Caleys and so in to Fraunce.[1]

Other chroniclers do little more than embroider this account. Fabyan, who seems to have drawn from the same source, expressed himself with only verbal differences.[2] Later chroniclers introduced diverting incidents. Best known is the "prety conceyt" related by Hall to show the "humilite of a kyng but more the fantasie of a woman." When a London widow, "muche aboundynge in substance and no lesse growen in yeres," gave twice as much as had been expected of her and was thereat "lovingly kyst" by the royal lips, she promptly added to the twenty pounds twenty pounds more.[3]

---

[1] C. L. Kingsford, *Chronicles of London* (Oxford, 1905), p. 186.

[2] *Ibid.*, p. xvii; R. Fabyan, *The New Chronicles of England and France*, H. Ellis, ed. (London, 1818), p. 664.

[3] [E. Hall], *The Union of the Two Noble and Illustre Famelies of Lancastre and York* (edition of 1548, London, 1809), p. 308.

Certain versions of the collection of the benevolence, however, let us see that all gifts were not entirely spontaneous. Hall relates that some contributors were moved "with shame, some with feare."[1] The continuator of the Croyland chronicle is sarcastic about this "nova et inaudita impositio muneris ut per benevolentiam quilibet daret id quod vellet, immo verius quod nollet."[2] While the benevolence was being collected and, as we shall see, other and heavier taxes were also being harvested, Margaret Paston wrote: "The Kyng goth so nere us in this cuntre [county] both to poorer and to ryche that I wote not how we shall lyff but yff the world amend."[3] The most detailed account of Edward's methods, however, is that of an Italian visitor, who in a letter of March 17, 1475 sketched them as follows:

The last four months [the king] has been very active and has discovered an excellent device to raise money. He has plucked out the feathers of his magpies without making them cry out. This autumn [he] went into the country from place to place and took information of how much each place could pay. He sent for them all, one by one, and told them that he wished to cross to conquer France and deluded them with other words. Finally, he has so contrived that he obtained money from everyone who had the value of 40 l. sterling and upwards. . . . From what I have heard some say, the king adopted this method. When anyone went before him, he gave him a welcome as if he had known him always. After some time he asked him what he could pay of his free will towards this expedition. If the man offered something proper he had his notary ready, who took down the name and the amount. If the king thought otherwise he told him, Such a one, who is poorer than you, has paid so much; you who are richer can easily pay more. And thus by fair words he brought him up to the mark; and in this way it is argued that he has extracted a very large amount of money.[4]

---

[1] Ibid.

[2] Historiae Croylandensis Continuatio, W. Fulman, ed., Rerum Anglicarum Scriptores (Oxford, 1684), pp. 451–593, p. 558.

[3] The Paston Letters, J. Gairdner, ed. (6 vols., London, 1904), vol. v, p. 233, May 23, 1475. Cf. below, p. 107.

[4] Calendar of State Papers . . . in the Archives . . . of Milan, A. B. Hinds, ed. (London, 1912), vol. i, p. 193, letter of Battesta Oldovini de Brugnato to Antonio de Bracellis.

It thus appears that behind the veil of genial persuasion
there was the somewhat stern countenance of one who
smiled or kissed only when offers were in proportion to the
substance of the contributor.

The Milanese letter notes the weeks during which the
benevolence was solicited and the holders of property who
were expected to contribute. Four months before mid-
March would carry us to November, 1474; and everyone
who had movables worth £40 or more was approached.
On both points we get confirmation from the Coventry
Leet Book. In this was transcribed a commission of December 21, 1474 to the mayor and eight other citizens of
Coventry, explaining at length the king's purpose to invade France and directing that well-disposed citizens who
had not already in the king's presence "shewed largely
unto us thair benivolence in this behalf" and whose names
were appended be urged to do so. Since the recent parliamentary grant could be used only for archers' wages, the
commission explained, other charges remained to be met,
such as wages of "men of armes, ordinances, artillarie,
shippes, vitall, carriage, [and] redy tresoure of money for
calueltees that necessarily will fall." Whatever contributions might be promised were to be recorded in sealed
"billes" which in turn were to be forwarded to the king
and were to remain with him, not being "delivered unto
the eschequier nor to any other Courte of Record." The
commissioners were to move the people so that February 1
should be the day of payment for the first half "of their
seid benivolences." Soon after that date the king would
pay "to every man reteigned in his armie a grete part of his
wages for the yere." May 1 should be the last day of payment for the other half, since at about that time he intended "to make his monsters." Three days after these
instructions had issued under the privy seal at Coventry,

other instructions were given under the signet, also at
Coventry, to the mayor and "Shirreffes" of the city. The
officials were directed to warn all citizens "being of the
lyvelode of x li by yere and above" and all thought to be
"of the haveur of c li. and above in movable goodes and
otherwise" to appear before the king the next Monday to
"understande our plesir." On Monday the names of men
answering to either qualification were to be certified in
writing "as for the very value of their said lyvelodes and
goodes."[1] These Coventry instructions assure us that the
king was in the city in person at the end of December,
1474, summoning before him citizens who were to be exhorted to contribute "benevolences" between February 1
and May 1, 1475. They reveal that the city authorities
were requested to supply official lists of prosperous citizens
whose wealth could be expressed either in incomes of £10 or
more or in movables worth £100 or upwards. While the
latter figure is greater than the £40 of the Milanese letter,
which says nothing about incomes, it may be that the
writer of the letter, confining himself to a single criterion
of wealth, was thinking of London, where the property
specification may have been different. What is clear, from
both accounts, is that an extraordinary income and property tax called by the new name of benevolence was exacted from men of substance between November, 1474 and
March, 1475 with some precision.

About this so-called first benevolence modern historians
tell us little more than can be learned from the chronicles,
the Milanese letter, and the Coventry Leet Book.[2] So far
as they have looked they have discovered few unprinted

[1] The Coventry Leet Book, M. D. Harris, ed. (London, 1907–13), pp. 409–413.
[2] W. Stubbs, The Constitutional History of England (3 vols., 4th–6th eds.,
Oxford, 1903–06), vol. iii, pp. 219, 281, 283; J. H. Ramsey, Lancaster and York
(2 vols., Oxford, 1892), vol. ii, pp. 402, 465; C. L. Schofield, The Life and Reign
of Edward the Fourth (2 vols., London, 1923), vol. ii, pp. 104–106, 385.

documentary sources. Ramsey found on the teller's roll of the Easter term of 1475 payments made "collectoribus benevolentie domino Regi concesse" and on the Michaelmas receipt roll of 1478 fifteen sums amounting together to £50 paid "de denariis domino Regi erga viagium suum in regnum Francie anno xv° de benevolentia sua concessis."[1] These items make it clear that not long before or after Easter, 1475 collectors were active in collecting the benevolence and that three years later small outstanding arrears were paid into the exchequer. Apparently the exchequer received nothing in 1475.

To discover how the money was accounted for at the moment we should recall Professor Tout's studies. From the records of the thirteenth and fourteenth centuries he has shown that on many occasions, and especially when the king himself made war outside of England, the finances of the campaign were administered in the wardrobe and recorded there.[2] The convention was still observed in 1430 when the young Henry went to France.[3] After that year no English king went to fight on French soil until 1475; but, when Edward iv then resumed the tradition, the tradition of the records was also in part resumed. So far as money was got, not by parliamentary grant but by gift, the receipts were recorded by the keeper of the household.

[1] Ramsey, *op. cit.*, vol. ii, p. 402, n. 4. His conjecture that "the proceeds of the benevolences seem to have been paid in to the war account with those of the legal taxes" is somewhat misleading.

[2] T. F. Tout, *Chapters in the Administrative History of Mediaeval England* (5 vols., Manchester, 1920–30), vol. ii, pp. 131–145; vol. iii, pp. 224–225; vol. iv, pp. 97–112.

[3] Public Record Office, E 101, 408/9 52/31. Sir John Hotoft is described in these accounts as "custos garderobe hospicii domini Regis ac thesaurius guerrarum suarum." His "recepte" from September 30, 1429 to May 24, 1431 were £47,097 18s. 2½d., of which £33,325 7s. 10d. came from the exchequer and the remainder from Queen Katherine for her household and from miscellaneous payments and credits. His expenses for military purposes during the same period were upwards of £20,000, the injured manuscript not disclosing the precise amount.

The household accounts for 1475 are not readily accessible. Originally they must have comprised "books of particulars," i. e. a detailed record of income and expenditure, some of it day by day, tendered to the exchequer at the end of the year by the keeper and by the controller of the household.[1] These valuable documents seem not to be preserved. The exchequer, however, had long had the custom of digesting the particulars of various sorts of accounts submitted to it and of enrolling them in abbreviated form. Such enrolled accounts are always of value in that they give a summary view of the finances of a year or of several years, although they omit many details which we are often eager to know about. It happens that the enrolled household accounts of the later years of Edward IV are in part in so ruinous a condition that apparently no one has had hopes of salvaging much from them. In general there is no need to try, since usually the books of particulars survive. For the year 1475, however, an incitement to do so arises from the desirability of learning something about the financing of Edward's expedition to France. Fortune favors us rather grudgingly. On the injured membranes which do record the digest of the account we can decipher the information on the following pages.

The marginal caption, the introduction, and the conclusion, it will be seen, survive intact. All note that the official designation of the money received was a "benevolencia." The second and the following items disclose that the money was paid in by several receivers, each answering for one or two counties (or for one of the three parts of Lincolnshire), the grouping of counties being much like that which prevailed in the naming of sheriffs. Both introduction and conclusion indicate that the total proceeds of the benevolence were £21,656 8s. 3d.

[1] Cf. below, p. 96–97.

RECEPTE BENEVOLENCIE DICTO REGI PER DIVERSOS SUBDITOS SUOS
INFRA REGNUM ANGLIE CONCESSE.[1]

Et de xxi^m dclvi *lis.* viii *s.* iii *d.* per ipsum receptis de diversis personis
subscriptis, Receptoribus benevolencie . . . regni Anglie concesse, vide-
licet,

	£	s.	d.
de Ricardo Jeny, Receptore benevolencie dicto domino Regi concesse per diversos . . . dicti domini Regis et guerrarum suarum	5946	16	7
de Henrico Marland et Jo . . . in com. Midd. concesse	689	2	5½
de Ricardo Haute, Armigero, Receptore benevolencie . . .	918	15	8
de Reginaldo Rokez . . .	..	13	4
de Willelmo Brent . . .	..	..	..
. . . Skynner et Waltero Forde . . .	..	..	..
de Roberto Berdesey et Roberto Skein . . . in hundredis de Kyngeston . . .	7	10	2
de Johanne Penley, Johanne Forstere et Johanne Whitebrede . . . in com. Norff. et Suff. concesse	2993	4	10
de Thoma Fowler . . . in com. Bedd. et Buk. concesse	320	8	2
de Guidone Wolston . . . in com. Northt. concesse, ad duas vices, viz., una vice £353 3s., alia vice £9 2s. 6d.	[362	5	6]
de Johanne Frysley . . . in com. Leyc. . . . una vice £141 12s. 6d., alia vice . . . 7½d.	..	..	..
de Ricardo Forestere, Receptore benevolencie eidem domino Regi per diversos subditos suos de Kesteven in com. Linc. concesse	..	..	8
de Hugone Moresby, Receptore [etc.] de Holand in com. Linc. . . . una vice, xxiii die Maii anno xv, £72 2s., alia vice, xxvii die Junii eodem anno, £231 9s. 1d.	[303	11	1]

[1] P.R.O., Enrolled Household Accts., E 361/7.

The text, except the names of the counties, is here extended, and the amounts are given in Arabic rather than Roman numerals. The omissions are for the most part those of the injured manuscript. The name of each receiver was undoubtedly followed by a phrase like that used for Kesteven.

	£.	s.	d.
de Nicholao Leven . . . de Lyndesey in com. Linc. concesse.	659	17	9
. . . in com. Nots. et Derby concesse ad vices, una vice, xxvi die Maii, . . . 10½d., alia vice, xxix die Dec. eodem anno, £70 8s. 4d.	. .	. .	. .
de Willelmo Wylkez . . . in com. Stafford concesse	240	0	0
de Johanne Forster . . . concesse	541	6	4
de Thoma Copote et Roberto Hagurston . . . et Berk. . . . una vice, xxiv Maie anno xv, £333 6s. 8d., alia vice [injured] 8d., alia vice, xxxi Maie anno xv, £50	. .	. .	. .
de Willelmo Collyng . . . in com. Wiltes. . . . una vice, xxx Maii . . . [alia vice] £16 8s. 6d.	. .	. .	. .
de Johanne Yong . . .	. .	. .	. .
de Henrico Boteler . . .	. .	. .	. .
. . . . . . in com. Glouc . . .	. .	. .	. .
. . . . . . in villa Bristoll concesse	800	0	0
de Egidio Dawbe . . . in com. Somer. et Dors. concesse	1323	15	7
. . . . . . in com. Devon. concesse	356	13	4
. . . . . . in com. Cornub. "	145	5	0
. . . . . . per diversos subditos suos de Scaccario suo et Recepta eiusdem Scaccarii concesse	45	10	0
. . . . . . per diversos subditos suos in eadem ville concesse	133	5	0
. . . . . . sicut cont[inentur] in predictis duobus primis libris ipsorum Custodis et Contrarotularii de particulis			

Summa   Totalis Receptarum benevolencie xxi^m dclvi *li.* viii *s.* iii *d.*

The ruinous condition of the membranes deprives us of certain information. In 11 instances — and this is most disturbing — the amounts paid in by the receivers are missing. In 2 of the 11 there is record of what were probably the 3 largest installments.[1] In contrast, the amounts

[1] In the case of Leics. and of Oxon. and Berks. Wholly or largely missing are the contributions of Kesteven, Notts. and Derby., Wilts., Glos., and five unnamed counties or pairs of counties.

paid in by 15 receivers are preserved. Along with the 3 installments from the counties the totals of which are incomplete and with £178 15s. 10d. from officials of the
exchequer and others at Westminster the assignable contributions amount to £16,304 18s., or to three-fourths of
the entire benevolence. Certain of these attributions, however, have to remain hypothetical, for it happens that 3
recorded contributions are without the names of the contributing counties. One of these names can be supplied without hesitation. It is that of the city of London. No other
county or counties would so appropriately have headed
the list; the entry is followed by that of Middlesex; the
receiver was the cofferer of the household, who was in close
touch with London;[1] the contribution is so much greater
than the combined one of 2 wealthy counties like Norfolk and Suffolk that no 2 other unnamed counties would
have made it. Another contribution can be assigned with
considerable probability to Essex and Hertfordshire. It is
the third one, amounting to £918 15s. 8d. The receiver in
this instance was Richard Haute, a man whose name appears often in the letters patent of 1472–76 and who was
always associated with Essex.[2] It is likely that Hertfordshire was grouped with Essex, since the list adopts the
grouping usual in the appointment of sheriffs and there is
no separate entry for Hertfordshire. The place of the entry in the list, following Middlesex, points to these 2
counties. The third large contribution for which the name
of the contributing county or counties is missing amounted
to £541 6s. 4d. Its place in the list is between Notting-

[1] P.R.O., E 101, 412/5, 6: household accounts for October 31, 13 Edw. IV to
September 30ff. and for September 30, 16 Edw. IV to September 30, 18 Edw. IV.

[2] In 1472 Haute was member of a commission of array for Essex; in 1474,
member of a commission to inquire into smuggling there; finally and most con-
vincingly, member of each of the seven commissions of the peace appointed for
Essex from July, 1472 to November, 1476 (*Calendar of Patent Rolls, 1467–1477*,
pp. 351, 490, 614).

hamshire, Derbyshire, and Staffordshire on the one hand
and Oxfordshire, Berkshire, and Wiltshire on the other.
The scribe seems to have been passing from north to south.
Warwickshire could appropriately have been noted at this
point, and the inclusion of Coventry would explain the
somewhat large contribution. But Warwickshire must
have been the county, the name and contribution of which
are missing but the receiver for which was Henry Boteler.
Several entries on the patent rolls refer him to this county.[1]
The receiver of the £541 6s. 4d., however, was John Forster. This name appears several times on the patent rolls
but perhaps not always designating the same man. Most
often Forster was active in the southeastern counties.[2]
From such of them as he was associated with we have the
contributions in the case of Middlesex, Bedfordshire, and
probably Essex and Hertfordshire. There remain Cambridgeshire and Huntingdonshire. Since these 2 do not
appear elsewhere in the list, since they were under the
same sheriff, and since the gift is proportionate to what
was given by other counties of the southeast, we may assume with considerable propriety that the contribution
should be attributed to them.

If these 3 attributions — to London, to Essex and Hertfordshire, to Cambridgeshire and Huntingdonshire — be
accepted, we have names attached to 14 single or joint
contributions.[3] Arranged geographically, the known con-

---

[1] *Ibid.*, pp. 403, 405, 490, 606, 639.

[2] In 1470 he was member of a commission of array for Huntingdonshire, and
in 1472 of similar commissions for Beds., Midds., Hunts., and Herts. In 1473
he was one of the commissioners directed to inquire into items which sheriffs were
neglecting in their returns in Cambs., Hunts., Herts. and Essex. In 1474 he
was commissioner along with others to inquire into the lands held by the late
Earl of Worcester in Hunts. From 1471 to 1475 he was six times commissioner
of the peace for Herts. and Hunts. (*ibid.*, pp. 199, 348–350, 406–407, 462, 617).

[3] Apart from the small contributions of the hundreds of Kingston, the officials of the exchequer, and certain men of Westminster.

tributors were: in the southeast, London, Middlesex, Essex and Hertfordshire, Norfolk and Suffolk, Cambridgeshire and Huntingdonshire; in the east and midlands, Holland, Lyndsey, Bedfordshire and Buckinghamshire, Northamptonshire, and Staffordshire; in the south and southwest, Somerset and Dorset, Devon, Cornwall, and the town of Bristol. Contributors, the amounts of whose gifts remain unknown, were, in the southeast, Kent, Sussex, and Surrey; in the east and midlands, Kesteven, Shropshire, Worcestershire, Warwickshire, and in part Leicestershire, Oxfordshire and Berkshire, Nottinghamshire and Derbyshire; in the south and southwest, Hampshire, Wiltshire, Gloucestershire, and Herefordshire. It is somewhat surprising that there is no place in the list for the 3 ridings of Yorkshire, for Lancashire, or for the counties farther north. Since none of the receivers seem to have been associated with any of these counties, it is likely that the north contributed nothing to the benevolence.

The impression given by a geographical survey of the contributions is that the counties of the southeast were by far the most liberal. Outstanding was the gift of the city of London, amounting to nearly 28 per cent of the total collected. Middlesex, Essex and Hertfordshire, Cambridgeshire and Huntingdonshire gave 10 per cent more of it; Norfolk and Suffolk another 14 per cent; and it is not unlikely that the gifts of Kent, Surrey, and Sussex constituted another 8 per cent. If so, this group of counties gave 60 per cent of the total benevolence. Nor was the southwest illiberal. The £800 given by Bristol was the urban contribution second to that of London, while Somerset and Dorset were among the largest county contributors. The gifts of the three along with those of Devon and Cornwall amounted to 13 per cent of all donations. If the unknown contributions of Hampshire, Wiltshire, Gloucestershire, and Herefordshire could be added, the gifts of the south-western counties probably would not fall short of 20 per cent of the total benevolence. This leaves relatively little to be attributed to the midland counties. The known gifts from Bedfordshire and Buckinghamshire, Northampton-shire, Holland, Lyndsey, and Staffordshire were only 9 per cent of the total; and the incomplete returns from Leices-tershire, Oxfordshire and Berkshire, Nottinghamshire and Derbyshire add but 2½ per cent more. It is unlikely that the further returns from the five last named counties (which must have been small) and the contributions of Kesteven, Shropshire, Warwickshire, and Worcestershire brought the total midland share in the benevolence to more than 20 per cent.

These regional contributions suggest that the incidence of the new tax differed from that of the fifteenth and tenth, the form usually assumed by extraordinary taxation throughout the fourteenth and fifteenth centuries. This, of course, is the implication of the documents of the Coven-try Leet Book and of the account of the Italian visitor. Both reveal the benevolence as virtually a tax on incomes of £10 and upwards or on movables worth £40 and more — or at least £100 and more. The fifteenth and tenth, however, was a tax on movables worth 5s. and upwards. In practice it fell largely upon livestock and grain, and in towns upon household effects and merchandise as well. It had been definitely apportioned in 1334, and since then, as between township and township, had been little changed.[1] Not only was it collected so as to bear somewhat heavily upon classes which had relatively little property, but its antiquated ratings took slight account of the economic

---

[1] J. F. Willard, "Sidelights upon the Assessment and Collection of Mediaeval Subsidies," *Transactions of the Royal Historical Society*, 3rd ser., vol. vii (1913), p. 167; "Surrey Taxation Returns," *Surrey Record Society*, no. xviii (London, 1922); E. Powell, *A Suffolk Hundred in the Year 1283* (Cambridge, 1910).

changes of one hundred and forty years. Dissatisfaction with it, or at least a desire to supplement it, was revealed by the resort to a poll tax in 1381 and to certain income taxes of the fifteenth century. In 1404, 1411, 1428, 1435, 1450, and 1472, incomes from lands, tenements, rents, and annuities were subjected to taxation, the rate and incidence varying on each occasion.[1] Since the income tax of 1472, like the benevolence of 1475, was contributed to support the expedition to France, and since two fifteenths and tenths were imposed for the same purpose, a brief account of the financial measures of 1472–75 is needed to disclose the relation of the new forms of taxation to the old. We shall find record of still another new device.

When Edward IV proposed to parliament in 1472 that he recover his lands in France, parliament offered to this end the maintenance of 13,000 archers for a year. Its first contribution in support of them was the income tax mentioned above. In an indenture of November 30 this was defined as "the x part of the value of a yere oonly of the issues and profittes of all maner Londes and Tenementes, Rentes, Fees, Annuyteez, Offices, Corrodies and Pencions." Exemption was granted only to lords of parliament and to spiritual persons holding lands "amortysed to eny Chirche or other place spirituell." The assessment was to be made by commissioners armed with powers of inquiry and with authority to name collectors. The proceeds were to be put in local safe-keeping until with the assent of parliament they might be withdrawn to pay the army as it set out. Payment was due at the Purification, 1473.[2] Three months after the latter date the Commons in an indenture of April 8 declared that, since returns were not

---

[1] *Rotuli Parliamentorum* (6 vols. [London, 1783]), vol. iii, pp. 546, 648; vol. iv, pp. 318, 486; vol. v, p. 172; vol. vi, pp. 4–8. I hope to describe these taxes elsewhere.   [2] *Ibid.*

in from certain shires, they had as yet no knowledge of "what the seid x[th] part amounteth unto." Explaining also that it was necessary to provide further for the wages of the 13,000 archers, they now granted a fifteenth and tenth of the customary sort, excepting the £6,000 which since 1446 had been remitted. The proceeds, like those of the income tax, were to be held in safe-keeping until the proclamation of the muster of the army. The date of payment, June 24, was deferred by the king until Michaelmas,[1] but a later indenture discloses that the tax was not collected as planned.

This later indenture, drawn up in a sixth session of parliament on July 18, 1474, explained that the income tax of 1472 had, soon after it was due, yielded £31,410 14s. 1½d., but that returns from five northern counties and certain smaller areas were not in even yet. We also learn that the fifteenth and tenth of 1473 had not been collected. Since the authorization of it would become void and the £31,410 harvested from the income tax would invert to the contributors if the king did not set out for France by Michaelmas, 1474, two necessary steps were taken at once. The date before which the king must depart was extended to June 24, 1476, and the fifteenth and tenth was regranted, being now made payable at Martinmas, 1474.[2]

Even so, provision for the expedition remained inadequate. The £31,410 from the income tax and the newly regranted fifteenth and tenth would together produce, the Commons computed, £62,094 4¼d. But the cost of 13,000 archers for a year at 6d. a day would be £118,625. Since the northern counties had thus far contributed nothing,

---

[1] *Ibid.*, pp. 39–41.
[2] *Ibid.*, pp. 113–114. There had been no returns from Cheshire, Northumberland, Cumberland, Westmorland, the bishopric of Durham, the town of Newcastle, the city of Lincoln, the wapentake of Ewecrosse, Yorks., and the hundred of Wormelowe, Herefs.

an adjustment was made in accordance with which they
would furnish and pay 590 archers. In return they were to
be excused from contributing to the income tax of 1472,
to the fifteenth and tenth payable at Martinmas, and
to any further assessment which might be required. In
terms of money they were credited with a contribution of
£5,383 15s. There remained £51,147 4s. 7¾d. still to be
found by the counties and towns which had already paid
the income tax and were about to pay a fifteenth and
tenth.[1] It was a large sum, and to raise it the Commons
devised a new method of assessment. This was the second
deviation from reliance upon a fifteenth and tenth made
by this parliament of many sessions.

This new method was a combination of the one normally
used in levying a fifteenth and tenth, of the one applied in
collecting the income tax of 1472 and of one not hitherto
elaborated. The money was

to be levied and perceyved severally [1] of the Goodes and Catalles ...
usuelly to the payment of xv[es] and x[es] chargeable ... and [2] of all
Londes, Tenementes, Annuytees, Corrodies, Rentes, Pensions and other ·
Possessions [defined as in 1472] ... the forsaid Goodes and Catailles ...
first to be taxed and charged afore any Londes or other Possessions
aforesaid, [3] the Goodes and Catalles of such persones not havyying any
or but litell Lond or other frehold nor to xv[e] and x[e] afore tyme but litell
or not charged, in ease and relyef of other persones to the said x[th] part
[the income tax] and other charges afore tyme gretly charged, specially
at this tyme [to] be chargeable and charged.[2]

The new tax was thus to fall most heavily upon the last
group, i. e. upon men who, having little land, had contributed only slightly to the income tax of 1472 and whose
movables were wont to yield little or nothing to the fifteenth and tenth as usually assessed. Normal contributors
to the fifteenth and tenth were also to contribute now, but
relatively less than usual. Most lightly to be taxed were

---

[1] *Ibid.*, p. 115.   [2] *Ibid.*, pp. 115–116.

men who had paid the income tax of 1472. The new group which emerges as subject to taxation in 1474 were men possessed of movable property acquired by themselves or their ancestors since 1334 but possessed of little land.

As it happened, the new tax of 1474 was never collected in accordance with the plan proposed. Half of it as granted was to have been payable on June 24, 1475, the other half at Martinmas following. When, however, parliament met in its seventh session on January 23, 1475, it was clear that the king would journey to France in the coming summer. Preparations were well under way.[1] Before Easter indentures could be signed with the captains and some £17,696 paid them as wages for themselves and their men for the first quarter.[2] The money must have come from the two parliamentary contributions already made to the expedition, the income tax of 1472 and the fifteenth and tenth payable at Martinmas last. On November 28 receivers had been appointed to take over the proceeds of the former;[3] and, although there had been a tendency during the intervening two years to dissipate the sums in safe-keeping, so that parliament had to act to recover them, they seem to have been largely paid over. As a new indenture described the receipts, "the which forseid xth part [the income tax] and [the] xv^e and x^e, at their severall daies paiable, been in substaunce levied and paied and part thereof to your Highnes delyvered."[4]

---

[1] *Cal. Pat. Rolls*, 1467–1477, pp. 474, 479, 492, 494–496.

[2] *Foedera* . . . T. Rymer, ed. (London, 1704–35), vol. xi, pp. 844–848. Since Rymer attributes the payments to "Exit. Annis 14 E. 4, Pen. Cler. Pell," he must have found them on the Michaelmas teller's roll.

[3] *Cal. Pat. Rolls, 1467–1477*, p. 496.

[4] *Rot. Parl.*, vol. vi, pp. 121, 151. The Michaelmas receipt roll of 14 Edw. IV (E 401/919) seems to show no receipts from a fifteenth and tenth at Martinmas, but does show receipts from a clerical tenth. If Edward did not collect the fifteenth and tenth then due, there was the more reason for requesting a benevolence.

As a result of this situation, a new indenture, probably drawn on March 14, 1475, concerned itself primarily with the £51,147 4s. 7¾d. which in the preceding summer the Commons had proposed to raise in the novel manner described above. Confronted now with the busy preparations for war and the immediate need for ready money, they confessed that there was no time in which to work out the new plan. "The fourme of the Levie," the new indenture declared, "is so diffuse and laborious that by likelihode the payment of the half of the same somme, paiable [on June 24] nowe next to come, cowed not by that tyme be convenyently levied and reared accordyng to the Graunte therof." The chancellor, moreover, on behalf of the king explained that the half was needed even before June 24. Whereat the Commons "lovyngly ponderyng and weiyng . . . sette a rather and a ner day" for its payment. "And for asmoch as wee remembre," they continued, "that the moost easy, redy and prone payment of any charge to be born within this Reame by the Commens of the same is by the Graunte of xv^es and x^es, the Levie whereof amongs your people is so usuell, although it be to theym full chargeable, that noon other fourme of levie resembleth therunto," the Commons commuted both halves of the £51,147 for a fifteenth and tenth to be paid "in the xvme of Ester nowe next comyng" and for three-fourths of a fifteenth and tenth payable at Martinmas.[1] In this way the carefully devised assessment of the preceding summer came to naught. Haste prevented the elaboration of the plan, and the Commons with regret fell back upon the customary tax, although it bore unfairly upon them — "although it be to theym full chargeable."

---

[1] *Ibid.*, pp. 151–152. The Easter receipt roll of 15 Edw. iv seems to show no receipts from a fifteenth and tenth. This matter, as well as the failure of the preceding receipt roll to record returns from a fifteenth and tenth, needs further investigation.

Despite the fact that the plan of the Commons for raising £51,147 remained unexecuted, it is not unlikely that it
influenced the king to resort to benevolences. The benevolences, to be sure, were supplementary to the grants made
for the archers, as Edward pointed out at Coventry. But,
since supplementary support likewise had to come from the
king's subjects, a wise administrator would arrange that
men not otherwise heavily taxed should contribute it. The
idea of reaching such persons had been the animating one
of the new tax of 1474. Actually the king adopted this idea
before the new tax fell due and applied it in his own way.
We have seen that he began his solicitations in November,
1474, and requested that gifts made him should be paid
one-half on February 1 next, one-half on May 1. The
household account reveals that the receivers paid over
much of what they collected in May.[1] When, therefore,
the Commons in March surveyed the financial situation,
this was not what they had in the preceding June expected
that it would be. The king had meanwhile solicited benevolences from a great number of his subjects, each of
whom enjoyed an income of £10 or more or possessed
movables to the value of £40 or upwards. Since he had employed a method which the Commons themselves had in
principle devised, they could the more readily abandon it
and fall back upon a fifteenth and tenth. While, therefore,
the fifteenth and tenth of November, 1474, and the quickly
following one of April, 1475, were taxes of the unreformed
sort, the benevolence paid almost concurrently with them
was a contribution two-thirds as great as either and came
from persons who might otherwise have contributed little to
the heavy taxation of the year. The idea of reaching them
had been formulated by the Commons before the king acted.

[1] Of the recorded dates of payment, five were in May, one in June, and one in
the following December. See above, pp. 96–97.

If the proposed but unlevied tax of 1474 professedly departed from the normal fifteenth and tenth by assessing incomes and movables which the latter did not reach, can we discover in what counties and towns such incomes and movables were particularly to be found? For, if the localities accord with those which especially paid the benevolence, we shall have found the home of the newer fortunes of the preceding century. Perhaps we shall then be able to suggest the origin of some of these fortunes.

The apportionment of the proposed tax of 1474 among the several counties and towns is noted in the indenture recorded on the parliament roll. The corresponding apportionment of the customary fifteenth and tenth, which at this time yielded some £31,000, may be got from the accounts of the collectors.[1] In making a comparison of the two we perceive at once that £51,147 is a sum equivalent to about one whole fifteenth and tenth and two-thirds of another for all counties except those of the north.[2] Hence, for purposes of comparison there should be placed, alongside the normal assessment of a county or town, three-fifths of the assessment proposed in 1474 for the same area. If this is done, significant divergences between the assessments disclose themselves. Certain counties and towns would have contributed at the new rating only from 75 per cent to 86 per cent of what they contributed to a fifteenth and tenth. Such were Norfolk, Huntingdonshire, Hamp-

---

[1] The sums due from the counties and towns had not been changed since 1334. In 1446 a remission of £6,000 was deducted *pro rata* (*Rot. Parl.*, vol. v, p. 69), leaving a total of a little more than £31,000 to be collected. The figures here used are those of the assessment of 1446 as recorded for the half-fifteenth and half-tenth due at Martinmas following (P.R.O., E 159/223; K. R. Memoranda Roll, 25 Henry VI).

[2] See above, p. 102, n. 3, for the counties excepted. The indenture of 1474 computes one-fifteenth and tenth for all counties and towns which had not compounded at £30,684.

shire, Wiltshire, Gloucestershire, Berkshire, Oxfordshire, Warwickshire, Rutland, the East Riding of Yorkshire, and the towns of Oxford and Shrewsbury. Others would have contributed from 86 per cent to 95 per cent as much — Cambridgeshire, Bedfordshire, Lyndsey, Northamptonshire, Nottinghamshire, Shropshire, Herefordshire, Dorset, and the towns of York and Bristol. In a few instances there would have been little change, the assessment being not more than 4 per cent below or 4 per cent above what was usual. Such was the case with Sussex, Holland, Buckinghamshire, Leicestershire, and Worcestershire. In other counties and towns, however, the new ratings compensated for any losses. Assessments were increased by from 5 per cent to 10 per cent in Kent, Surrey, Somerset, Cornwall, the North Riding of Yorkshire, and the town of Nottingham; by from 11 per cent to 25 per cent in Suffolk, Hertfordshire, Staffordshire, Derbyshire, and the cities of London and Salisbury; by 26 per cent to 50 per cent in Essex, Devon, the West Riding of Yorkshire, and the cities of Norwich and Coventry; finally by more than 50 per cent in Middlesex, the city of Worcester, and the borough of Southwark.

If we attempt to interpret these regional deviations from the established rating, we must remember that they may in a measure have been due to the assessment in the new tax of incomes from land as well as of hitherto untaxed movables. Since, however, the latter were to be taxed in preference to the former, we may perhaps conclude that increased ownership of movable property was primarily responsible for the divergences noted above. Increase in movable property, again, may in some instances have resulted from a development of agriculture. Certain regions may have come to have more livestock and grain than they had in 1334. Such may be the explanation of the higher rating of once backward areas like Staffordshire, Derby-shire, and the North Riding of Yorkshire. Intensified exploitation of the tin mines of Cornwall and Devon may explain in part the larger assessment of these counties. But in the case of other counties and of the towns another probable explanation is at hand. They were regions which had within a century undergone a pronounced industrial development.

In the latter half of the fourteenth century the woolen industry had forged ahead greatly, becoming the dominant one in England. Attendant upon its expansion was a shift-ing of the centers in which it was pursued. Certain towns, such as Oxford and York, declined, while others such as Norwich and Salisbury, prospered. In general there was a migration of woolen workers from larger towns to smaller ones and to large villages. In organization there took place a transition from the craft system to the so-called domestic system. New woolen-manufacturing areas appeared in the lower Cotswolds, especially in Somerset, in Suffolk and Essex, in Kent, and in the West Riding of Yorkshire.[1] All of these were now among the areas rated more highly to the tax of 1474 than they had been to fifteenths and tenths. Since there seems to be no reason for supposing that the in-come from land had increased in them when it had not, for example, in Norfolk or Northamptonshire, it is permissible to infer that the increased assessments reflected the in-creased industrial wealth of the counties in question. For the rating of Salisbury the explanation is similar, while in Norwich the worsted industry throve. Coventry had spe-cialized in the making of caps. London, in becoming the foremost port of the realm, had extended its prosperity to Southwark and to Middlesex. The treatment of Bristol,

---

[1] H. L. Gray, "The Production and Exportation of English Woolens in the Fourteenth Century," *Eng. Hist. Rev.*, vol. xxxix (1924), pp. 13-35.

however, is puzzling. There can be no doubt that the town had developed as a mercantile and industrial center during the preceding century, and its contribution to the benevolence of 1475 confirms this belief. Yet by the rating of 1474 it was to pay only 90 per cent of what it usually contributed to a lay tenth. Perhaps in some way it had secured favored treatment. Apart from this instance the new rating of towns and counties is largely what we should expect. It reflected to a considerable degree the economic changes which had taken place during a century.

What the regional assessment of the tax of 1474 reflected in a moderate degree, the benevolence of 1475 disclosed in a more pronounced manner. The king and his agents sought out the well-to-do in a rough and ready way, and their method was particularly applicable to the large towns and to industrial regions. Hence, London and Bristol became noteworthy contributors and Middlesex confessed to a prosperous suburban population. The contributions of most towns are not noted as such; but it is likely that the benevolence of Norfolk and Suffolk became a large one through the gifts of Norwich and the Suffolk cloth towns, and that of Somerset and Dorset a generous one through the gifts of the Cotswold cloth-making area. In Essex there was both a suburban population and thriving industrial towns and villages. Any precision in the relationship between large benevolences and areas of flourishing industry and trade should not be insisted upon. Possibly such relationship is more accurately indicated by the rating of 1474. But in so far as this rating and the returns for the benevolence agree in estimating the wealth of certain areas higher than the fifteenth and tenth had done, we may be assured that these areas were the ones which had prospered during the last century. That such prosperity was largely due to the development of the cloth industry is not improbable.

A final question remains. Was the benevolence a really new device in taxation, and was the one of 1475, as the chroniclers declare, the first benevolence? It has become clear that the idea of getting money from men little or not at all taxed to the fifteenth and tenth was not new. Six income taxes had already during the fifteenth century departed from the customary usage. In 1474 a comprehensive and presumably more equitable tax had been devised. To this the benevolence of 1475 owed certain of its features. In other respects also it had antecedents. Gifts made to the king to assist him in an emergency were not new phenomena. They were called *dona*, and with them are to be grouped a few *mutua*, or loans which were not repaid. In a brief paper the history of *dona* and of unpaid *mutua* in the fifteenth century cannot be told. But it may be pointed out that in 1461 Edward IV had profited by a *mutuum* of £11,000 which was not repaid, and in 1471 by a series of *dona* which altogether amounted to £18,964. On both occasions the contributions were made to meet the financial stringency which prevailed after the king's seizure of the throne and before a tax of the usual sort could be voted by parliament or convocation. Early in 1453 a like need of money had elicited a series of *dona*, all of them amounting to about £2,764, but some of them perhaps treated as loans demanding repayment. On rare occasions before this time, as in 1443 and 1449, a few gifts in money were made to the king. If we compare the *dona* and unpaid *mutua* earlier than 1475 with the benevolences of that year we find similarities and differences. Usually the former were relatively large and were contributed by a few persons — great ecclesiastics, titled laymen, or merchants. Yet in 1453 and in 1471 some came from unnamed people, described, for example, as the men of county Kent. In the latter we have precursors of the gifts of 1475.[1]

While, therefore, the emergency character of earlier *dona*, the non-repayment of them, sometimes the total income from them, and sometimes the humble givers of them are anticipatory of the benevolence of 1475, the latter none the less has other claims to be called the first of its kind. It was the first to be systematically solicited throughout a large part of the realm and to be contributed by large numbers of the king's subjects. It was the first to be collected by receivers appointed to that end and to be accounted for as a whole in a carefully drawn account. It was probably the first to be paid not into the exchequer but into the household. It was, above all, the first to exemplify, although in a somewhat impromptu manner, reform of an antiquated system of taxation. In this it supported the efforts of the Commons to supplement the fifteenth and tenth by an income tax on land and by a further tax on appropriately assessable movables. In eliciting contributions from fortunes which had arisen during the preceding century, probably largely through the development of industry and trade but hitherto little taxed, it made its best claim to novelty and to being "the first benyvolence."

[1] For our knowledge of *dona* and of unpaid *mutua* earlier than 1475 we are dependent upon the receipt rolls of the years mentioned above.

ENGLISH PUBLIC FINANCE AND THE NATIONAL STATE IN THE SIXTEENTH CENTURY

FREDERICK C. DIETZ

WHILE the extension of the scope of business over larger territorial areas which called the national state into being has been discussed in some detail, the technique of the establishment of centralized governments in place of feudal monarchies has been somewhat neglected. Fiscal history affords one avenue of approach to this problem. A study of public finance not only indicates the administrative measures actually adopted to enlarge the royal authority, but gives certain clues to the reasons for the resulting character of the new state organisms and for their failure to satisfy the sociological aims which certain of their ideological proponents had in mind.

In that forward thrust in the development of public administration in England which historians call the foundation of the national state, one of the characteristic qualities was the addition to the comparatively simple machinery of government of a more effective set of bureaus designed to secure real control at a distance from the capital. This development is particularly manifest in the realm of fiscal affairs, where the extension of royal authority through the centralized supervision of the Crown lands and the customs is indeed striking.

The most significant of the new departures was the appointment, in connection with newly acquired lands, of the general surveyors and the auditors of the land revenues, who rode around from estate to estate collecting the king's rents, examining the condition of the property, and issuing the requisite royal directions. It may be that these officials, whose introduction seems to have been planned by Richard III, provided the model for the still more important committee of high officials who, in Henry VII's reign, rode about the country in search of all those who were guilty of breaches of the peace, illegal entry, livery and maintenance, riots, abduction of wards, and other offenses which tended to disturb the country or to interfere with the fiscal rights of the Crown.

In connection with the customs the existence of an embryonic nonfeudal bureaucracy, dating from the period before the advent of Henry VII, intercepted the early introduction of a new system of general surveyors and auditors along the lines of the Tudor land offices. The centralization of authority in the customs was expressed by the enforced use of semi-national, and then national, valuations as a basis for the collection of rates of duties, by the Elizabethan integration of all ports outside London under the general surveyors of custom causes, and by the unified farms of the customs on a national basis under the Stuarts.

It is noteworthy that the ultimate audit control over the new royal officers was exercised in Henry VII's time by the king in person, and under his successors by committees with delegated royal powers. This development involved a purposeful neglect of the exchequer, where traditions and practices favored the sheriffs, bailiffs, and customers, with all their disintegrating localism. The exchequer system of elaborate parchment rolls, for instance, was not competent to provide that oversight from a distance which was a prerequisite of the new fiscal system. It was only after the king's money came into the collectors' hands that the exchequer checks were satisfactory. In the new scheme of things the minutiae of estate business behind the rents actually paid to the king were to be carefully watched. The introduction of easily handled paper account books in place of the parchment rolls, the use of Italian forms of bookkeeping, and the proper functioning of the itinerant inspectors would be easier in an entirely new organization. The Tudor fiscal committees were consequently developed into a series of revenue courts with separate treasuries attached, independent of the ancient course of the exchequer.

Royal commissions were used also to control many of the more important expenditures and disbursements, and such commissions continued to be used without formal institutionalization until after 1641. To assist the *ad hoc* commissioners, an office of the auditors of the prests [1] and foreign accounts appeared at a comparatively early period. When the new revenue courts, together with the office of the auditors of the prests, were finally amalgamated with the exchequer, their forms of procedure were retained within the resulting organization. Late in Elizabeth's reign the newer methods of audit were applied even to the customs, which had hitherto remained subject to the more ancient exchequer practice. As a result of such mergers and shifts, the exchequer itself became in most respects merely a Tudor commission functioning in behalf of the royal interest at the motivation of the king's will.

Even more suggestive than the study of typical Tudor administrative departments as revealing the processes attending the establishment of the national state is an investigation of the innovations in the functions of government. This process is somewhat obscured by the fact that

[1] Prests were advances of money to officials entrusted with its expenditure.

medieval traditions and institutions were, through changes of connotation and nuance, virtually transformed under the outward semblance of continued integrity. Much that was really new passed for what was in form old. Thus, from the time when Sir John Fortescue was chancellor to Edward IV, to that when the Earl of Middlesex was lord treasurer to James I, the practice of public, or rather royal, finance was conditioned by the traditional phrase that the king ordinarily must "live of his own." Every word in the phrase changed its meaning in the century and a half after the death of Edward IV. There were, of course, serious possibilities in the failure to recognize the new under cover of the old, and in critical times the medieval survivals might, and did, seriously hamper the Crown.

Of considerable significance in the persistence of remnants of medieval views, which was by no means confined to England, was the circumstance that the revolution of 1485 was only imperfectly realized. It is a truism that Henry VII founded the national monarchy in England as did Louis XI in France, and Ferdinand and Isabella in Spain. Yet it is equally important for the future that the first Tudor was unconscious of the cataclysmic quality of the movement which he initiated. Unaware of the high destiny of his house as the English builders of a new type of state, Henry VII stressed his rôle as the legitimate vehicle of the feudal kingship by the allegation of his headship of the house of Lancaster and of the analogous place of his queen in the house of York. Consequently he took over a good deal of the nomenclature of the feudal world and made it possible to carry over into the new order many precedents and traditions of the dead Plantagenet monarchy.

Antecedent to the actual development of the new national monarchy there were certain social and economic needs and desires which paved the way for its successful advent. Medieval rulers no longer adequately met the expanding requirements of English life. Sir John Fortescue, writing before 1485, envisaged a centralized monarchy, which should be powerful enough to put down the local tyrants, with their disorderly brawls and forced perversion of justice through the practice of livery and maintenance, administer justice equitably, and enforce peace and order everywhere throughout the land.

In the writings of the early-sixteenth-century publicists, such as Starkey, Forrest, Fish, and Brinklow, the demand for amplification of the government's functions is more highly elaborated. Old evils, already known in the fifteenth century, had become national in extent. The wrongs of enclosures and the low standards of social morality were apparent to these critics. Wealth was ill used, and the rich ate up the poor. Merchants exported necessities and imported only luxuries. The great enclosing lords made it impossible for the poor to live. The enhancing of rents and the increase of fines of leases caused the decay of the realm. The relations of the sexes left everything to be desired, and the conduct of priests, monks, and friars did not better current sexual evils.

The Church, having stressed regard for externals for too many centuries, had no real message for such troublous times. Her authority was so much decayed that she probably could not have enforced a new morality even if her leaders had seen the need for it. The only hope of salvation on a nationally extended scale lay in the king. The end of government was declared to be the promotion of the public good, and it was held that the functions of the state must be increased to set wrongs right.

> For chiefly your crown to this intent you wear
> Wrong to reform that equity may rule bear.

The king was to "perceive the commonwealth's noyance, and for the same to take ordynaunce." To this end all individuals and all institutions, including the Church itself, might be subordinated to the royal authority.

The climax of such views was reached in the notion of the organic state in which the king as head directed the activities — moral, religious, and economic — of all the members, who served him and owed all that they had to his protection and care. Such exalted views, frequently found even in the early seventeenth century, were of course little more than pious sighs for an ideal which had failed of realization.

The restoration of the golden age, which was merely the legalistically-minded sixteenth century's way of demanding positive social benefits at the hands of the king, was not unconsidered by the Tudors. Henry VII's legislative and administrative acts to suppress disorder, to expand industry and trade with royal aid, and to improve economic conditions are well known. His son's assumption of supreme control over the English church was stimulated in part by the same purpose, and the step was welcomed by contemporaries as a necessary preliminary to the preaching of a new social gospel. There was nothing, so far as the Tudor attitude went, which prevented the introduction of a modern type of all-controlling paternalistic state during the sixteenth century.

Nevertheless the national state founded by the Tudors and carried on by the Stuarts was not of this variety. In the actual work of the government as it affected the individual subject during the sixteenth century much attention was paid to treasons, riots, and breaches of the peace, to forgery, libel, and perjury, to "lewd and naughty words," to family quarrels, matrimonial disputes, and suits over land, to the control of the Church, the maintenance of uniformity, and the suppression of dissent, to enclosures, the relief of the poor, the avoidance of idleness, and the training of the young. While all these matters have social implications, the attitude of the Crown as the sixteenth century went on seems to have been determined more and more by considerations of the preservation of internal peace through the elimination of the causes of disturbance and the enforcement of outward unity in the interests of its own safety.

The failure of the well-ordered state of the Tudor-Stuart commonwealth to measure up to the most advanced thought of the day can be explained in considerable measure on fiscal grounds. From the very outset it was well understood that the desired type of government would be quite expensive. More than one writer went into an elaborate discussion of the necessity of the prince's being rich. He must have revenues adequate to meet all demands made upon him, and he must have sufficient income over and above his expenses to gather "some store for sudden events, either wars or dearth."

While more was expected of the king, skepticism about the value of state efforts persisted. Taxes, imprests, and imposts were generally believed to impoverish the realm "after the manner of France." There was no widespread faith that heavy payments by the people of the nation to the king would be anything else than wasted. Perhaps a better way of putting the situation would be to say that national feeling was still rather restricted and made headway only in the face of strong localisms. The county populations saw little advantage to themselves from the central government. They were willing to assume the costs of county affairs; let the king carry the burdens of his own business. Some writers were willing to grant the state a free hand in increasing its revenues, even to the point of conceding that the Crown might lawfully and with a safe conscience take taxes of its subjects. Yet this was not generally the case, and for practical purposes the whole period from 1485 to 1641 was a struggle over money between the king and his subjects.

In the last analysis, however, the realization of the high hopes of those who had hailed the national state as the dawn of a new day was thwarted less by inability to raise money than by the circumstance that money was required for other objectives. On the assumption that the heart is where the treasure is disposed, it seems that the real interest of the new national states was elsewhere than in domestic social polity. On the Continent the national monarchies were already engaged in the game of seizing each other's territory. After an initial episode in France, Henry vii consciously prevented England during his own reign from following other national states in conforming to the pattern of a power entity, intent upon enforcing its views upon its neighbors and consequently under the heaviest obligations of providing for its own defense. Given the circumstances of European life and England's position, it is hard to see how she could have continued permanently to avoid being induced to follow continental fashions. Henry viii had, however, no desire to continue his father's policy, although the most solemn adjurations to do so were addressed to him. Thus in the *Tree of Commonwealth*, written by Edmund Dudley while in prison during the first days of the young king's reign, Henry viii was urged to avoid wars, since "the commodities of this noble realm be so noble and with that so plenteous that they cannot be spended or all employed within the same, but necessarily there must be intercourse between this realm and the outward parts for the utterance thereof and specially for the wool and cloth, tin and lead, fell and hide." This plea for an international outlook as a necessity for foreign trade was backed up by the observation that "war is a marvellous consumer of treasure and riches: for I suppose a right great treasure is soon spent in a sharp war." Yet within a few years Henry VIII as the ally of Ferdinand plunged his country into war with France and definitely obligated himself to assume the heaviest commitments for defense and offense. Choice and necessity led his successors to continue in his course.

A simple comparison between the normal, peace-time armed-service budgets at various times between 1485 and 1641 is quite illuminating. In the latter part of his reign, Henry VII expended annually £1,200 for the wages of his private bodyguard of the yeomen of the guard. The sum of £88 a year was paid to the surveyor of the ordnance and his clerks. The keeping of Berwick and the east and middle marches against Scotland cost £2,500 a year. The wages of the garrison at Calais were about £10,000 annually, and certain small payments were made for the navy and for the English forces in Ireland.[1] A hundred years later the yeomen of the guard received £4,000 a year for wages and £1,222 for liveries. The more recently instituted gentlemen pensioners received £4,500 a year. The ordnance office had a budget of at least £10,000 annually. Calais fortunately had been lost. Berwick, where expenditures had just been reduced by James I, still needed £5,000 a year, and was to do so for some time to come. To other border stations and forts and garrisons,

---

[1] During the three years 1485, 1486, and 1487 the king's ships cost £1,841, or £600 a year. In the first year and a half of Henry VIII's reign the repair and building of ships and the purchase of bow staves amounted to £3,138. In the war periods 1492–93 and 1495–96 navy payments were more considerable; in other years, smaller. Irish revenues were said to be unable to meet the costs of the Irish garrison; but except in the years 1494–96 little money seems to have been sent to Ireland from England.

such as those at Land's End, St. Mary's, Portsmouth, and other points, £5,000 a year was allotted, and this was soon to be increased. There were English forces in the Low Countries, maintained at a charge of £25,000 a year, to guarantee the repayment by the Dutch of £40,000 a year, and the costs of the English occupation of Ireland, where during the recent wars Elizabeth had spent as much as £336,000 in a single year, averaged £70,000 a year for the first decade of James I's reign. The navy, which as late as the early years of Elizabeth's reign had occasionally kept within a peace-time appropriation of £6,000, now regularly required £40,000 annually for normal maintenance.

These figures, except those for Ireland, represent the peace-time military appropriations. In the event of war the expenditures of the new power-state skyrocketed remarkably. Figures here must be largely tentative, since it is impossible to determine all the extra disbursements which were due to war purposes. Definitely known expenditures in certain decades may, however, have certain relative values. In the critical ten years after 1491 Henry VII engaged in two wars, with France and Scotland, besides crushing several rebellions. His military operations cost something over £107,000 in addition to certain incidental charges for aid to the Duchess of Brittany of which the accounts are not available. Between 1541 and 1550 Henry VIII and Edward VI again fought France and Scotland. From the beginning of the first alarums in 1539 to the time of Henry VIII's death the Crown spent £2,134,000 for the building of fortifications in England and at Calais and Guisnes, for the charges of the navy and the siege, capture, and keeping of Boulogne, and for the war against Scotland. To this sum Edward VI's government added £1,386,000 between 1547 and 1550. Again, in the decade from 1591 to 1600 Elizabeth spent approximately £4,000,000 for her forces in Ireland, France, and the Low Countries and for the navy, with such little success that the drain continued through the last years of her own régime and into that of James I. As time went on wars became even costlier. In the single campaign of 1640 Charles I spent £570,000 in his failure to teach the Scots proper respect for his majesty.

There were two other factors by which the policies of any sixteenth-century king, however much concerned he might have been with a social program, would have been restricted. The first of these was the sixteenth-century price revolution, which worked so insidiously that even modern scholars tend to overlook its constant presence. There were also rising standards of taste and luxury, growing out of the increasing wealth of Europe, which the English court, following continental fashions, inevitably adopted. Conspicuous consumption was a real political factor. Few Englishmen would have been willing to forego it, lest the national honor, the king's dignity, and their own pride be injured. In the royal household alone, to use merely one of the great spending departments of the court for illustration, these two forces of rising prices and higher living standards drove up the cofferer's normal disbursements from a mere £13,000 in 1505–06 to £25,000 in 1538, £45,000 in 1545, £50,000 or £60,000 in the latter years of Elizabeth's reign (in spite of Burghley's thrift and care), and £70,000 during the latter part of that of James I. The same processes were at work to increase the pensions and annuities paid to courtiers and officials from £1,354 in 1506 to £102,000 in 1638.

Nor would a more detailed exposition of royal expenditures lead to a different conclusion from the one here indicated. The closest study of Crown disbursements from

1485 to 1641 reveals constantly growing outlays for military preparations and actual warfare, larger advances for exchanges of diplomatic agents, pyramiding appropriations for the royal court in connection with the household, wardrobe, chamber, buildings, and royal parks, and larger payments of pensions and annuities. Virtually nothing was spent by the state directly toward the realization of the social ends envisaged by the contemporary publicists. What was done along these lines was done by the local authorities or by the reorganized church. The English government in the sixteenth and early seventeenth centuries devoted practically all its resources toward its own maintenance or toward the military ends of the system of *Der Staat als Macht*. The irony of the business was that the support of the court and the upkeep of a skeleton fleet and insignificant military departments used up most of the Crown's resources. There was only a little left for the war chest, the accumulation of which was considered an important part of military activity. In the event of war, even second-class efforts completely disorganized the revenue system, compelled the alienation of capital resources, and heaped up debts.

It is only a partial explanation of the neglect of social aims in the Tudor-Stuart state to say that since the money available was sufficient only for the support of the court and military affairs, they alone were served and other matters were overlooked. A truer evaluation of the situation reveals an interesting mechanistic connection between the choice of purposes actually made by the Crown and the compulsion to that course provided by the traditions of fiscal policy.

Certain considerations of practical politics affecting Henry VII's fiscal program at the beginning of his régime colored the issue throughout the entire period. Owing to the rapid development of the spoils system during the fifteenth century, Henry VII received with the Crown only the smallest endowments. He also enjoyed the customs dues of the capital, the wool customs collected at Calais over and above the wages of the garrison and the mortgage payments due to the Staplers, and such sums collected in the ports outside London as the local officials were willing to disgorge.

There were theoretically three possible courses open to King Henry. These were the continuation of experiments with direct taxes, which so far had had no positive results, the extension of the policy of developing large landed estates, and the increase of the customs revenues. Henry VII tried all three devices. His greatest success was achieved in connection with the Crown lands, which, it may be noted, were widely recognized as the best endowment of the Crown. In his own person Henry VII was a congeries of local feudal lordships, as indeed his immediate predecessors were, only to a more limited extent. As the actual holder of the Lancastrian estates, the lands of York, the properties of Warwick and Spenser, and many another feudal holding, Henry VII was able to use his local feudal position to begin the task of making land the fiscal basis of the Tudor state. The general inclination to sanction such revenue devices as might satisfy class prejudices, such as the detestation of Henry's middle-class followers for the feudal baronage, gave great freedom to the king's activities. He was able to resume alienated royal domains, confiscate the lands of the "traitors" who had fought against him at Bosworth Field and of those who had taken part in the early rebellions of the reign, to revive fiscal feudal rights, such as marriage and wardship, and to insist upon the greatest extension of tenure *in capite* in the hope of eventual escheat to the Crown.

Public opinion regarding the monasteries, the bishops, and the Church in the sixteenth century made it possible for Henry's successors to continue his land policy by increasing the royal "livelihood" at their expense. After Elizabeth's last exchanges of less valuable parcels for the bishops' best properties and her last great attainders of the northern feudal nobles, the increase of Crown estates was still sought through such irritable devices as the search for assarts and purprestures (parcels once part of the king's domains and forests lost by encroachments) and the re-survey of the royal forests.

At the beginning of the Tudor régime the customs seemed less auspicious than the landed estates. The Calais revenues had for the most part perhaps permanently escaped royal control. More could be expected from London, where in 1507 the more adequate payment of customs dues was enforced by the substitution of an official scale of valuations in a book of rates in place of the merchants' declarations. Various trade treaties did something to stimulate the passage of goods through the custom-houses, and royal loans to merchants were designed to accomplish the same end. The increase of revenue from the customs by about 28 per cent between 1485 and 1509 was no mean achievement, but the real importance of the customs in the English fiscal system did not begin until the lands began to show the operation of a kind of law of diminishing returns in Mary's, Elizabeth's, and James I's reigns.

Although the more important categories of customs duties were granted by parliament, the customs, at least since Henry VII's reign, were considered as a virtual part of the king's own inheritance. This view was strengthened by the principle, reported by Dyer, adduced in connection with the suit of London merchants against impositions in

1559, that customs commenced with the king's control of the ports and his right to close them against the payment for a royal license to import and export goods. There were other possibilities in the discovery that the customs could be used to serve domestic business interests. Although some writers insisted that duties on exports were in reality paid by English artisans through the lowering of the prices of their products, it was generally believed that the customs outward were paid by the foreigners. Such dues were less harmful than the customs on imports paid by English merchants, which increased the cost of goods to the consuming public. Levies on necessities were bitterly resented, to such an extent that in 1610 Lord Salisbury removed the new impositions of 1608 in so far as they were laid upon the necessities of life. Duties on luxuries, however, especially those which might be produced at home, were positively popular. Gerard Malynes, the merchant economist, argued for a tariff to protect home industries on the ground that the highest function of the state was the maintenance of traffic. By this he meant the increase of national and individual wealth with the active help of the state. The bait he held out to secure this boon was that such assistance would make the subjects the more willing to pay for the support of the Crown. Finally, in the book of rates of 1610 industrial protection was openly avowed as a government policy as a kind of sugar coating to sweeten the pill of impositions.

Of greater immediate importance were the schedules to "equalize traffic," that is retaliatory duties or special levies on foreigners in the interest of the English merchant. Even Sir Edward Coke held that the king might lawfully levy countervailing duties to make equality in case of duties levied in foreign parts, since such duties were for the advancement of traffic, which was the life of every island, *pro bono publico.* When Lionel Cranfield somewhat later discovered that alien merchants were quasi-lawfully liable for an additional imposition of three pence in the pound beyond that paid by native merchants, he almost popularized the original exaction of 1608.

Under the cover of assertions of royal rights and the manipulation of customs duties to protect the native merchants and industrialists, opposition to new duties was disarmed. A vast extension of royal customs duties under the name of impositions was carried into effect without parliamentary sanction from Mary's time onward.

The political opponents of impositions feared that the income from the new customs dues would render the Crown financially independent and thus end the possibility of a financial readjustment which would involve the parliamentary control of the state. There never was much possibility of such productivity on the part of the impositions or other customs dues. For though the Crown income from the various types of customs went up remarkably, the increasing yield even when taken together with the lands and other revenues was never quite enough to provide for the needs of the court, the requirements of the services, and the rapacity of the courtiers.

It was more or less clearly recognized at least as early as Thomas Cromwell's time that even for such as were considered normal peace-time expenditures direct taxation afforded the only adequate basis for royal finance. On the other hand direct taxes were cordially disliked. In their older form of purveyance they aroused continual protests, which ended only with the abolition of purveyance by the Long Parliament. In their more recent guise of fifteenths and tenths and subsidies they were always unpopular. Fortescue raised his voice against them, granting their permissibility only in the event of war or some other extraordinary occasion. Under the constitution such direct taxes had the added difficulty of requiring parliamentary appropriation. Unfortunately for his system, in the formative years of the Tudor state Henry VII did not grapple with the problem of direct taxes. His very success in dealing with his lands and customs is perhaps a partial explanation of his neglect. Moreover, the opposition of his middle-class supporters to this method of raising revenue, as revealed in Fortescue's works and by several revolts directly attributable to efforts to collect taxes on Henry's own part, made the king loath to undertake radical innovations here. After a few cautious experiments, Henry VII left the matter of direct taxation pretty much where it had been under the Lancastrians. The nation was no more accustomed to meeting the expenses of its government by direct payment than it had been when Henry IV took the crown. Half a century after Henry VII's death John Hales, referring to Henry VII's experience, pointed out that "that way of gathering treasure is not always most safe for the Prince's surety; for we see many times the profit of such subsidies spent in appeasing the people that are moved to sedition partly by occasion of the same."

Little progress was made in the use of the fifteenth and tenth and the subsidy by Wolsey, whose gravest difficulties with parliament grew out of his attempts to secure grants in 1514, 1515, and 1523. In the disturbed third of a century after Wolsey's fall and again in the last fifteen years of Elizabeth's reign direct taxes were voted and collected often enough to inure the people to them. More than that, while the value of a single subsidy or a single fifteenth and tenth could not be raised and in fact depreciated, the number of grants in a single appropriation and the value of the sums annually taken from the people mounted steadily. It would seem as if by 1603 the payment of direct taxes should have been an habitual matter, and these taxes should have formed a regular portion of state revenues without regard for the necessity of a war before they could be obtained.

On at least two occasions the Crown had tried to get the parliament to make some acknowledgement of the inadequacy of the old notion of direct taxes as extraordinary war supplies. In 1566 Lord Chancellor Bacon made the suggestion that taxes should be voted for the payment of the Queen's debts. This novelty was so little liked by the Commons that the grant of this year was the smallest of Elizabeth's reign. Again in 1610, after the refusal of the nation to continue the heavy Elizabethan votes on the ground that the government no longer had the Spaniards, but only the Irish, left to deal with, James I sought to induce parliament to vote a subsidy to pay past debts, and to provide an annual "support" for the future. "Support and supply" as used by James I in 1610 was another way of asking that the king be given tax grants in peace as well as in war. This attempt, too, failed, and when the next grant but one was made, in 1624, a special commission was created with it, to see that it was spent for war purposes exclusively.

Even if fifteenths and tenths and subsidies could have been reduced to the status of regularly recurring taxes, they were in themselves unfitted to be made the foundation for a national fiscal system. The fifteenth and tenth was hopelessly stereotyped long before the Tudor era began. In 1334 it had assumed the form of a fixed tax on land, and since then it had been subject to no changes except diminution in yield to allow for "decays." The subsidy represented a Tudor attempt to levy on income from land or capital goods (personalty). In actual practice the subsidy tended to become little more than a land tax. It was difficult to add the names of new men to the subsidy books so as to bring new wealth within the scope of the tax. The subsidy thus became a fixed tax also, capable only of declining in yield as "subsidy men" decayed.

Ship money, the later non-parliamentary direct tax, represented an effort to escape from the limited incidence and fixed yield of the subsidy as well as from the reluctance of parliament to vote appropriations and the desire of its leaders to use grants to increase their political power. The Crown determined in advance the sum demanded and required new assessments, independent of the subsidy rates, to be made. Yet even in connection with ship money no effort was made to escape the military connotation of direct levies. Ship money was said to be collected for the maintenance of the fleet, and every penny actually was used for naval purposes. The fact that a large part of the potential revenues were justifiable and leviable only for military purposes perhaps helped to make military efforts one of the chief forms of state activity in the first period of the national system, from 1485 to 1641.

It was asserted by Hakewell in 1610 during a parliamentary attack upon James I's increase of his customs through the levy of impositions that each royal liability was covered by a corresponding source of revenue, and that the king might come to parliament for funds if his own were not sufficient. It should be noted that not only was this view directly contrary to established ideas, but it was disproved by events. For James made appeals for taxes on just such grounds and came face to face with the old disinclination of the nation to appropriate funds to cover his deficiencies.

Henry VII's regard for tradition and political expediency prevented the adoption at the beginning of the Tudor régime of a revenue system adequate for more than the briefest time. The main reliance was placed on lands and customs, and public taxation remained a war revenue measure. Rising costs of maintaining the court and the growing demands of the armed services in face of the European diplomatic situation left no funds for the adoption by the government of functions for which the times were crying out. The Crown's failure to make the state mean very much to the average individual made him loath at a later date to permit the abandonment of the medieval tradition that the king was entitled to ask for aid from his people only in the event of war.

At the same time certain aggressive political leaders saw the possibility of capitalizing the fiscal difficulties of the Crown and the ever present reluctance of the nation to pay taxes even for war by precipitating a conflict between the king and parliament. Parliament under such inspiration made the novel departure in the early years of Charles I's reign of refusing to respond to royal requests even for military appropriations in the face of a great war. The king's only possible recourse short of turning the government over to a group whose every action branded them as incompetent to act as the administrators of the state was to govern as an absolute ruler. Thus fiscal traditions, policies, and practices played an important part not only in determining the character of the first phase of the English national state but in terminating it in the bloody struggles of the Civil Wars.

ASPECTS OF ELIZABETHAN APPRENTICESHIP

MARGARET RANDOLPH GAY

THE Statute of Artificers of 1563, that "industrious longe lawe," is often considered as a great industrial code, the work of far-sighted statesmanship amalgamating earlier practices and legislation in an adaptation to present need. We can only imagine now, in the absence of adequate documentary evidence, the days of its passage through parliament: the appearance of witnesses from this or that industrial or mercantile group, town, or district; the opinions of the country gentry as they debated it in committee; the petitions from trades, the appeals to legal knowledge and to former statutes, and a steady pressure of government influence to put the bill through. There was ample room in its many-sidedness for both conflict and interweaving of interests.

The present study attempts an analysis of some of the forces behind the introduction and regulation of apprenticeship under both the Act of 1563 and the woolen-industry statutes of 1555 and 1557. The question of degree of enforcement will not here be considered. In the records of central and local courts [1] there is sufficient evidence of efforts at enforcement to raise certain questions: whether

---

[1] The present article is part of a larger study, in preparation, of the history of the 1563 apprenticeship clauses from the 16th to the 18th century. Manuscript sources have been chiefly the following: (a) Quarter Sessions records for fourteen counties chosen to form industrial or agricultural groups; (b) the Agenda Books and Memoranda Rolls of the King's Remembrancer of the Exchequer, from 1552 on; (c) the Coram Rege Rolls of the King's Bench, 1563–82 and scattered years in the 17th century — both (b) and (c) with chief reference to the selected counties; and (d) State Papers Domestic, Privy Council Records, and other miscellaneous manuscript material.

they were directed by or against particular groups, particular forms of industrial organization, and particular layers of economic life.

The apprenticeship provisions in the Statute of Artificers rested on traditional policies of the handicraft stage in town economy and were thus available instruments of opposition to that form of industrial organization, the putting-out system, already in town and country mingling with and superseding the handicraft.[1] The least narrowly restrictive was the requirement of a seven-year term of training. This had come to be a familiar institution in many towns and crafts;[2] it was first applied by statute to the worsted, and in the 1550's to the woolen, industry. In the Act of 1563 it was prescribed that none save those exercising in 1563 an

arte, mystery or manuall Occupacion [were] to sett up occupye use or exercyse any crafte . . . nowe used . . . within the Realme of England or Wales excepte he shall have bene brought uppe therin Seven yeres at the least as Apprentyce . . . nor to sett anye person on worke in suche . . . Occupacion beinge not a workeman at this day, except he shall have bene apprentyce as is aforesaid, orels having servyd as an Apprentyce . . . will becomme a Jorneyman or be hyred by the yere.[3]

The injunction of 1563 on masters to employ a fixed proportion of journeymen to apprentices[4] less closely fol-

---

[1] The term "putting-out" is used in preference to others well known, as "domestic" or "wholesale handicraft," in view of 16th-century usage in the acts of 1552 and 1557, "to put to" weaving, etc., and in the Statute of Artificers, § 20, "clothear that dothe put clothe to makynge and saile."

[2] There is no need to multiply references on this subject. It has been discussed in connection with the Statute by O. J. Dunlop (Dunlop and R. P. Denman, *English Apprenticeship and Child Labour*, New York, 1912). Enrolments of apprentices and freemen in town records, as at Leicester, Norwich, or Northampton (Ms. Books of Apprentices' Indentures), show that indentures for seven years or more were quite usual before 1563.

[3] 5 Eliz., c. 4, § 24.

[4] 5 Eliz., c. 4, § 26: in the trades of clothmaker, fuller, shearman, weaver, tailor, and shoemaker, one journeyman must be kept for the first three apprentices, and for each apprentice more than three a journeyman employed. This clause was adopted bodily from a statute of 1549 (3 & 4 Ed. VI, c. 22).

lowed gild precedent than did the act of 1555 which had
forbidden country weavers to keep more than two apprentices at one time, thus definitely limiting the size of the
individual master's establishment. Nevertheless the 1563
regulation expressed the handicraftsman's need to ensure
a foothold on every rung of the ladder to a mastership.

The sections of the Act which prescribed property
qualifications for apprenticeship to townsmen embodied
a definite governmental policy directed, not against the
migration of town artisans to the country, but against the
movement of agricultural labor into industrial occupations.[1] Earlier statutes and proposals for national reform
had a similar purpose: an act of 1406, and the "industrial
program" laid before parliament in 1559.[2] The Statute of
Artificers has, however, been considered as part of the attempts to check the decay of towns, then so frequently
alleged. The complaints of certain older centers which
were victims of a redistribution of population helped to
evoke a belief that population was decreasing, as did a like
movement in the eighteenth century. But urban concentration was an important contemporary phenomenon. It

---

[1] 5 Eliz., c. 4, §§ 19-23. In cities and corporate towns householders were
allowed to apprentice (beside their own sons) only the sons of freemen of cities
or corporate towns not husbandmen nor laborers; except that merchants, mercers, drapers, putting-out clothiers, and some others, were further restricted to
sons of forty-shilling freeholders. In market towns members of these occupations
could apprentice only sons of sixty-shilling freeholders, and other householders,
if they were not husbandmen or laborers, the sons of any except husbandmen or
laborers. Weavers in country districts (weaving for sale by the clothier) were
restricted to sons of sixty-shilling freeholders. There were no restrictions in
certain trades which must necessarily be located in the country: the "village
industries," potters, fullers of cloth.

[2] By the first (7 Hen. IV, c. 17), apprenticeship in city or borough was only
for the children of twenty-shilling freeholders. By the latter only the sons of
forty-shilling freeholders could anywhere be apprenticed, and none to a merchant unless his father's estate was of the annual value of £10 or his descent was
from a gentleman or merchant (R. H. Tawney and E. Power, *Tudor Economic
Documents*, London, 1924, vol. i, pp. 325ff.).

seems likely, in fact, that laments of decay in many cases arose as much from the contest between the enlarging economic area of the corporate town and its static political area as from any actual decline in economic activity.[1] The signs of this contest, and of increasing industrial and commercial activity in the countryside, appear in court prosecution under the seven-year apprenticeship law.

Apprenticeship regulation by the gild and town had had both an economic and a social purpose: the former determined by that belief in quality of workmanship and in limited production which belonged to a market of slowly changing extent, needs, and tastes; the latter the prevention of idleness. National apprenticeship regulation inherited both aims. So far as it was a policy originated or approved by the government it had a primarily social purpose based on political need. In the class dislocations and unrest of the preceding half century, political and social stability was the common hope, unemployment the common danger. Training gave each worker an assured place, and in youth kept him "under government;" that this supervision might be lifelong, corporations were to be favored above market towns and villages.

Preceding Elizabeth's accession, in that decade so lavish of bills and statutes for reform,[2] William Cecil had been for a time a member of parliament and for three years a secretary of state. It is possible that the Statute of Artificers is not only a distillation of public opinion, but the sum of

---

[1] Cf. Leland's description of Barnstaple: "The Suburbes be now more then the toun" (*The Itinerary of John Leland, 1538–43*, pts. i–iii, Lucy Toulmin Smith, ed., London, 1907, p. 169).

[2] *Commons Journals*, vol. i: 1547, bill for merchants, clothiers, and artificers to dwell in towns (p. 2), bill for bringing up poor men's children (p. 1); 1548, bill for the exercise of two handicrafts, bill for taking of apprentices (p. 6). There is frequent repetition of such measures. Some of the statutes were for the retaining of journeymen, 3 & 4 Ed. vi, c. 22; for retailing in corporate towns, 1 & 2 Philip & Mary, c. 7; and the cloth acts.

measures toward which Cecil himself had been working. He seems at any rate to have agreed with the general view.[1] The country gentleman thought it better to export raw wool "than [that] any clothiers should be set awork within the Realm . . . all these insurrections do stir by occasion of all these clothiers; for, when our clothiers lack vent over sea, there is great multitude . . . idle; . . . they . . . murmur . . . and . . . stir the poor commons . . . to a commotion."[2] A memorandum by Cecil in 1564 echoes this opinion:

the deminution of clothyng in this realme wer profittable to the same for manny causees; first, for that therby the tilladg . . . is notoriosly decayed . . . in that . . . the realme is dryven to be furnished with forrayn corne, . . . Secondly, . . . the people that depend uppon makyng of cloth ar of worse condition to be quyetly governed than the husband men. Thyrdly, by convertyng of so manny people to clothyng, the realme lacketh not only artificers, which wer wont to inhabitt all corporat townes, but also laborers for all comen workes.[3]

There could be no clearer statement of the ideas that seem to be behind the Statute of Artificers.

While Crown policy thus opposed for social reasons an uncontrolled expansion of the national industry, the nature of the market caused a similar opposition from economic interests. The market of the national cloth trade was wider, more varied and variable, than that of the town economy; but trade was all the more subject to intense competition and fluctuation. In a depression some producers blamed the sellers; the sellers, overproduction. The

[1] If the memorandum quoted in the text is not simply his abstract of another's arguments.

[2] *A Discourse of the Commonweal of this Realm of England*, E. Lamond, ed. (London, 1893), p. 88. This danger was always present to the minds of Elizabeth's Privy Council upon any stoppage of the cloth trade.

[3] Tawney and Power, *op. cit.*, pp. 45ff.: the memorandum is in favor of continued non-intercourse with Antwerp.

ideas of the town economy were current, and merchants, together with groups of producers, turned to apprenticeship as a means of restricting production and ensuring uniform quality of workmanship. The individual merchant undoubtedly in practice often attempted a flexible adaptation to demand, such as appears in instructions to a factor in the Turkey trade that "we are . . . to frame ourselves according to the desires of foreign nations," [1] but officially at any crisis in the cloth trade the trading companies upheld a traditional standardization. The Merchant Adventurers Company clearly was one of the main forces behind the first of the mid-sixteenth century series of cloth acts.[2] When in 1550 they were accused by clothiers of agreements lowering cloth prices, they answered that cloth lay unsold at Antwerp and was badly made. Other clothiers, probably those with competitors in mind whom they hungered to suppress, country rivals, perhaps, or retailers and wholesalers intermeddling with clothmaking, claimed that the low prices were the result of the late increases in the number of clothiers who made poor cloth, being untrained; there should be a law to restrict clothmaking to those with apprenticeship.[3] With the support of London clothworkers, drapers, merchant-tailors, shearmen, the act of 1552 was passed, standardizing anew the dimensions and weights of woolen cloths. Probably the same groups supported also the separate act requiring a seven-year apprenticeship for all who "weave or make or put to weaving or making" any

---

[1] E. Lipson, *History of the Woollen and Worsted Industries* (London, 1921), p. 85.

[2] As merchant exporters had been behind earlier standard-setting laws. In the 17th-century depressions, of 1616 and 1622, the Merchant Adventurers attributed the decay of the cloth trade in part to neglect of the laws for true clothmaking. (*Calendar of State Papers, Domestic*, Jas. I, vol. lxxxviii, nos. 41 and 97; Addenda, vol. xl, no. 128; vol. clxxx, no. 74.)

[3] Tawney and Power, *op. cit.*, vol. i, p. 184.

broad woolen cloth.[1] Drapers in the seventeenth century
gave a specious approval to apprenticeship for clothiers,
and praised the Act of 1563 as part of the "auncient
policie" to preserve true clothmaking, with an eye to their
own control of cloth-finishing.[2] That the Merchant Adventurers, at least officially, approved the apprenticeship
policy as well as direct cloth standardization is indicated
by the apparent coincidence of its adoption with years of
the Crown's financial dependence on the Company, in
1550–52. Two years later, clothiers of certain towns secured a modification of the apprenticeship law to apply
only to country clothiers; at the same time Mary was
restoring the Hanseatic merchants to favor with partial
privileges.[3] But the three years following were marked
both by the returning influence of the Adventurers[4] and
by new statutes for apprenticeship: the first, in 1555, for
a seven-year term for all weavers; the second, in 1557, a
revival of this term for all makers of woolen cloth or kerseys.[5] Neither Merchant Adventurers nor the cloth industry can have had any direct concern with the Act's addition of a general seven-year term, though town interests
may have shared in securing the property qualifications.
But study of the court cases indicates that behind the en-

---

[1] 5 & 6 Ed. VI, cc. 6 & 8. Cf. G. Unwin, *Studies in Economic History* (London,
1927), pp. 148, 186–187. This, however, does not analyze the connection in the
succeeding years between the history of the seven-year term and the Adventurers' relations with the Crown. Interests of the other London groups were to
some extent identical: some drapers engaged in cloth-finishing, some at this time
were members of the Merchant Adventurers; some of the Clothworkers Company were export agents.

[2] S. P. D., Jas. I, vol. cxxx, nos. 140 and 141, probably in 1622. The Drapers
of London, ostensibly on behalf of the "Drapers of England," complained of
clothiers who without a full apprenticeship dyed, dressed, and fulled cloth.

[3] Their privileges had been withdrawn in 1552 in favor of the Merchant Adventurers. The statute referred to was 1 Mar., stat. 3, c. 7.

[4] Unwin, *op. cit.*, p. 206.

[5] 2 & 3 P. & M., c. 11, § 7, and 4 & 5 P. & M., c. 5, § 22. Both acts, however,
in other respects favored the town clothiers, as well as the town weavers.

forcement of apprenticeship, and of certain other sections of the cloth acts, were mercantile influences utilizing these regulations for their own ends.

Analysis of the Westminster prosecutions requires a brief reference to the administrative machinery on which the enforcement of such laws depended. In the Exchequer and the King's Bench, suits on penal statutes were almost wholly in the hands of common informers who received a share of the penalty. The informer was a link in the none too strong chain of administrative concessionaires that bound the mass of laws into relation with the daily life they were designed to regulate. Such men did the work of salaried inspectors for a reward contingent on the uncertainties of legal process or on the racket they organized in a natural desire to obtain an assured income for protection of offenders against conviction. Some of them were deputy alnagers or deputy farmers of customs; most had their agents in the counties.[1] Some were employed as prosecutors on behalf of a group. London feltmakers, for example, endeavoring to further their craftsman interests, "put in trust" two Southwark feltmakers "for all suits that concern the said science;"[2] and these, between 1574 and 1578–79, brought a large number of informations against unapprenticed feltmakers in various counties.[3] Organizations must frequently have made use of such convenient agents; it would be natural to employ men who had trade affiliations with their employers. The fact that many of the

[1] The Wiltshire justices in 1620 reported to the Privy Council proceedings against informers in the county, some "the evill under-agentes of more notable Informers" of London (S. P. D., Jas. 1, vol. cxii, no. 14). Alliances of London and local informers occur in both Westminster and Quarter Sessions records.

[2] Unwin, *Industrial Organization in the 16th and 17th Centuries* (Oxford, 1904), pp. 133–134.

[3] Public Record Office, Excheq. Q. R. Memoranda Rolls, 16 Eliz., 20 & 21 Eliz.; mostly on the statute 8 Eliz., c. 11 (for felt-making).

informers in suits on the cloth acts and the Statute of
Artificers are mercers, merchants, drapers, clothworkers,
merchant-tailors, haberdashers, clothiers, or weavers,
from London and the clothing counties, suggests their
connection with whatever groups were prosecuting on
these statutes.

In tracing the course of informations on the cloth acts in
the Westminster courts, in addition to their apprenticeship provisions two other sections of the statutes of 1555
and 1557 have been fully tabulated: one the prohibition of
1557 on country clothmaking;[1] the other, the restriction on
the number of looms to be kept by country weavers and
clothmakers.[2]

Before 1560 there were few prosecutions under the cloth
acts; in 1553–54 only three apprenticeship informations for
the whole country under the act of 1552. With 1557 the
number of informations began to increase, but until 1560
there were none for unapprenticed clothmaking, and six for
unapprenticed weaving, some of which were from Essex;
for keeping an illegal number of looms, a dozen divided between Devon and Somerset.[3] From 1560 the amount of
prosecution markedly increased; the distribution of the
cases can be followed in the subjoined tables [4] — the cloth-
acts informations in three counties, and, after 1563,

---

[1] 4 & 5 P. & M., c. 5, § 21: none to make, weave, or row long or short woolen
cloths, kerseys, pinned whites, or plain straits except in cities, boroughs, corporate towns, or in market towns where for ten years clothmaking had been
established. Of the fourteen counties (cf. above, p. 134, n. 1), in Cheshire, Lancashire, and Yorkshire (except for a radius of twelve miles about York) wherever there had been clothmaking for twenty years it was allowed to continue.

[2] 2 & 3 P. & M., c. 11, §§ 1 & 2; outside cities, boroughs, corporate towns, and
market towns, clothmakers to keep only one loom in their own houses, and not
to let out looms, or houses for looms; weavers to keep only two looms.

[3] Excheq. Q. R. M. R., Agenda Books, vol. ii, 1 Mar., 2 & 3 P. & M., 3 & 4
P. & M., 4 & 5 P. & M., 1 Eliz.

[4] See below, pp. 162–163.

those for lack of legal apprenticeship under the Statute of Artificers [1] in five counties. The significant feature is the very large proportion from Devonshire, and in second place, Somerset. These counties are the center of prosecution under the cloth acts, but in Devon it should be noted how relatively few cases there are of unapprenticed clothmaking, in contrast to the county's lead in the other three offenses; while in the informations under the Act of 1563 it has, correspondingly, none against clothiers but far more than any other county against weavers. In Somerset the apprenticeship informations against clothmakers or clothiers, and those against weavers, are almost equally divided, but in Wiltshire prosecutions are, rather, against clothiers.[2] Offenders in the Devon cases of country industry are mostly described as weavers, but a number of clothmakers are keeping looms. It is uncertain whether the word "making" in the Devon informations refers to clothmaking proper or to weaving; in Somerset it seems to have the former meaning, and the prosecutions often include working or rowing cloth.

These differences correspond, so far as can be judged, to differences of industrial organization in the three counties. Contemporary references to the Devonshire woolen industry indicate that it was carried on chiefly by small, com-

---

[1] Space forbids the inclusion of the other eight counties (of the selected fourteen) which have some cases under either the cloth acts or the 1563 Act. The totals are as follows: 1560–1603, cloth acts, (a) for unapprenticed weaving, Essex 3; (b) for unapprenticed clothmaking, Essex 9, Worcs. 6, Lancs. 3, Warr. 3; (c) for country clothmaking, Essex 7; (d) for illegally keeping looms, Lancs. 4. 1563–1603, Statute of Artificers' seven-year term, West Riding abt. 11, Lancs. 24, Chesh. 4, Staffs. 19, Warr. 16, Leics. 8, Northts. 15, Notts. 4. So far as could be noted without careful count, elsewhere in England no county has more than about 16 cases on the two apprenticeship cases combined of the cloth acts, or more than 12 on the other two sections. For apprenticeship under the Statute of Artificers, cases are most numerous in London, Kent, and, to a less degree, in Suffolk, Surrey, and Sussex; in these counties offenders are chiefly retailers and victuallers. In none are there appreciable numbers in the cloth industry.

[2] And in the few Worcestershire prosecutions.

paratively independent producers, the series of processes related vertically by a chain of purchases and sales rather than by the radial dependence of the fully developed putting-out system.[1] By contemporaries it was likened to Yorkshire, and like Yorkshire had all grades of organization: the specialized independent spinner and the weaver who sold yarn or raw cloth in the market; the "meaner clothier" who differed from the weaver only in degree of specialization, borrowing his wool and selling his cloth "on the bare thred;"[2] the clothier who bought raw cloth and sent it to the fuller; the "rich clothiers" of centers like Tiverton,[3] men such as Peter Blundell, large putters-out, and smaller men, gentlemen, butchers, retailers, putting out small lots of wool or yarn, as the Westminster prosecutions reveal them; and weavers who were fullers, and fullers keeping looms.[4] In Somerset and in Wiltshire the industry was on a more developed putting-out basis, probably less so in west than in east Somerset or in Wiltshire, which like all the broadcloth counties was a stronghold of this form of organization.[5]

[1] The petition for reducing the standard weight of Devon kerseys, which was instrumental in securing the 1592 statute, explained that the clothiers were not to blame for kerseys lighter than standard, but the weavers and fullers from whom they bought. (Acts of the Privy Council, vol. xxii, p. 89, November 26, 1591.) Cf. also Thomas Westcote's description, in his *View of Devonshire, 1630* (Exeter, 1845), p. 61.

[2] Memorandum by the Staplers on the necessity of wool-broggers, 1614 (S. P. D., Jas. I, vol. lxxx, no. 13). It was difficult even in the 16th century to distinguish in usage between "clothier" and "weaver." Cf. the bill introduced in the Commons, 1558, "for weavers in Devon and Cornwall not to be called clothiers." (*Commons Journal*, vol. i, p. 54.)

[3] Tristram Risdon, *Survey of Devonshire* (London, 1714), p. 39.

[4] Like the Devon clothier prosecuted in 1563 for keeping two looms and in 1567 for unapprenticed weaving and fulling (Excheq. Q. R. M. R., Pasch. 5 Eliz., Rot. 80; Mich. 9 Eliz., Rot. 275).

[5] Yet even in Wiltshire there was a mixture: a weaver of Chippenham is described as weaving cloth for sale to the clothier (Wilts. Mss. Sessions Rolls, indictment at April Sessions, 3 Jas. I). Four weavers were claiming from a

Prosecutions from Devon and west Somerset are further differentiated from those in east Somerset and Wiltshire by the type of cloth which the offenders were producing, narrow cloths in Devon, mostly these with a few broadcloths in west Somerset, broadcloths in east Somerset and Wiltshire.[1] The narrow-cloth branch was Devon's specialty, comprising kerseys, white straits, and Tavistock cloths. Somerset narrow cloth seems to have been made in the half of the county west of a line from Bridgwater through Chard, and consisted of Taunton, Chard, and Bridgwater cloths,[2] Dunsters, straits, and types of kersey. Some clothiers in Chard and Taunton were making broadcloth, though it is doubtful whether this was identical with the east Somerset and Wiltshire variety.

A specialization among the informers followed the same divisions; those who prosecuted the one branch of manufacture left the other alone.

There are several apparent explanations for the marked preponderance of informations against the narrow-cloth producers of the southwestern district. The first and most obvious is that it represents an actually greater disregard of the laws. The narrow-cloth loom required only one

clothier of Malmesbury unpaid piece-work wages for yarn delivered to them; a clothman delivered yarn to a weaver (*ibid.*, Mich. Sess., 1 Jas. 1, indictment; Mich. Sess., 2 Jas. 1, examination for embezzling; May Sessions, 12 Jas. 1, another). In Somerset, presentments of the Viewers of Cloth for Taunton show that clothiers were putting out (Som. Mss. Sessions Indictment Rolls, no. 7, 1602–03).

[1] The cloth is specified only in informations for country or unapprenticed clothmaking, but it may be assumed from what is known of the localization of the manufacture that the same difference holds for all the informations.

[2] Taunton and Bridgwater cloths in the acts of 1552 and 1557 are called broadcloths, and by statute they were half as long and heavy, but as wide, as the broadcloth. In the Westminster informations, however, they are called both broad and narrow, sometimes kersey, and are valued at widely different prices. Evidently these names were applied to several varieties, but they were all a cheaper and probably somewhat smaller cloth than the true West of England broadcloth.

weaver, and in many cases little means and comparatively little skill;[1] for this reason narrow cloths would seem to have been better adapted than broadcloths to household production by families unapprenticed to the trade, like those of the local craftsmen and tradesmen, the laborers, husbandmen, and even parish clergy, who are prosecuted.[2] The very character of the Devon industry probably facilitated access to the purchase and disposal of small quantities of material and product; on the other hand, in counties where the putting-out system prevailed, the clothier made such independent access unnecessary for the small producer. The system itself, with the workers scattered over a country area, encouraged, rather than prevented, a neglect of apprenticeship. In any county, enforcement could be attempted only by the semi-organized craftsmen of the small towns, or the organizations of the incorporated town. Even if in consequence of a greater diffusion of the industry over the countryside in Devon, there was in fact more unapprenticed weaving supplementary to other occupations in this county than in eastern Somerset and in Wiltshire, there must have been more in the latter districts than the rarity of prosecutions from them would indicate. A truer index of the lack of law observance and the spread of a rural industry was the modification found necessary in 1576 of the country clothmaking prohibition in the 1557 act; the amendment permitted clothmaking in the country places where it had since grown up.[3]

Another explanation would ascribe the number in Devon

[1] Not all narrow cloth was a coarse grade requiring so much less skill than the broadcloth; Crediton kerseys were noted for their fine quality (Westcote, *op. cit.*, pp. 61 and 121). It was said in praise of the Essex bays that they equalled kerseys in fineness (S. P. D., Eliz., vol. ccl, no. 47).

[2] In Devon there were two rectors of country parishes sued for unapprenticed weaving, Excheq. Q. R. M. R., Trin. 8 Eliz., Rot. 53, and for country kersey-making, Mich. 7 Eliz., Rot. 229.

[3] 18 Eliz., c. 16, applying to Somerset, Wiltshire, and Gloucestershire.

and west Somerset to the chance presence of industrious informers. It is true that the Devonshire informations were mainly the work of a few men, particularly of one John Otterey, weaver of South Molton. But the common informer had an intelligence service that went beyond local bounds; Otterey was informing in Somerset and might as well have done so elsewhere in the west. Moreover, there were in all three counties as many London informers as provincial, and for their greater attention to offenders in the narrow-cloth branch there must certainly have been some cause.

The occurrence of the informations is not, of course, to be accounted for by one factor alone. Undoubtedly there are random elements, chance knowledge of an offense, individual jealousies. There may be a question how far local groups were the instigators of prosecution — groups of craftsmen, of clothiers, cloth-finishers, or merchants.[1] Their influence cannot be wholly excluded, but it is not a sufficient explanation. Elsewhere, where prosecution seems definitely attributable to the organized purpose of a craft group, the informations are of a character quite unlike the Devon and Somerset cases; they are sporadic, not continuous over several years, and they include offenses of a type scarcely occurring in the southwestern series. They are, moreover, rare among Westminster informations, appearing more often in the Sessions cases. For example, the Staffordshire Sessions records furnish evidence of an attempt by Walsall and West Bromwich nailmakers to suppress unapprenticed country nailers in the expanding metal-working district of south Staffordshire; the informers are two or three nailers of those towns, and one professional informer. But the only hint of this in the Exchequer are

[1] The scattered prosecutions in the western counties of offenders outside the woolen industry are too few for analysis.

two informations, one against a Sessions offender.[1] A few Exchequer prosecutions reflect friction at Manchester among dyers and clothworkers.[2] But there is no trace in the Exchequer cases of the short struggle in 1602–04 by master-weavers in west Wiltshire, organized in "fellowships" in the established clothing centers such as Trowbridge, Bradford, Westbury, Calne, to control the weavers of the adjacent country by apprenticeship informations at the Sessions, presentments by the Westbury hundred jury, and Sessions Orders for the weaving craft. Two master-weavers, who were the appointed searchers of cloth,[3] brought the informations, which were not only for unapprenticed weaving but for keeping apprentices without the legal proportion of journeymen, for apprenticing in a town the sons of husbandmen lacking the necessary estate, for employing unapprenticed journeymen.[4] Such offenses hardly appear in the Devon and Somerset Westminster prosecutions, in fact there are only two.[5] But they are precisely the offenses galling to the town handicraftsman, and their absence in Devon and Somerset suggests a lack of handicraft influence behind the informations.[6]

[1] Brought by the professional informer, who was a local man but not a nailer by trade; an instance of the employment of common informers by craft or trade groups. Cf. Staffs. Mss. Sessions Rolls, 33 Eliz. to 42 Eliz., and Excheq. Q. R. M. R., Mich. 37 Eliz., Rot. 198.

[2] Excheq. Q. R., Mich. 23 Eliz., Rot. 108–109; Pasch. 24 Eliz., Rot. 81; Pasch. 25 Eliz., Rot. 110; Mich. 25 Eliz., Rot. 123, 125–126; Hil. 26 Eliz., Rot. 78.

[3] Appointed according to the statute 39 Eliz., c. 20.

[4] Wilts. Mss. Sessions Minute Books, no. 2; Sessions Rolls, 44 Eliz. and 1 Jas. 1.

[5] Both from Devon, 1568 and 1582: (a) keeping apprentices without the legal property qualifications, (b) without journeymen. (Excheq. Q. R. M. R., Pasch. 10 Eliz., Rot. 330; Q. B. Cor. Reg. Rolls, Trin. 24 Eliz., Rot. 43.) They are very infrequent in all counties, an indication of how little craft groups made use of the Westminster courts.

[6] It is unfortunately not possible to compare the Westminster with the Sessions cases for Devon and Somerset; the 16th-century Sessions records in Devon are very scanty and those of Somerset have serious gaps. What evidence there is

It is difficult to see cause in Devon for prosecutions by clothiers of weavers or other clothiers. The weaver and clothier were not competitors, except so far as the small clothier was of the same status, and the share of this class has already been discussed. There was presumably no such strong jealousy, in the absence of a dispersed putting-out system, on the part of the town employer toward the country putter-out, as there was in some other counties, notably in Worcestershire,[1] where prosecutions against clothiers are probably to be ascribed to such rivalry. A few eastern Somerset and Wiltshire informations against clothmakers may have a similar cause — Peter Blackborowe, a clothier of Frome, prosecuted some of the larger broadcloth clothiers in his neighborhood for setting up in the country and without apprenticeship.[2] But their influential protests, backed by the justices of peace, secured consideration from the Privy Council and modification of the law.[3] If this was the attitude in the broadcloth district for which the statutes once sought by the clothiers had first been intended, it is not likely that the narrow-cloth makers would show greater eagerness in their application. Clothiers or cloth-finishers, however, in Taunton, Bridgwater, and Chard, may have been responsible for some

for Somerset indicates that apprenticeship suits were chiefly against bakers and small tradesmen, with a few in the woolen trades; and so also for Wiltshire, where informations in the woolen industry belong almost wholly to the group discussed in the text.

[1] Expressed in the Act of 1534 restricting clothmaking to certain large towns (25 Hen. VIII, c. 18); that of 1554 freeing town clothiers from apprenticeship; and generally for the clothing counties in the acts of 1555 and 1557.

[2] Excheq. Q. R. M. R., Pasch. 17 Eliz., Rot. 86, 94–98; Mich. 19 Eliz., Rot. 82, 88, 92; Hil. 20 Eliz., Rot. 64; Pasch. 20 Eliz., Rot. 74; Mich. 20 Eliz., Rot. 105. Blackborowe was partnered in prosecution by two or three weavers of Westbury and Bradford. The clothiers were described as making 500 to 1,000 broadcloths within the eleven months of prosecution.

[3] Above, p. 12. Cf. *Acts of the Privy Council*, Eliz., vol. ix, pp. 16, 73; vol. x, p. 28; Lansdowne Mss. 22, fol. 361; Excheq. Entry Books of Decrees and Orders, vol. v, 5 November, 17 Eliz.

prosecutions in that region, though many were brought by London informers against inhabitants of these towns.[1] Had town cloth-finishers in general had much share in the Westminster prosecutions, it is to be expected that these would have applied at least as often to unapprenticed fullers or dyers as to weavers; but there are very few suits against offenders in these crafts.

There was in the southwest one organization with the resources and unity essential to carrying on a long series of prosecutions; this was the Exeter "Company of Merchant Adventurers trading to France" and to Spain, which was chartered in 1559–60. The merchants of Totnes, Tiverton, Dartmouth, Collumpton, Barnstaple, Chard, Taunton, Lyme, had close and friendly connections with them.[2] Is it possible to find here the moving spirit behind the Westminster informations? If the local merchants were employing this indirect means of enforcing a standard of workmanship or of checking interlopers by prosecution of trading clothiers, or weavers who sold to merchants outside their company, it is curious that there should be no sign of this in Dorset, where kerseys were made, nor when other local Merchant Adventurers in clothing districts (at Bristol, Hull, or York) were attempting to exclude craftsmen and retailers from merchandising. The direct weapon against the unapprenticed merchant would have been prosecution under the Statute of Artificers. But only one such case has been observed,[3] although the Totnes merchants were proposing in 1581 that Exeter merchants and others

[1] Townsmen there had complained in 1555 of unapprenticed country clothmakers, weavers, fullers, shearers, who competed in their manufacture, and they had obtained an act requiring country cloth to be searched and sealed in one of the three towns (2 & 3 P. & M., c. 12). The Sessions records evidence some activity by the Viewers of Cloth against use of prohibited materials, but not of any campaign against unapprenticed or country makers.

[2] Wm. Cotton, *An Elizabethan Guild of the City of Exeter* (Exeter, 1873), *passim*.   [3] In Devon, 1592.

should join them in presenting a bill to prohibit country merchants, and the Exeter Company in 1584 agreed to this, adding that none should be merchants without a seven-year apprenticeship.[1] It must be inferred that provincial public opinion was opposed to the enforcement of this policy, as it was opposed to any narrowing in the channels of trade and employment; an attitude which strengthened the resistance of retailers, clothiers, and craftsmen to the exclusive policies of the Adventurers Companies.[2]

If the majority of informations could be shown to be against trading clothiers, clothmakers, weavers with interloping connections, it would lend strong support to a theory of local merchants' influence in the Westminster cases. But what slight evidence there is relates only to a few Somerset clothiers: of these one was a Taunton merchant who on one occasion acted as representative for the Exeter Merchants before the Privy Council to urge reduction of the new customs on English cloth in Brittany;[3] another was a Taunton clothier and merchant whose name appears in the records of the Exeter Company as a subscriber to Gilbert's voyage in 1586.[4] More indicative of

[1] Cotton, *op. cit.*, pp. 129–130, 159.

[2] As at Bristol, when the 1566 act conferred a monopoly on the Merchant Adventurers: the tuckers complained of decreased employment, and combined opposition to the act secured its repeal in 1571 (Unwin, *Studies in Economic History*, p. 197). There was a similar revocation of the drapers' monopoly at Shrewsbury in 1572 (by 14 Eliz., c. 12); both occurring in the depression following interruption to the Spanish trade.

[3] Cotton, *op. cit.*, p. 68: Thomas Pope, the younger. He was prosecuted for selling Taunton and Bridgwater cloths without search, the informer being one John Leake, London mercer and deputy alnager. (Excheq. Q. R. M. R., Pasch. 21 Eliz., Rot. 107; Hil. 24 Eliz., Rot. 250.)

[4] Cotton, *op. cit.*, p. 83: Simon Saunders. He was several times prosecuted in the Exchequer by John Leake and others for selling unsealed cloth, or exporting it uncustomed, and once in 1567 for country clothmaking near Taunton. (Q. B. Cor. Reg. Rolls, Trin. 9 Eliz., Rot. 25, and *passim*; Excheq. Q. R. M. R., *passim*.)

the western merchants' interests is the statute of 1585
which in regard to straits modified preceding legislation.
Mercantile influence is usually to be found behind standardizing regulations in the cloth industry, and in this
case it may have been that of Totnes merchants, since
straits were a specialty of Totnes and its neighborhood.[1]
The Act did away with standards for this cloth; thereafter
it was to be made in sizes agreeable to the merchant. But
the significant modification is the permission of country
clothmaking and weaving and the allowance of three looms
to all. Clearly merchants in this branch of the trade had
no wish to prosecute under the earlier laws restricting the
expansion of the industry.

The preceding discussion has attempted to state the
possibilities for and against the dominance of local forces in
the prosecution of offenses under the cloth acts and the
Statute of Artificers. The balance on the whole seems to
exclude local influences, mercantile or industrial, from a
principal part. From time to time attempts by individuals
or local groups to check competition perhaps coincided
with and reinforced the main course of prosecution, which
may be considered as a part of London's long-continued
struggle for commercial supremacy within the country.

In the sixteenth century this movement toward centralization is somewhat overshadowed in interest by the
effort of English, chiefly London, merchants to oust the
Hanseatics and other foreign traders. Though the Act of
1523, by which the foreign merchant was to be cut off from
direct contact with country producers of broadcloth, had
a definite effect in concentrating the export of undressed
cloth into London hands,[2] at the end of Henry VIII's reign

---

[1] Westcote, *op. cit.*, p. 61. The act referred to in the text is 28 Eliz., c. 18.
[2] 14 & 15 Hen. VIII, c. 1; G. Schanz, *Englische Handelspolitik gegen Ende des Mittelalters* (Leipzig, 1881), vol. i, p. 430.

one-half of the cloth export belonged to foreigners.[1] The larger part of the other half was undressed white cloth from Gloucestershire, Worcestershire, and Wiltshire, traded to the Low Countries and Germany by the London Merchant Adventurers; but in the export trade of English merchants of the outports and of foreign merchants other than the Hanseatic, narrow cloths, southwestern and northern, had a considerable share;[2] and the southwestern varieties found their chief market in France, Spain, and Portugal, outside the London Merchant Adventurers' sphere of influence. The southwestern outports, chief of which was Exeter, maintained through the sixteenth century a freedom from London domination greater than that of the ports near London and those trading to the Low Countries, Germany, or the Baltic.[3]

It cannot perhaps be said with certainty that the London Merchant Adventurers, having their privilege to export undressed white cloth, were "little interested in or actually indifferent to the exportation of . . . the lighter woollen fabrics, the new draperies, and others."[4] They, and other London groups interested primarily in the white cloth trade, recurrently show, in the sixteenth and seventeenth centuries, a jealously critical and restrictive attitude toward all fabrics, other than broadcloths, which invaded the export or domestic markets. John Leake, the London mercer and deputy alnager, who prosecuted in the Westminster courts for defective manufacture Somerset producers of narrow cloth, wrote in 1577 a memorandum on "deceits" in clothmaking. He exempts from criticism only

---

[1] Friis, A., *Alderman Cockayne's Project and the Cloth Trade* (London, 1927), pp. 45 and 47, based on Schanz's estimates.

[2] Cf., *ibid.*, p. 42, estimating from figures given by N. S. B. Gras, *The Early English Customs System* (Cambridge, Mass., 1918), that early in the 16th century foreign merchants exported a considerable amount of colored kerseys.

[3] Friis, *op. cit.*, pp. 20, 86, 115.   [4] *Ibid*, p. 61.

those "fine cloths" (from the western broadcloth counties) which are brought to market undressed.[1] A similar
complaint is voiced in the seventeenth century, by the
London Drapers, of defects in Devon, Hampshire, and
Chard kerseys, Devon bays, and kerseys from the North;[2]
while at the same time the Merchant Adventurers recommend as a remedy for the cloth-trade depression a reform in
clothmaking, especially that of the faulty new draperies,
and they point to the well-made Worcester cloth, supervised by a Corporation.[3]

Early in the sixteenth century English merchants attacked the position of the foreign merchant by means of the
Act of 1523, already mentioned; a hundred years later, the
foreigner is gone from the export trade, and it is the merchants of the outports with whom London disputes control, as in 1638 with Exeter over the so-called Spanish
cloth.[4] Prosecutions against southwestern narrow-cloth
producers seem to supply evidence of a hitherto little
noticed aspect of this competition.

While in 1606 the Merchant Adventurers' export of
narrow cloths from London to the Low Countries and Germany in Company ships was only about 8 per cent of their
total London export,[5] individual members of the Company

---

[1] S. P. D., Eliz., vol. cxi, no. 38, also vol. cclxxxvii, no. 96. In this criticism,
Leake specifically includes Taunton, Bridgwater, and Chard cloths, which were
dyed (and dressed?) before sale. He was most actively informing against producers of these cloths in 1577 and following years.

[2] S. P. D., Jas. I, vol. cxxx, no. 140.

[3] Ibid., no. 143. The Merchant Adventurers occasionally, it is true, are concerned lest faults in their chief export should prevent its sale; cf. for example
S. P. D., Jas. I., vol. lxxv, no. 85 (Privy Council instructions to justices to enforce search and sealing of cloth, Merchant Adventurers having complained of false
making); and their own orders for inspecting cloth in the merchant's hands, W. E.
Lingelbach, The Merchant Adventurers of England (Philadelphia, 1902), p. 129.

[4] S. P. D., Chas. I., vol. ccclxxx, no. 86.

[5] Friis, op. cit., p. 61. Compare John Wheeler's round figures as to other
cloths exported besides undressed whites, A Treatise of Commerce (New York,
1931), p. 335.

were trading in narrow cloths outside their privileged region. Apparently in the mid-sixteenth century they may
have made some claim to include Spain within their privileges, for the 1554 charter of the Chester Merchant Adventurers reserves the "franchises of the Society of Merchant
Adventurers frequenting Spain, Holland, Zeeland, Brabant,
and Flanders."[1] It was members of the London Merchant
Adventurers who proposed, twenty years later, the formation of the Spanish Company;[2] a twenty-year interval
during which there can be only conjecture as to the extent
and direction of their interests outside their own trading
sphere, or as to the unlicensed competition within their
markets of other types of cloth.[3] Into this twenty years
are concentrated nearly all the Westminster prosecutions
against the narrow-cloth producers of the southwest.

It might have been expected that the broadcloth counties would have had the larger number of informations on
the cloth acts, since the first two of these, in 1552 and 1555,
applied, in their restrictive clauses and their prescription of
apprenticeship, only to producers of broadcloth. But evidently no forces were at work to ensure limitations of production in this branch of cloth manufacture; had Merchant Adventurers, other London interests, or groups of
clothiers so directed, informers would have brought suit.
When, however, narrow cloths had been expressly included
in the legislation of 1557 prohibiting country clothmaking
and requiring apprenticeship for clothiers, prosecutions
began to increase, particularly in Devon and Somerset.

[1] C. Gross, *The Gild Merchant* (Oxford, 1890), pp. 360–363.
[2] Unwin, *Studies in Economic History*, p. 181: the Company of Merchants
trading to Spain and Portugal.
[3] In the absence of any study of customs figures for the second half of the
16th century, and of that intimate knowledge of the Company's policies and relations with local Adventurers' Companies which could be gained only from their
lost Court Books.

In the first years of Elizabeth's reign, the financial demands of the Crown upon the Merchant Adventurers were stimulating the Company to an increasingly exclusive membership policy,[1] and it may be suggested that this was an incentive to individual London merchants to enter the narrow-cloth trade. But in the southwest the trade was now more strongly organized with the formation of the Exeter Company, at the same time that trade with the Netherlands and Germany was subject to interruption and uncertainty. It seems possible that prior to London regulation of the Spanish and Portuguese trade by means of the Spanish Company London merchants were utilizing prosecution on the cloth acts and the Statute of Artificers to harass narrow-cloth producers and restrict production of the light woolens, either with a view to London dominance of the Exeter and southwestern merchants, or because the lighter types of cloth were invading their own markets. While those of the southwest had long been a manufacture sufficiently important to standardize, an absence of prosecutions against kersey-makers of Hampshire, Dorset, or the North points to a relatively greater expansion in the southwestern trade, a greater competition in the domestic market, and a greater increase in exportation of Devon kerseys and straits and Somerset light woolens. This is to some extent confirmed by John May's statement in 1613 that Yorkshire was imitating the Devonshire kerseys for the export trade,[2] and perhaps also by Leland's complete disregard, in the early sixteenth century, of the west Somerset cloth industry.[3] If domestic fashions were favor-

---

[1] Unwin, *Studies in Economic History*, pp. 165–168.

[2] John May, *A Declaration of the Estate of Clothing* (London, 1613), p. 32.

[3] *The Itinerary of John Leland, 1538–43*, pts. i–iii, pp. 101, 103–104, 166. Leland was impressed by the activity of the eastern clothing towns and villages, but hardly mentions clothmaking in the west except at Dunster. This may have been due, however, merely to a better acquaintance with the eastern section.

ing the narrow, lighter, and cheaper cloths more than broadcloth, London cloth-finishing, and wholesale and retail distributing, interests would regard the growth of narrow-cloth production with the jealousy shown in criticisms of their quality.[1]

Prosecutions against makers of these cloths continue with vigor till shortly after the trade with Spain stopped in 1569; and they are renewed chiefly at and around Exeter between 1578 and 1582, years in which the local branches of the Spanish Company, dominated by London, were struggling to establish their exclusive privileges against craftsmen and retailers. The decline in prosecutions following 1580 may perhaps be accounted for in part by the recognized footing London merchants had now obtained in the southwestern trade;[2] after 1586 the trade depression, and what appears to be a definite governmental intention to stop informations on penal statutes, explain the practical disappearance of all cases in the western counties.[3] The few prosecutions at the turn of the century are attributable to local inspiration.

In Essex and Norfolk there seems to have been a situation, similar to that in Devon and Somerset, in which an actual growth of industrial and commercial activity involved interests beyond local bounds. The Quarter Sessions records of Essex [4] contain evidence in numerous pre-

---

[1] See above, pp. 153–154.

[2] A comment by Peter Osborne, Lord Treasurer's Remembrancer, in 1579, suggests that western merchants were to some extent successfully subordinated to London, at least in the import trade in Spanish wool (Br. Mus., Lansdowne Mss. 29, no. 22).

[3] Council proceedings in 1586–87 reveal anxiety over popular discontent: in 1586 the Justices of Assize were instructed to direct justices of peace to stay proceedings on all commissions for penal statutes (*Acts P. C.*, Eliz., vol. xiv, p. 163; also as illustrative of the Council's attitude, *ibid.*, pp. 305 and 366).

[4] Unfortunately those of Norfolk are, in the 16th century, too fragmentary to furnish much evidence, as indictments and prosecutions are almost wholly lost from the Sessions Rolls.

sentments by hundred juries or individual informations, of an expansion in the victualling and retailing trades arousing the trade demarcation disputes traditional in town history, and friction between newcomers and the settled dealers of a town or village.[1] In several cases the offender is a recent arrival, perhaps a representative of that shifting mass of permanently migratory labor which filled the interstices of the economic structure.

Part of the Westminster prosecutions against retailers and victuallers in Essex and Norfolk may be, like the Sessions cases, the expression of growth; part probably result from the activity of informers attracted to the East Anglian granary by opportunities for profit on the middlemen statutes.[2] This would be especially likely in the years 1586–90 when bad harvests and high prices had stimulated the hostility of the great consuming center, London, toward the middleman and superfluous victualler. A number of the offenders may have been the aliens who filled this area, against whom trade conditions had also increased the antagonism.[3] But behind the East Anglian prosecutions against retailers were, probably, centralizing London influences as in the southwestern woolen industry. East Anglian worsteds and the young "new draperies" manufacture were outside the scope of the cloth acts; while much of the export trade in Essex short woolens was in

[1] Session records for the 16th century in the other fourteen counties are not sufficiently complete for a comparison, but in the 17th century, Norfolk and Essex maintain their lead in prosecutions against retailers and victuallers, except for Suffolk and other counties touching the London area; in the 16th century these show a concentration in 1586–90 like that in Norfolk and Essex.

[2] Against forestallers, regraters, ingrossers, exporters of grain. But in the Midlands wool-growing region a like activity of informers against wool-broggers was not accompanied by an increased apprenticeship prosecution of retailers.

[3] Cf. the draft of a bill in 1593 to prohibit aliens from retailing imports unless they had served a seven-year apprenticeship. (Hist. Mss. Com., Third Report, Appendix, House of Lords Mss., p. 8.)

London hands.[1] London wholesalers, however, in the seventeenth century endeavored to limit the country draper's independence,[2] and the prosecutions against Norfolk and Essex drapers and mercers seem to be a sixteenth-century symptom of the same movement. An industrial as well as a commercial interest was involved so far as London wholesalers were engaged in the finishing processes for stuffs and met competition from local drapers, mercers, and grocers in this line as well as in the export and domestic trade.[3]

Throughout England in the sixteenth century the apprenticeship law of 1563, observed by force of suitability and custom in some occupations and areas, was in others constantly neglected. The proportion of neglect to observance is not here the question, if indeed it is possible to answer. Certain conclusions have been suggested by watching the court record of the "national industrial code" in forty years of operation.

Fundamental in the relation of the Act to the economic changes of the period was the deflection of its force from national social ends to those of particular groups, of mercantile rather than industrial interests. In the local courts prosecutions reflect sporadically, but more accurately than at Westminster, the changing pressures of economic growth which brought new rivalries on the fringes of the towns, new demands in the villages, and induced occasional attempts to suppress competition on the part of local

[1] Friis, *op. cit.*, p. 21; at least this was true at the beginning of the 17th century. The woolen industry prosecutions in both counties seem to be due to local groups: Norwich craftsmen or drapers and Coggeshall clothiers.

[2] R. B. Westerfield, *Middlemen in English Business* (New Haven, 1915), p. 310.

[3] A Norwich grocer employed a servant who wove for him lace of worsted yarn: deposition of an embezzling silk-weaver in 1568, Norwich City Mss. Minute Books of Sessions, no. 4. It is not unlikely that local mercers, like their London confrères, were putters-out of yarn and silk to stuff-weavers.

groups or individuals, such as the mercers of Brentwood and Chelmsford,[1] the Staffordshire nailers, the Wiltshire weavers.[2] But in the Westminster courts it is only where a stronger influence than that of a local craft or trade is involved that the extent of prosecution corresponds to industrial or commercial expansion, so that in the national industry of cloth production both the cloth acts and the Statute of Artificers have little importance as an influence affecting industrial organization. Their potentialities as instruments of restriction on the putting-out system seem never in practice to have been realized. Little opposition is indeed discernible toward this invader of handicraft traditions, except when its extension from the town to the country awoke the resentment of town capitalists, or the employer's control of the instruments of production made obvious to the craftsman a dependence which was only latent in his control of the raw material. A rudimentary factory concentration of workers and tools sooner stirred the craftsman's opposition. Thus the Wiltshire master-weavers in the regulations they obtained from justices of the peace in 1603 restricted the "clothman" to keeping one loom and forbade any hiring out of looms; but while they insisted on apprenticeship for both journeymen and master-weavers, they required none for the clothier.[3]

But such opposition as there was to the putting-out system finds scanty expression in the court records, either local or central; the districts where Westminster prosecution in the woolen industry is greatest are districts with the least advanced form of putting-out organization. More-

[1] Essex Mss. Sessions Rolls, April Sess. 14 Eliz.

[2] The stimulus in some cases may have been the burden of taxation or poor relief.

[3] Wilts. Mss. Sessions Rolls, Mich. 1 Jas. 1; published in full in Hist. Mss. Com. Var. Coll., vol. i, pp. 74–75. A similar attitude is found among Suffolk weavers in 1539 (Unwin, *Studies in Economic History*, p. 272).

over, the apprenticeship regulations were least employed where they would have been most effective to check putting-out, against the unapprenticed clothier and the unapprenticed journeyman. Their slight use against the clothier was probably in part a result of the same public sentiment which may have tended to check prosecution of unapprenticed merchants. Whatever the prejudice of the country gentleman in the earlier sixteenth century had been against expansion of the cloth industry, succeeding generations of magistrates had to recognize the pivotal position of the clothier. "On his prosperity, and ability to give work to the poor, depended the social tranquillity of England."[1] In addition, there was the difficulty of defining a clothier's "exercise of a trade."[2] The rarity of prosecutions against the unapprenticed journeyman is but another indication of the small extent to which handicraft interests are represented in the attempted applications of the statutes. This lower layer of economic life was not touched by the London-inspired efforts at enforcement which in the southwest and in the east affected the upper employing and trading stratum and the middle layer of shopkeeper, victualler, small master, and home-worker.[3]

[1] Friis, *op. cit.*, p. 22. Thus the Suffolk justices in 1622 were unwilling to enforce the Act of 1563 against unapprenticed makers of new draperies, for fear of increasing depression and unemployment (S. P. D., Jas. 1, vol. cxxix, no. 59). In 1576 it was said that the cloth acts were not executed, since the magistrates "[per]ceaving what multitudes of pore do hang upon them have much favored ye matter" (S. P. D., Eliz., vol. cclxxxvii, no. 96).

[2] In Devon a husbandman was prosecuted for making kerseys without legal apprenticeship. He admitted lack of apprenticeship, but claimed that he had not made kerseys within the meaning of the statute: that he had bought them raw in the market and delivered them to the tucker, thereafter selling them. The court held that such buying and sale required no apprenticeship. (Excheq. Q. R. M. R., Hil. 22 Eliz., Rot. 65.)

[3] The term "home-worker" has been chosen to denote, however unsatisfactorily, that increasing part of the economic order made up of men who carried on a craft either within or outside a putting-out organization, but were independent of any traditional handicraft status as journeyman or small master.

INFORMATIONS IN THE EXCHEQUER, 1563–1603, AND IN THE
QUEEN'S BENCH, 1563–82

I

Cloth Acts

	Devon				Somerset				Wiltshire			
	A	B	C	D	A	B	C	D	A	B	C	D
1560–62	31	..	..	30	2	..	..	7	..	2	2	2
1563–65	57	2	45	22	24	13	14	·7	1	..	..	11
1566–70	24	12	71	13	7	16	37	3	..	..	2	..
1571–75	..	1	1	..	1	..	9	1	..	4	8	2
1576–80	8	5	32	7	..	10	4	..	..	4	..	1
1581–85	..	..	3	2	..	..	..	..	..	..	..	..
1586–90	..	..	..	..	..	..	..	..	..	1	..	..
1591–95	..	..	..	..	..	..	..	1	..	..	..	..
1596–00	5	2	..	..	..	..	..	..	..	..	..	..
1601–03	..	..	..	..	..	..	..	..	2	..	..	..
	125	22	152	94	34	39	64	19	3	11	12	16

Key: A — Weaving without apprenticeship, Act of 1555.
    B — Weaving, clothmaking, and rowing without apprenticeship, Act of 1557.
    C — Making cloth and kerseys in country places, Act of 1557.
    D — Keeping more than statutory number of looms, Act of 1555.

II

Seven-year term, Act of 1563

	Devon	Somerset	Wilts.	Worcs.	Essex	Norfolk
1563–65	2	6	2	3	2	4
1566–70	28	19	4	..	7	29
1571–75	2	5	18	5	2	10
1576–80	38	6	6	6	7	2
1581–85	5	6	3	2	16	6
1586–90	..	..	..	7	19	40
1591–95	1	..	..	1	1	1
1596–00	..	..	..	2	..	3
1601–03	1	2	3	..	2	..
	77	44	36	26	56	95

III

Distribution by trades, seven-year term, Act of 1563 [a]

	Devon[b]	Somerset	Wilts.	Worcs.	Essex	Norfolk[c]
clothier or clothmaker	..	6	5	8	1	1[d]
weaver	55	12	4	3	4	14[e]
dyer	4	3	3	..	3	..
clothmaker	..	1	..	..	..	..
shearman	..	..	..	1	..	3
fuller	1	1	4	1	..	..
tailor	..	..	2	..	4	9
draper	..	1	1	1	..	2
woolendraper	..	1	4	..	1	2
linendraper	..	..	..	..	3	1
mercer	2	2	..	1	5	6
haberdasher	..	1	..	..	..	2
grocer	..	3	..	..	3	2
chandler	..	2	1	1	7	1
miller	1	..	..	..	1	4
baker	3	2	2	1	3	10
brewer	..	1	2	..	8	14
butcher	1	2	6	..	2	3

[a] Omitted from the table are the prosecutions against offenders in leather trades, building trades, and metal trades, none of these groups having more than five in any county; also a few miscellaneous trades, ash-burner, potter, hosier, etc., with one or two prosecutions only. For other counties cf. above, p. 143, n. 1.

[b] Devon has one prosecution against a *merchant*.

[c] Norfolk has an additional prosecution, in retailing, against a *petty chapman*.

[d] "Maker of broadcloth, bays and says."

[e] And six linen-weavers.

MEDIEVAL SPANISH GILDS

JULIUS KLEIN

As EACH royal conqueror, in the centuries succeeding Alfonso VI's capture of Toledo in 1085, raised his pennants over the walls of some stronghold newly captured in the reconquest of Moorish Spain, the ever-present chroniclers, amid their glowing descriptions of the pageantry and exaltation of the historic event, in almost every case made note of one lowly but interesting detail. They were struck by the fact that the Moors had carefully segregated the craftsmen in streets or wards, according to their various callings and evidently with some definite, orderly administration of their common craft affairs.[1]

Certain circumstances of the life and environment of the Spanish kingdoms in their successive epochs were especially conducive to the development of craft organizations. First of all there were the various natural advantages and resources of the peninsula, particularly the abundance of those raw materials essential for vigorous industrial growth — extensive mineral deposits, exceptional clays and building stone, almost unlimited pastoral possibilities, and greatly diversified forest resources from the coniferous zones in the northwest to the sub-tropical region of the southeast. With excellent harbors adjoining major sea-lanes in every direction, widespread oversea commercial operations were inevitable, and it was no accident that

[1] Juan de Hinojosa, "La Asoc. profesional obrera" in *Revista católica de cuestiones sociales* (August, 1915). The Moors were not the first inhabitants of the peninsula or of Europe to follow this practice; but, as we shall see, theirs was the influence which gave the immediate impulse to the development of the Spanish gild system.

some of the earliest, most vigorous gild life of medieval Spain appeared among the seafaring folk on the Catalonian and Biscayan coasts.

Three other factors in the evolution of Spanish civilization had an immediate bearing upon the stimulation of the gild system. First, the peninsula was for long periods torn with the bitterest warfare, not simply among the various kingdoms and rival groups of nobility, where it was chronic throughout Europe in the Middle Ages, but particularly during the more than seven centuries of the wars of reconquest against the Moslem invaders. This made for the close concentration of life in walled cities where the restricted markets made imperative, especially during the thirteenth century and in certain areas of chronic hostilities, the very type of limitation upon competition within crafts and trades which was the essence of the gild. Secondly, the intermittent, often prolonged, campaigns also meant empty coffers for many a royal treasury, even after the expulsion of the Moslems, when imperial ambitions in the Old World and the New lured the Spanish sovereigns into many costly delusions of grandeur. The fiscal support of organized industrial and trade groups became precious indeed to more than one harassed monarch. Thirdly, the devout crusading fervor which inflamed the nation with each successive drive against the hated infidel supplied added incentive to that religious element which was so prominent in the early stages of gild life everywhere. The Spanish *cofradia* or fraternity, the predecessor of the gild, observed the ecclesiastical precepts common to such bodies throughout early medieval Europe with far more earnest, grim intensity than did its contemporaries in other lands. It was thus able to pass along to the gild a solidarity of organization which had much to do with the subsequent vigor of gild life in Spain.

In view of the rich natural resources of the peninsula, it was but natural that the Roman colonial authorities, beginning in the time of Julius Caesar, should set up in Spain various *collegia* or corporate groups of craftsmen for the systematic exploitation and control of mining, metal- and clay-working, quarrying, the making of textiles, the preparation of foodstuffs, and allied pursuits. But neither these organizations, nor any which may have been set up during the turbulent, confused Visigothic interlude of some three centuries between Roman and Moorish periods, can be accepted as definitely preliminary to the medieval gild system of Spain. There is no proof of unbroken continuity. Even if there were, the differences between the two earlier institutions and the gild were so fundamental as not to warrant placing them on any common basis other than in the broad category of groups of artisans. For example, although the Fuero Juzgo, the great Visigothic code, has ample evidence of handicraft activities,[1] it says nothing as to any definite, orderly groupings for purposes of craft control. It would seem very doubtful, therefore, whether the Germanic *gelda*, a religious rather than an industrial association of craftsmen, or any other comparable Gothic device ever appeared in Spain as a link between the Roman *collegia* and the medieval gild.[2]

In 711 began the series of swiftly surging invasions of the Moslems, who with amazing speed soon inundated the peninsula. Industry and commerce were at the outset, of

[1] E. g., leyes 4 and 12, lib. ix, tit. i.

[2] Among those who adhere to the belief of such continuity are Rodriguez Villa, "Reseña hist. de los Gremios" in *Almanaque del Museo de la Industria* (Madrid, 1871), p. 129; Tramoyeres, *Instituciones Gremiales en Valencia* (Valencia, 1889), p. 31; Eduardo Ibarra, "El Origen de las Universidades," *Real. Acad. Hist.* (Madrid); Perez Pujol, introduction to Tramoyeres, *op. cit.*, pp. 8–9. Perez Pujol, *Hist. instituciones sociales . . . Esp. goda*, implies that there were traces of the apprenticeship system under the Goths in Spain, but his evidence is inconclusive.

course, badly disrupted, but as the invaders consolidated their gains, decades and even generations elapsed between the successive campaigns, and consequently there was ample opportunity during these long intervals for the development of trade, not simply within the respective Christian and Moslem areas, but also between the two.[1] Furthermore, the Moors retained many phases of Christian economic and even religious life within their domains; but in addition, and quite independently, they influenced decidedly the future industrial development of the peninsula's civilization.[2]

They not only brought with them their priceless heritages of learning — in mathematics, astronomy, the ancient classics, and so forth — but made equally significant contributions along industrial lines as well. Their exceptional native talents in fine steel fabrication, ceramics, leatherwork, and textiles were soon brought to fullest flower by the abundance of Spanish raw materials essential for these favorite crafts of theirs.[3] It is no wonder, then, that James the Conqueror, as he rode through the streets of Valencia in 1238 on taking possession from the Moors, remarked upon the twenty or more sections of the city which had been allocated each to a different craft. It was quite natural that various groups of artisans, well organized into something very like gild units, were conspicuous among the Moorish inhabitants of Cordova who welcomed Sancho the Fat of Castile in 956 when he made

[1] Arch. Real. Acad. Hist., Madrid, Salazar Mss., vol. i, p. 36, cites documents of the Military Order of Calatrava (caj. 3, nos. 9, 10) of 1173 and 1182 granting the Order certain revenues levied on caravans "between Toledo and Cordova . . . trading with the Moors."

[2] In the same collection, Manuel Abella Mss., vol. viii: a 13th-century Moorish code of rules for markets, handicrafts, etc., which apparently served as a model for similar ordinances in various Christian cities after their recapture from the Moors.

[3] Cf. Riaño, *Industrial Arts in Spain* (Madrid, 1879).

his much heralded weight-reducing pilgrimage to the Jewish court physician of Abd-ar-rahman III. Indeed, the opinion seems to be general among historians that Moorish industries had actually advanced to the stage of gild organization — control of output, inspection, and determination of working conditions — or something closely approximating it.[1] But precise data on this point are unfortunately not available, save perhaps on apprenticeship regulations under group control, of which there are some evidences.[2]

It is significant that in those northern Castilian cities whence the Moslems were first evicted the early Christian town charters of the ninth, tenth, and eleventh centuries, though frequently referring to many crafts, give no indication of any organized groups of them. The inspection of wares, the establishment of weights and measures, and the determination of working conditions, among other usual perquisites of the gild, were in almost every case placed in the hands of the town council (*concejo* or *cabildo*).[3]

Indeed municipal institutions were well along in their development in medieval Christian Spain, before there was any indication of a definite gild system in control of industry. We have, then, in Spain a confirmation of the

[1] Notably Conde, *Hist. Dom. Arabe*, pt. iv, cap. 19; Rodriguez Villa, *op. cit.*

[2] Amador de los Rios, *Hist. de los Judios en Esp.*, vol. i, p. 154. Uña y Sarthou, *Asoc. obreras en Esp.*, p. 103. On the other hand, cf. Arch. Real. Acad. Hist., Madrid, Mss. 25–1–C 12, fol. 113: a privilege granted by Alfonso X to the clothmakers of Murcia shortly after its capture in 1243, to carry on their craft in their own homes with their assistants without any external control or administration.

[3] Muñoz y Romero, *Colec. de Fueros*, pp. 73, 124ff.; *España Sagrada*, vol. xxxviii, cap. xiv. These references are to *fueros*, or charters, from the 9th century down to that of 1020 of León. They mention many trades, including some instances where artisans worked in family groups, but nothing more. Indeed the León charter refers plainly to tax payments and other formalities by individual craftsmen, with no allusion whatever to associated action among them. The famous *fuero* of Sahagun (1084), one of the most detailed feudalistic documents in Spanish history, shows no sign whatever of organized crafts.

deduction of Charles Gross in connection with the origin of English municipal government, as to the lack of any substantial contribution thereto by the gild. It is not until the end of the twelfth or the beginning of the thirteenth century, after the reconquest had penetrated far down the peninsula and taken in all of the larger, industrially developed centers except Granada, that we come upon unmistakable evidences of artisan associations under Christian jurisdiction.

Whatever its antecedents — Roman, Gothic, or Moorish — the Spanish gild, like its contemporaries elsewhere, sprang from circumstances which would have produced it whether there had been any precedent of similar character in that region or not. As Sancho Seral, one of the best informed recent investigators of this subject has remarked, the Spanish gild was "fully explained by its epoch, justified by its social environment."[1] As production technique improved under the Moorish influences already referred to, the consumer and producer were no longer within the same household and the division of labor thus began. The craftsmen soon felt the "collectivistic" spirit of the time, which was stimulated by the proximity of members of the same calling within a common neighborhood. Such segregation afforded a ready basis for the next step in definite gild organization.[2] The latter arose only where and when indus-

[1] *El Gremio Zaragozano* (Saragossa, 1925). See also Minguijón, *Elementos de la Hist. del Derecho Esp.* (Saragossa, 1915), vol. iv, p. 92; Eduardo Hinojosa, *Hist. Derecho Esp.* (Madrid, 1883), vol. i, p. 263; Sales y Ferré, cited by Uña, *op. cit.*, p. 98. Uña, however, inclines to the theory of the continuity of Spanish gild life from Roman to medieval times.

[2] Incidentally, the segregation seems to have been a purely voluntary affair, a convenience for customers and craftsmen, and not the result of any mandate from local or royal authorities such as was evident in some other countries. Cf. Keutgen, cited by Maunier, *L'origine et la fonction écon. des villes* (Paris, 1910), p. 199; also von Below, *Probleme der Wirtschaftsgesch* (Tübingen, 1920), p. 299. Sancho Seral, *op. cit.*, p. 19, cites the case of a halberd-maker in Saragossa in the 15th century who had been expelled from the town quarter of his craft by his

try had become so well developed as to empower the artisans to group together for their mutual advantage, and especially for defense against other elements in a social order in which the lone individual was indeed helpless. And, as in other lands, here it was the craftsmen themselves who took the initiative without mandate from any over-lord.[1]

An important consequence of this early regionalization of crafts was the concentration of individual trades by parishes. The parochial unit, partly because of the centuries of religious fervor during the wars of reconquest, became to a peculiar degree the nucleus of Spanish community life. It follows, therefore, that as each craft set up an organization among its members there was an instinctive association of the group with some parish saint and chapel or shrine.[2] We thus find the religious element strongly affiliated almost at the outset with these trade groups, which appeared all over the peninsula under a variety of names, many of them with religious connotations: *congregaciones, sodalidades, hermandades, almoynes, caritats, basíliques,* and so on; but the most common term was that of *cofradia* or fraternity.[3]

The recurring fervor of crusading enthusiasm down to

colleagues and subsequently petitioned the city fathers to permit his return, "else his livelihood would be gravely impaired." Ortiz de Zuñiga, *Anales de Sevilla* (lib. ii, p. 1253), refers to the crafts having districted themselves in that city, evidently a heritage from Moorish times; there is also an indication of the distribution of traders by various nationalities — French, Genoese, Castilians, Catalonians, and so forth.

[1] Uña, *op. cit.*, p. 319; Bisson, *Hist. du Travail*, p. 8.

[2] Cf. Ramírez de Arellano, *Catálogo de artifices . . . en Toledo . . . en los archivos de sus parroquias* (Toledo, 1920).

[3] These earlier religious bodies of workers were most varied and numerous in Aragon; cf. *Colec. Docs. Arch. Corona Arag.*, Bofarull, ed., vol. xl, p. vi. See also "Antiguos Gremios de Huesca," Ricardo del Arco, ed., *Colec. Docs. par Hist. Arag.*, vol. vi (Saragossa, 1911). The last-named collection has a few of the earlier *cofradia* documents, but is mainly composed of gild ordinances of the 16th to 18th centuries, inclusive.

the evacuation of Granada by the Moors in 1492, and especially during the great drive of reconquest from 1212 to about 1260, did much to strengthen these semi-religious associations of workers, which were thus prolonged considerably beyond the period when similar bodies elsewhere in Europe had deteriorated to more or less perfunctory social groups. But it must not be assumed that the *cofradia* was simply a body of artisans with devotional purposes. Its members "did not unite to adore a saint; they united before the saint to accomplish certain political and social purposes."[1] Its objective was evidently group action by the industrial element so that it might take its place in the sharply classified social order of that day.

The *cofradia*, however, was still by no means a full-fledged gild organization. It was devoted almost solely in its earlier stages to mutual welfare, sick and funeral benefits, religious and civic ceremonials, and similar non-industrial purposes. It had none of the control functions and monopolistic objectives which distinguished the bona fide gild or *gremio* of later years. In a word, it closely approximated the early-eleventh-century craft fraternities of Cambridge, Abbotsbury, and Exeter.

It has been customary to refer to the *cofradia* as a sort of religious antecedent of the gild, to imply that somewhere along in the decades 1100–50 Spanish craftsmen began to organize themselves into religious clubs, which were gradually transformed some two centuries later into associations with predominantly industrial purposes. However, this

---

[1] Sancho Seral, *op. cit.*, p. 21; Uña, *op. cit.*, p. 141. Those "purposes" sometimes took on a military significance, as during the siege of Barcelona in 1359, when the *cofradias* organized the defense. Any sizeable insurrection, from that launched against Queen Urraca of Castile (1109–26) in Sahagun to the more serious revolts under Charles v by the *Germanía* of Valencia and the *comuneros* of Castile in 1519–21, were vigorously participated in by the craft fraternities. Cf. Muñoz y Romero, *op. cit.*, p. 302; Tramoyeres, *op. cit.*, pp. 97, 105–107.

simple and convenient formula, like a good many others, is not entirely accurate. Indeed, there were *cofradias* which already, as early as the first half of the twelfth century, had certain economic attributes usually associated only with bona fide gilds of a much later period. For instance, the *cofradia* of the shop-keepers of Soria was recognized by Alfonso VII (1126–57) as having not only certain religious functions, but also the privilege of choosing a provost and two judges to supervise certain local weights and measures.[1] Furthermore, any disputes within the craft membership were to be settled by special magistrates of the craftsmen themselves.[2]

The town charter of Oviedo of 1145 and that of Ledesma of about the same date recognized the organization of *cofradias* among the various crafts for industrial administrative purposes.[3] In 1200, Pedro II of Aragon incorporated in a comprehensive decree a series of earlier privileges as applied to craft fraternities in Barcelona along the same lines.[4] Similarly, the town charter of Escalona (1130) is interpreted by some writers as a warrant to the local artisans to include in the ordinances of their *cofradia* certain special industrial privileges.[5]

These instances depict a gradual development of various

---

[1] Loperraez, *Descrip. Obisp. Osma*, vol. i, p. 275; vol. ii, p. 245; Colmeiro, *Hist. Pol. Econ. Esp.* (Madrid, 1863), vol. ii, p. 316. This privilege was later extended to other *cofradias* of Soria by various sovereigns, notably Ferdinand III in 1239, who not only exempted their respective memberships from certain royal taxes in exchange for lump sum payments, but specified that their products were to be inspected by four or five of their own "good men" instead of by town officers. Cf. Loperraez, *op. cit.*, vol. iii, p. 60.

[2] Asso. *Hist. Econ. Polit. Aragon*, p. 214, indicates that the allocation of the *cofradia* of furriers in Saragossa to a certain quarter of the city in 1137 carried with it also certain arrangements for the self-regulation of their operations, the inspection of products, and so forth.

[3] Sanchez Ruano, *Fuero de Salamanca*, p. 160.

[4] Capmany, *Memorias . . . sobre la marina de Barcelona* (Barcelona, 1780), vol. i, p. 15.

[5] Muñoz y Romero, *op. cit.*, p. 485.

non-religious functions on the part of the *cofradia*, although it is well to note that one of the most important functions of the later craft gild, namely the control of weights and measures, was still largely in the hands of town officials during the twelfth and thirteenth centuries.[1]

It is, of course, out of the question to establish with any degree of precision the definite beginnings of the predominance of economic over religious and social purposes in these organizations. To say, as do some historians, that the religious *cofradia* was displaced in the early 1300's by a predominantly economic *gremio* or gild would be decidedly misleading. Indeed there were areas in Spain, the kingdom of Aragon for example, where the name *cofradia* was applied to craft associations right through their whole cycle, from their earliest emergence at the beginning of the twelfth century down to their collapse in the eighteenth. As a matter of fact, the term *gremio* does not occur in any of the Aragonese source materials consulted in the present study, and the documentation on gild life in that kingdom is unusually voluminous; although, of course, for purposes of convenience the term *gremio* is often utilized by modern writers in their descriptions of Aragonese industrial history.

In general, then, the title of *cofradia* cannot be taken to connote invariably a religious fraternity of craftsmen throughout medieval Spanish history.[2] The process of transformation from the industry of serfdom to that of the

---

[1] Cf. the town charters of Tudela (1117), Sahagun (1152), and Oviedo (1145), in Muñoz y Romero, *op. cit.*, *passim*. In the case of Oviedo the inhabitants were given permission to sell bread and cider " according to just measurements whenever they wished" under the supervision of a town official, the *merino de los hombres buenos*. Cf. also Martinez Vigal, *Colec. Hist. Ayunt. Oviedo*, pp. 9ff.

[2] In fact, quite apart from the Aragonese instance just cited, that term was often applied to other varieties of non-religious associations. For example, in Cáceres there was in the middle decades of the fourteenth century a *cofradia* of young sportsmen of the nobility made up only of "those gentlemen who had participated in bull fights." (Arch. Real. Acad. Hist., Madrid, Mss. 12–24–5, B 126.)

gild system was unquestionably facilitated by this interlude of religious association. In Catalonia, where gild life became especially vigorous during the rapid industrial and commercial rise of that section, there were during the first half of the twelfth century not only considerable numbers of craft fraternities with industrial functions but also even groups of masters of such organizations. In a way this development seems to have been similar to the English gild merchant in its earlier religious and social form. In the country as a whole, however, there is no evidence of a precise Spanish equivalent to that body. In England the gild merchant thrived longest in communities where the division of labor was more retarded, namely in smaller towns in the midst of rural districts; but in the case of the Spanish cities, whether because of their heritage of strong Moorish industrial advancement or for other reasons, there was little or no evidence of such general associations of the merchants in all lines of a given locality.[1]

It was not until the thirteenth century that there were widespread evidences of real craft organization for purposes of trade and industrial control, with all the gild attributes of standardization of product, classification of workers (as apprentices, journeymen, and masters), group control of raw material distribution, inspection of working conditions and output, and so forth. These were prescribed for each craft in great detail by the municipal authorities in the various town ordinances and charters of that period.

In addition to this close control of the municipal governments over the crafts, there were also certain functions

[1] Alcocer and Basanta de la Riva, *Fuentes Hist. Gremios . . . Valladolid* (Valladolid, 1921), cite a "medieval *cofradia*" in that city which was made up of representatives from forty-nine craft groups. The authors, however, do not present any specific documentary evidence as to the type or date of this organization.

operating in the opposite direction; in other words, there were instances of participation in the town administration by spokesmen of the various craft gilds.[1] Clearly such participation of craft members in municipal government under royal sanction indicated a definitely non-religious functioning of the *cofradias*, since the presence of their spokesmen on the various town councils was obviously intended for legislative and administrative action on commercial and industrial matters. In thus recognizing the rising economic importance of the *cofradia* the Crown had before it frequent precedents of royal favors to individual associations of craftsmen, usually in the shape of exemptions from royal taxes or from the jurisdiction of some Crown officer.[2]

The great thirteenth-century general code of Castilian law, namely *Las Siete Partidas* of Alfonso the Wise, and the corresponding general codes of Aragon, Valencia, and Catalonia, all go into great detail regarding standards of trade ethics, especially stipulating the punishment of fraud, without, however, making any reference to the use of the *cofradia* or any other craft group for that purpose. The whole tenor of these compilations is in defense of the consumer as against the crafts.[3]

[1] For example, the city council of Barcelona by decree of James I in 1257 was ordered to include among its membership a number of craft-gild representatives, which soon rose to 32 out of the total 100, an indication of the great influence of these industrial groups in the Catalonian capital. The same was true in Perpiñan, Lérida, Gerona, and other Catalonian cities. In Valencia in 1283, Peter I of Aragon included four representatives of each of the twenty-one craft gilds in the town council. (Cruilles, *Gremios de Valencia*, 1883, p. 10.)

[2] Capmany, *op. cit.*, vol. i, p. 16. Similar concessions were made to certain craftsmen of Valladolid by Ferdinand IV in 1297 and by Alfonso XI in 1331.

[3] For example, in 1283 royal confirmation was given to an earlier charter of the *cofradia* of the weavers of Soria in which sharp penalties were fixed for any artisan indulging in night work, not as a social evil, but because it afforded opportunity for concealment and fraud to the detriment of the consumer. Similar contemporaneous instances might be cited of royal stipulations regarding the qualities of cloth and accepted methods of manufacture. The penalty as a rule

The municipalities followed precedents in the royal codes and likewise established their control not simply over the qualities of workmanship among the various crafts, but even over the very existence of certain callings. In Cáceres in 1229, for instance, we find the town charter establishing punishment for any craftsman carrying on his vocation "sine mandato de concilio." Indeed, the town ordinances of this period were so detailed on the technical phases of industry that they might well be referred to as veritable codes of industrial policing.[1]

The gradual development of non-religious functions of the *cofradia* during the latter half of the thirteenth century evidently gave some concern to the Crown.[2] Social activities were broadened in many directions, even to the maintenance of drill corps and marching clubs ostensibly for purely social diversion. This development, however, be-

---

consisted of confiscation and burning the faulty product in the public market place. (Loperraez, *op. cit.*, vol. iii, p. 217.) The Partidas in general took no unfavorable attitude toward the artisans other than barring them from entry into the ranks of knighthood (pt. ii, tit. xxi, ley 2). The restrictive attitude toward industry referred to above was aimed rather at the masters of establishments. Although the Castilian code thus frowned on the industrial leaders of the country, in Aragon and Catalonia they were allowed to enter town councils, as already pointed out, and even had access to higher offices in the kingdom, indicative of the favorable status of industry which has prevailed in Catalonia from that day to this.

[1] The ordinance of Oviedo of 1245 required bakers to use a stipulated town seal in stamping each loaf of bread so as to identify the acceptable grades and to assure uniformity of product. The local ordinances of the same city of 1274 designated meat inspectors whose approval was required "in the interests of public health" before any meat could be offered for sale in the town. Similarly the town charter of Salamanca fixed restrictions on the sale of cutlery, established prices for leather and iron products, and so forth. The charters of Molina and Plasencia of the second half of the 13th century fixed prices and penalties for adulteration for a dozen or more trades. In the case of the latter city the ordinance stipulated that shoemakers, to take one typical example of extreme detail, must do their work so well "that the stitches would not come out until the sole wore through." There was also precise stipulation as to the thickness of leather to be used, the size of seams, and so forth. (Colmeiro, *op. cit.*, vol. i, p. 319.)

[2] See above, p. 171, n. 1. As early as the first quarter of the 12th century, the military potentiality of the *cofradia* was rather disquieting to the Crown.

gan to concern the political authorities; hence we have Alfonso X going so far in the charter of Sahagun (1255) as to prohibit all *confraderias* in that town.[1] Similarly the charter of León (1267) prohibited the maintenance of such organizations except on written permission from the bishop. James I also began a series of restrictive measures in Valencia and Aragon at about the same time.[2] It should be understood, however, that these restrictive measures were evidently the exception rather than the rule, since there are repeated instances of royal favors being granted directly to the *cofradias* of craftsmen in many cities, even to the extent at times of acceptance by the sovereign of honorary membership in some especially favored group.[3]

As indicated above, the economic as contrasted with the religious and social aspects of the *cofradia* were already well in evidence by the middle of the thirteenth century.[4]

---

[1] Muñoz de Romero, *op. cit.*, p. 313.

[2] Tramoyeres, *op. cit.*, p. 42.

[3] Ferdinand III (1217–52) and his Queen were honorary members of the tailors' *cofradia* of Seville. He had also given the members of the tanners' fraternity of Soria so many exemptions from the jurisdiction of the town authorities in the inspection of their wares that they likewise regarded him as one of their craft.

The earliest complete ordinances of a *cofradia* encountered in the present study are those of the silversmiths and iron-workers of Valencia dated 1298 (*Col. Docs. Ineds. Arch., Aragon*, vol. xi, pp. 23ff.). The document comprises many royal concessions to these craftsmen, who seem to have been the special favorites of the Crown, not only in this kingdom but throughout the peninsula, possibly because of the special interest of the royal household in the products of their workmanship.

[4] As a rule each group had an executive assembly or *cabildo* composed apparently of most of the more prominent members of the craft. This group designated four *jurados* or inspectors who carried out the industrial policing of the craft, levied fines, confiscated improper products, enforced work rules, and so forth. In Valencia the inspectors were named by the Crown and turned over a portion of their collections of fees to a town official, the *almotacen* or *mustafaz*, who supervised or observed such inspections in the interests of consumers. In some crafts, especially those affecting public health, such as the food trades, the city magistrates chose a small group of councillors, usually twelve, through whom the municipal authorities exercised control over the industry. In the case of larger crafts the *jurados* were aided in their tasks by various *veedores* or "ob-

Membership in the crafts was, according to all available evidences, entirely voluntary at least up to the early 1300's. By the end of the fourteenth century, however, obligatory membership and artisan classifications were evident in all parts of the peninsula.[1]

The thirteenth-century craft ordinances still retained many heritages of the earlier religious origins of the *cofradia*.[2] Numerous formalities of the organization were centered about the parochial church or neighborhood chapel. There were always careful provisions of alms for the poor and contributions toward the celebration of various saints' days. The *cofradias* were also conspicuous in combating the fearful pestilences which swept over the peninsula on various occasions, as for example that which devastated Seville in 1383. One incidental feature of interest is the fact that women members participated in the *cofradias* in various cities.

After the recapture of Cadiz in 1262, there was a lull of some two centuries in the drive of the reconquest, with the exception of the campaigns from 1327 to 1350 around Gibraltar. The Moors had been hemmed in behind the

servers." Occasionally they also called upon a small group of *prohombres* or veteran masters, who in some cases had retired from active operation. Uña (*op. cit.*, p. 134) analyzes the ordinance of the cobblers' *cofradia* of Burgos of 1259, bringing out numerous industrial stipulations. This definitely refutes the theory of Tramoyeres that there were no signs of conspicuously industrial functions in the bona fide *cofradia* of the 13th century.

[1] Uña, *op. cit.*, pp. 143ff.

[2] Related to this aspect of these organizations is the religious phase of the Mesta, the Castilian sheep-owners' association. That body was, of course, in no way associated with these various local crafts, since its membership was made up of participants in the industry all over the country and was in that respect almost the only example of a national industrial organization. Nevertheless, it too gave evidence of considerable devotional interest. A very elaborate portable altar was carried back and forth in the semi-annual migrations of the herdsmen, and impressive ceremonies were held at either end of the great journeys to and from the pastures in the northern mountains and the southern and western plains. The account books of the organization show careful semi-annual contributions to numerous religious funds and purposes.

mountain borders of the kingdom of Granada, where they held out until Ferdinand and Isabella raised their colors over the towers of the Alhambra on the morning of New Year's Day, 1492. Thus the Christian sovereigns, during the last two centuries of the Middle Ages, were able to devote more and more of their attention to the consolidation of their respective kingdoms and the upbuilding of trade and industry. The fourteenth and early fifteenth centuries were therefore filled with indications of progress of craft organizations all over the country.[1]

Indeed on more than one occasion there were evidences of real concern as to whether this craft movement was getting out of hand. James II of Aragon actually went so far in 1315 as to issue the notable decree *ut monopolia*, formally abolishing the industrial fraternities in his kingdom, evidently because of their threatened encroachment upon royal prerogatives. This was confirmed in various royal edicts in connection with town charters in which the *cofradias* were sharply singled out for their "disservice to the king and other peril to the people." [2] There were similar contemporaneous pronouncements in Castile, Aragon, Valencia, and Navarre.

But the trend of the gild movement was evidently too strong to be checked by such royal declarations.[3] Throughout the fourteenth century craft groups of all varieties from shepherds to surgeons in all parts of the country were formally recognized in such royal decrees, thus effectually

---

[1] *Docs. Ineds. Corona Arag.*, vol. xl, pp. 23ff.: ordinances of numerous Aragonese *cofradias* of this period.

[2] Charter of the town of Tudela in Muñoz y Romero, p. 423. See also Asso, *op. cit.*, p. 235.

[3] James II granted the right to organize a *cofradia* to the furriers of Saragossa only four years after his stern edict of prohibition of 1315. Similar grants were made to other trades in various cities in 1322, 1328, 1329, and 1336. The one of 1336 was a grant by Pedro IV of Aragon to the Jewish cobblers throughout that kingdom, permitting them to organize in a single craft fraternity.

nullifying the edicts of general prohibition. The latter apparently originated in part at least as a gesture of consideration to various municipal authorities and other groups more or less antagonistic to or jealous of the rising power of the crafts.

This widespread intrusion of the Crown into industrial regulation was evidenced in the royal responses at almost every meeting of the Castilian, Valencian, and Aragonese Cortes during the fourteenth century.[1] A good Castilian illustration of such centralized regulation was the decree of Peter the Cruel of 1351, the famous *Ordenamiento de Menestrales* or Ordinance of Artisans, which fixed wages, prices, and working conditions for a dozen or more crafts. His successor, Henry II, issued a similar ordinance early in his reign (1369–79).[2] Municipal authorities were in each case instructed to amplify these decrees with any necessary detailed local regulations. In some cases the Crown delegated to the town authorities the right to issue all necessary gild ordinances, carefully reserving, however, the right of final approval.[3] Thus the Crown and the municipalities everywhere utilized the craft organizations for purposes of administration and regulation of industry, and especially, of course, of taxes.

Probably the best example of such procedure was in the case of Barcelona, which was easily the industrial leader of Spain, then as now. By 1400 the city had some forty-five active craft groups, each with an elaborate series of char-

---

[1] For instance, the Valencia Cortes of 1348 confirmed the right of the Crown to indicate when and how the craft meetings were to be held. This was felt necessary because "unauthorized meetings had been followed by grave consequences." It was stipulated, furthermore, that all such meetings had to be confined strictly to the industrial interests of the craft. Cf. Cruilles, *op. cit.*, pp. 14–15.

[2] Cf. Sempere y Guarinos, *Hist. del Lujo*, p. 142; *Ords. Reales*, lib. vii, tit. v, ley 1.

[3] James II made such a grant to Barcelona in 1319, which was confirmed by Peter IV in 1337.

ters and ordinances.[1] The relationship between town authorities and gilds in Barcelona, to which reference has already been made, became by the latter part of the fourteenth century an even more intimate affair. That is, the representation of the gilds on the town council and in the various other units of the town government were more extensive, and as a consequence the gilds in turn were constantly the subject of legislative and administrative action on the part of the municipal authorities.[2]

In Aragon the gilds were not represented in the town governments as a rule; nevertheless the town councils, rather than the Crown, with rare exceptions [3] established their direct authority over the trade groups. As a rule the ordinances of the gilds in Aragonese cities during the fourteenth century acknowledged in the opening passages of those documents their indebtedness to the town officials, not the king, for the right to organize the craft in the interests of the citizens of the community. As the century progressed, the latter aspect was especially stressed in connection with the reservation of the craft for the residents of the community as against strangers from near-by cities and especially from foreign countries.

The progress made during the fourteenth century in the general strength of the gild movement naturally resulted in a marked elaboration of the external relations of the institution to the consumer, to other gilds, and to the municipal authorities. During this period various municipalities

[1] Some idea of the voluminous character of these 14th-century gild documents can be gained from the pages of Capmany, op. cit., vol. iii, pp. 321ff., and vol. iv, passim, in which are tabulated the gild codes of this variety from those of the silversmiths of 1301 to the ordinance of the provisions dealers' fraternity of 1395. See also Uña, op. cit., pp. 177–178.

[2] Cf. Juan de Hinojosa in Rev. Catal. de Cuest. Soc., January, 1916.

[3] One of the few such exceptions where the Crown intervened directly in Aragonese craft jurisdiction was in the case of the approval granted by Philip II to the ordinances of the fraternity of notaries of Saragossa in 1561, doubtless because of the semi-official character of their calling.

developed so-called *casas del peso*, or bureaux of weights and measures, in the functioning of which the respective gilds collaborated closely, sometimes even to the extent of designating one or more representatives who had joint authority with a corresponding number of town officials in controlling the measurements for a specified commodity. In the case of the larger seaboard towns *consulados del mar*, official trade promotion and control offices, were established to advance and regulate the commerce of the port. The local craft gilds were associated with these bodies with a view toward guaranteeing the quality of the export wares. In this field the Catalonian and Valencian ports led the way, which had not a little to do with the great success of the Mediterranean trade of those regions in the later Middle Ages. Aragonese political and commercial domination around the shores of the inland sea reached its peak in the 1440's, with consulates in fifty-five cities and trading footholds in nearly every important community around the Mediterranean.

In general, by the close of the fourteenth century the economic purposes of the craft groups had very largely crowded out their social and religious aspects, although such religious aspects as loyalty to the patron saint of the craft and the observance of certain religious ceremonials remained. As indicated above, the term *cofradia* was used in Aragon down to the nineteenth century to include both industrial and religious types of the craft associations. Elsewhere in the peninsula, however, the fifteenth century brought a gradual segregation as between the *cofradia* or fraternity with its major religious and social interests on the one hand and the *gremio* or gild with its very predominantly industrial interest on the other.[1]

---

[1] The religious aspects of the *cofradia* were carefully fostered and respected by local as well as central authorities, even when restrictive measures were

The *gremio* was already growing in power and prestige as the fourteenth century drew to a close. It had developed a marked specialization of internal structure: stricter disciplining of its members; the stipulation of detailed qualifications for their various gradations, working conditions, and so forth. Naturally there came with this an increasing insistence upon compulsory membership. First evidences of this occur in Valencia in 1392, where by town ordinance all silversmiths practicing their art in that place were required to be members of the gild.[1] Similar restrictions appeared shortly thereafter in Castilian cities, and it was not long before there came the inevitable testing and examination of candidates for each craft, which thus introduced the basic gild philosophy of monopoly control.

Thus the interrelationship among the three grades or classes within the ranks of the crafts, namely apprentices, journeymen, and masters, became much more definite as the gilds increased in strength and significance during the fifteenth century. The earliest indication of elaborate apprenticeship rules occurred in Valencia in 1443;[2] and, as usual, the Castilian gilds followed shortly thereafter.[3] There had, however, been evidences of recognition of the institution of apprenticeship at least as early as the middle of the thirteenth century, when Alfonso x, in *Las Siete Partidas*, referred to payment of a training fee to masters by their subordinates.[4] At about the same time James I gave master craftsmen in Valencia complete control of the

---

adopted against the industrial activities of those bodies. For example, when Charles v in 1528 at the Cortes of Monzón formally declared the abolition of *cofradias*, he specifically exempted their religious functions from the edict.

[1] Tramoyeres, *op. cit.*, p. 55.

[2] Uña, *op. cit.*, pp. 195–265.

[3] *Idem*, pp. 187–188, citing the membership rules of the cobblers and tailors of Burgos. Sancho Seral, *op. cit.*, p. 28, describes the compulsory examination by the town inspectors (*veedores*) of any would-be storekeepers.

[4] Pt. v, tit. viii, ley 11.

persons of their apprentices.[1] It was not until the 1380's that formal apprenticeship contracts made their appearance, usually between the boy's father and the employer.[2] At that time in such agreements the apprenticeship period was usually fixed for about five years, and the master was required to give "good and sufficient food, drink, clothing, and shoes, in sickness and in health," while the lad was being taught his trade. In Catalonia the term of service was usually three or four years; and in Castile there was, as usual, a lack of any definite stipulation of this sort until the last of the fifteenth century.

The tightening of control on the matter of apprenticeships came as the monopoly purposes of the gilds were clarified. During the early years of the reign of Ferdinand and Isabella, the apprentice had to show his baptismal certificates and full proof of *limpieza de sangre* or "purity of blood," thus excluding Jews, Moors, slaves, and converts, all of whom had previously not only been permitted to enter the gilds, but had indeed played a very important part in the industrial life of the nation.[3] The number of apprentices per master was carefully fixed, and there were very severe penalties levied upon any of the lads who dared abandon the master's house. Sons and sons-in-law of masters who entered the ranks of apprentices were usually given special consideration and priority.

After the apprenticeship, the years as a journeyman worker (*oficial*), usually two, were on a definitely fixed

---

[1] Tramoyeres, *op. cit.*, pp. 166–167.

[2] Sancho Seral, *op. cit.*, p. 33, n. Catalan and Urbiola, *Hist. Univ. Zarag.* (Saragossa, 1924), vol. ii, pp. 345–346, gives an interesting apprenticeship contract of 1385 for training in medicine and surgery.

[3] See above, p. 179, no. 3. Racial prejudice in craft matters was destined to become far more emphatic in later years. The Valencian cobblers' gild in 1597 barred from apprenticeship all negroes and "mulattoes of the color of quince marmalade because of the protests and disturbance which would result from the sight of such persons mingling with honorable and well dressed people."

wage carefully stipulated by the gild. The journeymen sometimes had their own associations. Their movements within the craft from one establishment to another were on a more privileged basis than those of the apprentices, although they were not allowed to leave as a rule on less than one month's notice. At the end of their approximately two years' experience as journeymen, the candidates were given examination for mastership. In some cities the successful candidates were required to put on an elaborate festive banquet for the gild masters; the cost of the meal was usually stipulated in the ordinances of the gild. The examinations as a rule were held at no fixed season, but every detail of them was precisely enumerated in these codes of the crafts.

The privileges of the masterships were painstakingly safeguarded. No master was allowed to have branch shops, evidently on the theory that this would impair the control of competition, which was, of course, the basic principle of the entire gild system in its later period. In some crafts there were brotherhoods (*hermandades*) among the gild masters of the same craft in different cities. Through these organizations the privilege of interchangeable membership was maintained.[1]

The great days of the Spanish gild system began to wane as the fifteenth century drew toward its close. The economic strength of the realms of the Crown of Aragon, the stronghold of the Spanish gild system, had reached its zenith in the reign of Alfonso v. After his death in 1458, the aggressive raids of Barbary corsairs and triumphs of the Turks around the Bosphorus gradually impaired the commercial prestige of the Aragonese in the eastern Mediterranean. With the unification of the kingdoms of the peninsula under Ferdinand and Isabella, there was

[1] Ricardo del Arco, *op. cit.*, p. xvi.

promptly launched a nation-wide campaign to co-ordinate the gild system with the general political policies and requirements of the monarchy. Steps were taken to accelerate the tendency toward requiring all artisans to have compulsory membership in gilds. Then came the association of unorganized craftsmen in minor pursuits into existing or new gild groupings. These measures were, of course, inspired not in the least with the idea of strengthening the gild set-up for its own sake, but solely in the interests of consolidating all available resources of the realm in the hands of the royal authority. Thus the overshadowing predominance of the Crown during the great days of Ferdinand and Isabella marks the beginning of the decline of gild autonomy in the field of industry.

A further factor in the weakening of the gild structure during this period was the aggressive drive of the Inquisition, which resulted in the expulsion of many skilled artisans, industrialists, and merchants among the Jews and Molsem converts. The sharp falling off in the industrial vigor of Barcelona, the major center of gild life in the peninsula, after the Inquisition had begun its work there in 1493 was directly attributed to this factor.[1]

Quantities of excessive regulatory measures were already beginning to accumulate at the turn of the sixteenth century; thus was inaugurated that overloading process which was finally to reduce the economic structure of Spain to ruins. The gild system during the closing years of the reign of Ferdinand and Isabella took on a more and more ponderous immobility with the increasingly complicated regulatory devices largely emanating from the Crown. Manuel Colmeiro, the outstanding economic his-

[1] Cf. Sampere y Miguel, *Barcelona en 1492*, a paper delivered before the Ateneo of Barcelona in 1892. King Ferdinand complained bitterly at a meeting of the Cortes of Tarazona in 1495 of the collapse of craft integrity and industrial zeal in the kingdom.

torian of his country, quite rightly holds that "although very few political writers ascribed the ruin of Spanish industry to the gilds, nothing is more certain." [1]

Doubtless other factors, political and social, contributed to that unhappy end, but the process of ossification became clearly evident as the royal autocracy undertook the political exploitation of the gilds. They had served an excellent purpose in the later Middle Ages in the regulation of trade during a period when some form of guidance was sorely needed — a period of great confusion, economic as well as political. They had contributed materially to the training of craftsmen, the preservation of some of the exceptional artisanship of the Moors, and the establishment of standards of production and commercial ethics at a time when the uncertainty of public authority provided no other media for that important responsibility.

But these were other times and other political environments, and the need for such an institution was unquestionably on the wane. Ferdinand and Isabella launched a multitude of gild ordinances and industrial codes, partly with a view toward unifying the nation, industrially as well as politically. Similar craft groups in different cities were brought together on a national basis, in some instances as a precedent making use of the long successful functioning of the Castilian Mesta, or corporation of sheep owners. The concentration of foreign trade through such royal agencies as the Consulado in Burgos, and subsequently the Casa de Contratación, in Seville, for the control of trade with the American colonies, served as useful examples of such nation-wide consolidation of trade and industrial control. National uniformity of production technique, prices, and trade policies was the evident objective, but it fell far short of attainment in spite of an endless stream of edicts, char-

[1] *Hist. Econ. Polit. Esp.* (Madrid, 1863), vol. ii, p. 237.

ters, and ordinances, which buried the industry and trade of the country under a stifling avalanche of regulatory and restrictive mandates.

The gild system was destined to continue for more than three centuries after the spectacular efforts of Ferdinand and Isabella — a long and sordid chronicle of decay and of royal exploitation almost unbroken by any relieving periods of temporary improvement. Never again after the autocracy took charge in the closing decades of the fifteenth century was the gild to enjoy such unhampered prestige, such vigorous supremacy over the industrial life of the nation.

SPANISH SHIPS AND SHIPPING IN THE SIXTEENTH AND SEVENTEENTH CENTURIES

ABBOTT PAYSON USHER

I

THE Biscayan coast of Spain was an important ship-building region in the Middle Ages, though we do not commonly hear much about it. By the fifteenth century, Biscayan-built ships were a dominant factor in the carrying trade between northern Spain and Flanders, and many Spanish-built vessels were sold abroad. The importance of the wool trade made this route one of the primary lanes of the Atlantic seaboard, and with fishing constituted a broad basis for the prosperity of the region. The Catalan coast was notable for its trade with both the Levant and Flanders, but ship-building seems to have been less vigorously developed. The local timber was of inferior quality, as in Andalusia, and was recognized to be ill suited to the construction of the larger vessels required on the longer voyages.

Gervasio de Artiñano attributes a rôle of large importance to these Biscayan shipyards.[1] He holds that these shipwrights took the initiative in building large merchant vessels and that the Venetians and Genoese were merely

[1] Gervasio de Artiñano y de Galdaçano, *La arquitectura naval española (en madera): bosquejo de sus condiciones y rasgos de su evolución* (Madrid, 1920), p. 50. He cites Fincham, *History of Naval Architecture.*

following in their footsteps. Although there was undoubtedly an important activity in this region as early as the thirteenth century, we have no evidence that Biscayan-built vessels attained the size that we know was achieved by the Genoese and the Venetians. The Biscayans must be given a larger place in the history of shipping than is frequently assigned to them, but there is no warrant for assigning them a position of leadership in the construction of large vessels or in the development of new types. Despite their situation on the Atlantic coast, they seem to have been closely identified with the traditions of ship-building common to the Mediterranean, and even in the sixteenth century produced no distinctive types.

The galleons and the unarmed merchant vessels that became so famous in the history of the Spanish Main were mere variations of types that were common to the Mediterranean. It is now generally recognized that the term "galleon" implies no distinctive features of hull design or rigging. In these respects, there is no difference between the galleon and the "ship:" the former is merely a merchantman armed with cannon. This use of the sailing vessel for naval warfare began early in the fifteenth century at Venice, in connection with the patrols sent out against pirates.[1] With the gradual change in the character of naval warfare made possible by the development of heavy ordnance, the armed sailing vessel steadily became a more important element both in naval warfare and in long-distance commerce. The term "galleon" appears in Venice in the fifteenth century, but it was not at first applied to the armed sailing ship with which it later became identified. The first Venetian galleons were ships designed "for use on the rivers in the land wars. They were high in

[1] F. C. Lane, Venetian Ships and Ship Builders, p. 7 (manuscript thesis, Harvard University Library).

the sides like round ships, but were like galleys in that they were rowed, the oars projecting through the sides."[1] Apparently, all the innovations that culminated in the galleon of the sixteenth century were at least Italian in origin, if not definitely Venetian. By the beginning of the seventeenth century Italian writers like Bartolomeo Crescentio and Pantero Pantera attempted to make some distinctions between the structure and rigging of ships and those of galleons, but no distinctions are valid for any long period or for the various ship-building centers that were constructing both.[2]

The caravel was developed by the Portuguese, and although the history of the type is by no means established in all details, there are strong grounds for presuming that it first appeared in the thirteenth century, achieved a characteristic form by the beginning of the sixteenth century, and was subsequently modified in a number of particulars.[3] The carracks and urcas, though frequently identified with Portugal, were originally Genoese and Flemish types which first came into use in Portugal by purchase from foreign yards, to be imitated subsequently by the Portuguese. Thus, even the peninsula as a whole contributed few major innovations to naval architecture.

The importance of the ship-building industry in Spain and Portugal was due primarily to the volume of tonnage they were capable of constructing rather than to any notable transformation of the primary types of vessels. The location of the Biscayan region favored eclecticism, and the conditions of Spanish trade required a wide range of types of merchant vessel. Escalante de Mendoza, writing

[1] *Ibid.*, p. 50.
[2] G. de Artiñano, *op. cit.*, pp. 97–98; Henrique Lopes de Mendonca, "Estudios sobre navios portugueses," *Memorias da Acad. Real das Sciencias de Lisboa,* ii classe, n. s., vol. vi, pt. i (1885), pp. 25–26.
[3] *Ibid.*, pp. 40–58.

in 1575, emphasizes this characteristic of Spanish naval architecture. The pilot in his dialogue says:

All those nations of which you have spoken hold these same opinions and each is right in a way, for each nation holds that it has invented the best form and model for ships that can be devised to navigate its waters and carry on the trades in which it is engaged. Such are the Venetians with their great carracks which are well fitted to resist and combat the Turks and Moors their neighbors and enemies. They carry large cargoes and freights to the regions with which Venice commonly trades.

The French build small and medium sized vessels that are good sailors at beating to the windward so that the vessels can enter and leave the small, shallow ports and go to Newfoundland for the fishing usually making the return trip in winter.

The Flemish build great, flat-bottomed urcas which draw very little water so that they can navigate among the banks of the famous Flemish channel. These vessels come to Spain loaded with great masts, timber, sail cloth, and other merchandise, returning with wool, wine, olive oil, dried fruits and other things.

The English likewise build very small vessels suited to their small ports. They bring to us their cloth and other merchandise and return loaded with wood, olive oils and the other commodities which they need just as the Flemish do.

The Portuguese build their vessels very strong, very large, and powerful, although they build no great number. They sail to the remote East Indies and take thither many people and necessary commodities. On those coasts they are powerful and capable of meeting the enemies with whom they contend in those waters and those lands, whence they bring back great cargoes of spices and other valuable merchandise as we see they do.

The Castilians endeavor to build both large and small vessels of every type and model to navigate every sea in the world, and to serve all the requirements that are served, by the ships of all the kingdoms and provinces which have been described individually.

But, however, it is recognized by all that the best ships were, in the past, commonly made in the channel at Bilbao in the province of Viscaya, although I believe that the business is now decayed, because they have made it a matter of profits and built ships that they did not intend to sail themselves, but to be sold for use in the western ocean. They sometimes built weak ships not having regard for the qualities they should possess. But despite all this it cannot be denied that the best masters, the best supplies of wood, nails, pitch, and hemp for the construction of vessels are to be found in Viscaya and the neighboring coasts. In general, they give vessels the best possible model, the most suitable dimensions, and at the lowest cost; so that they sail better, with less risk and danger than even the ships and galleons built in Lisbon which are more strongly built and more heavily armed than any others, as is required by their trade.[1]

These characterizations seem to be essentially sound for the date of writing, though they are not perhaps wholly just to the Low Countries, where the shipbuilders were certainly producing a wider range of types than Mendoza recognized. Spanish empiricism and eclecticism were not, however, wholly successful in meeting the new problems of oceanic commerce, and the Dutch innovations subjected the Spanish to increasing pressure of competition from the latter part of the sixteenth century. The petitions of the Cortez contain complaints of the use of foreign-built vessels in 1520, 1523, and again in 1559.[2] The ship-building industry on the Catalan coast was in such serious condition that a master shipbuilder with 300 workmen was sent from Bilbao in 1562 to reorganize the Catalan shipyards.[3] In 1563, an ordinance was issued reiterating the rules for giving native-build ships preferences in the trade to the New World, reaffirming the bounties for the construction of vessels of more than 600 *toneladas*, and granting bounties for the first time for ships ranging from 300 to 600 *toneladas*.[4] Even in 1575 Mendoza thought that the Biscayan shipyards were less prosperous than formerly. But apparently the industry found new stimulus, and, in the north at least, the latter part of the century seems to have been a

---

[1] Escalante de Mendoza, "I hinerario de navegación de los mares y hierras occidentales." Extracts in G. de Artiñano, *op. cit.*, p. 272. A full text, from a different manuscript, has been published by C. Fernandez Duro, *Disquisiciones Náuticas*, vol. v, pp. 413–515.

[2] Diego Clemencín, *Elogio de la reina católica Doña Isabel*, Memorias de la Real Academia de la Historia, vol. vi (Madrid, 1821), p. 260, n. 1; *Cortes de León y Castilla*, vol. iv, p. 377; Teofilo Guiard y Larrauri, *Historia del Consulado y Casa de Contratación de Bilbao y del Comercio de la Villa* (Bilbao, 1913), vol. i, p. 204, note.

[3] *Ibid.*, p. 206.　　　　　　　　　[4] *Ibid.*, p. 205, note.

period of relative prosperity. In 1583 there were 15,000 *toneladas* of shipping under construction in Biscaya, and in the next three years fifty vessels were ordered for the royal navy.[1] The defeat of the Armada did not check mercantile activity, and the shipyards continued active in the last decade of the century.

The meager material available affords a basis for presuming that the shipyards on the northern coast in the provinces of Santander, the Asturias, and Galicia suffered vicissitudes like the Biscayan yards, though they seem never to have constructed as many ships. There are many references to the low grade of shipping constructed in Andalusia and along the shores of the Gulf of Cadiz, especially in the Condado de Hiebla. The pine available around Seville was useful for interior finish and the superstructures, but there was no local timber suitable for the hulls of the larger vessels. There were two important repair yards, Borrego and Horcadas, on the river at Seville, but one must assume that the southern yards were in no position to make any substantial contribution to the tonnage required for long-distance trade. There was, of course, a considerable demand for fishing vessels and small coasters, which we may presume to have been met by local construction.

The first quarter of the seventeenth century was certainly a critical period for the ship-building industry. There were losses at sea which cast doubt upon the adequacy of the native-built ships. Considerable numbers of foreign-built ships were admitted to the registers for trade with the New World, and there were several attempts by ordinance to impose upon the builders new standards of construction and new proportions in respect of ships designed for the trade to the New World.

[1] *Ibid.*, p. 208.

The explanation of this situation presents a problem of the greatest interest. Were the difficulties encountered by the shipyards due to the minute regulations imposed upon the trade of the New World, to gradual exhaustion of the supplies of strategic raw materials, or to the increasing technical superiority of the Dutch shipbuilders? Without more specific study of ship-building in the various regions, we cannot answer these questions definitely; but there are strong grounds for presuming that the most important single factor in the decline of Spanish ship-building was the technical advance in Holland. The Dutch introduced new types. Shortly after 1570, one of the 30 to 40 ton fishing craft was developed on a larger scale as a cargo boat. This "boat" or "bus" is not very specifically described. Illustrations are available, but we have few details of the distinctive features of hull design or rigging.[1] This development was transitional. It constitutes the chief break between the older traditions and modern ship-building, for the full consequences of the change appear in the "flute" (*fluit, fleute, fliboot*), first produced at Hoorn in 1595.

The length of the vessel was considerably increased relatively to the main breadth, the old proportions of 3 to 3.5 times the main breadth being altered to a ratio of 4 to 1, which was soon increased further to 5 to 1 and even more. The rigging was also modified.[2] The castles were abandoned, too, so that the ship assumed a general appearance more in keeping with our notions of large sailing vessels. The type was not stabilized for nearly twenty years, but it quickly demonstrated its superiority over the older kinds of merchant vessel. Dimensions common in the seventeenth century were: length, 130 Amsterdam feet; breadth,

---

[1] B. Hagedorn, *Die Entwicklung der wichtigsten Schiffstypen bis ins 19 Jahrhundert* (Berlin, 1914), p. 93.

[2] *Ibid.*, pp. 102–103. The name appears somewhat earlier.

26.5 Amsterdam feet; depth, 13.4 Amsterdam feet. There were some specializations of type between the Norwegian lumber trade and the Baltic trade: for the former, the ship was built somewhat deeper. In capacity, these ships commonly ranged from 400 to 200 tons dead-weight.[1] The flute had a rounded stern like so many of the smaller Dutch vessels.

The convenience of the square stern was considerable in the larger vessels; and in the early sixteenth century the general features of the new type were combined with a square stern and a rigging somewhat closer to the old square rig than was common in the true flute. This type was called the "pinace."[2] It was subsequently modified and its name was changed so that the early pinnace disappeared from the seas; but it served as the model for the ships of the East India Company, and is thus in fact the progenitor of the modern square-rigged ship.[3] When dimensions were reduced it was called a "snow" (*snawship*).

In addition to this notable progress in ship design, the Dutch were also making advances in the organization and equipment of their dockyards. Unfortunately, we have little specific information for the important period 1590–1630, but the agents of Colbert give many details concerning the use of saws driven by windmills and the general use of cranes for moving timbers and placing masts. Miss Barbour has collected significant data on the relative costs of building in Holland and in England, which indicate astonishingly wide differences.[4]

---

[1] E. van Konijnenburg, *L'architecture navale depuis ses origines* (Bruxelles, n. d.), vol. i, p. 75; see also vol. ii, p. 148.

[2] Hagedorn, *op. cit.*, vol. i, p. 105. Plates, vol. iii, fig. 8 (1625), fig. 9 (1678).

[3] Konijnenburg, *op. cit.*, vol. i, p. 76. Plates in vol. ii, fig. 151, and vol. iii, fig. 11.

[4] Violet Barbour, "Dutch and English Merchant Shipping in the Seventeenth Century," *Economic History Review*, vol. ii, pp. 273–275.

During the critical years 1590–1630 the Spanish ship-wrights introduced few modifications in ship design and made little progress towards meeting the demands for improvement in the sailing qualities of vessels. The most significant statement is to be found in an anonymous treatise on ship-building written apparently a little after 1623.

The nation that has made the greatest progress in this art is Holland, which makes its ships very strong, elegant in design, and very light. They secure many advantages by giving a very broad floor, for in this way the ship is not deep in the water, and is easily careened, and is light. In Spain everyone used to build ships each after his fashion according to the measures desired by the ship master. Ships were made short by the keel, and for this reason they pitched heavily: the floor was narrow and the depth great, so that they shipped much water, and in entering or leaving ports with bars affording little water, they were lost, to the damage of their masters and the merchants who loaded cargo in them. To remedy these difficulties, Don Diego Brochero de Anaya, sometime Admiral in Chief of the Royal Atlantic Fleet (who governed the fleet for several years and was later in the Department, and Grand Prior of San Juan) took occasion to bring these difficulties to the attention of His Majesty Don Philip III (who is now in heaven). His Majesty had a committee assembled in 1609 composed of skilled persons who had experience with marine affairs and with ship building. After discussing these matters and the seriousness of the losses suffered by our people from making its ships without rule or reason, but by the eye and at the caprice of each builder, they drew up in 1611 a schedule of dimensions and specifications for the building of vessels from 100–1200 toneladas. When some ships had been built according to these ordinances, experience showed them to be defective because the keel was long and the breadth narrow as appears in the said ordinances. The same committee reassembled in 1613 with others who were summoned, and attempted to remedy this mistake by reducing the length a little and increasing the breadth. With these measures they proceeded to build ships for the Navy, but as the breadth was faulty all the ordinances were condemned and in 1618 new ones were drawn up and published in Madrid in that year. Many galleons were constructed on these principles which put to sea in His Majesty's service in 1619, 1621, and 1623 in the three squadrons of the provinces of Cantabria, Guipuzcoa, and the four towns of the coast in the mountains of Burgos. They were tested and remained in service to the satisfaction of His Majesty and his ministers, although they revealed some imperfections which were dangerous and prejudicial to the service, and to those who navigate them. The errors ought to be corrected, but there is no one to bring the matter to His Majesty's attention, although the danger is evident to the naked eye and is a matter of daily experience. So we will proceed with the present work.[1]

In the discussion that follows, the construction of a galleon of 1,200 *toneladas* is considered, so that it is evident that part of the problem consisted in the somewhat special difficulties created by the attempt to build large naval vessels. In Escalante's time (1575) it was recognized that the larger vessels presented a serious problem. Although shippers showed a preference for the largest ships, Escalante says that the ship of 500 *toneladas* is undoubtedly the safest; better than either the larger vessels or the smaller vessels. He regards the ships of less than 500 *toneladas* as safer than ships exceeding that size.[2] There is thus substantial basis for presuming that the Spanish shipbuilders were having difficulty in securing sarisfactory performance from their vessels as mercantile and naval demands became more exacting under the pressure of new requirements and intensified competition with foreign shipyards.

It is significant that a problem of this magnitude, which is explicitly recognized in the treatises and ordinances, resulted in no substantial modification of the merchant ship and galleon of the early sixteenth century. There seems to have been little effort made to do more than standardize an existing type, with relatively small improvements in the fundamental proportions. Table I presents the proportions recommended in various treatises and in the ordinances dealing with the West Indian galleons. There is some

[1] C. Fernandez Duro, "Diálogo entre un Vizcaíno y un Montañes sobre construccion de naves," *Disquisiciones Náuticas*, vol. vi (Madrid, 1881) [hereafter referred to as C. Fernandez Duro, "Diálogo"], pp. 108–109.

[2] G. de Artiñano, *op. cit.*, p. 104, note.

change in the interval between Escalante and Garrote, notably in the relation of the length of the keel to the length over all. But Garrote is still building a galleon which is hardly more than a modest improvement over the "nave" of Venetian and Genoese shipwrights of the fifteenth century.

TABLE I

PROPORTIONS RECOMMENDED FOR THE MAIN DIMENSIONS OF SHIPS [a]

	Length to breadth (breadth = 1)	Depth to breadth (breadth = 1)	Keel to breadth	Keel to length (length = 1)
Treatises of Escalante de Mendoza, 1575 .... 3.18			2.78	.715
Garcia de Palacio, 1587 .... 3.23	.65	2.125	.65
Thome Cano, 1611 .... 3.3	.5	2.56	.77
Ordinances in the Laws of the Indies:				
a. Galleon of about 500 *toneladas*				
1613 .... 3.45		2.7	.78
1618 .... 3.29		2.58	.78
1666 .... 3.54		2.85	.805
1679			
b. Galleon of 18 *codos* breadth				
1613 .... 3.42	.5	2.67	.78
1618 .... 3.28	.5	2.5	.78
1666	.47		
1679			
c. Galleon of about 800 *toneladas*				
1613 .... 3.3		2.55	.775
1618 .... 3.15		2.45	.78
1666 .... 3.51		2.86	.815
1679 .... 3.55	.48	2.92	.815
Treatise of Francisco Antonio Garrote, 1691 Galleon of 18 *codos* breadth .. 3.43	.39	3.00	.875

[a] G. de Artiñano, *op. cit.*, pp. 128–129.

Further evidence is available for the year 1625, as we have complete measurements of twenty-one vessels that were measured in the repair yards of Borrego and Horcadas at Seville, July 5, 1625. There is evidence that the attempts at standardization of type had not been completely successful, even if we make some allowance for differences in the age of the vessels. It would seem, too, that the builders were if anything in advance of the treatises and ordinances. These measurements are especially interesting, moreover, because they afford an opportunity for explicit comparison of the Spanish type with the new Dutch pinnace, one of which is described by Joseph Furtenbach in great detail.[1] Furtenbach gives the measurements of *Der Lotzmann* of Amsterdam. Konijnenburg gives a date of 1625 and identifies the ship as the pinnace type.[2] As it is impossible to discover what "palm" Furtenbach uses in his text, it is not possible to give equivalents in English measure. The primary measurements and ratios are given in table III. Owing to the possibility of differences in the manner of taking some of the measures, the dimensions of the Mediterranean polacca have been included, because the diagrams prevent any error in comparison. The lines of the two vessels, shown by Furtenbach, are profoundly different; but the differences are not readily described, unless the plates are available for study, and detailed comparison is not essential to the present purpose. The outstanding differences in proportions are in the ratios of length to breadth and of the floor to the depth. The Dutch vessel is longer and the cross section is full-bodied. Reference to the proportions of the Spanish vessels in table II gives us ratios of length to breadth ranging

[1] Joseph Furtenbach, *Architecture Navalis: das ist Von dem Schiff gebau* (Ulm, 1629), pp. 89–102 and plates 10–15.
[2] Konijnenburg, *op. cit.*, vol. i, p. 75; vol. iii, pp. 3–4, figs. 7, 8.

TABLE II

SHIPS MEASURED AT BORREGO AND HORCADAS JULY 5, 1625[a]

| Dimensions (English feet: 1 *codo real* = 1.88 Eng. ft.[b]) | | | | | Ratios of dimensions to each other | | | | Capacity (in *toneladas*) |
Breadth	Length	Depth	Floor	Keel	L-B (B = 1)	D-B (B = 1)	L-K (L = 1)	F-D (D = 1)	
36.2	114.2	18.8	16.9	90.8	3.16	.52	.80	.90	736
36.6	112.0	17.0	16.9	89.0	3.06	.46	.81	1.00	656
36.6	113.0	16.5	16.9	92.5	3.10	.45	.81	1.03	655
35.4	112.0	17.0	16.9	88.0	3.16	.48	.80	1.00	642
36.6	109.5	16.5	16.9	87.2	2.97	.45	.79	1.03	619.5
34.8	111.0	16.7	16.9	89.0	3.20	.475	.795	1.02	615
36.0	108.7	16.7	16.0	84.2	3.00	.46	.78	.95	605
34.8	111.0	16.5	16.0	89.0	3.18	.47	.80	.975	604
33.0	108.0	17.0	16.0	84.5	3.24	.51	.79	.94	584
32.4	103.0	17.3	15.0	83.0	3.16	.53	.805	.87	551.5
29.1	100.3	17.0	13.1	80.5	3.43	.57	.805	.77	470
32.3	94.0	16.0	15.0	79.4	2.88	.49	.84	1.06	456
30.4	95.3	16.0	13.6	77.5	3.14	.525	.805	.85	442
31.0	97.5	15.4	14.1	78.5	3.12	.495	.81	.92	441
28.2	98.5	16.3	13.1	76.5	3.46	.575	.78	.81	437.5
29.5	95.6	15.1	13.1	76.7	3.20	.57	.81	.87	404.75
27.7	94.6	15.1	13.1	76.0	3.95	.54	.81	.87	346
27.2	95.0	14.7	12.2	77.5	3.46	.535	.815	.84	357.75
29.0	93.0	13.8	12.2	73.6	3.16	.47	.80	.89	347
27.8	90.8	14.1	12.2	71.7	3.23	.505	.79	.86	341.5
30.1	90.2	13.7	13.1	71.7	3.00	.45	.80	.96	338.5

[a] A. G. I.: Sec. III, 41-1-2/13. The references to the Archivo General de las Indias, Seville, are cited here and subsequently as A. G. I. All references are to Sec. III, Casa de Contratación.

[b] G. de Artiñano gives 1 *codo real* as equivalent to .574 meter. This gives a value of 1.88 English feet. Paucton, *Métrologie*, gives values which make the *codo real* equal to 1.81 English feet.

from 2.97 to 3.46; to be compared with a ratio of 4.35 in the pinnace. We have ratios of floor to depth in the Spanish ships ranging from 1.06 to .77, as compared with a ratio of 1.34 in the pinnace. Subsequent experience has justified the change in these primary proportions, and we must needs wonder why the medieval tradition persisted so long. One must presume that differences in general conditions of

TABLE III

DIMENSIONS [a] OF A DUTCH PINNACE [b] AND OF A MEDITERRANEAN POLACCA

	Dutch Pinnace (palms)		Polacca (palms)	
Length	113	L = 4.35B [b]	85	L = 2.94B
Breadth				
a. on top deck	20		29	
b. on main deck	26			
c. 3 palms above floor	26			
Depth of hold	15	D = .58B [b]	13	D = .45B
Between decks	6		7	
Floor	20	F = 1.34D	12	F = .92D

[a] J. Furtenbach, *op. cit.*, pp. 92–93, 103.   [b] *Der Lotzmann* (1625).

navigation and in the size of ships most commonly employed minimized what seem to us to be errors in proportions. The fore and stern castles may have created internal strains that made it dangerous to attempt a longer vessel. At all events, the Spanish were clearly confining their attention to small refinements in the established type; and, as they still failed to secure wholly satisfactory performance at sea, it seems evident that technical insufficiencies must have played some vital part in the decline of shipbuilding and the loss of some of the carrying trade.

Without substantial study it would be hazardous to draw any conclusions in respect of the possible exhaustion or dearth of primary raw materials. Escalante in 1575 seems to assume that most of the materials used in construction were of native production, with the conspicuous exception of masts and spars which were even in his time imported from Prussia by way of Flanders. The best sails came from "Las Olonas de Pondavid," or "Pundavi," which it is unfortunately impossible to identify, though it seems to be a corruption of a French place name (Pont Aven). Next after these came the sails from Villa da Conde in Portugal.[1] By 1625-30 the situation was profoundly different. The Spanish yards were then dependent upon imports for tar and pitch, for masts, for hemp (both for cordage and for sails), and for finished sail-cloth. It was then admitted that masts and tar could not be produced in the kingdom, but the author believed that all the other products could be produced in Spain or in the Canaries and the Balearic Isles.[2] It is difficult to resist the inference that significant changes had taken place in the absolute or comparative advantages of Spain in the production of many naval stores and materials, but without detailed information it is impossible to determine the nature of the factors underlying these changes. The supply of hemp and its products seems to present the most interesting problem, as it was possible to produce hemp over wide areas in Spain and Portugal.[3]

The development of ship-building in the New World also affords evidence of the pressure to which the industry was subjected at home. Some vessels were built in the colonies as early as 1530 and the activity of the yards increased. A considerable proportion of the tonnage engaged in the colonial trade in the seventeenth century was probably

[1] G. de Artiñano, op. cit., p. 273.
[2] C. Fernandez Duro, "Diálogo," pp. 203-204.
[3] Ibid., pp. 204-206.

TABLE IV

PLACE OF CONSTRUCTION OF THE SEVILLE FLEETS [a]

	Spanish owned						Foreign owned				Total[b]	
	Built in Spain		Built in Indies		Built abroad		Built in Spain		Built abroad			
	No.	Toneladas	No.	Toneladas	No.	Toneladas	No.	Toneladas	No.	Toneladas	No.	Toneladas
1599	18	7,615	2	300	6	2320	1	120	16	3720	43	13,955
1598 [c]	9	2,550	1	200	2	850			5	1050	17	4,750
1600	12	3,090	6	1460					7	2030	25	7,480
1606 out	18	10,520	4	1350							22	11,870
in	19	8,760	5	1850							24	10,610
1610	40	18,780	20	5975								
1641-42			27	7060	5	452						
1643-44			16	4910	1	300						
1647	3	1,550	7	1830								
1648	1	400	6	1688								
1660	5	1,780	5	1486	1	450						
1689	5	1,464										
1701-02	8	1,872			7	1316						
1702-03	1	248			2	401						
1706	8	3,294			3	684						
1753-54	6	4864	4	1032	21	7658						

[a] References to sources appear in the notes on tonnage with tables V and VI.
[b] Total tonnage given in summary in the manuscript is corrected for Biscayan *tonelada* =1.2 *toneladas* of Seville.
[c] Assumed that the *felibotes* are of Spanish build.

built in the colonies. As our statistics are merely samples, it is dangerous to assume that the data for the decade 1640–50 are representative. The material on ship-building available in the documents used is presented in table IV. Foreign ships were admitted to the registers for a short period including the years 1599 to 1600, but commonly it was required that foreign-built ships should be owned and manned by Spaniards. The data available scarcely warrant drawing any conclusions, but there is a rather striking indication that the shipyards in the New World contributed an important proportion of the tonnage used in the seventeenth century; and, as it was a period of declining trade, one must presume that the authors of the treatises were not exaggerating the decline of activity in Spanish shipyards.

II

The Archive of the Indies possesses a remarkable mass of material on shipping to the New World. No systematic attempt has yet been made to utilize these records. In time taken from other studies at Seville, Mrs. E. J. Hamilton collected important samples of these shipping records which make it possible to establish the general trend of the physical volume of shipping between Spain and the New World.[1]

The use of the material for international comparisons makes it essential to ascertain the value of the *tonelada*, the

---

[1] The registers and bundles in the Archive include several distinct classes of material (Pedro Torres Lanzas, *Catalógo de Legajos del Archivo de Indias*, Biblioteca Colonial Americana, Seville, 1921, vol. vi, pp. 95–248): 707 bundles of registers of outgoing vessels, covering the years 1523 to 1782; 1054 bundles of registers of incoming vessels; 31 bundles of registers of ships going or coming between the New World and the Canaries; 5 registers listing the foregoing registers of ships in annual series, 1523–1783; 11 registers covering particular New World ports for Porto Rico in 1666 and various ports for different periods in the 18th century.

unit used in all these records. As in all countries, the unit
used for the computation of freight charges and port dues
was presumed to represent the dead-weight capacity of

TABLE V

SHIPS CLEARED FROM SPAIN FOR THE NEW WORLD

	Total for years given[a]	Annual average	Range	Approximate average size (in *toneladas*)	*Toneladas* per year
1506–15 [b]	286	28	17–41	200 [c]	5,600
1516–25 [b]	503	50	18–73		
1526–35 [b]	629	63	45–86		
1536–45 [b]	685	68	22–97		
1546–55 [b]	702	70	3–101		
	783	78	22–105		
1556–65 [d]	665	66	19–109	322 [e]	21,000
1566–75 [d]	649	64	31–93		
1576–79 [d]	171	63	30–48		
1586 [f]		62		264	17,010
		87		266	23,230
1600–04 [g]	276	55	33–90	360 [h]	19,800
1640–50 [i]	277	25	6–44	340 [l]	8,500
1670–80 [i]	196	17	0–42	296 [i]	4,650
1701–10 [j]	80	8	0–31	330	2,640
1720–35 (6 yrs.) [k]					4,162
1740–46 [k]	147	20	19–25	400 [m]	8,000
1765–77 [k]	524	40	25–61	400	16,000

[a] Permits were granted for fleets as follows: 1688, 4,000 *toneladas*; 1689, 2,400 *toneladas*; 1693, 3,500 *toneladas* (letters, A. G. I., 42–6–18/22, June 15, 1688, March 29, 1689, May 19, 1693).
[b] C. H. Haring, *Trade and Navigation between Spain and the Indies* (1918), p. 339 (Appendix viii).
[c] C. Fernandez Duro, *Armada española*, vol. i, p. 352. Fleet collected at Carthegena for the expedition to Oran, 1509. Rating as given for all vessels over 100 *toneladas*.
[d] A. G. I., 30–3–1/3 — continuation of the series given in Haring.
[e] *Ibid.*, 36–2–2/10. February 17, 1556.
[f] *Ibid.*, 41–1–1/12. The lists as given may contain some duplication: the smaller numbers are certainly free from any duplication; the larger number is somewhat doubtful, but more probable.
[g] *Ibid.*, 30–2–2/4.
[h] Average rating of 151 vessels for the years 1598–1606 (*ibid.*, 41–1–1/12; 41–1–2/13).
[i] *Ibid.*, 30–2–3/5.
[j] *Ibid.*, 30–2–5/6.
[k] *Ibid.*, 30–2–5/7.
[l] *Ibid.*, 42–6–9/13; 42–6–10/14.
[m] *Ibid.*, 30–2–5/7 — data for 41 vessels.

the vessel if loaded with freight of the approximate specific
gravity of grain, wine, oil, or salt. As the vessel could not
be loaded to the limits of her dead-weight capacity, if the
cargo were general merchandise and drygoods, all such

freight was charged in terms of arbitrarily determined units of weight or volume that were presumed to represent the cubic content that would be required by the standard unit of cargo in grain, wine, oil, or salt. The authorities at

TABLE VI

SHIPS ENTERING SPANISH PORTS FROM THE INDIES

	Total number for years given	Annual average	Range	Average *toneladas*	Total *toneladas*
1506–15 [a]	228	22	10–46	200 [c]	4,400
1516–25 [a]	283	28	10–47		
1526–35 [a]	361	36	17–47		
1536–45 [a]	510	51	28–68		
1546–55 [a]	595	59	24–84		
1556–65 [b]	528	52	35–68	322 [d]	16,700
1566–75 [b]	538	53	38–72		
1576–79 [b]	189	47	?		
1585–1603 (9 yrs.) [e]	569	63	32–94	284 [j]	17,900
1600–03 [e]	229	56	41–111	360	21,600
1640–50 [f]	298	29	5–49	340 [i]	9,850
1670–80 [f]	152	19	1–33	296	5,600
1701–10 [g]	67	7	0–18	330	2,310
1740–50 [h]	234	21	14–36	400	8,400
1755–64 [h]	273	27	16–40	400	10,800
1765–77 [h]	554	42	26–56	400	16,800

[a] C. H. Haring, *op. cit.*, p. 339 (Appendix viii); *ibid.*, p. 212, citing *Relaciones hist. y geog. de América Central*. The returns are from Nombre de Dios only, but seem to include the whole fleet.
[b] Data supplied by E. J. Hamilton. A. G. I., 30-2-1/3 — continuation of series given by Haring.
[c] C. Fernandez Duro, *Armada española*, vol. i, p. 352.
[d] A. G. I., 35-2-2/10 — data from 13 vessels at Seville, February 17, 1556.
[e] *Ibid.*, 30-2-2/4.
[f] *Ibid.*, 30-2-3/5.
[g] *Ibid.*, 30-2-4/6; additional tonnage figures: 19-2-189/10, 19-2-188/9, 19-2-190/11.
[h] *Ibid.*, 42-6-9/13, 42-6-10/14.
[j] *Ibid.*, 41-1-1/12.

Seville had lists of equivalents for the classes of goods most commonly shipped;[1] they were reckoned by bales, by cubic content, or by weight, as might seem most convenient. All these units were intended to occupy the same space as the

[1] G. de Artiñano y de Galdacano, *Historia del commercio con las Indias* (Barcelona, 1917), pp. 299–302.

standard two pipes of wine, which weighed about two thousand pounds.

The ratings of vessels were determined empirically in Spain prior to 1613 — sometimes by direct experience in loading the vessel with particular types of cargo, and sometimes by crude calculations from the main dimensions. The need of a rating, not dependent upon the statement of the owner, led to attempts to formulate rules for the computation of the cubic content of the hold. A unit that was originally conceived of as a direct statement of dead-weight capacity thus became in fact a unit of volume that was only roughly equivalent. The rating of vessels involves many elements of inaccuracy. Whatever method is used, it should be recognized that commercial and official ratings have been, and still are, arbitrary and empirical.[1]

The material from the registers of clearances and entrances is presented in tables v and vi. The total tonnage of shipping to the New World seems to have been smaller than has been supposed, and there is so consistent a trend that we may presume that its general character is fairly well determined even by this modest sample of the material. The average size of ships is probably smaller than many have supposed, because of the relatively large number of ships of less than 500 *toneladas*. The classification by size of the ships on the lists for the years 1586–95 affords decisive evidence on this phase of the shipping business. It was found that vessels of less than 300 *toneladas* were

[1] There is clear evidence that the *tonelada* was conceived of as a unit of dead-weight capability that was very nearly identical with the British ton. The measurement *tonelada* was officially 26 per cent larger than the British measurement ton, and there is no adequate explanation of this wide discrepancy between the two ratings. In the following tables it has been assumed that the *tonelada* and the English shipping ton are practically identical. Oil was rated in terms of the short ton and iron in terms of the long ton. The weight of two pipes of wine was somewhat in excess of the short ton, but less than the long ton if the weight of the casks was not included.

especially well suited to the requirements of the trade to Tierra Firma (Panama). The cargoes were largely dry-goods. The trade to New Spain (Mexico), however, was more conveniently carried on in the larger vessels, because there were cargoes of wine and fruits as well as the dry-goods.[1] Economy and safety thus led to the employment of a considerable number of the smaller vessels.

TABLE VII

CLASSIFICATION BY SIZE OF VARIOUS FLEETS AT SEVILLE, 1586–1595 [a]

Rating (in *toneladas*)	Number	Capacity (in *toneladas*)	Per cent of total capacity
over 700	2	1,400	2.8
600–699	7	4,250	8.8
500–599	13	6,825	14.2
400–499	28	10,270	21.4
300–399	26	8,330	17.3
200–299	46	10,210	21.2
100–199	48	6,900	14.3
	170	48,185	100.0

[a] A. G. I., 41–1–1/2.

It is of course desirable that we should be able to form some judgment of the relation between the trade to the New World and the total trade of Spain, but no wholly satisfactory material is available. We have, however, an enumeration of the ships entering Bilbao for the year August, 1598–August, 1599, and we have a statement by Thome Cano covering the merchant fleets of Spain and Portugal. The registers at Bilbao do not specify tonnage, but the types are given and the approximate tonnage can be estimated without large errors.

The proportion of large ships seems to be unusual, but without some specific evidence it would be hazardous to

[1] Officials of the Casa de Contratación to His Majesty's Council of the Indies, October 22, 1641 (A. G. I., 42–6–9/13; doc. no. 1, fols. 479–481).

presume any failure in the enumeration of vessels engaged in general commerce. The Newfoundland fishermen were certainly included, though it may be that some of the coast fishermen were not enumerated. Unless one presumes a very large trade at Seville, employed in the coasting trade of Europe, we must recognize that Bilbao was a more important port than Seville. The trade to the New

TABLE VIII

VESSELS ENTERING BILBAO

(August, 1598–August, 1599 [a])

Class	Number			Presumed rating (in *toneladas*)	Presumed capacity (in *toneladas*)		
	Spanish	Foreign	Total		Spanish	Foreign	Total
Ship (Nao)	102	46	148	300	30,600	13,800	44,400
Urca	2	30	32	400	800	12,000	12,800
Pinnace ..	89	18	107	80	7,120	1,440	8,560
Volante ..	6		6	40	240		240
Zabra.....	8		8	100	800		800
Felibotes .		5	5	150		750	750
Patache ..	1		1	60	60		60
Caravel ..		2	2	120		240	240
	208	101	309		39,620	28,230	67,850

[a] Guiard, *op. cit.*, vol. i, pp. 159–166. The foreign ships are determined partly by direct statement, and partly by the names of the owners. Some Portuguese vessels and possibly some from St. Jean de Luz may still be included as Spanish.

World was less important in volume than the northern trade in wool, naval stores, dried fruits, and metals.

In the treatise of Thome Cano, published in 1611, we have an estimate or reminiscence of Spanish shipping. Apropos of the decline of interest at the time of writing he says:

The truth of this would not be denied by anyone who had known and seen that twenty-five years ago more than one thousand large ships were owned in Spain, and that in Viscaya alone there were more than two hundred which made the voyage to Newfoundland for whales and codfish and to Flanders with wool, whereas today there is not even one.

In Galicia, the Asturias, and Montañas (Santander) there were more than two hundred pataches which made the voyage to Flanders, France, England, and Andalucia carrying their merchandise, and today there are none. In Portugal, there have always been more than four hundred large ships and one thousand five hundred caravels and "caravelones," from which the King Don Sebastian was able to select and assemble eight hundred and thirty sail for the ill-starred expedition to Africa, without utilizing any from other regions; and leaving sufficient provision for the voyages to India, San Thome, Brasil, Cape Verde, Guinea, Newfoundland and other places; whereas today there is scarcely a ship to be found in the Kingdom that belongs to citizens, beyond a few caravels hardly worth consideration. In Andalucia, we used to have more than four hundred ships: more than two hundred made the voyage to New Spain, Terra Firma, Honduras, and the Windward Islands, a single fleet amounting to more than seventy-seven vessels; the other two hundred made the voyage to the Canaries, to the Indies, the islands, and other regions, loaded with wine and merchandize.[1]

The passage is clearly not a statistical estimate, and the statements about Andalusia are obviously padded, despite the positive information indicated by the statement about the fleet of seventy-seven vessels; but the proportions are not without interest. The whole northern coast is put on a par with Andalusia, each being given two-fifths of the total number of ships. The remaining fifth is evidently credited to the Mediterranean coast. Assuming these proportions to be roughly correct, we may infer that the fleets to the New World would have represented one-fifth of the total tonnage. But the entries at Bilbao in 1598–99 show that Cano's estimate is in error. Almost twice the New World tonnage entered the port in Spanish bottoms. It is curious that Cano should have overestimated the shipping of Seville, a locality with which he had been closely associated, and should have been so nearly accurate in his estimate for Biscaya. If we take the shipping of the New World to be one-tenth of the total for Spain, we reach a

[1] Thome Cano, "Arte para fabricar, fortificar y apareiar naos, de guerra y merchante . . ." (1611). C. Fernandez Duro, "Diálogo," pp. 87–88.

total of about 200,000 *toneladas* for 1585. Estimates made for other countries would lead one to believe that this is perhaps high, but there is a strong presumption that the total merchant fleet of Spain amounted to more than 150,000 *toneladas* but rather less than 200,000 *toneladas*. We may say, then, that at the height of her maritime expansion, about 1585, Spain had a merchant fleet of about 175,000 tons (*toneladas*). In this event, she would have ranked a rather good second among the north European countries.

The tonnage of the merchant fleets of the northern countries is given by Walther Vogel as follows:

TONNAGE OF THE MERCHANT FLEETS IN 1570 [1]

	Tons
Netherlands	232,000
Germany	110,000
France	80,000
England	42,000

The records of the ships passing the Sound make the figure for the Netherlands seem a little low, and the figure for England is lower than the totals of either of the notable enumerations of ships made under Elizabeth: for 1572 we have a total of 50,816 tons, and for 1582 a total of 66,827 tons.[2] If Cano's estimate for Portugal is not more than twice as great as the reality, the peninsula as a whole must have had a fleet of 250,000 to 300,000 tons; and, as Portugal was held by the Spanish crown at this time, the two countries might legitimately be combined. They would

[1] Walther Vogel, "Zur grosse der Europaischen Handelsflötten im 15, 16, und 17 Jahrhundert," p. 331 in *Forschungen und Versuche zur Geschichte des Mittelalters und der Neuzeit. Festschrift Dietrich Schafer* (Jena, 1915).

[2] A. P. Usher, "The Growth of English Shipping, 1572–1922," *Quarterly Journal of Economics*, vol. xlii, p. 467.

have been fully equal to the Netherlands, as conceived by Vogel. It seems rather difficult to believe, however, that the Netherlands had not achieved a more nearly dominant position in the carrying trade even as early as 1585. Her progress must have been rapid in the period 1585–1630, which is marked by her greatest achievements in ship design. The decline of Spanish shipping was perceptible by 1600, though the pessimism of the authors of the treatises in that period was certainly not warranted by actual conditions. Bilbao was perhaps less prosperous than in the sixteenth century, but trade with Brittany and Nantes grew and partially replaced the losses in the trade to Flanders. The history of shipping thus reflects the general economic depression of the seventeenth and early eighteenth centuries. The relative severity of international competition in the carrying trade and in the ship-building industry doubtless contributed some positive influences of an unfavorable character, but the ship-building industry was itself affected by industrial conditions.

SPANISH MERCANTILISM
BEFORE 1700 [1]

EARL J. HAMILTON

Upon the accession of Ferdinand and Isabella (1475) chaos pervaded Castilian economy and politics. Debased coinage, moribund agriculture, decadent industry, stagnant commerce, and contumacious nobles gave full scope to the absolutism, centralization, and paternalism of the Catholic kings. The formation of modern Spain through the union of Castile and Aragon, the conquest of Granada, and the discovery of America were the most celebrated, but not the only notable, achievements of these sovereigns. They built roads and bridges, paved streets, supplied cities with water, promoted urban cleanliness and sanitation, constructed lighthouses, improved harbors, favored shipbuilding and navigation, stimulated commerce and industry, suppressed internal strife, reformed the administration of justice, and in countless other prosaic ways advanced

[1] Under the Hapsburgs, Spain was a federation of five autonomous kingdoms — Aragon, Castile, Catalonia, Navarre, and Valencia — invested with separate parliaments, constitutions, monetary systems, and customs tariffs. In this study attention is concentrated upon Castile, the kingdom which comprised more than 75 per cent of peninsular Spanish territory and almost 85 per cent of the population, say, at the end of the sixteenth century. Castile owned and governed the Hispanic colonies of the New World; and her language, race, and institutions have largely determined the character of modern Spain. Although I endeavor to differentiate between Castile and Spain, the reduced compass of the present paper sometimes necessitates identification of the two.

Most of the data for this study are a by-product of historical investigations of money, prices, and wages in Spanish archives and libraries in 1929–30 as a Fellow of the Social Science Research Council and in 1930–31 as Delegate for Spain, International Scientific Committee on Price History.

the economic condition of their kingdoms.[1] Clemencín lists 128 ordinances of the reign of Isabella (1475–1504) affecting the economic life of Castile.[2]

The spontaneous emergence of a coherent, symmetrical, and adaptive mercantile system in Spain under Ferdinand and Isabella was inevitable. The conquest of Granada and the acquisition of Aragon's important Mediterranean dominions fostered imperialism. The discovery of gold on Hispaniola, when a revolution in warfare and a protracted fall in commodity prices were magnifying the importance of treasure, evoked restrictions on commerce and colonial exclusionism. The preponderance of extractive industries and the dearth of manufactures aroused protectionist sentiment in a nation making rapid cultural advances. For the exploitation and protection of distant dominions a strong merchant marine was essential. Navigation acts and ship subsidies were the logical result. The Hapsburgs extended and modified, but did not radically alter, the mercantile system of the Catholic kings. And before the accession of Philip II every important mercantilist policy introduced by the Bourbons, with the exception of model factories and protective duties, had been adopted by Spain.

Adam Smith's criticism[3] focused attention upon the place of treasure in the theory and practice of mercantilism, and few questions have evoked either more discussion or less investigation of primary sources by subsequent economists and historians. Hence there is ample justification for careful inductive study of mercantilist theory and practice concerning specie in all leading countries, particularly Spain, the nation that received and attempted to re-

---

[1] Konrad Haebler, *Wirtschaftliche Blüte Spaniens im 16. Jahrhundert* (Berlin, 1888), pp. 6–8.

[2] Diego Clemencín, *Elógio de la Reina Católica Doña Isabel*, Memorias de la Real Academia de la Historia, vol. vi (Madrid, 1821), pp. 243–258.

[3] *Wealth of Nations* (London, 1776), bk. iv, chaps. i–iii, vii–viii.

tain the enormous influx of Mexican and Peruvian silver in the sixteenth and early seventeenth centuries. Following the lead of Spanish economists and statesmen, I shall subordinate other features of mercantilism to consideration of treasure.

Though monopolizing the mines of precious metals throughout the mercantilist period, Spain sought no less valiantly than other countries to amass and retain treasure. Of the diverse expedients for the accumulation of gold and silver, interdictions of specie exports were the first adopted. Although they antedated the mercantile system, the purpose of these prohibitions — promotion of economic strength and military power — was mercantilist.

In the Cortes of 1268 Alfonso x prohibited exports of gold and silver,[1] and the prohibition was repeated several times in the fourteenth and fifteenth centuries.[2] In 1442 John II required that all payments to the pope should be effected through either bills of exchange or shipment of commodities.[3] Exasperated by inveterate violation of the law against specie exports, on April 10, 1471, Henry IV added death to the penalty of confiscation of goods.[4] But this measure availed little. Complaining that their subjects — actuated by greed — had taken advantage of La Beltraneja's uprising to spirit treasure out of the realm, Ferdinand and Isabella on March 2, 1480 modified the

[1] *Cortes de León y Castilla* [hereafter referred to as *Cortes*] (Madrid, 1861), vol. i, p. 71. In the Cortes of 1258 Alfonso x prohibited the exportation of live stock (*ibid.*, p. 57).

[2] *Ibid.*, vol. i, p. 225; vol. ii (1863), pp. 433–439; Alonso Díaz de Montalvo, *Copilación de Leyes* (Burgos, 1488), lib. vi, tit. ix, leyes xviii, xx, xxii; Antonio Vives, *Moneda Castellana* (Madrid, 1901), p. 21.

[3] Alonso Díaz de Montalvo, *op. cit.*, lib. vi, tit. ix, ley xxi; *Recopilación de las Leyes destos Reynos* [hereafter referred to as *Recopilación*] (Madrid, 1640), lib. vi, tit. xviii, ley ii.

[4] *Cortes*, vol. iii (1866), p. 829.

legislation against specie exports and attempted to render it effective. For exporting less than five hundred *castellanos* the money and one-half the offender's goods were confiscated for the first offense. For the second offense, as well as for the first exportation of five hundred *castellanos* or more, a penalty of death and deprivation of all goods was fixed. These penalties were mandatory upon judges, and their Majesties warned that pardons would not be issued. A special oath by judges to enforce the law against specie exports was instituted, and officers were exhorted to be diligent in detecting infractions.[1] Repetition of this drastic measure in 1488 suggests difficulty of enforcement.

In June, 1515 the Cortes informed the Crown that a great scarcity of money had resulted from exportation and petitioned for relief.[2] On the following July 20 Ferdinand ordered that the laws against specie exports be preconized anew in ports and fairs; that trustworthy agents be appointed customs inspectors; that at least once in every four months all bankers and dealers in foreign exchange be required to exhibit their books and to satisfy royal agents that no money had been exported; and that officials throughout the kingdom ascertain and report the names of specie exporters, the amounts involved, and the ports through which money had passed.[3] During the reign of Charles v one of the demands of the revolting *Comuneros* and at least eight petitions in Cortes were directed against specie exports. In 1520,[4] 1524,[5] and 1534[6] the

---

[1] Biblioteca Nacional [hereafter referred to as BN], *Sección de Manuscritos*, Mss. 13,110; *Recopilación*, lib. vi, tit. xviii, ley i; Alonso Díaz de Montalvo, *op. cit.*, lib. vi, tit. ix, ley xxiii; *Cortes*, vol. iv (1882), pp. 157–159.

[2] *Ibid.*, p. 258.

[3] BN, *Sección de Manuscritos*, Mss. 13,112; *Recopilación*, lib. vi, tit. xviii, ley iii.

[4] Archivo del Ayuntamiento [hereafter referred to as AA], León, *Sección Primera*, 289.

[5] *Ibid.*, Cordova, *Moneda*, 2.   [6] *Ibid.*, *Moneda*, 3.

Emperor issued pragmatics interdicting the exportation of gold and silver, but he abolished the death penalty. Under Charles v pragmatics and petitions in Cortes recognized the prevalence of specie exports.

A law of 1552 promised immunity from prosecution and, as a reward, the treasure seized to exporters on commission who reported the crime.[1] In the same year the purchase of bullion by a foreigner, Morisco, or drayman (*arriero*) was forbidden.[2] Although frequent complaints of the Cortes [3] against the exportation of money attest that the mammoth streams of Mexican and Peruvian silver did not render Castile indifferent to the loss of treasure, the reign of Philip ii produced little legislation to curb the "evil."

In 1606 Medina del Campo ineffectually petitioned Philip ii to levy a duty of 8 per cent on exports of money and to transfer jurisdiction over violations of mercantilist restrictions on specie exports to the courts of the Inquisition, because, it was argued, these infractions strengthened the enemies of Catholicism.[4] On November 7, 1609, the Cortes voted to send representatives to the Council of Castile to insist upon exemplary punishment for the men recently apprehended at Écija in a conspiracy to export treasure.[5]

The drain of gold and silver precipitated by inordinate vellon inflation during the reigns of Philip iii and Philip iv and by the disparity between Spanish prices and those of other countries, in conjunction with the decreased inflow

---

[1] *Recopilación*, lib. vi, tit. xviii, ley iv.

[2] *Ibid.*, ley v.

[3] Apart from the efforts to stop the granting of licenses, not less than five petitions against the outflow of money were presented to the Crown.

[4] Raymond Bona, *Problème Mercantiliste en Espagne au XVIIe Siècle* (Bordeaux, 1911), pp. 123, 127–128.

[5] *Actas de las Cortes de Castilla* [hereafter referred to as *Actas*], vol. xxv (Madrid, 1905), p. 6.

of American treasure, rendered remedial legislation imperative. On October 14, 1624, Philip IV fixed a penalty of
death and the confiscation of goods for the exportation of
specie, intermediation or assistance in the export, or con-
nivance by a public official to permit violations of this law.
As one of the conditions for a levy of twelve million ducats
by the Cortes, on February 7, 1626, Philip IV contracted to
punish exporters of gold and silver as prescribed by law.[1]
Convinced that foreigners were smuggling counterfeit
vellon into the realm and withdrawing gold and silver, his
Majesty also provided the death penalty for importing
vellon or bringing it near Castilian coasts.[2] These penalties having proved ineffectual, on September 13, 1628,
Philip IV adopted more drastic measures. For smuggling,
acting as intermediary, or receiving foreign vellon his
Majesty provided that the offender be burned at the stake,
his goods confiscated, and his children rendered ineligible
for certain posts and benefices. An abortive attempt to
import or to accept foreign vellon became a capital offense.
Failure to report infractions of this law was punishable by
confiscation of goods and a term in the galleys.[3]

Besides the hated Flemish retainers whom Charles V
carried to Spain when he claimed the throne, his entourage
included Wolfgang Haller, agent of the Fuggers.[4] To
finance the purchase of the Roman crown two years later,
Charles V borrowed 543,000 florins from the Fuggers,
143,000 from the Welsers, and 165,000 from various Florentines and Genoese.[5] During the next two hundred years

---

[1] *Ibid.*, vol. xliv (1923), pp. 206–208.
[2] *Recopilación*, lib. vi, tit. xviii, ley lx.
[3] *Ibid.*, ley lxi.
[4] Konrad Haebler, *Die Geschichte der Fugger'schen Handlung in Spanien*
(Weimar, 1897), p. 42.
[5] R. Ehrenberg, *Capital and Finance in the Age of the Renaissance* (trans. by
H. M. Lucas, London, 1928), p. 77.

the Spanish Crown was always heavily indebted to alien money lenders. Perpetually involved in costly military campaigns in France, Italy, and Flanders, the Hapsburgs were ever dependent upon foreign capitalists for advances and transfers of funds. To enlist the aid of international bankers and to facilitate the support of armies abroad, it was necessary to grant copious licenses to export money. Few matters elicited more bitter complaints from the Cortes and reformers than did the privileges thus extended — chiefly to the Fuggers until their bankruptcy early in the reign of Philip IV and thereafter to Genoese and Florentines. That the permits to withdraw specie were against the public interest was freely charged and generally believed. Under Charles V the Cortes protested, and each successive Cortes urged Philip II — with ever increasing importunity — to grant few or no licenses. But these remonstrances elicited only carefully phrased explanations of the indispensability of permits and fragile promises to restrict their issue. For mere exhortation the Cortes of 1617–20 substituted a more effective policy. As a condition for the levy of eighteen million ducats a promise was exacted from the Crown not to permit bullion exports and to restrict licenses for monetary withdrawals to men who furnished the government foreign credit and the time limit of the permits to six months.[1] On September 13, 1628, Philip IV further circumscribed the granting of permits. Their issue was restricted to the Council of the Treasury and their amounts to 50 per cent of foreign advances. The name of the grantee, reason for issue, time limit, nontransferability, and port of exit became essential statements in all permits. Upon becoming effective, the licenses were surrendered; and customs officials rendered biennial reports

[1] *Actas*, vol. xxxii (1910), pp. 84, 142, 149, 533–534, 582.

to the Council of the Treasury on their utilization.[1] *A priori* expectation of the inefficacy of these measures is confirmed by repetition of the prohibitions against specie exports on September 15, 1642, and against transferability of permits on December 23, 1642.[2]

Castile was not alone in prohibiting exports of gold and silver. At least as early as 1374 treasure could be exported from the kingdom of Valencia only in exchange for essential food imports,[3] an exception made necessary by the dearth of wheat resulting from a "comparative advantage" in rice and fruit. This regulation remained in force until the eighteenth century. About 1625 the viceroy attempted to abridge the privilege of exporting specie in exchange for food by requiring a viceregal permit. But on complaint by the *Corts* of 1626, Philip IV deprived the viceroy of jurisdiction and instructed treasury officials to issue permits upon certificates by the *Sindich* of Valencia that staple food had been imported.[4] A request from the *Corts* of 1626 to repeal the law requiring official permits to transport treasure within the kingdom, because foreknowledge had caused the police to rob and kill transporters, was denied on the ground that internal freedom of specie shipment would foster illicit export.[5] In the Aragonese Cortes of 1626 previous prohibitions against the exportation of money were confirmed;[6] and on representation of the Cortes of 1646 that heavy exports of treasure from Aragon to France were impoverishing the former and enriching the latter, Philip IV decreed that the death penalty might be imposed in extreme cases.[7]

---

[1] *Recopilación*, lib. vi, tit. xviii, ley lxi.
[2] Real Academia de Historia, *Leyes y Cédulas de Castilla*, $\frac{8^2-23-5}{4499}$.
[3] *Furs de Valencia*, tomo i, fol. 31.
[4] *Furs, Capitols, Provisions e Actes de Corts de 1626* (Valencia, 1635), cap. x, fol. 10.   [5] *Ibid.*, fol. 12.
[6] *Fueros y Observancias de Aragón* [hereafter referred to as *Fueros*] (Saragossa, ?), pt. i, fol. 250.   [7] *Ibid.*, fol. 291.

Particularly significant is the fact that before 1700 complete freedom to ship treasure from one of the five Spanish kingdoms to another did not exist. From the standpoint of prohibitions against specie exports each kingdom seems to have differentiated little between the other four kingdoms and foreign countries.[1]

Perceiving that an adverse balance of trade with Navarre and the nations trading in the Biscayan ports was undermining the laws against the exportation of money, Ferdinand and Isabella enacted a "statute of employments" in 1491. All foreigners importing goods through the Biscayan ports or carrying them from Navarre into Castile were required to file an inventory, including a declaration of value, at the port of entry or nearest town and to give bond through a native for the exportation of Castilian goods of an equal value within twelve months. Failure to register imports or to furnish bond was tantamount to smuggling.[2] Natives of Álava, Guipuscoa, and Biscay were forbidden to carry specie to France, or even near the French frontier, for the purchase of meat or live stock.[3] Granting the petition of Fernando de Burgos, a representative of the Burgos Gild Merchants, on February 11, 1503, Ferdinand and Isabella restricted the entry of goods from Navarre to seven stipulated towns.[4] In answer to a petition of the Cortes in 1515 Ferdinand increased the number of customs houses and provided for the appointment of upright inspectors.[5] The Cortes of 1534 unsuccessfully petitioned Charles V not to permit a

---

[1] See, for example, *Furs, Capitols, Provisions, e Actes de Cort de 1626*, cap. xxxiii, fol. 13; *Fueros*, pt. i, fol. 250.

[2] *Recopilación*, lib. vi, tit. xviii, ley x; Maurice Ansiaux, "Histoire Économique de la Prospérité et de la Décadence de l'Espagne au XVIe et au XVIIe Siècles," *Revue d'Économie Politique*, vol. vii, p. 528.

[3] *Recopilación*, lib. vi, tit. xviii, ley xi.

[4] Diego Clemencín, *op. cit.*, pp. 257–258.

[5] BN, *Sección de Manuscritos*, Mss. 13,112.

foreign ship to unload at a Castilian port without first giving bond to withdraw the value of the cargo either in goods or foreign exchange within twelve months, nor to sail without a thorough inspection for prohibited exports.[1] Controversies over licenses for specie exports in the reign of Philip II diverted attention from the statute of employments, but the Cortes of 1617–20 conditioned a grant of eighteen million ducats upon a royal promise to require foreigners to accept goods, not reals, for commodities brought to Castile.[2] A law of September 13, 1628 extended the statute of employments to natives as well as foreigners, and directed every subject and resident alien engaged in foreign business to keep detailed accounts. For comparison, records of imports and exports were supplied by customs officials. Transporters of goods from ports of entry governed by the statute of employments into the interior were required to bear a certificate that the goods had been registered and a bond for countervailing exports posted.[3] In 1632 the Cortes made extension of the statute of employments — hitherto confined to Biscayan ports and the Navarrese frontier — to all Castilian ports of entry a condition for an increased tax levy.[4]

From the beginning of colonization every effort was made to stimulate the discovery and exploitation of gold and silver mines in America. Natives and colonists were guaranteed security of property in claims; tools and equipment were exempted from attachment for private debt; royal officials exercised paternal care over provisions in isolated mining districts; and, unlike the case in other in-

---

[1] *Cortes*, vol. iv, p. 616.
[2] *Actas*, vol. xxxii, pp. 272–274, 533.
[3] *Recopilación*, lib. vi, tit. xviii, ley lxi.
[4] *Ibid.*, ley lxiii. In 1606 Medina del Campo had unsuccessfully petitioned for a law restricting specie exports to 25 per cent of the value of imports (Raymond Bona, *op. cit.*, p. 127).

dustries, in gold and silver mining involuntary, but paid, Indian labor could be exploited. But the distant El Doradoes of New Spain and Peru could not themselves fulfill mercantilist dreams: the treasure must reach Castile. With this end in view every phase of handling and transporting bullion from the mouth of the American mine to the door of the Castilian mint fell under the strict surveillance of the government, and elaborate precautions were taken against leakage into other states. Legally, at least, foreigners were excluded from trade in the Indies, and emigration, even of Castilians,[1] was controlled by royal permits. In an effort to prevent exports of Peruvian treasure to other countries through Buenos Aires, Castile imposed destructive restrictions — limitations of tonnage, absolute prohibitions, and prohibitive duties — upon trade between Buenos Aires and Spain on the one hand and Peru on the other. Economic development of the River Plate region, one of the most fertile on earth, was needlessly retarded. Yet these measures found virile supporters in the House of Trade and Seville Gild Merchant. Fearing that American treasure would pass to the Orient, and thus be lost to Spain, Philip II prohibited trade between Peru and the Philippines; limited the tonnage, value of cargoes, and amount of specie that might pass between New Spain and the Philippines; interdicted imports of oriental goods from another colony into Peru; and severely restricted trade between Peru and New Spain.[2] Upon compulsory registration in the colonial port — abolished in 1660, but treasure imports were then insignificant — ship-

---

[1] Space does not permit consideration of the highly controverted date of admission of non-Castilian Spaniards. My opinion is that it is generally placed too early.

[2] *Recopilación de Leyes de Indias* [hereafter referred to as *Indias*] (Madrid, 1681), lib. ix, tit. xlv; W. L. Schurz, "Mexico, Peru, and the Manila Galleon," *Hispanic American Historical Review*, vol. i, pp. 395-402.

ments of specie passed into the control of a royal agent (sea captain or silver master), and if all went well they were delivered to owners in the House of Trade at Seville. To protect treasure against enemies and pirates, the system of convoyed fleets was instituted about the middle of the sixteenth century and regularized shortly afterward. Thus one mercantilist expedient defeated another. Irregular and infrequent sailings from Spain, inevitable concomitants of the fleet system, facilitated the inroads of Dutch, French, and English interlopers upon colonial exclusionism.

No greater error has made its way into economic literature than the thesis that after 1552 the enormous inflow of American bullion rendered Spain so indifferent to the export of specie that bimetallic ratios and monetary regulations were unaffected by mercantilist considerations.[1] Castile repeatedly altered the bimetallic ratio, weight, fineness, and tariff of gold and silver coins; deflated vellon; and prohibited imports of debased foreign money in an effort to curb the outflow of treasure. At least 75 per cent of the innumerable petitions in the Cortes and pragmatics affecting money in the sixteenth and seventeenth centuries stated specifically that limitation of specie exports was a goal. In the seventeenth century the Cortes and his Majecty's Councilors were attentive to and deluged with monetary schemes for the retention and attraction of treasure.[2]

For the explicit purpose of protecting domestic producers, in the Cortes of 1351 Pedro I prohibited the importation of wine from Aragon and Navarre into Castile.[3]

---

[1] See, for example, W. A. Shaw, *History of Currency* (London, 1896), pp. 110–111.

[2] Earl J. Hamilton, "Une Monnaie en Période de Révolution Économique: Or, Argent et Billon en Castille de 1501 à 1650," *Annales d'Histoire Économique et Sociale* (Mars et Mai, 1932), and "Monetary Inflation in Castile, 1598–1660," *Economic History*, vol. ii, pp. 178–211.

[3] *Cortes*, vol. ii, pp. 60–61.

In 1390 John I extended the prohibition to all nations and added death to the penalty of confiscation of goods.[1] The Catholic kings banned raw silk in 1500, but permitted the importation of fabrics.[2] The law of 1511 requiring foreign woolens to meet Castilian gild specifications[3] afforded indirect protection to domestic industry. Throughout the sixteenth century the Cortes protested against foreign trinkets, parasites which sucked away treasure, and several prohibitory pragmatics were issued.[4] In an effort to stimulate the final stages of manufacture — tailoring, for example, but not weaving — Philip IV interdicted imports of a wide variety of finished goods in 1623,[5] and the Aragonese Cortes of 1626 protected silk and woolen manufactures through exclusion of foreign fabrics.[6]

Heavy production of staple raw materials in Spain naturally incited legislative efforts to restrict exports in the interests of domestic manufacture. Before the end of Charles V's reign exports of flax, hemp, hides, leather, raw silk, iron ore, and iron had been prohibited. On August 14, 1551, the Emperor increased from one-third to one-half the proportion of wool intended for export which natives might purchase — at the exact cost to the exporter, including identical credit terms — for domestic fabrication.[7] In 1674 the manufacturers of Aragon argued before a committee representing the four Estates of the Aragonese Cortes that it would be preferable to burn surplus raw

---

[1] Manuel Colmeiro, *Historia de la Economía Política en España* (Madrid, 1863), vol. i, p. 382.

[2] *Recopilación*, lib. vi, tit. xviii, ley xlix.

[3] Manuel Colmeiro, *op. cit.*, vol. ii, p. 317.

[4] BN, *Raros*, 15,431; Raymond Bona, *op. cit.*, p. 86.

[5] *Recopilación*, lib. vi, tit. xviii, ley lxii.

[6] *Fueros*, pt. i, fol. 248; Ignacio de Asso, *Historia de la Economía Política de Aragón* (Saragossa, 1798), p. 289.

[7] Alonso Díaz de Montalvo, *op. cit.*, lib. vi, tit. ix, ley xliii; *Recopilación*, lib. vi, tit. xviii, ley xlvi.

material, apportioning the cost among manufacturers, rather than permit its export.[1] But legislation was not confined to mere conservation of raw materials. A great effort was made to increase the production of hemp and flax — imported in distressingly large quantities from France and Flanders — at home and in the Indies;[2] and colonial governors were instructed to foster shipment of brazilwood, hides, wool, and cochineal to the motherland.[3]

That the Mother Country exercised a liberal policy toward colonial industry and commerce cannot be gainsaid. From the beginning, woolen and silk manufactures, objects of great concern to the Hapsburgs and Spanish mercantilists, were permitted;[4] but in the seventeenth century his Majesty regarded exports to other colonies with disfavor.[5] The requirement in 1628 of a license from the Council of the Indies to establish a textile factory in America was explicitly designed to protect the Indians from involuntary exploitation,[6] but one cannot be sure that perverted administration of the law did not protect Castilian industry. Early prohibitions against the planting of vineyards in Peru were not enforced. In 1595 Philip II legalized the clandestine planting, and levied the moderate excise tax of 2 per cent of the annual production.[7] But in subsequent legislation the exportation of wine to Central American colonies was prohibited.[8] The interdiction of forced in-

---

[1] Manuel Colmeiro, *op. cit.*, vol. ii, p. 337.

[2] *Indias*, lib. iv, tit. xviii, ley xx; Raymond Bona, *op. cit.*, p. 51.

[3] *Indias*, lib. iv, tit. xvii, ley xvii, and tit. xviii, ley ii; C. H. Haring, *Trade and Navigation between Spain and the Indies* (Cambridge, 1918), pp. 31–32; W. Roscher, *The Spanish Colonial System* (trans. by E. G. Bourne, New York, 1904), pp. 42–43.
In 1614 ,when cultivation was permitted in the Indies, tobacco was added to this list (*Indias*, lib. iv, tit. xviii, ley iv).

[4] *Indias*, lib. iv, tit. xxvi, ley v; W. L. Schurz, *op. cit.*, pp. 393–394.

[5] *Indias*, lib. iv, tit. xxvi, ley iv.   [6] *Ibid.*, tit. xvi, ley i.

[7] *Ibid.*, tit. xvii, ley xviii.   [8] *Ibid.*, tit. xviii, leyes xv, xviii.

dustrial labor by Indians indicates that the Mother Country had less interest in colonial manufactures than in mining; but no elaborate attempt was made to prevent manufacture for domestic consumption, and so long as an industry did not compete with Castile in an external market it remained undisturbed. On the other hand, Castile exerted little effort to preserve the home market for her own colonial wares.[1] Intercolonial trade not considered injurious to Castilian interests, nor likely to facilitate the smuggling of treasure, was subject to low duties and few restrictions.

Protective duties found little place in either Castilian mercantilist theory or practice, and the same is true of Aragon. Revenue duties seldom rising above 10 per cent, whether on a specific or *ad valorem* basis, were levied in Castile and Aragon; but no deliberate attempt to favor exports over imports or to determine the character of either is discernible. Increases in the duties coincided with pressure upon public finance. Preferential treatment was not uniformly accorded the colonies or European dominions. In spite of protests from the mercantilists, most of whom advocated freedom of domestic trade, each of the five kingdoms differentiated little between the other four kingdoms and foreign nations.[2] In fact, Castile levied the same duty on goods brought into the Archbishopric of Seville from

[1] The prohibition, on August 29, 1503, of imports of brazilwood except from the Indies is a notable exception (*Indias*, lib. iv, tit. xvii, ley iii).

[2] See, for example, *Cortes*, vol. iv, p. 570; Manuel Colmeiro, *op. cit.*, vol. ii, pp. 262–264; *Recopilación*, lib. ix, tit. xxxii, leyes i–iii. Down to 1693 internal customs restrictions seriously interfered with the migration of the Mesta sheep herds (Julius Klein, *The Mesta*, Cambridge, 1920, pp. 31–32). In March, 1508 food bought in Valencia and carried into Castile for *Juana la Loca*, the Queen, paid an export duty on leaving the kingdom of Valencia (Archivo de Simancas, *Casa Real* [E. M.], 9–1). In February, 1555 convents in Valencia had to pay Aragon export duties on saffron bought in Saragossa (Archivo Regional de Valencia, *Conventos*, lbo. 11068). Near the end of the 17th century Aragon and Navarre waged a tariff war (*Fueros*, pt. iii, fol. 4).

the interior as on those from abroad;[1] and the customs system of southern Castile, based on the *almojarifazgo*, a Moorish survival, differed widely from that of the northern, western, and eastern provinces. The absence of a national system [2] and the general belief that farming of the customs to foreigners led to evasions of the duties largely explain the indifference of mercantilists and statesmen to a protective tariff.

The identification of money and wealth by Spanish mercantilists and statesmen in the sixteenth and seventeenth centuries could hardly be matched by any other nation.[3] Spanish poverty and monopoly of silver mines were reconciled by the conviction that mercantilist principles had never become effective, that American treasure had slipped away to other powers.

Particularly striking is the fact that Spanish mercantilists — unlike those of other countries — did not attribute the outflow of treasure to exorbitant quotations of foreign exchange, nor did significant public sentiment for artificial regulation of the exchange rates arise. The disparity between Spanish prices and those of other countries during the price revolution rendered international payments through drafts originating in commercial transactions relatively insignificant and kept the rate of exchange constantly at the specie-export point. Money was usually remitted abroad, and the attention of mercantilists seeking the causes of national disaster was diverted from foreign

[1] See, for instance, *Recopilación*, lib. ix, tit. xxii, ley ii.

[2] It seems that some places remote from customs houses enjoyed the *de facto* privilege of importing dutiable commodities free. The Cortes of 1579–82 petitioned for the abolition of certain customs houses recently established on the ground that the duties and administrative obstacles had greatly diminished imports of necessary food and merchandise (*Actas*, vol. vi, 1867, p. 812).

[3] See, for example, Juan Sempere y Guarinos, *Biblioteca Española Económico-Política*, vol. ii (Madrid, 1804), p. cxc; vol. iii (1804), pp. xcix, ciii, clxxxviii–cxcii, ccxvi; *Actas*, vol. viii (1866), pp. 52–53, 55; vol. xi (1886), p. 535.

exchange. Furthermore, in the sixteenth and seventeenth centuries relatively little Spanish economic literature emanated from business men. Bating the clergy and nobility, few Spaniards had sufficient education to compose a mercantilist tract; and the clergy had little inclination for economic speculation. The vast majority of outstanding Spanish mercantilists before 1700 were ecclesiastics, little acquainted with either the economic literature or life of financially advanced nations. Their profession afforded them scant opportunity to acquire the intricate economic knowledge requisite to fathom foreign exchange.

Recognizing the inadequacy of prohibitions against specie exports, Spanish mercantilists supported efforts to accumulate treasure through a favorable balance of trade. On March 1, 1558, shortly after the great revolution in Spanish prices precipitated by the influx of Mexican and Peruvian silver had initiated a heavy outflow of treasure, Luis Ortiz [1] presented to Philip II his *Memorial al Rey para que no Salga Dinero del Reino*,[2] for his day — or indeed any later day — a remarkably lucid and consistent formulation of the balance-of-trade doctrine. Estimating that from Spanish and West Indian raw material—particularly wool, silk, iron, and cochineal — costing foreign nations but 1 ducat, manufactures worth from 10 to 100 ducats were returned to Spain, Ortiz complained that Spaniards had suffered greater indignities from Europeans than had America from Spain. In exchange for treasure Spaniards gave the Indians goods and trinkets of much or little value;

---

[1] He described himself as a resident of Burgos and a *contador* (accountant) of his Majesty (BN, *Sección de Manuscritos*, Mss. 11,042, fol. 247).

[2] Manuel Colmeiro (*Biblioteca de Economistas Españoles*, new ed., Madrid, 1880, p. 131) speaks of Ortiz's *Memorial* as a *book*, and we know that Moncada and other economists were familiar with it. But diligent search at Madrid has failed to disclose a single copy. I have used two manuscript copies, both in the Sección de Manuscritos of the Biblioteca Nacional, Mss. nos. 6,487 and 11,042; the latter, apparently the better one, is cited below.

but through the purchase of manufactures from her own materials Spain was enriching other countries and becoming the laughing stock of nations.[1] Ortiz favored prohibitions, to become effective four years after promulgation, against imports of manufactures and exports of raw products. The four-year interval, renewable in case of necessity, would furnish producers and importers of raw materials a temporary market, facilitate the provision of necessary productive equipment, and increase the supply of artisans through immigration and training. In the preparatory period a 5 per cent duty should be levied on imports of raw material and 20 per cent on exports. The importation of foreign woolen, silk, and linen fabrics should be permitted for re-exportation only. To curb exports of specie — he estimated the loss to France alone at a million ducats annually — from the barren northeastern coast of Spain, Ortiz formulated elaborate plans to supply the region with grain, olive oil, meat, and wine produced in Castile or imported from friendly nations in exchange for manufactures.[2] Local authorities should encourage the planting of oak forests, for acorns would feed swine and curtail imports of pork into Castile.[3] Ortiz estimated the loss of specie exchanged for foreign books at 200,000 ducats a year, and urged his Majesty to prohibit the importation of profane books and induce the archbishop of Toledo and other prelates to ban imports of ecclesiastical publications.[4] The plenitude of wild bees in Spain attested fitness for the production of wax; yet Spain lost 500,000 ducats a year through wax imports. To stimulate domestic production, Ortiz recommended appropriate public honors for owners of twenty or more hives of bees.[5] According to Ortiz, the

---

[1] BN, Mss. 11,042, fol. 247. [2] *Ibid.*, fols. 258–260, 263.
[3] *Ibid.*, fol. 272. [4] *Ibid.*, fols. 255–257.
[5] *Ibid.*, fols. 257–258.

greatest single loss of treasure — 2,000,000 ducats a year — resulted from paper and linen imports. He favored not only domestic manufacture of these products, but the cultivation of sufficient flax and hemp to supply the raw material.[1]

Relying upon the indispensability of Spanish staples, Ortiz estimated that his prohibitory system would force foreigners to spend, instead of perhaps 1,000,000 ducats on Spanish raw products, 8,000,000 or 10,000,000 on manufactures. "It is impossible for raw materials worth more than 1 million ducats to come to Spain from other nations, and the balance must of necessity be returned to us in money." [2] After allowing for a loss on invisible items, such as papal dues, he estimated that Spain would attract 5,000,000 ducats a year from abroad.[3] Although arguing that the mere retention of Mexican and Peruvian bullion would render Spain the supreme temporal power, Ortiz — like later Spanish mercantilists — coveted the gold and silver of other nations.

The coexistence of excessive wool and silk prices and a dearth of money during recent wars puzzled Ortiz, and he predicted that after peace more money and higher prices would ensue.[4] Yet he expected the elimination of international transportation of raw materials and manufactures under his protective régime to lower Spanish prices. Apparently failing to perceive the incompatibility of indefinite accumulation of specie and the quantity theory of money, Ortiz naïvely asserted in a single sentence that if the balance of trade is favorable, "not only will money not leave, but will come from other kingdoms to these, and the excessive prices of commodities must necessarily fall." [5]

[1] *Ibid.*, fols. 253–255.
[2] *Ibid.*, fol. 247.
[3] *Ibid.*, fol. 250.
[4] *Ibid.*, fols. 252–253.
[5] *Ibid.*

All of Ortiz's *Memorial* cannot be related to over-estimation of treasure and desire to accumulate it. As in other mercantilist tracts, there is a residue of economic planning for the direct promotion of national productive power. For the civil disabilities penalizing mechanical pursuits, Ortiz would substitute public honors. He favored legislation requiring all boys under ten years of age, including the sons of grandees, to learn letters, a trade, or a craft. Every youth not engaged in productive manual labor who failed to meet this requirement at the age of eighteen would be deprived of citizenship.[1] To beautify the landscape, promote silk culture, and mitigate deforestation, Ortiz recommended the planting of mulberry and walnut trees along royal highways;[2] and he advanced schemes for improving flour mills and internal waterways.[3]

Particularly striking are the relative plethora of protests from the Cortes against specie exports and the dearth of notable mercantilist tracts in the second half of the sixteenth century. But in the seventeenth century a catastrophic decline in imports of American treasure, the heavy exports of gold and silver resulting from ruinous vellon inflation, utter economic decadence, and nascent realization that the hegemony of Europe was passing to other powers initiated many investigations by national committees and incited serious speculative inquiry, which became particularly intense in the reign of Philip IV, when conditions grew intolerable. In 1619 — the year that a Committee of Councilors appointed by Philip III consulted many economists while taking stock of the realm — Sancho de Moncada published his *Restauración Política de España*, in which, following the lead of Ortiz, he estimated the loss of specie through an unfavorable balance of trade, supported

[1] *Ibid.*, fol. 248.
[2] *Ibid.*, fols. 270–271.
[3] *Ibid.*, fols. 269–270.

prohibitions against imports of manufactures and restrictions on exports of raw material, and tried to arouse Spain from industrial and commercial lethargy. A favorable balance of trade would not only retain the output of American mines, but attract treasure from abroad. Moncada urged Spain to emulate France and Holland, countries without mines, in which, because of.industry and active commerce, gold and silver abounded. Although he attributed the price revolution in Spain to the influx of American treasure, Moncada did not recognize the antinomy of indefinite accumulation of money and a favorable balance of trade.

Among the notable mercantilist tracts [1] published in the reigns of Philip IV (1621–65) and Charles II (1665–1700) were *Arte Real para el Buen Govierno de los Reyes y Príncipes* (1623) by Gerónimo de Cevallos; *Conservación de Monarquías* (1626) by Pedro Fernández Navarrete; *Comercio Impedido* (1639) by José Pellicer de Ossau; *Idea de un Príncipe Político Cristiano* (1640) by Diego Saavedra Fajardo; *Memorial en Razón de la Despoblación, Pobreza, y Estirilidad de España* (1656) by Francisco Martínez Mata; *Motivos para Adelantar el Comercio, Fábricas, y Artes en Aragón* (1678) by Pedro Borruel; and *Memoriales* (1686) — particularly "Extensión Política y Económica" and "Zelador General" — by Miguel Alvarez Osorio y Redín.[2]

Varying widely in details and emphasis, these writers shared the prevalent mercantilist conception of treasure, recognized the futility of prohibitions against specie exports, and agreed that only a favorable balance of trade —

---

[1] This list does not exhaust even the outstanding mercantilist publications. In his *Biblioteca de Economistas Españoles*, Manuel Colmeiro lists dozens of mercantilist tracts of the 16th and 17th centuries.

[2] Bating Borruel's *Motivos*, important and well-selected excerpts of all the above works — for the most part, rare — are printed in Juan Sempere y Guarinos, *op. cit.*, vols. i–iv (1801–21).

fostered by restrictions on imports of manufactures and exports of raw materials, paternalistic regulation of industry, and zealous application to arts and commerce — could restore prosperity. Being familiar with the work of Moncada, most of these authors accepted the quantity theory of money, but failed to relate it to the balance-of-trade doctrine.

Discrimination against foreign ships began in Catalonia as early as 1227[1] and in Castile by 1398,[2] but systematic navigation acts were introduced by Ferdinand and Isabella. For the explicit purpose of averting the loss of treasure through shipping charges and increasing the potential supply of war vessels, they subsidized the operation of ships of six hundred or more *toneladas*, forbade the loading of foreign ships in Castilian ports when native bottoms were available, and prohibited the sale, gift, or hypothecation of vessels to foreigners.[3] Heedless to the demand of the revolting *Comuneros* in 1520 and the petition of the Cortes of 1523 for enforcement of the navigation acts, Charles v exempted England from the statutory discrimination against foreign ships;[4] and it seems that in practice, though not in principle, he discontinued ship subsidies. Upon complaint from the Cortes in 1560,

---

[1] Antonio de Capmany y Montpalau, *Memorias Históricas sobre la Marina, Comercio y Artes de la Antigua Ciudad de Barcelona* (Madrid, 1779), vol. ii, pp. 11–12.

The navigation act of 1227, limited to commerce between Barcelona and Alexandria and Céuta, prohibited the use of foreign bottoms when ships of Barcelona were available. Exceptions and lax enforcement largely nullified this law in the 14th century; but in the 15th the Sea-Consulate of Barcelona, by virtue of subsidies to the Crown, secured its re-enactment in a more stringent form (Robert S. Smith, "The Sea-Consulate in Aragon," manuscript, Ph.D. dissertation, Duke University Library, chap. iv).

[2] J. Goury du Roslan, *Essai sur l'Histoire Économique de l'Espagne* (Paris, ?), pp. 290–291.

[3] *Las Pramaticas del Reyno* (Alcalá de Henares, 1528), fols. 157–158; *Recopilación*, lib. vii, tit. x, leyes iii, vi–vii.

[4] Diego Clemencín, *op. cit.*, p. 260, n. 1; *Cortes*, vol. iv, p. 377.

Philip II revoked all exemptions from the navigation acts held by foreigners,[1] and in 1597 he increased the bounty for the construction of ships suitable for the India trade.[2] In an effort to coerce the rebellious Dutch provinces, Philip III closed the ports of Spain and Portugal to their ships and thus stimulated direct voyages to the East Indies.[3] A promise to build ships in Spain and America was an important factor in the grant of the monopoly of slave imports into the colonies to Domingo Grillo and Ambrosio Lomelin, Genoese, in 1662.[4]

From the very beginning, foreign ships and sailors were debarred from colonial navigation,[5] but these laws were never rigidly enforced.[6] From the reign of Philip II to 1700 a dearth of native vessels forced the admission — with ever increasing frequence — of foreign ships.[7] All of the Hapsburgs attempted to stimulate colonial ship-building, and few mercantilist efforts yielded greater results.[8] Regardless of the navigation acts, the exclusion of foreign ships from the Indies, and the promotion of navigation by the House of Trade,[9] no interest in shipping commensurate with the extension of the Spanish Empire

---

[1] *Recopilación*, lib. vii, tit. x, ley viii.

[2] *Indias*, lib. ix, tit. xxviii, ley ii.

[3] A. Wirminghaus, *Zwei Spanische Merkantilisten* (Jena, 1886), p. 63; Maurice Ansiaux, *op. cit.*, vol. vii, p. 1035.

[4] José Veitia Linage, *Norte de la Contratación de las Indias* (Seville, 1672), lib. i, p. 281.

[5] Rafael Antunez y Acevedo, *Memorias Históricas sobre la Legislación, y Gobierno del Comercio de los Españoles con sus Colonias* (Madrid, 1797), pp. 42-45, 269-270.

[6] Cf. I. A. Wright, "Rescates: with Special Reference to Cuba, 1599-1610," *Hispanic American Historical Review*, vol. iii, pp. 333-361.

[7] Rafael Antunez y Acevedo, *op. cit.*, pp. 48-49; José Veitia Linage, *op. cit.*, lib. ii, p. 104.

[8] Abbott Payson Usher, "Spanish Ships and Shipping in the Sixteenth and Seventeenth Centuries," above, pp. 203-205.

[9] For an excellent discussion of the study and development of navigation by the House of Trade, see C. H. Haring, *op. cit.*, chap. xii.

was manifested by the government; and no mercantilist desideratum received less attention from the economists.

In the seventeenth century a few Spanish writers recognized that national income should be measured in terms of goods and services, not by the store of treasure, and adumbrated a liberal commercial policy; but inasmuch as they exercised little or no influence upon contemporary or subsequent economic policy and speculation, we need not consider them here.

Little inclined toward pure speculation, Spanish mercantilists made no great contributions to economic theory; but, stimulated by deplorable retrogression in the seventeenth century, they formulated valuable precepts, largely or wholly dissociated from accumulation of treasure but conducive to economic strength and welfare. With prophetic vision they denounced most of the evils leading Spain to ruin — such as *latifundia*, primogeniture, mortmain, vagabondage, deforestation, redundance of ecclesiastics, contempt for manual labor and arts, indiscriminate alms, oppressive taxation, and excessive holidays. Their reform program comprised technological education, immigration of artisans, restoration of the coinage, extension of irrigation, and improvement of internal waterways. History records few instances of either such able diagnosis of fatal social ills by any group of moral philosophers or of such utter disregard by statesmen of sound advice.

In conclusion, let us examine some salient results of Spanish mercantilism. The rapid colonization of America was largely due to the gold and silver mines. Yet gravitation toward Zacatecas and Potosí led Castile to neglect vast expanses of the most fertile territory, like that of the River Plate region. The Seville monopoly and the fleet system — institutions largely designed to maximize and protect imports of bullion — rendered supplies inadequate and led to exorbitant prices for European merchandise, stimulated interloping, and created disaffection for the motherland even in the colonies directly served. In isolated and unimportant settlements conditions were still more deplorable; the home government endeavored to exclude foreign vessels and traders, but made no corresponding attempt to assure supplies from Spain. In the efforts to prevent exports of treasure to other countries and to maintain vested interests in the fleet system, Castile exhibited a callous disregard of colonial interests, particularly those of the Philippines and Buenos Aires.

Satisfactory data on the progress of Spanish manufactures are not available, but for a season industry seems to have obeyed the stimulus of rising prices. The resultant material prosperity facilitated the intellectual, artistic, and literary achievements of the golden age in Spain. But the disparity between Spanish prices and those of other nations, heightened by artificial accumulation of specie, handicapped export industry, naval construction, and navigation. Furthermore, the illusion of prosperity created by American gold and silver in the age of mercantilism was partially responsible for the aggressive foreign policy, contempt for manual arts, vagrancy, vagabondage, luxury, extravagance, and other phenomena which contributed to utter economic decadence in the seventeenth century.

The rôle of Spain in mercantilism equals that of England in laissez faire. With the eyes of the world focused upon her and American treasure pouring into her coffers, Spain approximated a laboratory as closely as is possible in most social sciences. The progress of European mercantilism in the seventeenth century, particularly the system of Colbert and Louis xiv, was stimulated by the correlation between imports of American gold and silver and

Spain's hegemony of Europe in the sixteenth century. The decadence of industry and the poverty of Spain after 1660 helped to discredit the prohibitive system, and when it became patent that export prohibitions were powerless to impound Mexican and Peruvian silver indefinitely in the face of an adverse trade balance, the attention of enlightened mercantilists and statesmen shifted to control of specie movements through the balance of trade. The price revolution in the sixteenth and seventeenth centuries, beginning in Spain and spreading to other nations as American treasure flowed out, gave rise to the quantity theory of money, a theory that ultimately shattered the dreams of indefinite accumulation of specie and contributed to the world-wide decline of mercantilism.

THE GENERAL BOARD OF HEALTH, 1848-1854

CLARENCE PERKINS

THE purpose of this paper is to give an account of the work of one of the less widely known institutions of mid-nineteenth-century English government — the General Board of Health. The Public Health Act of 1848, which established the Board, was enacted only after a long campaign against British ruling-class ignorance and indifference to the social welfare of the masses. The Industrial Revolution caused great concentration of population in the towns, where the people lived in almost unbelievable squalor. Obliged to live near their work, laborers had to pay outrageous rents for places in which no gentleman would keep his dog. There was no drainage and no adequate ventilation, light, or water supply in most working-class habitations. Epidemics such as cholera ran riot among people living in such conditions, and other diseases claimed a steady and exceedingly heavy toll. Upper-class Englishmen had the scantiest notion of how bad conditions were. The great cholera epidemics of 1831 and the following years served one useful purpose — they aroused such terror that it was somewhat less difficult for reformers to get the public ear for their programs.

It was a small but devoted band that insistently urged the need for thorough reforms. Dr. Southwood Smith, physician to the London Fever Hospital, the novelist Charles Dickens, Edwin Chadwick, for many years secretary for the Poor Law Commission which administered the

Poor Law Amendment Act of 1834, Lord Normandy, and Anthony Ashley Cooper, later Earl of Shaftesbury, were its chief members. They worked through private associations, especially the Health of Towns Association, publications, and parliamentary commissions to inform the public of the terrible conditions.

In May, 1838 a report was made to the Poor Law Commissioners by Dr. Arnot and Dr. Kay regarding the removable causes of disease. In the same year Dr. Southwood Smith reported the results of his personal investigations into the conditions in two London slum districts. In 1839 the House of Lords carried an address to the Queen for a commission to make inquiries into the health of towns. In 1840 a committee of the House of Commons was set to work and later made its report. Later Mr. Chadwick reported on the sanitary condition of the artisan population. In 1844 a commission appointed by the Peel Cabinet reported on like conditions.[1] These reports showed the most frightful overcrowding in nearly all the industrial centers. In Liverpool there were 7,860 damp, dirty, ill-ventilated cellars in which 39,000, or one-seventh of the town's population, slept.[2]

In many industrial towns there was a shameful lack of good water and consequent prevalence of filthy conditions as well as lack of ventilation. Even the dead jeopardized the health of the living. Scandalous tales were told of the overcrowding of urban cemeteries and the consequent stimulus to the spread of disease which exacted a heavy toll in normal years.[3] Dr. Southwood Smith in a "Report on the

---

[1] Hansard, *Parliamentary Debates*, 3rd ser. [hereafter cited as Hansard], vol. xci, cc. 617–618.

[2] *Ibid.*, vol. li, c. 1226.

[3] In St. Martin's graveyard, one acre in extent, 14,000 persons had been buried in the past ten years. In Enon Chapel, 50 ft. by 40 ft., 12,000 had been buried since 1823. These statements were made in a speech in the House of Commons, 1847. (*Ibid.*, vol. xciii, c. 733.)

Prevalence of Fever in Twenty Metropolitan Unions"
(1839) said "the effect is the same as if twenty to thirty
thousand people were annually taken out of their homes
and put to death."[1] The annual death loss from prevent-
able causes was greater than the losses in any modern war
in which Britain had taken part up to that time. Alco-
holism was widely prevalent among people who lived under
these conditions. Men, women, and children all craved
stimulant. Only a small fraction of the children had useful
instruction.[2]

Several efforts were made to secure reform legislation
previous to 1848. A Borough Improvement Bill and a
Drainage of Buildings Bill were voted by the Lords in
1841 and again in 1842, but failed to pass the Commons.
In 1844 a bill to regulate buildings in London became a law.
A bill to make better provision for the health of towns,
brought in by Viscount Morpeth, 1847, met with such
determined opposition in the Commons that no action was
taken.[3] Early in February, 1848, Viscount Morpeth again
brought in a Public Health Bill only slightly different from
that of the previous year. In spite of much factious opposition, it was pushed along — action being hastened, doubtless, by the rapid advance of the cholera epidemic toward
England[4] — and passed the Lords on July 27, 1848.[5]

The Act for Promoting the Public Health, as finally enacted, August 31, 1848, set up a General Board of Health
composed of one paid member, another without salary, and
the first commissioner of Woods and Forests. It was given
authority for only five years. On petition of one-tenth of
the ratepayers in any urban area, or if deaths there averaged over twenty-three per thousand, the Board might

[1] J. L. Hammond, *Lord Shaftesbury*, p. 156.
[2] Hansard, vol. li, c. 1232.   [3] *Ibid.*, vol. xciv, cc. 24–26.
[4] *Ibid.*, vol. c, c. 1175.   [5] *Ibid.*, c. 894.

send its superintending inspector to make public inquiry after due notice, get information, and make a public report with his recommendations.[1] If there was no local act of parliament in force setting up a local representative body to provide pavements, light, water, or other public improvements, then the Board might apply the Public Health Act by an Order in Council, fixing the limits of the district and prescribing the size of the local Board of Health, to be sanctioned by parliamentary act before it would be finally valid.[2] When the Act was applied to any town, management of the local improvements and the execution of the Act was turned over to a local Board of Health to be chosen by the ratepayers according to a system by which one vote was given to every ratepayer for every £50 of rateable property up to six votes.[3] The town council was to be the local board in districts consisting of one borough.[4] The one exception to the full power of the local board to employ and dismiss its own officers was the stipulation that its surveyor could be removed only with the approval of the General Board of Health.[5]

The local board received authority to plan and carry into execution a great variety of local improvements, such as water works, drainage works, sewers and sewage disposal plants, and cemeteries,[6] and, with the consent of the General Board of Health, to levy rates, and even to mortgage them, to get funds for these works.[7] Provision was made for the Commissioner of Public Works to advance money to local boards.[8] Where the rateable value of property was not over £10, or when the premises — or separate apartments — were let to tenants by the week or

---

[1] *Statutes at Large*, vol. lxxxviii, 11 & 12 Vict., c. 63, secs. 6, 8, 9.
[2] *Ibid.*, sec. 10.   [3] *Ibid.*, secs. 13, 20.
[4] *Ibid.*, sec. 12.   [5] *Ibid.*, sec. 37.
[6] *Ibid.*, secs. 41–45, 75, 76, 81–84.   [7] *Ibid.*, sec. 107.
[8] *Ibid.*, sec. 108.

month and the rents collected oftener than quarterly, the local board might compound with the owners and force them, rather than the tenants, to pay the rates. It might even reduce or remit payment of any rates on account of poverty.[1] The Act also laid down numerous requirements and regulations for sewers and house construction.[2] Offensive trades were not allowed in towns, lodging houses were to be regulated, cellar dwellings restricted, intramural interments checked, and objectionable cemeteries closed. It was for a rather elaborate framework of a new system of local government that the Public Health Act provided. Yet one who reads this long statute can hardly fail to notice that a very large number of its provisions were permissive rather than mandatory. Great pains were taken not to infringe local liberties and privileges; for example, no local board might construct new water works if any water company in the district was able and willing to supply water.[3] The cost of setting up this new system of local government was insignificant in comparison with the heavy expenses necessary to secure a private act of parliament for the establishment of a local government body.

Soon after the Public Health Act was passed, parliament voted a lesser bill called "The Nuisances and Contagious Diseases Act," which provided more effective powers for abating nuisances and checking the spread of contagious diseases. The Privy Council was empowered to authorize the General Board of Health to make the needed regulations. The bill became a law on September 4, 1848.[4]

No time was lost in appointing the members of the new Board of Health. Ashley Cooper took the unpaid membership, and Edwin C. Chadwick, who had been so active in the public health movement, became the salaried member.

[1] *Ibid.*, secs. 95–96.
[3] *Ibid.*, sec. 75.
[2] *Ibid.*, secs. 49, 51, 52–67.
[4] Hansard, vol. ci, c. 54.

Immediately the Board set to work. Its first task was to take steps to check the cholera epidemic, the arrival of which could be expected at any moment. Such physicians as Dr. Southwood Smith and Dr. Arnot had long regarded cholera as a filth disease — a pestilence to be checked by prevention rather than cured by medicine; and so the Board promptly drew up a set of regulations which were sent to the Boards of Guardians and the Parochial Boards in Scotland.[1] They were informed about the provisions of the Nuisances Removal Act and ordered to get information regarding the localities where disease had been frequent of late and to have the accumulated filth thoroughly cleared out. These instructions were published just barely in time, for the dread disease appeared in Hull and Sunderland before the Board's inspectors could leave for Hamburg, where they were to go for scientific data.[2] But in many cases the instructions were neglected owing to carelessness of the local authorities and the fact that the owners of ill-conditioned houses desired to save expense and were members of or had great influence with the local authorities. The Board sent out simple instructions for the treatment of cholera and urged local officers to provide for house-to-house visitation of the infected localities in order to find the sick among the poor, who otherwise would not seek a doctor's care until too late, and to fit up Houses of Refuge to care for well people who would otherwise fall victims to the disease in overcrowded tenements.[3]

Where the Board's instructions were carried out, the violence of the epidemic was greatly moderated. This was

[1] *Report of the General Board of Health* (1849), pp. 7-8, and *Regulations*, pp. i-viii.
[2] *Report of the General Board of Health* (1849), pp. 4-5.
[3] *Official Circulars of Public Documents and Information directed by the General Board of Health* [hereafter referred to as *Official Circulars*], nos. 1-6 (British Museum, PP. 2793), pp. 105-106.

conspicuously shown in Glasgow where the disease worked great havoc among the well-to-do, while poor people who were regularly visited largely escaped death.[1] Boards of Guardians often delayed action partly to economize. In the end this was extravagant; for example, from the small court in Bishopsgate Street, Peahen Court, Glasgow, the Parish of St. Ethelburga had received up to August 29, 1849 one widow and twelve cholera orphans, whose maintenance, until they were able to care for themselves, would cost the parish not less than £420, though £30 spent promptly in cleaning up the court would have prevented a single case of cholera occurring.[2] Where the early symptoms were dealt with energetically, almost no deaths resulted; but where this was not done, about 53 per cent of the patients died. Of course overcrowding and continued residence in damp buildings without ventilation sometimes counteracted all means of prevention.[3] In Sheffield excellent preventive measures taken in working-class localities resulted in lowering the deaths to 4 out of 2,969 cases observed in two weeks, while among wealthier people not cared for by these special measures there were 7 deaths out of a far smaller number of cases.[4]

The General Board reported that the lack of system in local government was a serious hindrance to its work. Divided responsibility among local authorities was very common. One set of authorities managed the water supply and another the sewage works, if any. Still other authorities often controlled house drainage and others had charge of surface cleansing. One set of men cleaned the main streets, others gave the courts and alleys such care as

[1] *Report of the General Board of Health* (1849), pp. 10–19.
[2] *Official Circulars*, p. 109.
[3] *Report of the General Board of Health* (1849), pp. 20–21.
[4] *Official Circulars*, p. 112.

they received. Even worse division of authority was to be found in London. In the more densely peopled districts, over 120 different local acts of parliament provided for the establishment of 80 distinct local jurisdictions many of which coincided with neither parish, union, nor police districts. In the parish of St. Pancras there were 16 separate paving boards acting under 29 acts of parliament. If a householder requested that the accumulated filth be cleaned up, no one could tell whose duty it was and every one of the 16 boards must be consulted before any steps could safely be taken, so jealous were local office holders of their prerogatives. This state of affairs inevitably caused inefficiency. The General Board of Health had no power to originate prosecutions for neglect or violation of its orders, and therefore no direct control over local Boards of Guardians except in case the coroner's inquest showed that they had grossly neglected their duty.[1] Often the Board of Guardians openly flouted the recommendations of the physicians and the orders of the Board of Health.[2]

All this was very galling to such enthusiastic social workers as Chadwick and Dr. Smith, who fully realized the need for quick action to save lives and could not understand the apathy of middle-class Englishmen. Almost from the beginning there was hostility between the Board and some local authorities, the Board working for greater simplicity and efficiency and the local authorities raising the cry of overcentralization and depotism in defense, they claimed, of local liberties which the central Board wished to abridge. The Board wished at once to set up in each town a unifying authority, a local board of health of the kind provided for by the Public Health Act where the act was applied to a

---

[1] *Report of the General Board of Health* (1849), pp. 23–27.
[2] For example, the Guardians of Whitechapel Union, November 18, 1849 (*ibid.*, p. 28).

town or borough; but the law officers declared that it had no right to do so.[1] It was this conflict between the desire of the General Board for efficiency and the opposition of local boards to central control that was destined to destroy the General Board of Health.

Before it was passed by parliament the Public Health Act got considerable publicity, and progressive minorities in many towns soon availed themselves of the chance it offered to better conditions of life for the common people.[2] The usual procedure was to get the signatures of the required 10 per cent of the local ratepayers and have the General Board of Health send a superintending inspector down to make an investigation. These civil engineers were not on a regular salary but were paid by the day, some three guineas and others only two guineas. Eight of them were thus employed occasionally in 1850. Two physicians were chosen as medical examining inspectors that year at three guineas a day and sixteen other doctors were temporary appointees at from one to two guineas a day when employed.[3]

The superintending inspector announced his coming some weeks in advance and on arrival held public hearings lasting several days. In company with several leading citizens, he made a thorough personal inspection of sanitary conditions in the town under investigation. During the first two or three years after the establishment of the General Board of Health the inspectors were kept very busy and often their reports were not printed and sent out for several months after the visit and hearings. Usually a copy of the report appeared in the local newspaper and

---

[1] *Report of the General Board of Health* (1849), pp. 24–25.

[2] *Gloucester Chronicle*, August 12, 1848.

[3] *Parliamentary Papers*, 1851, vol. xliii, "Return of Expenditures and Work of the General Board of Health to May 5, 1851," pp. 43–50.

often it led to much argument. A typical example of such a report is that of Edward Cresy who made a preliminary inquiry into conditions in Brighton in 1849.[1]

First the inspector stated the geological features, population, and vital statistics of the town, and the amount of illness and expenditures for outdoor relief of the poor in recent years. Second he described in detail those parts of the town where disease was most prevalent and gave his views as to causes, usually insufficient water supply and grossly inadequate sanitary facilities resulting in accumulation of filth. Third he described the local government, and later the congested and unsanitary burial grounds, the insufficient housing, the 54 slaughter-houses scattered all over the town, and the pigsties adjacent so the swine could eat the offal from the slaughter-houses. Before closing he came back to the lack of proper sewers and water supply, and estimated the cost of the improvements that he thought were needed. Finally he made his definite recommendations for reforms, one of which was the application of the Public Health Act to the town and the establishment of a local board of health. The local details differed in various reports, but approximately the same bad conditions were described by the superintending inspectors in several hundred reports examined by the writer.[2]

Local newspapers gave a wealth of detail in regard to the working of the Public Health Act. After a reasonable interval, unless extremely vigorous opposition developed, the

---

[1] *Report to the General Board of Health on a Preliminary Survey of Brighton by Edward Cresy* (1849) [British Museum, C. T. 157 (1)].

[2] In many towns where such strong opposition developed against the application of the Public Health Act that it was delayed, a second or even a third attempt was made by minorities determined on reform of bad sanitary conditions and a second inspector was sent to look into conditions. Numerous reports of these second visits testify to the determination of reforming groups. Had the General Board of Health only possessed longer tenure of power, far more could have been done for these towns.

General Board of Health issued a provisional order or authorized an order in council applying the Public Health Act to the town. Every provisional order then had to be confirmed by an act of parliament, though several might be confirmed by the same bill.[1] The confirmatory act usually fixed the number of members of the local board of health and the qualifications of members and arranged for their election by the qualified ratepayers.

The attitude of the common people toward the representatives of the General Board of Health was first marked by surprise and expressions of satisfaction, complaints of bad conditions well known to them, and finally urgent requests that something be done.[2] The poor were quite willing to pay for the prospective benefits from improvements. The middle-class people in most towns were quite ignorant of bad sanitary conditions prevalent in their own town, for the main streets were generally kept clean. At Gloucester the mayor and other gentlemen said they had no idea how filthy some parts of their city were.[3] In general the strongest opposition to the inspectors sent by the Board came from the owners of the worst tenements from which very high rents were obtained.[4] This opposition was partly due to the fact that much of this type of property was held by so-called owners who had leased the land for a few years and put up cheap houses. Previous local acts of parliament had often practically confiscated the rents of such property holders by exacting huge rates to pay in one year for works that did not increase the rentals at all. Actually the chief

---

[1] *Parliamentary Papers*, 1852–53, vol. iii, pp. 477–481; and *Statutes at Large*, 12 & 13 Vict., c. 94; 13 & 14 Vict., cc. 32, 90, 108; 14 & 15 Vict., cc. 80, 98, 103; 15 & 16 Vict., cc. 42, 69; 16 & 17 Vict., cc. 24, 126; 17 & 18 Vict., c. 53; 18 & 19 Vict., c. 125; 19 & 20 Vict., c. 26; 20 Vict., c. 3; 20 & 21 Vict., c. 22; and 21 & 22 Vict., c. 10.

[2] *General Board of Health Report* (1849), pp. 49ff.

[3] *Ibid.*, p. 53.

[4] *Ibid.*, p. 54.

works needed were cheaper than the purely temporary work previously done; for example, a good drain paid for in twenty to thirty annual installments as arranged by the Public Health Act was cheaper than cleaning the cesspool every year, and far better. After paying confiscatory rates property holders naturally demanded guarantees that the cost would not exceed the estimates and that the inspector be made responsible for the works.

Many small properties previously escaped rating because the occupiers were so poor and the owners feared that rating of these properties for the new works would lead to general rating. This caused many small occupiers to oppose the new works after petitioning for them at first. In many towns half the houses were thus exempted and the owners feared heavier burdens if the Public Health Act were applied.[1]

Some opposition to the Act arose from local boards about to be superseded, but less than was expected.[2] As might be looked for, the owners of existing water companies who profited by their monopoly of the water supply were not enthusiastic over the Public Health Act. Opposition came also from persons interested in business enterprises that were nuisances, such as slaughter-houses.[3] Strong opposition in some towns came from the clergy of the national church, who disliked to see their churchyards closed and the inflow of burial fees thus stopped.[4]

---

[1] *Ibid.*, p. 58.   [2] *Ibid.*, p. 59.   [3] *Ibid.*, p. 66.

[4] The Reverend Henry Luxmore, at a meeting held at Barnstaple in November, 1849, led the opposition in a long speech in which he said that "the present graveyard had been sufficient ever since the time of William the Conqueror" and insisted that it was still sufficient. He claimed no offensive odors came from it and that the demand for a new burial place came from greedy men who were forming a new cemetery company to make huge profits, charging ten to twenty pounds each for vaults. (*North Devon Journal*, November 22, 1849, and December 6, 1849, p. 6.) Other speakers, however, made it quite clear that the stench arising from the graveyard used since William the Conqueror's time was terrific.

Some of the protests against the centralizing tendencies of the Board were due to its insistence that its inspecting engineers be employed by the local boards to help plan and build their works. The General Board was convinced that paid specialists were needed to plan the works and that ordinary administrative bodies and local engineers were not competent in such matters. Shining examples of this were seen in expensive sewers incorrectly planned so that instead of emptying their contents out they merely created huge subterranean lakes of sewage under desirable residential sections. The General Board in 1849 frankly announced that, although its members did not believe in riding roughshod over local wishes, it would refuse to give full credit to selfish opposition of owners of the cheapest kind of rental property that most needed thorough reforms.[1]

There is much information in the local newspapers about the operation of the Public Health Act. From these sources we learn that in Gloucester, after the publication of an official report concerning conditions, the town council voted almost unanimously to ask the General Board to send a superintending inspector and put the Public Health Act in force.[2] The inspector, Mr. Edward Cresy, held his public hearings and gathered information early in December, 1848,[3] and Gloucester went under the Public Health Act among the first (August, 1849), the town council being constituted the local Board of Health.[4]

Public-spirited citizens of Barnstaple took advantage of the new Public Health Act and of the formal notices sent by the General Board to clean up the town and to call attention to unsanitary conditions. A public meeting was held, October 14, 1848, at which many speakers deplored

[1] *Report of the General Board of Health* (1849), p. 66.
[2] *Gloucester Chronicle*, October 7, 1848. One speaker showed that a petition for a special act would cost £500 and be slower than this procedure.
[3] *Ibid.*, December 10, 1848.   [4] *Ibid.*, September 1, 1849.

the defective sewers, lack of traps at the public sinks (to which most poor people had to go for water), the very scanty water supply, and the presence of such nuisances as a slaughter-house and very numerous pigsties in the town. The commissioners [1] stated that they had no means of providing more water as that was wholly in the hands of a private water company. Other speakers maintained that Barnstaple was a healthy town and poor people must have their pigs near their houses.[2] Next month the superintending inspector sent by the General Board came to Barnstaple and conducted hearings.[3] The public hearings were

[1] In 1811 the town had secured a special act of parliament setting up an elected body of commissioners to manage public improvements.

[2] *Barnstaple County and North Devon Advertiser*, October 19, 1848.

[3] The *North Devon Journal* for November 22, 1849 gave full details of the hearings. On the first day it was shown that the large suburb of Pilton had never been free from fever, and that sewage from the houses there ran down gutters into the open streets since there was no adequate public sewer. In Barnstaple many people used water from wells which received drainage from the churchyard, where the average number of burials for the past 30 years had been 93 a year. This burial ground had originally been level with the church floor, but was now 8 to 10 feet above it. One witness said that a grave could not be dug in the old churchyard without disturbing corpses, and that 15 years ago the grammar school boys used to play with human bones from it, the big bones being used as ball bats. They got these bones from a cellar, then and now known as the Charnel House, under the school adjoining the churchyard. Another witness testified that the water-company shares were vastly higher in price than formerly and that dividends were three times as great as they used to be, but the company would not give the town an adequate water supply.

On the second day of the hearings the official surveyor of the Improvement Commissioners described the drainage as fairly good, but other evidence showed that this was not true for the suburbs. On the third day the superintendent for the water company said that lack of supply was due to leakage. He admitted that the company did not filter its water and sometimes it was foul. The publisher of one of the local newspapers asked the superintendent about the company's capital and profits, but got no response. R. Arnold, a baker, stated that he bought water for his business from water carriers, sometimes paying as much as a shilling a day.

On the fifth day intramural burials were discussed. There was a decided disagreement in the testimony. The vicar denied many sensational accounts of vile odors emanating from the churchyard. The sexton stated that he always used a boring iron before digging a fresh grave to be sure that the ground was clear. But the testimony as a whole showed the need for closing the old cemeteries.

scarcely over before a crowded public meeting was held (November 22, 1849) to voice opposition to the Public Health Act.[1] Many of the most prominent ratepayers were present and took an active part.

The superintending inspector must have been very busy, for his report on Barnstaple was not published until the middle of June, 1850. He found that only one-sixth of the houses had pipes bringing water inside, and the supply was insufficient, nearly all the sewers needed replacement, and two of the seven burial grounds were very serious menaces to public health and the others soon likely to become so. Of course he recommended that the Public Health Act be applied to the whole borough.[2]

In the meantime the local authorities had begun to busy themselves with sewer construction, which had been long postponed, apparently to prevent the application of the Public Health Act.[3] On June 26, 1850 the town council had a meeting to consider the Report. The mayor favored getting a special act of parliament for the town to authorize its people to do what they wished. General sentiment opposed the Public Health Act and the result was a vote of thirteen to four against it.[4]

The local papers continued to print numerous letters pro and con — the more ably written ones favoring the Public Health Act;[5] but the political influences opposed to it were too strong. The local Tory representative in parliament exerted himself on behalf of the opposition[6] and apparently the General Board dared not apply the Act to Barnstaple. Near the close of 1850 the town council appointed

[1] *Ibid.*
[2] *Ibid.*, June 20, 1850, p. 4.
[3] *Ibid.*, June 20, 1850, p. 5; July 18, 1850; August 1, 1850.
[4] *Ibid.*, June 27, 1850, pp. 4–5.
[5] *Ibid.*, August 15, 1850, pp. 3, 6, 8.
[6] *Ibid.*, July 11, 1850, p. 5; May 15, 1851, p. 5; June 5, 1851, p. 4.

a committee to confer with the water company to get a better water supply, but the company's solicitor wrote in answer that an interview would be quite useless.[1] The water problem continued to be agitated in the summer of 1851, and the local council proposed getting a special parliamentary act and borrowing the needed money;[2] but no effective action was taken.[3] A committee recommended that water be taken from a tiny stream that was quite inadequate, and so assured the water company of the monopoly for another year.[4] After four years in which few of the abuses had been dealt with, another memorial was sent up, asking for the application of the Public Health Act.[5] A superintending inspector was again sent to investigate and report. There was much disorder created by opponents present at the hearings,[6] and up to the summer of 1854 the opposition was strong enough to prevent any action.[7] Probably the opposition might have tired more quickly had the General Board of Health been permanently established instead of for only five years.

[1] *Ibid.*, January 2, 1851, p. 5.

[2] *Ibid.*, July 24, 1851, pp. 4–5; and November 27, 1851.

[3] *Ibid.*, June 17, 1852, p. 5.   [4] *Ibid.*, March 10, 1853, p. 6.

[5] *Ibid.*, October 13, 1853, p. 5.   [6] *Ibid.*, December 1, 1853, pp. 3–4.

[7] *Ibid.*, April 20, 1854, p. 5. It may be of interest to note that Barnstaple was a borough in which political corruption in parliamentary elections was not uncommon. In the parliamentary election of 1852 the two Tory candidates won, but charges of bribery were so freely made that a parliamentary investigating commission was sent down (1853). The testimony taken in the course of its investigation (*ibid.*, September 1, 1853, pp. 2–5, and September 29, 1853, pp. 3–5) shows that the great majority of the voters of Barnstaple sold their votes in 1852. Six pounds each was a standard price paid for a considerable number. The agent of one of the Tory victors paid out £2,200. The other had been promised the electoral victory for £1,500, but the expense had run far beyond that amount. In the year 1784 it cost the winning candidate £1,632 to be elected to parliament from Barnstaple, if the assertion of the local editor may be believed. (*Ibid.*, September 29, 1853, p. 5.) In 1929 the writer had a conversation with the secretary of a former cabinet member in the course of which the latter said he recalled its being said in recent years that Barnstaple was still a borough where votes were bought.

In many towns, however, the people were well satisfied with the operation of the Act. Testimony from Exeter showed that the cost of the great improvements made there was very low, and the local board had no interference from the central Board.[1] In Rugby the cost of getting the Act was £127, and by June, 1853 half the houses in town had been drained and provided with a steady and good water supply. In Barnard Castle the cost of getting the Act was £116. Little compulsion had to be used in cleaning up and the water cost 3½d. per month for all classes of houses. In Tottenham a rate of 4½d. in the pound was paying for the water and the sewers, and the ratepayers reported that the improvements had greatly increased the value of the property. In Dover the total rate for water, sewers, and sinking fund was about 9d. in the pound. In June, 1853 the exact cost could not be determined in Launceston, Wolverhampton, Derby, Southampton, Wigan, Gateshead, Woolwich, and Salisbury, but the majority of the people were satisfied with the improvements made, and not only was there no complaint of interference from the central Board, but in several cases, such as Woolwich and Penrith, it was reported that the Board helped the local authorities to cut the costs of their improvements. In many towns it was reported that there was some opposition to the Act at first, but this soon disappeared when its benefits were realized. The testimony was unanimous that nowhere had the General Board done anything to increase costs for the local boards.[2]

Before the end of 1853 the Public Health Act had been applied to 182 places, to the marked advantage of the people. In many places, with the consent of the General Board of Health, the local board mortgaged the rates to provide the funds immediately to make the needed im-

[1] *Ibid.*, June 23, 1853, p. 6.   [2] *Ibid.*

provements, especially water supply and drainage. In this way the cost of the improvements was spread over a term of thirty years, thus making the annual cost slight, especially after taking account of the income from the water works. The writer has found no evidence of the unwarranted interference in local affairs by the central Board which was so commonly urged against it by parliamentary and local opponents.

Another valuable service rendered by the Board was helping towns which had not gone through the long and expensive process of getting a special act of parliament to provide the town with a corporate organization by which the ratepayers could easily manage such local municipal improvements as paving, lighting, drainage and water systems. The local boards of health set up by the Public Health Act served as an important step in the development of local self-government in the smaller English towns, many of which had never before had any. The facilities for setting up local boards of health survived the demise of the General Board of Health (1854). The statute called the Local Government Act (1858)[1] clearly followed the procedure employed by the Public Health Act of 1848 for setting up local boards to enable local government privileges to be obtained cheaply by public act of parliament instead of by the older and more expensive private act. But the sanction and approval of the General Board was not required after September 1, 1858.[2] The next year another statute made these arrangements perpetual.[3] In the following years the statutes contained many confirmations of provisional orders, altering boundaries and regulating the borrowing powers of specific local boards of health, now obviously become the active machinery of local government.

---

[1] *Statutes at Large*, 21 & 22 Vict., c. 98, sec. 12.
[2] *Ibid.*, sec. 8.   [3] *Ibid.*, 22 & 23 Vict., c. 3.

Besides its main work of applying the Public Health Act to numerous towns throughout England, dealing with the cholera epidemic, and enforcing the Nuisances Removal and Diseases Prevention Act, the General Board of Health took an active part in the work of providing London with an adequate sewer system and investigating the water supplies of the metropolis and the problem of intramural interments there. Several of its members were also members of the Metropolitan Sanitary Commission which made its first report on November 19, 1847[1] and two later reports in 1848.[2] The activity of its leaders, Ashley Cooper, Chadwick, and Dr. Southwood Smith, was prodigious. Of this a considerable body of reports bears witness.[3]

It was well that the General Board of Health was very active for its time was passing fast. Established for only five years, it was in a vulnerable position. Its opponents mustered their forces to prevent its continuance in power. Its status was unusual because it was not headed by a member of the Ministry and so was not directly responsible to parliament. Its active members were not in parliament, and Palmerston (1854) recommended that it be made subordinate to the Home Secretary.[4] Learned theorists insisted that the Board was a despotic institution and raised

---

[1] *Parliamentary Papers*, 1847-48, vol. xxxii, pp. 1-189.

[2] *Ibid.*, pp. 253-291, 341-369.

[3] "Report of the General Board of Health on the Supply of Water to the Metropolis," May 28, 1850, *Parliamentary Papers*, 1850, vol. xxii; "Report of Dr. Arthur Farr and Mr. Granger to the General Board of Health on 38 Metropolitan Workhouses," March 26, 1849, *ibid.*, 1850, vol. xxi; "Report of the General Board of Health on the Epidemic of Cholera of 1848-1849," *ibid.*; *General Board of Health Report on Quarantine* (London: H. M. S. Stationary Office, 1849).

The collection of Parliamentary Papers preserved in the British Museum contains numerous returns of expenditures and reports of work done; e. g. *Parliamentary Papers*, 1851, vols. xliii, liii, xxiii; 1852, vol. xx. Some extracts from the minutes of the proceedings of the General Board of Health are to be found in the British Museum (*Parliamentary Papers*, 1850, vol. xxii, pp. 965ff.), but the writer was not fortunate enough to find these in full.

[4] Hansard, vol. cxxxv, c. 973.

the cry of overcentralization. An Anti-centralization Society was founded, which called meetings in many large towns and pushed through resolutions in opposition to the General Board of Health. Friends of the Board urged in answer that almost all the powers granted to the local boards were merely permissive and that there was almost no interference with them by the central Board. Part of the opposition to the Board was due to dislike of Edwin Chadwick, who made little effort to conciliate those whom he regarded as benighted upholders of filth, disease, and death. He had been secretary of the Poor Law Commissions for many years, and there is no doubt that this commission had wielded despotic power to bring about needed reforms. In fact, it may be doubted whether the Poor Law Amendment Act of 1834 could have been effectively carried out without considerable centralization of power. But the General Board of Health was unlucky enough to inherit and suffer from the animosity aroused by the harsh enforcement of the Act of 1834. It was the more unfortunate because Chadwick, who became one of the most abused men in English public life, actually felt the keenest sympathy for the poor who suffered so acutely from the awful filth of English towns.

The General Board of Health had to meet the bitter opposition of powerful vested interests which had access to the most highly placed people. Not even Palmerston with his great personal popularity could check the wave of hostile feeling. He stated that the Board members had all placed their resignations in his hands and would retire from the Board whenever it was best for the public service.[1] He denied that the Board was tyrannical and showed that the local boards had cost each of nearly 200 towns about £200 apiece instead of the £2,000 that a special private

---

[1] *Ibid.*, cc. 977–978.

act of parliament would have cost. He tried to get the Board continued for two years more and urged that its members be wholly subject to the Home Secretary.[1] But Lord Seymour, who had been a member of the Board for the past year or more and a bitter enemy of Chadwick, led the opposition. He had seldom attended its meetings, but his antagonism carried weight and the bill to continue the Board for two years was postponed three months and so it was left to expire.[2] Chadwick was given a pension of £1,000 a year on his retirement, and the next Board of Health was put under a president who had to be a member of the House of Commons. This arrangement continued until 1857, when the Board was abolished as a separate department and its duties transferred to the Council Office to be performed by the Lord President with the aid of a committee of the Council.[3] Only a beginning had been made in cleaning up English towns, but it was a good beginning.

[1] *Ibid.*, vol. cxxxiv, c. 1417. The Board had already been continued one year beyond its original five years, but only because of the fears inspired by another cholera epidemic.

[2] *Ibid.*, vol. cxxxv, cc. 967–1005.

[3] *Ibid.*, vol. cxlv, cc. 196–197.

THE DIPLOMACY OF RICHARD COBDEN IN HIS COMMERCIAL NEGOTIATIONS WITH FRANCE

ARTHUR L. DUNHAM

AT A time when Anglo-French co-operation in economic matters is under constant discussion and is of vital concern to many nations, it is interesting to consider the methods by which one of the first economic covenants between France and England for a really constructive purpose was secretly arrived at. Neither of the two men who did most to create the Treaty of Commerce of 1860,[1] Chevalier and Cobden, had had any experience in diplomacy. Yet they did more than the diplomatic officers of either government to find their way through a maze of political, administrative, and financial problems of great difficulty and delicacy. Of the two, Cobden alone was well known in both countries, and in his own was immediately made the object of so great a chorus of praise that his countrymen have referred to the agreement ever since as the Cobden treaty.

There have been a few voices raised in criticism of Richard Cobden, and it has even been suggested that he worked for free trade in order to promote his own business interests and those of his friends and relatives in the cotton-printing industry. Such voices have been virtually unheard, however, and justly so, for their criticism has been malicious and unfounded; but they have served one useful purpose in

---

[1] A. L. Dunham, *The Anglo-French Treaty of Commerce of 1860* (Ann Arbor, Mich., 1930).

bringing out the fact that no British writer has made a fair and impartial study of Cobden's methods in diplomacy.[1] His two well-known biographers were both selected by his family and used chiefly the materials which that family put before them.[2] Their work, therefore, despite many excellent qualities, both historical and literary, is generally laudatory and never seriously critical. The chorus of praise has, consequently, continued. Nearly all of Cobden's fellow countrymen have felt that the material greatness of their empire was due largely to the policy of free trade of which he had been one of the greatest and most successful advocates.

On one point the admirers of Cobden are unquestionably right: the sincerity of his idealism. Cobden ruined himself and his family financially and seriously impaired his far from robust health in the long and arduous struggle for the repeal of the Corn Laws, and he showed the same spirit thirteen years later in his work for the French treaty. During a considerable part of the negotiations in the autumn of 1859 Cobden was confined to his bed or his room, yet his work continued unchecked. After the signing of the treaty he was obliged to go south for two months, and after the conclusion of the tariff conventions, in December, 1860, he went to Algeria for a much longer period.

Another significant example of Cobden's genuine idealism is seen in his long advocacy of international peace,

[1] C. J. Fuchs, *The Trade Policy of Great Britain* (London, 1905), pp. 8–10. Fuchs' statements are temperate and reasonable. More violent expressions of this idea can be found in the collections of pamphlets on the Anti-Corn Law League, especially those of German writers, in which the library of the London School of Economics is very rich.

Cobden himself hesitated to go to Paris in 1859 lest he be regarded as a salesman for British goods.

[2] John Morley, *The Life of Richard Cobden* (London, 1879), and J. A. Hobson, *Richard Cobden, the International Man* (London, 1918). The more recent book on Cobden by W. H. Dawson, published in 1927, adds nothing really new regarding his diplomacy.

which, to him, was an even greater incentive to negotiate a commercial agreement with France than was free trade. Regarding free trade as the only true principle in commerce, he yet sought its adoption by France chiefly because he thought an increase in international trade between France and England would make war between them almost impossible. The sincerity of his pacifism had been demonstrated by his continued opposition to the Crimean War, which cost him his seat in parliament and made him for some time intensely unpopular. Another example of this genuine longing for international peace is his long struggle against the pugnacious Palmerston as an advocate of increased armaments and of intervention abroad. This aspect of Cobden's idealism has rightly been emphasized by his second important biographer, Mr. Hobson, and in some of the Cobden lectures given under the auspices of the recently organized Cobden Dunford Memorial Association.

Cobden possessed also the zeal of the true crusader. He fought all his life against what he regarded as injustice, ignorance, and insincerity. One is sometimes tempted to wonder whether he did not regard opposition to his views in rather too many cases as the result of some such unworthy motive, or of some weakness such as mental inferiority or lack of courage; and whether some of the difficulties which he encountered in France were not due to this very excess of zealous idealism. How could such a mind fully understand the nimble-witted French who combine with their love of conversation a devotion to reason, logic, and the *juste milieu*? Cobden could not understand such qualities even when he encountered them among some of his own countrymen, such as Lord John Russell, whom he quite unjustly regarded either as one of his own opponents in the negotiations with France, or as an insincere and untrustworthy supporter. He never understood that beneath Lord John's bantering cynicism, which induced him to bestow upon the champion of free trade the epithet of "Unabashed Eloquence," lay a considerable amount of shrewdness and also of real idealism, as was shown by his interest in the Italian *risorgimento*.

The limitations of Cobden's virtues were responsible for several of his errors of judgment and the unfortunate impression of vanity or combativeness that he produced in the minds of some of his critics. In reality he admired Emperor Napoleon III, yet in his writings and speeches he was often unfair or unjust to him, or gave distorted impressions of him to others. He frequently referred to Napoleon as "my pupil," or "my attentive listener," showing that he mistook patience and courtesy for timidity and incompetence. He was firmly convinced that he had converted an ignorant sovereign to free trade, although on the very day of his first audience the Emperor had previously received, with Cobden's knowledge, the equally ardent Chevalier,[1] and although Napoleon had done more than any other sovereign since the great revolution to moderate the excesses of the national tariff. Without hesitation Cobden attributed the Emperor's reluctance to take a decisive step in the negotiations with England to a lack of the necessary courage which it was his mission to "screw up," whereas events soon showed that the political opposition to the scheme would be so serious that it must be carefully considered by any responsible statesman. When the rumor of a proposal by the Emperor of an alliance between France and England for intervention in Italy, which would have sidetracked or ruined his treaty of commerce, reached him, he believed it implicitly

---

[1] Cobden Papers, Cobden to Lord Palmerston, October 29, 1859. These papers are in the possession of the Cobden Family in London.

and had to be reassured of its falsity by Lord John Russell, Lord Cowley, and Gladstone.[1] On the other hand, when the Emperor asked Cobden's consent to submit the proposed treaty of commerce to the Corps Législatif and the Senate for ratification, he flatly refused and threatened to break off the negotiations. On that occasion his determination unquestionably saved the very life of the treaty.[2]

Of the French ministers the one whom Cobden saw most frequently was Eugene Rouher, the minister of Commerce. A shrewd lawyer and an equally skillful politician, Rouher became in later years so powerful that he received popularly the title of Vice-Emperor. In 1859, however, his position was not yet outstanding, and Cobden felt for him little of that distrust with which he regarded most politicians. During the secret negotiations their relations were notably cordial and there was every indication of almost complete mutual confidence. When the negotiations became more official there were, inevitably, more points of friction; yet far fewer of these involved Rouher than some of the other ministers, or even their sovereign, in the opinion of Cobden. Great cordiality prevailed again in the spring when they prepared for the great tariff hearings before the Conseil Supérieur du Commerce over which Rouher was to preside. Rouher told Cobden that he must have British witnesses to give evidence that would form a reliable basis for the duties in the tariff conventions that were to complete the treaty signed in the previous January. He said he could not rely upon the testimony of the French manufacturers. It was evidently partly in response to the wishes of Rouher that Cobden agreed to serve as chief

[1] Cobden Papers, Diary, vol. i, January 5 and 7, 1860. Also Cobden to Gladstone, January 7, in Gladstone Papers; in Foreign Office 27–1331; in Morley, *op. cit.*, p. 725; and in Despatches of Comte de Persigny in Archives du Min. des Affrs. Étr., 1860.

[2] Cobden to Rouher, January 10, 1860 (Archives Nationale, F 12–2684).

British commissioner in the negotiation of these conventions.

For some three months the hearings before the Conseil Supérieur continued, with Rouher and Chevalier sitting on the Council and Cobden and Chevalier preparing British evidence and instructing the witnesses. At what point Rouher decided the disposition to be made of the evidence produced at the hearings is uncertain, nor do we know whether he or some higher official was responsible for that decision. We do know, however, that the Council never was allowed to discuss the evidence, which was simply filed away in the archives of the French government until it was published some months after the signature of the tariff conventions in six ponderous volumes.[1] The great *enquête* so eagerly demanded by the French protectionists in fulfillment of the solemn promise of the Emperor had thus been held, but was treated as a farce because, while the manufacturers had been heard, their words were contemptuously ignored. Cobden gave no indication that he ever knew this, or that he ever had any warning of what use the French government really intended to make of the *enquête*. It seems impossible that he should not have known, yet the subject is not mentioned in his diary or correspondence, although Chevalier, a member of the Council, knew and must almost certainly have told him that all the work of preparing the evidence and coaching the witnesses had largely been wasted.

It may be that Cobden's knowledge of the trick played upon the French manufacturers and the indignity offered to the Conseil Supérieur by the suppression of its delibera-

---

[1] [Anon.], *Historique du traité de commerce de 1860 et des conventions complémentaires* (Paris, 1861), pp. 107–143. Much of the author's information was derived from the *Economist*. See also Ernest Feray, *Du traité de Commerce de 1860 avec l'Angleterre* (Paris, 1881), pp. 13–18.

tions had some effect in changing his attitude toward Rouher. Whatever the cause, however, there can be no doubt of the change in attitude. At virtually every session of the tariff commission Cobden disputed the statements of the French delegates, including Rouher, and challenged the validity of their evidence, often with warmth. It is true that Rouher always proposed a duty higher than the one he expected to get; yet his love of bargaining was typical of most Frenchmen and of most negotiators.[1] We know also that Rouher's real expectations were moderate and reasonable, and that he never sought to raise moderate duties to the legal limit of 30 per cent even though only an obligation of honor stood in his way. It is clear, furthermore, that much of the evidence which he used had been collected with unusual care and judgment by special agents of the French government and was, therefore, of unusual value. Yet there is no indication that Cobden ever showed appreciation of this. On the contrary, the tension at the sessions of the commission grew steadily greater until the climax was reached when Cobden accused the French delegates of violating a pledge given by Rouher, the minister of Commerce, and Baroche, the temporary minister of Foreign Affairs, in January, 1860, that the new French duties on raw materials would never exceed 10 per cent.[2] Rouher met this challenge with courtesy but firmness by calling a special session of the negotiators of the treaty, and producing the official correspondence which showed that the French ministers had promised only that the minimum duties on raw materials should approximate 10 per cent. Cobden was obliged to admit

[1] See the Procès Verbaux of the fifty-one sessions of the Tariff Commission (Ministre des Affaires Étrangères, Mémoires et Documents Anglaises, vol. xcv).

[2] Ministre des Affaires Étrangères, Mémoires et Documents Anglaises, vol. xciv; memoranda of Alexis de Clerq, annexes 6 and 7; Cobden to Baroche, January 13, and Baroche to Cobden, January 22, 1860.

formally his error and the incident was closed; yet one is left with a somewhat painful impression of an unnecessary accusation, since Rouher and his colleagues had more than lived up to their obligations, for according to the text of the treaty all duties, except those on iron and coal, could have been left at or increased to 30 per cent. The British had had to take the risk of the French using their advantage, but to their honor the French did not do so and respected fully the spirit of the treaty.

Cobden's discourtesy was undoubtedly due to the strain of overwork. His duties had been arduous enough for many months and his furious determination had made them more arduous still. We know from his letters and diary that he was even more exasperated with his own government than with the French. The amount of red tape required was enormous and nothing appears to have been done by the Board of Trade to ease the strain on its commission. Anyone would have been wearied by such a mass of technical details, and the strain was peculiarly great on an idealist and reformer like Cobden. In addition, Lord Palmerston suffered that summer another attack of belligerency and French invasionism, and by his indiscretions and insistence on increasing armaments produced a most unfortunate impression on French public opinion and thereby greatly increased the difficulties of Cobden in Paris.[1]

Cobden's relations with Gladstone illustrate even more clearly than his relations with Rouher his methods as a diplomat. The correspondence between them was full and frank throughout the negotiations for the commercial treaty from early in September, 1859, when Cobden first

[1] Hobson, *op. cit.*, p. 259. Quotations are given from Cobden's diary showing his own views of his treatment by the Board of Trade and Rouher's views of Palmerston's indiscretions.

spoke to Gladstone about Chevalier's proposal of a treaty, until the actual signature of the treaty late in January, 1860. Gladstone practically was put in charge of the negotiations by the Cabinet and Lord John Russell, the Foreign Secretary, rarely intervened except on the few occasions when official action was required, when he acted promptly and decisively. Gladstone also had charge of the treaty when it came before parliament for approval. His vigorous support and political skill were vital factors in the success of the project. Cobden recognized this and showed his confidence in Gladstone and his appreciation of that statesman's sympathetic interest. Yet, although usually well informed about British politics, and himself a speaker of conspicuous ability in parliament, Cobden never showed a full understanding of the difficulties that confronted Gladstone either in the Cabinet or the House, nor did he display his usual insight into the attitude of British public opinion.

Gladstone summed up the attitude of the Cabinet in a confidential letter to Cobden in which he said: "Your objects are to cement the friendship with France, and, next to this, to increase trade and reduce the enormous establishments (military and naval). Of those objects the first is faintly appreciated at this moment and by way of a cold abstraction, the other not at all. . . . A majority of the Cabinet is indifferent or averse. . . ."[1] In order to overcome some of these difficulties Gladstone felt that something must be done to reduce the striking disproportion between the concessions made by England in the proposed treaty and those made by France to England. One method upon which he insisted was the shortening of the interval

[1] Gladstone to Cobden, January 12, 1860 (Gladstone Papers). See also John Morley, *The Life of William Ewart Gladstone* (3 vols. in 2, London, 1913), vol. ii, p. 22. Cobden's letters to Gladstone as well as Gladstone's to him are in the Gladstone Papers at Hawarden Castle.

before the French concessions would take effect, which he
rightly regarded as important because England's concessions would take effect immediately upon the approval of
parliament.

Another point Gladstone made was that it would be unwise to drive the French too far in reducing their duties;
that in view of the existing French tariff the proposed
abolition of prohibitions and the decrease of duties to a
general level of 30 per cent were great achievements. Cobden had written that he was working hard to get the
French to reduce to a general level of 20 per cent and
thought he could succeed if the French were given three
years or more for the application of their concessions. As
an economist and free trader Cobden was right, but as a
diplomat he was making a serious error in judgment. He
yielded to the better judgment of the chancellor of the
Exchequer only because he must as an agent of the government, but he never modified his convictions, and he showed
such a lack of enthusiasm in carrying out Gladstone's
wishes that the negotiations might have been seriously
checked had it not been for the tactful activity of the
British ambassador to France, Lord Cowley.

On another important question, however, Cobden was
right and Gladstone clearly wrong. This was the reduction of the heavy duties levied by England on wine and
spirits, duties that were not only heavy, but so designed as
to favor the wines and spirits of Portugal and Spain, with
their high alcoholic content, as against the lighter products
of France. Gladstone was willing to grant a large decrease
in these duties in his new budget, but did not wish to have
it embodied in the treaty since, under the terms of a
promise made by Sir Robert Peel to the British distillers,
the Treasury would be obliged to pay them a large indemnity if the decrease were made through a treaty. Cob-

den reported that the French government attached the greatest importance to having the reduction of wine duties in the body of the treaty; in fact they considered this one provision worth all the others combined. It was their opinion that only through its inclusion in the treaty could they get the support of the great wine industry and its agricultural allies, and that they would need that support badly in their struggle with the industrial protectionists.

Cobden was anxious also to have the British duties on French wines made so low that they could be sold freely in England. He believed, quite sincerely, that the light French clarets and sauternes would do much to improve the health of the British nation, and that if they could be sold in England at a moderate price it would be an easy matter for them to be made so popular that they would drive out port and sherry. At the last moment Cobden induced Gladstone to have the reduction of duties on wines and spirits put into the body of the treaty, but he never succeeded in having British duties on wine made low enough to facilitate the sale of the lighter French wines on a large scale. He was unquestionably right in the importance he attached to this concession, and it is most regrettable that Gladstone was not willing to sacrifice a little revenue for the sake of a considerable increase in Anglo-French trade and a great increase in international goodwill.

As an international man, Cobden is seen at his best in his friendship with Michel Chevalier. He had several good friends in France and his friendships were rich and true, but the friendship with Chevalier was the most important because it was the very cornerstone of the commercial negotiations of 1859 and 1860. Chevalier was as ardent a pacifist and free trader as his English friend, but his economic ideas were less rigid. He was the first to see the necessity of negotiating a commercial treaty between France and England, and he had the vision of this agreement as the first link in a chain that should bind all Europe together in commercial freedom. He persuaded Cobden to propose a treaty of limited scope to Lord Palmerston in 1856, and one of much greater importance in 1859.[1] Throughout the negotiations the part played by Chevalier was vital. Although he worked almost entirely behind the scenes, his leadership of the free-trade school in France, his eminence as an economist, and the respect in which he was held by the Emperor and many of his ministers were invaluable.

Cobden has sometimes been accused of ignoring intentionally the value of the services rendered in the negotiations by Chevalier, and even of taking all the credit for their success to himself. While he was probably less modest than Chevalier, and while he did sometimes use the personal pronoun rather freely in speaking of the treaty, of the "conversion" of the Emperor, and of his own labors in the cause, his vanity was hardly excessive. His reputation for that and the rather widespread impression of his egotism have been caused chiefly by the work of his two admiring biographers and of the Cobden cult in England which has produced other high priests and thousands of worshippers.[2] Cobden himself was perfectly aware of the remarkable knowledge and ability of Chevalier; he knew as well as anyone that Chevalier's services were indispensable at almost every stage of the negotiations. He leaned heavily on Chevalier's sound judgment of men and policies and relied upon him constantly for his understanding of French psychology. All these obligations were recognized

[1] Dunham, *op. cit.*, chap. iii.

[2] Fuchs, *op. cit.*, p. 8: "His countrymen have pushed this admiration of him to a cult bordering on the ridiculous, and this has also hindered his English biographers from forming an impartial judgment of him."

by Cobden, as has been stated by Chevalier himself, who continued to be devoted to Cobden during the brief remainder of his life, and afterwards never lost an opportunity to pay tribute to Cobden's memory as that not only of a great statesman but also of a true and loyal friend.

A capacity for deep and rich friendships was, then, one of Cobden's greatest assets in diplomacy. Two of his most devoted friends helped him in the work on the French treaty — Chevalier, and John Bright, who advised both Cobden and Chevalier on occasions and was very useful when the treaty came before the House of Commons; while Cobden's correspondence with Gladstone was so frank and confidential that it can be called evidence of friendship even if the relationship never ripened into personal intimacy. Cobden was able also, through his ability and charm, to make interesting acquaintances that were of great value, and to produce a profound and lasting impression on the minds of many of the most influential persons with whom he came in contact. In this, as in his friendships, there was something deeper and more lasting than the ability to maintain pleasant relations through a wide circle of social acquaintances, such as is associated with the work of most diplomats. In these personal relationships his sincerity, his idealism, and his enthusiasm were vital forces, and his ability and persuasiveness in conversation completed the work begun by his more fundamental qualities.

His liabilities were largely the almost inevitable complements of his assets. His zeal and determination were frequently carried too far and led to undue concentration on his immediate objective and to the ignoring of all other considerations. There was thus often a certain lack of balance in his judgments, resulting from his inability to see at the same time many sides of the question, a quality requisite to statesmanship of the highest type. Excessive enthusiasm produced also the tendency to regard opposition as due either to some inferior motive or capacity, or to personal enmity. Thus he met the militaristic outbursts and distrust of Palmerston with outspoken opposition combined with personal resentment, and because of this he failed to make the impression in his struggle with that stateman that his idealism deserved. He was, in short, as impetuous, even if in a different way, as that statesman whom he denounced for his impetuosity. He could follow only the straight and narrow path, and because Palmerston would not, Cobden thought the truth was not in him.

The same resentment of opposition as personal, when it was not so intended, was the cause of his quarrel with Rouher and of the tension that made the sessions of the tariff commission so difficult. It was made worse by his lack of a sense of humor, so valuable a quality in diplomacy. Cobden could never make his opponents look ridiculous as could Disraeli when he accused Peel of stealing the clothes of the Whigs while they were bathing. Cobden could only have denounced the theft as evidence of moral unrighteousness. Every check encountered by Cobden was treated as serious, as almost a matter of life and death, where a little patience or subtlety might, by turning the enemy's position, have made an arduous frontal attack unnecessary. It can be said, therefore, that Cobden himself was responsible for many of the difficulties which he encountered.

Cobden, then, lacked many of the qualities usually deemed essential in diplomacy — suavity, subtlety, patience, and humor. But he lacked also one of the greatest diplomatic defects, cynicism. In him there was no well-concealed but evil intent, no *arrière pensée*. His aims and motives were honorable and clear to all who chose to see, and therein lay the key to his success. He suffered because of his defects and the limitations of his mind, and he needed desperately the help of his calmer and more patient friends such as Gladstone and Chevalier. Yet he was able to win and keep those friends through his transparent sincerity, his enthusiasm, and the loftiness and purity of his ideals; and through them and his own ability, he, the undiplomatic crusader, made the Anglo-French treaty a truly notable achievement in diplomacy.

BATA, CHIEF FIGURE IN THE WORLD'S SHOE INDUSTRY

BLANCHE HAZARD SPRAGUE

SIGNIFICANCE OF BATA OF CZECHOSLOVAKIA

IT IS an inadequate statement to call Thomas Bata the Ford of Europe who applied American principles of mass production to the shoe industry of Czechoslovakia. Bata was more than an efficient imitator: he was a creative force and an organizer. Besides being the one shoe producer and distributor whom England, Germany, and France, as well as the United States, feared as the competitor who leapt over tariff walls, Thomas Bata set the pace in the organization of the world's shoe industry.[1]

He appealed to his contemporaries because of his wide mental vision and discontent with old methods of small-scale production in separate shops where only a few men worked, as well as with the usual slow distribution by means of fairs and single sales. He marked, in sober economic history, the transition from the custom period to the putting-out or domestic period, where the entrepreneur with venture and capital enters the field to produce on a large scale for a wide market.

---

[1] The literature recorded already in card catalogues under Bata's name shows his rapidly increasing importance. He has been the object of bitter attack in such works as Rudolf Philip's *Der unbekannte Diktator Thomas Bata* (Vienna and Berlin, 1928). In *Neue Wege* (Prague, 1928) and *Baťa Myšlenky, Činy Život a Práce* (Prague, 1929) Antonin Cekota has shown himself a friendly and admiring biographer. Paul Devinat's careful research in *Working Conditions in a Rationalized Undertaking; the Bata System and its Social Consequences* (Geneva: International Labor Office, 1930) was a study undertaken in order to find a true analysis and judgment of Bata's work and methods, with their social consequences.

Thomas Bata's own country, now the independent Republic of Czechoslovakia, was part of Austria under the rule of the Hapsburgs when Bata was born, in 1876, right in the same farming country about Zlin in eastern Moravia where later his shoe factories were built. The people of his father's market town were peasants, "brought up in the fear of God, trained to work and suffer all hardships as they came, producing felt slippers and raising many children for the Austrian battlefields." They worked like serfs in the fields for the count who lived in the feudal castle [1] towering in the background.

Here Thomas Bata spent his boyhood. To this same region in our time he seemed like a kindly feudal lord of fascinating appearance and habits, and an exciting hero. To his workers no legendary hero could compare with the owner of an industrial plant in which 32,000 employees turn out 165,000 pairs of shoes daily to be sent to all corners of the earth. More than that, Bata released thousands of boys and girls and men and women from the heavy work in grain and beet fields where only a meager living could be earned through long days of exhausting work, the men and women alike going barefooted and back-bent about their labors. Now the younger generation in and around Zlin for a radius of forty-odd miles are working for what seems to them to be princely wages, with far shorter hours than those known by the people left behind on the farms. Other thousands of Czechs are employed in Bata's distribution organization, composed of 2,600 retail stores at home and abroad, whose sales forces are supervised carefully after being trained originally at Zlin.

Bata was conversant with the details of the government of Zlin, where he acted as the efficient and progressive

[1] In the summer of 1931 Bata bought this castle to use as a clubhouse for his employees.

mayor. He was a member of the provincial legislature of Moravia and served on several State committees, particularly on those concerned with transportation facilities. He was also one of the vice-presidents of the Europaische Wirtschafts-Union,[1] an international organization for securing European co-operation in politics and economics, which has its headquarters at The Hague. Thomas Bata thought of himself as a man of the future, a man of the world rather than of one nation or country, believing that patriotism does not exclude cosmopolitanism.

Production

Prague and Brno, the chief cities in Bohemia and Moravia, were proud of their citizen shoemakers, skilled in the craft of shoemaking since the Middle Ages. Most sons followed fathers in their craft. Every boy had to learn some trade and remain always in that same craft, duly certified, with his work officially inspected throughout his lifetime. So Thomas Bata, the son of a shoemaker, knew as a boy that he was to be a shoemaker always, and wished to be more than an ordinary one.

He learned the trade of shoemaking in his father's shop among journeymen and apprentices along with his brother and sister. Except that he sat on a four-legged stool while he worked as a boy at a low square table (familiar in European shoeshops even before the time of Hans Sachs), while his American prototype sat on a low bench with his tools and work beside him, Bata's early training must have been much like that of William L. Douglas, George E. Keith, or George F. Johnson, founders of some of the greatest shoe enterprises in the United States. He witnessed the growth and the transition of the shoe industry in

[1] Cf. *Europa 1929 Yearbook.*

Czechoslovakia from the custom shop of his father to the most highly specialized and rationalized factory in the world. As a boy, visiting his playmates' houses, he saw many survivals of the first stage, home production for family use. As a workman he was intimately associated with other stages,[1] i. e. the second, known as the custom, or bespoke, work stage, with its later phase of some retail sales-work; the third stage, the domestic, which was characterized by the putting-out system where the entrepreneur put out stock to shoemakers and helpers working in their homes, who in turn took their completed shoes back to the entrepreneur's central shop to be inspected and sold in wholesale lots; and the fourth stage, characterized by the factory system, in which, for the sake of greater speed and closer supervision, the workers were gathered under one roof. Bata's present so-called factory is a huge plant composed of factory buildings at Zlin. In it the organization is devoted to that mass production for volume distribution which may become the distinguishing characteristic of a new fifth stage of organization for the world's shoe industry.

The first T. & A. Bata Company was formed in 1894 when Thomas and his brother Anton with their sister Anna set up for themselves in a shoeshop with their maternal inheritance as capital. The firm made a canvas shoe that could be produced in quantity and at a low price. Unfortunately, before the first year of business closed Anton, the brother who could speak and write German [2] easily in

[1] Cf. B. E. Hazard, *The Organization of the Boot and Shoe Industry of Massachusetts before 1875* (Cambridge, Mass., 1921).

[2] In Vienna, where most of the Austrian shoe merchants were to be found, German was the prevailing language. The Bata boys had been born and brought up in Moravia, where Czechs formed 95 per cent of the population. A few years' schooling in Hradeste, nearer Prague, had given Anton his chance to learn German.

dealing with Viennese merchants, was called to do his conscript service in the Austrian army. Thomas and his sister, handicapped, worked on till they found themselves in bankruptcy. Within two years, however, every creditor was paid. They had studied ways of saving as well as of specializing, and advanced to a successful larger business by developing the domestic system, putting out material to workers who had no care or share in marketing the finished product. Many custom shoemakers proudly refused to leave their homes to work in the Bata central shop. The demand for custom work, either bespoke or extra sale, was passing, however. These old workers were losing out in the transition to the new domestic system in their midst.

Before long, Thomas Bata developed a second phase of the domestic system in his central shop, where he had workers specialize on operations instead of making a whole shoe. He had forty workers employed in their homes making linen shoes with leather soles, and ten men in his shop cutting and crowning while he searched for new and larger markets. He found one in a Viennese wholesaler who ordered several thousand pairs of canvas shoes. Thomas Bata dared to take the proffered order, but, realizing he could never manufacture this quantity by hand within the time limit, he went to Frankfort in Germany to buy machinery such as he had seen pictured. He bought the most important machines and filled the order successfully. Then the familiar history of the shoe industry was repeated. The machinery, though run by hand power, needed more space. The Bata company built a new factory, sixty by thirty feet in size, and steadily increased their production.

In 1904 Thomas, leaving Anton to run the factory, went with three of his workmen to the United States — to Lynn, the special center for medium-priced shoes in Massachusetts. There, employed as regular workmen, they studied at close range the American ways of production. Bata visited other industrial centers of the United States before he and his workers went home to Czechoslovakia via England and Germany, working for a while in shoe factories of both countries. Experienced in American methods and standards, and in those of Bata's chief European competitors, they returned to Zlin to reproduce American shoemaking conditions and output as far as they could. Like journeymen of the Middle Ages whose *Wanderjahre* prepared them for the future, these men learned and assimilated much, and later adapted to their own conditions many systems of American production.

In 1908 Thomas Bata became sole owner of the business but kept the firm name. Three years later his shoes went over the border, the first to be exported from Zlin to a foreign country. These went mostly to customers in the Orient, for whose trade Bata was specializing. According to government figures, the T. & A. Bata Company made 6,000 pairs of common, McKay-sewn, canvas shoes daily. It was a shoe which common people could afford to buy. Quantity production was what Bata had aimed to achieve and maintain, and export trade, he realized, would help tremendously.

The World War brought an enormous demand for army shoes and an attendant loss of regular markets for other boots and shoes. Thomas Bata carried on with army shoes, taking first an order for 50,000 pairs, keeping part of it for his own firm, and dividing the remainder among three other shoe firms in Zlin. His factory was under the Austrian military inspection, but was allowed to remain in Bata's ownership and control. He was making 10,000 pairs of war shoes daily with 5,000 workers in 1918. During the War he had mastered methods of high-speed mass production, and had procured both more capital and improved machinery.

When the World War was over, Bata faced the results of the over-expansion of war times. Even the machinery, hastily made and hard used, was of little use for peacetime production. With other shoe manufacturers of Bohemia and Moravia, he had to face the silent and almost unrealized transition that had been going on in the manufacture of shoes during the World War. Factories and machine methods would predominate henceforth in the Czechoslovak shoe centers. New markets had to be found for such mass production, since the old markets of Vienna and Budapest could not be shared by the new Republic of Czechoslovakia. Thomas Bata planned to acquire and maintain both domestic and foreign markets without the aid of middlemen.

First the T. & A. Bata Company announced a plan of opening stores in every city in Czechoslovakia, where their shoes were to be sold at one price to any and every buyer. By the year 1922, the worst year in Czechoslovak finances, with many business failures and much poverty, Bata deliberately cut his price "50 per cent off every pair!" "Crush high cost of living" became his slogan. Manufacturers and merchants derided him, but he sold his stock. He not only liquidated his assets, but won the gratitude of his government because he had come to his country's aid in the dangerous period of revaluation and stabilization of its currency, which had to be accompanied by a heavy fall in home prices. At the same time that Bata made known his cut in prices of shoes, he announced a reduction of 40 per cent in wages, to take effect in three weeks' time, but accompanied it with an immediate cut of 50 per cent in the prices of all necessities sold in the company stores, so that no one in the Bata plant suffered.

The result of Bata's example was prodigious in all parts
of the country. His competitors were expecting his down-
fall, but when they saw that people were buying his goods
eagerly they had to bring themselves to follow suit, and the
movement became general. Nor was Bata's business en-
dangered by this bold step. In 1923 he began to reorganize
his factory completely, and this process has been continuous: all machines and methods have been discarded
when better ones were found, and the Bata system of workshop autonomy has been steadily developing.

Thomas Bata's plant is enormous and novel; his organization alone is distinctive enough to make him famous.
Eighteen buildings, uniform in size and shape, contain 108
complete factory units. His system is a composite of the
industrial systems employed in manufacturing other articles besides shoes, from Ford's automobile to Beech-Nut
cans of pork and beans. Assimilated principles, with original mechanical embodiment, are used on all sides. Everywhere the conveyor system is in sight. Very simple driving
devices for power and fool-proof machinery are coupled
with carefully considered speed for the conveyor, since this
speed is based upon the physical and mental capacity for
rapid and exact work on the part of the individual worker.
In some factories all the machines are of American make,
largely those of the United Shoe Machinery Corporation,
now familiar to most shoe manufacturers in Europe; in
others a considerable number of Swiss and some German
machines are installed. Only the newest and best machinery is kept. A single style of shoe goes through the
processes at one time, and this extreme simplification
makes for speed, and eliminates mistakes both in handling
and in bookkeeping.

Throughout these factories the organization is charac-

terized by efficiency to the nth degree, and Bata's original-
ity shows up in stark relief against the background of our
American factories. For instance, all the cutting of leather
for both uppers and soles is done in three stock buildings,
where the parts are also skived and tagged. Then they are
distributed, by means of cables and baskets in an over-
head-carrier system, to the eighteen factory buildings
where the other operations are to be performed. Of course
the universal rule has been the cutting of upper leather and
fittings on the top floor of a factory in the best light, and
that of all sole leather in the basement unless the stock was
bought cut.

In the Bata plant, the factories where the actual shoemaking is done are not laid out like ours. Thomas Bata
improved on every known system. He improvised. Each
floor is divided into two units, each capable of turning
out 2,000 pairs of shoes a day. Work comes on a belt to
the girls sitting before the fitting benches, approaching on
their left in a wire basket carrier, at a speed suited to the
ability of the average worker. A girl takes out her stint of
perhaps six pieces, does her part of the fitting, whether
perforating, stitching, cementing, button-holing, or lacing,
and returns the pieces to the basket before it has passed out
of her reach to the next operator. She keeps, she has to
keep, the pace of the belt all day, handling her share of
those 4,000 separate shoes, doing her special work perfectly, and keeping no one waiting. There is no trade-
union official or agent to protest the pace for her. The belt
carries the baskets on to the other parts of the unit, stopping at each left elbow for a single operation until the
stitching, lasting, bottoming, polishing, and packing are
completed. This organization of the processes makes it
easy to figure the cost.

The workers have a five-day week of nine-hour days, with

an hour for dinner, the main meal of the Czech day. This is generally eaten in the Bata-plant cafeteria, at a cost of six or possibly ten cents. The day's wage [1] is based on the stint, not on the actual minutes or hours of work. If the work of the unit is not complete at five o'clock, the people of that unit stay at work sometimes for a half hour more, until it is complete. Even in the cutting of leather the amount expected, a thousand pairs a day, for instance, is posted over the machine. That is the worker's stint. It takes youth as well as peasant strength to keep the pace, and visiting shoe manufacturers from America are all impressed by the fact that the required youth and strength are seen everywhere.

Thousands of other workers in the Bata plant have never worked directly on a shoe. There are masons and carpenters, machinists, stable-keepers and printers, store-keepers and house matrons, bakers and butchers, within the vast walled enclosure. The high wall has guarded gates, so that the firm's property and secrets may be kept safe. Stretching out on one side beyond the walls are a recreation field, a running track, and open lawns and gardens. A large dormitory to house hundreds of boys, and another for girls, equally large, are near by. There is a company hospital equipped in the most modern, efficient manner. A dance hall and a moving-picture theater are combined in one building, with a cafeteria large enough to serve six thousand meals per hour. Here, too, the conveyor system is used in the display tables for food.

Apartment houses, double houses, and single houses are supplied for families. All are equipped with bathrooms and cellars, dining rooms, parlors, and bedrooms; they are heated from a central plant. The rent for such apartments

---

[1] The day's pay is for so many pairs receiving this particular operation; all additional pairs are credited as bonus work.

and houses ranges from 45 cents to 75 cents a week. With keen interest in his workers and with vivid memories of his own boyhood days when the wash tub and cradle were inconveniently near his father's work table and the boys' apprentice stools, leaving no space for privacy or company, Thomas Bata insisted on modern, attractive rooms in the houses he built for his employees, who, like him, have come from one-room, bare-walled, poorly heated cabins such as an American used in pioneer days.

Company stores supply the employees with all kinds of food and clothing at cost. The vegetables and fruits, as well as the milk and butter, come from the Bata farms, and the clothing is suitable for men and women of all classes and of varied incomes. Though Bata inculcated and demanded saving on the part of his employees, he never withheld luxuries from those who could afford them. There is plenty of trading. During the summer of 1931, a ten-story department store building and a ten-story warehouse were erected.

In the dormitories there are continuation-school classes for the apprentices.[1] For the public school, which includes all the children of Zlin between the ages of six and fourteen, Bata provided the funds; but it was not on his land, nor was it under his control. Like all schools in Czechoslovakia, the Zlin school is run not by the local but by the national government, working through the minister of Education.

Garages for the company trucks and cars and a hangar with a fleet of airplanes make an interesting display. Buses drawn by horses used to be sent out to the rural districts to bring laborers daily. Since at home on the farms only oxen were used, for work and for driving alike, the farmer lads

---

[1] Cf. Gustav Swamberg, *Trading under the laws of Czechoslovakia,* Trade Bulletin no. 444 of the United States Department of Commerce.

and lassies were delighted over their daily bus rides behind horses. Since 1930 only motor buses have been used, with attendant saving of time.

Roads about Zlin are becoming better each year, and Bata has advocated better roads throughout the whole district.[1] Sanitation is excellent in the city as well as in the Bata plant, and after Bata became mayor of Zlin all the necessary city improvements, even to electricity for lighting and gas for cooking, were acquired.

Bata gathered into his plant nearly every industry allied to that of shoe manufacture except the manufacture of textiles and paper. These he bought in huge quantities to supply his shops for six months at a time, thus being able here, as in the case of hides, rubber, and food supplies, to purchase so cheaply as to bring confusion and dismay to his competitors.

The Bata company seldom needs to go in search of labor, for an average of two hundred people daily ask for a chance to work. A rigid examination, including a questionnaire, is given to applicants, and a physical examination is required. A probationary period of two weeks is allowed, and at its close the worker is either rejected without explanation or accepted. Once allowed to become a "Bata-man," every worker has to accept without question the "Workshop Autonomy Principles." These may be summarized briefly as follows:

1. The worker's *mentality* is to be transformed from that of a man whose wages are his chief concern to that of a collaborator in the Bata plant. To effect this, he must be

---

[1] Not satisfied with the budget and plans for roads, Bata guaranteed better roads for the same money. He took over the work, promising to pay extra costs out of his own purse. Instead he returned a part of the budget after he had provided excellent roads.

given a chance to take the initiative in production. He will be urged to this by the desire for gain, and he must therefore share in the profits.

2. Again, the worker must take *personal responsibility* as well as interest. He must not only do his work perfectly and speedily, but must make the most economical use of materials, powers, and time.[1] To this end he is to be encouraged to suggest changes in machinery as well as in the design of shoes.

3. The worker's *co-operation* is vital to the success of the whole organization. This constitutes his chief relation to the firm and to his fellow workers, all of whom have identical interests in the production of the plant.

4. To protect these common interests, *delinquents* must be *disciplined*. Individual workers cannot be allowed tardiness or carelessness which affects the output of their mates. Fines and lowered wages often lead to the elimination of the worker who makes himself unprofitable to the group undertakings.

5. *Comparison of output* of the 108 identical factory units serves as a true and feasible standard of performance. Foremen and workmen are judging each other for the benefit of all. Since *rapid promotions* from bench to managerial positions occur frequently, often in the case of men under twenty-five years of age, every apprentice sees his opportunity not far ahead, and limited only by his own endeavors.

Some critics of the Bata system find the discipline in the factory inconsistent with the "gilded paternalism" which dominates life in the Bata community; yet Thomas Bata always called the hospital, cafeteria, and comfortable

[1] Fifty per cent of all savings made go to the employees. Fifty per cent of each workman's profits are kept by the firm to pay his share of losses, but 10 per cent interest is paid for its use.

homes not gifts, nor charity, but the legitimate means of securing that well-being of employees conducive to maximum work. He insisted that his workmen should save a part of their earnings. Since he believed that recreation and sleep were both necessary to efficient workmen he made provision for amusements and for long hours of sleep. Proper diet, he knew, is necessary for active workers, so he provided fresh vegetables and fruit in his stores and cafeteria. All these welfare units he reckoned as essential to an adequate supply of efficient labor for mass production.

DISTRIBUTION

Even as a boy, Thomas Bata perceived the need of selling the shoemaker's product, since his father had not been able to make a living on ordered custom work alone. He became familiar with the problem of distribution when he went to the Zlin Spring Fair to help his father display and sell "extra" shoes and slippers at his booth. When he went into business with his brother Anton, in 1894, he entered immediately upon the domestic system where he had to manage both production and sales. He looked to Vienna for markets as a rule, for that city, with Budapest, controlled most of the wholesale and retail trade in goods of all kinds manufactured in Bohemia and Moravia as well as the rest of Austria. When Czechoslovakia declared its independence and separated from Austria in 1918, it lost its former markets, or found them far less easy of access since frontiers and customs intervened. All Czech industries had to find new markets, chiefly outside their country. Their own people had become poor and were not more than 14,000,000 in number. They could buy no great amount of luxuries, such as jewelry and leather bags, beads, and pottery, which Bohemia and Moravia could manufacture and market to advantage in quantity in New York, London, and Paris. Many articles of export made in Czechoslovakia were never seen in native shops in those lean years.

Bata realized that complete neglect of the domestic market, however, would be a source of weakness. By the establishment of hundreds of retail stores throughout Czechoslovakia, he sold shoes to people who had never worn them before. Scarcely a village in the country was too small to escape his attention; and even where he maintained no retail store, advertisements were posted indicating where his nearest distributor was located and the low price for which shoes might be purchased there. In this way Bata developed almost every available inch of the domestic market, so that, even with the anomaly of having the largest shoe factory in Europe located in one of the smaller European countries, his plant is still in a position to withstand the vicissitudes of the export trade to good advantage.

To see one Bata store in Zlin or Prague, Berlin or Chicago, is to see them all in their fundamental idea, definitely evolved by Thomas Bata. The window display is attractive. Beautiful colors of leather, good styles, and plainly marked low prices all conspire to lure the customer to enter. He finds a rather long, narrow store fitted on three sides from floor to ceiling with lightly-fashioned wooden shelves,[1] made in the Bata plant at Zlin. The paper boxes on these shelves were made, labelled, and filled with shoes in the Zlin factories. The seats for customers, the fitting stools for the clerks, and the mirrors about the store have the same origin. The advertising posters on walls and in windows carry pictures and words adapted to whatever

---

[1] The newer stores have steel shelves.

people may read them, but were printed in Zlin or Prague. The customer in a store in Pekin sees a Chinese girl playing tennis, wearing Bata tennis shoes. The Bohemian girl in Prague fancies she sees herself in the young lady dancing at a well-known Carlsbad pavilion in Bata slippers.

In the back of each store is a repair shop where frail or stout shoes can be reconditioned in a short time. There is no longer need of taking old shoes to an ex-custom shoe-maker to be cobbled by hand. Herein lies another griev-ance of old custom shoemakers against Bata. In some of the larger stores even those few moments of waiting may be beguiled by radio music in the rest room, or by a visit to a skilled chiropodist in a secluded corner. Some stores in the larger cities are housed in buildings six to ten stories high, which have apartments for clerks and workmen on the upper floors above the store, besides rest rooms, offices, and repair shops. At Prague, Bata recently completed the world's largest shoe store, with eleven floors and covering almost half a large city block. Designed in the modernistic style, it is most attractive, with its entire front of chro-mium steel and glass. The interior and fixtures are equally modernistic and alluring.

Wherever a Bata shoe store is found, it is apt to be near other shoe stores, and the advertising signs in the Bata windows always set forth prices lower than those in the windows of competitors. The nationality of the sales force and, to a certain extent, the style and quality of shoes dis-played are in accord with the neighborhood.

Every manager of a Bata store, wherever it is, in either hemisphere, has been trained in Prague or Zlin, and goes back there frequently to report his selling conditions and to be instructed on the Bata projects. Every customer who takes a pair of shoes away from a Bata store carries on his paper-covered box or bundle the slogan, in the language of his country:

ALL SHOES GUARANTEED

BATA SHOES OF DISTINCTION

"WORN THE WORLD OVER"

"OUR CUSTOMER — OUR BOSS"

Paradoxical as it may seem, the declarations of Bata, Ltd., in the consular offices at Prague show that some of the world's greatest shoe-producing nations are among Czechoslovakia's best customers for shoes. The following table, selected from many, gives concisely the distribution of imports and exports in footwear by Czechoslovakia in 1926:

Sources of imports and destination of exports [a]	Czechoslovak imports Crowns [b]	Czechoslovak exports Crowns
Austria	968,000	22,785,000
Germany	862,000	112,137,000
United States	719,000	16,098,000
Great Britain	611,000	66,645,000
Netherlands	76,000	15,000,000
Jugoslavia	54,000	33,000,000
Denmark	12,000	28,000,000
India	...	7,206,000

[a] Other figures are given for Norway, Poland, Rumania, Switzerland, and Egypt.
[b] A crown equals about 3 cents in United States money.

Of this distribution Bata then had much the largest share, because his production had been outstripping that of all Czechoslovak shoe manufacturers since 1912. His factory, using 4,000 laborers to make 10,000 pairs daily in 1917, and 17,000 laborers to make 125,000 pairs in April, 1931, was employing by October of 1931 over 32,000 laborers to produce 165,000 pairs. Other factories in Czechoslovakia with workmen totalling 10,000 produced 30,000 pairs daily, and 34,000 scattered shoemakers working in their homes or shops produced another 34,000 pairs daily, making a total of 61,000 Czechoslovak workers who were producing 189,000 pairs daily in April of 1931, at the rate of 50,000,000 pairs a year. Of these, Bata's plant made 31,000 000.[1]

Of this output, from 25 to 30 per cent is exported either to his representatives in foreign countries or to the firm's retail stores. Bata tried to eliminate middlemen in his foreign as in his domestic trade. In Germany and Austria, Bata agents used to receive a 15 per cent commission and were given terms of net cash; they had to pay the freight. If they changed the terms, or the price, the interest or any discounts were deducted from their commission. Thus the agent assumed cash payment at full prices, besides all credit risks. Now agents receive from 2 to 10 per cent according to their separate contracts with Bata. In the United States all exports are sold for cash to one firm, the Atkinson Shoe Corporation of Boston, who have sixteen direct accounts with the large department stores distributed from the Atlantic to the Pacific. Just as in production, so in distribution Bata, Ltd., is protected against all losses, since definite people are carrying the responsibility which they cannot shift to the firm. Strict calculation and foresight are required in the amounts of shoes ordered. Practically all shoes now exported by the firm are sold to its representatives for cash.

Since Bata got cash payments, he could buy immense quantities of raw materials on a cash basis. This gave him a price so low that he could in turn undersell his competitors.

[1] These figures were given June 15, 1931 by Karl L. Rankin, United States commercial representative at Prague. Other figures given November 1, 1931 by John B. Atkinson of the Atkinson Shoe Corporation show Bata manufacturing at the rate of 60,000,000 pairs yearly, of which 1½ per cent come into the United States.

The Bata agents set up in their regions typical Bata stores. In the Far East there are stores in Soerabaya, Batavia, Semerang, Pandong, Singapore, Shanghai, and Penang, each displaying appropriate posters for its clientele. In Jugoslavia on October 1, 1931 there were 110 Bata retail shoe stores. In Poland, where Bata's first retail shoe store was opened in Warsaw in April, 1930, his firm has become the largest retailer of footwear, with twenty-two stores already in operation, and the sites for nine others secured. This competition is said to be playing havoc with the Polish shoe industry, since even with high tariff duties the Bata firm, with its increasing number of chain stores and superior business methods, is retailing shoes at a much lower figure than is paid for Polish shoes.

Holland, in January, 1930, had 20 Bata stores, and Egypt 7; Switzerland, in October, 1931, had 40, India had 80, Constantinople alone had 40, and the United States had 24. France has Bata stores in its eastern towns, and Great Britain, South America, and Africa all have a share in making up the tale outside of Czechoslovakia. Last August the Bata Shoe Company, Ltd., was formed in South Africa with its head office at Johannesburg — the Bata answer to that country's 30 per cent tariff to protect a vigorous growth of the South African shoe industry.

Bata, Ltd., led in the amount and value of shoes exported from Czechoslovakia, and that country in turn led other European countries in the export of shoes. In November of 1928 she was reported as ranking second in the world in the volume of her shoe exports, being surpassed only by England, the oldest shoe-exporting country of all. Czechoslovakia has now, however, surpassed even England by over a hundred million crowns (about $3,000,000). The United States, which in the past exported on the average six times as much as Czechoslovakia, had reduced her shoe exports during the first eight months of 1928 to a third of the value of Czechoslovakia's. Germany, who exported more than double the quantity which Czechoslovakia exported in 1924, exported about one-fourth as many in 1931.

It is with the two last-named countries that Czechoslovakia is fighting hardest, with each of them already on the defensive, as is shown by their response in tariff legislation and a bettering of their own organization of shoe production. At first sight, the fight in Germany seems to be just a part of the rivalry of a century — the Czech against the Teuton.[1] No one who knows the history of race struggles in Bohemia and Moravia would expect that Bata, the successful Czech industrialist who dared to rise out of an agricultural section of the country, would be received with kindness or even toleration by the German industrialists or bankers of Prague. Pride and problems in the new Republic of Czechoslovakia bound Teuton and Czech together in a semblance of political unity after 1918; but it was not till 1926 that financial co-operation was secured by the alliance of Jewish bankers with Bata and other Czechs.[2] This racial struggle makes it apparent why Thomas Bata was a Czechoslovak hero to his own people: he has been their champion.[3] The whole fight seems, however, to be just that inevitable one between two stages of production with an industrial revolution intervening. Thousands of solitary shoemakers doing hand work in their small shops

[1] Cf. *Handbook* prepared under direction of the Historical Section of the Foreign Office, G. W. Prothero, ed., no. 2, pp. 10–39.

[2] Dr. Frantisek Munk of Prague says that the progress of the Czechs in banking and industries was not really sudden. Ever since 1860, the Industrial Revolution has brought Czech country people gradually into cities, to become powerful bourgeoisie.

[3] Cf. Leo Pasvolsky, *Economic Nationalism of the Danubian States* (New York, 1928), pp. 199–200.

in Czechoslovakia joined in spirit with other thousands all over Austria and Germany. In 1928, cheap light footwear from the Bata factories in Czechoslovakia began to flood the German market, and because of its astoundingly low prices met ready sale in Germany.

German shoemakers, in both Germany and Austria, tried in vain to save themselves from the menace of Bata shoes by complaints or injunctions. Their salvation lay in reforms in production and distribution, and this was gradually perceived by the German shoe industry. Prices of shoes have been lowered and the operating costs of factories decreased, while quality and style have been improved and variety increased. Bata's competition seems to have led the German shoe production and distribution to their own reform, and to their re-establishment on a far sounder basis.[1]

At the close of the year 1931 Bata visited Erfurt, one of the chief production centers for men's shoes in Germany, and placed a large order with the Erfurter Mechanische Schuhfabrik. The finished shoes were to be delivered bearing the stamp "Bata Shoes — German Products." It was hoped that in this way the taste of German consumers would be better suited than by the Czechoslovak products, and that the German high import duty on men's footwear might be avoided.

The dread of European competition seems to have come to the United States in one bound with the Bata enterprise, not gradually with the growth of imports from other European countries. Neither the general public nor the rank and file of shoemakers in the United States had heard in 1928 any such expression of fear, yet many thousands of

---

[1] Meanwhile Bata, Ltd., ceased construction of a shoe plant in Upper Silesia.

shoes were coming every month from abroad. The record
for the calendar year of 1929 reads:

Country of origin	Men's and boys' Pairs	Women's and misses' Pairs	Children's Pairs	Total Pairs
Austria	5,307	365,012	4,243	374,562
Czechoslovakia	54,962	4,397,866	46,584	4,499,412
France	8,273	312,769	12,100	333,142
Germany	5,800	171,647	15,109	192,556
Switzerland	25	162,755	132,364	295,144
United Kingdom	291,645	54,795	36,002	382,442
Canada	50,242	23,686	438	74,366
Other countries	3,553	25,917	1,547	31,017
Total	419,807	5,514,447	248,387	6,182,641

Only Czechoslovakia, however, was carrying on mass
production, and exporting to the United States millions of
pairs to compete with ours.

For a century and a half Lynn had been exporting
women's medium-priced shoes that could be made in
quantity and sold easily to West Indian, South American,
and Mexican wholesalers.[1] Even after slipping, by 1900,
from first to second place in the United States as a shoe
producer, Lynn had seemed secure in her foreign and
domestic markets. By a strange twist of fate or of human
nature, Lynn, the one spot in the United States which is
suffering the most from Bata competition in medium-
priced shoes, is the one place where Thomas Bata the man
has been well known, cordially welcomed, and kindly
spoken of. He joined the Lynn Chamber of Commerce
upon his return to the United States in 1919, not as a
shoe-worker as in 1905, but as a manufacturer; and he
never relinquished that membership. Having bought two
adjoining buildings, he organized the Bata Shoe and

[1] Cf. Hazard, *op. cit.*, pp. 28–31, 37–39.

Leather Company with a capitalization of $100,000. With his brother John as president of the company and his youngest brother, Bohus, as manager, Thomas Bata started the production of shoes similar to those made in other Lynn district factories, with union shoemakers at union prices and under the restriction of Massachusetts industrial legislation and supervision. There, as manufacturer and distributor, he made his contacts with the shoe world of Massachusetts as it centered in Boston.[1] He tried out American tanned leathers and machinery; he discovered the tastes and fancies of American women, and maintained friendly relations with other shoe manufacturers.

Year	Sandals		Shoes		Slippers	
	Pairs	Dollars	Pairs	Dollars	Pairs	Dollars
1927	314,365	636,691	385,915	814,637	178,392	328,681
1928	646,228	1,281,562	1,210,487	2,850,912	505,034	1,138,978
1929	2,162,371	4,607,178	2,425,045	5,333,154	1,048,801	2,425,534
1930	1,119,272	2,446,270	1,016,420	2,140,895	897,449	1,971,154
1931 [a]	617,275	1,082,527	429,300	695,612	351,455	501,455

[a] January–March.

By 1923, when Thomas Bata made his great and drastic reorganization of the Zlin plant, he had given up the Lynn factory, shipped home much of his machinery and stock, and taken his Czech secretary back to Zlin — a valuable asset with her knowledge of American methods and distributors, and her facile use of both the English and Czech languages. Two years later Bata's novelty shoes, of a type to compete severely with Lynn shoes, began to come into the country in great quantities,[2] which large department stores in New York, Boston, and Chicago took by thousands of pairs a week.

[1] During the two or three years that the factory was in operation, however, Bata had to spend much of his time in Zlin because of the financial and industrial confusion.

[2] The declared Czechoslovak exports of shoes to the United States show the rapid increase. After June 18, 1930 they were dutiable.

The reaction, actual, probable, and possible, of these Czechoslovak exports, mainly from the Bata plant, was voiced by leaders of the organized shoe manufacturers of the United States at the tariff readjustment hearings in 1929. The same arguments and basic facts were recited by all the advocates [1] of a tariff, and Thomas Bata's power was the undertone heard in each speech, though his name was never mentioned. The speakers agreed that their fight was for the protection of labor, or a duty that would equalize the cost of labor, and not for the protection of inefficient workers or of antiquated machinery and methods. The tremendous increase in importation of shoes from Czechoslovakia was attributed to the adoption of methods used in American mass production, and efficient layout in shoe plant, plus management of high order and vision. The fact was emphasized that some foreign competitors (meaning Bata) had the fundamentals that Americans have, with management equal to the most efficient in this country, in addition to a wage schedule only one-third of ours and lower costs of materials. A duty of 25 per cent was recommended.

These arguments at the tariff hearings were countered by questions about the apparent success of western shoe concerns without tariff protection; these brought the reply that wages in western non-union centers were not so high, and that the shoes manufactured in them did not come into direct competition with foreign imports. Other questions implied that over-expansion and old-fashioned methods

[1] The speakers who carried most weight both with the Committee on Ways and Means and with the country at large were J. Franklin McElwain of Boston, representing the National Boot and Shoe Manufacturers Association, Harold C. Keith, president of the Walk-Over Company of Brockton, the most important exporter of shoes, controlling sixteen Walk-Over stores in Europe, and Mayor Bauer of Lynn, representing the Lynn Shoe Manufacturers Tariff Committee and the city — itself a victim of the Czechoslovakian competition, with many vacant factories, bankrupt firms, and thousands of unemployed shoe workers.

were the real cause of disaster, rather than foreign competition.

Finally Congress put a tariff of 20 per cent on imported shoes, effective in June, 1930. The first half of that year saw increased importation of Bata shoes, to take advantage of the remaining months of free entry. That same year, owing to depression or glutted markets, the shoe production of the United States fell off 57,000,000 pairs, women's shoes alone dropping off some 19,000,000 pairs. The 20 per cent tariff could not save this decline, nor stop importations from Czechoslovakia. From 1923 to 1929, that importation had mounted from 435 pairs of women's shoes to 4,397,000. Though the number decreased the latter half of 1930, the first three months of 1931 saw it rise to 617,275 pairs of sandals, 429,300 pairs of shoes, and 351,455 pairs of slippers, a total of 1,398,030, or nearly 6,000,000 a year.

The remedy sought by some American shoe manufacturers in 1931 was a higher tariff.[1] That advocated by others was greater efficiency in methods and savings in cost of production, though not at the expense of the shoemaker's wages. This group asked that the United States be allowed free hides, with retention of the present relatively low duty on shoes. Some manufacturers agreed with the opinion[2] that cutthroat competition to drive Bata out of the American market would be unwise, since Bata would not suffer; that co-operation, instead of competition, by an attempt at proper allocation of foreign markets would be better for both American and Bata interests in the world market. Already a healthy reaction

---

[1] An additional 10 per cent on McKay stitched shoes was recommended by the United States Federal Tariff Commission and approved by President Hoover on December 2, 1931, to become effective January 1, 1932.

[2] G. Hirschfeld in *Printers' Ink*, December 11, 1930.

is being seen in the United States, which is putting its own house in better order by improved methods of production and distribution. The German solution may be that of the United States also; she may try to out-Bata Bata.[1]

The International Shoe Company, by some unannounced changes and savings, was able in 1931 to reduce the prices of the previous year by 17 cents; and, by adding thousands of workers, to increase its output during the summer and fall of 1931 from 145,000 to 185,000 pairs daily. It does not fear the competition of Bata, Ltd., even if it should change its lines and specialties. The Endicott-Johnson Corporation announced in November, 1931 that orders on hand and increasing sales assured steady full-time work for 17,000 workers for the next two months. For the three months previous, their factories had been running at full capacity, turning out 130,000 pairs of shoes daily, or 780,-000 pairs each six-day week. This increase, in face of the world depression, makes it seems as though American producers of shoes similar to the Bata shoe were awake and progressive. Like Bata, these two largest American concerns have developed the organization of their shoe industry free from trade-union control, and on the lines of mass production for volume distribution. This raises the question whether small-scale production, combined with highly organized union conditions of labor and a too highly specialized product, does not constitute as great a source of weakness to Lynn as does Bata's competition.

Although the great shoe manufacturers who visited Bata's plant and were entertained in his home could not help liking him and admiring his keen, inventive, and ad-

---

[1] The Brockton newspapers of August 27, 1931 carried news of one such attempt. Work was to begin soon in a Brockton factory using the A. U. C. stuck-on process for making shoes. The inventor claimed that by eliminating forty-two operations he would create a new low price level and revolutionize the shoe industry.

venturing mind, they have naturally been prejudiced against him as a competitor. Yet there are other than shoe interests to be considered: the United States wants the Czechoslovak trade.[1]

Conclusion

Spectacular and swift in death as in life, Thomas Bata died on July 12, 1932 in an airplane crash. Three days later a funeral service, held in an open square of the Bata plant at Zlin, was attended by about twenty thousand of his employees, by Czechoslovakian citizens and friends, and by acquaintances from various parts of the world. Immediate news dispatches from the Bata management at Zlin said there were no debts to banks or private individuals, all taxes were paid, and the workmen's savings, estimated at $3,500,000, were guaranteed by bank deposits.

Bata's stock on hand in June had been published as amounting to 25,000,000 pairs of shoes valued at about $37,500,000. He had had to curtail his production in early summer, and blamed the closing of his foreign markets on the tariff barriers raised by Great Britain, Germany,

---

[1] When the United States minister to Czechoslovakia visited the Bata plant at Zlin in 1931, Bata welcomed him and his party by saying it was his greatest ambition to introduce American methods into Czechoslovakia, and confessed that he cherished particularly the enlightened egotism put into practice by such men as Ford and Filene. The American minister spoke in admiration of the rapidity with which Bata had built up this great industrial undertaking, and said his visit to Zlin was a part of his attempt to acquaint himself at first hand with Czechoslovakia's economic conditions.

Julius Klein, when director of the United States Bureau of Foreign and Domestic Commerce, in the introduction to his bulletin on Czechoslovakia, its industries, resources, trade, and finance, traced the expanding export trade which enabled her to import large quantities of our American specialties like autos and adding machines. This bulletin indicates the importance of a number of great industries in Czechoslovakia. The Skoda of Vilkovice iron and steel plant, which is larger than Bata's plant, employs about 30,000 workers on an average. Like Bata, it ships to the Far East, to South Africa, to South America, and to the United States.

France, South Africa, and the United States. These countries found it necessary to shut out the shoes of this Czech who rocketed from obscurity. His death leads to the conjecture: "Will the industry he founded continue with such force, voracious as ever for world markets? For a short time, perhaps. Eventually it will dwindle. Bata was its brains, the dynamo, the illimitable vision and ambition. These qualities are not transmitted nor bequeathed to heirs and subordinates. They died with Bata as they have died with many another strong man before him." [1]

Thomas Bata was one who thought "in wholesale terms;" he wanted world trade instead of national trade. President Masaryk of Czechoslovakia has spoken freely of Bata's great and increasing influence on the economic prospects of Europe. Norman Hapgood,[2] visiting Bata at Zlin, found him impatient of national and continental boundaries, heard him reckon the low price of shoes if all such boundaries were abolished or forgotten and every person out of the hundreds of millions in the world had two pairs of shoes a year. Besides believing in a world market for mass production, Bata was looking forward to a United States of Europe in the economic sense and visualizing the air as a far better area for commerce than the land-separated oceans. He believed in a future for his industrial triumph; and his will pledged his associates to carry on the policies on which he had conducted the business. "Never think of yourselves, but put all your strength and all your interest into the common welfare."

Perhaps it is for ideas like these which work as leaven in the world's industrial lump that Thomas Bata will be best remembered in future years, though he may be called always "the wizard shoemaker of Zlin."

---

[1] Editorial in the *Brockton Enterprise*, July 14, 1932.
[2] Cf. Hapgood, "Europe's Henry Ford — Shoemaker Bata," *New York Times*, March 8, 1931.

THE ORGANIZATION OF THE TEXTILE INDUSTRIES IN JAPAN

D. H. BUCHANAN

BECAUSE of the success of her exclusion policy, Japan was subjected later and more suddenly than any other country to the economic currents of the modern world. The various stages of economic organization came to her with much more overlapping than they came to the Occident. Here the most modern mechanical equipment competes with the implements of the Pharaohs, and the industrial and commercial organization of world economy meets that of the self-sufficing feudal manor.

The textile industry was the first to be transformed in Europe, and it has been the first to adopt the factory in the Orient. This industry in Japan presents, perhaps, the best cross-section which any country offers of the series of industrial stages which the West passed through in achieving its modern industrial and commercial civilization. It is the purpose of this article to give some glimpses of the situation as it now appears in the Japanese textile industry. In order to do this effectively it will be necessary to describe briefly the earlier situation.

Modern industrial development in Japan has extended to the production of cotton, silk, hemp, wool, and rayon, but we shall be concerned in the main with cotton and silk production. While development has been chiefly in these two lines of manufacture, not all their phases have received the same attention. Before the restoration in 1868, the lord of Satsuma had ordered equipment for a small

cotton-spinning mill from England and the Tokugawa sho-
gunate had been negotiating for the establishment of a mill
in Tokyo.[1] About 1880 the Emperor's government established in different parts of the country ten cotton-spinning
mills, which were sold to private companies as rapidly as
they proved successful. The government also saw the
need of improved silk reeling, and in 1872 established a
modern filature which became a model for the entire country. Business men soon saw that the greatest comparative
advantages were in the production of yarns and threads —
raw materials, if you please — rather than in the weaving
of cloth. The government was also concerned about the
foreign-trade situation. It was necessary to import new
equipment from the Occident, and certain consumers'
goods came in rapidly. During the first decade after the
restoration 36 per cent of all imports were cotton yarns
and cloth. The problem of balancing these imports with
exports was serious. Raw silk was the largest export, and
there was a great desire to increase this and lessen the cotton imports.

The government also encouraged both woolen and
hempen manufacture by modern methods, the former with
an eye to military supplies. But neither could compete
with cotton or silk for the investment of business capital.
It was the introduction of these new power industries, together with the gradual transformation of the market and
of the attitudes of the people, which combined with the
old situation to produce the striking modern contrasts.

Before the opening of the country in 1868 the textile industry was widely scattered. Both cotton and hemp were
grown in nearly all the provinces, indeed in almost every
village and on almost every farm. Perhaps 80 per cent of

---

[1] H. Nishi, "Die Baumwollspinnerei in Japan," *Zeitschrift für der gesamte
Staatswissenschaft*, Ergänzungsheft xl (1911), pp. 56, 59.

the people were directly dependent on the land, and almost every family had its patch of cotton, the lint from which was worked up in and for the household. Simple tools not unlike those used in Europe had been in vogue for generations [1] — a pair of small wooden rollers removed the seeds from the lint, and the great bow was used for carding. The better grades were converted into yarn on a spinning wheel, while the poorer qualities provided padding for mattresses, cushions, comforters, and winter clothing. The yarn was woven on hand looms into cloth for family use. Dyeing — often from home-grown materials such as indigo and madder — was commonly done at home.

Hemp was likewise locally grown and woven to meet local needs. Rein reports in 1874–75 that "the most common clothing of the country people is made of a coarse [home-made] hemp fabric, colored blue with indigo[2] . . . which is everywhere grown for the purpose." [3]

Silk was produced in many parts of the country, and the common people used small amounts of the poorer qualities. Reeling was a common agricultural household industry, and the thread could also be cleaned, prepared, and woven in the home. In that unscientific period many silk-worms were improperly developed or were bred from poor "seed" and produced irregular filaments. Some cocoons were cut by the escaping moths and others entangled by two worms which had spun themselves into a great double cocoon. The outer and inner filaments, even from the best cocoons, were thin and generally tangled. This poor material was sometimes, by much labor, made into real finery for the farm people. There are no means of knowing what

[1] *Ibid.*, pp. 48–50.

[2] J. J. Rein, *The Industries of Japan* (1889), p. 378.

[3] *Idem, Japan, Travels and Researches* (1888), p. 408. See also B. H. Chamberlain, *Things Japanese* (1905), p. 431.

share of the country's textiles were thus produced by families for their own use, but it was a very large share.

At the same time there was a large amount of specialization in all these types of manufacture. Niigata and the ancient city of Nara were famed for the manufacture of *jofu*, a very delightful hempen cloth for summer wear. It was, and still is, dyed into most attractive patterns, among the most popular of which are those in gracefully waving autumn grasses, suggesting coolness, or the matchless Japanese idealization of breaking waves. Its production was by hand and by either independent families or persons working at the behest of merchants. In either case the merchants must have handled its distribution.

Cotton manufacture was also highly developed in certain communities. It seems, however, that it was much less specialized than was either fine hemp or silk weaving. While "the summer clothing of the more prosperous classes and of the inhabitants of cities generally has been [from 1600] mainly of cotton," the people "have never expended upon it any real art." [1] Cotton not used on the farm was sometimes spun there and sold to the weaving centers. Some raw cotton was sold to persons who put it out to families for spinning. Some weaving was done in the farm homes for local sale to consumers and to dealers, but most weaving for sale was handled by specialists, either independent families or persons working for putters-out. Kurume in northern Kyushu and Sakai and Himeji near Kobe and Osaka were great cotton trading and manufacturing centers. Morioka and Ashikaga in the north were also noted for this manufacture.

Silk manufacture was far more specialized. Silk was the clothing of the élite, and had long been made up into highly artistic products. It required the touch not only of the

---

[1] Rein, *The Industries of Japan*, pp. 378, 379.

craftsman but of the artist, and in its patterns are preserved many of the finest creations of this gifted race.[1] We have seen that silk reeling was widely done by the people who grew the worms, but dyeing and weaving were highly centralized. Kyoto, the ancient capital, has been for centuries the chief seat of these industries as well as of the other fine arts of the country. Here were the court and its numerous retainers, and here, during the long peace of the Tokugawa régime when Japanese arts saw their greatest development, came with their retinues the shogun from Tokyo and feudal lords and chieftains from all parts of the country. They added to the large local demand a demand for many art goods which were purchased as presents for friends and favorites back home. Other important centers of silk manufacture were Hakata, in northern Kyushu, Yonezawa, far to the north, Kiryu and Ashikaga, about seventy miles northwest from Tokyo, Fukui and Ishikawa (provinces now known for export silk), and Nagahama on the shore of Lake Biwa.

Fine artistic work was called for in many different uses. The decorations of palaces, castles, temples, and shrines, as well as court, religious, and ceremonial costumes, demanded rich brocades. Gold and silver threads were used with an elaborate array of colors and shades. Numerous lesser people of the knightly and wealthier classes also used much silk for dress and household purposes. Japanese women wore a great deal of silk, some of which was exquisitely made. The principal dress, the kimono, was of silk, and in winter in the lightly constructed unheated Japanese houses both men and women wore many layers of long clothes which were, especially for men, very full. But the most elaborate item of clothing was the woman's sash.

[1] An excellent collection of these has been preserved, in spite of fires, by the weavers' gild of Nishijin, Kyoto.

Often a foot or more in width, these were generally woven in elaborate designs with numerous colors. This called for a complicated loom, and the one in use was quite similar to those used in Europe and India. The sash industry was conducted in a large number of household shops, some of which were independent; but in many the workers used raw materials put out by men with ability to organize and market and capital to invest.

These centers also produced large amounts of plainer silk goods for kimonos, undergarments, and household use, which required much less skill. In many grades modest designs were woven in with dyed yarns, but for the clothing of younger women, and especially of children, the patterns were bolder. These, as well as those containing solid colors, for the formal clothes of older persons, were produced by dyeing in the piece. Stencil dyeing was highly developed, especially in Kyoto, where it is still supposed that the waters of the famous Kamogawa River add much to its success. Kyoto was the chief center for the finest goods, but the others mentioned produced as well large amounts of undyed cloth and the lower grades of figured fabrics. Nearly all these were produced in small household shops, some belonging to farmers, in which the artisans were either independent or received wages from a putter-out of raw materials.

Such was the situation when the country was opened to western trade and influence. Since then there have been marked changes, but progress has been most irregular. In some departments it has been revolutionary, in others scarcely noticeable.

Japanese statistics, especially for the uses of historical study, are for our purpose notoriously poor. It is not that the Japanese did not keep records, but that a different set of facts was emphasized. After the organization of the new central government there was a keen demand for information, but it took a long time to build up a new agency moved by the scientific rather than the traditional spirit. While increasingly elaborate figures were published, it was decades before they could be called more than "intelligent guesses." But the personnel of the various departments in Tokyo has rapidly improved and statistics have now become fairly reliable.

Another difficulty is that the information gathered and published has steadily changed. In the early days, statistics of households engaged in textile manufacturing and information as to whether or not they were independent or dependent upon a capitalist were given. Later, only factories were included. The bases for these figures have also been modified. At first they were classified according to the number of persons employed; but that has now been changed, as, for instance, in the case of weaving places, to looms employed. For the present study it is possible to use only certain typical figures and to supplement these by observations and inquiries. The statistics used are from the statistical reports of the central governmental departments. In only a few cases has it seemed necessary to give specific references; where statistics are from other sources, those sources are given.

In cotton spinning the old methods have been rapidly displaced, and Japan has become one of the leading cotton-spinning countries of the world. This industry is conducted on the most advanced factory lines with the best of machinery and highly skilled labor, and is managed by very large but very capable corporations. Furthermore, there exists a highly effective trade organization in the Japan Cotton Spinners Association. Both woolen and hempen spinning have also gone over to the factory system, and are conducted by corporations on an extensive scale. Rayon manufacturing, which is a new industry to the country, is not yet highly successful but is carried on in strictly modern plants on a large scale. Except that coal-tar dyes have been introduced and some simple mechanical equipment adopted, preparing, bleaching, and dyeing have been done mainly by the old methods. But the main stronghold of the ancient system, in both equipment and organization, has been weaving. Much cloth is woven in great factories on the most up-to-date automatic looms; but much is also woven in isolated households on primitive hand looms. Between these extremes we find almost every possible variation.

The household system in its entirety, that is the producing and manufacturing of materials for household consumption, still prevails in three of the main kinds of textiles. Farm families still frequently grow cotton for household purposes; in the more backward districts this is often actually spun, woven, and dyed. The same is true of hempen cloth, of which the farmers' "blue jeans" are still often made. Rural families reel or convert into "floss" silk considerable amounts of their poorer cocoons, and a part of this is made up into cloth for their own use; it is "the nice thing" for a rural family to present a guest with a piece of silk so produced.

Little outside labor or capital is brought in for this kind of production. Labor is frequently hired, but it is usually unspecialized farm labor. When specialized skill or machinery is required it is usually for a separate stage in manufacture utilized only by producers for sale.

The household weaving of factory-spun yarn, especially of cotton yarn, for domestic consumption is far more common than household spinning. Up to the time of the World War it was the usual thing for country women to make a large share of the family clothing in this way. But the increasing employment of country people in industrial and commercial establishments has reduced the amount of spare time and has also raised the standards of taste until the more uniform factory-woven and dyed cloth is demanded. At any rate, this type of industry is characteristic now only of the more backward rural communities.

Production by independent handicraftsmen of textiles for sale is of long standing in Japan. This work is generally performed in a part of the dwelling house, and is therefore called *kanai kogyo*, literally "industry inside the house." [1] Perhaps more than 10 per cent of the raw silk is still thus reeled,[2] though increasing percentages come from the factory filatures which also become steadily larger. This is practically the only type of yarn which is produced on a commercial scale outside the factories.

As for weaving, it is impossible to arrive at exact information as to the status of work carried on; but it is possible to see the direction in which the tide is moving. Until very recently a large share of the weaving and dyeing was done in households rather than in factories, and a goodly proportion of these households conducted independent businesses. In 1912 roughly 700,000 persons were employed in weaving, of whom 30 per cent, employed on 29.4 per cent of the looms engaged, were in this category. In the same year in Yamanashi Ken 90 per cent of the looms were thus managed. Such households have in the main used hand looms, so that for the country as a whole their output is proportionally less.

While the conditions indicated in the table opposite were much affected by the World War, and while these figures are

---

[1] Some twenty years ago official statistics for this business were discontinued.

[2] In 1922 the proportion of hand-reeled silk was 15 per cent and the average number of basins used by such producers was 1.4. Commonly there is one person per basin.

not quite strictly comparable, it is clear that the independent household industry was still of great importance in 1920. There were such independent weavers in all the prefectures, though only a few in the north. This type was much

STATISTICS OF WEAVING IN JAPAN [a]

(Cotton, silk, hemp, and their mixtures)

ESTABLISHMENTS

	Factories of over 10 workers [or looms][b]	Domestic [c] handicraft workshops	Putting-out capitalists	Piece-workers in home workshops	Total
1912	5,159	134,771	11,385	276,321	427,636
1915	3,967	190,646	10,291	212,976	417,880
1920	6,110	259,046	14,111	227,190	506,457

LOOMS

1912 Power	100,506	4,668	1,176	5,306	111,656
Hand	60,349	211,191	21,545	328,298	621,383
1915 Power	116,591	6,880	2,128	3,990	129,589
Hand	41,403	228,795	17,896	251,874	539,968
1920 Power	225,919	26,185	5,173	23,866	281,143
Hand	41,078	292,332	14,321	284,396	632,127
1923 Power					342,588
Hand [b]					355,793
1929 Power					406,849
Hand [b]					202,880

WORKERS

1912	148,093	216,266	20,738	312,601	697,698
1915	153,805	178,843	24,482	266,271	693,406
1920	242,546	339,011	28,240	321,127	930,924

[a] Adapted from figures given in the 29th and the 37th *Annual Statistical Report of the Department of Agriculture and Commerce* and the 6th *Annual Statistical Report of the Department of Commerce and Industry.*
[b] The figures for factories for 1923 and 1929 apply to factories employing ten or more looms; those for 1912, 1915, and 1920 apply to factories employing ten or more workers.
[c] For 1912 the figures are given as applying to households engaged in *kanai-kogyo*, and it is stated that they are "independent." For 1915 and 1920 this classification is lacking; instead there is one for independent establishments employing less than ten persons. Since earlier classifications included under factories only those employing more than ten persons, those employing less than ten seem to be a continuation of the *kanai-kogyo* under a different name.

more prominent in silk-weaving than in cotton-weaving centers. Kyoto, the home of the silk industry, had many independent weavers but few factories and power looms, while Osaka, the home of the cotton industry, had many factories but few independent craftsmen and hand looms. In the production of *habutai* silk for export this independent industry was very prominent. Five of the leading provinces in independent household weaving, employing 23,540 hands, had three times as many persons at that work in independent as in dependent households, and lacked few of having half as many in independent households as they had in factories. In Fukushima Ken persons thus working were nearly half the total. While a large share of this was doubtless subsidiary work by agriculturists, these families produced over one-sixth of the total value output of *habutai*. In the production of cotton cloth, on the other hand, the situation was quite different even in 1912. The weaving of cotton blankets, calico, cotton flannel, cotton sail-cloth, cotton crêpe, and towelling was practically all done either in factories or under the putting-out system by household workers. Cotton weaving was done either under the putting-out system or in the factory; but silk weaving, with its expensive materials and elaborate patterns, especially where marketing was easy, as in Kyoto, Kiryu, or Yonezawa, could be successfully carried through by a household. Such organization was less characteristic of woolen weaving, which had been imported as a factory industry, but a great deal of both woolen and hempen cloth was still so produced in 1912.

While the factories have become more important, the traditional type of organization has by no means been completely eclipsed. The silk-weavers' gild of Kyoto found in 1927 that 40.3 per cent of the weaving families of that city were of this independent class. It appears that this type prevails where the hand loom is employed, but in 1930 the weavers' gild of Ashikaga found that 17 per cent of the power-loom factories there were independent and 9 per cent partially so.

Since 1923 woolen weaving has been brought into this part of the picture. This is mainly due to a tariff, called the luxury tariff, of 100 per cent put on woolen fabrics. The Japanese now use large amounts of woolen cloth for clothing; men in business and professional life, as well as students, are largely so dressed. Women have held to their traditional costume but school children, both boys and girls, are often dressed in woolens. In order to guard the trade balance and the exchange rate the government laid this duty. Before that time there had been in the neighborhood of Ichinomiya, near Nagoya, a considerable production of woolen cloth by hand looms. The development of electric power and the high import tariff has induced these people to take up production in their homes on power looms. One may ride for miles about Ichinomiya through densely settled rural villages in which a large majority of the houses have weaving sheds attached, each accommodating from one to five wide looms. Many of the weavers are independent and produce for independent sale, continuing even when they must hold their products for a market. In 1920 about one-third of these small craftsmen were independent, and it may be supposed that as many or more are independent still. In 1929 there were 435 little factories in that Ken with less than 10 looms each. These factories contained 2,025 power looms and 304 hand looms, or an average per factory of 0.7 hand looms and 4.6 power looms.

The industries subsidiary to weaving have likewise generally remained on a small scale. Since it is the business of these concerns to do work for cloth producers or dealers, there is not the same degree of independence which an autonomous weaver enjoys. Like weaving, dyeing has not passed over to the factory stage. But many of the lesser advantages of the machine system, such as power equipment, steam, and hot water, are possible even in a small shop. Much of the yarn and cloth produced in large factories has been dyed in small workshops. In 1912 the figures for factories and domestic workshops were 216 and 2,627 respectively; but the average number of persons employed in a factory was only 22, while the average per domestic workshop was 2.6. The War and post-War boom saw a great development in this industry but it remained on a small non-factory scale. In five years the number of establishments was multiplied more than seven times, to 20,001, the average number of hands being practically the same as in 1912. In 1929 the number had fallen to 12,000 establishments which were slightly larger on the average, with 4.2 persons each. There are a few modern plants for this work, and it appears that they will be permanent. Most of them are in the neighborhood of Tokyo and Osaka, and are concerned primarily with cotton dyeing and printing. Recently one of the largest of the cotton-spinning companies established what is said to be one of the most modern bleaching, dyeing, and printing works in existence. It is operated wholly by Japanese and seems fully successful. Interestingly enough, it has been located on the Yodogawa, which comes from the same source as the Kamogawa, already mentioned in connection with Kyoto dyeing.

The putting-out system has long existed in Japan, and there are well-defined terms regarding it. The merchant-capitalist of Europe is described in characters which mean "original" weaver. In the vernacular he is referred to as *de-bata*, which means "sending-out weaver," or as *moto-ori* or *moto-bata*, each of which means "main-stem" or "root" weaver. Japanese statistics formerly included information as to these households, and the Japanese rendered the word into English as "investors." Households which receive the raw materials and do weaving for wages are referred to by characters meaning "wage-weaving" households. In the vernacular they are called *chin-bata*, which means "weavers for wages." A weaver who is independent financially but who secures raw materials and patterns and perhaps markets his product through a larger *moto-bata* is called a *shita-bata*, which means "lower weaver." The separate terms applied to the putting-out weaver suggest the different relations between him and the other weavers. To the weaver on wages he is a *de-bata*, "putter-out," while to the man who merely works through him he is the *moto-bata* or *moto-ori*, the central stock on which weaving is supported. The functions of this person differ somewhat from those of the merchant-capitalist in Europe and in India. In Japan it is exceptional for him to be a dealer in cloth; he is called a "producer," and between him and the buyer there is commonly an intermediary, called *naka-dachi*, "stand-between."

This putting-out industry was important in the areas specializing in textiles in old Japan, and has continued so in the modern period. It appears, indeed, to have greatly increased after the opening of the country, especially in cotton manufacture. While cotton spinning was being taken over from the households into the new factories, weaving was also being reorganized. This was a revolutionary movement only in that the production of cloth became organized by *de-bata* to a larger extent on commercial lines. The amounts of cloth produced and consumed were much increased.[1]

The figures given on page 313 show the importance of this type of work in the weaving industry, where its greatest significance lies. While the great growth of weaving in

---

[1] There are no adequate figures for proving this, but observers generally agree that a marked advance has occurred.

factories, especially by cotton-spinning companies, is of the greatest importance, the putting-out system is still very remarkable. In 1920 over one-tenth of the power looms were employed by the putters-out in their own places and in the homes of their employees, and a still larger number and proportion of hand looms, exceeded only by the hand looms worked by independent households, were worked in the same way. In 1912 there were 5,159 weaving factories employed on cotton, silk, and hemp and their mixtures, using an average of 31 looms each; but there were 11,385 putters-out, employing an average of 31 looms each on the same materials. In 1920 the factories had increased in slightly less proportion than the putters-out but the numbers of looms worked had swung in favor of the factory. The average factory employed 43.6 looms, while the average putter-out employed only 23.2 looms. These *de-bata* tended to use hand rather than power looms, but their total was 22 per cent larger than the total of looms in factories of more than 10 workers.

But this system is tending to be of less importance. The number of hand looms employed has dropped, until in 1929 it was only one-third that in 1912, while power looms had increased to four times as many as in 1912. This is especially true in cotton manufacturing, which is very rapidly going over to the large-factory system. The looms operated by members of the Japan Cotton Spinners Association have doubled since 1918; all are in large factories, and these are driving the hand looms out of business.

In the weaving of silk and the various mixtures of silk, rayon, and cotton, however, the putting-out system remains, even though power looms have been adopted. The first use of power looms did not mean the factory as opposed to the putting-out system. Indeed it was often the putting-out weavers who first recognized the advantages of the power looms and who had the capital to purchase them. The plentiful supply of cheap electricity in Japan has made it easy for these men to start small factories for themselves and to lend money for the purchase of a few looms by their more energetic piece-wage workers, who continue to weave on the wage system. Hamamatsu, a cotton-weaving center, and Ashikaga, where chiefly silk and rayon are woven, illustrate the different stages of development in the two industries. In Hamamatsu in 1928[1] there were 1,678 factories and workshops using 29,389 power looms, 172 hand looms, and 880 foot looms, with only 18 per cent of the factories and 13 per cent of the looms on wage work; whereas of 972 power-using factories and workshops in Ashikaga in 1930, 720 or 74 per cent of the factories, employing 50 per cent of the looms, were on wage work and 90 more were partially so.[2] Generally it is the larger power mills which are independent, and even in silk weaving these contain the larger proportion of power looms. Yet many shops using only two or three looms are wholly independent and very successful. In Kiryu one silk mill of 70 looms was working on wages for a *de-bata* in 1928. The great disadvantage which Japanese textile men associate with the power loom and the factory is that it is impossible to reduce production in slack times without suffering positive loss.

Different *de-bata* follow different practices regarding the amount of their work which is put out. Some put the yarn out to a bleacher or dyer, then the warp to a warper and beamer, and the weft to a pirn winder, then the whole to a weaver, and, finally, the cloth to a finisher. Others approach nearer the factory system and conduct all these processes except the first and the last in their own shops,

---

[1] Figures furnished by the Hamamatsu weavers' gild.
[2] Figures furnished by the Ashikaga weavers' gild.

where some weaving is also done. This latter practice is more nearly typical of silk weaving in Japan now. In more highly specialized work, as in Kyoto silk weaving, there may be no weaving done in the *de-bata's* home shop. In Kyoto the *de-bata* commonly provides the loom for the *chin-bata*, and in a few cases furnishes him with a house. In nearly all cases he is in the position of creditor. In the country districts the hand loom is usually owned by the family, but modern power looms are more likely to be owned by the *de-bata* or to involve an additional debt to him.

In Kyoto in 1928 the largest *de-bata* was putting out work to between 150 and 160 looms. Ten Kyoto *de-bata* put out to over 100 looms each, and about 30 put out to over 50 looms each. These few big men employed only slightly more than one-fourth of the looms so working;[1] others employed smaller numbers down to one or two. In Ashikaga there are 2,059 members of the weavers' gild, not including those who work for wages. Of this number 850 are *de-bata*; about 100 of these have weaving factories of their own, leaving a large number who put out all their weaving. Some have the preparing processes done outside, while many have part of them done on their own premises. One of these factories contains 122 power looms employed on medium-grade silk goods. Besides this the owner puts out work to some 200 looms, a part of which are power looms. Another has 62 looms and puts out no work; while a third has one factory with 48 looms, and another with 12 looms, and also gives out work to 60 *chin-bata*. In 1927 there were in this neighborhood 6,056 power looms in just 500 establishments, of which 325 contained less than 10 looms each while 2 had more than 300. The following table

[1] Information from the Nishijin weavers' gild.

gives the figures for the years 1922, 1924, 1927, and 1930, indicating both distribution and rapid growth.[1]

POWER LOOM FACTORIES AND WORKSHOPS IN ASHIKAGA

Looms employed	1922	1924	1927	1930
Under 10	51	83	325	..
10– 20	26	50	128	..
20– 30	8	18	16	..
30– 40	4	17	10	..
40– 50	6	2	3	..
50–100	9	12	13	..
100–200	2	2	2	..
200–300	0	1	1	..
Over 300	2	2	2	..
Total	108	187	500	972
Total looms	2,577	3,648	6,056	9,739

In 1928 about 400 of the smaller establishments, containing roughly 1,500 power looms, besides over half of the 10,000 hand looms in the district, were also worked under the *chin-bata* or wage system.

Most *de-bata* in silk weaving specialize in some particular product. The main division is between goods for export and goods for home consumption. *Kasuri* is a kind of silk cloth whose figures result from both the warp and the weft yarn being dyed in patches before it is woven. This requires very careful work from the beginning of dyeing through beaming and weaving; Izumi's business in Kiryu is typical. He has a large dwelling house of which about half the first floor is made into a factory. All dyeing and preparing is done in this shop, and twelve wooden hand looms are operated by as many girls. Since the patterns must be carefully executed by placing the weft thread at

[1] Figures furnished by the Ashikaga weavers' gild.

just the correct place, no flying shuttle can be used; indeed the weaver uses a dozen or more small shuttles, and many of the weft threads must be caught by both ends and placed in position. This man also puts out prepared materials to several hand looms operated by *chin-bata*.

A few *de-bata* are also raw-material dealers. This is conspicuously the case in Chichibu, Saitama Ken, where some raw-yarn dealers have long put out yarn to *shita-bata* (lower weavers), who put them out further to *chin-bata*; the same practice prevails in Fukui city. In a few cases *de-bata* are engaged in some other branch of the business such as dyeing or cloth brokerage. Still others are landlords, which is quite natural since this business has been an important part of village economy. One of the larger *de-bata* between Ashikaga and Kiryu, Mr. Ito, is a large landlord. He puts out materials only to farmers, many of them his own tenants. He now has 150 hand looms in about 60 houses, working largely with rayon. All the preparing except dyeing and throwing is done by hired labor on his own premises. The main floor of a big Japanese country house is usually divided into two parts, one of which is the dwelling, while the other has only a hard dirt floor and serves as kitchen, storeroom, and general workroom on stormy days; sometimes one corner stables a horse. Ito's house has been made into both a factory and a storeroom. The dirt floor has been replaced by cement, and an additional room has been added for the preparatory machinery. The great rooms are piled with bundles of silk and rayon from the dealers, dyed yarn back from the dyers, and finished goods which come in constantly from the weavers. Ito's wife has a modern desk in the dining-room, and there she receives finished work, gives out raw materials, and makes the proper entries in her own and the other person's book. But here too the power loom is making way. Ito has already installed 4 power looms and is building a shed for 20 more.

Until twenty years ago the *chin-bata* establishments were generally the homes of the poorer farm families and of wage workmen about the smaller towns. These were simple places of one or two rooms, containing one or two hand looms, where mother or daughter added a few *sen* to the daily income. They are still much the same, except that in some of them an electric motor and power looms have been installed.[1] There is now something of a capital investment, and the owner of the looms urges steadier work.

The table on page 313 gives figures for these wage-working families. They were evidently disappearing rapidly until the War-time boom. While statistics are lacking for recent years, the figures are certainly much lower than in 1920. Power looms in factories have rendered the old hand looms in homes more and more nearly obsolete, though the number of wage weavers working on power looms is still smaller. Usually these have been purchased by the *de-bata* for whom the work is done. With power equipment it becomes profitable to make weaving the main rather than a mere subsidiary employment. Thus the little factory tends to be enlarged by the bringing in of one or two relatives or other employees.

At this point we reach the parting of the ways. Many *de-bata* have established central factories for the preparing processes and also for weaving. Since the *de-bata* provides most of the capital for the wage-working shops under him, it is often more desirable to place such looms in his own factory and perhaps put an energetic wage weaver in charge. It is a question which little factories shall expand

[1] Japanese villages are almost all supplied with electricity. Even twenty years ago very few villages were without electric light.

into great ones and which shall perhaps disappear. Frequently a wage-working factory succeeds in rising; but generally it is one operated by an independent weaving family or by a *de-bata* that advances. There is a tendency in all types of weaving to keep the number of hands in a factory below ten [1] in order to avoid the restrictions of the factory law. Of 1,506 factories and workshops in Hamamatsu using power looms only 159 came under the factory law; [2] yet this is a district in which cotton weaving is developing on a large scale. In the entire country, places where cotton is woven with less than 10 looms each declined by 38 per cent between 1923 and 1929, but these were still 93 per cent of all establishments weaving cotton. Over 90 per cent of all places where silk and silk mixtures are woven employ less than 5 looms, though these small places decreased by 35 per cent between 1923 and 1929. Yet in both cotton and silk weaving the large factories, employing more than 50 looms, steadily increase. While there is a great desire among smaller concerns to avoid the factory law, there are such advantages in large-scale operations that those who are able to do so intend to set up large establishments.

The table opposite shows the number of weaving places (now called factories) of different sizes and the number of looms of each kind employed in each category.

The larger concerns which are legally classed as factories vary greatly. Many are best described as "factory-like workshops" since, although they use power machinery, they are only half factories; others are strictly modern in every respect. Silk reeling and throwing are often done in establishments operated by hand or water power. The machinery is often of wood, and the wearing joints soon

[1] Below fifteen until the law was changed in 1923.
[2] Figures furnished by the Hamamatsu weavers' gild.

indicate the lack of balance and loss of motion characteristic of the entire shop. Raw materials and finished products may be stored in the office, and the accounts are
only simple records made on soft paper with a writing
brush.

For a very long period of development several features
of the earlier system generally remain in these concerns.

WEAVING FACTORIES AND LOOMS

Cotton

Number of looms	Number of factories		Power looms		Hand looms	
	1923	1929	1923	1929	1923	1929
Under 10	112,453	69,821	10,249	9,691	141,584	79,156
10–50	4,506	3,859	79,904	81,943	12,135	4,403
Over 50	1,020	1,054	153,144	185,131	5,681	2,495
Total	117,979	74,734	243,297	276,765	159,400	86,054

Silk and silk-cotton mixtures

Number of looms	Number of factories		Power looms		Hand looms	
	1923	1929	1923	1929	1923	1929
Under 5	117,099	75,944	12,679	14,820	144,886	87,163
5–10	3,217	3,568	10,517	18,222	10,520	5,992
10–50	2,323	3,236	36,214	53,631	8,417	5,108
Over 50	296	359	27,736	39,176	1,071	927
Total	122,935	83,107	87,146	125,849	164,894	99,190

It is not to be imagined, for instance, that a weaving factory should perform all the processes under its own roof.
Such work as bleaching, dyeing, warping, winding, and
finishing may be put out to other persons on piece rates;
and even when they are undertaken by the mill itself it is
not uncommon for them to be contracted out to men who,
though they do them in the owner's factory, work under
what is essentially the putting-out system. The small fac-

tory owner is likely to postpone as long as possible the full
management of all the processes; yet in this respect the
Japanese industrialists have been more aggressive than
most Orientals. Imbued with the *samurai* spirit, they have
not shrunk from complete management of the largest
concerns.

Smaller factories are owned by individuals, partnerships,
and limited partnerships, while larger ones are usually
owned by corporations. The latter are frequently closely
controlled and highly efficient. Labor administration, like
factory management, is an adaptation of western methods
to Japanese customs. In small factories family members
and relatives form a large share of the hands, while employees proper are hired on terms similar to those which
have prevailed in agriculture. Eighty per cent of the textile laborers are young women, generally hired for terms of
one to three years at yearly wages. Remuneration includes board, room, the customary gifts of two kimonos at
certain festivals, and a money payment. The best factories also hire girls on long contract and treat them pa-
ternally, but this is partly because most of the girls are
young and away from home for the first time. It is also
necessary to provide living quarters and supervision.
These features are in some degree survivals of feudalism,
but they preserve certain humane elements which western
individualism often lacks. It is not certain that the larger
mills are backward in this respect.

What of the future? The large-factory system has taken
over nearly all the making of yarns and threads, and has
made great inroads on plain weaving. The usual economy
of large-scale operation inevitably drives the successful
owner towards expansion, and it seems that the factory
may occupy the entire field. Yet it is by no means settled
that this result will be even slowly reached. Besides the

dense population already accustomed to a combination of agricultural and textile operations, there is the fact that electrical power allows diffusion while steam demanded concentration. Will the love of the soil and the country-side, combined with the insistent demand for a higher standard of living, move the Japanese to force to a successful conclusion this union of the farm with power industry?

This combination seems most likely to succeed in the silk-weaving industry. But what of rayon? Will it permanently increase the demand for real silk as a mixture, or will it permanently displace silk? Japan now produces large amounts of rayon and weaves it mixed with silk and cotton. This provides an appeal to the large, new middle-class demand rather than to the narrower aristocratic market formerly catered to. Will the Japanese follow the Occident (which no longer wears the laces, velvets, braids, and embroideries of the day when power machinery was first put in factories) and modify their clothing in keeping with the economies of the factory system? Will they give up their richly wrought fabrics for the cheaper and plainer power-woven materials? A change in this direction seems now unquestionably in progress, but can it smother the love for those exquisite creations of the craftsmen of Nishijin? These are too much a part of Japanese tradition to be wholly forgotten; the conquest will not be sudden.

The advance of the factory has followed no logical plan, but has gone forward wherever it found resistance weakest. In some areas its rule is now complete, while in others its influence is negligible. In still other regions it joins in friendly co-operation with its former adversary, and in some the two have formed a union which may yet result in the birth of a new creation.

THE BRITISH NORTH AMERICAN PROVINCES BEFORE CONFEDERATION —TRADE AND TARIFFS

J. C. HEMMEON

For those of my readers who are not familiar with the Canadian political and economic situation at and shortly before the confederation of the British North American Provinces in 1867, a few preliminary words of explanation seem desirable. Previous to 1841 these provinces consisted of British Columbia, Upper Canada, Lower Canada, New Brunswick, Prince Edward Island, Nova Scotia, and Newfoundland. Each of these provinces was quite independent one of the other, though of course they were all subject to the sovereign power of Great Britain through governors sent out from that country and through the secretary of State for the Colonies. In Upper Canada the population was predominantly English speaking, while in Lower Canada the majority was of French descent with French as the mother tongue. Much discontent had arisen in these two provinces, partly the result of ill feeling and jealousy over fiscal and other problems, partly the result of the lack of responsible government and the arbitrary actions of the British governors and the British Colonial Office. In 1841 the two provinces were united to form the Province of Canada, and in 1867 a larger federal union was accomplished. This union, which was called the Dominion of Canada, included the Province of Canada, which was redivided for local purposes into Ontario and Quebec, and, in addition, the Maritime Provinces of New Brunswick and Nova Scotia were cajoled or forced into the federation, to be followed a little later by Prince Edward Island and British Columbia. Still later the North West Territories were acquired. Newfoundland refused to join the federation and still prefers to remain outside the family circle; while British Columbia was so far away and so inaccessible until the Canadian Pacific Railway was completed that I have not included her in this brief study.

It is perhaps unnecessary to offer any apology for a study of trade and tariffs as they existed in what are now the Maritime Provinces of Canada before their union with the dominant partners, Ontario and Quebec, in 1867. Certainly no apology is necessary to the student of economic history, but, in this particular case, such a study may be of help to those who are not economic historians but are concerned with certain problems which confront Canadians today. There are many Maritime Province people who are of the opinion that the political and economic union has accomplished little, since 1867, that has been useful to them, and much that has been disastrous. They say that the protective "National Policy," adopted in 1879, and since then made more highly protective, has compelled them to buy in a limited and expensive market while it has not made available a compensating market where they may sell their own products. By way of further explanation they say that their own goods are not needed to any extent in Quebec, Ontario, and the western provinces, while the goods that they need have to be purchased in those provinces at prices much higher than those which prevail in the competitive markets of the world.

There is little doubt that their statements are to a certain extent true, but their case would be much stronger if it were possible to show the exact amount of the trade between the Maritime Provinces and the rest of Canada.

This cannot be done because the necessary statistics are not available. I am quite aware that some statistical work has been done, but the conclusions reached are necessarily based on stray facts and guesses. Some light can, I think, be thrown on this problem by facts and figures at our disposal while the provinces of the Dominion were politically independent and while, at the same time, they benefited from a small measure of reciprocal free trade in raw materials. With the exception of this limited amount of free trade the provinces of what is now the Dominion of Canada treated each other before 1867 as independent nations now do. For example, Nova Scotia imposed duties on goods imported from the Province of Canada as she imposed duties on goods produced in Russia. This makes it possible for us to state the exact nature and extent of the trade before 1867 between any and all of the provinces which then existed and which now form part of the Dominion of Canada. I am fully aware that with increased population, better transportation facilities, and the abolition of tariff barriers, trade between the provinces has increased greatly, but I am also of the opinion that, from a study of the period when the provinces treated each other no better than they did the rest of the world, it is possible to arrive at certain general conclusions concerning natural trade channels which will help us in determining, to some extent, the justice of the claim that the Maritime Provinces were forced into an unholy and unprofitable alliance with the rest of Canada and, more particularly, with the so-called central provinces of Ontario and Quebec.

There is no doubt that before 1867 and until that date there were considerable differences in the duties imposed by the provinces on imported commodities, but it is very difficult to say what these differences amounted to. The old Province of Canada had adopted the practice of imposing ad valorem duties as a substitute for specific duties, while the other provinces were still in the habit of using specific duties to a considerable extent. This makes comparison between the tariffs of the various provinces difficult, particularly since prices at that time are often impossible to determine. There is no doubt that the tariff rates of Canada were higher than those of the Maritime Provinces, though the difference has been exaggerated; it is to be explained largely by the fact that the Province of Canada had undertaken a very ambitious policy of canal and railway construction, though at the same time there is no doubt that the desire to afford protection to home industries was a factor of some importance. On the other hand the Maritime Provinces were less advanced industrially, their expenditures were comparatively not so great, and they depended primarily on trade and shipping to support their inhabitants.

Under the Canadian tariff act goods were listed in nine schedules. In three of these specific duties predominated, though not to the exclusion of ad valorem duties. Some of these duties, especially those on luxuries and on commodities not produced in the province, were very high. The prevailing rate of duty on most manufactured goods and on goods not otherwise specified was 15 per cent, a very moderate rate in comparison with that which prevails in the tariffs of today. Foods were generally subject to rather high specific duties but wheat was duty free. In Nova Scotia most of the duties were specific and rather high on luxuries, but not so high as in the Province of Canada. The not-otherwise-specified rate was 10 per cent, and there was little or no incidental protection afforded by these duties. In New Brunswick the duties were a little higher than in Nova Scotia, the not-otherwise-specified rate — which was the rate that was collected on most manufactured commodities — being 12½ per cent. The fact that the rates in New Brunswick were rather higher than in Nova Scotia is to be attributed to a more extensive railroad program and to financial deficits. Rates in Prince Edward Island and Newfoundland were much the same as in Nova Scotia. It is not my desire to burden my readers with details, and, for that reason, I have considered it better not to quote specific rates but rather to attempt a general and comparative impression. In order to make this impression rather more detailed and concrete, I have appended some figures which show, in a general way, the rates of duty that prevailed in the different provinces in 1861.

	Canada	Nova Scotia	New Brunswick	Prince Edward Island	Newfoundland
Proportion of duties collected to value of all imports..........	11	7¾	9½	8½	7½
Proportion of duties collected to value of dutiable imports	19	11⅜	13¾	10¾	12½

Provision was also made by the different provinces for the admission free of duty of many primary products originating in these provinces. The products so named were much the same as those listed under the Elgin Reciprocity Treaty, which was in operation from 1854 to 1866. It is important that this fact be noted, because the existence of what were practically similar relations between the different British provinces and between those provinces and the United States makes it much easier to arrive at conclusions that are positive, since the facts upon which these conclusions are based need not be qualified on account of the existence of varying and different causal factors.

As early as 1824, James Stuart, who had been solicitor-general of Lower Canada (Quebec) wrote:

There is absolutely no intercourse whatever between the Canadas and New Brunswick. An immense wilderness separates the inhabited parts of both and they have no interchangeable commodities admitting of any trade between them by sea. Nova Scotia is remote and is only accessible from the Canadas by land through New Brunswick and keeps up a small trade with Lower Canada by the Gulf of St. Lawrence in productions of the West Indies. Between Lower Canada and Prince Edward Island there is hardly any communication whatever.

This statement of Stuart's may be accepted as largely true, in so far as it points out that there was little or no trade between Canada and the Maritime Provinces because there were few "interchangeable commodities." Their separation by "an immense wilderness" was not nearly so important a cause, for the water route — open for the larger part of the year — was cheap and easily navigable; the people of the Maritime Provinces were (and still are) bold navigators attached to the sea, and were at that time in possession of a large mercantile marine which was widely scattered over the seven seas. Had opportunity for trade with Canada offered, had there, in other words, existed any amount of "interchangeable commodities," they would have been among the first to avail themselves of such an opportunity. Not long after Stuart made his pronouncement, the provinces of Lower Canada and Nova Scotia offered a substantial subsidy to a steamship line to run between Halifax and the city of Quebec. One steamer, the *Royal William*, was in operation for two seasons and was then withdrawn as a result of lack of business.

The larger part of the trade of the Province of Canada was with Great Britain and the United States. It was almost equally divided between these two countries, but in

1867, and for some time before and after that date, imports to Canada from Great Britain exceeded imports from the United States, while precisely the opposite was true of Canadian exports, a state of affairs which has been reversed within recent years. Trade with the other British provinces was almost negligible. Such trade as existed was carried on by the St. Lawrence River, though a little went through Portland by water and rail.

The imports and exports of the Province of Canada for the fiscal year ending June 30, 1867, are shown in the following table:

	Imports	Exports
Great Britain	$34,260,509	$14,962,504
Maritime Provinces	1,108,373	3,549,197
United States	20,272,907	25,583,800
France	1,711,151	266,987

Nova Scotia is credited with more than half of the Canadian imports from the Maritime Provinces, but much of these consisted of sugar and molasses carried from the West Indies in Nova Scotian vessels. The most important imports of products originating in Nova Scotia consisted of fish, fish oil, and coal. Newfoundland was responsible for about one-quarter of the Maritime Province export trade to Canada — principally fish and fish oil. New Brunswick and Prince Edward Island sent fish in small quantities. It will be noticed that, although the trade between the Province of Canada and the Maritime Provinces was comparatively small, the value of Canadian exports to these provinces was much greater than the value of Canadian imports from them. This is a characteristic which undoubtedly exists at the present time although, since the trade is now domestic, it is impossible to say how the old ratio has changed or whether it has changed at all. If a guess is allowable, it is probably the case that the Maritime Provinces import a much larger proportion from the old Province of Canada than they export to it, this being a result of the much higher protective tariff that now prevails; whereas the Maritime Provinces have very few products that are needed in the rest of Canada, nor are these products protected by duties that are adequate to secure them a market in the central portions of the Dominion. In 1866 the principal Canadian exports to the Maritime Provinces consisted of flour, other agricultural products, such as butter and lard, and a small quantity of manufactured goods.

Most of the trade — both export and import — of the Maritime Provinces was with Great Britain and the United States. The export trade to Great Britain consisted largely of raw materials, of which lumber, ships, and a few agricultural products were the most important, while the return trade was largely in manufactured goods including cutlery, woolens, and certain luxuries. The export trade to the United States was also composed largely of raw products such as coal, fish, gypsum, and lumber, while the import trade was much more varied. Nova Scotia imported flour, corn and oatmeal, pork, hams, and tobacco, all of which paid no duty under the Reciprocity Treaty. Dutiable imports consisted of hardware, iron, cutlery, cotton, and leather goods. Free goods imported by New Brunswick from the United States consisted of flour, salted foods, oatmeal, and corn and rye flour; while the dutiable commodities were drygoods, tea, spirits, wines, ales, hardware, tobacco, leather, and molasses. Prince Edward Island imported from the United States flour, which was free, as well as hardware, cutlery, leather, tea, and molasses, all of which were dutiable. In the case of each of these three provinces the value of the flour imported was greater than the value of all other imports.

The trade of the Maritime Provinces with each other, although not nearly so important as that with Great Britain and the United States, was much greater than that with Canada. For the most part they exchanged with each other such natural products as each province produced most cheaply. Nova Scotia exported coal, gypsum, fish, and some forest products, receiving in exchange agricultural commodities, horses, and cattle from Prince Edward Island and New Brunswick. Trade with Newfoundland was not important. Such trade as existed consisted largely of fish and fish oil exported from Newfoundland, while the principal imports to the island were food products. Trade between the Maritime Provinces and the West Indies ranked next in value after trade with Great Britain and the United States, and was much more important than trade with the Province of Canada. The Maritime Provinces imported from the West Indies large quantities of sugar, molasses, and rum, for which they exchanged fish, fish oil, and some agricultural products.

A comparison of exports and imports of the three Maritime Provinces of Nova Scotia, New Brunswick, and Prince Edward Island shows the extent to which the value of commodities imported exceeded the value of commodities exported. This is particularly marked in the case of Nova Scotia. For the year ending September 30, 1866, the value of commodities imported into that province was $14,381,008, while the value of commodities exported was only $8,043,095. This so-called unfavorable balance of trade is to be explained by the fact that Nova Scotia as well as the other Maritime Provinces had a large fleet of sailing vessels busily engaged in transporting commodities between foreign countries. The tonnage owned and registered in the several provinces in 1866 was as follows: Nova Scotia, 400,895; New Brunswick, 233,945; Quebec (seagoing craft), 144,989; and Ontario and Quebec (lake and river vessels), 80,000. I am quite aware that these figures are not accurate nor in many cases commensurable, owing to the fact that no great care was exercised to strike from the list those vessels that were lost or sold, and also because of varying and careless methods in measuring tonnage. Moreover, all of the provinces did a considerable export business in vessels which ordinarily found a ready market abroad, principally in Great Britain, and these vessels are not listed among commodities exported. This is but natural, since vessels sold abroad were not in many cases exported specifically for that purpose, nor, as I have noted above, was the sale abroad likely to be recorded.

I am inclined to think that this study of trade relations between the Maritime Provinces, the Province of Canada, and other countries, at the latest date when it is possible to present figures, are of some help in establishing the claim that the union of 1867 has been harmful to the Maritime Provinces to the extent that it has deflected their natural trade into other and less desirable channels. It has in addition compelled them to buy in a highly protected and costly market, while it has not afforded a similar market where they may sell their products. Of course this is not the whole story. The change from wooden vessels to iron and later to steel steamers was a terrible blow to the principal industry of the Maritime Provinces and particularly to Nova Scotia. The people of these provinces have been charged with a lack of vision in that they failed to foresee the change that was coming, and a lack of initiative in failing to take advantage of this change when it was finally brought home to them; but that is another and an equally sad story for the provinces by the sea.

SOME RECENT ECONOMIC CHANGES IN CANADA

W. W. McLAREN

With a population of slightly over ten million living on an area that is nominally greater than that of the United States and richly endowed with certain natural resources, Canada in the past decade has raised herself to the fifth place among the trading nations of the world. The United States, the United Kingdom, Germany, and France surpass her in the total value of their foreign trade. The per capita foreign trade of Canada in 1928 was $124, while that of the United States was $36.26. Moreover, Canada's production is not overloaded with primary goods. In 1929 the manufactures exceeded the raw products in value by 50 per cent. Even with this large preponderance of manufactures, at least half of Canada's imports are in the form of finished goods. The prospects, therefore, are bright for the further development of certain Canadian industries, especially the metallurgical and chemical, as the home market is still so largely supplied by imports from other countries. In so far as additional protection will encourage growth in these branches of industry, the present government seems more than willing to co-operate.

Likewise, Canada's balance of international payments during the past decade demonstrates the growing strength of her position. During the War period, there came into the country about $1,250,000,000 for the purchase of Canadian products, and during the same period large investments of foreign capital were made in Canada, mainly by citizens of the United States. The industries thus developed contributed enormously to Canada's production in the decade since 1920. Furthermore, the abundant harvests of the early years of that decade created a foundation for prosperity both in the agricultural regions of the West and in the industrial East.

These factors combined caused an unprecedented accumulation of savings which were used by financial institutions and individuals, not only to finance domestic capital needs, but also to avail themselves of opportunities for profitable investment abroad. Thus, after 1923, we had on balance an export of capital to our credit, though at the same time other countries, particularly the United States, continued to invest large sums in the Dominion.[1]

Like the United States, the Dominion of Canada has had a "favorable" balance of merchandise trade throughout the decade, with the single exception of the year 1921. The total favorable trade balance amounted approximately to $1,200,000,000 between 1920 and 1929. This sum, plus some $370,000,000 repaid by Great Britain, constituted the major share of Canada's credits which have been used to establish her creditor position in international finance. The magnitude of Canada's net investments abroad was estimated in 1930 to be approximately $1,800,000,000, made up of direct investments in Latin America and the United States, the purchase of foreign securities and the repurchase of Canadian securities held abroad, and loans on call in New York.

In the two years since 1930, Canada has suffered with the rest of the world from the effects of the depression. Her merchandise exports and imports have declined about 25 per cent, and some of the invisible items of her balance of payments have likewise diminished. Capital move-

[1] *The Canada Year Book* (Ottawa: Dominion Bureau of Statistics, 1930), p. 586.

ments into the country have been greatly stimulated by the new tariff legislation of 1930 and 1931, and the favorable balance of merchandise trade which had persisted for a decade was reversed in the fiscal year 1930–31, but it is expected that in 1932 a favorable balance of merchandise trade will be re-established.

The Great War, which may be said without any doubt to have furnished the impetus for the Dominion's rapid progress since 1914, saddled Canada with a vast burden of debt which in the main was not represented by offsetting assets. At the end of the fiscal year 1913–14, the Dominion's net debt was $336,000,000. Broadly speaking, it was a debt incurred for productive purposes, and 90 per cent of it was payable in London. Six years later, the total net debt of the Dominion was $2,600,000,000, and in 1929 $2,225,000,000, divided among London, New York, and Canada, in the ratio of 2.6, 2.2, and 18. The annual interest on the national debt was $124,900,000 in 1929. In the decade under consideration, the principal of the national debt was reduced by nearly $400,000,000 and the annual interest charge by more than $15,000,000.

This picture of Canada's public indebtedness is not complete, however, without including the obligations of the provinces and the municipalities. In 1928, the bonded debt of the nine provinces was approximately $750,000,-000, and that of the municipalities slightly over $1,000,-000,000. Much of this provincial and municipal debt was incurred in the construction or purchase of public-utility enterprises, for in Canada (and especially Ontario) the public utilities are frequently municipally owned. Since many of these enterprises are operated so as to show a profit sufficient to meet the interest and depreciation charges on the plant, the tax burden is correspondingly lightened.

To meet the interest charges on this indebtedness of the three groups of public bodies, as well as to pay the running expenses, the taxation system in Canada has been transformed since 1914.

Referring, in the first place, to the system of taxation of the Dominion, the short session of parliament in August, 1914 increased the customs and excise duties levied on a variety of commodities, including coffee, sugar, spirituous liquors, and tobacco. The following year an additional 5 per cent was added to the customs duties imposed on goods imported under the British Preferential Tariff and 7½ per cent on all other imports.

In the same year a variety of stamp taxes were imposed. In 1916 the Business Profits War Tax was set up, and the following year the Income Tax Law was enacted. Both of these taxes were increased in 1918, and in 1919 the Income Tax was again increased and its application widened. In 1920, a surtax on all incomes over $5,000 per annum was imposed, as well as a sales tax on certain commodities. The so-called War Taxes in the fiscal year 1921 provided a revenue of $168,000,000, and for the first time in history the receipts from customs duties were deposed from their position as the primary source of the Dominion's revenue. The total receipts from taxation in the Dominion increased from $126,000,000 in 1914 to $294,000,000 in 1920, and to $396,000,000 in 1928. The War Taxes reached their maximum in 1924 and have since declined, as the levies on sales, incomes, and War profits have been either reduced or abrogated; but the receipts from customs and excise duties have steadily increased until in 1929 they furnished five-eighths of the total income from taxation, or $250,000,000.

The expenditures of the Dominion during the War and in the decade since 1920 reached a fairly stable equilibrium by 1924, but at a magnitude nearly three times as great as the pre-War figure. In the five-year period before 1914, the annual average expenditure of the Dominion was about $130,000,000; since 1924 it has been approximately $370,-000,000. The peak of the national expenditures was reached in 1920 and amounted to $786,000,000. This huge total was made up of $346,000,000 for war and demobilization purposes, $114,000,000 for capital expenditures and advances to railways, and $107,000,000 as interest on the national debt. In 1929, the expenditures of the Dominion were $378,000,000, the two largest items being $125,000,-000 for interest on the national debt and $44,000,000 for pensions to War veterans.

In this same period the per capita burden of taxation, which had been $16.40 in 1914, had more than doubled in 1920, and in 1929 amounted to $40.41. The cost of the War and of the development since 1920, with its accompanying expansion of the national debt, is shown by the figures of per capita total disbursements. In 1920, the per capita disbursements amounted to $91.07, but by 1929 the repayment of the War debt and the refunding operations had so reduced the interest charges that the per capita total disbursements had fallen to $38.62, or nearly $2.00 less than similar figures for revenues from taxation. If the total per capita receipts from taxation and other sources are contrasted with the total per capita disbursements, the figures are $46.97 and $38.62 respectively. So far as these figures may be cited as a valid proof, it is apparent that the Dominion Government was in a position in 1929 to use a little more than $8.00 per capita per annum for the reduction of the national debt, or for other purposes. The reduction of the debt in the fiscal year 1928–29 was approximately $52,000,000,[1] and during the decade 1920–29

[1] *Ibid.*, p. 809.

approximately $275,000,000. Nevertheless, the national debt of Canada still amounts to about $2,225,000,000. At the rate of amortization accomplished during the past decade, it will take eighty years to complete the repayment, though a calculation of this kind is certain to be upset by the march of events. The continued rapid growth of Canada's population, and the exploitation of her natural resources at an accelerating pace, will be certain to shorten the period. On the other hand, events of a different kind involving large accessions to the debt might greatly prolong the period.

In the second place, the funded debt of the nine provinces of Canada amounted in 1928 to about $750,000,000. The ordinary revenue of the provinces was $168,000,000 in 1928, as compared with $92,000,000 in 1920. The expenditures for the same years were $166,000,000 and $54,000,000 respectively.

Prior to 1900 provincial finance had been relatively simple. The revenues were made up of Dominion subsidies provided by section 118 of the British North America Act of 1867, plus income arising out of the sale of natural resources and fees received for performing services for their citizens. With the beginning of the century, a great increase in functions of government in many of the provinces caused the older and simpler financial plan to be no longer adequate. Even in 1916, the receipts from provincial taxes amounted to a mere $16,000,000, but by 1928 that figure had grown to more than $90,000,000 — an almost sixfold increase. This change in the receipts from provincial taxation was largely due to the appearance of the automobile and the adoption of government control of the sale of liquors in the majority of the provinces. The provincial governments in 1928 derived from permits to drive automobiles and trucks nearly $19,000,000, from gasoline taxes almost $10,000,000, and from the profits of the liquor control over $22,000,000. On the average, the total receipts and expenditures of the provinces amounted to a little over $18 per capita.

In the third place, the municipalities of the Dominion, with a bonded debt of a billion dollars, must be considered. In a young, growing country the municipalities have labored with the almost Herculean task of keeping up with the demands of the population for educational and other public services. To meet the expense of these services, almost their only source of revenue is the tax on the assessed value of real property, though in some cases personal property is also levied upon. Under these circumstances, capital expenditures for schools, water-works, sewers, streets, and pavements have been defrayed by loans; hence the fact that the total bonded debt of the municipalities is larger than that of the provinces by $250,000,000. In the sixty-seven cities of Canada, each with a population of 10,000 or more, approximately 40 per cent of the people reside. The receipts and expenditures of these cities in 1928 were approximately $225,000,000, and involved a per capita tax of $56. The statistics for the smaller municipalities are not avabilable, but for the urban people of the Dominion, defined as those residents in cities of 10,000 or more inhabitants, the total per capita burden of taxation, including federal, provincial, and municipal taxes, aggregated approximately $114.41. The total taxes paid into the coffers of the federal, provincial, and municipal governments [1] in 1928 aggregated approximately $760,000,000, or nearly 12 per cent of the national income, which was estimated for that year at $5,600,000,000.[2] For the year 1927, the national wealth of Canada, exclusive of undeveloped

---

[1] Figures are given only for municipalities of 10,000 or more inhabitants.
[2] *The Canada Year Book* (1930), p. 831.

natural resources, was estimated at $27,668,000,000.[1] The
contrast between this figure and that of the debt of all
public bodies, $4,000,000,000, shows that Canada has
mortgaged her birthright to the extent of about 15 per
cent.

At the beginning of this chapter it was pointed out that
Canada has achieved great importance in foreign trade.
Not only is this true of Canada as a national unit, but of
Canadians as individuals, for their per capita participation
in foreign trade in 1928 was greater than that of the inhabitants of the United Kingdom, and more than three
times as large as was the case in the United States. The
per capita foreign-trade figure in Canada is surpassed only
by New Zealand, Australia, and Denmark.

The explanation of these foreign-trade figures, as far as
exports are concerned, may be found in the richness of the
natural resources — farms, forests, and mines — which are
being exploited, and in the rapid growth of certain manufacturing industries, particularly wood products and paper;
but other factors, which are of great importance, are to be
found in the railroad and highway network, the extensive
system of canals, the excellent banking facilities, and the
energy and resourcefulness of the people who operate
them.

The size of the import trade is explained by the bringing
in of raw materials, such as cotton and wool, for further
manufacture, and of capital goods for the development of
manufacturing industries, the mechanization of agriculture
and mining, and the development of water-power resources.

The trade of Canada is easily visualized from the statistics of exports and imports. Over 47 per cent of the value

[1] *Ibid.*, p. 827.

of her exports in 1928–29 consisted of agricultural and vegetable products. The value figure was $646,500,000. Wood, wood products, and paper supplied 21 per cent of the exports, or $288,600,000 in value; animals and their products 12 per cent, or $158,750,000; and non-ferrous metals and their products 8 per cent, or $112,650,000. These figures demonstrate that Canada is still exploiting her land, forests, and mines, and selling the products abroad in either unfinished or finished form.

Of Canada's imports, 27 per cent, or $346,600,000 in value, consists of iron and its products, mainly machinery and structural forms; 18 per cent, or $233,100,000, are supplied by agriculture and vegetable products; 16 per cent, or $206,400,000, by textiles and textile products, both raw cotton and wool and highly finished cotton, wool, and silk fabrics and knit goods; 13 per cent, or $175,000,000, by nonmetallic minerals and their products. In these imports, Canada is seen as a country with a huge consumption of raw materials for her manufactures and a rapidly expanding development of plant and machinery. A further element of the picture is supplied by the large imports of vegetables and fruits. Canadians are now consuming fresh vegetables in winter as well as tropical fruits the year round.

The picture of Canada thus drawn from the trade figures tallies in most respects with our traditional ideas — a country with more than half of its people engaged in farming, mining, lumbering, and trapping. But in addition to this rapid and profitable exploitation of the gifts of nature, there are even more rapidly expanding secondary industries. These manufactures explain the importation not only of raw sugar, raw cotton, and wool, but also of machinery and other iron products. The great service industries like transportation, both inland and ocean, commerce, and banking must not be forgotten if the modern situation in Canada is to be understood.

It is to this second element of the picture that we now turn. Canada adopted a protectionist policy in 1878, and has pursued it continuously since that time. The rates of customs duties have steadily risen and the policy of protection is no longer seriously questioned by any important political group in the country. Nevertheless, Canada's tariff history displays many interesting variations from the protectionist norm to which we have become accustomed in the United States during the past sixty years, due mainly to her membership in the British Commonwealth of Nations. As long ago as 1859, Canada had obtained from the Government of Great Britain at least tacit consent to the doctrine that the Canadian parliament had the right to adjust the taxation of the people in the way it deemed best. However, in 1897, with the election of Sir Wilfrid Laurier and the Liberal party to power, a "reciprocal" tariff, one-eighth lower than the general tariff, was enacted and at once applied to the imports from the United Kingdom. The following year the rate of preference to imports from Great Britain was increased to 25 per cent and in 1900 to 33⅓ per cent.

Behind these preferences extended to Great Britain, though they appear to require no other explanation than the loyalty and gratitude of the people of the Dominion, there was another motive. Although it is true that the parliament of Great Britain ceased, after 1859, to enact tariff laws for Canada, or to modify in the interests of her trade such laws as the parliament of Canada saw fit to pass, it is likewise true that commercial treaties negotiated by Great Britain included in their scope the colonies and the dominions, and by the operation of the most-favored-nation clauses which these treaties contained it was impossible for Canada to regulate completely her commercial policy. The Canadian prime minister in 1897 took to London to the celebration of the Diamond Jubilee of Queen Victoria the new reciprocal tariff as a gift from a grateful colony. The gift was received with the greatest enthusiasm by the press, and the British parliament was under the necessity of accepting it even though acceptance meant denouncing her commercial treaties with Germany and Belgium if she was to retain the benefits of the Canadian preference for her exporters. Without any fear of contradiction it may be said, therefore, that the reciprocal tariff of 1897, while it seemed a free gift to the Mother Country, was the price which Canada paid for liberty to regulate not only her *fiscal* but her *commercial* policy.

It is not to be imagined that even in 1897 there was any disposition in Canada to give up the national policy of protection inaugurated in 1878, nor is the enlargement of the preference rate in 1898 and again in 1900 to be interpreted as a modification of the protectionist sentiment. In 1904 the horizontal rate of the British preference was abolished and a new schedule of duties on imports from Great Britain was drawn up. In 1907 a third schedule, the intermediate, was added to the British preferential and the general tariffs. This intermediate tariff was created as a basis of negotiation with foreign countries in the interests of Canadian trade. In this form the tariff legislation has stood ever since, though the rates of duties have been modified, i. e. both increased and decreased, in all three categories.

This new power of control over her commercial policy has been exercised freely by Canada since the War. In 1920 the British West Indies were granted rates even lower than those of the British preferential tariff. In 1928, by Order in Council of June 26, the British preferential tariff was extended to Newfoundland. In July, 1931, a treaty was negotiated with Australia setting up mutual preference in the trade between the two countries.

Even greater activity, and perhaps more significant in the light of Dominion autonomy in the control of her commercial policy, has centered around the intermediate tariff. As a result of voluntary adherence to treaties of amity and commerce negotiated by Great Britain with foreign countries, or trade agreements between Canada and certain foreign countries, the intermediate tariff applies to products imported from France, her colonies and protectorates, Belgium, Italy, the Netherlands, Argentina, Colombia, Cuba, Denmark, Japan, Norway, Spain, Switzerland, Venezuela, the Baltic states, the succession states of Central Europe, Portugal, and others.

The reverberations of Canada's control of her commercial policy have not yet come to an end. During the decade beginning in 1920, almost every year witnessed some act of parliament which modified the application of the tariff upon imports from some foreign country. The liberalizing effect of this legislation has been to encourage external trade, and the volume of imports and exports has increased. But the trade routes traversed by the imports have remained much the same. The United States and Great Britain continue to be the principal sources of the imports. From the rest of the world, Canada's imports have increased in value during the decade by about $58,-000,000, or 72.6 per cent, but her exports to countries other than the United Kingdom and the United States have grown in value some $226,000,000, or 222.2 per cent. As the flow of goods to the United States has been impeded by our tariff barriers or the diminishing needs of our markets for Canada's products, the surplus has entered new trade routes to other markets. To this extent the application of the intermediate tariff levies on goods has encouraged the demand for Canadian products.

In recent Canadian tariff history there are two questions on which debate has centered. One is the British preference, the other is the adoption of a "Canada first" protectionist tariff. The failure of the British preference materially to increase imports from Great Britain, and the complete failure of the general tariff to prevent a rapid increase of imports from the United States, called into question the continuance of the preference. The growing domination of the Canadian market by American imports, coupled with the prohibitive levies of the Smoot-Hawley tariff on certain of Canada's exports, and the recession of business as the deflation of 1930 advanced, accounts for the Bennett tariff of 1931.

In 1896, the year before the British preference was adopted, imports from the United Kingdom amounted to $32,800,000, or 31.1 per cent of the total imports. In the same year, Canada's imports from the United States were valued at $53,500,000, or 50.8 per cent of the total. Ten years later, the proportion of the import trade originating in the United Kingdom had fallen to 24 per cent, and in 1929 to 15.3 per cent, whereas the imports from the United States had increased to 59.6 per cent and 68.6 per cent for the two years in question. The value of the imports from the United Kingdom showed large absolute increases due to the growth of Canada's needs for machinery and other finished goods. But the significant figures for our purpose are to be found in the percentages of the imports coming from Great Britain and the United States respectively.

To have all the facts of the trade situation before us, the destination of Canadian exports should be added. In 1896, 57.1 per cent of Canada's exports were taken by the United Kingdom, 34.4 per cent by the United States, and 4.7 per cent by other foreign countries. In 1929, the percentages had materially changed: 31.8 per cent to the United Kingdom, 36.7 per cent to the United States, and 24 per cent to other foreign countries. Canada's trade with the other parts of the Empire has always been of small magnitude, with a tendency to increase. In 1896, of her imports 2.2 per cent and of her exports 3.7 per cent originated or were

FOREIGN TRADE OF CANADA [a]

Fiscal Years, 1896–1929

(value in thousands of dollars)

Imports	United Kingdom	Per cent	Other British Empire	Per cent	United States	Per cent	Other Foreign Countries	Per cent
1896	32,824	31.1	2,388	2.2	53,529	50.8	16,618	15.8
1906	69,183	24.4	14,605	5.1	169,256	59.6	30,694	10.9
1914	132,070	21.3	22,456	3.6	396,302	64.0	68,365	11.0
1922	117,135	15.7	31,973	4.3	515,958	69.0	82,736	11.0
1929	194,100	15.3	63,319	5.0	868,012	68.6	140,247	11.1
Exports								
1896	62,717	57.1	4,048	3.7	37,284	34.4	5,152	4.7
1906	127,456	54.1	10,964	4.6	83,546	35.5	13,516	5.8
1914	215,253	49.8	23,388	5.4	163,372	37.9	29,573	6.8
1922	299,361	40.4	46,473	6.3	292,588	39.5	101,816	13.8
1929	433,875	31.8	102,251	7.5	499,612	36.7	327,970	24.0

[a] Compiled from *The Canada Year Book* (1930), pp. 466, 469.

destined for the Empire; in 1929, the proportions had become respectively 5 per cent and 7.5 per cent.

From the Canadian point of view, the most remunerative of her activities in connection with foreign trade has been the extension of the advantages of the intermediate tariff to countries outside of the Empire. The extension of the British preference to the Empire has netted little in the way of additional outlets for Canadian products. Even in the case of the United Kingdom the preference has not prevented a steady proportionate decline of the market for Canadian products. The general tariff rates applied to goods coming from the United States have not been materially changed since 1907, and yet the balance of merchandise trade between the two countries has grown steadily more unfavorable to the Canadians. As a result of this experience, Canadians naturally regard the British preference as more than a partial failure, and have begun to question the wisdom of continuing it longer. Similarly, the trade figures explain the hostile attitude of Canadians to all traditional schemes for an Imperial preference. Furthermore, the slow growth of exports to the United States, as compared with the rapid increase of trade with other foreign countries, has called for a revision upward of the general tariff rates on imports from the United States. High as they have been, these rates have not served to prevent a steady increase of imports from the United States — a fact which can be explained partly by the investment in Canada of nearly $4,000,000,000 of American capital, and partly by the proximity and well-established connections of the two countries. In spite of the undoubted advantages of these interchanges of goods between the two neighbors — advantages which were distinctly reduced in 1930 by the Smoot-Hawley tariff with its prohibitive levies on milk and cream, feeders and stockers, fresh vegetables, wheat, and several other commodities — the Bennett tariff was enacted in 1931 as a means of reducing the imports from the United States.

The Liberal Government yielded to this pressure to some slight extent in 1930, and the changes proposed by the Government were announced in the Budget Speech in May. The so-called "countervailing duties" on sixteen commodities constituted the principal item for discussion, though numerous other changes, both increases and decreases of the rates, were announced. The object of a countervailing duty is to impose the same rate upon an article imported into Canada from another country as that country imposes upon the article when imported from Canada. For example, wheat was an article of commerce between Canada and the United States. Under the Canadian general tariff, the rate had been 12 cents a bushel and the rate under the American tariff 42 cents. The new tariff proposal was that wheat should enter free of duty, provided that "if any country imposes upon wheat produced in, and imported from, Canada rates of duty higher than are enumerated in this item, equivalent rates of duty shall be imposed upon wheat entering Canada from such country."

The debate in parliament was particularly bitter, not on the ground that the countervailing duties were too high, but because, as Mr. Bennett, now the prime minister, said, the "measure of protection that the farmers of this country . . . are to receive is to depend, not upon our conception of their requirements, but upon the conception that other countries may have of the requirements of their own people."

In due time the new duties were enacted into law, but before sufficient time had elapsed to give any hint of their effects, a general election threw the Liberal Government out of office and installed the Conservatives under Mr. Bennett.

In September, 1930 the new parliament was called together in special session to deal with two questions: first, the relief of unemployment, and second, the amendment of the tariff. When the amendments to the Customs Act were introduced, it was clear that the framers of the changes had in mind the "Canada first" policy of which so much had been made during the election campaign. Not only were higher rates of duty imposed upon 166 items, but the "countervailing duties" were dropped. A new and more effective form was given to the anti-dumping clause, and power was given the Governor in Council to "prohibit the importation into Canada of any goods exported directly or indirectly from any country not a contracting party to the Treaty of Versailles."

A further clause was added to the Customs Act which provided that "in the event of the producers of goods in Canada increasing prices in consequence of the imposition of any duty under the provisions of this act, the Governor in Council may reduce or remove such duty."

The debate on the amendment centered around not the increased rates but the anti-dumping clause, the embargo provision, and the proviso that prices should not be raised by the Canadian producers as a consequence of the increased rates of duty on imports.

The royal assent was given to the Customs Act as amended on September 22, and parliament was prorogued to enable the prime minister and his colleagues to proceed to England for the meeting of the Imperial Economic Conference.

When parliament met again in March, 1931, the debate [1] on the Address gave the prime minister an opportunity to discuss the project for Empire trade which he had presented to the Economic Conference, and gave the Opposition an occasion for criticism not only of the Canadian proposals but also of the revision of the rates of customs duties enacted at the special session of parliament in September, 1930. This debate is of special interest in connection with continuation of the British preference. Speaking in parliament on March 17, the prime minister said, "I had made known . . . just what the policy of the Govern-

[1] *Debates of the House of Commons, Dominion of Canada, 1931*, vol. i, pp. 7–101.

ment was and would be at that conference, namely, an effort to secure reciprocal preferences within the Empire." On the same occasion, the prime minister stated that at the second plenary meeting of the conference he had "endeavoured to point out that reciprocal trade agreements were absolutely essential for the preservation and maintenance of the economic life of our Empire." Quoting from the minutes of the conference, his remarks were, in part: "I rejoice that the Government of Canada finds, in the Empire scheme I have to propose, the surest promise that its duty to its own country will be fulfilled. For we believe that through the broadening of the home markets of Empire states to Empire products, every unit of this Empire will benefit."

The Canadian proposal was rejected, or at least a decision on it was postponed until a later date. Mr. Snowden, the chancellor of the Exchequer, speaking in the House of Commons, interpreted the Canadian proposal as a demand upon Britain to change her fiscal policy so that preferential rates could be given to produce which the Dominions sent to Britain. He described the Canadian proposal as follows:

The only proposal put before the conference by the Dominions was Mr. Bennett's, whose offer was, "I am not going to reduce the tariff against the United Kingdom but I will raise the tariff against the foreigner by ten per cent of the present rate. . . . If you will tax foreign wheat I will give you, not reciprocity, but I will keep the tariff against this country as it was." That tariff was a prohibitive tariff. Both Mr. Bennett and Mr. Scullin (the Australian Prime Minister) were perfectly honest when they said their policy was to give preference to British imports where they must import these goods, but where British goods competed with Canadian or Australian goods, then they would impose a duty as protection for their own goods.

The Canadian "Empire scheme" was wrecked upon the rock of Britain's traditional fiscal policy. As the chancellor of the Exchequer vehemently declared: "An unfounded rumor has appeared in the press that the government is considering an all-round 10 per cent import duty for revenue purposes. No government in which I am in charge of the national finances will ever give serious consideration to such a proposal." But the last word on the "Empire scheme" has not been uttered. Before a year had elapsed, Mr. Snowden was no longer chancellor of the Exchequer, a National Government was in office, and specie payments were suspended. The process of altering the fiscal system of the United Kingdom has made huge strides during the past year, and in part in the direction suggested by Mr. Bennett. A 10 per cent ad valorem duty has been imposed upon imports entering Great Britain from other than Empire states, and yet the part of the British free-trade policy which the Canadian prime minister was specifically attacking still stands unimpaired, for wheat is still on the free list.[1] Whether the Dominion during the Ottawa conference will be able to force foodstuffs off the British free list remains to be seen; but one thing seems certain, that as long as the "Canada first" policy prevails, the Dominion will not offer, as a *quid pro quo*, a modification of the rates imposed upon imports from Great Britain if by so doing the Dominion manufactures are exposed to serious competition from similar British goods.

[1] Since this was written a duty of 3 shillings a quarter on wheat from other than Empire sources has been imposed by the British Parliament.

AMERICAN MATERIALISM:
AN ECONOMIST'S INTERPRETATION

CHESTER W. WRIGHT

FROM the early decades of this country's independence, when inquisitive travelers ventured across the ocean, curious to learn what sort of society was arising in the New World under democratic ideals, down to the present, when recent arrivals are enviously anxious to discover the secrets of the country's prosperity, the charge of being materialistic has perhaps been the most common of the varied characteristics which these visitors have attributed to the American people. Whether the facts justify the characterization or not is a question hardly susceptible of definite proof and may always remain a matter of opinion. The lack of a clear agreement as to just what the term materialistic implies has only added to the uncertainty involved. But, since so many foreigners substantially agree upon the point and so many American critics accept the same view, it will be assumed, for the purpose of this essay, that there is some justification for the charge, at least in the sense in which the term is subsequently defined. It will then be our object to suggest an explanation of the phenomenon as seen in the light of economic history.

First of all, it will serve to lessen some of the ambiguities which have surrounded the use of the term materialism as employed in this connection if we examine the concept with which it is commonly contrasted. A non-materialistic society may be one where relatively more stress is placed upon (1) cultural or (2) non-cultural activities. The first of these may in turn be subdivided into (*a*) cultural activities of the type requiring a minimum of material goods, the life of thought and contemplation or religious devotion, as that of the ascetic, the Buddhist ideal, the monastic or the simple life, and (*b*) cultural activities as more commonly conceived of in the western world, which require considerable material means for their support, such as the pursuit of art, literature, the drama, music, etc. The second class, the non-cultural activities, may also be subdivided on the same basis into (*a*) the life of inertia and idleness, maintained with a minimum of material goods, and (*b*) the life devoted to the more sensuous pleasures which generally require considerable material means for their support. Bearing in mind this four-fold classification of non-materialistic modes of living, our next step is to inquire which of these were most stressed by foreigners as lacking in American life and formed the basis for their characterization of Americans as materialistic.

To be brief, it may be said that most of these foreign travelers found all four of the non-materialistic modes of living neglected or but slightly developed in the United States. A life of idleness was almost unheard of, and there was general agreement that the people were extremely active, energetic, and industrious. Nor, until recently, did the foreign traveler find much evidence of the less cultural mode of living in which sport, social frivolity, and the more sensuous forms of pleasure played an appreciable part. The southern planter with his good living, hospitality, and sports was the nearest approach to be seen; but elsewhere such activities were little in evidence, especially in sections where Puritanical and Quaker influences predominated. Though there was general agreement among the commentators that neither of these two forms of non-cultural and non-economic modes of living was much in evidence, still, it was not this that was much stressed as a reason for characterizing the people as materialistic. The main basis for the charge was the backward state of the more cultural activities.

Yet of the two forms of cultural activities, as classified above, it is very noticeable that the one chiefly dwelt upon by these commentators as lacking was not that of the simple life devoted to thought and contemplation. In fact, it is seldom that this is so much as noted. On the other hand, nearly all the stress is placed on the relatively undeveloped pursuit of the various arts. Moreover, the emphasis on this point seems to have increased as the nineteenth century advanced. To summarize: the American people were characterized as materialistic because, on the one hand, their activities were so exclusively devoted to business. On the other hand, of the four non-cultural modes of living, which in consequence were relatively neglected, two were seldom mentioned; and of the remaining two — both of which, it should be noted, commonly required means for their support — the one really stressed as undeveloped was the pursuit of the cultural arts. But before proceeding to the explanation of the phenomenon some additional qualifications, mainly of a limiting type, are necessary; for much has been assumed as implied by the characterization of materialism which was not ordinarily included in the term as employed by the critics.

It is not infrequently assumed, for example, that the charge of materialism also implied the trait of miserliness; yet it was seldom that this trait was either explicitly charged, or even implied, against the Americans. Extravagant expenditure for luxurious forms of living was not common, at least not before the last of the nineteenth century. Yet Americans did not closely count the pennies spent as did many classes in Europe, and mere miserly hoarding was much less common than in the Old World. Money might be saved to expand a business or to take advantage of other business opportunities, and this process might be continued long after the fortune accumulated had passed the sum necessary to provide for the most extravagant wants. But the activity was kept up as a game — often the only game known — where the main objective was success through victory over rivals, with the accompanying prestige, while the additional wealth was a minor consideration. That mere miserliness was not involved is further indicated by the fact that few people faced the loss of fortune with less concern than Americans, and certainly no nationality has been more free in giving or has given with less thought of ulterior reward.

A more important misconception is found in the common assumption that the materialism with which Americans were charged implied a lack of high ideals. Admittedly, as the previous analysis suggests, it did imply that the development of the cultural arts ranked low among the ideals which motivated the American people. But, after all, there are other ideals which can be ranked even higher on the basis of their contribution to social well-being. Among such may be listed the ideals of liberty; of democracy political, economic, and social; of religious freedom; and of humanitarianism with its all-inclusive social uplift — all of which, it might well be claimed, have been much more powerful forces in America than in the Old World. In the emphasis upon such objectives America has been outstandingly a nation of idealists. As the exponent of these high ideals the United States has led the world — should we add? — at least to the close of the nineteenth century. Nor did the foreign critics commonly deny the fact. It was, indeed, to see how a people professing such ideals were progressing that many foreign travelers journeyed across the ocean, especially during the first half of the century. Not a few were high in their praise of the country's institutions and life as developed under these ideals. Others criticized, either lacking sympathy with some of the ideals or asserting, not without a measure of truth, that the people seldom lived up to their ideals in practise. These ideals reflected the high aspirations of a youthful nation which it was hoped might be attained in a world comparatively free from the trammels of the old institutions and traditions which dominated Europe. If some of the means adopted to further their attainment indicated a lack of that sophistication born of long experience in endeavors to govern mankind, it could be charged to the enthusiasm of youth. Despite the prevalent materialism the American people could not be characterized as lacking in high ideals, at least of a certain type. The foreign critics in general tacitly admitted as much; for those who wrote adverse criticisms rather than praise did so chiefly on the ground that the ideals were too high to be practicable.

One final point remains to be suggested further to clarify what was involved in this charge of materialism. Practically all of the foreign commentators who made this criticism appear to have come from the upper middle or upper classes abroad. Furthermore, what little fairly close contact they had with Americans was ordinarily with those occupying much the same rank in the social order. Thus the comparison drawn on this point between Americans and Europeans was chiefly between those in the upper social strata. The very fact that the only two forms of non-materialistic activities which were commonly noted as lacking in American life were the two requiring the greatest material means for their support made this comparison almost inevitable. Neither in Europe nor in America were the lower classes possessed of the means for such activities.

Had the comparison been extended to include the lower social strata the difference between the Old World and the New in this respect would have been far less marked; though we may presume that the common tendency of lower groups to imitate the upper, so far as means permit, would still have resulted in some differences. Certainly it is significant that the comments of immigrants seldom even mention such a difference. Rather, they insistently dwell upon the economic opportunities and the pervading spirit of democracy.

As thus narrowed down and clarified the materialism charged against the American people, which it is our object to explain, is found to consist of the assertion that Americans of the upper classes devoted a relatively large proportion of their life to business and a relatively small proportion of their time to the pursuits of a well-endowed leisure, chiefly the cultural arts. Neither miserliness nor a lack of high ideals was implied, and the comparison was not commonly applied to the lower classes. In the search for an explanation of the phenomenon, to which we now turn, it is clear that since such social characteristics are a product of the social environment, including the influences inherited from the past, it is there that the explanation must be sought. And as a comparison is involved, this must cover the social environment bearing upon the point in both America and Europe. The latter will be considered first.

Since religious faith may be presumed to have an important influence in shaping men's ideals, despite the fact that practise may fall so far below professions, we will first view the European background from this angle. Christianity, as developed under the Catholic Church, was the religion which in the course of the Middle Ages came to be almost universally accepted in western Europe. Its original and essential spirit was certainly non-materialistic, opposed to the laying up of goods in this world and stressing the mode of living which would secure salvation in the world to come. The biblical description of the difficulties which would beset a rich man's efforts to enter into the kingdom of heaven and other similar warnings need no repetition. Moreover, it would appear that these precepts were not without some appreciable influence on the actual mode of life during the Middle Ages. After all, the comforts and pleasures which material means could provide in those days were relatively few, and acceptance of the simple life was thus made easier. Besides, the opportunities to acquire wealth through the ordinary modes of getting a living were extremely limited. Also, the chance that anyone who succeeded in accumulating wealth would enjoy the fruits thereof was most uncertain. The destruction and plunder of constant warfare, robbery, and innumerable forms of extortion only too frequently placed the property of the weak at the mercy of the strong. Furthermore, life itself was also most uncertain and relatively brief; for, in addition to the various causes of violent death, there was ever lurking disease or the sweep of the pestilence against which man was still powerless. And over all hung that terrible uncertainty — the Judgment Day which was to usher in the end of the world.

By the early part of the second millennium of the Christian era developments began to take place which, slowly but steadily, wrought a marked change in these conditions. Commerce began to expand and had a stimulating effect on other economic activities. In this revival the Italian city states took the lead; and, ere long, there arose within them an aristocratic group of great wealth, chiefly acquired in banking and trade. The humanistic revival culminating in the Renaissance greatly altered the outlook on life, and increasingly concern as to salvation in the future was forgotten in the enjoyment of this world's pleasures. The Christian ideal of simple living became more and more difficult to live up to, even for the clergy. The Church itself found its authority on the wane. Even the semblance of its unity had vanished with the final split between Rome and Constantinople, and growing signs of dissension now appeared in different parts of the west, finally culminating in the Reformation. Among the resulting Protestant sects, though most marked in those of Calvinistic origin, the doctrines relating to various forms of economic activity reflected an attitude very different from that which had been theretofore upheld by the Church of Rome. The taking of interest was justified; thrift was praised; and success in the accumulation of wealth, it was held, might be a means of contributing to the glory of God. But wasteful and pleasure-seeking modes of life were still condemned and a more insistent stress placed upon insuring salvation in the life to come.

We need not here enter into the controversy whether the Protestant ethic was the original and primary cause for this shift in attitude or whether the shift was due fundamentally to changes in underlying economic conditions. That there was a close interaction seems clear, and which was the primary motivating force is unimportant for our purposes. But it is important to bear in mind certain of the economic changes which were contemporaneous with, or followed, the advent of modern history.

After the discovery of the ocean route to the Far East with its riches and of the New World with its store of precious metals commerce expanded rapidly, economic activities in general were stimulated, and we enter a new period when the whole tempo of economic life proceeded at a faster pace — a pace which has been accelerating as each new century has dawned. Thus there arose opportunities for accumulating wealth through strictly business activities that in time became infinitely more numerous and vastly greater than had theretofore been available. As the centuries passed wealth and property rights became better protected; devastating wars became less frequent; and plunder, robbery, and endless petty warfare almost disappeared. Wealth and accumulated capital began to assume a more important rôle in the struggles and successes of both nations and individuals.

The outlook on life also was gradually altered. As the rationalistic attitude spread and scientific knowledge grew, the end of the world seemed less imminent and the fires of hell less certain. Life itself became more secure and the span of existence was steadily extended. Meanwhile the material means for satisfying human wants were rapidly augmented. Things which in earlier centuries were luxuries for kings not infrequently became necessities for the masses, while for the wealthy new luxuries were developed in a profusion beyond the dreams of earlier generations. Thus, as the allurements of life in this world grew and concern for the future life waned, the spirit of gain, apparently always only latent and simply needing a favorable environment in which to grow, blossomed forth exuberantly. Despite the essential teachings of its avowed faith, the western world, with growing avidity, sought the material goods contributing to the pleasures of mundane existence.

The reaction of these developments on the upper classes, the groups that had theretofore enjoyed the relatively greater proportion of this world's goods, is of interest for the light which it throws on our problem. A tendency to disparage the accumulation of wealth had never been conspicuous among most of these groups. But the means they employed to acquire wealth had in the main consisted of various forms of exploitation based upon power and force rather than that of ordinary business enterprise. The great castes that in earlier centuries dominated the social order, such as the nobility, the clergy, and the bureaucracy, were little loath to take advantage of their position to add to their possessions. Moreover, the families belonging to these castes were, as a whole, fairly strongly intrenched in their position, despite the evil fate that overtook some. Wealth once acquired was often handed down from generation to generation through a long succession. In countries where primogeniture and entail were common this helped to maintain fortunes intact. Younger sons who suffered thereby sought preferment in government service, the army, or the Church, but seldom in business, for trade was socially taboo among the upper classes. This Old World caste attitude toward business, so markedly in contrast with that which developed in America, is important for our thesis.

Obviously it was easy for castes which acquired most of their wealth by other means to look down upon those engaged in business. It involved little sacrifice and gave added social prestige. And whatever sacrifice might have been involved was greatly reduced by various means of getting around the objection. Investments in business undertakings on the grand scale seem to have had little stigma attached to them, and actual management could be delegated to commoners. Landed estates, the chief source of income for many, fell without the proscription. Though not quite ideal, marriage with a rich merchant's heiress was a way to wealth which some, at least, were willing to adopt. Furthermore, there was a constant seepage into the aristocracy from the group of wealthy commoners through the granting of titles to those whose wealth was found serviceable to king or country.

In spite of the risks attendant upon broad generalizations so on intangible a subject, it seems clear that this attitude existed throughout most of western Europe; though its actual influence varied greatly as between different countries and different periods. In Italy in the late Middle Ages, where many of the ruling families of the city states had risen out of the merchant and banking class, it was less marked. Perhaps Spain represented the most extreme case, where the nobility were at one time forbidden to engage in business and where even today the social condemnation of such action is powerful. In France, Germany, and Austria, with their strong caste heritage from feudalism, royalty, and bureaucracy, this attitude remained extremely influential, at least well into the nineteenth century. Distinctly more liberal were Holland and England, the two countries which, after the decline of Mediterranean trade and the Italian city states, soon took the lead in the expansion of European commerce. The social scorn implied in the continental characterization of eighteenth-century England as a nation of tradesmen is well known, as is Voltaire's surprise at finding men of business so prominent among the upper classes. It was in England that the economic developments previously noted wrought the most marked change.[1] But throughout Europe, as a large class of newly rich commoners developed out of the new opportunities for acquiring wealth and as mere wealth became a relatively greater power, some among the older castes gradually succumbed to the temptation of business. Others, already possessing large means, lacking opportunity and ability to take advantage of the new openings, or still merely dominated by caste tradition, often as a defense mechanism, insisted the more strongly on the old social taboo. Notwithstanding the

[1] As illustrative of the point see *The Antiquity, Honor and Dignity of Trade* ... by a Peer of England [James Caulfield, ed.] (Westminster, 1813), especially p. 34.

steady modification of the general attitude, to be a "trades-man" put one outside the pale of many groups throughout the nineteenth century, even in England.

Despite the widespread social taboo upon engaging in business that prevailed among the upper classes in Europe, the high ideal of the simple life won little favor, and the mode of living commonly followed was one requiring very substantial material means for its support. This wealth, as has been indicated, was generally obtained by ways that did not commonly involve active personal participation in business enterprise, no matter what the original source of the wealth. Also, the strongly intrenched position of these castes enabled most of them to retain rights and privileges from which much of their income was obtained and to hand down their accumulated wealth for generation after generation. This latter fact is important because the development of cultural modes of living is greatly facilitated when wealth is held in a family for more than one generation. It requires means to provide the leisure requisite to develop an interest in, and a capacity to engage in, such pursuits, as well as to carry them on. The difficulties confronting the aspiring newly rich, because of this fact, are well known. But when two or more generations of a family possess the requisite means for cultural activities and establish a tradition for maintaining them it has something of a self-perpetuating influence. That such conditions did tend to develop a traditional mode of living involving at least some of these cultural activities among the upper classes of Europe is evident. But that their wealth was also used to maintain activities of a non-cultural type is also obvious. Sports, frivolity, society, and many other of the more fleeting and sensual forms of pleasure doubtless required a much larger proportion of their income among most of these groups.

We have seen that it was chiefly these two forms of activity, the cultural and the more frivolous or sensual, traditionally maintained among the upper classes of Europe and supported by wealth, that foreigners found relatively undeveloped in America, though the former was most stressed in their criticisms. What conditions peculiar to the American social environment tended to create this difference in modes of living is the question to which we next turn.

Of considerable importance among these conditions was the selective process determining those who migrated to America. While the reasons for seeking a home in the New World varied and often were complex, there can be no doubt but that economic considerations — the hope of bettering their material condition — constituted the dominating motive for migration. In the seventeenth and early eighteenth centuries religious motives may have been dominant among certain groups such as the Puritans, the Quakers, or the Huguenots; but even these were not unmindful of gain, and the influence of the religious motive rapidly dwindled as time went on. Occasionally, among still smaller groups, political ideals were prominent; with some simply the spirit of adventure. Increasingly predominant with each new century, it was the appeal of a new Eldorado which attracted the groups by which America was peopled — a materialistic objective. And this meant, as a corollary, that these immigrants came almost exclusively from the less well-to-do classes, generally from among the poor or, at best, the lower middle class. Most of them were common laborers, farm hands, artisans, or mechanics. Among them lack of means had of necessity prevented any appreciable development of cultural tastes and pursuits, to say nothing of indulgence in the less cultural forms of luxurious expenditure. A society starting on such a foundation could hardly be expected to evolve a highly cultural life in a brief period.

Moreover, it is important to note that what we may consider as the original foundation provided by the immigration of colonial times was greatly increased by an ever-growing stream throughout the nineteenth century. Thus American society was constantly being abnormally augmented almost entirely at the lower cultural levels. How significant this was is best indicated by the fact that the native whites of native parentage have made up little more than half of the total population of the country. Nor, in this connection, should we overlook the important negro element, varying from a fifth to a tenth of the total population, only freed from slavery within the memory of some yet living, and still burdened with many handicaps.

The effects of this lack of cultural traditions among those who migrated to America were intensified by influences that in the long run were of even greater importance. These arose out of the economic environment in which these people found themselves and out of the age in the world's history in which they lived. The immigrants came to America primarily to improve their economic condition, and, for most of them, America proved to be in fact a land of golden opportunity. Fortunes were not made overnight; hard work, energy, and perseverance were required of most. But they were an ambitious and energetic people, or they would not have made the venture; and in time their labor was fairly certain to be well rewarded. It was the reports of success which they sent home to relatives and friends that induced an ever-increasing stream to follow in their wake.

The basic factors contributing to the economic advancement of these people were certain underlying economic conditions and the facilities which science and invention were making available. The former may be summed up as consisting of cheap and varied natural resources, a scarcity of labor, and great freedom of economic initiative and opportunity. The influence of the latter was most marked from the time of the Industrial Revolution on, when technological advance proceeded at a rate unparalleled in history and made the nineteenth century stand out as pre-eminently the age of material progress. With the rich resources of a virgin continent before them and possessing technological equipment for the opening up of these resources such as man had never dreamed of theretofore, the American people turned their whole energies to the development of this unparalleled opportunity. Ambitious, active, imbued with the spirit of work, and enjoying almost unlimited freedom of action, they so wrought that within a century and a half a new and relatively weak country was raised to the position of the richest and most powerful nation on earth, while its people attained the highest standard of living that the world has ever known.

In such an environment and such an age it is not surprising that the social taboo upon engaging in business, so widespread in Europe, found little upon which to thrive when transplanted in America. Traces can be found in the colonial period, perhaps most frequently among the planter aristocracy of the South, where it lingered longest; but as the vigorous life of the nineteenth century advanced even this practically disappeared. Doubtless the fact that people of English origin and ideals dominated the land and that in England this traditional attitude was being undermined much more rapidly than on the Continent were influential. The marked power of the Puritan, Calvinistic, and other strongly religious groups was similarly significant. To the Puritan, work was almost a sacred obligation, while a life of luxury and leisure was a device of Satan leading straight to hell. Plain living and high thinking constituted his ideal, but the high thinking must be on religious lines. Writing in 1835 of the Puritan progeny, an acute French observer remarked:

He [the American] has no conception of living without a profession, even when his family is rich, for he sees nobody about him not engaged in business. The man of leisure is a variety of the human species of which the Yankee does not suspect the existence, and he knows that if rich today, his father may be ruined tomorrow. . . . The habits of life are those of an exclusively working people. From the moment he gets up, the American is at his work, and he is engaged in it till the hour of sleep. Pleasure is never permitted to interrupt his business; public affairs only have the right to occupy a few moments.[1]

Thus the New World came to adopt an attitude the very reverse of that of the Old World; business was looked up to as pre-eminently respectable, while a life of leisure was likely to face social condemnation.

Another extremely important factor in the situation was the democratic spirit that pervaded the whole social order. Although it was not until the nineteenth century that this attained its full growth, yet even in colonial times, despite the Old World heritage, the social order was far more democratic than in Europe. This was only in line with the trend of the age, but the frontier environment greatly stimulated its development in the New World. The upheavals of the revolutionary period seriously weakened what remained of aristocratic tradition, and in the second quarter of the nineteenth century, save for the planter aristocracy and the blot of slavery, democracy was triumphant in both the political and the social order.

Thus the castes that dominated European nations were ruthlessly eliminated. A titled aristocracy was banned by the Constitution. Whatever special influence the clergy

[1] Michael Chevalier, *Society, Manners and Politics in the United States* (Boston, 1839), p. 283.

had enjoyed in the early colonial period disappeared with the final disestablishment of the churches, so there was no ecclesiastical hierarchy. The resolute determination to maintain only the smallest possible standing army prevented the rise of a military caste. The low pay and uncertain tenure of public office under the spoils system were effective checks upon the growth of a bureaucracy. The opportunities for getting a good living by non-business means, which the Old World provided in such profusion for these castes, were almost non-existent in the United States, and only in a few cases did appreciable power or social prestige attach to membership in these groups. In the absence of such opportunities and in the presence of dazzling opportunities in business, with no concomitant social taboo, the acquisition of wealth became the quickest and surest means to power and social prestige. To a far greater extent than in Europe, men of ability were drawn into business, and, in turn, these men of business dominated the whole social order.

This democratic society, with its comparative absence of caste and its fluid nature, provided a stimulus to ambition and action. The old mediaeval idea that man was born to a given vocation divinely ordained and that he should not strive to rise above the station in life in which his lot was cast, which checked the ambitions and energies of subdued and servile masses in Europe, found little acceptance here, though revived in the late defense of slavery. To quote our French commentator again:

In general, the American is little disposed to be contented; his idea of equality is to be inferior to none, but he endeavors to rise only in one direction. His only means, and the object of his whole thought, is to subdue the material world, or, in other words, it is industry in its various branches, business, speculation, work, action. To this sole object everything is made subordinate, education, politics, private and public life.[1]

[1] Chevalier, *op. cit.*, p. 277.

The incentives to accumulate wealth were strengthened by the comparative security of property rights. Except as it might be involved in business enterprise, there was little exploitation of the masses by the classes. Except in the South during the Civil War, there was never widespread destruction of property by war. The political institutions set up to protect property rights provided a strong bulwark, and wealth once gained, though subject to the great vicissitudes of business, was otherwise relatively secure.

While all these characteristics of the American environment help to explain the great absorption of the people in business, there were certain other conditions which tended to check the growth of cultural pursuits. Mention has previously been made of the relative poverty and lack of a tradition of cultural pursuits among those who came to America and of the constant addition to this large element in the population down to 1914, both significant because it requires time as well as wealth to develop such activities. But in America, though wealth might be rapidly acquired by some, there was far less stability of the family fortune than in Europe and less chance that the accumulation would be handed down unimpaired to succeeding generations. Though quickly made in a rapidly developing and highly speculative society, fortunes could disappear with almost equal speed. The general recognition of the fact is shown in the first quotation from Chevalier, and the old adage that it was "but three generations from shirt-sleeves to shirt-sleeves" suggests a common experience. The sources of income were distinctly less stable than those of the English aristocracy. Furthermore, the final elimination after the Revolution of the remaining vestiges of primogeniture and entail, together with the marked hostility towards perpetuities, hastened the dispersion of estates that might otherwise have remained intact.

A similar result followed the freedom with which those who made money spent it or gave it away. "Easy come, easy go," fully applied to the American newly rich. But it is also to be remembered that this was a period of unparalleled advance in the general standard of living. Much of the rising incomes that might otherwise have been employed to maintain cultural activities was diverted to secure the endless number of new or improved devices and services contributing to less cultural satisfactions. At the same time the desire to provide for these wants, for either one's self or one's children, supplied a reason for continuing longer in business to accumulate a larger fortune.

Still another influence tending to delay the development of the cultural life is to be found in the great preponderance of the rural element in the population. Many of the institutions depended upon to foster the arts can only be supported through the concentration of wealth found in large cities. Urban life also provides the close contacts tending to stimulate and to hasten the spread of cultural pursuits. In America, living on a farm involved much greater isolation even than it did in Europe; nor was there in American rural districts any cultural influence equal to that of the castes of Europe on their landed estates. Also, although the average American farmer was much better off materially than the mass of the agricultural classes in Europe, he seldom acquired a fortune and his life was one of long hours of unremitting toil. Finally, it is to be noted that in the urban centers, where the environment was more favorable to the development of the arts, the growth of population, in so far as it was not due to the cities' natural increase, was a product of two streams, one from the rural districts and one from abroad — but both lacking a cultural heritage.

Thus far our effort to explain American materialism, as first defined, has dealt in comparisons between the European and the American environment of earlier generations. Yet further evidence in support of the suggestions advanced is to be found in tendencies observable on each continent among the present generation.

In Europe the predominent position and power of the old castes is on the wane, sinking before the ever-rising spirit of democracy and the growing power of wealth accumulated in business. Particularly noticeable is the transformation on the Continent since the upheavals incident to the World War. Deprived of special privileges and family heritages which made possible a life of leisure, cultural or otherwise, many members of the aristocracy have finally resorted to the pursuit of business. Meanwhile the power of the wealthy bourgeoisie has risen; opportunities, position, and social prestige hitherto denied are increasingly conferred upon them. The old social taboo upon engaging in business is being undermined more rapidly than ever before. Yet the old tradition of the pursuits of the gentleman still persists and, if means permit, these pursuits are carried on by the bourgeoisie as well as the castes. But an active business pursuit is increasingly common among those that now constitute the dominant classes. In this last respect Europe is rapidly adopting one characteristic of America's materialism.

In America, on the other hand, we see increasing signs that the combined factors of accumulated wealth and the passage of time in which this wealth is handed down to succeeding generations are producing groups in whose lives the pursuits of leisure, including those of the cultural arts, play an increasingly prominent part. The business man takes more time off for sport, for travel, for amusements, and for the arts; he more frequently retires instead of waiting to drop dead in the harness. If the newly rich adopt an unintelligent patronage of the arts as a form of ostentation or for social prestige it at least implies a certain recognition of the standing of such pursuits. Moreover, it is one means by which in time a genuine appreciation of the arts is developed. The children of the well-to-do now find the day when they set forth to earn a living increasingly postponed by the lengthening of the educational process. And, despite the strong nineteenth-century trend of our curricula toward "practical" subjects — both a result and in turn a cause of our materialism — an increasing element of cultural studies is now being provided, and also pursued. Notwithstanding the bitter comments of our own critics, impatient of the slow rate of progress and often failing to appreciate what has been accomplished, the younger generation is entering active life with a larger interest in, and a greater ability to follow, the cultural pursuits than ever before. To repeat: the process requires time as well as means; America is only newly rich and most of its people only a generation or so from a frontier environment. The cultures of ancient Athens, mediaeval Florence, and modern Paris were not evolved in a single generation; and in our admiration for the product we too commonly overlook the servitude, the exploitation, and the suppression of human aspirations upon which, at least in part, they were built up. If our own cultural life is still backward, we may yet hope that its bases, despite all the defects, have greater potentialities for human well-being than had those of old. Though the cultural growth be slow, it is in evidence; so that as regards this characteristic American materialism is being modified in favor of European standards.

Our comparisons of the social heritage and environment of Europe and America have been sketched in with broad generalizations presenting sharp contrasts of black and white, though a more extended and detailed study would indicate the need for many modifications and a more general use of neutral tones. But if, in essentials, the analysis be sound, the conclusion that follows can be briefly summarized. American materialism as defined—consisting of an excessive absorption in business, on the one hand, and an undue neglect of the pursuits of leisure, chiefly those of the arts, on the other hand — was fundamentally a product of the age and the environment in which the nation evolved. In world history the age, especially the nineteenth century — and most of America was not settled before then — was characterized by phenomenal economic progress and by the rapid spread of democratic ideals and institutions. The environment was a virgin continent offering unequalled economic opportunity and practical freedom from Old World institutions to establish such a social order as the settlers might desire. The settlers, mainly derived from the masses rather than the classes, were primarily interested in improving their economic condition, and finally evolved a democratic social order in which business was pre-eminently respectable; and the castes with their special privileges, which in Europe had been the main support of the tradition of cultural pursuits, were practically exterminated. The so-called American materialism thus evolved was fundamentally a reflection of the characteristics of the age. Like so many so-called American traits, it was American only because America afforded the best environment for the pure and unfettered development of these characteristics. As the ancient heritage of the Old World crumbles before the spirit of the modern age and business becomes a common and respectable activity of the upper classes, Europe approaches America. In the New World, as wealth accumulates and is handed down from generation to generation, providing the material basis for the development of cultural tastes and traditions, America approaches Europe. Thus time will dispel the differentiation.

THE RISE OF THE FACTORY IN THE AMERICAN CARPET MANUFACTURE

ARTHUR HARRISON COLE

THE development of the carpet industry in the United States to the stage of factory production has many points of interest for the economic historian. Not only did it involve a rapid supercession of imported fabrics — a feature in which the early protective tariffs seem to have played a significant part — but the course of development itself differed appreciably from that of either the early cotton- or wool-cloth industries. Moreover, we have to do here with an industry which is in various respects peculiarly American. It was in this country that a broad use of wool floor-coverings first arose — a phenomenon of the 'twenties and 'thirties, which in fact forecast new standards of living; and the manufacture of wool carpeting early took on the characteristic of large-scale operation so typical of American industry.

The use of wool floor-covering in the Colonial period was, of course, narrowly restricted. Floors were for the most part bare, although in some parts of the country sand and rushes were utilized to relieve or soften the severity of bare boarding. Rag rugs and an occasional piece of imported carpeting were the only forms of wool floor-covering employed, and these were limited to use in the parlor or living-room and at bedsides, even in the more prosperous homes.[1] In the period between the Revolution and 1830,

[1] "May 13, 1795: — At one o'clock to-day I called at General Washington's ... a small brick house on the left side of High St. . . . I was conducted up a

there seems to have been a marked increase in the use of floor-coverings, though just when it came about is uncertain. It appears to have been particularly rapid in the period of good times which, following the somewhat false prosperity of the years immediately after the 'Peace of Ghent, characterized the 'twenties.

The course of importations in the period before the 'thirties reveals an expanding trade in carpetings beginning late in the Colonial era and markedly enlarging in the first decades of the nineteenth century. From the time when the item of "Irish Rugs" was an object of value in an inventory in 1637 to the days just before the Revolution when Mrs. Margaret B. Livingston, wife of Judge Livingston, owned thirty-six yards of "Broussells carpet with Border," imported fabrics of this type appear now and then in Colonial records; although it is doubtful whether all of these imported carpetings were for use as floor-coverings — since at that time such articles were employed also as decorations for tables.[1] At all events, the trade may be characterized as one of a minor luxury type.

The first information we have regarding regular importation of carpets relates to the firm of J. Alexander & Com-

---

neat but rather narrow staircase, carpeted in the middle, and was shown into a middling-sized, well-furnished drawing-room. . . . The floor was carpeted." Thus wrote Thomas Twining. (See his letters published in 1894 as *Travels in America One Hundred Years Ago*.) Obviously, even in such a household as that of the Washingtons, a carpeted stairway or room was something unusual enough to cause comment. Madame Benjamin Franklin wrote to her distinguished husband a description of her carpets in 1765 in a letter which is reprinted in J. F. Watson's *Annals of Philadelphia* (1857), vol. i, p. 206.

As late as 1800 carpets were "known" in the houses of only a few families in such places as Ridgefield, Connecticut, and "were all home-made, the warp consisting of woolen yarn and the woof of lists and old woolen cloth, cut into strips and sewed together at the ends." (S. G. Goodrich, *Recollections of a Life Time*, 1856, vol. i, p. 74.)

[1] W. B. Weeden, *Economic and Social History of New England: 1620–1789* (1890), vol. ii, p. 878; H. E. Smith, *Colonial Days and Ways* (1900), p. 204; J. T. Scharf and T. Westcott in their *History of Philadelphia: 1609–1884* (1884),

pany, whose advertisement appeared in the *New York Gazette*, June 30, 1760. The merchandise offered for sale included a large variety of textiles — "check handkerchiefs, linens . . . Lawn and Minonettes" — but it also listed the article of "Scot's Carpets." During the next year, these merchants added Turkey carpets, and in 1763 announced that they had "imported some English and Scot's carpets and Hair cloth for Stairs and Passages." [1] Subsequently such items are to be found in the newsprints of the period with increasing frequency, although it is not until substantially later — around 1815–20 — that there is any regularity in the appearance of such notices.

Outstanding in this import trade was the "Scot" or Kidderminster carpeting — called "ingrain" in this country — while second came the inferior variety called Venetian, differing from the former only in having a vegetable (probably jute) warp instead of a woolen one. These represent the plainest of woven wool floor-coverings, being substantially but heavy woolen cloths. As late as 1825 — when import data by varieties first become available — ingrains and Venetians contributed 502,000 square yards out of a total of 590,000. Meanwhile, to be sure, other types had begun to make their appearance — Brussels, Wilton, Turkey, and tufted rugs; and, after competition from domestic manufacture had grown more severe, these carpetings became characteristic of the import trade. At

vol. ii, p. 877, state that carpets were introduced into that city about 1750 but "did not come so speedily in general use."

It is traditionally, though erroneously, reported that the first carpet used in a private house in this country was found in that of Captain Kidd, the famous pirate, who was executed in 1701. This was thought to have been a small Eastern rug which he had taken from one of his prizes. (W. Lord, Jr., "History of the Carpet Industry" in *The American Carpet and Upholstery Trade*, vol. x, 1892, pp. 676, 769; and also *Wool and Manufactures of Wool*, 1887, p. liii.)

[1] S. Knapp, "American Carpets" in C. M. Depew's *One Hundred Years of American Commerce* (1895), vol. ii, p. 486.

first, however, prospective American producers had to meet chiefly the flood of ingrain fabrics.

Yet, looking at the matter in another way, this flood presented an opportunity. The domestic demand for a relatively simple textile product was growing rapidly. While absolute quantities of domestic consumption, of course, cannot be ascertained, we do know that as early as 1788 Brissot de Warville commented on the extravagant use of carpeting by Americans who spread them even in summer! "They sacrifice reason and utility to show. The Quakers have likewise carpets; but the rigourous ones blame this practice. . . . One [who] was offended at finding the passage from the door to the staircase covered with a carpet, would not enter the house; he said . . . it was better to clothe the poor than to clothe the earth." [1] We know that the interruption of trade before the War of 1812 was a source of difficulty to Kidderminster manufacturers; [2] and that by 1825–28 importations of ingrain and Venetian averaged 625,000 square yards. Here, indeed, was an opening for American enterprise.

The meagerness of carpet consumption in the Colonial and early post-Colonial days was reflected in methods of manufacture. Production was carried through in a very simple manner. Evidence exists that nearly all the domes-

---

[1] J. P. Brissot de Warville, *New Travels in the United States of America: Performed in 1788* (2 vols., London, 1794), vol. i, p. 270.

[2] Herbert Brougham remarked that "at Kidderminster where a great carpet manufacture is almost entirely destroyed . . . the poor . . . were forced to part with . . . even the clothes off their backs, to raise food, until the pawnbrokers . . . refused to issue any more tickets." "If the trade [with America] was opened, it would materially relieve the town" of which "a very considerable proportion of the manufacture has been for America." See the discussion on Herbert Brougham's "Motion on the Present State of Commerce and Manufactures and the Repeal of the Orders in Council" in *Hansard's Parliamentary Debates*, 2nd ser. (1812), vol. xxiii, col. 493, and in the *Reports of Committees* in the British Parliamentary Papers for 1812. See also *Niles' Weekly Register*, vol. iv (1813), p. 138.

tic output came from the households which consumed the finished article. The weaving accounts kept by George Washington, for instance, covering the years 1767–70, show two items of carpets — one, 23½ and the other, 12 yards long — manufactured for use in his family;[1] and Tench Coxe reported that in the first three-quarters of 1791 some 512 yards of carpeting were produced "in a family way" in Providence, Rhode Island.[2] Premiums for carpets not uncommonly were offered at the fairs and agricultural exhibitions which came to be held widely in the New England and middle States, and even for as late a period as the 'twenties and 'thirties notices of home-made carpeting exhibited at these annual gatherings are to be found. At the fair of 1821 in Pittsfield, Massachusetts, Mrs. Perkins and her four daughters displayed their joint manufacture for the preceding year — a product which, in addition to woolen and linen cloth, included 53 yards of "carpetting;" and in 1830, when the Society for the Promotion of Agriculture and Domestic Manufactures; in Washington County, Pennsylvania, held an exhibition, carpets and hearth rugs were shown among other household productions.[3] There is likewise an occasional note in McLane's Report of 1832 on household manufacture of carpeting — for example, that more than half of the carpeting used in certain New Hampshire towns was produced in the families of the communities.[4]

So considerable were household manufactures that at times the product passed into general trade. In 1791,

---

[1] V. S. Clark, *History of Manufactures in the United States: 1607–1860* (1916), Appendix vii, p. 602.

[2] T. Coxe, *View of the United States of America: 1787–94* (1795), p. 227.

[3] *Niles' Weekly Register*, vol. xxii (1822), p. 266; S. Hazard, *Register of Pennsylvania*, vol. ii (1828), p. 328. See also *Niles' Weekly Register*, vol. xxi (1821), p. 308, and vol. xxiii (1822), p. 181.

[4] L. McLane, *Documents Relative to the Manufactures in the United States* (1832), vol. i, pp. 623, 625 (22nd Cong., 1st sess., House Executive Document, no. 308).

a Mrs. Susannah Shepard of Wrentham, Massachusetts, bought a chaise for which she made payment with goods of her own handicraft, and among these articles were 14 yards and 2 "nails" of carpeting for which she received £2 2s.[1] As late as 1832, a family in New Hampshire was reported to be turning out 1,000 yards of carpeting annually; McLane's Report gave the domestic manufacture of carpeting for the town of Gilmanton, New Hampshire, for the previous year as 10,000 yards, and in four counties in that State the amount of carpeting manufactured, which was "made mostly in families" and which was "sold in other States," was said to have exceeded the amount of the foreign article consumed.[2] On the whole, however, evidence pointing to a large household production of carpeting for sale purposes is scanty; and I am inclined to think that goods derived in this manner formed no substantial part of the domestic supply.

An alternative phase of manufacture was that by professional weavers who worked up material either on the order of customers or possibly with no incentive beyond their own initiative. By the latter decades of the Colonial period, there were indeed handicraftsmen in the woolen-cloth industry who, using either apparatus in their own shops or the looms of their patrons, "wove up" wool on order. Possibly these woolen-cloth weavers may also have taken over the fabrication of carpets for customers. In fact, it is definitely asserted that in the middle of the eighteenth century, yarn carpets were made and sold by village weavers;[3] and Tryon states that after the ordinary loom

---

[1] W. R. Bagnall, *The Textile Industries of the United States* (1893), p. 174.

[2] McLane, *op. cit.*, vol. i, pp. 585, 628. See also pp. 661 and 682.

[3] Smith, *op. cit.*, p. 14. Miss Smith's testimony is considerably weakened by the fact that elsewhere she states that "carpets were seldom woven at home" (*op. cit.*, p. 243) — an assertion which is surely erroneous unless she means to exclude rag carpeting.

had gone out of general use for woolen cloth, "carpets for a neighborhood were woven by some member of the community" — presumably a specialized handicraftsman.[1] The available evidence is too meager for positive conclusions, but I am inclined to be dubious as to the real importance of manufacture by handicraftsmen as far as domestic supply in the early decades is concerned.

One exception, however, must be made to the last statement. In the carpet manufacture, as in other branches of the textile industry, the Philadelphia district held a peculiar position. There the handicraft organization grew to appreciable dimensions, and continued to flourish long after factories had come to dominate the situation elsewhere. As early as 1811, there were said to be 4,000 hand looms in operation in Philadelphia upon fabrics of various sorts; and, while it is impossible to estimate with any approximation of exactness the number engaged upon carpets, possibly, as Kendrick says, there was "a goodly proportion" thus employed.[2] References to this type of operation appear from time to time in subsequent years, as in Benton and Barry's survey of the wool manufacture, made in 1836;[3] while as late as 1860 we find published a most complete description of the system as it existed in 1857 — a system which probably had changed little from

---

[1] R. M. Tryon, *Household Manufactures in the United States: 1640–1860* (1917), p. 216.

[2] J. R. Kendrick, *Annual Report* of the Secretary of Internal Affairs for Pennsylvania (1889), pt. iii, p. D2.

The report by the fragmentary *Census* of 1810 of a production of 9,034 yards of carpeting and coverlets suggests a fairly important industry in that area. See *A Statement of the Arts and Manufactures of the United States* (1810), pt. iii, reprinted in the "Digest of Manufactures" in *State Papers on Finance*, vol. ii, p. 691. See also *Niles' Weekly Register*, vol. vi (1814), p. 324.

[3] C. Benton and S. F. Barry, *A Statistical View of the Number of Sheep and the American Wool Manufacture* (1837), p. 121: "There are also many weavers in and about the city of Philadelphia who operate looms by hand, in the manufacture of jeans, carpets and other goods of which wool is a component."

earlier decades.[1] Work was "distributed among a large number of weavers" who were dependent upon the "manufacturers" for directing the industry. The "individual manufacturers," who numbered about a hundred, furnished employment to at least 1,500 hand-loom weavers. Some of these producers operated on a distinctly large scale, the most important being reported as keeping 150 looms busy; but obviously, with only 1,500 looms in the aggregate, many others must have had scarcely 10 weavers looking to them for direction. Seemingly, the relationship between employer and workers was that common in the "putting-out" system. The weavers owned their looms and tackle, and the employer furnished the material although at times the workers seem to have taken over the purchase of raw materials for themselves. This arrangement is indicated, at least, with regard to the production of the lowest quality of goods — rag and list carpets — in which a difference in compensation was made depending on whether or not the weavers supplied their own chain or warp.

The size of the individual weaving shop also varied. Perhaps the typical shop contained a single loom — or at most two. This is stated to have been the case frequently in the "low" end of the business; but many weavers both here and in the higher sections did set up additional apparatus. In the rag and list branch, the number of looms per shop is specifically said to have run as high as eight, although "rarely" to have exceeded that figure. If, as was not improbably the case, such establishments in the more respectable section of the industry contained ten or a dozen, sometimes even fifteen or twenty looms, we find a rather odd arrangement — neither falling within the simpler variety of handicraft system proper, nor yet, be-

[1] E. T. Freedley, *Philadelphia and its Manufactures: 1857* (1860), p. 239.

cause of the unusual size of the shops, conforming to the customarily accepted notion of the "putting-out" system. Otherwise, to be sure, the indicia of the "domestic" system appear: the superintendence of the work by the "individual manufacturer;" his complete control of marketing the product; the payment of work by the piece; and the existence under the immediate eye of the producer of a central shop where the yarns were prepared for distribution to the weavers.[1]

Prior to the domination of the domestic market by factory-made goods, therefore, there were two chief sources of supply. In the northern part of the country, household manufacture was the general rule, broken only here and there by the existence of a more advanced industrial form; while in Philadelphia there had developed a sort of putting-out system, which by its organization and scope of operations appears to have been producing for a market much larger than the district itself. Possibly carpets of Philadelphia manufacture were sent both north and south, especially into the growing coastal cities; and perhaps this development in the first decades of the nineteenth century gave encouragement to those enterprising men who sought to replace foreign importations with domestic production carried through on a scale never before contemplated.

As in the case of cotton or wool, the point at which the manufacture of carpets succeeded in attaining the factory basis is somewhat dubious. Dallas remarked in 1816 that carpets "have not been the objects of American capital,

---

[1] As regards the central shops, it may be noted that Freedley speaks in that year (1859) of the employment of 1,000 winders, dyers, warpers, etc., "in addition to the weavers" (*ibid.*, p. 239).

This organization is similarly described by Kendrick at a much later date: "Procuring his yarns dyed and ready for weaving, he [the weaver] would begin on a roll of carpet and in a few days deliver it to the central factory fully finished and ready for market" (Kendrick, *op. cit.*, p. D5).

industry, and enterprise, to any important degree;"[1] yet at an early period individuals are mentioned as connected with the production of carpeting — a fact that seems to indicate the existence of sizable establishments under their control. It is alleged, for example, that one William Calverly made carpets in Philadelphia as early as 1775. It was stated, in fact, that he made the first carpets ever manufactured in the United States.[2] Although such hardly could have been the case, perhaps the reference implies the earliest shop devoted solely to the production of carpeting, or the initial manufacture of a type of fabric — possibly ingrain — different from the rag rugs or yarn carpets theretofore known in the American industry. In view, however, of the subsequent form of development in the Philadelphia district, it seems probable that Calverly's establishment was merely an early instance of a handicraft shop.

Whatever may have been the character or size of Calverly's enterprise, the manufactory of one William P. Sprague, which was set up in 1791, was hailed anew as the beginning of a Philadelphia carpet industry; and, in this case, the product made is mentioned — Turkish and Axminster carpets.[3] Sprague's plant, however, was probably but a small shop similar to those which, by 1811, could boast an aggregate of 4,000 hand looms. Subsequently, other individual manufactories appeared elsewhere. Henry Wansey, a Wiltshire clothier, who travelled in this country in 1794, wrote of "a cotton and carpet manufactory at

[1] A. J. Dallas, "Report of the Treasury Department on Tariff Duties on Imports," February 12, 1816, in *State Papers on Finance*, vol. iii, p. 90.

[2] J. J. MacFarlane, *Manufacturing in Philadelphia: 1683-1912* (1912), p. 22; Bagnall, *op. cit.*, p. 169.

[3] J. L. Bishop, *A History of American Manufactures from 1608 to 1860* (3rd ed., 1868), vol. ii, p. 31; A. S. Bolles, *Industrial History of the United States* (1879), p. 394.

Worcester (Massachusetts), carried on by Peter Stowell & Company with a good capital."[1] Peter and Ebenezar Stowell were said to make "fine carpets," and at one time had in operation six looms "of their own invention and construction."[2] Establishments outside the Philadelphia area must have been few in number, however, so rarely does one find mention of individual names connected with the manufacture of carpets in the days before 1820. In no case, moreover, within or without the Philadelphia district, is the evidence clear of an establishment in the factory form.

The decade of 1825–35 was the heyday of the American carpet industry, and it marks the period when the factory form of organization became dominant. In the period before 1825, to be sure, instances are noted of the erection of new mills — mills which were quite obviously factories. In Philadelphia by 1810, Isaac Macaulay had bought an interest in John Dorsey's floor oil-cloth factory — established in 1807 — and prepared "to carry on the manufacture on a more extensive scale." In 1815 he removed to the old Hamilton mansion on Bush Hill and established his factory there. His success in making floor oil-cloths was so great that he was induced to undertake the manufacture of carpets; workmen were imported from Kidderminster, England, and the carpet looms set up in the old Hamilton

---

[1] H. Wansey, *The Journal of an Excursion to the United States of North America in the Summer of 1794* (1796), p. 48.

[2] W. Lincoln, *History of Worcester* (1837), pp. 321–322.

C. G. Washburn states that Cornelius Stowell, the father of Peter and Ebenezar, began as early as 1790 to manufacture woolen goods, print calicoes, and dye and dress woolen goods; and that among the products was the item of carpets. Apparently, carpet production was a small factor until 1804, when it did assume importance.

It may be noted in passing that goods of their production are said to have been the first carpets used in the State House in Boston. See C. G. Washburn, "Manufacturing and Mechanical Industries of Worcester" in *History of Worcester County, Massachusetts*, D. H. Hurd, ed. (1889), vol. ii, p. 1596.

mansion. New buildings had been put up which "extended as far north on Schuylkill Fifth St. as Morris St.," and "here Macaulay spun his own yarn for carpets." In 1821, he made the "ingrain carpetings for the State Capitol at Harrisburg." It is said also "that in this establishment were woven the first Brussels carpets made in the United States."[1] And now we begin to find a number of factories appearing in States farther north. In New York, John and Nicholas Haight set up a manufacture of mixed cotton-warp and woolen-weft carpets by which they were said in 1821 to employ "several hundred persons."[2] In 1824, mills were erected at Great Falls, New Hampshire, in which carpeting and certain woolen cloths were made; while mills producing nothing but carpets appeared at about the same date in Thompsonville, Connecticut; Medway, Massachusetts; and Jersey City, New Jersey. The last, devoted solely to ingrain carpeting, was alleged in 1827 to employ 100 hands in weaving alone, while spinning and preparing of the yarn — really in a separate establishment at Little Falls — employed yet another hundred persons.[3]

The years 1827 through 1831, however, stand out as exceptional even in a period when carpet manufactories were rising in places as distant as Gorham, Maine, and Wheeling, West Virginia. These four or five years saw launched enterprises which, under favorable auspices, survived the competition of subsequent decades, and from which may be traced in an unbroken line concerns important or predominant in the present American industry. These were the Tariff Manufacturing Company, at Sims-

[1] Scharf and Westcott, *op. cit.*, vol. iii, pp. 2231–2235; P. A. Hall, *The Rug and Carpet Industry of Philadelphia* (1917), p. 1; *Niles' Weekly Register*, vol. xxi (1821), pp. 148 and 288; vol. xlii (1832), p. 91.

[2] *Ibid.*, vol. xxi (1821), p. 213.

[3] *Ibid.*, vol. xxx (1826), p. 282; vol. xxxiii (1827), p. 208.

bury, Connecticut; the Hartford Manufacturing Company, which was established at Thompsonville, Connecticut; and the Lowell Manufacturing Company at Lowell, Massachusetts.[1] Of these the Tariff and Hartford concerns have since become amalgamated with other similar units to form the Bigelow-Sanford Company of today; while the Lowell Manufacturing Company constituted an important integral part in the formation of the present Roxbury Carpet Company. Among the items particularly noteworthy with regard to these mills is the scale upon which they were begun. The Tariff plant, launched in 1827 and backed by H. K. Knight & Company, drygoods merchants of New York City, had acquired by 1832 a capital of $123,000 and a working staff of 136 persons. The Hartford Manufactory, organized in 1828 by Orrin Thompson of the firm of Andrews, Thompson & Company — also a distributing agency in New York City — claimed by 1833 a capital of $215,000 and a staff of 100 employees. The plant was started with 50 hand looms devoted to two-ply ingrains, and by 1833 had added a new building for the production of three-ply fabrics.[2] Greatest, however, was the Lowell concern which, incorporated in 1828 for cotton manufacture, bought the plant of the Medway enterprise, mentioned above, and organized production on a scale undreamed of a few years before.[3] In 1832, accord-

[1] There is considerable confusion even in contemporary accounts as to the names of these establishments. The "Tariff Manufacturing Company," established at Simsbury, was often called the "Simsbury Company," whereas later, when the town of Tariffville was set up, the firm was sometimes spoken of as the "Tariffville Company." The same is true for the "Hartford Manufactory." Located in a part of Enfield which later became Thompsonville, it is frequently referred to by one or the other of these names. More confusion occurs later in 1854, when the two companies, the Tariff and Hartford — now owned by the same group of men — were re-organized under a new charter and called the "Hartford Carpet Company."

[2] J. R. Commons, ed., *Documentary History of American Industrial Society* (1910), vol. iv, Suppl., pp. 17–21.

[3] C. Cowley, *Handbook of Business in Lowell* (1856), p. 86.

ing to McLane's Report of that year, the Lowell Company was turning out 110,000 yards of ingrain and Brussels carpeting and tufted rugs, and providing work in this production for 153 employees — men, women, and boys.[1]

The erection of these three large mills would be startling enough for an industry so young, but it appears that they were only the leaders in a broad development. One can list a dozen concerns of substantial size which made their bow in the years around 1830. Among them would be included the plant of Andrew & William McCallum — emigrants from Scotland — who began the manufacture of carpets in Philadelphia in 1831 — starting an enterprise which for fifty or seventy-five years had an important place in the Philadelphia industry. Likewise, there were the mills at New Haven, Connecticut; Martinsburg, Virginia; Baltimore, Maryland; Steubenville, Ohio; Framingham, Massachusetts; and three in Columbia County, New York.[2] Subsequently, the factories became too numerous to mention.

The result of such a rapid expansion is evident in censuses of the wool manufacture — Pitkin's in 1834, Benton and Barry's in 1836, and Graham's in 1845. The two former reported 18 to 20 factories which were interested in

---

[1] By 1845 this last mill possessed 50 power and 40 hand looms and was manufacturing 7,000 yards of carpeting per week, or something like 360,000 yards per annum (H. A. Miles, *Lowell as It Was and as It Is*, 1845, p. 51).

[2] Other mills might be reported for the following localities: Catskill and Rochester, New York; Norwich, Connecticut; Cumberland and Huntingdon Counties, Pennsylvania; Bergen City, New Jersey; and Wrentham, Massachusetts.

Sources of data upon the establishments among these latter mills include Bishop, *op. cit.*, vol. ii, pp. 318, 339; J. H. Temple, *History of Framingham* (1887), p. 16; *Census* of 1860, vol. iii, pp. liv–lix; Scharf and Westcott, *op. cit.*, vol. iii, p. 2309; Hazard, *op. cit.*, vol. iv (1829), p. 93, and vol. v (1830), p. 192; *Niles' Weekly Register*, vol. xxxvii (1829), p. 8; S. Fay, "Carpet Weaving and the Lowell Manufacturing Company" in the *Bulletin of the National Association of Wool Manufacturers*, vol. v (1874–75), pp. 17–18; and McLane, *op. cit.*, vol. i, pp. 16, 338, 386, 980, 1039, and vol. ii, pp. 171, 427.

whole or in part in carpet production; while Graham listed 56 mills in half of which the product was entirely carpets, rugs, and carpeting, and in half of which carpet production was a part of the regular output.[1] Of the capacity of the carpet manufactories, variously measured by these writers, Pitkin reported that there were "at least" 511 carpet looms in the 18 to 20 factories just mentioned — and now we know these data to be seriously defective; Benton and Barry gave 61 sets of carding machinery in 18 carpet mills; while Graham reported 135 sets of cards in the 56 mills producing carpets.[2]

Among the factors which may be offered as explaining this rather extraordinary growth, two seem to be particularly significant — aid from the manufacture of wool cloths, and the influence of rising tariffs. To be sure, the increasing prosperity of the country was a necessary precedent. Possibly also, the success of the handicraft shops in the Philadelphia area lent encouragement; but the two forces just mentioned claim particular attention.[3]

[1] T. Pitkin, *A Statistical View of the Commerce of the United States of America* (1835), p. 492; Benton and Barry, *op. cit.*, pp. 111-124; *Statistics of the Woolen Manufactories in the United States*, W. H. Graham, ed. (1846), *passim*; and S. N. D. North, "Century of American Wool Manufacture" in the *Bulletin of the National Association of Wool Manufacturers*, vol. xxiv (1894), pp. 331-332.

[2] The measurement, "sets of cards," was one commonly employed in the woolen-cloth manufacture to indicate the size of an establishment. There was in the earlier days a more or less direct ratio between the number of carding units and the spinning or weaving capacity of the mill. In so far as the carpet mills spun their own yarns, and did not employ cotton, jute, or linen yarns, the same basis of comparison would be fairly satisfactory for this industry. More recently, the capacity of carpet mills has been wholly estimated by the number of looms, since many carpet mills do not now spin their own wool yarns, nor is their consumption of materials so largely now confined to yarns of this type as was true 75 or 100 years ago.

[3] The situation with respect to raw materials gave the industry at least no support. The wools employed for carpeting, then as now, came chiefly from abroad. In some of the tariffs of this period a duty was laid upon coarse wools, and so would have constituted an impediment to the growth of the carpet manufacture. However, the rates on such wools were low; and obviously the industry overcame such handicaps as these rates contributed.

Aid from the wool-cloth manufacture was twofold. First should be indicated the evolution of machinery for the preparation of woolen yarns. The machinery employed for this purpose in the carpet industry was borrowed from the wool-cloth manufacture where it was first utilized. For the production of carpet yarns, the machinery did not differ from that required for making yarns for broadcloths or cassimeres. Indeed, carpet yarns were of simpler manufacture because of their coarse character. Therefore, especially in the case of carding machines and spinning apparatus, there was already developed a mechanical equipment for these processes which served as a point of departure for factory growth in carpet production.

However, it is worth noting that the rise of the factory in the carpet industry took place without aid from technological advance in carpet machinery proper, that is, on the weaving end. There had been developed no loom or finishing apparatus which differed from that available to the household or handicraft producers. The carpet looms of the period were exceedingly simple devices, if compared with the elaborate equipment to be found in the modern mill. They were essentially of the plain-loom type on which all wool fabrics could be produced, except that construction had to be heavier to care for the coarser yarns employed and the weight of the manufactured product. "The setting beam, with which the weavers packed the fulling yarns one against the other, after each passage of the shuttle, was a heavy 4-inch square piece of pine, which greatly taxed the arms of the operative. The treadle, too, kept one foot and leg in constant operation." [1] The work was so exacting of physical energy, the posture was so hard, and the whole body of the operator so fully engaged that women were poorly suited to the occupation, and we

[1] Kendrick, *op. cit.*, pp. D10–11.

find little or no mention of them as carpet weavers until power machinery was introduced. It was upon this treadle type of loom that ingrain and Venetian carpetings were produced, while Brussels carpeting apparently was manufactured upon a similar loom differing only in minor details. In the Brussels production some provision had to be made for raising the loops of the pile — a technical requirement met through the insertion by hand of wires over which the threads were drawn, and which were withdrawn after shots of filling yarn had bound the loops into place.

The production of ingrain carpeting involved the use of some device for introducing the pattern into the fabric. Knowledge of the Jacquard mechanism spread from abroad to this country in the early 1820's, and was almost universally applied in the fabrication of ingrain carpets. The only variant method was a loom in which the control of the warp yarns was secured by means of a cylinder studded with pegs by which heddles were operated to separate the warp threads into suitable divisions. The device is first mentioned in connection with the American industry at approximately 1830 and, like the Jacquard apparatus, was used apparently only in connection with hand looms.

To be sure, attempts were instituted to employ power in connection with carpet weaving. In 1837 there was exhibited at the Franklin Institute some ingrain carpeting woven on a power loom invented by Alfred Jenks of Bridesburg, Pennsylvania. This early loom is said to have had sixteen shuttle boxes, eight on each side, and in numerous regards to have anticipated the use of power as applied to weaving ingrains at a later date. About 1840, Nicholas Haight, manager of the New Jersey and Little Falls Carpet Companies, is reported to have invented an ingrain power loom; and in 1842, one Alexander Calderhead of

Philadelphia exhibited his power carpet loom at the aforesaid Franklin Institute. None of these inventions, however, seems to have been particularly successful in actual
use, nor to have made any significant impression on the
weaving practice of the time. Although a few of Jenks'
looms were bought by the McCallums of the Glen Echo
Mills in Philadelphia, apparently their utilization did not
prove profitable, as the use of power appears not to have
been adopted by other mills.[1]

In short, carpet weaving in a factory form was developed on the basis of hand-driven devices, and remained
dependent upon hand technique even when the industry
had developed to a sizable scale. Thus the Hartford Manufacturing Company was launched in 1828 with fifty hand
looms to which another fifty were added in 1841; and the
Lowell Manufacturing Company had hand looms alone
when it was producing yearly 140,000 yards of carpeting.
Power-driven apparatus in weaving came only with the
Bigelow inventions of the 'forties and 'fifties — twenty
years after the carpet manufacture had attained factory
organization.

The manufacture of carpeting in conjunction with other
wool products was another source of strength to the carpet
industry. The establishment of the Stowells in Worcester began in connection with other work; the Tariffville
Manufacturing Company made a substantial quantity of
linseys; while the two larger mills in Pennsylvania — an
area always known for its mixed manufactures — were
listed by Graham as manufacturing respectively "carpets,
rugs, and sattinets" and "flannels, also carpeting."[2]
Occasionally, too, one finds mention of early factories that

---

[1] *Ibid.*, pp. D12 and D14; *Journal of the Franklin Institute*, 3rd ser., vol. iv
(1842), pp. 103–104, and vol. vii (1844), pp. 110–111.

[2] Graham, *op. cit.*, pp. 41 and 147.

may have produced for "custom." Thus, the *Census* of 1820 listed a factory large enough to use 8,000 to 10,000 pounds of wool and operate eight looms — with the comment that "the work is done principally for customers." [1] Yet it is to be remarked that many of the new carpet mills were devoted solely to the manufacture of floor coverings with which they supplied a wide market. Among these were the Hartford Company, the Gorham Company in Maine, and the Framingham plant.

The relative suddenness of expansion in the American carpet manufacture cannot be attributed to the culmination of the broken commercial relations with England in 1807–15, which played an important rôle in the rise of both the cotton-cloth and wool-cloth sections of the textile industry. The distance of the United States from foreign sources of carpet supplies, combined with the relatively heavy character of the article, to be sure, must be regarded always to have given a greater degree of protection than was enjoyed by other portions of the textile trades. Perhaps under any circumstances it would have suffered less competitive inferiority than the latter. Nevertheless, the enhancement of formal protection in the shape of tariff duties must be posited as contributing appreciably to the launching of carpet production in the 'twenties and 'thirties. Tariff duties on carpets had risen from 5 per cent ad valorem in 1789 to 15 per cent in 1794 — at which figure the tax remained for thirty years. [2] With the tariff of 1824 came a change to specific duties — a form of duty which would be bound to have increasing benefit to the

---

[1] *Census* of 1820: *Digest of the Accounts of the Manufacturing Establishment in the United States and their Manufactures* (Washington, D. C.: Gales & Seaton, 1823), p. 12.

[2] The tariff of 1816 carried a duty of 25 per cent ad valorem upon all woolen goods except certain items including "woolen rugs" — the latter probably being subject to a catch-all clause imposing a duty of 15 per cent.

domestic industry if the latter could lower its costs. This change of 1824 was followed by a further advance four years later; and the new level was largely sustained in the tariff act of 1832.[1] Thus for nearly a decade the domestic carpet manufacture enjoyed a new and considerable protection against foreign importation. Hezekiah Niles, for one, regarded the carpet manufacture as "being established" in 1828 by virtue of the tariff just enacted,[2] and surely the coincidence of this higher protection with the enlarging domestic output of 1824–32 was not mere chance.

All in all, whatever the underlying causes of the sudden expansion in production, unquestionably the industry was thriving in these decades. In 1791, Hamilton had been able to say little for the carpet manufacture except that some "beginnings had been made" in this fabrication. He suggested an additional duty of 2½ per cent on carpets and carpeting as a means of securing money for premiums on wool growing, and stated that this was an increase "to which the nature of the article suggests no objection and which may at the same time furnish a motive the more to the fabrication of them at home."[3] As late as 1816, Dallas placed carpets and carpeting in his third class of industries — "those so slightly cultivated [in

---

[1] Rates in the tariff of 1824 ran from 50 cents per square yard for Brussels, Turkey, and Wilton carpets to 25 cents per square yard on Venetian, "ingrin," and mixed carpets. These were increased in 1828 to 70 cents per square yard for the former, while Venetian and "ingrain" paid 40 cents per square yard, and mixed fabrics 32 cents per square yard. Corresponding rates in the tariff of 1832 were 63 cents, 35 cents, and 25 cents ad valorem. The average value of importations in the first class was $1.46 per square yard in 1832, and in the second 67½ cents. Accordingly, such duties provided a protection of something like 45 per cent ad valorem for Brussels production and even more for the important ingrain and Venetian manufactures.

[2] *Niles' Weekly Register*, vol. xxxiv (1828), p. 410: "The superior kind of carpets," he said, "are about to be manufactured at sundry places, especially at Medway and Lowell." See also the *Census* of 1860, vol. iii, pp. lv–lvi.

[3] Hamilton's Report in F. W. Taussig, *State Papers and the Tariff* (1893), p. 99.

the United States] as to leave the demand of the country wholly, or almost wholly, dependent on foreign sources of supply." [1] Yet fifteen years later, despite no striking advances in technique and no introduction of new types of carpeting, the domestic industry had expanded several-fold and acquired what seems to have been a firm footing on the factory basis of production. [2]

Noteworthy in this development was the lack of intermediate industrial stages — unless one takes the Philadelphia experience to be applicable to the country as a whole. Generally speaking, the production of carpeting was restricted to household manufacture until the factory arose to turn out different and superior types for domestic consumption. Although in a few cases — particularly in the Philadelphia area — a number of mills may have grown from shops concerned at one time with handicraft production or with supervision over scattered hand-loom weavers, the majority of the mills, and especially those which later came to dominate the industry, were launched at once on a factory basis. The way of their development was prepared by no intermediate form of organization such as that which occurred in the rise of factories for wool cloth proper, or in certain other products such as boots and shoes. When the time came for carpets to be manufactured on any considerable scale, their production commonly took on at once the factory form of organization.

Likewise, it is notable that the trend of factory growth early was strong towards large-scale operation — prophetic of the trend in the carpet industry since that time.

---

[1] Dallas, *op. cit.*, vol. iii, pp. 89–90. See also *Niles' Weekly Register*, vol. ix (1816), p. 441.

[2] If space permitted, evidence could be presented to show that already by the 'thirties the American mills had been able to drive from the domestic market foreign goods of the low and medium grades, especially two-ply ingrain, and to make some beginning in the production of finer fabrics, e. g., Brussels carpeting.

Small mills there were, of course, but almost from the start the dominant elements in domestic manufacture were the establishments like the Hartford, Tariff, and Lowell mills which were launched on a strikingly large-scale basis. The Tariff mill, it will be recalled, in 1832 had a working staff of 136 persons, the Hartford one of 157, and the Lowell a group of 153 employees. By 1836 the Poughkeepsie carpet factory could boast 70 men employees, and there were several which fell in the intermediate class of 40 to 60 hands. With such a running start, and with the subsequent development of steadily widening consumption and of ever more complicated and costly weaving apparatus, it is no wonder that a hundred years later we find carpet mills rivalling in size the largest units in the whole textile industry and a domestic carpet manufacture dominated by two or three extraordinarily large and powerful concerns.

PIONEER BANKING IN ALABAMA

WILLIAM O. SCROGGS

When Alabama was admitted into the Union in 1819, a great migration to this region from the older seaboard States had been in progress for a decade. A territorial census, palpably incomplete, was taken in 1818 and indicated a population of 67,594. The more carefully taken federal census of 1820 gave the number of inhabitants as 127,901. Between 1820 and 1830 the population increased 141 per cent, and from 1830 to 1840 it increased 61 per cent.

The inrush of settlers just as the machinery of the State government began to operate had a far-reaching effect on the development of the State's banking system. The rapidly increasing demand for goods of all sorts and the inadequate facilities for their transportation into the interior caused prices to rise sharply and stimulated speculation. In 1817 flour sold for $20 a barrel at the chief points of distribution.[1] Public lands were also sold at fancy prices, and on credit. The federal government offered some of the choicest tracts for sale to the highest bidders, and the fertility of the soil, together with the high price of cotton, gave these lands great value in the eyes of the purchasers. The prices of good river lowlands ranged from $160 to $170 per acre.[2]

Next to lands, the largest investment was in slaves. It is to be noted that while the white population increased 123 per cent from 1820 to 1830, the negro population in this

---

[1] *Niles' Weekly Register*, vol. xii (1817), p. 341.
[2] *Ibid.*, vol. xiii (1817–18), p. 16; vol. xiv (1818), p. 8.

decade increased 182 per cent. In 1830, 46 per cent of the population was negro. The white population was almost wholly native-born and predominantly of Scotch-Irish descent. It consisted largely of immigrants from Georgia, the Carolinas, Tennessee, and Virginia, who had left the exhausted cotton and tobacco lands of the old estates for the virgin soil of the Southwest.

In 1840, a generation after the beginning of the settlement of the State, 94 per cent of the inhabitants engaged in gainful occupations were following agriculture, 4 per cent were following trades and manufactures, and the remaining 2 per cent were about equally divided between commerce and the professions. The population, therefore, was rural. In 1830 Mobile, the largest town in the State, had only 3,190 inhabitants.

The main business of the people was the raising of cotton with slave labor. In 1821 the State produced 20,000 bales; in 1826, 40,000 bales; in 1834, 170,000 bales, and in that year its output was equalled only by that of Mississippi. The cultivation of cotton required capital; but of this the newly arrived settlers had very little, and such as they had was employed at first mainly in the purchase of land. Slaves and plantation supplies had to be obtained on time payments or with borrowed funds, and most of the planters were in debt. The available amount of private credit was wholly inadequate for the development of the country on a scale commensurate with the growth of its population. Under such conditions the use of the credit of the State came in due course to be regarded as a proper method of supplementing the credit supplied by individuals. This brief description of economic and social conditions in the State during the early years of its history will make it easier to understand how an individualistic frontier population came to embark on such a socialistic venture as a banking system under State ownership and management.

The first bank to be chartered within the present limits of Alabama was incorporated on December 11, 1816 by the legislature of the Mississippi Territory.[1] This was the Planters' and Mechanics' Bank, of Huntsville. It is significant that the charter authorized the territorial government to subscribe to 500 shares of the capital stock. Although these shares were never taken by the Territory, this provision in the charter reveals an inclination toward a policy of government banking which some years later was to have important effects on the finances of the State.

Several other provisions of the charter throw light on conditions in the frontier community. The stockholders were permitted to pay their subscriptions in installments — a clear indication of the scarcity of liquid capital. The voting power of the stockholders diminished as the number of shares they held increased. A holder of five shares or less was entitled to one vote for each share, while the holder of a hundred shares could cast only one-third of a vote per share. No stockholder, regardless of the number of his shares, was allowed more than a hundred votes, and no share would confer voting rights until held for three months.

Further efforts to insure a democratic management of the institution appear in regulations forbiddind directors to hold office for more than three years in succession and stipulating that not more than three-quarters of the directorate were to be in office for two successive years. The pioneer legislators seem to have had a real dread of a money power and a fear that the management of the bank might fall into the hands of a chosen few.

---

[1] At that time the present States of Alabama and Mississippi were united under a single territorial government.

With the inflow of settlers, the demand for banking facilities increased. On February 13, 1818, the territorial legislature incorporated the Tombeckbe Bank at Saint Stephens, which was then the seat of the government. The provisions of the charter were similar to those prescribed for the bank at Huntsville, but this time it was stipulated that two-fifths of the capital stock should be reserved for subscription by the Territory.[1]

On November 20, 1818 the Bank of Mobile was incorporated with an authorized capital of $500,000, one-fifth of which was to be reserved for the Territory.[2] The following day the legislature enacted a new law with regard to the sale of stock by the newly established banks at Huntsville and Saint Stephens. Not more than 5 shares were to be allotted to a purchaser at any one time, and his purchases during the first six days of the sale were restricted to 20 shares. The purpose was to give small investors a chance to obtain an interest in the banks before the wealthier citizens bought the shares in larger amounts. Even more drastic was the provision limiting profits from the sale of the stock to 10 per cent. The excess, if any, was to go to the local academies in the towns where the banks were situated. That the stock of one of these banks was in sufficient demand to command a premium is attested by the payment of $1,850 as excess profits to Green Academy by the bank at Huntsville.[3] If anyone became rich through his investment in the territorial banks, it would not be through legislative favoritism.

The Territory never took advantage of its opportunity to hold stock in any of the banks, as funds for this purpose

---

[1] *Acts Passed at the First Session of the First General Assembly of the Alabama Territory*, February 13, 1818.

[2] *Acts Passed at the Second Session of the First General Assembly of the Alabama Territory*, November 20, 1818.

[3] *Alabama Republican*, August 3, 1821.

were not available. On December 14, 1819 Alabama became a State, and the establishment of a State-owned bank soon became an important public question. The effects of the financial crisis of 1817 were still in evidence in the Southwest, and business was greatly hampered by a disordered currency. On June 16, 1820 the bank at Huntsville suspended specie payments, and this aroused great indignation and distrust of privately managed banks. There had also been a general suspension of specie payments by banks in Tennessee, whose notes had formed a large part of the circulating medium in northern Alabama. The State treasury at the same time refused to receive any but specie-basis bank notes in the payment of taxes, and this caused further hardship to many citizens.

The general distrust of private banks, combined with the urgent need of credit, led the people to look to the State to furnish what could not be obtained through private enterprise. It was clearly the intention of the framers of the constitution that the State should go into the business of banking, for that document provided that "one State bank may be established, with such number of branches as the general assembly may from time to time deem expedient." The constitution also stipulated that, if any private commercial banks were established, at least two-fifths of the capital should be reserved to the State, and that the State should have a voice in their management equal to its share of the bank's stock.

The legislature lost no time in incorporating, in 1820, the Bank of the State of Alabama, with an authorized capital of $2,000,000. The State was to supply two-fifths of the capital and private stockholders the rest, and the institution was to commence operations as soon as $100,000 of the capital had been paid in in specie. The minimum capital was never subscribed, and the plan came to naught.

Meantime, the monetary stringency became so acute that in 1821 the legislature authorized an issue of non-interest-bearing treasury notes in small denominations, ranging from 12½ to 75 cents. These were issued in payment of warrants drawn on the treasury, and were receivable by the State in the payment of all public dues. To support the credit of this issue, the governor was authorized to obtain a loan from any specie-paying bank in the State up to 50 per cent of the face value of the notes outstanding.[1]

This requirement of a bank loan as a "cover" for the notes served as a check upon possible inflation, and they circulated at par and brought needed relief to the treasury. By 1823 the improvement in the State's fiscal condition permitted their retirement, but the State had been brought nearer to a system of public banking as a result of this experience.

When the legislature convened in 1823 Governor Israel Pickens had a new plan for a State bank. He pointed out the improbability of obtaining sufficient capital for such a bank by relying on private subscriptions, as only a small portion of the authorized capital stock of any of the banks had ever been subscribed for. There was no disposable capital; the people of the State were indebted to the federal government for their lands to the amount of $5,000,000, and about one-fifth of this was being paid into the United States treasury every year. Fully half of the annual receipts for cotton were expended in the purchase of public lands, and a good part of the remainder went to purchase imported articles of consumption. Under such circumstances, therefore, only those could subscribe for new banking stock who had access to the vaults of the old banks, and the new bank would practically be owned by

[1] *Acts . . . of the State of Alabama . . . 1821*, p. 95.

one or more of the previously chartered institutions. It would be merely one of the old banks with a new name in a new place, "without additional capacity for doing good, and with the enlarged power and extended sphere for doing mischief."

We have an example [said the governor] of one institution purely and entirely *public*, both as respects *capital* and *direction*, continuing through years of war and peace in successful and creditable operation. The State bank of South Carolina is a source of great profit, dispensing almost entirely with the necessity of taxation, while it has given essential aid in useful internal improvements, and, which is still more important, furnishing at the same time a circulation regulated with a regard to no other than the general interest. It is a question worthy of inquiring how far this favorable example is susceptible of successful imitation.

The important problem was how to get funds for this venture. Governor Pickens called attention to the sixteenth sections granted to the townships for educational purposes. If the sale of these were competently conducted it would produce a fund of several millions, and this sum, if converted into banking capital, would under careful management give more regular and durable returns to the school fund and cause the townships less trouble than would the usual method of leasing.[1]

The legislature at once gave its attention to the establishment of a bank, and on December 20, 1823 the Bank of the State of Alabama was duly created. The faith and credit of the State were pledged for its support. The capital, to which no limit was set, was to consist entirely of public funds, as follows. (1) The money derived from the sale or rent of the lands granted to the State for a university. This institution was to receive in return for such funds State stock or certificates of indebtedness bearing interest at 6 per cent. (2) The money received from the

[1] Message, 1823.

"three per cent fund." [1] The dividends from this fund,
after its conversion into banking capital, were to be devoted to the building of roads and canals, the improvement
of rivers, or to the increase of its principal. (3) The proceeds of the 1,620 acres granted to the State for the establishment of its seat of government. The dividends from
this fund were to be applied to objects connected with the
seat of government, or devoted to increasing the principal.
(4) All moneys arising from the lease of the salt springs in
the State donated by the national government. (5) The
proceeds of all escheats to the State. (6) All other public
funds which the State might acquire, provided that their
investment was authorized by law. (7) State stock, with
interest not exceeding 6 per cent. All money in the treasury
at any time was pledged for the payment of the interest,
and the various special funds, except the university and
3 per cent funds, which were held in trust, were to be
pledged to secure the principal of the stock, and thus to
maintain the faith and credit of the State.

Such was the manner in which capital was to be obtained
for the new bank. The proceeds of the sales of the sixteenth sections were not included, as Governor Pickens
had recommended. These funds, however, were later converted into banking capital. The preamble of the act
stated that it was "highly important to provide for the
safe and profitable investment of such funds as may now
or hereafter be in the possession of the State, and to secure
to the community, as far as may be, the benefits of an extended and undepreciating currency."

The president and directors of the State bank were to be
chosen annually by a joint vote of both houses of the legislature, and were empowered to issue notes not under the

[1] Three per cent of the proceeds of the sale of public lands in the State by
the federal government, given to the State for internal improvements.

denomination of a dollar, which were to be receivable in the payment of public dues. The sums to be lent were to be apportioned among the counties of the State according to their representation in the general assembly, and the counties were to be notified of the amounts their citizens were entitled to borrow. If within sixty days the citizens of any county failed to apply for the whole amount to which they were entitled, the residue might be discounted to any citizens who applied, provided, of course, that they could give proper security. In short, the bank was to be conducted for the benefit of all the people. Any citizen with good security was to be accommodated, but the note he presented for discount was required to have the endorsement of two good names, and the bank officials were not allowed to endorse for one another.[1]

In 1825 the bank began operations at Cahawba, and the next year was removed to Tuscaloosa, the new capital of the State. There were many difficulties to contend with at first, owing to the wide circulation of the depreciated Tennessee currency, but the report to the legislature on November 24, 1826 showed that the bank was holding its own. There was no inflation of note issues. The amount of debts then due the bank was quite large; but, as one of the objects was to furnish the planters with credit, it is not surprising that it should have loaned over half a million dollars in such a short time. It was only doing the work expected of it.

Conditions in 1827 were not so satisfactory. The Tombeckbe Bank failed in May, and this prevented many citizens from taking advantage of a deduction which was then allowed by the federal government in payments for lands, and which expired in July. The federal land office rejected the paper of this bank, and it circulated elsewhere only at a

[1] *Acts ... of the State of Alabama ... 1823*, p. 1.

heavy discount. Besides this misfortune, the planters for two years had suffered from drought, raising only a fraction of their normal crops, and the price of cotton had fallen from about 21 cents in 1825 to 9½ cents in 1827. It was necessary, therefore, for the State bank to extend its accommodations to a point almost hazardous. There was an enormous increase of note issues. By the end of 1828, however, the circulation had been contracted within safe limits, and the indebtedness to the bank had been slightly decreased.

On January 12, 1828 a second issue of State stock to the amount of $100,000 was authorized in order to increase the capital of the bank and meet the necessities of the planters. Three days later the legislature authorized the sale of the sixteenth sections, the proceeds of which were to be converted into banking capital. The way in which the bank had been managed up to this time was encouraging the State to plunge in more heavily.

There is nothing to indicate reckless management until 1830, when the debts due the bank more than doubled those of the preceding year, increasing from $614,157 to $1,249,843. In the meantime the profits of the bank were being used to increase the bank stock, and in this way considerable sums were being added to the principal of the trust funds. The interest on the State loan was readily paid by the bank, and when the payment of the first $100,000 of stock became due on October 1, 1834 it was promptly made.[1]

In 1832 the establishment of branches of the State bank began, and, as each new branch was authorized by the legislature, an additional issue of State bonds was sanctioned to provide the new institution with capital. The

---

[1] *Southern Advocate*, November 11, 1834; *Acts . . . of the State of Alabama . . . 1834*, no. 62.

dates on which issues were authorized, and the amounts specified, are as follows:

December 20, 1823, to increase capital of State bank		$100,000
January 12, 1828, to increase capital of State bank		100,000
" 21, 1832, to establish a branch at Montgomery ...		300,000
November 16, 1832, to establish a branch at Decatur		1,000,000
December 4, 1832, to establish a branch at Mobile		2,000,000
" 12, 1832, to increase capital at Montgomery		500,000
January 10, 1835, to increase capital at Decatur		500,000
" 10, 1835, for stock in Bank of Mobile		740,000
" 10, 1835, to establish a branch at Huntsville		500,000
" 9, 1836, to increase capital at Huntsville		500,000
" 9, 1836, to increase capital at Mobile		1,000,000
" 9, 1836, to increase capital at Tuscaloosa		500,000
" 9, 1836, to increase capital at Montgomery		700,000
June 30, 1837, to enable the banks to resume specie payments		5,000,000
December 23, 1837, further to assist banks		2,500,000
Total amount authorized to December 23, 1837		$15,940,000
Total amount of bonds sold (1823–40)		$10,959,556

The greater portion of the bonds were sold in London and New York, but a small number were disposed of in New Orleans. The rate of interest varied from 5 to 6 per cent. In addition to borrowing for its own banks, the State subscribed for stock in the local bank at Mobile to the amount of $600,000, as it was entitled to do under the constitution.

The growth of the bonded debt as a result of these investments is shown by the following figures:[1]

1824	$100,000	1836	$6,318,000
1830	200,000	1837	7,378,000
1832	500,000	1838	10,259,000
1833	4,000,000	1839	10,859,000

[1] The debt in 1839 represents the total amount of bonds sold for banking purposes, less $100,000 in bonds redeemed in 1828. Most writers on this subject have fallen into the error of supposing that all bonds authorized by the legislature were actually sold, and have stated the debt in round numbers at fifteen millions. See, for example, Knox, *History of Banking*, p. 596.

For the first six years of its history the State bank was conservatively managed, but as the speculative fever began to pervade the Southwest in the 'thirties, caution was thrown to the winds. Every section of the State now had its branch bank, and this was run almost independently of the main bank at Tuscaloosa. As the credit of American States was good and Alabama could borrow easily, her banks seemed to have unlimited means, and the discounting of notes proceeded merrily. Then came the evils of an inflated circulation. A fair idea of the reckless issue of paper money may be obtained from the following table, showing the relative amount of specie to circulation and deposits for the period from January 1, 1835 to May 1, 1837:

State bank	1 to 5.19
Mobile branch	1 to 7.03
Montgomery branch	1 to 9.43
Decatur branch	1 to 9.49
Huntsville branch	1 to 6.76

In Alabama the generally unfavorable conditions of the time were aggravated by the undue influence of the legislature in the management of the bank. As already stated, the president and directors were chosen annually by the legislators, and the baneful influence of politics early became apparent. The actual working of the system was somewhat as follows. A candidate for the legislature would promise to get accommodations at the bank for his constituents if elected. After his election he would be beset by aspirants for directorships in the banks and would make an agreement with them whereby they would get his vote provided that they would afford his political clientèle ample opportunities to obtain loans from the bank. If the directors refused to accommodate his constituency, they would lose his vote at the next election. Thus the legislator, the bank director, and the voter each got what he desired; but the banks suffered.

Strange to say, although the director received no compensation for his services, there was always a lively scramble for the office, and the legislature was besieged at every session by whole troops of candidates. There were seventy-two directors to be elected for five banks, and it was utterly impossible for a member of the legislature to have a personal knowledge of the host of candidates to select from, and if he had that knowledge, he was virtually compelled to log-roll in every election. Every county was anxious to have one or more directors in some of the banks, and to effect this the delegation from that county had to swap votes enough to elect their directors.[1]

In his *Reminiscences of Public Men in Alabama*, William C. Garrett relates an amusing incident connected with the election of bank directors. In the midst of a session a legislator died, and his colleagues, as a mark of respect to his memory, wore a band of crêpe on their coat sleeves. As this became the distinguishing mark of a member of the legislature, everyone wearing the badge became a recipient of attentions from the candidates for directorships. A clever stranger, who happened to be in Tuscaloosa at the time, placed the usual sign of mourning on his arm and for several days was elaborately fêted by the candidates, until the imposture was discovered.

As to the directors themselves, each was dependent on the rest for the favors he desired to obtain from the bank; and, in deciding on the paper presented by any of his colleagues, he virtually passed on his own. Not only was political favoritism shown in making loans, but notes were often discounted in the most careless fashion imaginable.

[1] *North Alabamian*, February 9, 1838.

An extreme instance of carelessness was discovered in 1841 by the commissioners appointed to examine the branch at Montgomery. One note for $750 was signed by William S. Crenshaw and endorsed by James and Joseph Crenshaw. The signer, it was discovered, was ten years old and lived in Georgia. Joseph Crenshaw, one of the endorsers, was his father and had no property, while the other endorser, James Crenshaw, was a brother of the signer and lacked a few months of being four years old. A second note for the same amount was signed, presumably, by the four-year-old son, James, and endorsed by his father and ten-year-old brother. A third note, also for $750, was signed by the father and endorsed by the two minor sons; and all three notes had been recommended for discount by a member of the legislature.[1]

In spite of loose management the banks continued to declare dividends until 1842, but it is impossible to state whether these always represented genuine profits. On January 10, 1835 the State bank and branches were ordered to create a sinking fund from their profits after paying current expenses and the interest on the bonds. In 1836 direct taxation for State purposes was abolished, and the legislature ordered that the expenses of the State government should be paid from the bank's profits. The dream of the bank's founders seemed now to be on the point of realization. The law-makers deemed it entirely practi-

[1] *Report* of the Bank Commissioners, 1841. The minute book of the Montgomery branch throws much light on the way in which the directors conducted their business. On February 18, 1835, for example, at a meeting of the board it was resolved that notes offered for discount should be taken up in the order in which they were entered on the offering book, allowing to each director the privilege of calling up two cases out of order. Before the meeting was over, however, it was resolved that the notes of directors, ex-directors, members, and ex-members of the legislature should be called up at any time upon the motion of a member of the board. (Ms., State Department of Archives and History, Montgomery, Minute Book, Branch of the Bank of the State of Alabama at Montgomery.)

cable that the institution should discharge the interest and principal of the State debt and at the same time free the people from the burdens of taxation. Unfortunately, while Alabama was making these preparations for fair weather a hurricane was approaching. This was the Panic of 1837.

In the autumn of 1836 the discounting of notes that had been proceeding so rapidly received a check, and the State bank and its branches were making frantic efforts to get specie. On September 9, 1836 the cashier of the Montgomery branch wrote to a New York banker: "We are out of circulation and out of funds in every direction but New York. Money is said to be unusually scarce in Mobile and New Orleans, and I much fear that *all* will not be able to stand it."[1] This was a sign of the approaching storm. Six months later it struck in full force. Each of the State-owned banks in April, 1837 found it necessary to cease redeeming the notes of its sister institutions and was hard put to it to redeem its own. The banks continued, however, to receive each other's notes on deposit and to return to the depositors notes of the description they had placed in the bank.[2] On May 8, 1837 President Whiting, of the Montgomery branch, wrote: "The demand on us for specie has continued without abatement for a week, until the last two days. I am afraid it will be renewed again before long."[3] Two days later this bank suspended specie payments.[4] On the 12th all the Mobile banks suspended; the Decatur branch followed five days later, and by the 25th not a bank in the State paid specie for its notes.[5]

[1] Ms., State Department of Archives and History, Letter Book, Montgomery Branch of the State Bank, Cater to Wyman, September 7, 1836.

[2] *Ibid.*, Whiting to Hallett, April 24, 1837; Whiting to Ingersoll, April 30, 1837.

[3] *Ibid.*, Whiting to Hallett, May 8, 1837.

[4] *North Alabamian*, June 23, 1837.

[5] *Ibid.*, May 26, 1837; June 23, 1837.

The citizens naturally looked to legislation as a remedy. Many regarded the policy of contracting circulation, now adopted by the banks, as a prime cause of all the evils. Public meetings were held in various parts of the State to discuss measures of relief. One of the earliest of these was held in Mobile before the sharpest distress had been experienced. Resolutions were adopted opposing any special legislative action. A few days later, however, a second meeting was called, which adopted resolutions demanding an immediate assembling of the legislature, and the issue of bonds, or of post notes receivable in the payment of debt. The financial stringency must have developed very suddenly to produce this marked change of sentiment in such a short time. On May 13, 1837 Governor Clement C. Clay yielded to the popular demand and summoned the Alabama legislature to meet in June.

The banks, having suspended specie payments, were now at the mercy of the legislature, which, according to the articles of incorporation, could either approve the suspension or declare the charters forfeited. By an act approved June 30, 1837 the suspension was legalized, and various other measures of relief were provided. The notes of the State bank and branches were to be received in the payment of public dues, notwithstanding such suspension. The banks were to continue their discounting operations, but were required henceforth to give a preference to those applicants who had received no previous accommodation, or who had met their obligations promptly. Especially important was the provision that all banks, State and private, should within twelve months procure an amount of specie equal to one-eighth their capital, and increase the amount to one-fifth their capital by July 1, 1840, and to one-fourth by July 1, 1841. To obtain this specie for the State banks, the governor was authorized to issue $5,000,-

ooo in bonds. In the parent bank and each of its four branches was to be placed $1,000,000 of these bonds, one-half to be sold for specie, which was to be deposited in the banks, and the rest to be sold for funds equivalent to specie, which were to be placed in New York as a fund subject to the drafts of the bank for whose benefit the bonds had been sold.

The banks were required henceforth to issue and keep in circulation their bills and notes to an amount equal to their capital. With this requirement was a series of provisions for the relief of the bank debtors. All debts were to be divided into three parts, with one part to be paid each year until the whole amount was discharged. The first payment was to be 25 per cent of the debt, and the remaining 75 per cent was to be divided equally between the payments of the second and third years. Every debtor taking advantage of this extension clause was excluded from further accommodations if he owed as much as $2,000, until his indebtedness was discharged.

The circulation of the bank and its branches had increased from $7,000,000 to $10,000,000 between November, 1836 and February, 1837, and by the first of June following had been contracted to $5,699,236, thus showing that over $4,000,000 in bank notes had been withdrawn within four months. This sudden contraction, it was claimed, was due to constant runs on the banks.[1] The Montgomery branch was so thoroughly drained of specie that when the time drew near for its payment of the semi-annual interest on its bonds it did not have sufficient gold on hand and tried to borrow the sum from its sister banks. This proved impossible, as they were in similar straits. The amount needed was $20,000, and the bank had in its vaults only $19,500. It succeeded, however, in borrowing

[1] *Ibid.*, June 30, 1837.

$500 elsewhere, and by surrendering the last of its gold prevented a default and preserved the good name of the State.[1]

The bank officials seem to have made conscientious efforts throughout 1838 to resume specie payments, but there is little to indicate that the debtor class really desired it. The more that "rag money" depreciated, the more the bank debtors would profit; and the legislature, bowing to the popular will, had sought to make this money abundant.[2] At the end of 1837 the debts due the State bank and branches had reached the sum of $20,144,794, and of this amount $5,074,082, or over 25 per cent, was due from the citizens of Mobile County alone. In three other counties — Madison, Montgomery, and Morgan— the indebtedness reached a total of $4,187,134.[3]

When one recalls that by the act of June, 1837 the first installment, or 25 per cent of the bank debts, that is $5,000,-000, had to be paid within the year, and that this sum was little short of the amount of bank notes in circulation, it will readily appear that the requirements of the law could not be fulfilled. It became necessary, therefore, for the State to extend further indulgence.

The reports of the commissioners appointed to examine the banks give a clear idea of the condition into which these institutions had fallen. In 1838 there were 55,000

[1] Ms., State Department of Archives and History, Letter Book, Montgomery Branch, Whiting to Armstrong, September 22, 1837; Whiting to Mead, October 19, 1837.

[2] Jacksonville *Republican*, May 10, 1838. A writer in the Mobile *Chronicle*, styling himself "A Planter," voiced the popular sentiment as follows: "My humble views are that the banks should not think of resuming specie payments for the present, but should go on to discount liberally. Our money answers all our domestic purposes, and the banks could discount as well now to their own profit as ever and [keep] hands off till we could make another crop at least. . . . But close your doors upon us now, order suit, and . . . *we are gone, and many —to Texas.*" See *North Alabamian*, April 20, 1838.

[3] *Report of the Joint Committee Appointed to Examine the Bank of the State of Alabama and Its Branches*, 1837.

voters in the State, and of these 11,611 were at that time
indebted to the banks. Of this number 880 were indebted
to from two to four banks. Curiously enough, there was
complaint that the banks were limiting their accommodations to a chosen few; and the financial stringency of the
time was widely attributed to this cause! In spite of the
large number of citizens who had been accommodated at
the banks, however, a few were being favored at the expense of the rest; for in this year the presidents and directors alone were liable for $1,093,179 and ex-directors for
$2,179,508. Ninety others had received loans to the
amount of $3,054,433. The direct and contingent in-
debtedness of the legislators in 1840 was reported as
follows:

State bank	$74,975
Montgomery branch	81,118
Huntsville branch.................................	18,973 [a]
Decatur branch...................................	83,937
Mobile branch......................	444,756
	$703,759

[a] In the report of this branch only the direct, and not the contingent, liabilities of the legislators
are given.

It thus appears that in the abuses of bank administration the directors themselves had taken a more prominent
part than had the legislators. Some attempt at reform had
already been made by reducing the amounts for which the
directors might become liable. At the session of 1839 a
series of acts was passed to effect more thorough reforms.
The number of directors was reduced to six for each bank,
and neither they nor the president might henceforth become liable to their bank in any manner. Compensation
was provided for the directors, in the hope that this would
check their tendency to recompense themselves at the ex-

pense of the bank.[1] At the following session legislators were forbidden to endorse or stand as security on any paper presented at the main bank at Tuscaloosa, though they were not debarred from receiving accommodations for their own benefit.[2] Salutary as these measures were, they came too late.

Since 1836 the banks had been compelled to shoulder the expenses of the State government, and this burden came at a time when they were least able to bear it. Moreover, the expenses of the government increased at a rapid rate when they no longer had to be met by taxation, and the prospect of the banks being able to extricate themselves from their difficulties grew more and more hopeless. To bring about reform required much courage and sacrifice, so closely were politicians and planters alike involved in the system. But reform agitation began as early as 1840, when William L. Yancey, the editor of the Wetumpka *Argus*, began to advocate the separation of banks and State and the restoration of the school, university, and internal improvement funds to their proper functions. Benjamin Fitzpatrick, in 1841, became a Democratic candidate for governor on an anti-bank platform, and was supported by Yancey. He was elected, although many staunch Democrats threatened to bolt. The Democratic politicians were chary of grappling with the bank problem too strenuously for fear of splitting the party and giving the Whigs not only control of the State government but also the State's electoral vote in the next Presidential election.

The four years of Governor Fitzpatrick's administration mark a long stride in the return to normal conditions, though the reforms were not accomplished without opposition from a minority of the Democrats, united with the

---

[1] *Acts ... of the State of Alabama ... 1839*, February 2, 1839.
[2] *Acts ... of the State of Alabama ... 1840*, February 3, 1840.

Whigs. In 1842–43 the four branch banks were placed in liquidation, and in 1844 the same treatment was extended to the parent bank. On January 9, 1843 the total indebtedness to the banks was $16,401,873, classified as follows: good, $8,852,136; bad, $5,501,493; doubtful, $2,048,244. A year later the grand total was reduced by little more than $1,000,000, being now $15,324,793. Of this sum the good debts amounted to $7,429,800, the bad to $5,335,538, and the doubtful to $2,559,455.[1]

In 1846 all the assets of the State bank and its branches were vested in three commissioners and trustees,[2] who were to close up the business of these institutions and employ such funds as were available to the redemption of State bonds. In 1848 this work was entrusted to a single commissioner, Francis S. Lyon. He met with unexpected success. By pushing the collection of debts due the bank, he reduced the bonded debt to $4,484,667 in 1853, and to $4,231,889 in 1855. During the next five years the principal was gradually reduced to $3,445,000, a sum that forms part of the present indebtedness of the State and is an ever-present reminder of the days of pioneer banking under State management. Not only the principal of the debt, amounting approximately to $10,000,000, had to be dealt with, but also an annual interest charge of $500,000, and the interest on the school and university funds (about $100,000 a year) had to be met promptly. Over $1,500,000 in notes of the State bank were also to be redeemed. The interest payments were made promptly, and the circulation was reduced from $1,600,000 in 1847 to $291,237 in 1853.

There was only one bank of issue left in the State when the State's banks were closed, and its notes were insuffi-

---

[1] See *Report* of the Bank Commissioners for 1843 and 1844.
[2] *Acts . . . of the State of Alabama . . . 1845–46*, no. 2.

cient for the needs of the community. It was found expedient, therefore, to allow a limited amount of the old bank currency to remain in circulation. These notes were receivable for public dues, and as a sum no greater than the taxes for a single year was ever outstanding at any given time, they circulated at par with specie, or very nearly so. Nearly all the expenses of the State government were paid with this form of money, which would return to the treasury in the payment of taxes and other public dues. As the receipts from 1848 to 1860 usually exceeded expenditures, a large surplus accumulated in the treasury; but as this was in the form of an inconvertible paper currency, it was only an evidence of so much debt redeemed. In 1859 over a million dollars of this currency was burned.

After 1855 very little was accomplished in reducing the bonded debt, as the available assets of the banks were nearly exhausted, and it became increasingly difficult to purchase outstanding State bonds as they became less numerous, many being held in various parts of Europe by families and trust estates. In 1868, twenty-three years after the State bank and its branches had gone into liquidation, their books were finally closed. The experiment with a State-owned banking system had been costly, but the material losses were offset in some measure by the expansion which the banks brought about in the State's economic development.

FACTORS IN THE EARLY PITTSBURGH IRON INDUSTRY

LOUIS C. HUNTER

THAT Pittsburgh was destined by nature for a rôle of industrial importance is evident to all those for whom maps have meaning. Topography and geology worked persistently for this place. The early military importance of Pittsburgh's site arose from the same circumstances that assured it a civilian career of prominence. The wedge of land at the confluence of the Allegheny and Monongahela rivers was a point of strategic importance for the movement of men and materials, for whatever purpose, between important geographic sections. The wealth of coal which underlay the once thickly wooded hills made possible an industrial growth which transportation facilities alone could not have assured. But there was more than geographic determinism in the career of this city. Had the conquest and occupation of the continent by settlers followed another course than that from east to west a different destiny would have been decreed for Pittsburgh. An occupation of the continent by Europeans via the Gulf of Mexico and the Mississippi or, less conceivably, by oriental peoples thrusting eastward from the Pacific would probably have preserved Pittsburgh's Golden Triangle in as primeval a state as that in which the first French explorers found it. In this event the whole course of the economic development of the country would have been radically altered, at least with respect to the location of industrial and commercial foci and the course of trade. The development of trans-Appalachian transportation and trade might well have been delayed until after the coming of the railroads had destroyed the potential value of Pittsburgh's situation as a point of trans-shipment between trans-montane highways and western rivers. The rich ore and coal fields of the upper Mississippi Valley would have been in course of exploitation for decades before those of western Pennsylvania received significant attention, and the iron industry of the Middle West would no doubt early have become intrenched to an extent beyond the power of Pittsburgh coal to alter.

Without positing so marked a distortion of events in order to display the human influences shaping the economic history of Pittsburgh, suppose either that the French had maintained their hold on the trans-Appalachian West or that the English, in the treaty of 1783, had succeeded in fixing the western boundary of the young republic along the line of the Appalachian mountains. The political barrier would have taken away in part or entirely those commercial and industrial advantages which the mountains, in conjunction with the western waterways, gave to Pittsburgh. Situated as Pittsburgh was in the path of westward expansion, business came to it and flowed through it with a minimum of effort on the part of its citizens.

It would require no great ingenuity to assemble other "might-have-beens" in the economic history of the Ohio Valley and of Pittsburgh contingent upon the alteration of the human elements in the situation. These elements being what they were, Pittsburgh's industrial growth was based upon two great natural advantages: a high-grade and easily accessible mineral fuel in limitless amount and a strategic position upon the Mississippi-Ohio river system which formed the basis of internal commerce in the trans-Appalachian West until the Civil War. The importance of these two factors was early recognized. Almost every description of early Pittsburgh dwelt in glowing terms upon them. The traveller from the East on approaching Pittsburgh was first made conscious of its presence by the heavy pall of sooty smoke which six days in the week lay heavily over the town. This product of imperfect combustion was at once the symbol of Pittsburgh's prosperity, evidence of one of the material bases of her industry, and the defiler of the landscape. If the sensitive observer was repelled by these by-products of industry and wealth, he was no less aroused to enthusiasm when, from the eminence of Coal Hill, he viewed the panorama spread before him of the three rivers, Monongahela, Allegheny, and Ohio, in their setting of enclosing hills. Here was a scene that appealed to merchant and manufacturer as powerfully as to the artist, for rivers in the pre-railroad age, when overland transport at its best was both tedious and expensive, had a meaning for men that has long been lost. River transportation after the introduction of the steamboat was synonymous with ease, cheapness, and speed of carriage. Whatever the navigation hazards and deficiencies of the western rivers, they formed a connected and extensive system of water roads over which freight could be floated or propelled at a cost remarkably low for the time. It would be difficult to determine which of these natural gifts, rivers or coal, contributed most to the development of modern Pittsburgh. It would not, perhaps, be inaccurate to say that before 1850 the western rivers were a more vital factor than coal in the economic development of Pittsburgh but that after this date, with the rapid extension of railroad facilities and the decline of river traffic, it was coal that maintained and advanced her industrial position.

So long and so prominently has the name of Pittsburgh been associated with coal, iron, and industry that the commercial basis of her early development is often forgotten. The commercial potentialities of the site were a principal cause for its early military occupation. With the advance of settlers into the trans-Appalachian West, physiographic, economic, and political factors combined to converge the westward movement upon the Ohio Valley. The village of Pittsburgh was in the path of this migration and could scarcely have avoided commercial prominence. To the western settlers commercial communication with the eastern seaboard was as important as the connection with the Mother Country had been to their colonial forbears. The settler brought with him needs for manufactured goods and other commodities which could not be met by the industrially undeveloped and agriculturally limited West. To satisfy these needs and profit thereby became the burning desire not only of individuals but of villages, cities, and States. During the early decades the westward movement and the resulting commerce followed particularly the routes across the middle Appalachians which connected the seaboard with the upper reaches of the Ohio and its tributaries. The traffic through Pennsylvania to points of shipment on the Monongahela and upper Ohio rivers was especially heavy. So long as the prevailing methods of transportation required the trans-shipment of goods passing between the mountain regions and the lowlands of the interior, Pittsburgh at the head of the navigable waters of the Ohio Valley had but to take toll of the passing stream.

The pre-eminence of the all-Pennsylvania route to the West did not last long. Other commercial routes between the seaboard and the interior rose to importance and gained an increasing share of the traffic. Before long New

York, with the aid of the Erie Canal, out-distanced Philadelphia, whose position was weakened on the other side by the commercial enterprise of Baltimore. Despite these defections the western trade via Pennsylvania grew steadily, and with it the commercial activities and wealth of Philadelphia and Pittsburgh. From an early date, moreover, a portion of Baltimore's trade with the West passed through Pittsburgh. The Pennsylvania interests were active in improving their commercial connections with the West. In the early 'thirties canal communication was established between Pittsburgh and Philadelphia and in the next decade between Pittsburgh and Lake Erie. In the early 'fifties Pittsburgh secured railway contact with Philadelphia, and through a feverish display of energy was joined by various projects to the rapidly growing railway network of the West. The success of the commercial interests of Pittsburgh in obtaining the latest mode of transport facilities both with the West and with the East enabled them for a time to maintain their hold on the trade between these two sections. But it soon proved to be their undoing by depriving Pittsburgh of its original and primary reason for existence as a commercial depot and point of trans-shipment between the trans-Appalachian routes and the western rivers. With the extension of the railroads serving Pittsburgh, arrangements were made for through, unbroken shipments accompanied by pro-rating agreements. These were followed by end-to-end consolidations of the railroads which, with the accompanying decline of river traffic, brought to a close the essentially commercial phase of Pittsburgh's development.

From its early beginnings at Pittsburgh, manufacturing had benefited greatly from the city's position as an entrepôt in the important East-West trade. Commercial enterprise did much to clear the ground and smooth the

way for the establishment and growth of manufacturing
industries. Old channels of transportation were improved
and new ones were created. Roads, steamboats, canals,
and railroads were built and improved and transportation
service of increasing regularity and reliability was provided. Commercial contacts were made and markets developed. Branch houses and agencies were established and
good will was created. Banking and exchange facilities
were developed in response to commercial needs. Pittsburgh through her commercial connections was kept in
close touch with the needs and requirements of the different parts of the western country for manufactured goods.
Country merchants and buyers from all parts of the West
passed through Pittsburgh on their annual trips to the
East, stopped overnight, found stores and warehouses
heavily stocked with imported goods and native manufactures, and concluded part or all of their purchases here.
The news and fame of Pittsburgh manufactures was carried by the mercantile profession to all parts of the country. One of the most important results of this independent
commercial life was the accumulation of a large fund of
capital available for investment in manufacturing enterprises. The mercantile professions were the most important source of capital, outside the industry itself, for the
Pittsburgh iron industry of the ante-bellum period.

In the creation and development of the numerous agencies of transportation and commerce which in turn fostered
the growth of manufacturing at this point, Pittsburgh commercial enterprise and capital did not stand alone. Pittsburgh was but one link in the chain of interests extending
from the Atlantic seaboard to the Ohio Valley that participated in and profited from the East-West trade that took
the Pennsylvania route. The maintenance and extension
of the ways and means by which this trade flourished fell

on all of the commercial interests concerned. Roads, canals, and railroads were built and capital and credit were supplied through the combined efforts of these extensive interests in a measure greatly beyond the capacity of a frontier commercial and industrial community such as Pittsburgh to provide. Manufacturing once under way at Pittsburgh contributed to the same end.

Favored as Pittsburgh was by abundant fuel, navigable waterways connecting the city with a vast interior basin in rapid process of settlement, and extensive marketing facilities made available by the capital and enterprise of Philadelphia and her commercial allies, the growth of its manufactures was inevitable. Two factors were of primary importance in determining the kinds of manufactures to be established at Pittsburgh: the availability of the requisite raw materials and the cost of transporting the finished articles from the East or Europe to the western country. Freight charges from Philadelphia to Pittsburgh were twelve cents a pound in 1786, five cents a pound as late as 1818, and it was not until the Pennsylvania Canal was fully in operation in the middle 'thirties that rates declined to one cent a pound. The extreme difficulties of carriage across the Appalachian barrier had from the beginning of the migration to the West forced emigrants to reduce their furniture and equipment to a minimum and, so far as possible, to convert their possessions into cash before their departure. Manufacturing at Pittsburgh received its first significant impulse from the business of outfitting emigrants preparatory to the last and easier stages of travel by river and overland to their new homes. When settled they continued to look to Pittsburgh for supplies of goods which proved so expensive to bring across the mountains. Pittsburgh therefore came to concern herself pre-eminently with the fabrication of heavy and bulky goods that were difficult and costly to import from the East, the mountain barrier giving her substantial protection from competition from the older industrial districts. "Pittsburgh manufactures," a phrase which obtained wide currency in the western country, came to be largely synonymous with "heavy manufactures," especially with those composed entirely or in large part of iron.

Curiously enough, at the outset of an industrial career which was early to win for Pittsburgh the somewhat exaggerated title of "the Birmingham of America," neither of the basic raw materials of the iron manufacture as conducted in the late eighteenth and early nineteenth centuries in this country was available in practicable amounts at or in the neighborhood of the future Iron City. The few scanty surface deposits of iron ore in the vicinity were inadequate as a basis for even very minor operations. Mineral coal, although early discovered and utilized at Pittsburgh, was in the early nineteenth century in this country regarded as entirely unsuited for use in the basic processes of iron-making. These depended exclusively upon charcoal for fuel. The extensive character of charcoal manufacture, the annual product of thousands of acres of woodland being required to supply a single blast furnace or forge with fuel, confined the production of iron from the ore to small rural iron-works located in the less settled districts where woodland was plentiful and cheap. The iron manufacture, therefore, cannot be regarded as native to Pittsburgh; it was gradually built up through a process of importation by which successive stages in the manufacture of iron, beginning with the final ones, were transferred from the countryside to this urban center. The progress of this transfer was dependent upon success in the use of mineral coal as fuel in the different metallurgical operations and in the economical concentration at this point of supplies of crude iron in its various forms.

The first iron manufacturer at Pittsburgh was the blacksmith. He began where his successor of a century later was to leave off, with iron in the completely refined form of wrought bar. With wrought iron in the convenient sizes long known as merchant bar obtained from the rural forges of central Pennsylvania this craftsman forged and wrought the diverse finished articles needed by a new and growing country: horseshoes, wagon tires and ironwork, nails, plough irons, and the numerous kinds of tools and implements needed by emigrant, trader, or farmer. With the establishment of the first rolling mills at Pittsburgh we have the first important step in the process by which the different stages in the manufacture of wrought iron were transferred one by one from the rural districts until at length, in the 'sixties and 'seventies of the nineteenth century, the article was made entirely at this central location from the primary raw materials. Iron which previously had been brought to Pittsburgh in the form of merchant bar was now imported in the form of large slabs of wrought iron called blooms. In the rolling mill these slabs were easily and cheaply reduced to the various sizes of merchant-bar and sheet iron for the convenient use of the fabricator of finished iron wares. The next step in the centralization of the iron manufacture was the transfer of the secondary refining processes to this point. Iron at this stage came to Pittsburgh in the form of cast pigs, the product of the rural charcoal blast furnaces. The refining of the pig iron which previously had been effected in the rural forges was now performed in the refinery fires and puddling furnaces which became regular equipment at most of the rolling mills. The first rolling mill was established at Pittsburgh in 1812, and seven years later puddling was introduced for the first time. Puddling spread slowly and as late as 1836 the amount of blooms consumed by the rolling mills was twice that of pig iron. By the middle of the century, however, five-sixths of the crude iron consumed in the Pittsburgh rolling mills was received in the form of pig iron.

Not until two score years after the introduction of the secondary refining processes at Pittsburgh was the initial process in the manufacture of iron, the reduction of iron ore in the blast furnace, undertaken at Pittsburgh. The year 1859 marked the erection of Pittsburgh's first blast furnace by one of the leading rolling mill companies, and the success of this first experiment led to the general introduction of the manufacture of pig iron at this point by rolling mills and independent operators. With this final step effected, the evolution was complete; the iron manufacture in all its stages was at length conducted at Pittsburgh.

While the centralization of the iron manufacture at Pittsburgh was encouraged by some conditions it was materially retarded by others. The part which Pittsburgh's fuel resources and favorable commercial situation played in stimulating the industrial growth of the city has already been suggested and will bear some elaboration. Mineral coal possessed important advantages over charcoal for industrial purposes. It was more compact in character, requiring less space for transportation and storage. It was less friable and suffered less both from handling and exposure to the weather. The cost of mining coal as conducted in this region was much less than the cost of preparing charcoal. Finally, the concentrated character of coal beds as contrasted with the extensive character of the charcoal supply was a factor of the greatest importance for the centralization of industry and the conduct of large-scale operations. A coal mine of a few acres in extent would produce as much fuel as hundreds of acres of average wood-land. The superior quality of Pittsburgh coal also favored the growth of the iron manufacture at this point. While coal was widely distributed in the region between the Appalachians and the Mississippi River, that in western Pennsylvania associated with the name of Pittsburgh was superior alike for metallurgical and general industrial uses to most of the coal resources developed in the western country in the ante-bellum period. The development of rival industrial centers was discouraged by this fact and by the necessity which many of these centers in the Ohio and Mississippi valleys were under of importing fuel from the Pittsburgh district.

Pittsburgh's favorable position on the western rivers afforded her iron manufacturers convenient and cheap access not only to markets but also to supplies of crude iron which were lacking in the vicinity. Her first supplies of iron were drawn from the Juniata region of central Pennsylvania, which remained to the end the principal source of bloom iron. The Allegheny and Monongahela valleys early became the seat of an important blast-furnace industry, and together they constituted the most important supply district for the Pittsburgh rolling mills prior to 1850. Practically all the crude iron produced in these valleys was borne cheaply in flatboats to the Pittsburgh market on the seasonal floods. As the Pittsburgh iron industry in its expansion found these supplies inadequate, the western waterways and the steamboat enabled it to draw upon the iron districts of Ohio, Kentucky, Tennessee, and even distant Missouri.

A concentrated and cheap supply of fuel, and convenient access both to markets and to supplies of crude iron, made iron-manufacturing possible at Pittsburgh on a steadily increasing scale. To the other industrial advantages of this site were added the economies which followed from large-scale production. The size of the rural iron-works of this period and the scale of their operations were limited by the narrow radius within which supplies of raw materials could economically be obtained. When the charcoal supply or, less frequently, the ore supply within practicable reach of the iron-works was exhausted, the latter would have to be dismantled and in large part abandoned. Because of the difficulties of transportation in the unsettled regions where these iron-works were usually located, and where the means of transport were commonly confined to such crude roads as the iron-master himself could afford to construct, the radius of supply was very limited and the scale of operations correspondingly small. These circumstances prevented the rural iron-master from obtaining the general benefits which follow from large-scale operations; and they prevented him in particular from securing the advantages of the newer technique which involved more elaborate equipment than the scale of his operations warranted. Even steam power, which was used exclusively in the Pittsburgh iron industry from the establishment of the first rolling mill, was but slowly introduced, and then on a scale necessarily small, in the rural iron-works. The increase in the product of the rural iron industry was effected mainly by the multiplication of the number of furnaces and forges and only in small degree by the increase in the size of the individual plant. On the other hand, the average annual consumption of crude iron per rolling mill at Pittsburgh increased from 814 tons in 1826 to 6,670 tons in 1857, or more than eightfold in three decades.

These industrial advantages of Pittsburgh were offset materially by difficulties which were only slowly overcome and which greatly retarded the centralization of the iron manufacture at this point. There were, in the first place, the added costs of transporting iron in its cruder and bulkier forms to Pittsburgh with the transfer of the different stages of the manufacture to this point. As the manufacture of iron was conducted in the United States about 1820, a ton of merchant bar was equivalent to about 1⅛ tons of blooms, 1½ tons of pig iron, or 4½ to 6 tons of iron ore plus the amount of limestone used as flux in the blast furnace. In 1818, $70 per ton was paid for the carriage of iron from the Juniata region to Pittsburgh. The handicap imposed upon the urban iron manufacturer in assembling crude iron, as computed from the above figures, would amount to nearly $9.00 per ton of bar iron if crude iron was imported in the form of blooms, $35 per ton if the refinement of pig iron was undertaken, and from $250 to $350, as a broad estimate, if the entire manufacture of iron from the ore was intended. The weight of the handicap imposed must be estimated in connection with the price of bar iron at this time, which was at Pittsburgh from $200 to $210 per ton. The comparatively small difference in weight of equivalent amounts of bar and bloom iron encouraged the early establishment at Pittsburgh of the final process of the iron manufacture in which blooms were reduced to merchant bar. The wide difference in weight of equivalent amounts of bar iron and iron ore goes far to explain the late introduction at Pittsburgh of the pig-iron manufacture. Every step taken in the improvement of the means and in the reduction of the costs of transportation lowered the handicap under which the Pittsburgh manufacturer labored in competition with the rural iron-master. The improvement of overland transportation through the construction of turnpikes, canals, and railroads, and of inland waterway transport by the development of river steamboats and lake steamers, is an integral part of the history of the Pittsburgh iron industry. The latter in its growth had to wait upon the progress of the former.

More serious than the problems of transportation connected with the introduction of new stages of the iron manufacture at Pittsburgh — problems which, after all, were the concern of all branches of industry and were not to be solved by any one of them — were those associated with the new manufacturing technique and fuel. Balanced against the economies resulting from the use of mineral coal and from the adoption of new methods of refining and forging were the harmful effects of these innovations upon the quality of the finished iron. Mineral coal contained impurities which rendered it greatly inferior to charcoal for metallurgical purposes. These impurities if communicated to the iron in course of manufacture lowered its quality and limited its usefulness. The degree of contamination depended upon the directness of the contact between the coal and the iron and upon the state of the latter at the particular stage of manufacture. Molten iron absorbed impurities far more readily than solid iron at red or white heat. The early introduction at Pittsburgh of the reverberatory type of furnace for heating slab or bar iron and for use in puddling materially reduced this problem. It was the reverberatory furnace in fact which made possible the substitution of mineral coal for charcoal. In this furnace the fuel and heating chambers were separated and the only contact between fuel and iron was through the hot gases and through small particles of coal and ash carried by the draft into the heating chamber.

The degree of contamination of iron in the form of slabs or bars while being heated in the reverberatory furnace was scarcely appreciable if the heating was conducted with care. In the puddling process, however, the iron was in a molten or semi-molten state much of the time, and consequently it absorbed in significant amount the impurities contained in and conveyed by the hot gases. Improvements in the puddling process lowered but did not eliminate the fuel hazard. Puddled iron in time obtained a secure position for itself in the iron market, but in the early decades of its manufacture it made but slow progress in competition with the more highly regarded product of the charcoal forge. While the reverberatory furnace thus made possible the introduction at Pittsburgh of the more advanced stages of the iron manufacture, the primary process of reducing iron ore to pig iron in the blast-furnace continued without substantial change of equipment or practice. The ore was reduced to molten metal, then as today, in direct contact with the fuel. A maximum communication of the impurities of the coal to the iron was the result. Mineral-coal pig iron met with a very unfavorable reception from Pittsburgh iron manufacturers, who were in consequence very slow to embark upon its manufacture themselves. Although modifications of blast-furnace construction and practice improved the quality of pig iron made with coal, charcoal pig iron was slow to lose its preeminence in the iron market. Quite apart from the character of the fuel used, the new processes for refining and forging iron as conducted in the rolling mill were injurious to the quality of the iron. This resulted partly from the fact that the new processes encouraged the use of a lower grade of crude iron than could be used successfully in the rural forge. In addition, rolling was generally held to be not as satisfactory a method of compacting and shaping iron as the more primitive and costly method of hammering; and puddling produced a grade of iron inferior to that of the process it superseded.

Thus the introduction at Pittsburgh of the various stages of iron manufacture was regulated by considerations of technique affecting the quality of the product as well as by the conditions controlling the improvement of transportation. Quality is a relative matter, and it would be more exact to describe the product of the new technique not as inferior but as less useful. Prior to 1850 the demand for iron in the trans-Appalachian West arose principally from the needs and requirements of the pioneer agricultural economy of this region, needs which were met to a large extent directly by forges and rolling mills without the mediation of manufactories of finished articles. The principal consumers of wrought iron were blacksmiths, who forged and wrought bar iron into a wide variety of uses to meet the needs of farmer and wagoner. Many a farmer was his own blacksmith. Consequently a grade of iron was required that could be put to many uses and that could easily be wrought by the common blacksmith with his average skill and simple equipment. These requirements could be met only by a high-grade iron of all-round merit, specifications which were most adequately filled by the product of the rural charcoal forge. The acceptability of bar iron made from charcoal blooms in the rolling mill was only slightly less; and with the perfecting of the puddling process, using charcoal pig iron, the use of puddled bar increased steadily, stimulated by its lower cost. As the manufacture of finished articles of iron was withdrawn from the village and rural smithy and concentrated in factories using elaborate equipment and mechanical power to produce a single article or a limited range of articles, the character of the demand for iron changed. Instead of a high-grade iron of general merit, the manufacturer desired a grade of iron which would meet satisfactorily the conditions of fabrication and use of a particular article. With the specialized equipment and skill at his command he could often successfully utilize a grade of iron which in the hands of the common blacksmith would prove useless. To use iron possessing other qualities than were required for the particular purpose was found to be both unnecessary and costly. Gradually it was discovered that no grade of iron was without its uses. A "low grade" of iron was less useful than a "high grade" of iron only in that it could be put to fewer uses successfully. A low grade of iron would serve some use or uses probably as well as a high-grade iron; in some instances it was actually shown to be superior to the latter. The coal-smelted pig iron which the Pittsburgh manufacturers of merchant bar and sheet iron rejected so decisively in the late 'forties was found to make excellent rails. The early raw-coal pig iron of eastern Ohio was said to be superior to charcoal pig iron in the making of stoves and light castings. The problems which faced the Pittsburgh iron manufacturer as a result of the harmful effects of the new technique and fuel were solved, therefore, not only by technical improvements but by the changing character of the demand for iron, which increasingly emphasized quantity production to specification and low cost at the expense of high general merit in the product.

As a result of very favorable natural and economic factors and of technical progress, the growth of the early Pittsburgh iron industry was rapid. In the three decades between 1826 and 1857, the total annual consumption of crude iron by the rolling mills increased twenty-three fold. In this rapid progress Pittsburgh met with competition from three sources: the western country itself, principally Ohio, Kentucky, Tennessee, and Missouri; the north Atlantic seaboard; and Europe, mainly Great Britain. The numerous rural blast furnaces in the western States did not compete with the Pittsburgh manufactories but supplied them with crude iron. Of forges producing wrought iron there were never very many in the West, and in the face of competition from the rolling mills they steadily declined in importance. In the early 'thirties there were but a few rolling mills scattered through the entire Mississippi Valley west of Pennsylvania, but these increased during the following decades until, in the late 'fifties, they numbered more than forty, twice the number at Pittsburgh. Most of these were to be found scattered along the Ohio River from Wheeling to Paducah, Wheeling and Cincinnati being the most important centers. There were in addition a small group of rolling mills at St. Louis, and others along the Cumberland River, the Great Lakes, and at some inland points. Despite their number the total product of these western rolling mills, if we exclude rails which Pittsburgh did not manufacture, was less than the product of the Pittsburgh rolling mills.

It is difficult to separate eastern competition from that of Great Britain, inasmuch as the eastern rolling mills frequently worked with British crude iron as raw material. In addition to the direct competition with the products of eastern and British iron-works there was indirect competition resulting from the sale in western markets of hardware of eastern or foreign origin made wholly or in part of iron. Pittsburgh iron manufacturers were protected from competition from the older iron districts by the additional transportation charges borne by the latter in reaching the western markets. Further protection from foreign competition was given by the tariff, which during the half century prior to the Civil War averaged as high as freight charges between Philadelphia and Pittsburgh. There were three routes by which eastern and British iron could reach the western markets: by the routes across the middle Appalachians from Philadelphia and Baltimore to the Ohio River; by sea to New Orleans and thence up the Mississippi River and its tributaries; and by the Erie

Canal-Great Lakes route. Very little outside iron, however, found a market in those portions of the Ohio Valley
most accessible to the East by the first route. Some kinds
of iron, particularly nails and rails, reached the West in
significant amounts via New Orleans. It was in the regions tributary to the Great Lakes and made so accessible
to the East by the Erie Canal and lake steamers that Pittsburgh felt eastern and foreign competition most severely.
The opening of canal communication between Pittsburgh
and Cleveland on Lake Erie in 1840 enabled Pittsburgh
iron manufacturers to share a market from which they had
largely been excluded since the completion of the Erie
Canal. Shipments of Pittsburgh iron to the Lakes country
increased rapidly in the succeeding decades.

On the whole, it may be said that Pittsburgh iron manufacturers, although at times aroused on the tariff issue,
were not greatly disturbed by the fact or prospect of British competition. More important than the protection
afforded either by the Appalachian barrier or the tariff was
the difference in the character of British and Pittsburgh
iron. British iron of the kinds which found large sale in
this country was for the most part characterized by quantity production for industrial uses, by a limited range of
usefulness, and by cheapness. The market which Pittsburgh supplied was, as we have seen, predominantly agricultural and required a high-grade article of general usefulness. The distinctive product of Pittsburgh was merchant
bar, that of Great Britain was rails. Although the manufacture of rails was undertaken at a number of places in the
West prior to 1860, Pittsburgh made no serious effort to
develop this branch of the industry and was not positively
affected by the extensive sale and use of British rails in
market areas otherwise dominated by her. According to a
contemporary writer, an authority on the iron trade and a

protectionist, the amount of foreign iron other than rails consumed in the West and Southwest during the 'fifties was insignificant.

The story of the pioneer age of the Pittsburgh iron industry has to be told largely in terms of the operation and interaction of impersonal forces, natural, economic, and technological. The personalities of the industry left small impression upon succeeding generations, and achieved an obscure immortality only in the yellowed leaves of old directories and newspaper files. The early Pittsburgh iron industry has had no Smiles and perhaps deserved none, although it could provide plenty of inspiration for an Alger. It produced neither famous men nor famous organizations. Several of the companies prominent in the first half of the nineteenth century outlived the century but were at length either absorbed or overshadowed by the mammoth aggregations of the Age of Big Business. The early Pittsburgh iron industry had its outstanding figures, its Shoenbergers, Spangs, Shorbs, and Browns, but these names are distinguished for the strength of character and the length of service of the men who bore them, as well as for the high reputation of the products associated with them, rather than for any notable achievements in the scale, organization, or technology of production. The early Pittsburgh iron manufacturers contributed scarcely anything of significance to the technical and metallurgical progress of the industry. In the introduction of new processes and equipment their record for pioneering is better. Both the forging of iron by grooved rolls and the puddling process secured a substantial foothold in this country first at Pittsburgh. In the western country, Pittsburgh led in the improvement and extension of these processes with respect both to the scale and efficiency of operations and to the quality of the product. The pioneer work in the use of bitumin-

ous coal in the blast furnace, however, was done elsewhere. More than two decades elapsed after the first
successful smelting of iron with bituminous coal in western
Maryland and western Pennsylvania before this process
was introduced at Pittsburgh in connection with the first
blast furnace erected at this point. Lack of enterprise, as
well as the difficulties of obtaining a supply of iron ore, was
in some measure responsible for this delay. The introduction of the new blast-furnace fuel among the manufacturers
of pig iron was, moreover, discouraged and delayed by the
refusal of the Pittsburgh iron manufacturers for some years
to use the new product in the manufacture of wrought iron.
Their reasons for rejecting raw-coal and coke pig iron as
unsuited to their purposes carried weight, yet iron manufacturers elsewhere were successful in converting this grade
of crude iron into marketable wrought iron.. Pittsburgh
iron manufacturers showed a further lack of enterprise in
their slowness to meet the most significant of the new industrial demands for iron. The railroad was the first great
modern industry to impose upon the iron industry the new
requirements of specialization of quality combined with
low cost. Although in 1857 there were twelve rolling mills
in the trans-Appalachian West engaged in the manufacture
of rails and producing a substantial share of the country's
total product, Pittsburgh did not at this date have a single
mill engaged in this branch of the manufacture.

Such conservatism as Pittsburgh iron manufacturers dis-
played toward the close of the ante-bellum period should
not be allowed to obscure the very substantial achievements of the earlier decades. That the men responsible for
the growth of the industry showed no technological genius
is not surprising. Most of them were trained in commercial
rather than mechanical pursuits. The region was industrially new, and men possessing technical skill and knowl-

edge were comparatively scarce. Nor was there much occasion or need for technological genius in the early decades of the industry. The revolution of the technology of the iron manufacture had already been effected in England, and the task which confronted the iron manufacturers in this country was the adoption and adaptation of these innovations within the limits fixed by the character of local materials and existing needs. This the early Pittsburgh iron manufacturers did for that increasingly important section of the iron industry in this country whose growth was based on bituminous coal as fuel. Their pioneering, though not conspicuous, was none the less necessary because it was adaptive rather than creative in character.

ECONOMIC BEGINNINGS OF THE BOSTON AND ALBANY RAILROAD, 1831-1867

CHARLES L. HODGE

THE slow but significant westward drift of population and trade after the Revolution emphasized the dearth of natural facilities for inland transportation in Massachusetts. The uneven, rocky surface of the State is tilted to the west, ending in the almost abrupt wall of the Berkshires; few of its numerous streams are navigable for any considerable distance, and the most important exception — the Connecticut — flows southward on a line approximately one hundred miles from the coast.

The close rivalry which had existed since Colonial days between Boston and New York City for supremacy in the export trade lent to the acquisition of the newly opened Ohio region trade a peculiar significance. New York City was nearer than Boston by fifty miles to this great reservoir of raw materials, and had in addition the incomparable advantage of the Hudson River, navigable for heavy boats as far north as Albany.

The profits to be realized in opening a cheap and easy means of communication between Boston and Albany appealed strongly to the speculative temper of the times, and as early as 1791 plans for a canal were promoted by a group of persons under the leadership of General Henry Knox. Two routes were surveyed as far as the Connecticut River, and the following year Knox and his associates, having received a charter from the State, were incorpo-

rated under the name of "The Proprietors of the Massachusetts Canal."[1] The magnitude of the project was,
however, beyond the slender resources of the promoters, if
not of the State itself, just emerging from the financial
burdens of the war; and the experience served to discourage
further active interest in the subject until 1825.

That year marked the completion of the Erie Canal by
the State of New York, linking up the Hudson River at
Albany with the Great Lakes at Buffalo. The prosecution
of that work had been observed with alarm by the merchants of Boston, and early in the year the State legislature
hurriedly passed a bill authorizing the appointment of
three commissioners to ascertain the practicability of constructing a canal from "Boston Harbor . . . to some point
on the Hudson River . . . in the vicinity of the junction of
the Erie Canal with that river."[2] Although no instrumental surveys appear to have been made west of the
Connecticut River, the commissioners and their distinguished engineer, Colonel Loammi Baldwin, reported the
following year a recommendation for the immediate construction by the State of a canal to Albany, the estimated
cost being $6,000,000.[3] While the commissioners were en-
gaged in their labors a new chapter in the history of transportation was being written in England by the eventful
opening of the Stockton and Darlington Railway. No
better commentary could be had on the desperate determination of Massachusetts to break through the western

---

[1] *Resolves of the General Court of the Commonwealth of Massachusetts* [hereafter
referred to as *Resolves*], act of March 10, 1792.

[2] *Ibid.*, act of February 25, 1825.

[3] *Report . . . for a Survey of . . . Routes . . . from Boston to Albany* (reprint,
Boston, January 11, 1826). It is difficult to understand the signing of this remarkable document by a man of Baldwin's reputation except on the grounds of
contagious optimism. The technical problems, as apparent from the surveys,
were staggering. The plans called for a total rise and fall of 3,281 feet and a
4-mile tunnel through the Berkshires.

barriers than the official recommendation of Governor Lincoln to the commissioners in June, 1825 to consider the feasibility of this new mode of transportation as a possible alternative to canalization.[1] Notwithstanding their failure to entertain the suggestion, public sympathy in favor of a railway grew astoundingly, threatening to plunge both projects into the vortex of partisan politics. Moreover, the threatened rupture served to raise a dangerous question of precedent: whether, apart from the uncertainty attaching to the expense and practical results of the rival means, the State could consistently engage in the business of general transportation.

After sundry attempts to secure further action had failed, a select committee were at length appointed late in the year 1826 to enquire into the "practicability and expediency of constructing a Railway from Boston . . . to the Hudson River, at or near Albany." As no appropriations were made, the committee pursued their investigations by means of circulars sent throughout the State. On this basis, and by much reference to English experience, they were able to report, in 1827, unanimously in favor of construction.[2] Thereupon the legislature authorized the appointment of two commissioners and an engineer to make the necessary instrumental surveys, and appropriated $10,000 for the purpose.[3] Their report, made January 29, 1828,[4] is noteworthy for its wealth of data.[5] Comparative costs of canals and railways led the com-

[1] *Resolves*, message of the governor to the June session of the legislature, 1825.

[2] *Massachusetts House Documents* [hereafter referred to as *H. D.*], no. 13, 1827.

[3] *Resolves*, no. 4 in vol. cxcvii, June 14, 1827.

[4] *Massachusetts Senate Documents* [hereafter referred to as *S. D.*], report no. 5, 1828. Copies were printed for distribution.

[5] The tables on production and distribution of commodities, particularly manufactured and semi-manufactured goods, as well as other statistics, throw valuable light on the economic conditions obtaining at the beginning of the Industrial revolution in New England.

missioners to recommend a horse-drawn railway as preferable to either steam populsion or canals. The solid ability of the report carried great conviction. It definitely settled the issue between canal and railway, and by virtue of the popular enthusiasm which it engendered, constrained the legislature to face the question of State versus private construction. To this end a "Board of Directors of Internal Improvement" was appointed to determine upon what principles the railroad system should be introduced into the State.[1] Authority was conferred to receive land grants and other contributions, to engage two engineers, and to make provisional arrangements with the State of New York in respect to such part of the line as would traverse that State.[2]

The year 1828 was passed in running surveys in both States to locate eligible routes. Three distinct lines were run: the first (known as the southern route) led from Boston to Worcester, through Springfield to West Stockbridge (State line), thence by way of Chatham to Albany. This was selected over the more northerly routes, and was substantially that taken by the Boston and Worcester and the Western railroads at a later date. The total distance was 200½ miles.[3]

Many influential men of the times, notably Nathan Hale, Emory Washburn, and Theodore Sedgwick, had devoted themselves to the task of arousing popular agitation for construction of the railroad,[4] and this visible evidence

[1] *Resolves*, act of March 11, 1828.
[2] The New York Legislature at Albany, over the protests of New York City representatives, pledged itself by an act of April 15, 1828 to construct or permit construction of a railway from the Massachusetts State line to Albany.
[3] *Journal of the Senate of New York*, 52nd sess.; and *Report on Railway Surveys . . . Boston to the Hudson River*, by James F. Baldwin, Engineer (Boston, 1828).
[4] Liberal use was made of the press and pamphlets: Washburn's first articles appeared in the Worcester *Aegis*, November, 1826; Sedgwick's pamphlet in 1828. The most effective of Hale's many contributions consisted of a series of six lengthy articles in his paper, the *Boston Advertiser*, issues of January 5 to February 2, 1827, being later reprinted in pamphlet form.

of active interest by the State in securing a western outlet intensified an already formidable public sympathy. Notwithstanding the growing pressure of private opinion, and despite the insistence by the governor on definite action, the legislature, having exhausted the recourse of new surveys, declined to commit itself further. All attempts during the ensuing two years to induce State construction having failed, and the patience of the business community being at length exhausted, petitions were presented for the incorporation by private persons of the "Boston and Worcester Railroad" with rights to construct a railway from Boston to Worcester. The incorporators had two objects in mind in thus embarking upon the construction of part of the proposed line. It was felt in the first place that the existing business between the two towns which then moved by road fully justified the investment of private capital in a rival and cheaper means of transport; and as the distance was but forty-four miles the required capital could be successfully raised. In the second place the completion and profitable operation of a portion of the great line westward would encourage the State to construct at a later date the more difficult and costly remainder.

The State was not unwilling to be thus relieved of a troublesome subject and the required act was passed with but slight opposition. The charter contained the following provisions: the capital stock was definitely limited to 10,000 shares of $100 each; the company was granted the right of eminent domain, even over existing highways; all damages arising out of wilful obstruction were recoverable by it in treble the amount thereof; the exclusiveness of its franchise was guaranteed for thirty years; complete and unlimited authority was vested in it to determine every phase of its policy, including rates; it was provided that such rates as it might charge should not yield a revenue in excess of 10 per cent of the value of the investment, the State reserving the right, in case of excess after ten years, of revising the rates for the succeeding ten years; and at the end of twenty years or at any time thereafter the State might purchase the road upon payment of all costs plus 10 per cent interest.[1]

The corporation's engineer was John M. Fessenden, who had made a study of the Stockton and Darlington and had been connected with the first lines in New York. His report recommended the southern route and estimated the cost of construction at $884,000, with $34,000 for annual cost of operation.[2] Work was commenced early in 1832 and the line to Worcester completed in July, 1835.[3] The actual cost had risen to $1,319,000 and the capital stock to $1,500,000.

Receipts from operation of the line during the next two years amply justified the financial expectations of its owners, but notwithstanding, hopes of inducing the legislature to construct the remainder of the route proved disappointing. Moreover, it had granted the franchise in 1833 to several directors of the Boston and Worcester who had incorporated as the "Western Railroad Corporation."[4] The charter provided for a capital of not less than 10,000 shares nor more than 20,000 shares of $100 each; and in case subscriptions exceeded the maximum issue, holders of Boston and Worcester stock were to be given preference up to the amount of such holdings. In other respects the provisions were similar to those of the Worcester charter. The magnitude of the project was now more clearly apparent, and the incorporators of the Western Railroad were loath to

[1] *An Act to Establish the Boston and Worcester Railroad* (reprint, Boston, 1831).
[2] *Report of the Engineer to the Stockholders, 1832* (reprint, Boston, 1833).
[3] S. D., no. 49, 1836, Fourth Annual Report to the Legislature, p. 1.
[4] S. D., no. 27, 1833.

exercise a privilege which appeared more than likely to result in financial loss. In consequence, no action was taken until late in the year 1834, when subscription books were opened in Springfield, Worcester, and some of the intermediate towns. The gesture was half-hearted, and would not have been made but for the pressure of certain events.

In that year the State of New York granted a charter to the "Castleton and West Stockbridge Railroad Company" (later the Albany and West Stockbridge) to form a connecting link between Albany and the western termination of the Western Railroad. At the same time a competitive line known as the "Hudson and West Stockbridge," the stock of which was held principally in New York City, obtained a similar charter; and shortly thereafter an offer was made by certain Wall Street interests to take up the entire capital stock of the Western. The offer was promptly rejected as an attempt to prevent actual construction; nevertheless it doubtless played a part in forcing the opening of the subscription books.[1] The resulting failure was a forceful proof of the almost universal doubt concerning the financial future of the line; nor were there lacking many who now questioned its technical practicability.

Early in 1835 a new danger appeared in the shape of a projected road from Hartford, Connecticut, to Worcester, for which a charter was granted by the State of Connecticut.[2] The promoters of this line proposed to extend it from Hartford to Albany in the west and to New York City in the south; and they lost little time in placing an engineer in the field.[3] To combat this move a public convention was

[1] *Historical Memoir of the Western Railroad* by George Bliss (Springfield, 1863), p. 22.
[2] *Ibid.*, pp. 25–27.
[3] The affairs of this company, known as the Hartford and Worcester Railroad, are detailed at some length in Bliss's work.

called on July 2, 1835 in Worcester, to which were invited the interested parties of both projects, the governor of Massachusetts presiding. The conference failed to effect a compromise of differences, and all the participants departed, in order to see who would be first in the field.[1] The books of the Western were again opened, and this time a determined effort was made to secure pledges. Only about half of the shares were subscribed, and these in small lots. Nothing daunted, the incorporators assembled another public meeting, this time in Faneuil Hall, to appeal for subscriptions. Committees were appointed to make a door-to-door canvass in every town along the proposed route. Every class was appealed to. Even the clergy were exhorted to deliver sermons on the patriotic duty of building the Western. By these means the total number of shares disposed of was raised to 18,300, leaving a deficiency of 1,700.[2] New meetings were held and fresh committees appointed, and at length on December 5, by dint of persuasion and entreaty, the full amount was subscribed. How difficult the task had been is shown by the fact that there were over 2,300 subscribers (an average of less than 9 shares per individual), most of the holdings being in lots of from one to 4 shares, and the bulk of all subscriptions having been obtained from the middle classes and from common laborers.[3]

Capable engineers having been secured and surveys run, grading was commenced in mid-winter of 1836–37. To defray expenses two instalments of $5.00 each had been levied on stock subscriptions, but collection proved difficult. Approximately 10 per cent of all subscriptions were

[1] Three distinct routes other than those proposed by the Hartford and the Western groups were strongly supported at the convention.

[2] G. Bliss, *op. cit.*, pp. 28–29. Also *Boston Weekly Messenger*, August 20, 1835.

[3] *H. D.*, no. 16, 1836.

defaulted, and many who met the first payment declined to pay the second on the ground that they had been prevailed upon to subscribe on the understanding that they could surrender their stock after the initial payment of $5.00. It was found possible to secure new purchasers for but a portion of the unpaid shares, and the company was rescued from this embarrassment only by cash donations, the donors preferring not to obligate themselves further by taking stock.[1]

This experience had not been wholly unexpected by the directors. Early in 1836 they had caused a petition to be presented to the legislature praying for the incorporation of a bank to be known as "The Western Railroad Bank" with a capital of $5,000,000, the stock of which was to be subscribed in every county of the State, the bank to purchase and hold, as part of its reserve, stock in the Western Railroad, and the customary bank tax to be paid for twenty years to the treasury of the Western Railroad rather than to the State.[2] This was a bold and well calculated stroke. Experience had taught the directors of the Western that little assistance could be expected by direct appeal to the legislature. The failure of the federal government to renew the charter of the Bank of the United States at this time, by raising the fear of general credit stringency, had made the idea of large State banks peculiarly acceptable, and the support of the "cheap money" faction in the legislature was thus enlisted in the cause of the Western Railroad.

Before the general excitement occasioned by this petition had subsided, another lengthy memorial was presented in favor of the establishment of a $10,000,000 "State Bank of Massachusetts," half of the stock to be subscribed by the State, the bank to have the power of

---

[1] G. Bliss, *op. cit.*, p. 35.   [2] *H. D.*, no. 16, 1836.

note issue and of establishing branches and to be required to subscribe to 10,000 shares of Western Railroad stock.[1] A favorable report on the bill by the Committee on Banking threw the conservative element into a panic, as it soon became evident that the united strength of the two parties supporting the bill would secure its passage. In order to break up the alliance it was necessary to yield to the Western petitions for aid, and a bill originated by the Democrats [2] was hurriedly passed providing for subscription by the State to $1,000,000 of Western Railroad stock, whereupon support of the bank bill by the railroad party was withdrawn.

Two provisions of the subsidy bill are worthy of note as having an important bearing on subsequent events. These were, first, that no assessments were to be paid by the State on its stock subscriptions until 75 per cent of the same assessment had been paid by the private stockholders; and second, that three of the directors of the Western were to be appointed by the State.

The work of grading the road preparatory to laying the rails had progressed for a distance of less than twenty miles when business of every description was brought to a virtual standstill by the paralyzing crisis of 1837. General bank suspension and a strangling of credit were followed by widespread distress and failure; and the inability of the Western stockholders to meet the third and fourth instalments again plunged the road into difficulties. Moreover, it was now seen that the cost as originally estimated would have to be revised to $4,000,000, whereas but $3,000,000 (including the State's portion) was subscribed. The State, being now involved as a large stockholder, was forced to

[1] *Ibid.*, no. 43, 1836.
[2] *Resolves,* April 4, 1836, *An Act in Aid of the Western Railroad Corporation,* reprinted in *First Annual Report to Stockholders.*

come again to the rescue.[1] The 75 per cent clause was amended, and further aid to the amount of $2,100,000 was assured by the sale of State scrip in England, the proceeds to be applied to construction of the Western and the property of the road mortgaged to the State as security.[2]

Six assessments having finally been paid by the private stockholders only after prolonged and unavoidable delinquency, and the stringency of the depression continuing into 1838-39, it became evident that no substantial collection of the remaining fourteen assessments could be looked for. This, less premiums on the sale of the State scrip, left a new deficiency of $1,200,000, and further State aid was the only recourse. The repeated necessities of the road had, however, put the legislature out of temper, and important concessions were necessary to secure the additional scrip: four of the nine directors were to be appointed by the State, which also reserved the right to purchase the line at any time thereafter upon payment of cost to the private stockholders plus 7 per cent interest, less dividends.[3]

Meanwhile further difficulties had developed in another quarter. The Albany and West Stockbridge Railroad had done nothing by way of construction, and subscriptions to its stock (including that of the city of Albany) were in any event inadequate. Repeated representations by the Western interests having failed to secure action, a proposal was offered to the Albany company to "aid" it in the construction of its line.[4] Under the terms of the agreement, as

[1] *An Act to Aid the Construction of the Western Railroad* (February 1, 1838), reprinted in *Third Annual Report to Stockholders*.

[2] One per cent was to be deducted from receipts each year to constitute a sinking fund for retirement, interest likewise to be paid out of earnings.

[3] *S. D.*, no. 35, 1839.

[4] It was felt that a direct offer to purchase the franchise of the Albany company would be met with refusal; and the subscriptions to stock by the city of Albany would be withdrawn in the event of ownership by a Massachusetts corporation.

reached April 23, 1840,[1] the city of Albany subscribed to $650,000 of stock, paying for the same with its scrip, bearing 6 per cent interest to be paid by the Western as rent of the road and the principal to be redeemed out of earnings, such bond redemption entitling the Western to receive equivalent amounts of stock. The Albany company retained its corporate identity but gave the Western exclusive control under permanent contract, the latter road to construct, equip, and operate the Albany line.[2]

The resources of the Western were inadequate at the time to carry out the terms of the contract, and the city of Albany was subsequently prevailed upon to extend the amount of its aid to $1,000,000.[3] This in turn proving insufficient, the Massachusetts legislature was again petitioned, and a final loan of State credit in the sum of $1,000,000 obtained.[4] The last obstacle was now removed, and the work of completing the road went forward rapidly, Albany being reached on December 21, 1841.[5]

Some aspects of the construction as well as the operating problems in the early days of the roads deserve a brief mention. The original plan of the Worcester called for wooden rails covered with a thin strip of iron. Actual construction,

---

[1] *Articles of Agreement* — reprinted as an appendix to *S. D.*, no. 35, 1841.

[2] As the private stockholders of the Albany transferred their shares to the amount subscribed to by the city, the cost of this valuable property right to the Western amounted to the cost of drawing up the contract — about ten dollars. The Albany bonds were eventually redeemed through the operation of a sinking fund established for the purpose.

[3] *Journal of the Senate of New York*, act of May 26, 1841, Report of the directors of the Albany and West Stockbridge to the legislature of New York, January 22, 1842.

[4] *S. D.*, no. 35, 1841. Sinking-fund provisions were similar to those provided in the first loan. As interest and principal were paid punctually by the road, the State lost nothing by granting its credit. Perhaps for this reason the four State directors adopted a policy of entrusting the management of the road to the private owners with a minimum of official interference — a policy continued to the end.

[5] *Sixth Annual Report to Legislature*, 1842.

however, was begun with an English wrought-iron edge rail about 9 feet in length and weighing 40 pounds. This did not stand up well, and both replacements and the second track were of the T pattern, weighing 60 pounds and about 19 feet in length. The method of laying the first rails was as follows: a trench was dug beneath each rail and filled with gravel and loose stone; the ends of the wooden cross-ties were embedded in the gravel and the whole tamped firm; the rails, resting in heavy cast-iron "chairs," were then spiked down. Approximately two-thirds of the line (27 miles) was straight-away and about 17 miles level; the total rise and fall in 44 miles was 714 feet, the maximum grade 30 feet to the mile, and the shortest radius of curvature 600 feet for 900 feet.[1]

On the Western, conditions necessitated high grades and sharp curves. Sixty-three miles were straight-away, with 118 miles of curves, the worst being 1,042 feet in 1,500, 955 in 910, and 882 in 490 feet; only 7 miles were level, 107 miles of a total of 156 having grades in excess of any on the Worcester, and the "ruling grade" (at Washington summit) being 83 feet per mile for $1\frac{1}{2}$ miles, with a 5 degree uncompensated curve. A single track of T pattern rail weighing $56\frac{1}{2}$ pounds was originally laid. The rails were supported on chairs spiked to wooden cross-ties, but unlike the Worcester road the ties were in turn fastened to longitudinal sills of wood, with 4 additional sills under the rail joints, and the entire understructure embedded in packed gravel and stone. Deep cuts, high embankments, and numerous bridges were further characteristics.[2]

These physical differences between the carriers made for much higher operating expenses on the Western; moreover

[1] *Report of the Engineer to the Stockholders*, 1834–35; *S. D.*, no. 33, 1838; *Eleventh Annual Report to Stockholders* (Boston and Worcester), 1842.

[2] *Report of the Engineer to the Stockholders*, 1838–39 and 1841–42; and *Sixth Annual Report to Stockholders* and *Eighth Annual Report to Stockholders* (Western).

the severe New England winters and heavy spring freshets in the mountains raised traffic problems against which, on the whole, the Worcester did not have to contend. A further difference lay in the population density of the country traversed and the relative proportion of manufactured goods to agricultural products offered as freight. All these considerations greatly favored the Worcester, and it was therefore perhaps but natural that irreconcilably divergent policies of rate making should ensue. Way traffic was heavy on the Worcester, making the construction of branch lines necessary from the very beginning.[1] It had no effective competition at any point, the stage coaches and wagon traffic being hopelessly outclassed. Likewise, business between Boston and Worcester was sufficient to assure it a profit without the necessity of taking a single passenger or ton of freight from the Western. The policy early evolved by the Worcester management as a result of these conditions — and never wholly relinquished — might be said to be one of "customary" rates, low enough to discourage stage and wagon competition, but with little attempt at achieving a flexibility designed to attract new business or to swell the volume of the old. A rate structure and classification having been established and the results found profitable, the tendency was toward crystallization and "natural growth."

The principal points of business for the Western were Springfield and Albany, and at both cheap water competition was effective. The road was therefore compelled to charge what the traffic would bear. Rates to way stations where competition was not serious were fixed relatively higher, but even here the generally low value of the class of freight secured discouraged high rates. The Western there-

---

[1] Commutation service to and from Boston had become an important source of revenue as early as 1838.

fore embarked upon an aggressive policy of low rate manipulation in an effort to "create" business in volume. In the course of such experimentation, rates were sometimes changed as many as three or four times within a year, and goods moved from one classification to another.[1] Low-grade commodities were hauled at less than cost, provided some return above prime or direct expenses was secured; some were moved at less than this in order to encourage the growth of a volume such as would ultimately justify the rate.[2]

The long through haul to Boston was essential to the Western, but such business could be secured at the level of the competitive rates only on condition that the Worcester accept the transfer at less than its own established rate. This it was willing, within limits, to do, as its own profit was thereby augmented; but with the Western's theories of low and experimental rates it was not in sympathy, declining to haul any class of merchandise below cost of service, and generally opposing variations in rates even when above such cost. It was inevitable, therefore, that the two roads should come into sharp conflict over the level of the joint rate and their respective shares in it.

Upon the opening of the Western to Springfield in 1839, an agreement had been effected with the Worcester company regarding the division of the through passenger fare, which was fixed at $3.75.[3] The fare from Boston to Worcester was then $1.50. On through passengers, however, the Worcester company was to receive $1.25 and the Western $2.50, or approximately 2.7 cents and 4.3 cents per mile respectively.[4] After six months, however, or between April 1, 1840 and January 1, 1844, the through rate to Spring-

[1] The effort to secure bread for transportation is an example in point.
[2] Such as "special rates" on lime, gravel, etc.
[3] *Eighth Annual Report to Stockholders* (Boston and Worcester), 1840.
[4] *Tenth Annual Report to Stockholders* (Western), 1845, pp. 28–29.

field was reduced to $3.00, the Western absorbing the whole reduction.[1]

The opening of the Western to Albany in 1842 necessitated a new arrangement. Moreover, neither company had professed itself wholly satisfied with the results obtained under the contract of 1839. Accordingly, the Western proposed a new contract on both passenger and freight through business, under which the Worcester was to be allowed a fixed sum per passenger and per ton, the Western to have authority to vary the through rate according to the exigencies of business conditions, thus making its returns variable. The chief reasons underlying such a principle of division, according to the Western, were: (1) that a discrimination should be made in favor of the Western because of the fact that it gave the Worcester new business, such business being gathered in small amounts along the whole line, but delivered in the mass to Worcester; (2) that the expense of construction and operation of the Western were necessarily greater per mile than that of the Worcester; (3) that the legislature, foreseeing such differences in cost, had in consequence reserved to itself the right to fix the tolls which the Worcester might charge on business passing over it from other lines.[2]

The Worcester declined acceptance of the principles advanced by the Western, and after much delay in attempting to reach agreement, the latter road in January, 1844 petitioned the legislature to settle the controversy by granting it authority to enter upon and use the Worcester at rates of toll to be prescribed by the legislature.[3] Before a bill could be reported, however, both roads agreed to arbitrate their differences, and the legislature dropped the

[1] *Eighth Annual Report to Legislature* (Western), 1844, pp. 10–11.
[2] *Tenth Annual Report to Stockholders* (Western), 1845, pp. 18–30.
[3] *Ibid.*, p. 30.

matter. The arbitrators, after a full hearing, handed down their decision in May, 1844, sustaining in part the contentions of the Western, and fixing the share of the Worcester at $1.10 per passenger and $1.26 per ton of freight on the joint business; provided, however, that should the Western increase the through rate, the share of the Worcester was to be increased proportionally.[1]

The award was bitterly assailed by the Worcester management.[2] Late in the year tactics of embarrassment were resorted to. The fare from Boston to Worcester was then $1.50. This was reduced to $1.25, making it to the interest of through passengers to purchase separate tickets over the two lines.[3] The Western thereupon reduced the through rate by the same amount and called upon the Worcester to take its proportional reduction in the division of through receipts. As the award had not specifically provided for a reduction of the through rate,[4] the Worcester declined to accept a reduction of its share, and on January 15, 1845 gave notice of its intention to terminate the award, and to submit a new proposition, which was done on January 23. It provided for mutual determination of the joint rate, the share of each carrier to be based upon the principle of equal net profit per mile on such business.[5] The Western objected, on the grounds that the difference in accounting practice would yield divergent results, and that the method was not only complicated, but even if properly administered would subject the income of both carriers to undesirable fluctuation; above all, it denied the principal

---

[1] *Award of the Arbitrators*, May 21, 1844, reprinted in *S. D.*, no. 9, 1846.
[2] *Thirteenth Annual Report to Stockholders* (Boston and Worcester) pp. 6–18.
[3] *Tenth Annual Report to Stockholders* (Western), pp. 28–29.
[4] Obviously within the intent of the award.
[5] *Proposition submitted — for the mutual regulation of the joint reprinted fares and freights*, annexed to *Thirteenth Annual Report to Legislature* (Western), 1845, pp. 37–39.

contentions of the Western as set forth in the previous dispute.[1]

Agreement proving impossible, the Western again sought relief from the legislature.[2] That body, however, influenced by the consideration that other carriers in the State might be similarly situated, and not wishing to involve the government in the regulation of private business, refused a specific remedy, but passed a general law [3] empowering the Supreme Court to appoint three commissioners to determine, upon application, all such disputes, such awards to be binding for the space of one year.

While the suit instituted by the Western under this act was pending,[4] new proposals were offered by each company in an effort to avoid a lengthy and expensive litigation. That of the Western contemplated the establishment of an "equated mile" as the basis of division of the joint rate, for the purpose of which computation the length of the Worcester was to be assumed to be 40 miles, that of the Western 170.[5] The Worcester offered as a counter proposal a pro rata per-actual-mile division of the gross joint receipts, after first deducting certain handling charges.[6] Complete failure to compromise these differences brought forth a proposal from the business community to unite the carriers under one management.

In pursuance of this suggestion committees were formed from the directorates of the lines to consider the matter, which on December 18, 1845 rendered a joint report unanimously recommending consolidation.[7] At a meeting of

---

[1] *Ibid.*   [2] *S. D.*, no. 105, 1845.
[3] *S. D.*, no. 106, 1845.
[4] *Eleventh Annual Report to Stockholders* (Western), 1846, pp. 21–22.
[5] *Fourteenth Annual Report to Stockholders* (Boston and Worcester), 1846.
[6] *Ibid.*
[7] *Report of the Committees of the Boston and Worcester and Western . . . on the Subject of Uniting . . .* (Boston), 1846.

the stockholders of the Western the report was approved and the president instructed to open the necessary negotiations with the Worcester. The latter company, however, tabled the joint report and refused to consider the matter further.[1] This action left no recourse but to reopen the rate dispute.

As a result, the "Contract of 1846" was drawn up, recognizing the right of the Western to a division of joint receipts in excess of a pro rata per mile basis. This was accomplished by deducting 10 cents per passenger and 12 cents per ton from the pro rata share of the Worcester, plus a lump sum of $2,000 per year, and adding the same to the pro rata share of the Western.[2]

This contract, having expired in 1849, was renewed with slight emendations[3] until 1855, when an audit by the Western convinced that company that the method employed since 1846 in computing its share was at variance with the terms of the contract.[4] Again it became necessary to resort to arbitration. The referee decided in favor of the Worcester, whereupon the Western promptly terminated the contract. Provisional arrangements in 1856 and 1857 for the conduct of joint business served only to increase the mutual animosity; and in the latter year the legislature passed an act obligating one road to receive passengers and freight from another under such terms as should be decided upon by commissioners appointed by the Supreme Court.[5]

Upon petitions of both carriers under this act, a new award was made in 1858, the terms of which so incensed

[1] *Proceedings of Stockholders of the Boston and Worcester* . . . (Boston), January 12, 1846.

[2] *Twenty-sixth Annual Report to Stockholders* (Western), 1860, pp. 6–7.

[3] G. Twitchell Papers, Baker Library, Harvard University.

[4] *Twenty-third Annual Report to Stockholders* (Western), 1858, pp. 7–8.

[5] *Resolves*, act of May 30, 1857.

the Western that it immediately offered $25,000 to the Worcester to abrogate the decision and instituted suit to set it aside.[1] The award attempted to establish as a basis of division the principle of pro rata division of business originating at each station, rather than that of total joint receipts.[2] It was hoped thus to obviate certain anomalies which existed at some stations because of discrepancies between way and through rates.

Immediately upon expiration of this award in 1860, the controversy was resumed with renewed bitterness. Numerous complaints by merchants of obstruction to shipments led the Boston Board of Trade to seek a settlement, which it finally secured in 1862 by arbitration;[3] but the experience convinced that body that no permanent solution either in the interests of the people or of the carriers was possible except through consolidation.[4] The decision reversed the previous one, establishing a division according to the aggregate of passengers and tons carried one mile, and was therefore eminently unsatisfactory to the Worcester company. The Western, anticipating the refusal of the Worcester to renew this contract upon its expiration, petitioned the State for a charter to extend its line to Boston in direct competition with the Worcester.[5] This threat was sufficient to force the latter to agree to a joint committee to decide upon what terms a union of the roads might be effected,[6] but upon subsequent application to the

[1] Supplement to *Twenty-fifth Annual Report to Stockholders* (Western), 1860, pp. 1–9; *Twenty-sixth Annual Report to Stockholders* (Western), 1861, pp. 5–19. Cf. *Thirtieth Annual Report to Stockholders* (Boston and Worcester), 1860, pp. 28–37.

[2] *Ibid.*, pp. 22–28.

[3] *Report of the Select Committee of the Boston Board of Trade*... (Boston), 1862.

[4] *Ibid.*, pp. 26–46. The language is Catalinian in character.

[5] *Twenty-ninth Annual Report to Stockholders* (Western), 1864, pp. 17–22.

[6] *Thirty-fourth Annual Report to Stockholders* (Boston and Worcester), 1863, pp. 7–8. The general body of Boston and Worcester stockholders were favorably inclined to a union, though the directors as a whole seem not to have been.

legislature for a bill granting the necessary authority, the measure was defeated.[1]

Despite this unexpected reversal, it was apparent that union was not far off. The business communities served by the roads were exasperated to the point of open censure (particularly of the Worcester) at the prospect of further disruptions; the legislature was restive, the stockholders weary of bearing the cost and odium of the struggle.

The danger of further rupture in 1867 was sufficient to set in motion these cumulated forces, and an exasperated legislature passed a bill "authorizing and requiring" the Western Railroad to extend its line to Boston in the event the Worcester refused within three months' time to sell, lease, or consolidate its road with that of the Western.[2] The Worcester had no alternative but to accede, and on December 16, 1867 the Boston and Worcester and the Western ceased to exist and the Boston and Albany Railroad rose in their place.

Measured in terms of the primary purpose of its early proponents, the railroad westward failed to achieve any large measure of success. Of the total volume of tonnage transported from 1842 to 1867, something less than 7 per cent could be classified as export business. Water and rail transport to New York City were shorter by fifty miles and correspondingly cheaper;[3] the expansion of the railway net quickly diverted the Canadian trade to other lines,[4]

---

[1] *Thirtieth Annual Report to Stockholders* (Western), 1865, pp. 6–7. It was subsequently alleged that secret opposition of the Worcester directors had defeated the bill.

[2] *Resolves*, act of May 24, 1867, reprinted in *Thirty-eighth Annual Report to Stockholders* (Boston and Worcester) and *Thirty-third Annual Report to Stockholders* (Western).

[3] *Statements . . . Before the Committee on Railroads and Canals (Mass. Legislature) . . . on the Petition . . . for Consolidation . . .* (Boston, 1864), p. 10.

[4] *Twenty-fourth Annual Report to Stockholders* (Boston and Worcester), 1853, pp. 9–15.

TABLE I

WESTERN RAILROAD PASSENGER AND FREIGHT VOLUMES, 1842–63 [a]

Year	Number of passengers	Tons of freight	Tons one mile
1842	265,000 [b]	...	...
1848	371,883	265,542	24,656,129
1853	618,027	324,883	28,153,554
1858	484,277	437,896	33,043,106
1863	654,214	663,927	53,808,561

[a] Western *Annual Report to Stockholders* for years specified.
[b] Estimated.

TABLE II

BOSTON AND WORCESTER AND WESTERN RAILROADS: INCOME AND
DIVIDENDS, 1842–67 [a]

Year	Boston and Worcester			Western			Boston and Worcester and Western
	Gross income	Net income	Dividends (in per cent)	Gross income	Net income	Dividends (in per cent)	Total net income
1842	$349,000	$181,000	8	$513,000	$247,000	o	$428,000
1847	722,000	340,000	9	1,325,000	649,000	8	989,000
1852	759,000	349,000	7	1,339,000	657,000	6½	1,006,000
1857	1,019,000	406,000	7	1,910,000	1,084,000	8	1,490,000
1862	1,006,000	490,000	8	2,096,000	1,110,000	8	1,600,000
1867	1,943,000	728,000	15	4,087,000	2,837,000	10	3,565,000

[a] Boston and Worcester and Western *Annual Report to Stockholders* for years specified.

TABLE III

BOSTON AND WORCESTER AND WESTERN RAILROADS: NUMBER OF
CARS [a] AND ENGINES, 1842–67 [b]

Year	Number Passenger Cars			Number Freight Cars			Number Engines		
	Boston and Worcester	Western	Total	Boston and Worcester	Western	Total	Boston and Worcester	Western	Total
1842 ...	39	..	..	568	..	..	18	..	..
1847 ...	78	75	153	460	1,906	2,366	20	49	69
1852 ...	200	86	286	742	1,752	2,494	26	59	85
1857 ...	..	90	..	..	2,138	..	..	72	..
1862 ...	91[c]	90	181	674[c]	2,376	3,050	30	72	102
1867 ...	122	102	224	773	3,130	3,903	36	88	124

[a] Figures for freight cars reduced as nearly as possible to "cars of equal capacity."
[b] *Annual Report to Stockholders* for years specified.
[c] Western was supplying cars to Worcester by agreement.

TABLE IV

WESTERN RAILROAD: BARRELS OF FLOUR FROM ALBANY, 1842–67 [a]

Year	To Boston	To other Stations	Total
1842	85,986	86,124	172,110
1847	513,851	188,649	702,500
1852	231,546	254,793	486,339
1857	198,870	207,390	406,260
1862	567,968	328,862	896,830
1867	592,874	352,626	945,500

[a] Western *Report to Legislature*, 1867. Flour shipments are a rough index of the growing dependence on other than local agriculture. Large error, however, is occasioned by the varying quantities shipped by water.

and as late as 1867 the Western stated that lack of facilities in Boston hampered an export business that might be developed to 13,000 tons per month.[1]

The contribution of the line to the internal development of the State, however, was of signal importance. The early pre-eminence and success of the Worcester and the Western made them in many respects a pattern for later roads, and present-day engineering technique has been able to make but slight alteration of a roadway laid nearly a hundred years ago. For approximately a quarter of a century it was the single direct means of communication with the West; the decline of agricultural pursuits in favor of the vigorous and more profitable factory system was thereby in large part made practicable. While it is impossible to measure the precise influence of a railroad on the economic growth of the communities it serves, some rough notion of the internal progress which the lines from Boston to Albany helped to create may be gathered from their own financial records and the volume of their business. The brief tables on pages 467–468 will perhaps best summarize the results achieved by the Boston and Worcester and the Western.

[1] *Thirty-second Annual Report to Stockholders* (Western), 1867, p. 7.

FREE TRADE AND THE OREGON QUESTION, 1842-1846

THOMAS P. MARTIN

THE common or joint struggle for free trade as against protection in Great Britain and the United States which had its beginnings in the so-called alliance between certain Liberty party leaders in the latter country and members of the Anti-Corn Law League in the other[1] had its ending in momentous transactions which because not formally connected have never been well understood in their relations to each other. The repeal of the Corn Laws, the enactment of the Walker Tariff, the settlement of the Oregon question, and one might add the annexation of Texas and the beginnings of the Mexican War with what came in its train, have generally been treated as separate incidents in national history. Even in the last number of *The American Historical Review* a writer[2] deals with "British Party Politics and the Oregon Treaty" as if facts and factors in economic history common to the complementary sections or "interests" of Great Britain and the United States played almost no part at all in British politics. Without attempting to engage in any controversy whatsoever, the present writer purposes here to show how the "alliance" mentioned

[1] For the inception of this alliance see my "Upper Mississippi Valley in Anglo-American Anti-Slavery and Free Trade Relations, 1837–1842," in *Mississippi Valley Historical Review*, vol. xv, no. 2 (September, 1928), pp. 204–220.

[2] Frederick Merk, in vol. xxxvii, no. 4 (July, 1932), pp. 653–677.

above was perfected, and how the subsequent agitation grew into a sectional or "interest" co-operation [1] passing national boundaries and compelling rational adjustments.

I

The Anti-Corn Law activities of the Liberty party during the fall, winter, and spring of 1840–41 greatly interested Richard Cobden, who just then was rapidly rising to leadership in the Anti-Corn Law League, and Joseph Sturge, the Birmingham grain dealer, who in addition to being a leader in the League was virtually the head of the new British and Foreign Anti-Slavery Society. Consequently Cobden asked Sturge to write a public letter to the League's membership emphasizing "the importance of cleaving to the *true* principle of *immediate abolition*." Sturge, however, wished to visit the United States, and Cobden had to beg him to remain in England to make the most of the visit of the American "missionaries" whom Leavitt and Elizur Wright, Jr., predicted would be sent.

Now this is a glorious field of operations for you. There are more human beings in bonds in North America than in all the rest of the *Christian* world, and we by our corn laws throw the entire power over the legislature into the hands of the *slave owners*. What a splendid theme this would make for O'Connell and Brougham in the Anti-Corn Law debate, if you were in London to urge the subject on their attention at the meeting of deputies. [It is now] more than ever necessary that we should cling to our principle, when parties (I mean the two great political parties) are so nearly balanced that both are beginning to turn their eye towards us. The Whigs are trying to *use* the League; and there are so many of our supporters who are mere partisans that I am afraid they will break our ranks, unless such men as you should keep us together.[2]

[1] See the late Professor Frederick J. Turner's *Frontier in American History* (a collection of his essays) and articles of later date.

No attempt is made to give footnote references to obvious sources which are easily available in any research library.

[2] Henry Richard, *Joseph Sturge* (London, 1864), pp. 277–278.

That an analogous political situation existed with reference to the Liberty party in the United States, Sturge was soon to learn. In spite of Cobden's remonstrances, Sturge sailed for America, landed at New York April 3, and entered at once upon various projects which brought him into frequent and intimate contact with Leavitt and Wright, two arch-politicians of the Liberty party. Sturge promised Leavitt before he sailed, August 1, that he would soon secure and send back to him full details regarding the Corn Law question in England. Moreover, he had meanwhile met (at Buffalo, New York, early in July) John Curtis of Ohio, the "missionary" who was then on his way from the Unionville Convention to England, and had thereby gained almost at first hand important information regarding the intents and purposes of the Anti-Slavery "wheat interest" in the West.[1] The political situation was tersely described by Leavitt in a letter to Sturge, August 6, intended perhaps for perusal by Cobden.

It is expected there will be a convention at Cleveland, Ohio, next month, or in October [in accordance with plans made at Unionville]; and it will probably be then necessary for us to determine on our own course of policy with regard to the Tariff; that is, whether we shall resolve to adhere strictly to free trade, let England do as she may, or whether we shall write in the retaliatory principle with our Government, to lower our duties as fast as England lowers hers. The latter has many advantages and appeals strongly to national pride. . . . There will be a strong effort to raise a national party on this basis; and the abolitionists will be greatly beset to join it, perhaps to head it.[2]

Armed with Leavitt's letter, which admirably re-enforced the main point of Curtis's lectures to League audiences — that the West might turn to protection if the Corn Laws were not repealed — Sturge became very active

[1] Joseph Sturge, *Visit to America in 1841* (1842).
[2] *The Emancipator* (New York), September 9, 1841; and *The Patriot* (London), October 4, 1841.

among free-trade leaders, obviously with Cobden's approval, for Cobden wrote to Bright (November 7): "Sturge will attend the meeting of deputies, and intends to propose a motion for testing the House upon total and immediate repeal early next Session. He ought to be supported. We must know our friends." [1] Sturge did indeed attend the meeting of the Anti-Corn Law deputies in Manchester a week later, but it required the diplomacy of Francis Place, the London labor leader, to put Sturge's proposal in acceptable form. In the end a resolution was adopted that "it was desirable that efforts should be made by our friends in the house of commons as soon after its meeting as possible to procure a Total and Immediate repeal of the Corn Laws." [2]

Apparently this proved to be acceptable also to the Ohio "wheat interest" convention which, called by Salmon P. Chase, at length met during the last days of the year at Columbus. Under the leadership of Chase, who seems to have been inspired by Joshua Leavitt, this convention in its turn adopted resolutions embracing the free-trade doctrines which Leavitt for two years had been preaching with tongue and pen.[3] Of course, it did not represent all of the Liberty party; and the party as a whole was not committed to free trade. The responsible heads of the party, like James G. Birney, its candidate for president, had to be careful not to drive away anti-slavery, protectionist Whigs who were drifting towards them; but it is clear that Liberty party men used the free-trade argument whenever

[1] John Bright Papers, copy of a letter from Richard Cobden to John Bright, November 7, 1841 (furnished through the kindness of Mrs. H. C. Darbishire).

[2] British Museum, Additional Mss. 35,151, f. 351, Place to Cobden, November 15, 1841.

[3] "Proceedings of the Liberty Convention of the State of Ohio," December 29–30, 1841, in *The Philanthropist* (Cincinnati), January 5, and reprint, January 12, 1842.

and wherever it might possibly do good. For all practical purposes the "alliance" between Liberty-party and Anti-Corn Law League men was effective.[1]

II

The southern free traders were not idle. The decline of the Democratic party after the Panic of 1837, the persistent agitation of the Whigs for a return to protection, and the Whig victory in the presidential election of 1840 had made them uneasy. The Compromise Tariff Act of 1833, by which duties were being gradually reduced over a period of ten years, was obviously in jeopardy. Southern minds naturally reverted to nullification as a last resort; but Calhoun was not alarmed. He believed the Whig tenure of office would not last long and hoped he would be able to capture the presidency in the next election (1844).[2] Others were not so sanguine; and, moreover, free-trade activities on the part of northern Abolitionists were a distinct novelty. Bennett's *New York Herald* had described the "very curious meeting" at Vocal Hall in New York, October 23, 1840, at which Joshua Leavitt delivered his free-

[1] "Our indefatigable friend Joshua Leavitt has presented a voluminous petition to Congress praying for something nearly equivalent to *free trade* with Great Britain in case of the abolition of the Corn Laws, it gives a history of the Anti-Corn Law movement &c. It was well received by many of our statesmen and its prayer was only rejected by a *party* vote of the Whigs, all the Democrats in the Senate voting for it. . . . Great and excellent meetings of the Liberty party have been held in Ohio, Maine, and Vermont. Our prospects are brightening in this department of our Enterprise." John Greenleaf Whittier to Joseph Sturge, August 12, 1842 (furnished through the kindness of Mr. Joseph Sturge, Jr., of Birmingham, England).

Whittier's reference is to Leavitt's second "Wheat Memorial." See U. S. Senate Documents, 27th Cong., 2nd sess., no. 339 (160 pages, including index); see Cobden's reference to it in his second speech in Parliament (*Hansard's Parliamentary Debates*, 3rd ser., vol. lix, cols. 793–796).

[2] See John George Van Deusen, *Economic Bases of Disunion in South Carolina* (1928), chap. ii; and J. C. Calhoun to J. H. Hammond, September 24, 1841, in *Calhoun Correspondence*, Jameson, ed. (1899), pp. 489–493.

trade-for-free-labor speech; and it had denounced the activities of Joseph Sturge, who in 1841 had brought a British and Foreign Anti-Slavery Society "Address," signed by Thomas Clarkson, to be presented to the president of the United States. *The National Intelligencer* had published full accounts of John Curtis's lecturing in England under the auspices of the Anti-Corn Law League.

Anti-bellum records of southern opinion are not over-abundant,[1] but one may safely conjecture that it was thought it would not do to let Liberty party-Abolitionist Yankees appear as the sole champions of the West in efforts to open the markets of Great Britain to western grain, flour, and provisions. Whether with such a train of reasoning or not, General Duff Green, veteran journalist with western as well as southern connections, friend of James Gordon Bennett, and political ally of Calhoun, went to England in the late fall of 1841 on one of the strangest missions in the history of American foreign relations.

General Green arrived in London about December 1, 1841, while John Curtis was still actively lecturing in connection with the Anti-Corn Law League. Sir Robert Peel's Government had recently come into office and had formulated a policy of conciliation with other governments and peoples. Lord Ashburton had been fixed upon for a special mission to the United States to settle the dangerous northern or Maine boundary question. But Lord Aberdeen, Foreign Secretary, had complicated the situation, so far as General Green was concerned, by negotiating the so-called Quintuple Treaty with continental

---

[1] See speech by Henry A. Wise in Congress, January 25, 1842, attacking John Quincy Adams and charging that an English party was at work in the country; also Governor Gilmer's message to the Virginia legislature charging that the British were "backing" Birney and Morris, reviewed in *The Philanthropist*, January 29, 1842.

powers, including France, for the suppression of the African slave trade. Consequently, Green dashed off to Paris to foment opposition to French ratification. It was spring before he returned to London. Then he published a series of articles on the economic and international aspects of the anti-slavery movement for the enlightenment of British public opinion.[1]

According to General Green, the anti-slavery movement was neither in the United States nor in Great Britain the philanthropic, humanitarian movement which its leaders proclaimed it to be. As early as 1817, John Quincy Adams while minister to England had advised Edward Coles to settle in Illinois and to help steer the West into political and economic relations with the East, away from its connections with the South, in order to put an end to slave-holder domination of national affairs. Since then Abolitionists had pursued that policy and had even appealed to British anti-slavery people for aid.[2] In Great Britain Richard Cobden had pointed out, as early as 1835, the serious character of American commercial competition; and the government had resorted to "visit and search," ostensibly for the suppression of the African slave trade but really for the protection of the carrying trade "beyond the Cape of Good Hope." Efforts had been made to destroy American credit in London and to "substitute" East Indian for American cotton. "And all this was done under the pretense of a horror for the slave trade, and com-

[1] My first sketch of General Duff Green's venture abroad was published in *The Courier-Journal* (Louisville), April 15, 1923, sec. 3, p. 11, in a series of special articles on "Nineteenth Century History." See Professor St. George L. Sioussat's reference to these in *American Secretaries of State*, vol. v (1928), p. 399; also his "Duff Green's 'England and the United States,' with an Introductory Study of American Opposition to the Quintuple Treaty of 1841," in *Proceedings of the American Antiquarian Society for October, 1930.*

[2] See "Some International Aspects of the Anti-Slavery Movement, 1818–1823," in *Journal of Economic and Business History*, vol. i, no. 1 (November, 1928), pp. 137–148.

passion for the poor negroes." Now the British through the anti-slavery party would abolish slavery in the United States, Cuba, and Brazil and by so doing raise costs of production in those countries above those in the East Indies. Green questioned whether it was politic to do this. The chief market for western produce was in the South which in turn found its market for cotton in Great Britain. Together the South and the West determined the tariff policy of the United States, valued by Great Britain as a market for manufactured goods. The West was beginning to produce a surplus for export overseas and to resent exclusion from British markets by the Corn Laws. Would it not be better for Great Britain to conciliate both the South and the West by dropping the "anti-slavery" policy and repealing the Corn Laws?

In due time Cobden characteristically undertook the instruction of Green in the art of dealing with British "interests" (or sections). In Manchester,

your object should be to prove the capability & readiness of the U. S. to do a greatly increased amount of business provided our corn law was repealed. . . . The American securities are chiefly held by Capitalists in London or elsewhere, *not in Manchester*. But I think you are likely to find the City people (in London) quite alive to the subject of the State-debts, & if you can shew them as I think you can easily do that the repeal of the corn-law would enable the States to pay their debts the Lombart St & Threadneedle St people will cooperate with the Manchester men in opposing the corn law.[1]

It ought to be made clear to them that the best way of making the States liquidate their debts is to offer them a market here for their produce. The City people have some notions about the Federal Government assuming the State debts, & other impracticable projects. Their minds ought to be disabused of any such delusive hopes, & taught to look to a Free trade in breadstuffs. Could you indoctrinate Mr Alsazer, the writer of the Times City article, with these views it would be half the battle.[2]

---

[1] Duff Green Papers, Library of Congress, Richard Cobden to Duff Green, August 28, 1842.

[2] *Ibid.*, September 7, 1842.

Green naturally had formulated his own plans for securing a manifestation of British interest in American produce,[1] but he co-operated with British free traders as well as he could and supplied the kind of information they desired about the West. Thus the basic argument of Leavitt, Curtis, Elizur Wright, Jr., and their school of anti-slavery followers, that the West (which they intended to "occupy") was indeed a great agricultural section complementary to British manufacturing and financial sections which should be freed from the handicap of the Corn Laws, was confirmed by a free-trade apostle of the pro-slavery interests of the South.

III

Peel reduced the sliding scale of the Corn Laws, in 1842, to a level equivalent to the Whig eight-shilling fixed-duty proposal of 1834. American protectionists denounced it as a discrimination and urged retaliation; but Cobden probably went too far in asserting that it was the cause of the enactment of the Whig tariff of 1842.[2]

Next came great relative changes in business conditions. The pacific diplomacy of Peel's Government removed the immediate risk of war with the United States and brought back trade with the Near and Far East;[3] while the Ameri-

[1] *Ibid.*, Duff Green to his wife, September 1, 1842.

[2] News of Tyler's approval of the tariff bill and of the American ratification of the Webster-Ashburton Treaty reached England September 15. Something like a panic followed; and Cobden immediately threw blame on the Government. On the Continent, Friederich List, in *Allgemeine Zeitung*, rejoiced and urged the Zollverein to raise its duties. Aberdeen, foreseeing difficulties, was anxious to secure the settlement of the Oregon boundary; but the Tyler administration played for time.

[3] Recovery began in the latter part of November (see Peel Papers, British Museum, Goulburn to Peel, November 24, 1842, enclosing letter by William Cotton of the Bank of England). Conservative reports of it were decried by Cobden in a letter to J. B. Smith, December 5, 1842, in J. B. Smith Papers, Manchester Free Public Library.

can tariff of 1842 was productive of nothing, unless it was a deepening of the business depression during the next year, for the bottom was not reached before the middle of the next summer.[1] Pioneer farmers were sent trekking across the plains and the mountains; and the numbers which went to the Oregon country soon made the northwestern boundary as serious a question with Great Britain as the northeastern had been.[2] Those who remained behind had the satisfaction, however, of seeing their surplus produce invade the British markets in spite of the Corn Laws. It is not too much to say that this experience, enjoyed by free traders in Great Britain as a confirmation of the statements of Curtis and Green as well as by farmers in the West, produced a deep conviction among the latter, many of whom were Whigs, that "American" and other systems of protection could be and at that time were injurious.[3] Indeed General Green, who was again in London in 1843 when alarming "Oregon" rumors began to arrive, declared to the government that the interest of the West in Oregon would cool if Great Britain in good time would

[1] See Arthur H. Cole, "Wholesale Prices in the United States, 1825–1845," in *Review of Economic Statistics*, vol. viii, no. 2 (April, 1926), pp. 69–84. The reaction of 1844 almost cancelled the recovery from the previous decline.

[2] Joseph Schafer, "Oregon Pioneers and American Diplomacy," in *Essays ... Dedicated to Frederick Jackson Turner* (1910), pp. 35–55; and Frederick Merk, "The Oregon Pioneers and the Boundary," in *American Historical Review*, vol. xxix, no. 4 (July, 1924), pp. 681–699.

[3] On January 27, 1845, Dr. Gamaliel Bailey in retrospect declared in *The Herald* (Cincinnati), "A more liberal policy on the part of England would awaken a better feeling on this side of the Atlantic.

"The change in her Tariff, which took place in 1842, slight as it was, by opening to some extent a new market for western produce, disposed the people of the West to liberal means of commercial policy. Let this change be followed up, by such a modification of the Corn Law as will admit our corn and wheat into the English market, at reasonable duties, and in a short time you would scarcely find an advocate of a high protective Tariff throughout the whole West. . . ."

The Democrats (low tariff) won congressional elections, in the fall of 1842, in New York, Pennsylvania, and Ohio, to the great alarm of protectionist Whigs. See *Niles' National Register* (Baltimore), November–December, 1842, *passim*.

show willingness to enter upon the negotiation of a treaty for the admission of American grain and provisions.[1]

In America the campaign of 1844 got an early start. The conventions and campaigns of 1843, while the depression was most severely felt, set the chief issues. Strangely enough, a second General Anti-Slavery Convention held in London that summer produced the first great stir. Lewis Tappan of New York and Stephen Pearl Andrews of Texas, who had formerly been in the pay of Joseph Sturge on a mission to Havana, revealed a plan for effecting compensated emancipation in the Lone Star Republic and apparently secured the approval, if not the support, of the British government. Consequently, General Duff Green and Ashbel Smith, the Texas minister in London, professed alarm and precipitated a movement on the part of the Tyler administration for immediate annexation.[2] In history this has obscured the manifestation of free-trade influence, which was impressive, in that Convention; for both Joshua Leavitt and Richard Cobden (delegate of the

[1] Duff Green Papers, Library of Congress, Duff Green to Peel, June 27, 1843 (draft). Green declared that Calhoun and other southern senators had supported the Webster-Ashburton Treaty, "because they believed it would lead to further negotiations adjusting satisfactorily the commercial and political relations of the two Governments;" while Benton and the Van Burenites had opposed it and had kept alive the spirit of territorial controversy by bringing forward the Oregon bill. "Arrangements have been made whereby powerful influences in the several states, of the Union will act in concert, in favor of a treaty with England providing for the adjustment of the North Western boundary and an exchange of our respective products on terms of reciprocal and mutual benefits. . . ."

[2] In September, N. W. Senior undertook to caution and guide Green, as Cobden had done. "You must not attempt to obtain from any British statesman a disavowal of the wish that Slavery should cease in Texas. You might as well have attempted to get such a disavowai from Dr. Channing. Nor must you attempt to use, as an argument in favor of your view of the Oregon question, the fact that your countrymen believe their claim to be best. . . . The Whigs will aid you in abolishing differential & protective duties, & in referring any claim to arbitration. But any argument that is obviously sophistical will not only do no good, but will do harm. . . ." (Duff Green Papers, Library of Congress, Senior to Green, September 8, 1843.)

Manchester Anti-Slavery Society) were there joining in an effort to put an end to the Convention's policy of urging fiscal discriminations against slave-grown produce and in favor of free-grown produce.[1] The Oregon question, first made political by a preliminary convention at Cincinnati, July, 1843, was cleverly combined with the Texas question the next May in the Baltimore Democratic National Convention.[2] The Liberty party steered clear of the Oregon question, denounced the project for the annexation of Texas, and maintained an anti-slavery attitude without giving too much offence, but took good care to emphasize that it would use all its influence and exert its utmost energies to extend markets for the products of free labor, now largely "confined to the non-paying markets of the slave States."[3] Blind insistence on protection and Clay's uncertain attitude towards annexation were fatal to the Whigs. The Liberty party gained free-trade and anti-slavery votes at their expense, particularly in western New York; and the victory went to the low-tariff Democrats, who had placed at the head of their ticket James K. Polk of Tennessee.[4]

[1] The Anti-Slavery Reporter (London), June 21, 1843, pp. 103–106; and The Patriot (London), June 26, 1843. It was charged that free trade had weakened the anti-slavery movement; and the historian, W. L. Mathieson, remarked in his Great Britain and the Slave Trade (1929), pp. 85–88, about the "waning zeal" which was noticeable even in John Bright. See, also, "Aspect of Affairs in Great Britain," an interesting editorial possibly inspired by Duff Green, in The New York Herald, July 21, 1843.

[2] The proceedings of the Baltimore Convention of 1844 apparently were not published separately. See Niles' National Register (Baltimore), June 1, 1844; and other contemporary newspaper accounts; also D. W. Howe, "The Mississippi Valley in the Movement for Fifty-Four Forty or Fight," in Mississippi Valley Historical Association Proceedings, vol. v, pp. 99–116; and C. E. Persinger, "The 'Bargain of 1844' as the Origin of the Wilmot Proviso" in American Historical Association Report for 1911, vol. i, pp. 189–195.

[3] See reports of the Liberty party Convention at Buffalo, in The Emancipator (New York), September 7 and 14, 1843.

[4] Edward Channing, History of the United States, vol. v, pp. 543–545.

IV

Little if anything has been written about the significance in world politics of the American election of 1844, though it marked a definite return to democratic ideals in America at a time when the Old World was saddled with reaction, and liberals were preparing for the revolution which eventually came in 1848. The apprehensions of conservatives did not find much open expression; but liberal interests, especially the commercial ones in Great Britain, commented hopefully. In their view territorial questions (Texas and Oregon) had been quite overshadowed by the tariff question, during the last six weeks of the campaign; and they freely predicted that there would be no war over Oregon if the Corn Laws were repealed and the American tariff of 1842 were revised. In other words, they believed free trade would keep the peace. Intelligent conservatives agreed with the liberals in this.[1]

But both sides overlooked the mischief that could be

---

[1] On November 30, 1844, both *The Economist* (London) and *The League* (London) pointed to the Whig victory in Ohio, the State from which John Curtis had come, and tried to put the onus on the Peel Government. "The men of Ohio," declared *The League*, "have voted not so much against Free Trade, in the success of which no portion of the Union is more directly interested, as against the unsuccessful efforts to open trade." *The Economist* observed, "We open our ports to the cotton and rice of the south, and we there find every disposition to appreciate the advantages of our superior manufactures. We close our ports against the corn of the north . . . and they readily join those who are more immediately interested in excluding our goods from the American market." *The League's* "joy at the success of a Free-Trader" (Polk) was "not a little dashed" by his alleged opinions regarding slavery. "We are always grieved to find any section of Free Traders who do not fully carry out their own principles: Free Trade includes Free Labour, and must, in its results, lead to the perfect emancipation of industry in all its forms."

Representative Thomas J. Henley, of Indiana, in a speech to the House, December 22, 1844, quoted extensive opinions of the British conservative press, particularly of *The Times* (London) and *The Liverpool Mail*; also, of the Liberal press, particularly *Dublin Freeman's Journal*. See *Congressional Globe*, 28th Cong., 2nd sess., vol. xiv, Appendix, pp. 74–78. Another interesting speech is that by Thomas L. Clingman, of North Carolina (*ibid.*, pp. 114–120).

worked by the disgruntled "all of Oregon" men in the new Congress who let no grass grow under their feet. The Congress had hardly been organized when William ("Foghorn") Allen, of Ohio, opened the question in the Senate, while a colleague pressed the matter in the House. It remained for Aaron V. Brown, of Tennessee, a close friend of the president-elect and chairman of the Committee on Territories, to put the matter in a truly alarming state. He managed apparently to keep the Oregon question quiet until the Texas question was virtually settled by arrangements for annexation, and then, during the week of January 27, he rushed a bill for the occupation of Oregon through the House and carried it with a vote of 140 to 59.[1]

The Oregon debates in Congress, brief though they were, were full of language uncomplimentary to the British, which John Bull found wounding to his *amour propre*. In the person of the premier, Sir Robert Peel, John Bull swelled with hardly suppressed anger and professed to believe the situation serious.[2] Clearly his government was faced by an American democracy recently victorious over conservatives at the polls, a democracy which was inaugurating its return to office with a vigorous twist of the British lion's tail, partly to conciliate a delegation of "all of Oregon" men from the region north of the Ohio. Then came the new president's assertion, in the inaugural address of March 4, that "our title to the country of the Oregon is 'clear and unquestionable,'" which, though not formally addressed to Great Britain, clearly called for an answer. That answer was not long in forthcoming. With a vessel waiting in the Mersey to take the news over

[1] *Ibid.*, pp. 17, 36–37, 48–49; and Appendix, pp. 44–50. A. V. Brown's work is recorded on pp. 197ff.

[2] Peel to Aberdeen, February 23, 1845, Aberdeen Papers, British Museum, selections privately printed (copy in Library of Congress). Sir Samuel O'Malley proposed, March 1, to take over a large body of Irish and hold the Oregon country (Peel Papers, British Museum, vol. ccclxxxi, f. 286).

promptly to the United States, Peel and Aberdeen declared to both the Commons and the Lords, with the hearty approval of the Opposition, that the British had rights in the Oregon matter "clear and unquestionable" which they were "resolved" and "prepared" to maintain.[1] For the time this satisfied the British sense of national honor and pleased the Old World conservatives. In turn it may have caused people in America to pause and to consider the responsibilities of their position (at least, the British fondly believed that it made Polk look very foolish); but it had a ridiculous aspect when it was seen from contemporary American newspapers that there had been no such excitement in the United States as Polk's address had produced in Great Britain.[2]

V

The spring and summer of 1845 was a busy time for those who had charge of British and American foreign relations. Peel and Aberdeen became hopelessly involved in

[1] *Hansard's Parliamentary Debates*, 3rd ser., vol. lxxix, cols. 120–124, 193–199. Meanwhile *Punch* vouchsafed with characteristic seriousness that "the Bible on which Mr. Polk took the Presidential oath was very handsomely bound for the purpose in the skin of a negro." Quoted by *The Times* (London), April 7, 1845.

[2] British business interests, more inclined to be liberal than conservative, pointed to other than territorial topics in President Polk's Inaugural Address. Even *The Circular to Bankers*, which represented country-bank interests and was highly regarded by Sir James Graham, Home Secretary, declared that Polk had distinctly repudiated protection. *The Economist* and *The League* predicted that the new Administration would turn to low tariffs and that the low-tariff party (southern) and commercial interests (eastern) as well as the grain-growing West would oppose war over the Oregon question. These intuitions were correct. The new president, on March 10, turned to the South for a minister to Great Britain, offering the post successively to John C. Calhoun, F. H. Elmore, and F. W. Pickens — all of South Carolina; while Duff Green urged Calhoun to accept it with full power to settle the Oregon question and negotiate a commercial treaty. The post was ultimately accepted by Louis McLane, president of the Baltimore and Ohio Railroad, which was extending its lines to the wheat fields of the West. McLane had already seen service at St. James, in 1830, when he had negotiated with the "Tories" a treaty for the opening of the British West Indian trade. The news of his appointment was received in Great Britain with much satisfaction.

the swirl of British and Old World politics, Peel seeking to build up his country's military and naval strength and Aberdeen seeking to diminish the foreign menace by courting the friendship of France through Guizot.[1] In all this there was little but hostility towards the United States. But other forces were checking the tendency. Encouraged by the vigorously worded low-tariff paragraphs in the president's inaugural address, free traders in both countries were endeavoring to steer their respective governments towards the common end desired — speedy adjustments of territorial questions and removals of barriers to free trade. By the end of May all British talk of war with the United States subsided; and, as the weather continued cold, rainy, and unpromising, the Corn Laws literally became the question of the hour. Debates in parliament, May 26–28 and June 10, seemed definitely to forecast that the repeal of the Corn Laws was only a question of time; and Cobden's joy almost carried him beyond bounds.[2]

During the summer came the terrible blight which destroyed the potato crops of western Europe as well as those of Great Britain and Ireland; and it became certain by the middle of October that the United States was the only considerable and dependable source for plentiful supplies of food.[3] Indeed it seemed that the British Isles had suddenly been pushed off the continental shelf and anchored in the middle of the Atlantic, as dependent upon the United States for food supplies as they had ever been for raw cotton. Polk with his cat o'nine tails and the detestable Yankees seemed terribly near, especially when Pakenham, the British minister in Washington, got him-

---

[1] The Duke of Wellington to Aberdeen, March 1, 1845, Aberdeen Papers, British Museum, selections privately printed, illuminates the British problem.

[2] See below, p. 487, n. 1.

[3] See numerous reports in the British press, October 15 to November 15, 1845; and Peel Papers for the same period, especially November 3.

self into a diplomatic tangle by uncivilly rejecting without reference to his home government the administration's offer to settle the Oregon boundary on the forty-ninth parallel from the Rocky Mountains to the sea.[1]

On the American side, the changing British situation was met with distinctly complimentary developments. Before the end of March, business in the West was feeling the stimulating influence of foreign demand, and the press began to describe in happy phrases the movement of grain and provisions from West to East and the building of railroads (particularly the Baltimore and Ohio) from the East into the West for freight.[2] When in May, Thomas Ritchie began publishing *The Daily Union,* a new administration organ, in Washington, the troublesome Oregon question was deftly set aside until attention could be called to the significance of the free-trade movement in Great Britain.[3] Upon reading the parliamentary debates

[1] The Oregon negotiations had been resumed in Washington, July 12, 1845, between Secretary Buchanan and the British minister, Pakenham, under the eye of President Polk. See cartoon in *Punch* (London), vol. x, p. 155.

[2] See *Hunt's Merchants' Magazine* (New York), vol. xii, no. 4 (April, 1845). Dr. Gamaliel Bailey's *Herald and Philanthropist* (Cincinnati) declared, April 2, "the British market is becoming more and more important to the free West every year. The reduction of the English tariff, on several articles of Western produce, has already done much in quickening industry, and raising prices. . . . The supply of good beef for our Home market is quite small enough, owing to the large amount purchased for foreign ports.

"The intelligence brought by the Cambria is most cheering to our Western farmers and lard oil manufacturers. Henceforth, it seems, Lard and Lard Oil are to be admitted into Great Britain free of duty! . . . The supply of sperm oil is altogether insufficient to meet the demand. . . ."

On May 7, the *Herald and Philanthropist* looked forward to the repeal of the Corn Laws. "It is useless to look for greatly increased demand in the South; so long as slavery is continued there, the Southern market [will] be a limited and unsafe one. Slaves are meagre consumers of wheat. But when the slave system shall have given place to Free Labor, the Southern demand for breadstuffs will increase." An echo of the Wilberforce argument of 1822!

[3] See *The Union* (Washington), *passim;* and *The American Review* (Whig), August, 1845. It is hoped that Professor C. H. Ambler's *Thomas Ritchie: A Study in Virginia Politics* (1913) will be followed by a study of the great editor's work in Washington.

of May 26–28 and June 10, Ritchie was convinced, as was
Cobden at the time,[1] that the repeal of the Corn Laws was
certain to come,[2] though meanwhile he had found it necessary to answer the British press on Oregon. In conjunction
with George Bancroft and Robert J. Walker, "Father"
Ritchie launched, on July 1, a veritable crusade against
the tariff; while Dr. Gamaliel Bailey, Liberty-party editor
of the Cincinnati *Herald and Philanthropist*, pictured the
advantages of free trade to the anti-slavery West, predicting that in the event of the repeal of the Corn Laws "the
Western people will gradually part with their hostile feelings" on the Oregon question.[3] Not until after Pakenham
had hopelessly blundered, as indicated above, and the
failure of food crops in the Old World was known, did
"Father" Ritchie as the spokeman of his party definitely
change his course. Then falling in with the president's
wishes, he began to prepare the American public for the
strong paragraphs on Oregon which Polk was to insert in
his forthcoming first message to Congress.[4]

As the terrible autumn of 1845 advanced Lord Aberdeen
came to see his problem clearly. He must secure, if possible, a settlement of the Oregon boundary on the basis of
the forty-ninth parallel; because, if the Corn Laws were to
be repealed (as seemed certain) and great quantities of
food purchased from the United States and paid for with
British manufactures (as they should be), threatening
clouds of war must be dispelled and the American tariff of
1842 reduced. Consequently he began early in October to
move, presenting first a long-standing British grievance

---

[1] Letters from Richard Cobden to J. B. Smith, May 29, 1845, in J. B. Smith
Papers, Manchester Free Public Library, and from Sir George Murray to Peel,
June 21, 1845, in the Peel Papers, transmitting a lengthy extract from a Cobden
letter of May 29, which Peel in reply to Murray ironically described as having
"all the air of a genuine letter."

[2] *The Union*, July 5, 1845.　　　　　　　　[3] *Ibid.*, July 9, 1845.

[4] *Polk's Diary*, Quaife, ed., vol. i, p. 66.

against the American duties on rolled and hammered iron, as a protest against the tariff, but at the same time preparing the way for a settlement of rough-rice claims which South Carolinians justly held against the British. For during the summer Robert Barnwell Rhett had assured him that, if those rough-rice claims were put in train of settlement, he would make a vigorous attack upon the tariff and, if necessary, "renew the *Nullification* vote in South Carolina, which he had formerly proposed, and which had produced such serious consequences." [1]

Whether Lord Aberdeen had given private assurances or not, Rhett had returned to the United States, September 6, and was already raising a formidable anti-tariff agitation in the South. Indeed it gained such impetus that it interfered with "Father" Ritchie's editorial campaign on the Oregon question, mentioned above; and *The Charleston Mercury* bluntly remarked that southern statesmen were not ready to maintain, at a cost of two million bales of cotton per annum, "that we have a 'clear and unquestionable title' to every foot of ground in a territory which we have consented to occupy in common with the other claimant for twenty years." [2]

[1] As early as August 25, 1845 Aberdeen had discussed both questions — iron and rice — and had mentioned Rhett's view, in a letter to Peel. See Peel Papers; see, also, Aberdeen to Peel, September 17, 1845, Aberdeen Papers, selections privately printed; and Aberdeen to Pakenham, October 6, 1845 (draft), Foreign Office 5/423, no. 66.

[2] *Polk's Diary* (Quaife ed.), vol. i, pp. 17, 21–22; Polk Papers, Library of Congress, Buchanan to McLane, private and personal, September 13, 1845 (copy); R. K. Crallé to Calhoun, September 23, 1845, *Calhoun Correspondence*, p. 1053; and files of *The Daily Union* (Washington) and *The Charleston Mercury*, especially the issues of October 11 to November 11, inclusive, 1845. *The National Intelligencer* (Whig, Washington) and *The Cincinnati Gazette* (Whig), of the same time, make interesting comments on the controversy. Dr. Gamaliel Bailey's *Herald and Philanthropist* (Cincinnati), Liberty-party organ, reveals interesting jealousy of southern advances to the West at the Memphis Commercial Convention. Possibly the Democratic Convention of Hamilton County, Ohio, November 11, 1845, which devoted its attention particularly to an

Thus it came about that a vigorous discussion of the tariff as well as the Oregon question was kept up until Congress met in December; and the tariff paragraphs in the president's message, together with Robert J. Walker's strong argument against the tariff, in his report as secretary of the Treasury, which accompanied the message, were read with as much interest as were those on Oregon. In Great Britain, *The Times* (London) reflected much public opinion by remarking that there was nothing new on the Oregon question in the message, but on the tariff it "exhibits a sympathy with our own Ministerial intentions as marvellous as it is auspicious of international amity."[1] This is not to say, however, that some conservatives and their friends in Europe who did not understand the powerful influence of economic factors in British and American politics were not terribly alarmed over the prospect of war. Even Peel in a note to Aberdeen advised "silence and preparation;"[2] while the King of Belgium, "full of our disputes with the United States," was "most anxious that every effort should be employed to solve these difficulties by peaceable means." "This he desires for his own sake as well as ours, the turbulent spirits of this country, as of France, as of the whole Continent, being, as he says bent upon seeing us and the Americans at war."[3] Europe was indeed approaching the Revolution of 1848. But Aberdeen declared he had never been afraid of the Oregon question and felt confident that it would soon be settled, either by arbitration or direct negotiation.[4] In formulating his

anti-tariff memorial to Congress rather than to internal improvements was a sort of rival of the Memphis Convention.

[1] *The Times* (London), December 24, 1845.

[2] Peel Papers, Peel to Aberdeen, December 26, 1845 (draft).

[3] *Ibid.*, Leopold to Peel, December 27, 1845.

[4] *Ibid.*, Aberdeen to Peel, December 28, 1845; Aberdeen Papers, Aberdeen to Everett, January 3, 1846 (draft): theory that the repeal of the Corn Laws will win the West.

plans for the opening of parliament, Peel declared, "The admission of Maize will I believe go far to promote a settlement of Oregon."[1] This is enough to show what the policy of the British government was with reference to Oregon from that time.

In Washington, free-trade interests worked for the pacific settlement of the Oregon question as a part of the general program to reduce the tariff. John C. Calhoun, supported as he was by Robert Barnwell Rhett and his fellow nullifiers of South Carolina, wielded a tremendous influence in this direction in the Senate; but he should not be given too much credit, for many worked independently towards the same end. Pakenham declared that Archer of Virginia, Corcoran (the banker), and Benton of Missouri had "officiously" approached him with assurances that, if England would offer to accept the forty-ninth parallel, the whole of Vancouver's Island, etc., the administration would refer the proposition to the Senate, and the Senate would approve it "without much opposition."[2] Space does not here permit the setting forth in detail of what happened in Congress. Noisy demands for "all of Oregon" obviously lacked unanimous support from the West. After much deliberation, playing for time, and hunting around for inoffensive phrases and words, the Senate opened the way for a settlement by giving notice to terminate existing agreements with reference to Oregon, "with a view to a speedy and amicable settlement." This done, Great Britain made a proposal, which was duly referred to the Senate and accepted, locating the boundary along the forty-ninth parallel. The Walker Tariff Bill (reducing

[1] Peel Papers, Peel to Lord Francis Egerton, secret, January 6, 1846 (draft). See, also, "Peel and Polk," in *Punch* (London), vol. x, p. 155, cited above.

[2] Pakenham to Aberdeen, no. 138, December 29, 1845, and same to same, separate and confidential, same date, Foreign Office 5/430.

rates to a "revenue" basis) became law; while the British government proceeded with the repeal of the Corn Laws. (The Texas question was allowed to resolve itself in the annexation of Texas to the United States.) Everywhere English-speaking peoples rejoiced, except among the defeated partisans who were disgruntled; and there was ushered in an era of Anglo-American peace, good will, and free trade, which during the next fifteen years (with slight exception) operated greatly to strengthen the North and the West, and the north of England, against the day of southern secession and a war for the division of the Union.

SOME ECONOMIC ASPECTS OF THE LIGHT AND POWER INDUSTRY[1]

C. O. RUGGLES

THERE have been striking changes in the light and power industry in this country within the past twenty years, and especially in the extent to which these public utilities are supplying power to industry.

The federal census of electrical industries has been taken at quinquennial intervals since 1902; our latest statistics therefore are for the year 1927. Within the twenty-five-year period from 1902 to 1927 the growth in output and in capacity of the light and power industry has been accompanied by a continual increase in mechanization and in the size of both the individual plant and the generating units. These changes in turn have brought a marked decrease in the number of utility establishments, especially in the period from 1917 to 1927. In comparing 1927 and 1902, we find that the number of kilowatt hours generated was 30 times as large at the later date; the kilowatt capacity of generations, 21 times; the horse-power of prime movers, 19 times; the value of plant and equipment, 18 times; and the number of persons employed, 8 times. The customers were 11 times as numerous in 1927 as in 1907.[2] Even more striking has been the decrease in the same period of the number of those establishments which generate all or a

---

[1] With the consent of the editors, the writer has drawn freely on some of his previous articles in the *Harvard Business Review* (January, 1924), and in the *American Economic Review, Supplement* (March, 1929).

[2] The number of customers was not reported in 1902; see *United States Census of Electrical Industries* (1927), p. 17.

part of their energy, as distinguished from those operated entirely on purchased energy. The number of central stations generating all or a part of their energy decreased 28 per cent from 1902 to 1927.[1] If the stations which purchase all their energy are considered, the census data show that there were 227 such stations in 1907, the first year in which such information was collected. The number of such stations has steadily increased since that time, reaching 2,004 in 1927, almost a tenfold increase within a twenty-year period. Obviously these changes were in turn the result of

TABLE I

CENTRAL ELECTRIC LIGHT AND POWER ESTABLISHMENTS

Year	Total	Commercial	Municipal
1927	4,335	2,137	2,198
1922	6,355	3,774	2,581
1917	6,542	4,224	2,318
1912	5,221	3,659	1,562
1907	4,714	3,462	1,252
1902	3,620	2,805	815

the scrapping of small inefficient plants and the growth of large central stations.

While the number of central electric-light and power establishments increased from 1902 to 1917, they have decreased markedly since that date, as table 1 shows. If municipal plants are excluded and commercial plants alone are considered, the facts show that there was a decrease of 49.4 per cent.

When electricity first came into use in the early 'eighties it had to compete with gas, first for illumination and later for industrial uses. The much greater convenience of

[1] *Ibid.* In 1902 there were 3,620 central stations generating all or a part of their energy. The number of such central stations reached a maximum in 1917 when there were 5,124. By 1927 the number was but 2,331.

electricity for lighting gave the early central stations an advantage in securing that business, and the early managers of electric utilities appear to have considered it their goal. At first, central-station managers did not have adequate appreciation of the importance of the power phase of their business. Most of their attention was given to the lighting business. The national association through which executives exchanged ideas was named the "National Electric Light Association;" even in the late 'eighties only a small minority of the members of this association had any real vision of the possibilities of the development of the market for power, and at that time the Association had no committee on power. Many central stations had for some time little or no daylight load, and as late as 1907 many of them were embarrassed when the high-efficiency lamps made their appearance and threatened to cut down the consumption of electricity, even though these stations were securing a substantial increase in customers. Such an increase might mean higher cost of plant and of operation, but with each customer using high-efficiency lamps, and hence consuming less energy, the companies were facing inefficient use of plant unless their market could be extended. The introduction of high-efficiency lamps, therefore, stimulated the industry to develop a power load.

While electric motors are much older than the electrical industry, they at first depended for their supply of current upon primary batteries, consuming costly chemicals, and could consequently have no commercial significance in industry. Some important factors in the development of the electrical industry were to change this condition; the perfection of the dynamo and its use also as a motor when electrical energy was supplied were items of prime importance. About the middle or late 'eighties it became clear that alternating current was to be of much significance in making long-distance transmission feasible. This in turn wrought revolutionary changes in the electrical manufacturing business, and laid the foundation for the use of electrical energy, not only in the manufacturing plants located near a central station but also in those between two and three hundred miles distant from the point of generation. All the early electrical manufacturers had originally built equipment to generate and use direct current. The proportion of the kilowatt capacity of alternating-current generators to the total kilowatt capacity increased from 67.8 per cent in 1907 to 98.9 per cent in 1927. This represents the advantages which alternating current has over direct current in connection with long-distance transmission and transformation from one voltage to another.[1] The foregoing changes played an important rôle in the development of the wholesale market for power.[2]

In attempting to sell power to industries, central stations were faced with the problem of continuity of service. This, in turn, meant that a central station was compelled to have sufficient stand-by plant to provide against emergencies, or to be interconnected with other plants which

[1] The use of the thyratron tube now appears to offer possibilities of even greater long-distance transmission by means of direct current.

[2] The electrical census of 1927 divided the consumers into a much larger number of classes than had any previous census. Instead of the two groups "lighting" and "power" shown for 1922, the sales reported showed domestic service (residential consumption), sales for "small light and power (retail)," sales for "large light and power (wholesale)," and sales for farm service. Some of the reporting companies failed to indicate the class of service. In such instances the aggregates of these figures are shown under the designation "Undistributed by class of service." Adjusting the census data on this basis, domestic customers in 1927 constituted 83.1 per cent of the total number although they consumed but 13.2 per cent of the total sales; those consuming electricity for light and power at retail constituted 14.4 per cent of total customers consuming but 19.1 per cent of total sales; all other customers, which included the wholesale customers, equalled but 2.5 per cent of the total number of customers, but they consumed 52.6 per cent of total sales. This group consisted chiefly of large industries which purchased power from central stations rather than generate it themselves. (See *United State Census of Electrical Industries*, 1927, pp. 35–36.)

could furnish it with power in case of a breakdown. Fortunately the use of alternating current, making possible the transmission of electricity over long distances, in turn made the plan of interconnection feasible. Thus industries could depend upon service even from central stations which were dependent upon water power available only in certain months in the year or during years of ample rainfall. Such central stations were able to prevent a shutdown by being interconnected with central-station steam plants.

The degree to which the manufacturing industries have electrified and the extent to which they have purchased electrical energy from central stations is shown in table II. The first census for which data are available on the horsepower of electric motors in relation to the total installed primary power in manufacturing industries was that of 1899. In that year, the total horse-power of electric motors was 4.9 per cent of total installed primary power; for the census of 1929, it was 82 per cent. Of the total installed primary power used in 1899 but 1.8 per cent of it was operated by purchased electricity, while 3.1 per cent was operated by current generated by the industries. By 1929 53.1 per cent was operated by purchased energy, while but 28.9 per cent was operated by electricity generated by the industries. The horse-power of the motors in manufacturing industries run by purchased energy compared with the horse-power of those run by energy generated within the industries is shown graphically in the chart on p. 498. It will be seen that industries first purchased more electrical energy than they generated during the World War. This was partly because under the orders of the Fuel Administration some industries found it almost impossible to obtain coal. In other instances, the business was expanding in such an abnormal fashion that business men turned

TABLE II

POWER IN UNITED STATES — MANUFACTURING INDUSTRIES ᵃ

All industries	Number of establishments reporting power equipment	Total rated capacity (H.P.)	Electric motors driven by purchased current		Electric motors driven by current generated in establishments reporting		Per cent total installed primary power represented by H.P. of electric motors	Per cent of H.P. Electric motors run by	
			Number	H.P.	Number	H.P.		Purchased power	Current generated in establishments
1899	133,418	10,097,893	....ᵇ	182,562	16,891	310,374	4.88	1.81	3.07
1904	134,181	13,487,707	....ᵇ	441,589	73,119	1,150,886	11.80	3.27	8.53
1909	185,042	18,675,376	199,309	1,749,031	189,545	3,068,109	25.80	9.37	16.43
1914	205,590	22,547,574	452,102	3,917,655	320,260	4,929,967	39.24	17.38	21.86
1919	222,942	29,323,653	976,278	9,282,541	486,805	6,968,950	55.42	31.65	23.77
1923	173,415	33,092,222	1,425,492	13,364,298	616,387	8,821,403	67.04	40.38	26.66
1925	167,533	35,766,944	1,723,539	15,864,638	772,411	10,254,658	73.03	44.36	28.67
1927	174,118	38,825,681	2,151,675	19,132,310	790,810	11,219,979	78.18	48.28	28.90
1929	193,969	42,931,061	2,724,843	22,775,664	852,432	12,376,376	81.88	53.05	28.83

ᵃ Figures for the years 1899, 1904, 1909, 1914, taken from the *Abstract of Census of Manufactures* (1914), p. 491; figures for the years 1919, 1923, 1925, 1927, taken from the *Census of Manufactures* (1927), p. 1270. ᵇ Figures not available.

to the central stations for electrical energy, assuming that within a year or two the peak demand for such service would diminish rapidly. The accompanying diagram shows also that the tendency for industries to purchase electricity rather than generate it was merely accelerated by the war.

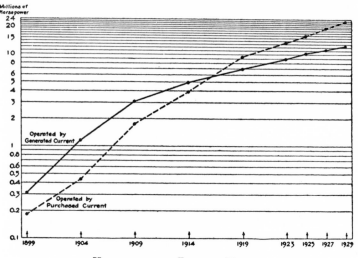

HORSE-POWER OF ELECTRIC MOTORS

The cost of electrical energy has been greatly reduced by the improvement in load factor, thus affecting the necessary capital outlay and operating costs. The diversity in demand which a big central station is able to realize because not all of its consumers use current at the same time gives it an advantage over an industry which generates current merely for its own use. Since the fixed costs in the central-station business are substantial, the number of hours per day of use of maximum capacity of the plant is a real factor in keeping down the cost of generation. This fundamental factor goes far toward explaining why many industries find it more economical to purchase energy from a central station than to generate it.

With large-scale generation of power and long-distance transmission came a chain of events which made it inevitable that the power and light industry should extend beyond the limits of municipalities and spread out over wide areas, even ignoring State boundaries. American industries know no State lines. The provision of the federal constitution which prohibits tariffs among the States has brought about an industrial and commercial development in this country which is destined in turn to have an important effect upon the power business itself.

Many of the small central stations were very inefficient, and in many instances did not furnish a twenty-four-hour service. The change which has taken place is reflected in figures which have already been quoted, showing that, while there was a substantial increase in the number of central stations in every period covered by the federal census up to the year 1917, there was a decrease of 49.4 per cent in the number of commercial stations from 1917 to 1927.

Sometimes the combination or consolidation of utility properties takes the form of a combination of different utilities in the same community under one management. In other instances there has been the formation of holding companies which have undertaken financial and operating functions; occasionally a group of more or less related utilities in one section of the country are controlled in this manner, or widely scattered properties which have no relationship whatever are brought under one management. There are also companies which purchase control of various utilities and then issue their own securities, based upon collateral security; they thus bring about a distribution of risk, but make no contribution whatever to the problems of management.

The growth of the electrical industry, some phases of which have been very briefly sketched, has helped to bring about the electrification of industry; the growth of the electrical industry, in turn, has been made possible by the wider market for electricity which the electrification of industry has helped to supply. The prospect of greater economic possibilities for the electrical industry brought about a keen interest on the part of the public in utility securities in the decade following the World War, thus stimulating promoters and speculators to enter this field.

The operation of the power industry on a large scale, starting in local consolidations and later developing into vast interconnected systems, offered the opportunity for the development of the public-utility holding company which is such a prominent factor in the public-utility field at the present time. It would not be possible within the limits of this discussion to present more than a brief enumeration of some of the advantages and disadvantages of holding companies in this field.

These holding companies are able to bring about savings, for example, in financing, construction, mass purchasing, expert services in engineering, accounting, management, and improvement of the quality and reliability of the service, and in making it available on a twenty-four-hour basis even to rural areas. On the other hand, local operating companies which are controlled by holding companies are not in a position to make competitive contracts. Nor does the public have adequate means under present regulation of knowing the terms of the contracts between the holding company and the subsidiary. This is strikingly true in the instances where the holding company is incorporated in a different State from that in which the subsidiary operates, or where there has been a pyramiding of a series of holding companies by means of which each controls the one just below it. In the latter instances, the operating company which serves the community is very far removed from the top holding company, which really controls its policies and dictates the terms of the contracts made with it.

While distinct advantages, both in the reduced cost of generating electrical energy and in the improved character of the service, have been realized through the centralization of the light and power business and through the interconnection of these centralized systems, there are, on the other hand, some difficult problems presented for solution as a result of such developments. Space limits the consideration which may be given to these problems to a brief discussion of the effect: (1) on rate making, (2) on the so-called fair return, and (3) on the character of the regulation itself.

Before electric central stations had spread beyond the limits of the cities in which they were located, rates were made upon a so-called municipal basis. Now, however, with one power station serving a large number of different communities, the question has arisen as to what constitutes a proper basis upon which to fix rates. Places which are located near the generating plants of a central-station system sometimes argue that they should have a very much lower rate than is given to places, say, two hundred miles away. Obviously the question of rate making for light and power is not as simple as it formerly was. The Interstate Commerce Commission, while it has followed no hard and fast rule, has ordinarily held that a place should not be robbed of its geographical advantages in rate making. This might argue for rates for communities situated near hydro-electric central stations lower than would be given to localities on the circumference of the circle served by such a plant. But the development within the electrical industry itself may in turn vitally affect the manner in which a *group rate theory* ought to be applied. Do the so-called natural advantages, on which the Interstate Commerce Commission has placed some reliance, change in meaning and hence in application with fundamental changes in the generation and transmission of electricity? Should "natural geographical advantages" be interpreted to mean that "representative" central station, to use the English economist Marshall's term, through which the maximum of external and internal economies can be realized? If this last question is to be answered in the affirmative, then it will be necessary to modify some of our early rate theories. If the municipal basis has almost completely disappeared in the generation and transmission of electricity, should not the municipal basis of rate making also go into the limbo? The Wisconsin Supreme Court held in 1922 [1] that under Wisconsin law it was necessary for the Wisconsin Railroad Commission to make rates for electricity in that State on a municipal basis. The Wisconsin legislature has since changed the Wisconsin law [2] so as to permit rates to be made in that State on a group or loop basis. Recently a federal court in Indiana has held that under Indiana law light and power rates must be determined on a municipal rather than a regional basis.[3]

It ought to be clear that a central electric station serving 100 communities might be able to generate electricity at a much lower cost than if it served but 10 communities. Indeed the very reason why it might be able to generate and transmit energy at a low cost would be because the serving

---

[1] City of Eau Claire et al *v*. R. R. Commission et al, *Public Utility Reports* [hereafter referred to as *P. U. R.*], 1922 D, 666.

[2] Subsection 2 of sec. 196.03, Statutes, 1929 reads: "For rate-making purposes the commission may consider two or more municipalities as a regional unit where the same public utility serves said municipalities, if in its opinion the public interest so requires."

[3] *United States Daily*, vol. vi, p. 2871 (February 19, 1932).

of the other 90 communities would enable it to realize a maximum of economies. To argue, then, that the rates to near-by cities should be based upon the distribution or transmission costs is to ignore the important fact that the cost of generating the energy would doubtless be much higher were it not that the central station was being operated on a large scale and supplying all cities within the area which the company found it advantageous to serve.

The foregoing argument does not mean that there should be no differences in the rates of different localities served by the same central station. Nor does it mean that so-called "state-wide uniform" rates now being adopted in some States [1] are necessarily sound. In some instances such rates may be justified, but in others there may be little basis for them, either from the point of view of the public utility or from that of the public. The mapping out of territories for rate-making purposes must be done with consideration of all the external and internal economies resulting from the very fact that the larger group of communities is being served by the same central station, and also in the light of the cost of substitute fuels available to industries within a given region. This will probably mean that the plan of dividing the individual consumers of a central station into classes for rate-making purposes must now be followed out in a logical and equitable classification of communities. Obviously each group of localities would present its own peculiarities, and rate structures would need to be worked out on the merits involved.[2] One thing, however, seems certain: since the basis for the generation and transmission of electrical energy has grown far be-

[1] In the States of Alabama and Georgia rates have been made on a statewide uniform basis. *P. U. R.*, 1929A, 458; *P. U. R.*, 1931E, 449.

[2] For an interesting case see Dallas Power and Light Co. *v.* Carrington, Texas Court of Appeals, 245 S. W. 1046.

yond municipal limits, the rate structure must now conform to the fundamental economics of the new situation.

As to the fair return to which a light and power company may be entitled, the changes of the last twenty years present some vital considerations. Statistics for the generation of electricity indicate that since the light and power companies are furnishing electrical energy to many important industries, they are much more affected by business depression than were the predecessor companies, engaged mainly in the lighting business. In other words, a distinct element of risk has been introduced into the light and power business by its taking on as customers large industries which may in times of depression curtail or even shut off altogether the current they consume. This, in turn, means that the period of time by which to determine whether a light and power company is receiving a fair return will need to be considered in terms of the business cycle.[1] Moreover, with the shift of industry away from the generation of its own power, the central station must be ready to serve large industries during times of prosperity, and yet be prepared to weather periods of depression; it must make heavy capital investment to be ready to serve the peak load, yet must be prepared to absorb the loss it will encounter with a marked decrease in demand from large industrial consumers. It may be questioned whether there is a sound basis for commission and court decisions to ignore consideration of past losses or past profits in determining a fair rate of return.

In view of the fact that the element of risk has been introduced into the light and power industry through its

---

[1] Some of our States have heretofore considered the calendar or fiscal year as the proper basis, or, if the law has not so specified, some commissions and court decisions have assumed a year as a satisfactory period. This may have been satisfactory where there was little difference from year to year in the character and volume of a company's business.

service to industries, it ought to be clear that a very high grade of management will be necessary for this utility in the future. This will require vision on the part of central-station management to build plants sufficiently ahead of needs to be able to meet the increased demands of industry, and yet not overbuild them. There ought to be increasing interest in stimulating efficiency in the management of this utility and in providing a penalty for inefficiency.

Finally, attention may be turned to the effect which the changes described are likely to have upon the character of regulation itself. In the light of the previous analysis and discussion, it would appear that the issues involved are far beyond municipal jurisdiction, and in some phases of the business beyond the jurisdiction of the States.

There are two ways of obtaining a profit out of public utilities: one is through efficient operation; the other is through financial manipulation of utility securities. Our system of regulation should be such as to encourage the former and curb the latter. The savings made possible through scrapping of small utility plants and the linking of communities into an interconnected system served by very large generating stations have offered opportunities for the effective use of both of these methods.

"It would appear that that portion of the power industry which cannot run away from its job, that is the local operating company, would be embarrassed if the pyramiding of utility securities should ultimately result in shaking the confidence of the investing public in public utility securities." [1] This possible danger was pointed out before the panic of 1929 by some of the committees of the Investment Banking Association. Holding companies should

[1] C. O. Ruggles, "Regulation of Electric Light and Power Utilities," *Proceedings of the 41st annual meeting of the American Economic Association*, vol. xix, no. 1 (March, 1929), p. 183.

furnish reports to the investing public which will show the financial condition of *each* of its subsidiaries. On the basis of the reports which some of the holding companies now issue, it is impossible for an investor to form an accurate and intelligent judgment. Probably the exorbitant price which holding companies have in some instances paid for utility properties accounts for their preference for financial statements that do not show the facts with reference to individual subsidiary companies.

The existence of a twilight zone between State and federal jurisdiction makes it difficult if not impossible to secure effective regulation of certain phases of the power business, and it encourages on the part of promoters and speculators in the light and power industry certain activities in which the public has a vital interest. There is no longer any doubt of the municipality's inability to control the affairs of a big utility which serves several hundred cities. The question now in the foreground is whether State regulation is adequate or whether we must have in addition some form of federal control.

There are two extreme views concerning the rôle of State commissions in the scheme of utility regulation: one is that these commissions have utterly failed in their attempts to regulate public utilities; the other is that these commissions are entirely adequate to regulate the business of utilities other than railroads, and that it is quite unnecessary to provide federal regulation of any sort within the field. A careful analysis of the situation will show that neither of these views is tenable.

There is no rhyme or reason in the arrangement whereby about four-fifths of the State commissions consist of three members each. Style or custom appears to have brought this about; there is no such uniformity in the magnitude of the problems confronting these various commissions. In some jurisdictions the membership should be increased, or at least the technical staff should be much enlarged. The staffs of too many of the State commissions are wholly inadequate. Not only should the number of experts be increased, but more of them should have a better understanding of the complex economic and business problems, which have become so important since the organization of these commissions. Experts should be better paid, and should be given assurance of an opportunity for a satisfactory career. The commissioners themselves are underpaid; their average salary is about $5,000. One commission pays salaries of but $2,000 to members other than the chairman. Only three commissions in the country furnish anything like an adequate remuneration for men of ability. Moreover, the term of the commissioners is too short, and, while reappointments or re-elections occur, there is not sufficient continuity of personnel to ensure effective public service. In a number of instances the commissions have no control over most of the public utilities other than railroads, and in other instances where their jurisdiction does cover all utilities, their power to regulate is definitely circumscribed.

If, then, the regulation of utilities by State commission has not been as effective as it should have been, the reasons already suggested go far in furnishing the explanation. Many of the State commissions have performed excellent service.

Attention may now be turned to the other claim, that the State commissions are adequate to the task of regulating utilities other than carriers and that no federal agency is needed. Those who hold this view frequently point out that only a minor part of the total electrical energy generated crosses State lines. It is necessary to examine somewhat closely the facts concerning the interstate movement of power if the significance of the problem which it presents is to be understood.[1]

While the interstate transmission of electrical energy is not large compared with the total amount generated in the United States, this percentage does not tell the whole story. The interstate business is of distinct importance in a number of areas throughout the country, and will probably be of much greater importance in the near future. Moreover, a decision of the United States Supreme Court is to the effect that a State may not regulate rates for electricity which enters into interstate commerce, even though this be a relatively unimportant part of a central station's business.[2]

---

[1] It is true that of the whole amount of the electrical energy generated in the United States, only 9.6 per cent of it crossed State lines in 1926. This fact is brought out in the study on interstate transmission of power made by the Harvard Bureau of Business Research (*Interstate Transmission of Power by the Electric Light and Power Companies in 1926*, Harvard Bureau of Business Research, December, 1927, Bulletin no. 68). The electrical census for 1927 showed that for commercial establishments, not including municipal plants, 13.9 per cent of all current generated and purchased crossed State lines. From data collected by the National Electric Light Association in 1926, 1928, and 1929, it found the amount of electricity crossing State lines for each of those years to be 8.9 per cent, 10.7 per cent and 11.8 per cent (see statistical bulletins of the National Electric Light Association, no. 1, December, 1927, and no. 5, June, 1930). The Federal Trade Commission made a study for the year 1929 in which it found that the amount of power that was exported across State lines, including the Canadian and Mexican borders, equalled 13.42 per cent of all electrical energy generated in the United States. Likewise that power imported in the same manner constituted 17.57 per cent of the total. (See Senate Docket, no. 238, 71st Cong., 3rd sess. These percentages were computed by deducting all energy that entered into interstate movement more than once. See page xi.)

[2] Three cases are of interest in this connection. The first two were concerned with the movement of gas across State lines and the third with interstate transmission of electricity.

In 1920 in Pennsylvania Gas Company *v.* Public Service Commission (252 U. S. 23, *P. U. R.*, 1920 E, 18) the gas company transmitted natural gas by a main pipe line from the source of supply in Pennsylvania to a point of distribution in a city in New York, which subdivided the gas there, and sold at retail to local consumers supplied by pipes laid through the streets of the city. In holding that the New York Public Service Commission might regulate the rate charged to these consumers, the court said that while a State may not "directly" regulate or bur-

From the statements of the court in the Public Service Commission of Rhode Island *v.* the Attleboro Steam and Electric Company [1] decision it would appear that even

den interstate commerce, it may in some instances, until the subject matter is regulated by Congress, pass laws "indirectly" affecting such commerce, when needed to protect or regulate matters of local interest; that the thing which the New York commission had undertaken to regulate, while part of an interstate transmission, was "local in its nature," pertaining to the furnishing of gas to local consumers, and the service rendered to them was "essentially local," being similar to that of a local plant furnishing gas to consumers in a city; and that such "local service" was not of the character which required general and uniform regulation of rates by congressional action, even if the local rates might "affect the interstate business of the company."

In the so-called Kansas Natural Gas Company, decided in 1924 (265 U. S. 298; *P. U. R.*, 1924 E, 78), the company, whose business was principally interstate, transported natural gas by continuous pipe lines from wells in Oklahoma and Kansas into Missouri, and there sold and delivered it to the distributing companies, which then sold and delivered it to local consumers. The court held that the local rates were not in controversy; that the State had no right to regulate the rates at which the gas was sold at wholesale to the local companies; that, while in the absence of congressional action a State might generally enact laws of internal police, although they had an indirect effect upon interstate commerce, "the commerce clause of the Constitution, of its own force, restrained the states from imposing direct burdens upon interstate commerce"; that a State enactment imposing such a "direct burden" must fall, "being a direct restraint of that which in the absence of federal regulation should be free." The court further maintained that the sale and delivery to the distributing companies was "an inseparable part of a transaction in interstate commerce — not local but essentially national in character — and enforcement of a selling price in such a transaction places a direct burden upon such commerce inconsistent with that freedom of interstate trade which it was the purpose of the commerce clause to secure and preserve."

The Public Service Commission of Rhode Island *v.* the Attleboro Steam and Electric Company was decided in January, 1927 (273 U. S. 83, *P. U. R.*, 1927 B, 348). The Rhode Island Public Utilities Commission attempted to raise the rates for electricity furnished by the Narragansett Electric Lighting Company at Providence to the Attleboro Massachusetts Steam and Electric Company. The Rhode Island Commission ordered this advance in rates on the ground that the business was being done at a loss and was therefore a burden on Rhode Island consumers for the benefit of those in Massachusetts. The commission contended that its action was in harmony with the decision of the United States Supreme Court in the Pennsylvania Gas case, in that its action affected interstate commerce only incidentally and indirectly. The interstate transmission of the Narragansett Electric Lighting Company was but 3 per cent of its total business. But the Supreme Court held that this case was ruled by the Kansas Gas case rather than by the Pennsylvania Gas case.

[1] See the last paragraph of the note above.

State regulation as recognized in the Pennsylvania Gas case would doubtless be permitted to apply only within very narrow limits. If, therefore, the Massachusetts commission were to attempt a reduction of rates within the State which would make it impossible for the Attleboro Company to pay the interstate price charged by the Narragansett Company without selling at a loss, the protection afforded under the fifth and the fourteenth amendments would probably be invoked by the utility. Furthermore, if a local company makes various sorts of payments to a holding company in another State, the State in which the subsidiary company operates may not be able to secure from the holding company adequate information to enable it to secure effective regulation of the subsidiary. It is possible that the decision of the Supreme Court in Smith *v.* Illinois Bell Telephone Company [1] and in the Western Distributing Company *v.* Public Service Commission [2] may strengthen the State commissions in their efforts to determine the facts concerning the costs of materials or services furnished by parent companies to local utilities, but this does not mean that the State may prevent the subsidiary from making such payment for materials, services, and the like.

It is clear that a parent or holding company which has control over the affairs of operating companies located in a dozen or more States may be vitally affecting the interests of the consumers of these companies, although the operating companies might be engaged in generating electrical energy which would be consumed wholly within the State where it was generated. Moreover, there are many holding companies which maintain that they are not public utilities, and in the absence of federal regulation on this

[1] 282 U. S. 133, 1930; *P. U. R.*, 1931 A, 1.
[2] 52 Supreme Court, 283 (1932).

subject, it will doubtless be difficult to regulate them effectively.

From an economic and business point of view there is no blinking the fact that the economies which holding companies have made possible in the service they have rendered to their subsidiaries have in some instances been substantial, but in others may well be doubted. There should be some way of determining the contribution which holding companies make to the efficiency of operation of subsidiary companies, and this should be taken into consideration in determining both rates and rate of return. It is not reasonable that parent or holding companies which maintain that they are not public utilities, thus escaping all regulation, should control the operating expenses, financing, and management policies of public utility operating companies.

In our efforts to regulate public utilities we have been so anxious to give private initiative full sway that we have really taken away much of the incentive toward efficiency in management. Fortunately, there are a few State commissions to which this statement does not apply, at least not without some modification; these attempt to take efficiency of management into consideration in determining a fair rate of return. A previous study by the writer [1] showed that some commissions did not believe that the rate of return should be uniform for all companies, but should be measured in each case by the efficiency of management and the character of service, and that a utility rendering excellent service at low rates should be entitled to reap a reward for its enterprise by being permitted to earn more than the normal rate of return; likewise, that one rendering inefficient service should not be permitted

[1] "Problems of Public Utility Rate Regulation and Fair Return," *Journal of Political Economy*, October, 1924, p. 543.

to advance its rates in order to obtain a normal rate of return until it had improved its service.[1]

Unfortunately, the commissions which hold the foregoing theory are decidedly in the minority and even those who do are unable to carry it out because of the inadequacy of their technical staffs. The majority of our State commissions tend to reduce rates to a certain level for all utilities in a given class, regardless of efficiency of management or character of service rendered. The general rule is to reduce rates if the management succeeds in making such savings in cost of operation as to increase revenue noticeably.

We have doubtless drifted into this unfortunate position because we have been slow to apply measuring rods to public utility management and service. This has doubtless been due to fear that such action might lead to an attempt by the commissions to substitute their judgment for that of the management. While there is no doubt that regulation has definitely limited management in many ways, and that much of this interference has been upheld by the courts, it is also true that interference with management where the decision must rest largely upon judgment rather than upon easily determined facts would not be permitted by the courts.

It will be said that there can be no dependable measure by which management or service may be gauged; but dependable comparative data along these lines are now being used effectively even at long range by the management and engineering organizations in control of their various subsidiaries, and something worth while along this line ought to be undertaken by the State commissions.

The upheaval of prices which came as a result of the World War brought about a situation in which much of the time of managers of the utilities and of the commissions

[1] *Ibid.* For further references, see note, p. 557.

was spent wrangling over valuation, and now with falling
prices it is probable that this performance will be repeated.
Too little consideration has been given to character of
service and costs of operation, which reflect efficiency or inefficiency in management. Items in costs of operation
which have been given scant consideration would, if capitalized, be of more significance than the difference resulting
from the use of a particular formula used to find so-called
fair value. Moreover, time spent in careful studies of
operating costs would stimulate better management, improve the character of service, and enable commissions to
determine the extent to which a premium or a penalty
should be applied in gauging the rate of return to be allowed to a utility. At present we are attempting too much
regulation of profits; we are encouraging the utilities to
make the rate base as high as possible, and to permit costs
of operation to absorb sufficient revenue to keep the rate of
return at a level which will not give rise to a demand for a
rate reduction. While utility commissions should not play
the rôle of directors of utility companies and thus supplant
management by regulation, they should determine some
standards of management. Management should be given
a comparatively free hand, but it must also be held responsible for results. If the economies made possible by holding
or management organizations are real, it ought to be possible to measure them, at least approximately. At present
it is in many instances uncertain whether the payments
made by a subsidiary to a holding company are in line with
the contributions made to the management of the subsidiary; therein lies an outstanding objection to the present
plan of reducing the rates of all utilities to a certain level
regardless of efficiency or inefficiency in management. It
does not require much intelligence to carry on such regulation. And unless the public is willing to recognize the need

for higher caliber men as commissioners aided by adequate technical staffs, including more men who understand the economic and business problems involved, there will be little hope for success along the lines here suggested.

If the foregoing analysis of the situation is sound, it would appear that the following conclusions with reference to the regulation of the light and power industry are justified:

(1) State commissions should be materially strengthened, and their jurisdiction extended so that in all States they will have the power to regulate utilities other than railroads. Moreover, the power to regulate these utilities, once jurisdiction over them has been granted, should not be circumscribed as it is in some States at the present time. Many of the regulatory problems of this industry require that all the light of local intelligence be focused upon them. Therefore, the bulk of the regulation of these utilities will doubtless continue in the hands of the State commissions.

(2) Federal regulation is necessary to cope with the problems clearly beyond the control of the States; [1] what form of this control would be most effective is not so clear. There have been proposals that the State commissions shall act as federal agencies in the regulation of such affairs. While this proposal has some merit, it is not easy to see how disputes between two State commissions over the transmission of electrical energy could be settled without the intervention of some federal agency. The Federal Power Commission, which already has limited authority in this field, has recently been reorganized and given somewhat more control over certain power companies. The Transportation Act of 1920 gave legal sanction to co-

[1] I am indebted to a former student, Professor Donald C. Power, LL.B., Ohio State University, for data concerning this subject in an unpublished thesis for the master's degree at Ohio State University in 1927, on the subject of "Future Interstate Regulation of the Electric Light and Power Industry."

operation between the States and the federal government, but in this case the Interstate Commerce Commission has sufficient power to bring recalcitrant States into line. State compacts have also been suggested, but this method would be slow and cumbersome, and would be unsuited to the everyday problems of these dynamic utilities.

Objection will of course be raised to the creation of any more regulating commissions, and especially of federal commissions. The State commissioners themselves will oppose federal regulation, yet the question may be raised whether federal control of utility activities lying between State and federal jurisdiction may not have the wholesome effect of keeping many utility problems within the jurisdiction of the State commissions. Moreover, federal regulation would probably stimulate the States to improve the character of their commissions in a field in which they have a real opportunity for the major work of regulation. Objection will also be raised to federal regulation on the ground that it simply means more red tape. But it is not easy to understand how utilities which have expanded their kilowatt capacity 20 times in a twenty-year period, and increased their own employees by nearly 730 per cent, can be regulated by the same number or type of agencies as were in existence when the industry was much less complex. Moreover, these utilities appear to be pursuing a somewhat different course from that followed by the railroads, and are attempting to secure large numbers of highly trained men. If brains are needed, and to a far greater extent, within the industry itself, an increase both in the number and in the quality of the regulatory bodies would also be a normal development.

In view of the fact that the business of the electric power and light utilities involves many technical problems which should be studied at close range, federal regional commissions would be superior to a highly centralized control such as we have developed under the Interstate Commerce Commission for railroads.[1] In addition to federal regional commissions, a federal public-utility commission should be provided the jurisdiction of which would be limited to cases appealed from the former. Whatever federal agencies are proposed for the control of utilities other than railroads deserve to be given some such study as was given to banking by the National Monetary Commission, previous to the adoption of the Federal Reserve Banking law. It is high time to begin such a study, which should lead to the strengthening of the State commissions and to a constructive program of federal regulation of those activities of power utilities over which the States can have no jurisdiction. Regulation, both by the State and by the federal government, should give some promise of encouraging initiative in management, but both operating companies and parent organizations should be held responsible for results. Public-utility rates and the rate of return allowed to public utilities should be determined in accordance with the contributions which they make toward efficiency in management and the maintenance of satisfactory service.

---

[1] It is of some interest that the Interstate Commerce Commission in its annual report for 1928 requested Congress to exempt the operation of electric railways from its jurisdiction, except those electric roads which exchange standard freight equipment with steam roads and join with steam roads in through interstate freight rates.

SOME INTIMATE HISTORY FROM THE LAST YEARS OF A SEVENTY-FOUR YEAR OLD BUSINESS

S. O. MARTIN

In 1857 a peddler, whom we will call John Morse, began a business which in 1926, under the administration of his son Richard Morse, reached a sales volume of approximately thirty millions of dollars. For the kind of business done this was a large figure, and so far ahead of that of its nearest competitor that description of the nature of the business would identify at once its real name.

It was a business more of distribution than production, and involved service problems of selection and installation. Sales were frequently in large initial units, made on a basis of installment payments, with replacement and supplementary orders subsequent to the initial order for smaller amounts handled on current terms.

Family diligence and thrift, with sustained attention to detail and development of service, were responsible for the steady growth of this business. The younger Morse had more advantages and a broader outlook than his father. For example, it is reported that the elder Morse apparently never fully accepted the policy of one price (neither did his successors in large contracts), and in later days, as individual transactions became larger and more numerous, his assistance in negotiating them was not always sought.

After nearly forty years, the original co-partnership of John Morse & Company was succeeded in 1896 by the corporation Richard Morse & Company, which developed the business successfully and increasingly along its original general lines until, about 1919, it began the acquisition of the businesses of some of its suppliers, and to that degree became a business somewhat more of production than formerly, though with emphasis as before on distribution.

In 1925, however, began mergers with competitors as well as suppliers, and it is in this period from 1925 to 1931 that the financial events about to be narrated took place.

The Morse business had concentrated first on the market in its home city and gradually radiated therefrom into adjacent territory, so that its market was a natural economic one. In two other centers, one a thousand miles and the other five hundred miles away, similar businesses had developed to proportions that were respectable, but by no means as large as those of Morse. An important commercial bank in the more distant city was an out-of-town banker for Morse, and, in close co-operation with a private banking house which later sponsored some of the most spectacular investment trust flotations, was the main instrument in effecting these mergers for Morse. Acts of this bank constitute the occasion for this article.

Late in 1925 a corporation, Richard Morse, Stokes & Company, Inc. — with a comma after Morse — was organized in a State other than that of Richard Morse & Company. The *comma* is important because several years later a corporation with the same name, but with a *hyphen* after Morse, was organized in a third State. This later "hyphen" corporation became a subsidiary of the original Richard Morse & Company, whereas the earlier "comma" corporation was organized to acquire the common stock of Richard Morse & Company and all the assets of Stokes Bros., Inc. The bank entered through another corporation which we will call A, owned on an approximately equal basis by itself and a third corporation which we will call B. Corporation B was in turn controlled by the dominant stockholding and management interest of the bank. Later one of the investment trusts, referred to above, also became interested in corporation B. Corporation A then purchased approximately the entire capital stock of Richard Morse & Company for a price about 70 per cent higher than its book value plus a promotion expense of about $400,000, and also bought all the assets of Stokes Bros., Inc.

The Morse stock was exchanged for participating, no-par, non-voting preferred of the "comma" corporation and the Stokes assets for common stock of the latter, so that when the transaction was completed corporation A (owned by the bank and others, as indicated above) owned practically all the stock, preferred and common, of Richard Morse, Stokes & Company, Inc., which in turn owned all the common stock of Richard Morse & Company and assets of Stokes Bros., Inc., at a total cost of about $9,500,000. Total combined assets were reported as about $24,000,000 and combined sales as about $26,000,000, and net earnings one year later were recorded as $1,700,000. Thereby Richard Morse personally had received a very high cash payment for his stock, and had ceased to have any proprietary interest in the business, just as it had joined operations with a new concern in a new territory.

Two months later, during the last of 1925, Richard Morse & Company sold an issue of $6,000,000 in 6 per cent debentures to the bank for 90, which the bank sold to the public for 98½, whereby a profit of a half-million was made for the bank, interest on which, for ten years, was to be paid by the corporation Richard Morse & Company. The floating debt of about $5,000,000 was funded and the working capital was increased by the same amount.

Early in 1926, through a pool which it organized, corporation A traded in the common stock of Richard Morse, Stokes & Company, Inc., at prices ranging from $9.00 to $14. Its book value was about $15 and earnings about $1.50 per share.

The original Morse company at this time acquired the other business, referred to above, in the city about 500 miles away, continuing its name and corporate structure. This business, which had begun over forty years before as a producer rather than distributor, developed the distribution for its own product, which in its field was regarded as the quality leader. In its zeal it had erected a new and splendidly equipped plant, capable, it is reported, of supplying the needs of the entire United States and some of the outside world besides, without any production whatever by competitors. This resulted in subsequent heavy burdens of unused plant capacity.

Additional working capital and purchase money being required for this acquisition, the bank purchased 40,000 shares of 7 per cent cumulative preferred, par $100, from the original Morse corporation at $93, and sold them to the public for $100, making a further profit of $280,000. Of course, this meant that the Morse corporation must pay dividends of 7 per cent on $280,000 for an indefinite period. Warrants accompanied this purchase permitting the future purchase of 320,000 shares of Morse common at prices less than book value. Of these, 260,000 were offered to the public with the preferred stock. In less than a year a profit of about $800,000 in cash had been made by the bank, with charges therefor imposed upon future Morse operations of $50,000 a year; warrants to purchase 60,000 shares of common at less than a book-value price had also been acquired as a bonus. At about the same time the "comma" corporation (Richard Morse, Stokes & Company, Inc.) sold the Stokes assets to the original Morse corporation for additional Morse common stock, so that the former now held nothing but capital stock of Richard Morse & Company.

Six months later, in the spring of 1927, the bank purchased about 140,000 shares of participating preferred stock of the "comma" corporation from corporation A, which it sold to the public at a profit of nearly $250,000. Deducting expense, the bank turned back to corporation A a profit of $165,000. The ownership of this corporation has been noted above (pp. 518–519).

The largest and most radical expansion came in the fall of 1927. The original Morse corporation acquired a chain of factories at widely separated locations, together with several chains of retail stores in one general area; at least eleven corporations were involved, and the total purchase price was slightly more than $9,000,000. This was practically the last expansion, although in 1929 the "comma" corporation acquired the assets of another retail chain in receivership for cash. Some of the intricacies of this move are not clear, but the main motive stated by the bank was the quest for management. With his release from proprietary interest in the hereditary business, Richard Morse had acquired such proprietary interest in several personal real-estate ventures. Bank loans had shown a tendency to rise and freeze in the conglomeration of Morse companies. Sales seemed to increase no faster than assets. Earnings per share of preferred were shrinking one-half, and those of common four-fifths — the next year to become nil.

There were two principals in the group of businesses just acquired. One was regarded as of the super-selling type, "a train-load lot man," and the other as of the steady treasurer type. In this deal, above mentioned, they sold to Richard Morse & Company plants in businesses of very doubtful earning power at full book value, when plants of a similar nature elsewhere could not be mortgaged for 25 per cent of their appraised value, and bought back from the bank, through its corporation A, control of the common stock of the "comma" corporation for about $3,300,000, thereby securing control of the Morse conglomeration for a price equal to about one-half of the over-valuation at which they had sold their own plants to the Morse group. At the same time they became chief executives of the "comma" corporation under a three-year contract at very liberal salaries, with a three-year voting trust controlled by the bank running coincident with the contract.

This whole transaction was extremely complicated, and when the new management of the bank came in, three years later, it was unable to trace entries beyond a certain point because of missing records. These two principals were on intimate personal terms with the controlling interest of the bank under the old management.

Both the original Morse corporation and the new principals of the "comma" corporation by the beginning of 1928 were heavily indebted to various banks, and to remedy this situation the bank dealt with in this article introduced into the situation a new corporation, which became the center of financial activities between the bank and the Morse group for the remaining three and one-half years.

In the pigeon-hole of the bank's general counsel had lain for two years the charter of a corporation known as the European and American Development Corporation, soon to be known to the initiate of bank and Morse circles as "E & A."

Before continuing with E & A, we may mention that an effort has been made to introduce no more corporate complexity into this narrative than is necessary to maintain the thread of events. The tortuousness of the actual corporate situation it would be hard to exaggerate. With the arrival of E & A upon the scene the group of corporations of the original Morse corporation (Richard Morse & Company, 1896) contained 37 units, and within eighteen months was to contain 45, all incorporated under the laws of eight States. At the head of these various units since 1925 was the "comma" corporation, and shortly thereafter the Morse Stokes Holding Corporation stood at the head of them all. In addition there was at least one corporation, which we may call C, jointly owned by the bank and the aforesaid investment trust, which seems to have been created to buy certain assets from the Morse group for cash supplied by the bank and investment trust; to pay off in 1929 the inevitable bank loan of Morse corporation of $5,000,000 to the bank; to supply $1,000,000 of working capital; and, after conveying these assets to four corporations (organized in three States), to be itself wound up.

A chart as large as a wall map was employed by lawyers at the last to follow this bewildering corporate structure of a business which had in sixty-two years reached a volume of $15,000,000 with but practically one corporation. Some of this maze seems to have developed from opportunism, that is, meeting an immediate situation without looking ahead; some of it may be explained by the response of a member of the bank's counsel who was asked how to meet a new situation: "Perhaps we shall have to fix it so no one can understand it."

We return to E & A, brought from its pigeon-hole in early 1928. This concern still retained its paid-in capital of

$300, though it was about to buy more than $13,000,000 (face) of installment obligations, and retained its director-ate, composed of lawyers, in the office of the bank's counsel. But there was added to it from the bank's staff an accountant-treasurer and his secretarial assistant.

E & A was a subsidiary of a corporation, which we will call D, which like A and C was owned in part by the bank, and like B and C in part by the aforesaid investment trust.

E & A was a corporate vehicle nominally for making liquid masses of installment paper taken by Morse for the more-than-current-financing orders referred to at the beginning of this article. Since the bank lent to E & A the funds with which it bought the above Morse paper, and in part owned E & A, which had almost no capital ($300), there was really only a substitution of names for the same loans, except that E & A bore the aspect of a finance corporation with separate corporate responsibility and accounting. It could also charge a higher rate of interest (and did at first), could handle paper of a character not appealing to banks or bank examiners, and could provide facilities for easy withdrawal, substitution, and change better than a bank department, and could impound that paper as specific security for the bank.

It might, of course, be somewhat embarrassing for the bank, as trustee for the holders of Morse debentures which it had sold to these holders (above, pp. 519–520), to direct and enable a bank subsidiary to buy Morse receivable paper that was backing Morse debentures, acting for the bank in its capacity as a creditor rather than as trustee. It seems to have been borne in mind, however, that E & A might be only a temporary repository for much of the Morse paper, until it could be taken over by special independent finance companies, one of which did in fact take over for a time $5,000,000 worth of Morse paper from E &

A, the bank in turn buying $5,000,000 worth of this company's 5 per cent three-year notes for 96¼. Most of this paper eventually came back to E & A because part of the various series remained in default 60 continuous days, contrary to the contract between E & A and the finance company.

Basic contracts between E & A and the Morse companies were executed early in 1928, and again in the middle of 1930; by them E & A "purchased" the paper at 90 per cent of the principal amount without any notification to makers, the Morse companies continuing collections thereon as agents for E & A, though the latter might notify makers of change of ownership of their notes at will and do its own collecting. In either case, the cost of credit investigation and of collecting was borne by Morse.

Under certain conditions, return was to be made to Morse by E & A of "differences between amount so collected and received . . . and amount originally paid" by E & A. Though the mention of the word interest was scrupulously avoided, there was provision for payment by Morse to E & A on average outstandings owed to E & A for the preceding month at the rate of 10 per cent per annum "as final adjustment of the purchase price of paper purchased hereunder." In the second contract (1930) this was changed to read so that this payment to E & A of not less than 6 per cent or more than 10 per cent on daily averages should be "for its services in connection with said paper." In the first contract, this service charge might become a credit to Morse if all paper with E & A were repurchased by Morse; but in the second contract, credit under such circumstances was provided for only by excess of collections over aggregate of purchases plus disbursements and expense.

In view of some of the above clauses, together with that in the second contract, whereby cash and/or paper in excess of 110 per cent of total sums paid by E & A was to be released to Morse, even a layman might doubt if a complete "purchase" of paper had been made. Was the paper "sold" or "pledged?" The preponderant legal opinion was that there was no "sale." The chief opponents of this view were counsel for the bank who drew the contracts. This, of course, was an issue of importance, since if E & A, for the bank, had merely "loaned" to the Morse companies for interest disguised as "service charges" against a "pledge" of installment paper still owned by Morse, instead of "purchasing" that paper from Morse for E & A as owner, then that paper remained a part of the assets of Morse for the benefit of other creditors of Morse as well as for the bank, despite the fact that the bank had lent E & A $11,600,000 in real cash to "purchase" this paper.

Furthermore, the "hyphen" corporation Richard Morse-Stokes Company, Inc. (above, pp. 518–519), had not been made and never was made a party to these contracts, though it was one of the main Morse corporations in relations with creditors, the "comma" corporation, Richard Morse, Stokes & Company, Inc., having become only an owner of stock of Richard Morse & Company, which in turn owned the "hyphen" corporation. Failure to insist on the signature of the "hyphen" corporation to the contracts is not yet understood. The whole attitude of E & A toward the Morse companies was decidedly liberal. Under the contracts, finance charges imposed upon note-makers by Morse in addition to prices of goods and services could have been deducted from the paper by E & A before purchasing, but it was not done. Lagging in substituting new paper for that representing goods that had been repossessed was permitted; and no accounting for the proceeds of sales of repossessed goods was demanded. In fact, relations between the bank and the Morse companies through E & A in the last two years of the latter's existence were so lenient as still to cause speculation as to where the true center of interest of the old management of the bank was located, or whether pressure of other matters caused laxness, or if possibly the two principals of the chief merger (above, pp. 521–522) now operating the Morse group had not some lever of action on the principals of the bank of more than a business nature.

Before the execution in the middle of 1930 of the second E & A-Morse contract just referred to, consolidated Morse developments were ominous. Earnings, greatly reduced the preceding year, had now (1929) become nil. Collections made for E & A by Morse were at once absorbed by Morse, new paper being "sold" therefor to E & A; the bank's loan to E & A had thereby become a revolving one. "Service charges" of E & A to Morse had been reduced from 10 per cent to 8 per cent, to 7 per cent, and finally, in July, 1930, to 6 per cent. After August 1, 1930 these service charges had to be paid in more paper instead of in cash. In August, 1929 the affairs of the Morse companies had become so incomprehensible that an outside firm of auditors and appraisers was employed by E & A to make a thorough investigation, which required several months to complete; again, strange to note, the costs, which eventually totaled more than $100,000, were met by E & A.

While this audit was in progress, came the financial crash of October, 1929, and in the next month the last corporation was organized (the Morse Stokes Holding Corporation), the senior securities of which were to be exchanged for at least 80 per cent of the debentures and stocks of the original Morse corporation and the "comma"

corporation. For junior securities, principals of the bank
and the investment trust fed in various securities and
guarantees of a fifth corporation, here called E, as an additional support to the senior securities. Over 80 per cent of
this exchange having been effected by April, 1930, the
Morse Stokes Holding Corporation acquired the "comma"
corporation from the two principals of the last merger
(above, pp. 521–522), but a group of individuals had to
guarantee them against $1,500,000 loss in accepting junior
securities of the new holding corporation before the exchange was finally effected.

Nor did all seem well with the bank. To the local clearing house in the fall of 1930 a report was made by the bank
on its loan to E & A which listed every individual series of
notes "purchased" by E & A from the Morse companies.
To this report reference will be made later. Within two
months, new interests had bought into the bank, and then
entered a new management which applied themselves to
various problems, including the E & A-Morse situation.
Early in 1931, it was foreseen by this new management
that a receivership for the Morse companies was probably
inevitable, and the problem of assuring to E & A all proceeds from paper which Morse may have "sold," but very
likely only "pledged" (above, pp. 525–527) to E & A, was
indeed a pressing one, with over $11,500,000 in cash lent
to E & A by the bank.

Time was needed for the new managers to investigate
and grasp a situation by no means obvious in its character, and in the meantime a debenture coupon of Morse
had been met by an advance of cash by the Morse Stokes
Holding Corporation against the pledge of open accounts
receivable by the Morse group, and by certain claims on
the government stated to have been allowed by the gov-

ernment but afterwards found not to have been. Over
70 per cent of these debentures were in the possession of
Morse Stokes Holding Corporation, and less than 30 per
cent, or about $1,300,000, were in the hands of the public.
These debenture holders were entitled to an explanation,
and it was soon made to them by the new bank management frankly and fully; they saw that after all real cash
had been paid by the bank through E & A for installment
notes payable to Morse, much of which — much more than
the total amount of their debentures — would never return to the bank, so that presumably they were better off
than they would have been if the Morse notes had not
been "purchased." Eventually co-operation was secured
from them and the general creditors of Morse, as will be
noted later.

The last six months of this seventy-four year old business were months of diligent investigation, analysis, and
action. The report to the clearing house showed that series
of notes covering about 700 separate transactions, representing about 625 separate legal makers, had been sold by
Morse companies to E & A; these totaled slightly over
$9,000,000, of which 45 totaled slightly over $6,000,000.
Of these 45 there were 16 "in default," totaling nearly
$2,500,000, or practically five-sixths of the total of slightly
over $3,000,000 reported "in default."

It was soon found, however, that the definitions of "in
default," "past due," and "current" as reported to the
clearing house were rather technical. Only that portion of
a series which was past due was so carried. The unma-
tured remainder was carried as "current," which did not
correspond to correct financial practice or to the E & A
contract, which clearly defined "current" to refer to the
paper of a solvent primary obligor, "no part of which nor

any installment thereof shall be in default in any respect." Furthermore, even when makers were in financial difficulties or had given new extension notes, such paper, because it had not yet matured, was also carried as "current." It accordingly became advisable to add to the report, as still questionable, a figure of slightly more than $2,000,000, making the unsatisfactory paper amount to about $6,300,000 out of a total of all paper of $9,000,000 plus. Of this paper 230 items out of about 550 represented obligations of $2,500 upward, totaling $8,500,000, while about 320 with obligations of less than $2,500 totaled slightly over $300,000. Of the former, 130-odd makers with notes totaling nearly $6,000,000 were in four cities in the eastern half of the United States, and the next 20-odd makers, in order of size of debts, increased the cities represented from four to eleven, to include the western half of the United States, and the total of obligations from $6,000,000 to $7,200,000. The maximum single maker was $900,000, and next were $500,000, $455,000, $367,000, $366,000, $227,000, and so on to include 9 more makers of $100,000 or more debt, all 14 of whom were in difficulties with paper non-current ranging from that extended to that wiped out by bankruptcy and totaling over $3,800,000.

So much for the foregoing Morse paper, which may be called wholesale paper. There was also a large block of retail paper, representing over 40,000 makers who were customers of a chain of retail stores owned by a subsidiary of Morse, and its subsidiaries, who were paying weekly and monthly installments on past and current purchases.

This retail paper totaled about $4,700,000, averaging slightly less than $120 per maker. Although E & A received monthly reports of collections, repossessions, and new sales contracts, these came through Morse, with whom were all of E & A's relations concerning this paper, although several officers of Morse and the chains were identical. Much of the wholesale paper was of a residual character; that is, it had not proved acceptable to the old-line finance companies, and was therefore carried by Morse of necessity. Early in 1928, one month after the conclusion of the E & A contract, it was found that out of nearly $12,000,000 worth of wholesale paper purchased by E & A by that contract nearly $3,800,000 was reported as "past due" because in arrears; over three years later, in May, 1931, out of $4,300,000 reported "in default" over $2,400,000 had been acquired in that first purchase. Of the retail paper slightly over $1,400,000 was included in the first purchase, increasing to nearly $5,000,000 at the time of the second contract (mid-1930).

The exhaustive audit referred to before (above, pp. 527–528) had resulted in a reserve of $1,500,000 being set up on the books of the chain a year earlier (mid-1929) for retail paper, then totaling nearly $5,250,000. Early in 1931 this reserve had declined to a little over $1,400,000 for retail paper, totaling first $4,800,000, and then being re-accounted as $4,700,000; but since in 1929, 26 per cent of the paper had made no payment for four months, and in 1931 this percentage had risen to 35, the above reserve was increased, for computing recoveries, to $1,800,000, or 38 per cent of the total retail paper.

In other words, at the very beginning the bank paid Morse, through E & A, about $2,000,000 more than it should have paid for combined wholesale and retail notes receivable with face totaling slightly over $13,300,000; which fact it could have ascertained from information then available. Although the error of the bank is evident, this detailing of it gives an inkling of some of the troubles of the Morse business.

The new management of the bank found the original loan to E & A of $11,600,000 reduced only $80,000 in three years, though it had been as high as $13,300,000. For it, E & A had received $13,300,000 and $15,150,000 respectively in Morse wholesale and retail paper, and still had $13,800,000 of it. In the meantime, some 1,300 series of notes had been paid and retired as new series were substituted for them, so that instead of describing the bank loan to E & A as frozen, we might more accurately call it an involuntary revolving loan. What it really was and amounted to can soon be shown. The following payments had been made by E & A to the bank in its first three years under the contract:

On principal	$ 80,000
As interest	1,717,000
Dividends [sic] (difference between "service charges" and interest)	100,000
Total cash returned permanently to the bank ..	$1,897,000

Had interest and dividend been applied, the original loan of $11,600,000 would have become a loan without interest of $9,703,000.

(This, of course, was not done; the interest and dividend were treated as bank income so that if they were now applied to principal a corresponding charge to the surplus of the bank would be required.)

Yet during this period E & A had made:

Cash collections totaling	$6,427,000
Service charges totaling	1,759,000
Total cash receipts of E & A to January, 1931	$8,186,000

From an original loan of		$11,600,000
deduct the above interest, dividend, and reduction of principal	$1,897,000	
Plus E & A expense for period	119,000	
Plus average cash balance	40,000	2,056,000

And it is seen that there was left in the Morse companies a revolving loan without interest for more than three years of $9,544,000

So, despite the profit to the bank from debenture and stock sales and trustee fees, possibly altogether a million dollars or so, the final balance, as far as the bank itself was concerned, was decidedly unfavorable.

What the final recoveries would be from the $13,800,000 total of paper naturally became the subject of lively investigating and estimating. Omitting the various computations and methods, from facts already indicated (above, pp. 529–531), it seemed unlikely that more than $6,000,-000 would be realized. The tale is not yet told, but over $2,500,000 was realized in 1931, of which not much more than $1,500,000 went directly to the bank in cash. Over $250,000 went into expense and the remainder into advances and investments with the view of increasing ultimate recoveries.

The only way to collect the sums mentioned above was to stop the Morse companies from losing money. They were leaking at every joint at the rate of over $2,000,000 a year. This led to a receivership in mid-1931. The business founded and fostered by John Morse and developed by his son Richard had come to an end, though a new company organized by debenture holders and creditors employing the Morse name, with a fraction of the old capital and a few members of the former organization, is starting again in the original home city with a future admittedly uncertain.

A former credit official of Morse described the situation succinctly when he said: "I can remember when an order for $10,000 requiring credit caused a huddle of the officers for days before being accepted, and the business earned a million a year. Then suddenly orders for $100,000 and more were accepted as part of the day's business." The American obsession for expansion — for more volume and territory rather than perfection — gained sway. More capital was available — at a cost. The fact that, no matter how solid the credit check was, there must also be some distribution of risk — some ratio to capital and surplus not to be exceeded — did not seem to be understood, and it frequently has been ignored by others, even bankers. Some sharp practices are reported to have crept in, though never a shadow has been cast on the reputation of Richard Morse, who, with the collapse of his real estate, is now as poor as his father was seventy-four years ago.

The bank, in the triple rôle of underwriter, trustee, and creditor, contemplated the profits from the exercise of these functions complacently, and permitted Richard Morse to lose his proprietary status and become a salaried manager. His successors, though grandiose and loosely knit, exerted a strange influence over the bank. The bank was either so partial to them or so involved that E & A almost seems to have been a private loan office to Morse companies under the management of the two principals of the large merger, thus making the fall more inevitable and less reparable.

This is not an isolated case. It is in some respects a typical, though extreme, illustration of what was going on in the United States — and possibly elsewhere — after the War, especially from 1924 to 1929. This period the economic historian may some day describe not only as one of excessive speculation but also as one abounding in economic and financial illusions.

AMERICAN POLITICS AT THE CROSSROADS

A. N. HOLCOMBE

AMERICAN politics was originally rustic politics. It could not have been otherwise. The people of the original States lived for the most part in the open country and were chiefly occupied in the cultivation of the soil. In eight of the original States, at the first census, there was no city or town with as many as 8,000 inhabitants. In the whole United States the proportion of the population dwelling in places of less than 8,000 inhabitants was over 96 per cent. There were only five cities or towns with more than 10,000 inhabitants. The largest of these, New York, contained somewhat more than 30,000 inhabitants; Philadelphia contained nearly as many. Boston numbered only 18,000 inhabitants; Charleston, 16,000; and Baltimore, 13,000. These were the only urban areas whose voters could have dominated congressional districts under the apportionment of seats in the Congress of the United States, following the first federal census. At least 100 of the 105 congressmen in President Washington's time lived in small towns or villages or in the open country. The average population per congressman at the apportionment following the first census was 33,000. Not all States were divided into districts for the election of congressmen under the early apportionment acts, but, whether congressmen were elected by districts or at large, urban interests could have exerted no great influence in national politics. We do not need to be assured by Jefferson that, though "the inhabitants of the commercial cities are as different in sentiment and character from the country people as any two distinct nations, and are clamorous against the order of things established by the agricultural interest," and "though by command of newspapers they make a great deal of noise," they "have little effect on the direction of policy." [1] There can be no question of the predominance of "the agricultural interest" in American politics during the Jeffersonian régime.

The subordination of urban interests and points of view continued during the period of Jacksonian democracy. Jackson himself explained the situation as clearly as anybody when, in his first annual message to Congress, December 8, 1829, he declared: "The agricultural interest of our country is so essentially connected with every other and so superior in importance to them all that it is scarcely necessary to invite to it your particular attention. It is principally as manufactures and commerce tend to increase the value of agricultural productions and to extend their application to the wants and comforts of society that they deserve the fostering care of Government." [2] The census of 1820, the first in which there was any count of the number of persons engaged in agriculture, commerce, and manufactures, reported over 2,000,000 as engaged in agriculture, about 350,000 were credited to manufactures, and less than 75,000 were credited to commerce. These proportions varied somewhat in different sections of the country, but agriculture led all the rest everywhere. In Massachusetts, then the leading manufacturing State, the number engaged in manufactures was a little over one-half as great as that engaged in agriculture. In New York it was about one-quarter as great. In Virginia the agricultural population

---

[1] See *The Writings of Thomas Jefferson* (Ford's edition), vol. iv, p. 463.
[2] *Messages and Papers of the Presidents*, vol. ii, p. 450.

was eight times as numerous, in South Carolina twenty-five times as numerous as that reported to be engaged in manufactures. Doubtless the accuracy of these figures leaves something to be desired, but their general significance is incontestable. As late as 1840, when a more careful census of occupations was taken, agriculture was still the leading occupation in every State except Rhode Island. In the country as a whole persons engaged in agriculture outnumbered those engaged in manufactures almost five to one.

The predominance of "the agricultural interest" in Jackson's time as in Jefferson's is clearly reflected in the distribution of seats in the Congress of the United States between urban and rural areas. During Jackson's presidency, by the apportionment following the census of 1830, there were 240 congressman, and the average number of inhabitants in a congressional district was at first 47,700. There were only four cities large enough to be entitled to more than a single congressman, New York, Philadelphia, Baltimore, and Boston. There were only three or four others, New Orleans, Charleston, Cincinnati, and Albany, whose voters could have dominated the congressional district in which they were situated. Altogether not more than a score of the 240 members were elected from these urban districts. There were eleven other cities of more than 10,000 population, and perhaps some of less than that number of inhabitants, whose voters may have been sufficiently influential to make their representatives in Congress responsive in some measure to urban as well as rural interests, but the total number of urban and semi-urban districts could hardly have exceeded one-eighth of the whole. At least 85 and perhaps more than 90 per cent of the congressmen must have been dependent upon rural voters for their election and must have remained largely under the influence of rural interests. There were great differences of opinion among the rural voters concerning the measures which their interests required, but none concerning the soundness of the proposition which Jackson, like Jefferson, made the foundation of his policy. The mixed farmers of the North, the cotton planters of the South, the grain growers of the West, all had their special interests to look after, but most of them had the same general interest in putting agriculture ahead of manufactures and commerce. Rival statesmen, notably Clay, Calhoun, and Webster, held their own opinions concerning the manner in which manufactures and commerce could best be made serviceable to agriculture, and combated Jackson's measures in the light of the special interests of their respective sections; but in all sections rustic politics continued to prevail over that kind of politics which may be described as urbane.[1]

The century which has passed since Jackson became president has witnessed a rapid gain by the urban population and a slower growth by the rural. In Jackson's time the industrial revolution was just beginning in the United States. The factory system of industry was in process of introduction. Transportation facilities were on the verge of rapid improvement, The great migration to the cities was impending. By 1900 there were 545 cities of 8,000

[1] "Urbanity," as distinguished from "rusticity," was doubtless not confined to cities and towns of more than 10,000 population a century ago any more than now. The inhabitants of many smaller places must have possessed the chief characteristics which distinguish the majority of the inhabitants of cities with respect to habits, manners, and character. Wherever the line between town and country may be drawn, the limitations of censuses of population ensure that it will be drawn arbitrarily. The census of 1840 was less imperfect than its predecessors and made possible a reliable estimate of the population in all places of more than 2,000 population. Upon the basis of that estimate, seven-eighths of the American people still resided in smaller places or in the open country. See George Tucker, *Progress of the United States in Population and Wealth in Fifty Years, as exhibited by the Decennial Census* (New York, 1843), p. 134.

inhabitants or more in the United States. Yet two-thirds of the people still resided in smaller places or in the open country. The World War marked the final emergence of the cities as the places of residence of a majority of the American people and the passing of the rural population into second place. In 1920 the population of what the census authorities defined as rural territory, including incorporated places of less than 2,500 inhabitants, had fallen to 48.6 per cent of the total. By the most recent census the rural population is estimated at under 44 per cent. Over 12 per cent of the people now live in cities of more than 1,000,000 inhabitants; over 17 per cent, in cities of less than 1,000,000 but more than 100,000; and nearly 18 per cent in small cities with populations exceeding 10,000. The balance between urban and rural population lies in the places with between 5,000 and 10,000 inhabitants. If all the inhabitants of incorporated places with up to 5,000 inhabitants are counted as rural, the rural population is still in a minority.

The question arises, whether American politics can continue to be rustic politics. If the majority of the American people now live in cities, must not American politics become more urbane than rustic? And if American politics is destined to become more urbane, how different may it be expected to be from the rustic politics which has hitherto prevailed?

The growth of population in town and country may be conveniently measured by the methods employed by the census. These methods clearly reveal the increasing concentration of the population in cities. In 1910, 45.8 per cent of the population resided in urban territory, and 54.2 per cent in rural territory. In 1930 the urban population formed 56.2 per cent of the total, and the rural population had declined to only 43.8 per cent. But these methods of measurement do not reveal the relative importance of the urban and rural population in American politics. Political strength is measured by votes, and in national politics the votes which count are the votes which choose presidential electors for the Electoral College and fill seats in the Congress. The political significance of the increasing concentration of population in cities depends upon the distribution of the urban population among the States and among the congressional districts into which the States are divided. It is evident that the accidents of political geography will prevent any close correspondence between the distribution of population between town and country and the distribution of seats in Congress between urban and rural States and districts. All the States contain both urban and rural inhabitants, but the proportions between the two vary widely in different States. Since the urban population is more concentrated than the rural, it may control less than its share of the States and of the districts. A majority of the people may live in cities and yet be unable to control a majority of the seats in the federal Senate and House of Representatives. This is a matter to be inquired into before attempting to appraise the influence of the urban population in federal elections and to determine the extent to which American politics may be expected to become more urbane and less rustic.

The first fact of political importance concerning the concentration of population in cities is this, that a large majority of the urban population is located in a minority of the States. Though a majority of the whole population of the United States is urban, according to the census of 1930, in only 21 of the 48 States is a majority of the population urban, and in several of these the urban population exceeds the rural by no more than a slender margin. It is evident that a majority of the senators of the United States are dependent for their election upon bodies of voters which are still predominantly rural in composition. The urban States, however, include a disproportionate number of the more populous States. Hence, although the senators from the urban States are outnumbered by the senators from the rural States, there are more presidential electors from the former than from the latter. Under the new apportionment, following the last census, the 21 urban States have 310 votes in the Electoral College, a clear majority of the total number of 531. The political importance of the urban States in presidential elections, measured by the number of votes in the Electoral College, exceeds that of the rural States, but in the Senate it is the rural States which seem still to be the more important. Moreover, at the present rate of growth of cities the urban States will remain in a minority in the Senate for a long time. Minnesota is the one rural State in which the urban population seems certain to outnumber the rural by the time the next census is taken, and Texas is the only other State in which such a result seems even possible. It is unlikely therefore that a majority of the population will be reported urban in a majority of the States before 1950, if the States remain unchanged in number and boundaries, and the now established predominance of the urban States in the Electoral College will not extend to the Senate for another twenty years. Hence, rustic politics may be expected to characterize the Senate long after presidential politics becomes comparatively urbane.

The second fact of political importance concerning the concentration of population in cities is that the urban and rural populations are distributed very unevenly among the congressional districts. The average population of the 435 congressional districts, as established upon the basis of the census of 1930, is 280,000. If the seats in Congress could

be distributed exactly in accordance with the distribution
of population between city and country, the urban population would now have 244 seats instead of the 199 to
which they would have been entitled by a similar distribution under the census of 1910. The representation of the
rural population would be reduced from 236 to 191. But
only thirty cities contain enough inhabitants to form one
or more congressional districts within the city limits, and
most of the cities must be combined with more or less extensive rural areas in order to form full-sized congressional
districts. On the other hand, it would be difficult to find a
compact territory anywhere, containing 280,000 rural inhabitants, without any urban population within its limits.
Many congressional districts must contain both urban and
rural areas, and the political importance of the urban and
rural population, measured by the number of seats which
they might control in the Congress, will depend considerably on the actual lay-out of the districts. It is possible to
form only a rough estimate of the distribution of seats between urban and rural interests by means of the census
returns relating to the distribution of population between
city and country. It is necessary, however, to attempt
such an estimate, in order to ascertain where the balance
of power lies in national politics.

The most significant material furnished by the census
of 1930, which can be used for estimating the number of
urban congressional districts, is that relating to so-called
metropolitan districts. These districts are designed to
show the magnitude of each of the principal areas of urban
population, regardless of the actual city limits, by including in a single total both the population of the central city
itself and that of the suburbs or urbanized areas surrounding it. In some cases the population of two or more cities,
located in close proximity, together with that of their

suburbs, is combined in a single metropolitan district. Ninety-five such metropolitan districts were reported at the census of 1930, each having an aggregate population of 100,000 or more and containing one or more central cities of at least 50,000 inhabitants. These metropolitan districts contained approximately 54,500,000 inhabitants, or, excluding the District of Columbia, which is not represented in the Congress, not quite 54,000,000. The total rural population of the United States, including that of incorporated places with less than 2,500 inhabitants, was reported at 52,820,000, or only slightly less than the metropolitan. That left almost 14,500,000 residing in urban areas outside the metropolitan districts. Evidently the balance of power between metropolitan and rural voters lay with this part of the population. If it could be assumed that the urban population outside the metropolitan districts were distributed evenly throughout the country, it would follow that all but the smallest metropolitan districts would have sufficient inhabitants to enable each of them to dominate a congressional district. In other words, the total urban population in a congressional district containing one of these metropolitan districts, as defined by the census, would ordinarily outnumber the rural population that might be combined with it to form a congressional district. The rest of the urban population would presumably be so distributed among the other congressional districts as to be swamped by the rural population. Twenty-two of the metropolitan districts, which were populous enough to be entitled to two or more congressmen each, would, under a fair districting of the States in which they are situated, receive a total of at least 125 seats in Congress. Adding one seat for each of the other metropolitan districts, the grand total of congressional districts, dominated by urban voters, should exceed 195 and almost reach 200. That would leave between 235 and 240 congressional districts which might be dominated by the rural voters. Upon the basis of such calculations rustic politics would seem likely to prevail over urbane in the federal House of Representatives as well as in the Senate.

In fact the excess of rural over urban congressional districts is greater than would appear even from these calculations. This is partly the consequence of the manner in which the urban population outside of the metropolitan districts is actually distributed over the country, and partly the consequence of a widespread disposition to favor the rural population in the districting of the States. The extent to which the congressional districts, as they exist, discriminate against the urban population can be ascertained only by a study of the actual lay-out of the districts within the several States.

The new apportionment of representatives in Congress, following the census of 1930, was the first in twenty years. No apportionment was made following the census of 1920, largely, it may be suspected, because of the opposition of rural States to a reduction in their representation.[1] Since the total membership of the House was kept at the same number as before, it was necessary to increase the average population of a congressional district from 211,000 to 280,000, and also to make extensive transfers of seats from the slow-growing to the fast-growing States. Twenty-seven members were taken from 21 slow-growing States and added to the representation of 11 fast-growing States. The representation of the other 16 States remained unchanged. Under the new apportionment 8 urban States

[1] A reapportionment bill actually passed the House in 1921, but was defeated in the Senate. Subsequently a controversy developed over the method of apportionment. See Edward V. Huntington, "Methods of Apportionment in Congress," *American Political Science Review*, vol. xxv, no. 4 (November, 1931), pp. 961–965.

gained 22 seats, and 6 others lost 9. Three rural States gained 5 seats and 15 others lost 18. Redistricting within the States should increase still further the gains of the urban areas at the expense of the rural. In fact, however, a number of the States have been slow to perform the requisite redistricting, and it may be necessary to elect their representatives in the seventy-third Congress at large. In other States disputes over the redistricting provoked appeals to the courts to determine the validity of redistricting acts, and the actual lay-out of the seats remains uncertain. In these States it is necessary to construct a theoretically fair lay-out of the districts under the new apportionment in order to ascertain what results may be expected from the redistribution of seats between urban and rural areas. The actual or presumable results of the redistribution of seats under the new apportionment do, however, let in a flood of light upon the urbanization of American politics.

For the purpose of measuring the distribution of congressional districts between the urban and rural population, the districts may be divided into six classes. The first class comprises those districts formed by the division of metropolitan areas populous enough to obtain more than one representative in Congress. These districts will generally be composed exclusively of urban residents, and their representatives in Congress should be responsive to a strictly urban electorate. In some cases metropolitan congressional districts include rural areas and in a few of these the rural population may outnumber the urban. In such cases the district is excluded from the first class and assigned to a class corresponding to its demographical character. The second class comprises all other districts which should generally be dominated by urban voters. Among these are all the congressional districts containing the metropolitan districts, as defined by the census, which are not included in the first class and which possess a central city of at least 100,000 inhabitants and a total population of at least 150,000, together with other districts containing two or more cities of at least 50,000 inhabitants and a total urban population which forms a clear majority of the whole population of the district. Classes III and IV comprise those districts in which urban and rural population is so commingled that it is impracticable to classify them definitely as either urban or rural. In class III are placed such of these districts as contain at least one city of more than 50,000 inhabitants, and in class IV all districts, not placed in a higher class, which contain a city of more than 25,000 inhabitants. In many of these districts the urban population is numerous, and in some it may even be predominant. But their ascendancy must be precarious. In others the urban population may be a minor fraction of the total. It is difficult to determine at what point the urban population becomes so definitely inferior in importance that the district should be classified as rural. Perhaps districts which contain no city of as many as 50,000 inhabitants would be generally dominated by the rural voters. This must almost certainly be the case if the district contains no city of more than 25,000 inhabitants, and the line may perhaps best be drawn at that point. It is convenient to divide the definitely rural districts into two classes. The first of these, class v, comprises those districts containing at least one city of as many as 10,000 inhabitants; the second, class vi, comprises the remainder of the districts, no one of which contains a city of as many as 10,000 inhabitants. There can be no question of the thoroughly rural character of this last class of districts.

The distribution of the 435 congressional districts, following the reapportionment based upon the census of

1930, between these six classes is shown in the table below. The districts are those determined by law in thirty-nine States [1] and in the other nine are based upon a theoretically fair districting in accordance with the rules previously prescribed by Congress.

CLASSIFICATION OF CONGRESSIONAL DISTRICTS

1932

(by political sections and distribution of population between city and country)

Section [a]	Urban		Mixed		Rural		Total
	I	II	III	IV	V	VI	
Northeast	69	16	16	12	9	0	122
Middle West	33	12	22	34	22	1	124
Upper South	9	8	13	13	23	7	73
Lower South	2	9	14	13	29	6	73
Far West	14	4	5	9	9	2	43
Total	127	49	70	81	92	16	435

[a] The Northeast section comprises the six New England States and the three North Atlantic States. The Middle West section comprises the five States of the old Northwest, together with six States of the newer Northwest beyond the Mississippi, extending from the Canadian border to Iowa and Kansas. The Upper South comprises five Middle Atlantic States, extending from Delaware to North Carolina, and four South Central States, Kentucky, Tennessee, Missouri, and Oklahoma. The Lower South comprises the eight States extending from South Carolina to Arkansas and Texas. The Far West comprises the eleven States of the Rocky Mountain and Pacific Coast sections. For the basis of this sectional classification, see my *The Political Parties of Today* (New York, 1924; 2nd ed., 1925), Appendix A.

The urban districts outnumber the rural districts by 176 to 108, but fall considerably short of the total to which the urban population would be entitled, if proportionate representation were possible. The urban population would receive little more than its fair proportion of the total

[1] In two of these States, Minnesota and New York, the redistricting was done by joint resolution of the State legislature without the approval of the governor and has been attacked in the courts. In the former State the highest court has pronounced the redistricting valid, and in the latter the inferior courts have pronounced it invalid. A final decision can be reached only in the Supreme Court of the United States. In Illinois the redistricting act, though approved by the governor, has been attacked in the courts and declared invalid in the court of first instance. An appeal is pending. In this case the ground of attack was the alleged unfairness of the redistricting rather than, as in the former cases, the procedure adopted by the legislature.

number of districts, if the districts in class III were added
to those in classes I and II, but such treatment of the class
III districts is clearly not justified by their character. The
class IV districts might with more propriety be included
with the districts in classes V and VI, in which case the rural
population would have approximately the representation
to which it would be entitled, if proportionate representation were possible. The balance of power between the
definitely urban and definitely rural districts is located in
the districts falling in class III. It is evident that the urban
population has a strong, but not as yet a clearly preponderant, voice in the House of Representatives. The rural
population is losing its grip upon the lower branch of the
Congress, but has not yet definitely lost the superiority
which it had always possessed prior to the World War.
Clearly, however, the old order is giving way to the new,
and the balance between rural and urban interests is about
to turn in favor of the latter.

To determine the rate at which the preponderance of
power in the lower branch of the Congress is shifting from
country to city districts, it is necessary to compare the distribution of districts under the latest apportionment with
that under the preceding apportionment. The same classification of districts can be used for the apportionment
based upon the census of 1910 as for that based upon the
census of 1930.

Twenty years ago the definitely rural districts outnumbered the definitely urban by 192 to 120. In the last
two decades the latter classes have gained 56 districts,
while the former have lost 84. The class VI rural districts
alone have been reduced from 83 to 16. In Washington's
time these strongly rural districts accounted for 100 out of
a total of 105 members of Congress. In Jackson's time
they accounted for at least 200 out of 240. At the begin-

ning of Wilson's administration they still accounted for nearly as many congressmen as the metropolitan districts. Now they are almost wiped off the political map. Another decade, marked by the same trend toward the cities as in the past, will give the urban population a definite superiority in the lower branch of the Congress. That means a predominant voice in two of the three political branches of the federal government. It means the passing of rustic politics and the coming of the brand of politics which has been characterized as urbane.

CLASSIFICATION OF CONGRESSIONAL DISTRICTS

1912

(by political sections and distribution of population between city and country)

Section	Urban		Mixed		Rural		Total
	I	II	III	IV	V	VI	
Northeast	58	11	17	20	14	3	123
Middle West	21	6	17	27	38	18	127
Upper South	7	5	5	9	24	28	78
Lower South	2	2	8	11	22	29	74
Far West	4	4	3	6	11	5	33
Total	92	28	50	73	109	83	435

There remains to be considered the probable differences between rustic and urbane politics.

It has always been believed that the influence of urban populations upon the conduct of government would be very different from that of rural, and in the early years of the Republic the prevailing supposition was that the change from rustic to urbane politics would be decidedly a change for the worse. Jefferson's opinions are well known. Writing in 1787 from Paris to his friend Madison, he predicted [1] that "when we get piled upon one another in large cities, as in Europe, we shall become as corrupt as they."

[1] *The Writings of Thomas Jefferson*, vol. iv, p. 479.

Thirteen years later, writing from Monticello to his friend Benjamin Rush, he declared: [1] " I view great cities as pestilential to the morals, the health, and the liberties of man. True, they nourish some of the elegant arts, but the useful ones can thrive elsewhere, and less perfection in the others, with more health, virtue, and freedom, would be my choice." This prejudice against cities, or rather predilection for the country, continued to characterize the dominant opinion among American politicians throughout the nineteenth century. In Jackson's time a discerning French writer, Alexis de Tocqueville, made a careful study of American politics and returned to his own land to write a book filled with discriminating praise of American institutions. But, though he found much to admire in America, he viewed the growth of cities with unconcealed alarm. Among the principal causes which, he believed, tended to maintain the republican form of government, he listed the absence of a great capital city. Then he added a memorable warning. [2]

The United States have no metropolis; but they already contain several large cities. Philadelphia reckoned 161,000 inhabitants, and New York 202,000, in the year 1830. The lower orders which inhabit these cities constitute a rabble even more formidable than the populace of European towns . . . within the last few months serious riots have broken out in Philadelphia and New York. Disturbances of this kind are unknown in the rest of the country, which is nowise alarmed by them, because the population of the cities has hitherto exercised neither power nor influence over the rural districts. Nevertheless, I look upon the size of certain American cities, and especially on the nature of their population, as a real danger which threatens the future security of the [republic]; and I venture to predict that [it] will perish from this circumstance, unless the government succeeds in creating an armed force, which, while it remains under the control of the majority of the nation, will be independent of the town population, and able to repress its excesses.

[1] *Ibid.*, vol. vii, p. 459.
[2] De Tocqueville, *Democracy in America*, vol. i, p. 370.

A half century later, in Cleveland's time, another discerning foreign observer, James Bryce, made another careful study of American politics, and, like De Tocqueville, recorded his opinions in an immortal book. Bryce also was distrustful of the influence of cities. "The growth of cities," he wrote,[1] "has been among the most significant and least fortunate changes in the character of the population of the United States."

Now the result which Jefferson dreaded, and from which De Tocqueville predicted the direct consequences, and the imminence of which Bryce lamented, has come to pass. A great part of the American people are "piled upon one another in large cities," and the armed forces of the government are no longer under the control of a majority of the nation, "independent of the town population." American politics is at the crossways, and the urban population, politically speaking, is coming of age. Rustic politics is known by the record it has made in the past. But the past does not so clearly reveal the character of urbane politics. The record of the urban populations in local government has given municipal politics a bad name. "There is no denying," Bryce declared,[2] "that the government of cities is the one conspicuous failure of the United States." But the government of cities has been improved since Bryce wrote. Moreover, urbane politics means something more than merely municipal politics.

The rise of cities has caused their peoples to make new demands upon their governments. The city-dweller can look to his local government for many services which the farmer or planter must provide for himself or go without. Water, light, heat, power, local transportation, drainage, protection of persons and property against fire and other

[1] Bryce, *The American Commonwealth* (1910 ed.), vol. i, p. 628.
[2] *Ibid.*, p. 642.

casualties, to mention only a few of the leading wants of people everywhere, must ordinarily be provided by the country-dweller for himself, whereas the city-dweller is dependent upon collective rather than individual enterprise, operating through the local government or corporations under its supervision. The office and factory worker is also dependent upon community activities of many kinds for the occupational security and efficiency which the farmer, planter, or rancher must obtain for the most part by himself alone. These fundamental differences between life in the city and life in the country create corresponding differences between the city-dweller's attitude toward government and that which prevails in rural areas. The city-dweller wants a vigorous, enterprising, and serviceable government; the farmer or planter tends to be more easily satisfied with one which undertakes less, provided that it interferes with him less. The former will support an expensive government, if it is high-powered and efficient; the latter prefers one that is economical, even though comparatively inert.

The growth of cities, therefore, and the accompanying expansion of governmental activities mean more than a mere growth also of the citizen's stake in the administration of public affairs. They mean a revolution in the attitude of the individual toward his government. This revolution applies not only to the attitude toward local government. It extends also to the city-dwellers' attitude towards their governments in State and nation.[1] The demands of modern urban society upon government ensure that the urbane politics of the future will be something radically different from both the rustic and the municipal politics of the past.

[1] See my *State Government in the United States* (3rd ed.), chap. vi, "The Peoples of the States."

The transformation of rustic into urbane politics will be characterized chiefly, it may be expected, by the development of a new science of public administration. The leading characteristics of the "rustic" administrative system were: (1) the independence of administrative officers of one another and the decentralization of administration; (2) a settled tradition of political interference with the administration of public business; and (3) reliance upon the popular election of administrative officers and upon the judicial review of administrative acts to protect the public against the abuse of administrative power. Under such an administrative system, especially if judges as well as administrative officers are elected by the people, efficient administration depends largely upon public sentiment in the various administrative areas and upon the responsiveness of the processes of nomination and election to such sentiment. Democracy and administration are confused, and, despite the constitutional distribution of powers between the several departments of government, administration as well as legislation becomes deeply involved in politics. The unsuitability of the "rustic" administrative system for modern urban society has long been recognized and efforts to correct its defects have been repeatedly made by urban reformers.[1] An "urbane" administrative system will be founded upon a clear distinction between "politics" in the narrow sense of the word and administration. It will readjust the relations between the chief executive and the other political branches of government, on the one hand, and the principal administrative officers on the other. It will introduce and strengthen the "merit" system for all ranks of the administrative personnel. It will reorganize the courts, where necessary, and take them "out of politics." The genius of urbane politics will lie in

---

[1] *Ibid.*, chap. xviii, "Democracy and Administration."

its respect for a new version of the old American doctrine of the separation of powers. Its most characteristic product will be a new distribution of power between politicians and administrators.

It is a profound mistake to suppose that the change from rustic to urbane politics will be necessarily a change for the worse. The supremacy of urbane politics will be accompanied by an unprecedented growth of public services. The creation of such services means the creation also of a great force of administrative officers. This is what many critics of modern political tendencies call bureaucracy. They have gone to much trouble to give bureaucracy a bad name. And it must be admitted that bureaucracy deserves a bad name, when it gets out of hand and becomes inefficient and oppressive. The great problem of urbane politics is to popularize expert administration without destroying its efficiency or unduly impairing its power, that is, to make bureaucracy responsible. The creation of responsible bureaucracy may appear to be irreconcilable with the American tradition that popular government should also be constitutional government, that is, a government of laws and not of men. If so, it is a deceptive appearance. The laws are not self-executing. For their enforcement they are dependent upon the acts of men. Somewhere discretion must be exercised. Rustic politics placed discretion largely in the hands of politicians and of judges. The activities of the politicians always added a personal touch to the government of laws. Judges professed to act more exclusively under the guidance of law, but the judicial review of legislative and administrative acts, which the nature of the rustic political system made an important part of their work, necessarily involved a wide discretion in the interpretation of law. It is desirable in modern urbane society that politicians and judges should share their discretionary powers more freely with administrative officers. That is the essence of the urbane administrative system which a responsible bureaucracy alone can operate. The enforcement of administrative responsibility, like that of judicial responsibility, will be, in the last analysis, the task of an enlightened public opinion. The foundation of any system of politics must ever be the system of education. Of no kind of politics is this more true than of the urbane politics of the future in America.

The transition from rustic to urbane politics will be but one phase of the era of change which seems to be impending. That we stand upon the threshold of great changes in American life has been a frequent topic of comment since the close of the World War and especially since the collapse of the post-War period of prosperity. By none have the implications of change been explained more lucidly than by Mr. Walter Lippmann. Writing in a recent issue of the New York *Herald-Tribune*,[1] he declares:

It would be naïve to think that men can or will be satisfied with the kind of life which they now have. They know, and every one knows, that invention and technical skill have opened up possibilities of security and plenty which are to a grievous extent unused or perverted. The awful paradox of our time, that there should be want in the midst of abundance, is self-evident proof that the prevailing political and economic arrangements and policies and methods of administering affairs are deeply and seriously at fault. A period of great changes is not merely indicated. It is certain.

Experimentation with new forms of collective effort appears to be the inevitable concomitant of a city-dwellers' world. Political experimentation should be no less promising than the other kinds of experimentation destined to accompany the adaptation of the institutions of the age

[1] Walter Lippmann, "Selecting a Successor to Holmes," *Herald Tribune* (New York), January 21, 1932.

that is passing to the needs of the age that is to be. Rustic politics, however well it may have served a rural people in the past, cannot meet the requirements of an urbanized age. Only urbane politics can meet those requirements. Now that the time for urbane politics approaches, its coming should be viewed with no less confidence than that with which Jefferson and Jackson viewed the dominance of the political scene by "the agricultural interest" a century and more ago.

THE EVOLUTION OF REPARATION IDEAS[1]

ELEANOR LANSING DULLES

As soon as the thunder of guns subsided on the Western Front the battle of financiers and politicians began. Already suggestions of the coming conflict had stirred up feelings which were to make reasonable deliberation almost impossible. There were wild forecasts of indemnities in various countries and high-sounding principles were formulated as a basis for the settlement. In fact even the more moderate statements grew out of the abnormal conditions which had prevailed, and all estimates of values and capacities to pay were distorted by the unusual conditions in production and consumption of wealth which had accompanied the war.

Nevertheless, from the beginning certain men had seen the nature of the economic relations involved. Their views were not widely followed by any large number until practical experiments had been made by forceful seizure, artificial protections and stimulants, payments by loans, and the transfer of wealth to creditor governments by means of an export surplus from Germany. These dramatic and costly experiments led to an evolution of practical policies which lagged behind theoretical understanding by an interval of approximately two years.

The reparation question was to concern millions of people and occupy the thought of scores of statesmen. Not only the sturdy peasants returning to their trench-scarred

[1] Edwin F. Gay, "War Loans or Subsidies," *Foreign Affairs*, April, 1926. In this article Professor Gay suggests the importance of the historical analysis of the sequence of ideas, an analysis which cannot be complete for many years.

villages, and half-starved Germans trying to reconstruct a wasted economic system, but millions of other people clamored for a settlement in the name of justice, or in the hope for increased wealth. Thus the question became, from the beginning, highly controversial. It called out the worst types of political effort and at the same time led to the evolution of new economic principles. It was to be dominated by practical expediency and yet was to be influenced by some of the best economic thinking of the time. The result was a confusion of ideas which was to bring privation and discouragement to many countries, intensify one of the worst depressions in history,[1] and bring the complicated structure of western industrialism to the verge of collapse.

The history of the reparation problem is long and complicated; volumes have been written and many more will be needed to explain the various episodes. There can be no attempt here to describe the succession of conferences, running close to fifty in number. Such an exposition would call for an explanation of political and budgetary considerations in more than seven countries, and a careful scrutiny of conditions in Germany. Moreover, the final verdict will have to wait on the passage of time.

It is possible, however, to isolate certain aspects of the question, and to trace the development of the understanding of the influences surrounding German payment through three major crises, and to distinguish four dominating ideas. These were the more conspicuous stages in the evolution of the question, which was marked by many minor events and decisions. The outstanding periods are generally recognized to be the years dominated by the Peace Conference, from 1918 to 1923; those of the Dawes Plan, from 1924 to 1929; the Young Plan era, from 1929 to 1931; and 1931 and

[1] *Report*, Special Advisory Committee (Basle, December 23, 1931), p. 19.

after. Each of these stages was influenced by a major group of ideas and a host of minority opinions, while under these fluctuating waves of opinion there was a steady growth of understanding that large transfers of wealth were impossible merely on the basis of political claims.

This gradual development of theory and its recognition in political circles was the result of brilliant analysis on the part of certain economists and of conspicuous happenings in the world of commerce and exchange. Such names as those of Keynes, Taussig, Ohlin, Moulton, Rist, Young, Stamp, and a host of others can be cited to indicate the level of the intellectual effort brought to bear on the question. The result has been seen in the formulation of the concepts of exchange values, international investments, the difference between external and internal obligations, the elasticity of foreign commerce, the problems of creditor countries, and the analysis of price structures. Moreover, a new and significant institution has been built up to help solve the practical problems of international capital movements, that is, the Bank for International Settlements.

The progress of political policy was discouraging when placed beside the brilliant achievements in theory. In every instance the pressure on Germany was relaxed only after the destructive effects had become glaringly evident. Moreover, the desire for less political distortion in the economic system was usually concealed under phrases which emphasized war bitterness and piled accusations of bad faith on claims that justice had not been accomplished.

The first of the four major stages in the reparation problem dates from before the armistice to just before the formulation of the Dawes Plan, in 1923. It is characterized, as are the others, by conflicting majority and minority opinions. From the beginning a number of economists and statesmen explained the difficulties in collecting from Germany, but their assertions were overwhelmed by the clamor for retribution. The idea written into most of the agreements and ultimatums was that of "direct appropriation of wealth." It was reasoned that the right of conquest was enough, and that economic mechanisms and the customary interchange could be ignored in circumstances which gave the victor power to extract promises of large payments.

This naïve concept of the nature of economic facts is applicable to primitive societies which derive their wealth from the productivity of nature and which do not engage in an extensive interchange of goods. It implies a low standard of living, lack of division of labor, and small surpluses to be used for barter or commerce. It is an idea of wealth which applies to an era before the development of money or credit, and which leaves out of account the complicated interweaving of past and future, and of widely separate areas. In fact, it ignores the essential characteristics of the modern world.

This idea of direct appropriation implies various hypotheses in regard to both paying and receiving countries. There were, first, in regard to Germany, certain underlying assumptions not usually made articulate that there existed a large amount of *surplus* wealth [1] or that it was desirable, for various reasons, to press down the German standard of living to a low point. These hypotheses were the unexpressed basis for the specific attempts to acquire goods formerly needed to maintain the German people.

---

[1] The statistical basis was found in the pre-War estimates of German wealth. The figures set forth by Herr Helfferich in 1913 in his book *Deutschlands Volkwohlstand* had exerted a great influence in Paris and in the subsequent conferences. The figures given for the annual income, 41,000 million reichsmarks, were taken as a starting point and a substantial fraction allocated as possible reparation payment. There is no doubt that a picture of a large and powerful empire, rich in resources, industrial equipment, man-power, and gold had dazzled politicians who were not yet in a position to count the cost of war in any country.

Further than this, in respect to paying countries, it was assumed that the surplus so transferred would be absorbed without disturbing the division of labor within countries or between countries, and without dangerously affecting capital relations. These assumptions, implicit in early decisions, proved to be counter to underlying economic facts. It soon became evident that the application of robber-baron policies, feasible in primitive economies, was impossible in more complicated situations.

A small but notable minority did indeed contend against the prevailing views, but their arguments were not generally known at the time of the signing of the treaty. Notes drawn up in Paris which explained the complicated factors which would interfere with large payments from Germany were, to a large extent, ignored. One of these notes, which was made available later in Mr. Baruch's account of the Paris Conferences, asserted that large payments could be made only from an excess of exports, and by virtue of a reduced standard of living and increased productivity in Germany, it warned that "Germany would become the workshop of the world. Not only would the world's markets be opened to the goods made in Germany, but the economic life of the world would necessarily adjust itself to the dependence on German service."[1] It continued by indicating that Germany might ultimately gain an advantage by the resulting extension of trade.

It was generally known that J. M. Keynes was dissatisfied with the progress of the negotiations and resigned from the British delegation because of the direction affairs were taking. His protest, the first to stimulate widespread questioning of the practicability of the treaty, was most effectively expressed, in the *Economic Consequences of the*

[1] J. F. Dulles, memorandum presented to the Peace Conference. See Bernard M. Baruch, *The Making of the Reparation and Economic Sections of the Treaty* (New York, 1920), pp. 48, 49.

Peace, in 1920. He gave an indication of the twofold nature of the problem in explaining the difference between a surplus which Germany could produce at home and the annual tribute which she could pay abroad, and in his protest against "reducing Germany to servitude" pointed to political difficulties which were to render collection well-nigh impossible. Thus he piled up arguments and evidence against the treaty, and prophesied with a validity which came later to receive universal recognition that "it is only the extreme immoderation, and indeed the technical impossibility, of the treaty's demands which may save the situation in the long-run."[1]

Many of the legal questions in connection with the treaty raised by Mr. Keynes are still open to debate; in fact, the question of justice will probably continue to defy solution. But the economic opinions which he outlined were held at the close of the war by a small group of thinkers, and spread from these few in ever-widening circles. This growth of understanding was slow, and the loss of resources, credit, and courage in Germany was extremely rapid. Thus it was not possible to achieve the practical adjustment which would yield the greatest possible payment to creditor countries. In fact, the sums which Germany had offered in 1919[2] became too large for her to pay in 1932. The failure to readjust the demands to economic possibilities was, therefore, detrimental to creditors as well as to debtors, for the loss to international credit was one which fell upon both.

One reason for the false dependence on the simple view of the extraction of tribute was based on comparisons with

[1] J. M. Keynes, *The Economic Consequences of the Peace* (New York, 1920), p. 82. See also pp. 208, 225.

[2] The first sum offered, 25,000 million dollars, was equivalent to approximately 7,500 million dollars after allowance for deductions and non-inclusion of interest, according to Mr. Keynes (*op. cit.*, p. 223).

the experience in France in 1871. This was a natural line of thought, but left out of account basic economic facts. The difference in the size of indemnities is of the utmost importance. In 1919 the figures indicated under the indeterminate conditions outlined for Germany totaled more than 31,000 million dollars. In contrast to this the indemnity paid by France after a shorter and less costly war was one billion dollars.

The destructive forces loosed by this false reasoning brought about their inevitable results. The treaty signed on June 28, 1919 came into effect in January, 1920, but even before this date certain properties were turned over to the creditor nations by Germany. Immediately serious difficulties emerged. There were protests from those who did not wish this ceded property to compete with domestic production, a feeling intensified by the fear that German services would be accepted under special arrangements which would make it difficult for labor in the receiving countries to maintain wage levels. These objections from many quarters were not conspicuously brought forward at this time, but showed a dawning realization of unwise tampering with the normal workings of a laissez-faire régime generally assumed to exist.

The second year of peace was characterized by growing difficulties in the field of reparation. Five notable conferences were held to discuss various aspects.[1] On these occasions attempts to adjust details of payment did not influence the basic ideas. Feeling was aroused in Germany at the Reparation Commission's valuation of appropriated property.[2] The distortion of economic relations,

---

[1] The main conferences in 1920 were those of May 15, Hythe; June 21, Boulogne; July 5, Spa; September 24, Brussels; and December 16, Brussels.

[2] Max Sering, *Germany under the Dawes Plan* (London, 1929), pp. 28–33. Germany paid 4,000 million dollars in 1920 and 1921, which was a time of widespread economic depression.

however, was only in its beginning, and the progress of theory was negligible.

The year 1921 was the date set for further large German payments. Early in January difficulties began to develop and the first of a series of conferences was called.[1] Deliveries in various commodities during the two years after the war had totaled, according to some estimates, 4,000 million dollars, but Germany was called on to make further large deliveries in kind and cash payments beginning in May, 1921. The Paris resolutions set these sums at 650 million dollars, in addition to 10 per cent of her exports, and excluding her obligation for a large capital sum (138,000 million reichsmarks). This was accepted under threat of the occupation of the Ruhr, and it was not until the first of May that Germany was declared in default for delay in payment.

Germany's claim that these payments could not be met was considered in creditor countries to be deliberate defiance. This assumption was the result of the idea that wealth could be extracted on a large scale merely on the basis of legal claims, and of lack of knowledge as to the amounts obtained. While it is impossible to value these sums to the satisfaction of both Germany and the Allies, it is nevertheless true that the wealth already transferred was large in view of the losses which Germany had sustained; these amounts approached the limit of tolerance of the economic system.

The fourth year of payment, 1923, was to bring into the foreground the problem of transfer officially recognized in 1924. Even though the practical consequences of economic changes became conspicuous the theoretical interpretation

[1] The principal meetings during this year were those of January 24, Paris; March 1, London; April 9, London; May 5, Allied ultimatum to Germany; October 6, Wiesbaden; and December 18, London.

had to wait for further proof. Indeed for the next two years the general interpretation of German economic phenomena — particularly the currency, prices, and exchange difficulties — was based on accusations of deliberate depreciation. The fact that in the first half of 1922 commodity prices and the cost of foreign exchange increased faster than the volume of currency in circulation escaped general notice.[1]

CHANGES IN THE GERMAN SITUATION DURING 1922

(1913 = 100)

	Foreign exchange	Commodity prices	Volume of money	Cost of living
January	45.5	36.7	20.5	20.4
July	118.0	100.6	33.5	53.9

It was natural, therefore, that the general atmosphere of hostility which surrounded the question should stimulate the belief that Germany was attempting financial default.

A different interpretation of German conditions was brought forward by the Bankers' Committee in June, 1922. They emphasized the precarious state of German credit and indicated that no large loan could be floated unless creditor countries were willing to co-operate in the flotation of the securities and unless German rehabilitation should be assured.[2] They failed in their desire to put forward concrete recommendations because the French members of the Committee objected to the conditions which the others held to be essential, that is, the reduction of German payments. This delayed reconstruction plans until the meeting of the Dawes Experts, although the findings of the Committee influenced the evolution of opinion. A

[1] J. W. Angell, *The Recovery of Germany* (New York, 1929), p. 336.
[2] *New York Times*, June 11, 1922. See text of the Committee's *Report*.

number of other notable events indicated a recognition of the inter-relation of the reparation, debt, and currency problems with more general economic questions. Unfortunately, political forces were still moving in divergent directions. Some of the meetings and statements in 1922 which bore on the situation were:

January	6	Cannes, Conference on reparation.
February	28	Frankfurt, Socialist Conference discusses reparation.
April	10	Genoa, Conference on finance and currency.
May	24	Paris meeting of Bankers' Committee on reparation; failed to agree, June 12.
July	12	German application for a moratorium until the end of 1922.
August	1	The Balfour note on the British position.
"	7	London, Allied conference of Prime Ministers to discuss reparation.

Thus attention was scattered over a wide field and everywhere abnormal conditions were evident. In some quarters there was a tendency to link these disturbances with the War-indemnity problem, whereas in other quarters such views were interpreted as "pro-German propaganda."

The dramatic invasion of the Ruhr followed quickly on the events of 1922, and was a concrete indication of the "direct appropriation" concept of reparation. It was the culmination of those arguments which assumed that a surplus existed and could be transferred if the will or the force existed. Thus the French and the Belgians marched into the smoke.filled coal regions of Germany to take wealth legally theirs under the treaties, but never proved to be available under economic laws. The result was political resistance and economic complications which had not been dreamed of. Then at last the significance of the costs of exploiting the mines in relation to the estimated surplus became evident to collector nations. The coal raised under

French supervision did not, in fact, yield the expected profit; the wages and administration expenses, as well as passive resistance, cut down the gains. This was a stormy period. The slow progress in understanding was extremely costly as the series of distressing events in the post-War years indicates. The outstanding events in 1923 were:

January	1	Announcement of new reparation proposals by Germany.
"	2	Paris, discussion.
"	11	Ruhr occupation.
March	16	Beginning of German passive resistance.
May	2	New German proposals — rejected later.
August	2	Allied note on reparation.
"	11	Cessation of deliveries in kind to Allies.
September	26	Cessation of passive resistance in Ruhr.
October	24	Germany requests examination of capacity to pay.
November	15	Mark stabilization.
"	23	M. I. C. U. M. (Mission Interalliée de Contrôle des usines et des mines) agreement reached.
"	30	Reparation Commission appoints two committees of experts.

Thus one phase was ended and another opened, with two startling phenomena — the Ruhr occupation, and the collapse of the mark.

In 1923 an additional contribution to the theory of the subject was made by the book of Professor Moulton and Dr. McGuire.[1] It emphasized the necessity of an exportable surplus, and made the concept fairly familiar to those who were already beginning to see the difficulties involved in the task of collection. The arguments which they marshaled were impressive, and if their analysis was in some respects too rigid and under-emphasized the discounting and lending possibilities, their main position was undoubtedly right.

[1] H. G. Moulton and C. E. McGuire, *Germany's Capacity to Pay; a Study of the Reparation Problem.*

There were, thus, a number of new ideas to aid the Paris Committees that met under Mr. Dawes and Sir Reginald McKenna. The conclusions embodied in the plan issued in April, 1924 were a valuable contribution to the theory of international finance. The transfer theory in particular was given more definite formulation and was, for the first time, widely recognized. Luckily for the later solution of German difficulties, constructive experiments in finance had been conducted in Hungary and Austria under the guidance of the League of Nations. As the result of their work, the idea of separating "transfer" from "collection" was clearly stated, and special exchange protections were set up to permit currency stabilization. Moreover, loans were negotiated to aid in the process of recovery.[1] Guided by this work, the Dawes Experts gave a new emphasis to certain aspects of international finance: a recognition of the importance of currency speculation, and the need for transfer protection. At the same time, the necessity of a sound reconstruction of German economic conditions was placed in the foreground. The separation of payment in Germany from payment abroad had a very great political significance in that it made it more difficult to declare Germany in default. Her problem was limited to handling her budget in such a way that revenues could be deposited in the Reichsbank to the account of the Agent General. This meant that if Germany could increase production, and cut down consumption in an endeavor to discharge reparation agreements, the value of the mark would not suffer.

This emphasis on transfer as separate from collection and the various special protections introduced strength-

[1] The names of Sir Arthur Salter, Jeremiah Smith, Sir Walter Layton, Professor Charles Rist, Pierre Quesnay, Jean Monet, and various associates are remembered in these countries because of their skilful handling of baffling problems.

ened doubts already existing as to the emergence of an export surplus. It indicated to those who had misunderstood the inflationary processes in Germany that the mark was in an extremely vulnerable position. In short, it crystallized the new developments in the theory of currency problems and gave them the stamp of official approval. At the same time it served to arouse faith in Germany and stimulated the surprising flow of funds in the next few years. Once the simpler ideas of conquest and seizure had been abandoned and new efforts directed along economic channels, the idea went abroad that Germany could and would recover. So it came about that the Dawes loan was only the first of a series put at the disposal of the German economy, and a short period of prosperity followed.

Then, again, the gold clause and the prosperity index paid tribute to the more complex analysis of international economic relations. These clauses were protections designed to lessen the strain, but they were provisions which were to allow for the change of payments both upward and downward, and so to assure some adjustment to economic fluctuations. Several decades of business-cycle study and recent rapid value changes had paved the way for this arrangement. An increase in the value of gold would obviously alter payment conditions; more goods would be required to meet the same nominal debt; and an improvement in German conditions would make possible the payment of larger sums through exports.

The Dawes Plan was a notable step forward, an expression of the new attitude toward reparation which had taken the place of earlier doctrines based mainly on desire. It was seen that Germany could pay large sums only as the result of great productivity, and could make those available only through commercial or investment channels. Unfortunately, not all the points at which the strain would come were clearly seen, and the wishes of politicians and economists made it easy for them to misunderstand the events after 1924 as a second phase of reparation began with the vigorous recovery.

It was, paradoxically, the very soundness of the ideas behind the Dawes Plan in 1924 which led in 1929 to the substitution of a new plan. The statements of the Experts and the protections granted to Germany served as an invitation to foreign lenders to furnish funds without fear that claims on Germany would be met in depreciated marks. Moreover, the prospect of rapid reconstruction of German industry and finance made it natural for lenders to rush to Berlin with tempting offers which were rarely refused. The inflow of capital was based on the expectation that normal industrial and financial life would be safeguarded. The annuities set down in the Plan were duly met by the German government, but the payments in marks did not cause noticeable transfer difficulties because special arrangements led investors to feel that it was safe to place money in Germany.

This was a time of genuine recovery, and, as often, prosperity blurred the clearer vision which had characterized 1924. Funds put at the disposal of municipalities, industries, and other borrowers led to a contradictory state of affairs. On the one hand, they made possible the rationalization of German industry and improvements in housing and social services. On the other hand, they piled up obligations to pay abroad large sums as interest and principal. The direct effect was that foreign exchange was available in the Reichsbank even though the balance of trade continued to be unfavorable. There is little wonder that those who took a more optimistic view of economic trends came to think that the transfer problem had been exaggerated. There was only a small minority who remembered the warnings in the Dawes Plan that "loan operations may disguise the position . . . they cannot alter it. . . . If Reparation can be paid . . . it can only be paid abroad by means of an economic surplus in the country s activities."[1] The new and more cheerful view pointed to the possible continuance of productive loans for some time.

Such optimism, unusual in post-War years, was borne out by events in Germany for a short period. There was a temporary interruption to the succession of conferences and hostile demonstrations on the part of creditors and debtors; payments under the Dawes Plan were made in full; in 1925 the economic boom in Germany was at its high point, and in 1926 there was an export surplus. The explanation was put forward in some quarters to the effect that, in this borrowing, Germany was like a "young country" and could absorb large funds in productive uses even at high rates of interest. The Reports issued by the Agent General indicated sound currency conditions and improvements in industry and trade, and only later began to warn of certain unsound budget practices and the use of borrowed money for "unproductive" ends. Economic opportunities diverted attention temporarily from the deep-rooted political unrest, and the more critical economists were silenced by the turn of events.[2]

Thus the third idea of the methods by which reparation could be paid began to develop out of the plan which formulated the second theory. The vast improvement in Germany which came with the Dawes Plan gave currency to the concept of discharging reparation payments through security operations. In the main financial centers, imaginations were fired with the possibility of a rapid expansion

---

[1] *The Dawes Report* (World Peace Foundation, Boston, 1924), p. 375.

[2] Most of the debt agreements with the United States were signed in 1925 and 1926.

on the basis of large credit facilities, and this kind of thinking was applied to the situation in Germany. Unfortunately, in the case of business as well as political borrowing, the rapid increase of obligations was limited by the slower development of marketing possibilities. Because of this discrepancy the increase of debts under the Dawes Plan at a ratio represented by a compound-interest curve proved to be unsound.

The Dawes Experts had not outlined a definitive settlement, but a trial period in which German capacity to pay had been safeguarded. During these years the rapid acceleration of German activity led observers to think that the time was ripe to fix a definite total. This thought was the result, in part, of fears that the prosperity index might increase German payments, and also of the desire to be free of occupation in the Rhineland and of foreign commissions in Berlin. On the other hand, the French were anxious to have a part of the political debt turned into commercial payments by the issue of securities. Meanwhile, Mr. Gilbert had indicated that the moment for a definite settlement had arrived. Many motives, therefore, lay behind the Geneva resolution of September 16, 1928 calling for a new conference. Steps were immediately taken to appoint experts to arrive at a "final and definitive settlement." The delegates assembled in Paris in February, 1929, just as the reversal of economic sentiment and values was about to change conditions in the entire world.

The theories embodied in the Young Plan had been foreshadowed by preceding conditions, just as those which were formulated in the Dawes Plan had been expressed by a growing number of observers before 1924. In both cases, the main concepts were modified to take account of political forces and compromise was necessary many times during the stormy sessions in Paris. Nevertheless, the central idea stands out clearly. It is apparent that the continuance of loans was counted on to ease the burden of payments, since no substantial export surplus had been available during the operation of the Dawes Plan. In no other way was it possible for the annuities to be "assimilated to commercial and financial obligations." Moreover, the Experts asserted boldly that "the total amount of the annuity proposed . . . can in fact be both paid and transferred by Germany."

Thus, although the Young Plan makes various references to exports as important, it is obvious that its main conclusions were valid only if loans were expected to continue. No other interpretation is possible in the light of the failure to secure an export surplus during the preceding years. All the phrases which refer to the expansion of commerce are based on the assumption that the more favorable conditions that came with Germany's ability to borrow would continue, and they were colored in some measure by the inflationary plans brought forward by Germans and others who hoped for the inauguration of ambitious schemes in "backward regions." These suggestions had little practical influence on the concrete measures outlined.

Nevertheless, the expansion of commerce and the development of backward regions was suggested several times in the first descriptive outline of the Bank for International Settlements. Some of these ideas persisted even in the Statutes of the Bank. As stated in the Young Plan they were extremely general: "We envisaged the possibility of a financial institution that should be prepared to promote the increase of world trade by financing projects, particularly in undeveloped countries, which might not be attempted through the ordinary existing channels."[1]   Dr.

---

[1] The Report of the Committee of Experts on Reparations (the Young Plan), His Majesty's Stationery Office, Cmd. 3343, p. 9.

Schacht had been insistent on the inclusion of these phrases in the Plan and also the shorter provision in article 3 of the Statutes. He had, perhaps, anticipated that they might afford a basis for the German claim that creditor countries had not fulfilled their obligations under treaties which included these agreements. In contradiction to such vague suggestions, a careful consideration of the functions, resources, and spirit of the new bank made it evident that there could be no action under this heading for a long time.

There was to be no delay, however, in the first steps to assimilate reparation payments into the complex fabric of non-political debts. Bonds were to be floated so that the securities could pass into the hands of individuals scattered over many countries. Some hoped that a large share of the German obligations could be held in this way. In fact, press discussions referred to bonds totaling 3,000 million dollars, indicating that such a high percentage of "commercialization" would spread the burden of War costs over wide space and time. The first move in the direction of the Young loan indicated, however, that the discounting of reparation in this way was to be extremely difficult. Thus the third theory of the manner of payment received official expression and widespread recognition just at the time when its fallibility was to be revealed by the reversal in financial conditions.

The inevitable breakdown was not anticipated by those who stressed the "young country" analogy and misunderstood the high interest rates in Germany. These rates were not so much a sign of the large earnings on capital as an indication of the serious shortage of savings and fear of risks. There was, therefore, bitter disappointment over the Young loan. The amounts offered to the public were smaller than some had hoped. And in addition to this, only two-thirds represented a commercialization, for it was found that Germany needed one-third of the amount to strengthen her financial position. In spite of these modifications of the original ideas, the value of the new securities fell sharply from the issue price on all the markets where they were quoted. This decline occurred, despite the high yield and special safeguards, because of a growing doubt on the part of the public as to the soundness of investments in Germany.

Although lenders considered security operations as a means of financing imports into Germany, these loans were, in a sense, a means of building up Germany's productive machinery and thus laying the basis for a future expansion of exports. The paradox of furthering a possible competition by means of capital supplied to Germany in a time of need was not clearly recognized because it did not show immediate results.

This distrust of German conditions and the increasing depression in the world in general handicapped the Bank for International Settlements and prevented extensive action on its part in assisting capital movements or reparation. The Bank was a well-constructed international trustee and agent for loans, but the whole idea of international lending had become temporarily discredited, and the Bank could do nothing to stem the tide of sentiment. The reversal of estimates went beyond the reasonable appraisal of Germany's capacity to pay, and in itself decreased credit and created transfer difficulties. Opinion which had been over-optimistic became suddenly hopelessly pessimistic. Thus the moratorium of 1931 became a necessity, and further reductions of a drastic nature were inevitable.

The theories which had been applied to reparation payments included a number of elaborations of the classical theory of international finance which were modified to show ways in which the general principles would apply to Germany. Thus, between the two extreme views, that of indefinite borrowing and discounting on the one hand, and that of an immediate and equivalent export surplus on the other, there were a number of more moderate ones. These indicated how German economic life would adjust itself to foreign demands, through changes in bank policy, taxation, productive efficiency, currency value, or loans. One or several of these changes would certainly work in the direction of increasing German exports, according to the arguments set forth. Most of these discussions did indeed describe the course of events in some one of the various phases through which Germany passed.

The difficulty with these theories, as they were viewed during the severe crises that came with the 1931 breakdown of payments, was not that they were false but that they did not warn of the secondary effects which came with excessive strain. Thus the deflationary tendency in Germany did bring export surpluses after borrowing ceased, but the influence on other countries was to accentuate the severe depression. Moreover, the decrease in German purchasing power put more goods at the disposal of creditor countries, but the accompanying effect on prices and credit disturbed economic life everywhere. For this reason the method of paying by exports aroused objections almost as soon as this method was apparent in 1930 and 1931.

Moreover, other threats to economic security were observed as the pressure in Germany stirred revolt. Even though the payments abroad in 1930 and 1931 were not large from some points of view, they had grave results in view of the feeling of oppression which existed. It was realized at last that the incentive to pay diminished rapidly as the original agreement became remote and the resistance of the rising generation became a formidable factor.

Once more there was a tendency for the views of politicians and economists to converge. The fourth stage of opinion was reached when the collapse of credit and the competition of exports threatened the world with a prolonged depression of prices. In this dark picture reparation payments appeared both as cause and as effect. The dilemma of the creditor nations brought about a grave situation and the round of conferences began again;[1] most politicians recognized the need for sweeping reductions in the interest of both paying and receiving nations. The fourth phase dates, in fact, from the flotation of the Young loan and the raising of the United States tariff walls in the spring of 1930.

The process of readjustment which took place in 1931 and 1932 involved a general change in attitude towards the present and future. The failure of the Young loan was coincident with a catastrophic decline of security values. It was suddenly realized that distant profits had been too heavily discounted. Whereas it had been argued in reference to Germany, and to various types of business enterprises, that continued investments were sound, it was suddenly realized that the assumption of expanding markets, low costs, and large-scale production was highly uncertain.

The deflation of reparation hopes was partly a cause and partly a result of this general movement. Those who claim that reparation could have been paid at Dawes or Young Plan figures during prosperous times leave out of account the depressing effect of such payments. Those who attribute the collapse in values to the reparation blunders

---

[1] These conferences were: 1929, the Young Conference, the first Hague Conference, Baden-Baden Bank organization committee; 1930, the second Hague Conference, and committees to put the Bank for International Settlements in operation; 1931, the conferences to arrange the "Hoover debt holiday," the freezing of German credits, and the Special Advisory Committee in Basle.

ignore the mistakes and exaggerations which were distorting the economic system at many points. Neither the amount paid as reparation nor the nature of its influence on economic practices is adequate to explain the dislocations of 1929 to 1932. On the other hand, the political threats and economic abnormalities which grew out of claims on Germany did much to interfere with confidence, credit, and the pursuit of normal projects.

In each of the four phases of the problem, public opinion and the action of statesmen had lagged behind the practical requirements of the situation by about two years. The plans of 1919 had been protested against by a small minority, and met the first serious check in 1921 when the direct appropriation of goods on a large scale ceased. The difficulties of transfer, which became apparent in 1921 and 1922, were formally expressed in the Dawes Plan of 1924. The possibilities of lending, which were manifest in the tremendous flow of capital toward Germany in 1925 and 1926, were fundamental to the Young Plan in 1929. The breakdown of lending and the failure of exports as payment mechanisms were widely recognized in 1929 and 1930, but a permanent adjustment was not officially sought until after the meeting of the Special Advisory Committee in December, 1931.

Meanwhile economic thinking, which had been so richly developed during Napoleonic times, was greatly advanced as the result of these later post-War difficulties. In the first place, it was evident that the simpler means of acquiring wealth could not be used in extracting large sums under modern conditions. The hopes of 1919 were defeated by the destructive inflation in Germany and the decline of transferable wealth. In the second place, the efforts in 1924 to protect exchanges and assure recovery resulted, not in exports, but in large loans. Then, in the third phase which was notable for the Young Plan in 1929, the expectation of easy adjustment through continued loans was followed by the collapse of credit and declining prices. The final phase of this period was characterized by the export surpluses which had been expected earlier, but was overshadowed by the deflation of prices and the growing desire to lessen reparation pressure on capital and commerce.

The tangled web of economic and political forces brought Europe to a tragic impasse. On the one hand Germany sincerely felt the nation was fighting for life in the attempt to throw off this financial burden. On the other hand, creditor countries thought that the revised claims would not fully cover their war damage. Economists, for their part, could point to the four stages of practical experience to show the dangers latent in large political payments. Even the sums called for under the Young Plan were too large to pass through normal financial channels, and threatened the stability of currency and credit. The solution was still highly uncertain in 1932, despite the clear relief into which certain facts had been thrown. Unfortunately there was a further stage of understanding to be reached, and the cost of such knowledge was high in terms of human suffering.

TYPES OF CAPITALISM

N. S. B. GRAS

In the nineteenth century an interest in capital and capitalism was gradually developed by socialists, who gave more attention to the subject than any other group. In their thinking, capitalism has appeared to be predominantly a system for the increase of fortunes and power at the expense of the workers. It comes near to being a synonym for exploitation. Although there is no good reason for denying the exploitation of workers at times, it will be apparent from what follows that this is no essential part of capitalism. The exploitation arises out of individualism and not out of capitalism. It is individualism that should be contrasted with socialism. Indeed a system of using capital is as necessary to socialism or communism as to individualism.

Many have been the efforts made to define capital — most of them useful. There is no thought of adding to the list here, but it is expected that out of a consideration of the different systems that have been developed in history will come a clearer understanding of what capitalism is and how it serves mankind.

Werner Sombart gave an historical turn to the subject of capitalism in his *Der moderne Kapitalismus*, first published in 1902. In a later work, *Der Bourgeois* (1913), he dealt with a pre-capitalist stage in history, setting forth the idea that, at the dawn and early beginning of society, man was as God made him. There was a restfulness that could be counted on and sufficient for existence according to custom; traditionalism reigned in this early static society; and there were values in use but none in exchange. The general concept reflects somewhat the ideas of Hesiod, Ovid, and Virgil. A close examination would probably show the picture to be mostly wrong.

The early as well as the later part of human development was absolutely dependent upon capital and the use of capital. To be sure, labor and land might be regarded as of greater importance, though this view would be hard to prove. Just as man is differentiated from the other animals by the use of fire, so is he to be distinguished from them by the accumulation of capital. Many animals collect objects, particularly of food, but none, so far as I am aware, for the purpose of production.

The capital of early man in the form of productive equipment was not large in amount but it was vital in its use. It consisted of weapons and tools for collecting objects of food and shelter, for hunting and fishing, and gradually for the cultivation of the soil. Archaeological and anthropological remains display more of these commodities than of anything else. Stone axes and arrowheads are among the earliest remains of man. Bone needles, earthen pots, and bronze knives are other examples. Numerous additional articles might be placed in the long list of goods belonging to early man's productive equipment.

Later came the hoe, the spade, the flail, the sword, the plow, the anvil, and what not. As we contemplate these and similar commodities, which in one form or another are commonly basic even today, we are inclined to rate highly the capital goods of early days.

The point is not to emphasize, much less to exaggerate, but to understand, the function of this equipment. In order to obtain an income from it man had to use it himself. He could not loan it or invest it for an income. He could, of course, loan it and often did so, but he did not obtain any material reward for his loan. The ideal was to help a kinsman or fellow-villager by a loan. This was caught up by the Church Fathers in the declining days of the Roman Empire and crystallized into dogma. So long as the village stage of economy prevailed, there could be but little objection to the doctrine.

Many early peoples became pastoral nomads, having large flocks of sheep and goats and herds of cattle and horses. Sometimes they possessed carts and wagons to aid them in their long seasonal migrations in pursuit of green pastures. I see no reason why we should not regard such nomads as highly capitalistic. They owned no land, though they had something like a dominance over vast stretches of territory. They worked in tending their animals but the labor was far from drudgery. Accordingly, their system seems to have been more a capital than a land or labor system. Indeed the animals might be roughly compared to the slaves in the capitalistic system of the ancient world and even to the power machines of today which, though they need attention, do most of the work and produce most of our goods and services.

The capital that a man or family in this early stage could command for his production arose through his own efforts. He could not borrow to any great extent or attract investment. Today we speak of plowing part of the profits back into the business. This was the original method of accumulation. Indeed throughout human history this seems to have been the main reliance, though it has been rivaled by other systems, as we shall see. Henry Ford secured a small loan when he started his production, the loan coming through the purchase of shares by other people. But later he bought off all shareholders, paying for the shares out of earnings. Ford has plowed back earnings and built up an enormous surplus that stands like a gigantic industrial fortress in our midst.

Other great corporations in America, while possessing the ordinary capital structure of common and preferred stock and bonds, have accumulated immense surpluses — partly out of war profits. These surpluses became a factor in the speculative loan market that culminated in the crisis of 1929. And since that time they have helped prevent the usual disasters that, in a period of prolonged depression, would have occurred to at least some of the firms in question.

We have become accustomed to think of the provider of capital and the user of capital as distinct. In the earliest type of capitalism, which we have just been considering, however, the user and the provider were one and the same person. Demand and supply were worked out within the one person or family group, which bears all the risk and takes all the profit or suffers all the loss. This system of capitalism was self-generating, or *autogenous*, as indeed we may label it.

The autogenous system of capitalism came to be rivaled by the *direct putting-out system*. In this new system the provider of capital and the user were different persons, but they were in direct contact with one another. The provider put out his capital directly to the user. Supply and demand were no longer united but they were not far apart.

This type of capitalism arose when money was coming to be a means of exchange as well as a measure of value, that is, very largely, when convenient coined money was taking the place of the awkward money by weight. All this occurred when town economy was supplanting village economy. Historically this has happened many times in the experience of the Mediterranean region. The most recent beginning came in the period about 1100–1300. The development then begun has proved to be continuous to the present time.

During the Middle Ages the Jews were the best-known examples of providers of capital. They loaned money to landlords, to officials of Church and state, and to business men. Incidentally, be it noted, they were permitted to charge 43 1/3 per cent per annum, a rate that was probably not on the whole excessive in view of the risks they ran, the sums they had to pay for protection, and the social ostracism to which they were subject. The Lombards and Cahorsines were their rivals to fame. Generally, merchants of whatever creed or nationality, who were rich from trade or nearing retirement, and mercantile families which possessed an accumulated capital and high credit, turned to money-lending as a profitable and far from strenuous occupation. The opposition of the Church to the loaning of money at interest is well known. Since most of the lending was surreptitious, the records are not voluminous, but they are sufficiently ample to make the main facts clear, that money was loaned, hard money withal — golden bezants, silver florins, golden gulden and golden ducats, French crowns and English nobles.

Another kind of loan was made under the guise of a temporary partnership. A merchant venturing out to sea (or setting off by land with a pack train) would form a partnership with a provider of capital who himself stayed at home. Sombart thought of such a provider as a landlord who had amassed his capital through the accumulation of urban rents, but landlords were spenders and not savers and the evidence for their participation in foreign trade seems to be lacking, as the studies of Heinen and Strieder have shown for Venice and Augsburg, respectively. It was much more likely that such providers were themselves business men, either retired or seeking additional sources of income.

These temporary partnerships were formed for but one

voyage or undertaking. At the end of the venture a settlement was made according to the original agreement. The
amount that each party contributed was returned, together with the appropriate share of the profits, if profits
had been earned. In the sea partnership, probably the
most common in Italy in the twelfth century, the division
of function was not so clear-cut as in the accommodation
partnership. In the sea partnership the stay-at-home
capitalist provided two-thirds of the capital required for
the voyage, while the traveling merchant provided one-
third. They shared the profits or losses equally. In the
accommodation partnership, however, the stay-at-home
capitalist provided all the capital and received three-
quarters of the profits. In this case the traveling merchant
was the simple user of the capital.

In both of these kinds of partnership the capitalist
sought an income without using directly the capital he invested: he sought to escape from the earliest type of capitalism. Likewise, the traveling merchant, as entrepreneur
and user of capital, sought to escape from the earliest type
in which he would have had to provide all the capital and
bear all the risk.

Besides the temporary partnership there was the partnership for a stated period — three or more years. Often
the partners were members of a single family; sometimes
they were unrelated by blood or marriage; and sometimes
they were mixed partnerships of two or more kinsmen and
one or more non-relatives. We see these partnerships well
developed in the Mediterranean and western European
countries by the fourteenth century. It might be that the
partners were all providers of capital and entrepreneurs as
well. In this case the partnership would belong to the
earliest or *autogenous* type. But it often happened that one
partner contributed all (or almost all) of the capital. Such

a provider of capital might be a wholesaler who wanted to help a retailer to set up a store or an artisan to establish or maintain a workshop. In each case there would be an ulterior motive to the investment: the provider of capital would want to derive an income, to be sure, but he would also want to gain in another way. He would want to sell his wares to the retail partnership and buy from the manufacturing partnership. But apart from these were partnerships entered into by rich and retired business men purely for the sake of a return on investment without any further effort on their part. In such cases the sharing of risk was probably decidedly subordinate to the provision of capital in the mind of the operating partner.

One way of sharing risk systematically in the period about 1350-1800 was for capitalists to underwrite marine ventures. Various persons with capital to invest or with credit that was good would agree to bear the risk of a voyage to the extent of, say, £50 or £100 or more. A score or more would write their names under the statement of the details of the enterprise; in short they would underwrite the insurance. At first this was probably a matter of mutual accommodation, later just a source of gain through the bearing of the risk. At first this underwriting might be done anywhere, later it was in the office of a broker who collected a fee for his work. This is the historic origin of marine insurance, and illustrates the direct putting-out system of capitalism, except that it was credit that was put up rather than actual capital.

An even older form, and one found today, was the loan on bottomry. In this case a person fitting out a ship would float a loan to be repaid with interest if the ship arrived safely in port. The corresponding respondentia loan was floated on the cargo. In both cases the provider of the capital bore heavy risk and received 25 per cent, more or less, on the principal of the loan, if the ship succeeded in reaching port.

As the Middle Ages drew near to a close, the joint-stock company came into existence. The providers of capital might be entrusted with the management or they might hold themselves aloof from it. Those stockholders who were noblemen, women, children, retired merchants, or merchants seeking an income apart from their regular business were simply the providers of capital. Gradually, in the seventeenth and following centuries, an increasingly large number of business men came to rely upon dividends from investment as the source of their livelihood. A relatively small number of stockholders were interested in actual management, much of which, an increasing amount in fact, was entrusted to paid officers.

At first the joint-stock company was confined to mining and public banking. Then it was used in foreign trade, notably in the sixteenth and seventeenth centuries. In the eighteenth century it was extended to transportation and in the next century to manufacturing, communication, storage, retailing, and so on. But, of course, as is well known, the victory of the joint-stock company came after 1850 in England and especially on the Continent. It is remarkable that this form of business organization, particularly the incorporated company, was more readily accepted in America than elsewhere. But we are interested chiefly in the fact that the joint-stock company enabled an investor to put directly into business such capital as he had and secure an income from it with the minimum of supervision. If the company issued bonds, he might purchase these, thereby obtaining from the same concern both interest and dividends.

The third type in the development of capitalism is the *indirect putting-out system*: the provider of capital entrusts his capital not to the user but to a money middleman who in turn passes it on to the user. The chief example of the money middleman is the banker but there are also insurance companies and investment trusts that perform a similar function. This money middleman corresponds chiefly to the wholesaler in general trade. Indeed in the development of capitalism and trade there is a close general parallelism. In the earliest type of each there is personal or family self-sufficiency to a large extent. In the second type, in town economy, there is a rapid development of the retail trade — in selling goods and in putting out capital. In the third type, the selling of goods and the putting out of capital are done indirectly, by means of middlemen who stand in between the producer of goods and the provider of capital on the one hand and the user of the goods and of the capital on the other.

The beginning of this third type goes back to the private bankers of town economy and accordingly does not lag far behind the second type in getting under way. But, whereas the direct putting-out system developed rapidly, the indirect system made but little headway until much later.

Private bankers arose in early town economy but flourished only in developed town economy and in modern times. Some of the money-changers and money-lenders became bankers when they took money on deposit and loaned it out to others. Probably the most common development, however, was for merchants to receive deposits and make loans. Often in old age or in the second generation of a family they gave up general mercantile functions in favor of banking. There is no question concerning this far-off beginning of the *indirect putting-out system*, but that beginning was only the tiny rivulet of a flow that was to become a great river at a later date.

Public commercial banks followed the private bankers

by about three centuries. These banks were joint-stock incorporated companies that necessarily had some official connection, but this did not prevent them from becoming general commercial banks. The first of such institutions were city banks, the Bank of Deposit in Barcelona, 1401, the Bank of St. George in Genoa, 1407, the Bank of the Rialto in Venice, 1587, the Bank of Amsterdam in 1609, and the Bank of Hamburg in 1619. The national banks arose somewhat later — the Bank of Sweden, 1688, the Bank of England, 1694, the Bank of Scotland, 1695, the first Bank of the United States, 1791, and the Bank of France, 1803.

For centuries the commercial banks were passive in their relation to their clients. They received deposits and made loans in a more or less routine fashion. When they had satisfied themselves that the borrowers were good risks, their responsibility ceased. Many banks are, of course, not far beyond this stage today, including English banks, which, however, since the Great War, are being shown a somewhat different type of leadership by the Bank of England.

It was German banks which pioneered in a dramatic way in the direction of a more active kind of banking. Lacking capital and seeing great possibilities of economic development after the formation of the Empire, the German banks were forced to do something different, if they were to make their meager resources cover the ground of the new opportunities. Accordingly, these banks got together in groups or *consortia* to finance the iron and steel industry, the electrical industry, the shipping trade, commerce in the Orient or in South America, and so on. In this way they made the most of what they had. In order to avoid the dangers of over-extension they insisted on some voice in the management of many of the firms to which they loaned money or extended credit. Often this control was exercised through the interlocking of directorates.

In America a similar type of banking arose in Wall Street. In the relation of Jay Cooke and Company, of Philadelphia, New York, and Washington, to the Northern Pacific Railroad Company during the years 1869–73, we see something of this system. This banking house floated the stocks and bonds of the Northern Pacific and exercised a measure of control over it, though the control was neither effective nor wise. After 1893 the firm of J. P. Morgan and Company began to influence railroads, steamships, and manufacturing concerns through the control of financing. At least one of the drives was to bring about the greater efficiency of the industries in question, particularly in the direction of the elimination or the mitigation of disastrous competition. The power of the firm of Morgan was considerably impaired by the establishment of the Federal Reserve System, which enthroned commercial banks still largely holding to a passive policy. But in due time that system, or at least the chief member banks of the system, have developed in the direction of an active as distinct from a passive policy.

One of the phenomenal developments of the modern era of business, that is, since 1800, has been the increase in the categories of money middlemen. Savings banks got their start in the early part of the century — in England in 1804 and in America in 1817. Private investment banks have grown up gradually in America, following the War of 1812–15. At first they performed such various functions as buying gold and silver, handling bills of exchange, transferring money and credit from place to place, discounting bank notes, and selling lottery tickets. Gradually the sale, and later the floating, of securities came to occupy their chief attention. Such banks were usually partnerships and such they are today; they usually possessed offices in more than one city as is also the case today.

In America, after the Civil War, there developed both trust companies and safe-deposit companies. Both of these have occupied prominent places in the financial structure of the country. The trust company has taken over functions of advice and initiative in investment, formerly performed by lawyers and trustees. Such a company comes pretty near to eliminating the work involved in putting out capital. It takes over the investment of funds and handles the dividends and interest resulting therefrom. It is now possible for a capitalist, commonly an heir, to divest himself of all responsibilities connected with his capital. His task thereupon becomes one of expenditure. This is not entirely new to society, for in remote times merchants and municipalities cared for the capital of women and children; but now there is a well-developed mechanism for doing this work with no element of charity connected with it at all.

There are also investment managers, both unincorporated partnerships and corporations, which perform much the same functions as trust companies. For a fixed fee they invest and reinvest funds, but unlike the trust companies they have no pecuniary interest, or very little interest, in the type of security that they purchase for their clients. In addition, there are investment counselors who merely advise their customers what to buy and when to sell, leaving to the customers the actual task of making the purchases and sales.

Insurance companies are products of the eighteenth century, but many of their policies and practices were developed in the nineteenth century. These companies take the risks of business and of life. They receive money and pay it out. They combine genuine insurance with savings in the case of endowment policies — in the United States since the 1850's. Enormous sums are paid to these companies daily in the form of premiums, which must constantly be invested in stocks and especially in bonds and mortgages.

In the business of putting out capital today there are various links in the chain between the provider and the user of capital. Ordinarily the user sells the security — a whole issue of millions in typical cases — to the wholesaler. This wholesaler is frequently an originator, either as an independent firm or in a syndicate with other firms. The wholesaler then sells to retailers or to large consumers. These consumers of securities, whether they buy from retailers or wholesalers, are, of course, the providers of the capital in question. Thus the business of providing capital has been developed along the same lines as general commerce.

Now, into this world of money middlemen has recently come a stranger, the investment trust. This institution buys securities of various kinds and in large amounts. In turn, it sells its certificates to investors, large and small. Like the various institutions which we have been considering, this one is also a money middleman. It receives money and pays out money. It is engaged in the business of putting out the capital of one person (or firm) to another person (or firm) to use. It offers to the investor special knowledge of securities, continuous management, and (often) diversification of investment. At first the banks in America were hostile; later they themselves established investment trusts with varying degrees of success. Just as some banks follow a passive policy and some an active policy, so some investment trusts are passive while others are formed to manage the firms in whose stock they have invested.

Of course, this present treatment is a mere outline. At every point there are questions of moment which must be passed over and developments that promise changes of business policy and management. For instance, the large American corporation has tended to build up a fund to be used for operating expenses; this fund has freed it from reliance upon loans from commercial banks. The operating fund in question has been the result of savings in a period of prosperity or of long-term securities floated at a favorable opportunity. The big commercial banks in America have met the new situation in part by turning to the security business. If they cannot make the commercial loan in the form of discounted paper, they can at least participate in the floating of the security which provides the corporation in question with a larger working capital.

The main thesis of this article is that in the first type of capitalism the ownership, control, and use of capital are united in one person or family; in the second type, ownership and a large measure of control are vested in the one person or class, while the use is lodged in a second person or group; in the third type, we find ownership, control, and use all separated. In this third type, the money middleman has control and with it the responsibilities of managing an intricate and delicate money-credit mechanism.

The implications of the development of this third type of capitalism — capitalism par excellence — are numerous and far-reaching. First, the new system has brought greater security to the provider of capital, because of the superior knowledge and greater experience of the money middleman. What effect this has had upon the amount of saving and upon the rate of return is not to be stated with any feeling of certainty. Second, the new type of capitalism has increased the availability of capital for the user, possibly, it will be found, to a dangerous extent. Third, business now has to bear the expense of a money-middle-man service made up of the fees and profits of these middle-men. I know of no way in which we can estimate the net benefits to business. Fourth, there has been developing in this money-middleman business a degree of credit which comes near to establishing a *credit*, instead of a *money*, economy. Behind the business of the industrial concerns are intangible assets; in the bits of paper which represent equities, and in the pieces of paper which are called money and checks, there is a degree of credit that is as challenging to the imagination, some believe, as to our civilization it-self. But still I think that we must at least call this new order not credit economy but *money-credit* economy, for we find that money is still an ultimate factor in the situation. Fifth, there has arisen a degree of centralization of control on the part of a relatively small number of money middle-men that has startled some of our political thinkers. I am personally not so fearful of the extent of the control in it-self as in the fact that the ownership of capital is divorced from its control and the fact that there has not been de-veloped a means of making effective the centralized control by money middlemen. If this control by money middlemen does not prove in the long run capable of measuring up to the needs of society, then socialization is a likely solution.

We may perhaps end with the opening theme — the re-lation of capitalism to socialism. These two systems are not to be contrasted at all. Capitalism has been the neces-sary means of getting a living. It could have been de-veloped along the lines of individualism or of socialism. Actually the choice that mankind has made has been along individualistic lines, with some local and temporary excep-tions. The time might come, however, when socialization would prove to be a better system than individualism. We should then enter a new condition of capitalism as follows:

TYPES OF CAPITALISM

Individualistic
    Autogenous
    Direct putting-out
    Indirect putting-out
Socialistic.

We have had not a little to record about money, stocks, and bonds. We should again call to mind that these instruments are but the outward symbols of the real agents of production — tools, buildings, raw materials, and other equipment. Obviously these would be as necessary to a socialist state as to an individualistic state. Socialism would be a means of control of business. The earlier system for the *direct putting-out* of capital would disappear along with the newer *indirect putting-out system* with its class of money middlemen. The chief issue is the socialistic control of capital *vs.* the *indirect putting-out system*. There is no challenge to capitalism but to the form of capitalism that dominates today. American preference is decidedly of the nature of a compromise: the *indirect putting-out system* is to be allowed to work out its own salvation, but the nation will supervise its operations.

THE MANAGERIAL FACTOR IN MARKETING

MELVIN T. COPELAND

The only trades which it seems possible for a joint stock company to carry on successfully, without an exclusive privilege, are those of which all the operations are capable of being reduced to what is called a routine, or to such uniformity of method as admits of little or no variation. Of this kind is, first, the banking trade; secondly, the trade of insurance from fire, and from sea risk and capture in time of war; thirdly, the trade of making and maintaining a navigable cut or canal; and, fourthly, the similar trade of bringing water for the supply of a great city. . . .

The joint stock companies, which are established for the public-spirited purpose of promoting some particular manufacture, over and above managing their own affairs ill, to the diminution of the general stock of the society, can in other respects scarcely ever fail to do more harm than good. Notwithstanding the most upright intentions, the unavoidable partiality of their directors to particular branches of the manufacture, of which the undertakers mislead and impose upon them, is a real discouragement to the rest, and necessarily breaks, more or less, that natural proportion which would otherwise establish itself between judicious industry and profit, and which, to the general industry of the country, is of all encouragement the greatest and the most effectual.[1]

The revolution of industry and commerce that has been taking place since the third quarter of the eighteenth century, when Adam Smith wrote his *Wealth of Nations*, has been conditioned not only on the invention of new machines, the application of power on a large scale, the refined division of labor, and the aggregation of large capital

[1] Adam Smith, *The Wealth of Nations*, bk. v, chap. i, pt. iii, art. i.

funds, but also on the development of the art of management. It is to that intangible but vital factor of management that I propose to direct my attention in this paper,
and I shall deal chiefly with the managerial factor in
marketing.

Adam Smith was skeptical of the possibilities of the successful application of the corporate form of organization,
outside of the four trades that he cited as being susceptible
of reduction to routine. His skepticism arose primarily
from the difficulties inherent in the management of an enterprise, not strictly routine in character, when not under
the watchful and observant eye of a proprietor guided by
intelligent self-interest. Nevertheless, those difficulties
have been overcome. Methods of executive control have
been devised without which the remarkable technical inventions of the last century and a half could not have been
utilized successfully.

Adam Smith recognized the problem of management.
He realized the lack of balance of interest and judgment in
the average man, especially when working for others. He
recognized, in a general way at least, the limitations on the
ability of a single human mind to comprehend the perplex-
ing details and the interacting variables which constantly
are influencing the welfare of a particular business enterprise large in scale, non-routine in character. He realized the jeopardy resulting to investors' capital from ill-
management. These difficulties have been ever-present in
the growth of large-scale businesses — the larger the scale,
in fact, the more serious the problems of management have
become. Nevertheless the economies of large-scale operations have been sufficient to induce the devising of means
for managing successfully capitalistic enterprises far too
large to be kept under the eye of a single proprietor. In
some instances, furthermore, large-scale management,

through subdivision of duties and specialization of managerial tasks, has enjoyed substantial advantages over management by individual proprietors. This has been conspicuously true in the field of marketing.

While new forms of business organization and new methods of management were developing, of course, during the first stage of the Industrial Revolution, that period was characterized especially by the mechanization of industry; attention was focussed primarily on production problems. For nearly a century after the factory type of industry was introduced, furthermore, the enterprises generally were under the close supervision of their owners, either individual proprietors, partners, or active holders of closely held stock. In the latter half of the nineteenth century, however, a second stage in the Industrial Revolution was reached. Then the corporate form of organization became more common in manufacturing businesses, with increasingly widespread public participation in ownership. In this stage the problems of business management came more and more to the forefront; many business undertakings became altogether too large for detailed personal supervision by the owners. In this second stage marketing activities also began to receive more attention, but progress in management came more slowly in marketing than in manufacturing. In manufacturing, the development of the art of management was a process of slow evolution; the discretionary power vested in foremen, for example, was supplanted only gradually by effective methods of planning, instruction, and centralized control of employment and of operations. In selling, however, manufacturers continued to vest discretionary power in their representatives long after some degree of effective control had been set up in the factories.

An especially enlightening account of manufacturers'

sales methods in England was published in *Hunt's Merchants' Magazine*[1] in 1839. In part it was as follows:

> Not an uninteresting feature of the internal traffic of Great Britain, is the system commonly styled commercial travelling. This institution, though now in its wane, is still exercised to a very considerable extent throughout the United Kingdom. Almost every commercial house there, of any note, employs one or more agents, whose business it is to travel about the country and procure custom for their principals. The commercial traveller, (as the agent is denominated,) is generally a young and very shrewd individual, possessing great suavity of manner, and a remarkable ability to suit himself readily to all the varied moods of his very various customers. Furnished by his principals with choice samples of their goods, he steps into his chaise or the stage, and with a light heart commences his circuit. It is not considered unusual if nearly a year elapses before he returns to his employers. At each town upon his route, he tarries at the principal inn, where he is sure to find a hearty welcome. After thus ensconcing himself in comfortable quarters, he arranges his samples, and, if it be forenoon, puts them under his arm and issues forth to visit the shopkeepers in the place. Wherever he goes, he is met with cordiality. Like all travellers, he is full of anecdote, and has at his command the rarest news of the time. None are more glad to see him than the shopkeepers' wives and daughters. To these he imparts the most recent scandal and the latest fashions, and affords them subjects for gossip until his next visit to the town. To the tradesman he lauds his samples with all the eloquence and ingenuity of which he is capable, and seldom leaves them without making considerable bargains in behalf of his principals. He then collects moneys due on former purchases, and, if in convenient shape, forwards the funds, together with his customers' orders for goods, by mail, to his employers.
>
> Nearly the whole of the country trade is managed by the commercial travellers. Each has his list of customers, who recognize his house only in him. Of them his principals are comparatively ignorant. To the discretion of the agent, it is left to determine who shall have credit, and to what amount that credit shall extend. . . .
>
> As Commercial Travelling has its benefits, so also has it its evils; and if its merits and demerits are weighed against each other, the first will kick the beam. In the first place, it may be urged, that it is not legitimately the province of the seller to carry his shop to the buyer; (as in truth he does when he sends to him his salesman and patterns.) It is reversing the natural order of things. It tends to demean the seller, and to create an inequality between the parties, honorable to neither.

[1] *Hunt's Merchants' Magazine*, vol. i (1839), p. 37.

Another objection to this description of agency is, that it invests the agents with undue control. The principals are necessarily obliged to give them free rein, and cannot always check them at discretion. Every travelling agent holds no inconsiderable portion of the funds, as well as the credit and reputation of his house, at his beck, and his slightest dereliction from the duty which he owes it, must, of course, influence all these unfavorably. As before stated, the customers know his house only in him, and it would require but little adroitness, on his part, to transfer their patronage wherever he listed. This influence is oftentimes abused. The natural, respective powers of principal and agent are confounded, and it is too often the case that the latter is dictator to the former. It is unnecessary to cite other objections to this description of trade, as it must be evident already, that it is a departure from the natural course. It is a diverticle, too, which is injurious to the character of commerce; tending, as it does, to debase it to the same estimation in which it was held in the feudal ages, and to render the name of merchant and trader synonymous with terms of contempt. In nowise can it be sanctioned by a clear-headed policy, and now that the communication between town and city is made so easy by the means of steam, there is no reason why it should not fall into entire disuse.

The foregoing statement is noteworthy not only for its picturesque account of the state of the art of salesmanship a century ago but especially because it illustrates the discretion then granted to sales representatives in guiding and controlling their individual activities and in handling credits and collections. The objection raised to the extent of the discretion vested in the salesmen, without control from headquarters, was based on grounds that were essentially the same as those on which Adam Smith objected to joint-stock companies outside a limited field, namely the undue jeopardizing of the interests and capital of the principals. Such risks were undertaken, of course, only because of the pressure to secure sufficiently wide markets to permit the economical operation of factories. The gains from factory production more than offset the risks and disadvantages of entrusting marketing activities to loosely supervised sales representatives.

The effect of the introduction of steam transportation,

furthermore, was quite the opposite of what was predicted by the author of the statement quoted. Steam transportation facilitated such further rapid expansion of factory production that the pressure for wider and ever wider markets continued. Hence sales activities were increased rather than lessened, a tendency which has continued down to the present day, especially in America.

How long manufacturers continued generally to grant such discretionary privileges to their sales representatives is a question that remains open for careful research. It is worth noting that some instances of that sort are still to be found even in America, where most progress in the art of sales management has occurred. In 1926, for example, we came across a small gear-manufacturing company in the eastern part of the United States which employed three salesmen with only the loosest sort of supervision [1] and a paper company [2] which employed thirty salesmen with similarly loose control; each salesman decided where and when he would solicit orders, subject only to the qualification that he should not approach prospective customers on fellow salesmen's lists. Various other examples, only a little less extreme, could be cited.

In general, however, the last twenty-five years have witnessed notable progress in the development of effective methods of guiding and controlling the activities of large, far-flung sales organizations. A domestic sales organization of five or six hundred traveling men is not at all uncommon in the United States at the present time, and some of the companies also have extensive sales organizations in foreign markets. The success with which the activities of these sales crews are planned and supervised probably would astonish Adam Smith, were he able to return to the

[1] "Exton Gear Company," *Harvard Business Reports*, vol. vi, p. 56.
[2] "Antrim Paper Company," *Harvard Business Reports*, vol. vi, p. 288.

mortal realm, nearly as greatly as the machinery with which the merchandise is produced for sale.

The direction and supervision of the activities of a traveling salesforce are far more difficult in certain respects than the control of a factory organization. The salesmen are scattered far beyond the range of the manager's eye, each dealing with ever-changing conditions and the omnipresent factor of human actions and reactions. The task of sales solicitation remains individualistic and partly emotional; it cannot be fully standardized.

How is it, then, that effective management of a large traveling salesforce typically has been accomplished, in spite of the limitations to standardization?

The first major step toward effective sales management presumably came from a recognition that it was a distinct function which could be separated from other functions of business administration. That step was part of the general evolution of the management of business enterprises, whereby the various tasks originally performed by the individual proprietor were split up into a series of specialized activities. The keeping of accounts was turned over to a bookkeeper; the bookkeeper eventually became an accountant; and the head accountant evolved into a controller, with a growing paraphernalia of budgets. The supervision of manufacturing activities was turned over to a factory manager, who acquired a staff of foremen and various other assistants and a ritual of operations. The handling of financial matters became the special task of a treasurer. Along with the recognition of such specialized functions as factory management, accounting, and finance came also the setting up of a sales manager.

Out of this evolution has developed what is termed organization and executive control. Specialized managerial tasks have been split off from other tasks or from those of the general manager. Each of these tasks has been assigned to a subordinate executive, with a definite statement of responsibility and authority. Means have been devised for checking up on the fulfillment of the responsibilities, so that the activities of all subordinate executives can be coordinated by the chief executive of the enterprise, who is responsible to the board of directors. Such is the situation typically in a well-managed business. How and when the principles of business organization developed, how and when the various steps in this evolution occurred, is an unexplored field for historical research.

The early sales managers apparently were in practically all cases men who had been salesmen and who were given the positions because of their outstanding ability to sell merchandise. That is still a very common situation. Such sales managers have been expected primarily to instruct and inspire the men under their charge in the art of salesmanship, and, usually, to handle by themselves the solicitation of orders from large customers. The early sales manager thus was supposedly a super-salesman, keeping close watch personally over the operations of the men under his charge. Later, as the size of the sales crews increased, and, also, as the general problems of management began to receive more careful study, the managerial aspects of the function began to assume more and more importance. The chief advances in real sales management have come during the last generation and are still in the process of evolution. It is as a result of these recent developments that means have been found for guiding and controlling the activities of a large number of salesmen operating over a wide market area.

The function of sales management, in the more advanced stage of its development, has required for its successful performance the ability to analyze complex situations, to exercise broad foresight in planning, to formulate decisions judiciously, and to use the tools of executive control, as well as to deal with the personal problems of selling. In other words the tasks of the modern sales manager involve planning and policy determination and execution as well as superior salesmanship. Examples of policy questions which must be dealt with by a sales manager, to select only a few at random, are as follows. Shall the product be distributed through wholesalers or directly to retailers? Shall distribution be sought intensively through a large number of retailers or shall a selection be made? Shall the product be trademarked? What terms and discounts shall be offered? Such questions of marketing policy are legion. They have become more numerous and more complex, of course, with the expansion of markets, and with the occurrence of revolutionary changes in the distribution field. The consideration and treatment of such questions constitute a major part of the managerial function of marketing. The provision of operating methods for assuring the carrying out of sales policies and plans by widely dispersed crews of traveling salesmen constitutes another major task in sales management.

One step in attaining effective management of sales personnel under modern conditions of marketing has been careful selection and training of salesmen. To cite a specific example, a company which employs about 300 salesmen for soliciting orders from retailers and for promotional work had a turnover of about 10 per cent annually in its salesforce prior to 1926. In other words, it had to hire about 30 new men each year to maintain its full quota. The cost to the company, through loss of sales during the transition and through various expenses incident to starting a new man, amounted to over $3,000 for each new man hired. In 1926 the company adopted a plan for more careful selection of its new salesmen, with reference to their individual qualifications, previous experience, and fitness for the particular territories in which they were to work. This procedure was based upon a thorough analysis of the company's previous experience with its salesmen. After the candidates had been selected under this new arrangement, the men were given a course of training before they were sent into the field. As a result, the turnover in the company's salesforce was reduced to less than 10 salesmen a year. The company saved upwards of $50,000 annually by this means, and of course secured a more effective sales crew. Various other companies have been developing improved methods for selecting and training their salesmen in order to reduce costs and to attain more effective discipline.

In training salesmen several companies attempted about twenty years ago to have their salesmen learn standardized sales talks, so-called. That resulted, naturally, in parroting, with unhappy effects on sales; consequently that type of instruction disappeared almost more rapidly than it came. Routine had been carried too far. The best practice at the present time is to give new salesmen adequate information regarding the merchandise that they are to sell and also to instruct them regarding the best methods of presenting the most salient points of the merchandise to prospective purchasers. The instruction of new salesmen, furthermore, is supplemented by frequent advice and instructions to all salesmen while in the field and oftentimes by assembling all or a portion of the salesforce periodically at headquarters for personal conference. Education is superseding mere emotional inspiration by the sales manager; as a result "bally-hoo" methods are being replaced by a higher type of salesmanship. The more careful methods of selecting and training salesmen, which are thus developing, are facilitating the successful management of large sales organizations.

The final aspect of sales management to be considered is the means of controlling the salesmen. Whereas the traveling salesman, in the early stages of the development of large-scale marketing, was largely his own boss, the tendency in recent years has been toward clearer and more precise definition of his task. At the same time better means have been devised for judging his performance. In defining the salesman's task, the territory in which he is to work has been specified precisely and in some instances lists of prospective customers to whom he is expected to sell have been prepared. Routes of travel have been studied, furthermore, so that each salesman can be advised regarding the most economical scheduling of his trip.

In order to work out the detailed plans for directing the activities of the traveling salesmen, market analyses, utilizing both published data and results of private surveys, have come into vogue. More and more comprehensive records of past performance also have been accumulated by individual companies. From these analyses and records it has been possible to set up standards of performance with which the results attained by each salesman can be compared, with allowance for peculiar conditions in different territories.

One manufacturing company, for example, recently divided its market in the United States into 44 districts for control purposes. Its sales in each district were compared with the number of white families, of income-tax returns, and of automobiles, and with various other market indices. In one district its average sales for a five-year period were $18.90 per 100 white families and in another comparable district $11.45. Similar differences were revealed between other districts and on the basis of comparison with other indices. The company now compares its sales in each district for each current six-month period with the more significant indices and thus has a continual guide to the accomplishments of the various members of its sales-force. This is only one simple illustration, very briefly stated. Many others, with much more complicated details, could be cited. Without going into the numerous and varied problems concerned with different types of sales organization, salesmen's reports, customer records, incentive methods of compensation, and all the other paraphernalia of modern sales management, however, suffice it to point out that the developments in statistical technique and the collection of statistical data of various sorts, both public and private, have furnished tools for the supervision of the activities of salesmen operating hundreds or thousands of miles away from the eye of the manager. The law of averages has helped materially to provide the means for guiding and controlling the activities of far-flung sales organizations.

As a result of the development of these managerial tools, the work of traveling salesmen in well-managed companies at the present time is closely scrutinized and the employer no longer finds it necessary to rely upon the personalities of individual salesmen or to trust to their discretion to anything like the extent that was common only a generation ago. This makes possible, of course, the successful operation of far larger sales organizations than safely could have been undertaken by primitive methods. Inasmuch as the scope of the available market has been a limiting factor in the growth of various enterprises, the improvement in methods of sales management has played a prominent part in the growth or formation of larger industrial units.

The foregoing statement is not presumed to be a complete and comprehensive picture of the task of sales management. It is intended rather to indicate some of the chief means by which the principals of a business enterprise have been able to organize and control intelligently a salesforce large enough to cultivate a broad market. It is intended to suggest the means by which the frailities of human nature that weighed so heavily in Adam Smith's mind have been surmounted in this human task of sales solicitation.

In wholesale trade the corporate form of organization also has developed, although the partnership has continued to hold an especially prominent place. Problems of management in a wholesale business are akin to those of the factory in so far as they pertain to the warehousing of stocks of goods. They are similar to those of a manufacturer's sales organization in the field of sales solicitation. Wholesale trade in itself, however, has not contributed largely to the progress in scientific sales management.

When we turn to the retail field we find that there during the last forty years the corporate form of organization has made particularly rapid progress. The capitalistic system has developed in the field of retailing in two major types of enterprise — the department store, and the chain store. These businesses started out as proprietorships or partnerships, but presently they attained such a large scale of operations as to call for incorporation.

Probably the first department store to be established anywhere in the world was the Bon Marché in Paris, which began operations in 1852.[1] The sales of the store in the first year were 450,000 francs; in 1863 they had risen to 7,000,000 francs; in 1877, 67,000,000 francs; and in 1900, 150,000,000 francs. Other department stores soon followed in Paris. The Louvre was founded in 1855,[2] Printemps in 1865, and others thereafter. In London were

[1] A. Saint-Martin, *Les Grands Magazins*, p. 30.   [2] *Ibid.*, p. 31.

established such department stores as Harrod's and White-ley's. In the United States, R. H. Macy Company was started in New York in 1858 [1] and Houghton & Dutton in Boston in 1872. The Jordan Marsh Company began opera-tions in Boston in the 'fifties. John Wanamaker opened a men's clothing store in Philadelphia in 1861 and in 1877 he added lines of women's garments and drygoods.[2]

The founding of department stores began a revolution in retail trade. It is noteworthy that this movement got un-der way, on a modest scale, in several countries at about the same time, 1852 to 1875. Although there were some local differences, broadly speaking, the department stores started in the various countries were strikingly similar in character, a fact which indicates that industrial, commer-cial, and social conditions had reached a stage favorable to the expansion of such enterprises. Without detracting from the genius of the entrepreneurs of this new type of business, it can be averred safely that fundamentally the department stores were successful because of favorable conditions. The variety of factory-made merchandise pressing for a market, especially perhaps, the introduction of ready-to-wear garments following the invention of the sewing machine; the accelerated speed of transporting goods to market by means of railroads and steamships; the introduction of telegraphic methods of communication which made market news quickly available; the rise in the purchasing power of the factory class and of the middle class of consumers; the increasing freedom and independ-ence of women, both in spending the family income and in accepting employment — such factors operating exten-sively throughout the industrial countries of the western world favored the growth of large-scale retailing.

[1] Paul T. Cherington, *The Wool Industry*, p. 225.
[2] Joseph H. Appel, *The Business Biography of John Wanamaker*, pp. 41, 80.

After 1890 the expansion of electric street car lines and other means of rapid transit greatly accelerated the growth of department stores, by bringing many more people within easy reach of urban trading centers. The stores thereby were made accessible to much larger numbers of consumers. Their market areas were widened. The introduction of new methods of paper manufacturing, which made possible cheap newspapers, gave added impetus to department-store growth after 1890 by providing means for advertising economically to large numbers of consumers.

While taking advantage of the favorable conditions, the department stores also promoted their own success by means of the policies adopted and the organization developed. At the outset the department stores in both Europe and America adopted a fixed-price policy and marked the prices on the goods.[1] Previously it had been common for a customer to haggle with the retailer over the price to be paid for an article. Under the new type of retailing, the price of any article was the same to all customers at any one time in each store. Such a price policy obviously was essential for large-scale retailing, since sales people in a large establishment could not safely be entrusted with discretion in price haggling. The one-price policy also was welcome to customers and served as a means of attracting trade. The early department stores likewise undertook to sell at low prices and to turn over their stock rapidly. Their low prices caused so much alarm to the unit stores in France and Germany that the small shopkeepers succeeded in having discriminatory taxes im-

[1] A. Saint-Martin, *op. cit.*, p. 30; J. Wernicke, *Warenhaus, Industrie und Mittelstand*, p. 40. In the United States a one-price policy was featured by some stores in New York as early as 1842, but the greatest impetus to the general observance of this policy in retail trade probably was given by John Wanamaker. See Joseph H. Appel, *op. cit.*, pp. 53–54.

posed on department stores; nevertheless they continued to grow.

The changes in price policies and in merchandising policies that have occurred in department-store retailing is another interesting topic for research. I wish, however, to direct attention here again to the managerial problems which arose in this type of large-scale retailing, where companies with annual sales of upwards of a million dollars each and thousands of employees are numerous. Without the solution of these managerial problems this type of institution would not have attained large success. To operate enterprises of this magnitude successfully it obviously has been necessary to develop methods of executive control which were not even dreamed of in Adam Smith's day or for decades thereafter.

When department stores were first established each department ordinarily was in competition with unit stores selling the same sort of goods. The shoe department competed with shoe stores, the piece-goods department with drygoods stores, the furniture department with furniture stores, and so on. This condition still exists, but the department store has at least partially superseded the unit stores in retailing numerous lines of merchandise. This situation obviously gives rise to the question: what advantage did a department store possess over unit stores competing with its departments? The answer, it seems to me, is that because of its size it could advertise more effectively; it could build up an institutional reputation, which was mutually advantageous to the various departments; it had financial resources which permitted it to meet an emergency that might arise in any particular department, without jeopardizing the entire business; and, above all, it gave an opportunity for more effective performance of the managerial function in retailing.

In operating a unit retail store, no matter how small, the proprietor must perform a variety of managerial functions. He must act as buyer, forecasting demand, judging price trends, and assuming market risks. He must be a financier, providing capital, and using it wisely if he is to be successful. He must grant credit and make collections, unless he sells only for cash. If he has any assistance, he must hire and train employees. He needs to have a knowledge of accounting. He must understand how to price merchandise to meet competition and still gain a profit. He must be a salesman; and often he attempts to advertise. Proficiency in so many diverse activities is required for the successful management of a retail store that it is little wonder that failures of small retail establishments have been numerous for many years. The rewards to be gained hardly could have attracted into the unit-store field a large number of men capable of coping effectively with such a range of managerial problems. The advantages of self-interest and personal supervision by a proprietor could not offset the obstacles to the successful performance of diverse managerial functions as other means of management were inaugurated and perfected.

The department store has subdivided the labor of management. Accounting, finance, credit, advertising, and usually employment are each centralized under the supervision of a trained specialist. The buying, selling, and pricing functions for each merchandise department originally were entrusted to an executive, ordinarily termed a departmental "buyer." During recent years more control over the activities of the buyers has been established in most department stores through merchandise managers and by means of specially devised systems, such as the so-called "retail method of inventory." Here as elsewhere, of course, the introduction and improvement of office appliances — the mechanizing of the office — has facilitated the technical progress of methods of executive control.

In department stores, as in the sales departments of manufacturing companies, therefore, the organization of the managerial function has superseded the watchful eye of a proprietor. The subdivision of the labor of management, the definition of tasks, the instructions to subordinates as to how their tasks should be performed, leaving them as little discretion as circumstances permit, the establishment of standards of performance, and frequent reports of results secured for comparison with those standards have provided machinery for administering the affairs of large, complicated marketing enterprises, with policy-making executives in supreme command. The result has been not only that large-scale operations have become practical but also that those operations on the average are handled better than an individual proprietor typically handles his affairs.

The chain store constitutes another form of capitalistic retail enterprise. Whereas the department store combines the retailing of a wide variety of goods under one roof with the merchandise department as the control unit, the chain-store system scatters its selling units over a wide market. The department store must attract consumers from a broad area to a shopping center; the chain-store system typically takes its stores to the points where consumers find it most convenient to make their purchases. Broadly speaking, the two types of enterprise are non-competing,[1] catering to different buying habits of consumers. The habits of consumers in buying merchandise sold in chain stores, however, vary for different types of

[1] This statement is open to qualification in that recently chain-store systems have come into existence which compete with certain departments which are typical of department stores. Whither this new trend may lead is an open question.

goods and this factor, together with certain other considerations, results in varying degrees of intensity in the location of branches; in the drug and grocery trades, for example, a single chain locates numerous stores within a single urban area, whereas in the shoe, clothing, or variety goods business each chain has only one or at most a few stores within such an area.

As in the case of most other marketing activities, a comprehensive history of chain stores has not been compiled, although Dr. Julius Hirsch in *Die Filial Betriebe im Detail Handel* gives an account of early chain-store developments in Continental Europe. In France, Les Etablissements Economiques, a grocery chain, was started in Rheims in 1866[1] and began immediately to open branches. It was followed soon thereafter by Dock's Remois, a chain formed in self-defense by wholesalers and retailers in Rheims. In Belgium, Delhaize Freres & Cie., operating Le Lion chain of grocery stores, was established in 1867.[2] A brother of the founder of that company withdrew from its employ in 1872 to start another chain — Ad. Delhaize & Cie. In Germany, Kaiser Kaffee Geschäft, G.m.b.H., began to develop in the lower Rhine district in the early 'eighties, and grew into a large chain. In all these countries chain stores subsequently developed in various other trades. In England, too, such chains as Lipton's, Ltd., Home and Colonial Stores, Maypole Dairy Company, Eastman's Ltd. (meats), Boot's Cash Chemists, Freeman, Hardy & Willis (shoes), Imperial Tobacco Company, and numerous other chains grew up.

In the United States the foundation of the Great Atlantic & Pacific Tea Company (groceries) was laid in 1858; on February 1, 1931, the company had 15,737 stores, with aggregate sales during the year ending on that date of

---

[1] Julius Hirsch, *Die Filial Betriebe im Detail Handel*, p. 73.　　[2] *Ibid.*, p. 66.

$1,065,806, 885. F. W. Woolworth opened his first variety store in 1878; in 1930 the company bearing his name had 1881 stores in the United States and Canada with total sales of $289,288,605. These were the beginnings of the chain-store movement in the United States. Growth was slow until after 1900; in fact 1910 is probably a better date for marking the acceleration in chain-store expansion in this country. After 1921 the rate of growth was further accelerated. The United States Census of Distribution reported that in 1929 chain-store companies handled a business amounting to $10,771,984,034. This was 21.5 per cent of the total retail trade. In some trades the ratio of chain-store sales to total sales was of course much higher than the average — groceries and meats, 33.3 per cent; shoes, 46.2 per cent; variety goods, 93.2 per cent.[1]

The total volume of sales of two of the pioneer chain-store companies in 1930 already has been cited. The sales of a few of the other large chain-store companies in the United States in 1930 were as follows: American Stores Company, $142,770,477 (2,728 stores); Kroger Grocery and Baking Company, $267,094,345; J. C. Penney Company, $192,939,362; S. S. Kresge Company, $150,508,126 (654 stores); Melville Shoe Corporation, $28,654,300 (484 stores); and Walgreen Company, $51,647,115.

As in the case of department stores, it apparently is significant that chain-store enterprises began to appear independently at about the same time in both Europe and America, for the most part in the same lines of trade, and to develop analogous types of organization and methods of control. This coincidence suggests that the similarity in conditions in the various industrial countries fostered the growth of chain stores as well as of department stores.

[1] "The Government Counts the Chains Store by Store," *Chain Store Age*, January, 1932, p. 23.

In chain-store enterprises, as in department stores, a division of the labor of management has taken place. Certain functions, namely buying, accounting, financing, employment, and advertising, usually are placed in the hands of special executives and managed from headquarters, where a warehouse also is operated to perform the wholesale task of supplying goods to the retail stores. Selling, therefore, is the chief task left to the employees in the stores.

In competition with independent unit stores, the chain stores in certain trades, such as the grocery business, have been enabled to reduce their expenses by eliminating credit and delivery service, but in other trades, such as drugs and variety goods, this sort of economy has had little influence on chain-store growth. The chains generally have taken over the wholesaling function, and in recent years the large chains often have enjoyed preferential concessions in prices from manufacturers. The chief advantages of the chain stores over unit stores, however, have accrued from the standardization of store layouts, standardization of stocks of merchandise, and especially the division of the labor of management, with expert planning, guidance, and control. The unit-store proprietor has the benefit of self-interest and personal supervision of his capital — Adam Smith's "general stock," but he cannot handle all the complicated problems of management as well or as economically as it can be done under the chain-store system.

In interpreting the chain-store development and in viewing its potential developments, the central point on which attention is to be focussed is the manner in which the managerial functions are performed. Other things being anywhere near equal, the superior form of management will survive. The methods of administering marketing activities still are far from perfect, but the trend is clear.

Inasmuch as marketing activities are chiefly personal, in contrast to manufacturing activities which involve utilization of machinery and power, consideration of the development of the managerial factor in marketing brings out with especial emphasis the part that the intangible factors of the division of the labor of management, systematic analysis and planning, and co-ordination of supervision and control have played in the development of the capitalistic system of industry. Adam Smith's emphasis on the importance of reducing operations to routine for the successful conduct of business affairs on a corporate scale was inherently sound. He did not foresee, however, the possibility in the development of the art and later the science of management which permits the segregation or division of tasks of administration into those which can be sufficiently standardized for delegation to subordinates and those which require discretion. Those which can be sufficiently standardized to permit of delegation predominate. For them, plans can be budgeted, explicit instructions drawn up, and a system of reports and records provided to test accomplishment. The major discretionary tasks thus become few in number in any one enterprise and can be vested in one or a few individuals, whose accomplishments also can be judged at least at intervals of some length.

In these developments of the managerial function in marketing, especial importance attaches to the part that statistical records have come to play. These statistics comprise the records of an individual company's own operations, market surveys and analyses, trade association reports, university studies, government compilations, and various other records. From these materials it has become possible to establish standards of performance and to ascertain trends with a degree of precision that was incomprehensible only a generation ago. These statistical records have furnished invaluable tools for the management of marketing activities. Incidentally, they also are becoming a fertile source for the study of economic history.

This consideration of the managerial factor in marketing suggests, finally, certain broad implications. Adam Smith and his followers built a social philosophy around the individual, supposedly guided by intelligent self-interest. Such a philosophy was natural for a period of geographical and industrial pioneering such as occurred during the seventeenth, eighteenth, and nineteenth centuries. The pioneer, whether on the frontier of civilization or in manufacturing or retailing, necessarily was a resourceful, hardy individual, sometimes ruthless in his methods, self-reliant, and distrustful of untried strangers. He must conquer to survive. The frontier stage has passed, however, both in world settlement and in industrial and commercial development. Just as it has become difficult for a man to go off to the backwoods and start a little farm for himself, so is it becoming increasingly hard for a man to start a little business with meager resources. The individual still is important and self-interest a powerful economic force; but the individual has become part of a complex social group. Now the individual typically must reconcile himself to working within an organization subject to managerial direction and control. The old philosophy, glorifying the individual, still tends to dominate much of our economic thought, but it cannot restore the frontier.

A new social philosophy is in the process of development. We are hardly conscious of it, but it manifests itself within individual business organizations, in trade associations, and in various other situations. This new philosophy is based on group interests, group loyalties, group rewards, and group discipline — group discipline being the keystone. In the course of this development it is to be expected that there will emerge a clearer understanding of the qualities needed for effective business administration, a better perception of the social obligations which administrative authority imposes, and a greater appreciation of the social values of real managerial ability.

DEMAND AS A FACTOR IN THE INDUSTRIAL REVOLUTION

ELIZABETH WATERMAN GILBOY

I

In the field of economic history as well as that of economic theory there has been a tendency to overemphasize the factor of supply. Precisely as the classical economists were inclined to accept demand as given and constant, most of the economic historians of the nineteenth century concerned themselves with a detailed analysis of changes in the technique of production, the decay and expansion of certain industries, the effects of power machinery upon production, and so on. Little attention has been paid to changes in the nature of demand, even to the undoubted extension of demand, and especially is it true that the mechanism by which these changes occurred has been overlooked. Labor, as well, has been considered rather as a factor in production than as the major portion of the consuming public. When demand has been touched upon at all, it was usually dealt with in vague and general terms, with reference to Adam Smith's theory of the extension of the market. Exceptions occur, of course. Mrs. Knowles, Hobson, and a few others were well aware of the significance of developments of the demand factor with respect to the Industrial Revolution. But even they made little attempt to analyze the structure of internal demand; rather they stressed the increase of commerce, and the opening of new markets in undeveloped countries.

Obviously the factory system with its complicated industrial mechanism cannot function profitably without a large and growing demand ready and willing to absorb its products as fast as they are produced. The factory form of organization was not new. It had existed in ancient Rome, again in mediaeval Florence, and at various times in England and on the Continent, previous to the Industrial Revolution. Before the eighteenth century, however, the factory had never become typical. It existed sporadically to provide a few articles of luxury for the upper classes. The thesis of this essay is, indeed, that the factory could not become typical until demand had been extended and had become sufficiently flexible throughout the entire population to consume the products of large-scale industry. In other words, the Industrial Revolution presupposes a concomitant development and extension of consumption.[1]

The "extension of the market" school, as those writers who emphasize the phrase of Adam Smith might be called, do not go so far as to examine consumption standards. Why should new countries made accessible to English goods by the expansion of commerce and the greater facilities of transportation have been eager to buy the output of the factories? Why, again, should the home population suddenly afford a market for a greater number of products? These questions have been unanswered for the most part.

Lewinski, for example, explains the origin of the Industrial Revolution in Belgium by the typical "extension of the market" approach. The growth of the market for

---

[1] I am greatly indebted to Professor Gay for pointing out to me the importance of the analysis of consumption in connection with the Industrial Revolution. He is, in fact, the only person known to me who has stated the above hypothesis definitely and clearly, though not in print. I owe to him the impetus which started me upon the investigation of demand, not only in connection with the Industrial Revolution, but in general.

Belgian goods was due to the growth of population within
the country, primarily, and to the extension of the external
market resulting from political alliances, first with France
and later with Holland.[1] He places emphasis upon the increase in population as indicating an increase in demand
which forced industry to adopt new production methods,
largely because of the action of diminishing returns.[2] It is
difficult to see why an increase of population as such should
necessarily lead to an increase in demand. The result
might just as plausibly be a decrease in the standard of
living of the population. The pressure of population upon
subsistence, reducing the standard of living of the majority
of the population to a bare minimum of existence, is a doctrine which has been familiarized by Malthus and Ricardo.
And it has been a fact in the case of China, and, until recently, of India. If population increase were in itself a
sufficient reason for increasing demand, calling forth more
highly developed methods of production, the Industrial
Revolution ought to be in an advanced stage in both India
and China. Increase in population cannot by itself increase demand except in the case of a people with a standard of living so firmly intrenched that any lowering of the
standard is implacably resisted. Then the increase in
numbers may well serve as a stimulus to the discovery of
profitable means of improving the technique of production.
Undoubtedly this is what occurred in Belgium, although it
is not brought out by Lewinski. Even when population
increase does increase demand, it is not usually the most
important aspect of the change in demand and probably
would not alone lead to extensive industrial reorganization. An expansion of the standard of living of the population, as well as the growth of new wants, is necessary.

[1] *L'Evolution Industrielle de la Belgique* (1911).
[2] *Ibid.*, p. 58.

Mrs. Knowles and the Hammonds seem to have had some such process in mind when they selected commerce as the cause of the Industrial Revolution in England.[1] They point to the new commodities introduced into general consumption as a result of seventeenth- and eighteenth-century commerce, and admit that an increase in the general demand of the population took place at the same time. The process by which this widespread increase in demand occurred, however, is not analyzed; and it may be pointed out in passing that the Hammonds' implicit admission of a rise in the standard of living of the population as a whole in eighteenth-century England is somewhat inconsistent with their theory of increasing misery of the working classes after 1750.

An unusual emphasis upon the significance of demand is to be found in Hobson's *Evolution of Modern Capitalism*. His fourth essential condition for the development of capitalism is "the existence of large, accessible markets *with populations willing and economically able to consume the products of capitalist industry*."[2] If these markets do not have populations willing and able to consume industrial products on a large scale, the type of business made widespread by the Industrial Revolution cannot exist. Hobson is aware of this and also makes consumption an integral part of his theory of over-saving as the cause of business cycles. That theory cannot be examined here, but it is of some interest to note Hobson's stress upon the part played by demand. It is made apparent again in his treatment of wages, in which he examines the justification of high wages from the point of view of the consumption of the workers and of the community as a whole.

Pillai comes very near to the point of view of the present

[1] L. Knowles, *The Industrial and Commercial Revolutions in Great Britain* . . . (1924); T. and B. Hammond, *The Rise of Modern Capitalism* (1925).
[2] See p. 2.

paper in the initial pages of his study of the Industrial Revolution in India. He contends that the extremely slow penetration of modern industrialism into India is due to the difficulties of changing the standards of consumption of the general population.[1] Probably there are still other authors besides those mentioned here who have recognized the significance of demand. None of them, however, pay any attention to the process by which demand changes. Hobson comes nearest to analyzing the mechanism by which changes in demand occur, but even he deals with the term in a rather vague way and links his analysis to an idealistic scheme of social progress.

It is therefore the task of the present essay, in so far as it can be done within the limits of a brief paper, to sketch the relation between changes in demand and changes in the technique of production. The theoretical argument will be illustrated principally, but not entirely, by the situation in England in the eighteenth century, at the time when the radical industrial changes which are classed under the heading of the Industrial Revolution were taking place.

II

The theory is simple. It may be briefly stated thus: necessary concomitants of the growth of large-scale production, and especially of its initial stages, are (1) changes in the shape of the demand schedule, to use Marshallian terminology,[2] or in the nature of demand, of the various

---

[1] *Economic Conditions in India* (1925).

[2] For the benefit of the general reader not versed in Marshallian economics, it may be explained that "demand schedule" is the term for a hypothetical list of prices and quantities, expressing the relation between the number of units of a commodity which an individual or a group *would* buy and the price per unit, at any one time under given conditions. Mathematically, price is usually expressed as a variable function of quantity. The standard of living of a person or group may be looked upon as composed of a series of interrelated schedules of this sort, all of which may change in shape and position, affecting other schedules in so doing.

layers of consumption within the general population; (2) a shift in the demand schedules of the group, or an increase in demand; (3) the introduction of new wants; and (4) mobility of individuals within and between the various classes of the population. In other words, the tastes of the population are changed both in nature and in quantity, new commodities are incorporated into the consumption of the group, and there is considerable shifting between the members of the various groups within the community. If any one of these factors is present, the others are likely to emerge. They are all interrelated. They mark a society which is socially unstable, in which standards of living are changing, and in which class lines are not clearly drawn.

A society in which the standards of consumption of a majority of the population are fixed and stable, wherein people are contented with what they have and desire nothing more, scarcely provides fertile soil for the sowing of industrial changes. Even an increase in population may have little effect in stimulating methods of production. If diminishing returns set in, the excess population may emigrate or die of starvation or plague, or war may ensue. New production methods *may* be invented, especially with a net population increase, but as a rule a complete overturn of the social structure is needed as well. The continued social stability of mediaeval life is a case in point; then the standard of living of each class was fixed by custom and tradition, and centuries elapsed before this stability could be broken down.

In order that a shift in the demand schedule may occur, individuals must be able to buy more units of a commodity at the same price, or the same amount of the commodity at a higher price. In other words, the entire schedule must shift upwards, indicating a greater buying power. There must therefore be an increase in the real income of the population. Real wages must rise, either through a decrease in prices or through a rise in money income, so that the majority of the population have more to spend.

The spread of new wants throughout the majority of the population is one of the most active forces leading to changes in standards of consumption. The introduction of new commodities leads people possessed of an economic surplus to try this and that, and finally to include many new articles in their customary standard of life.[1] If the economic surplus is not at hand, supposed necessaries may be neglected in order to obtain novelties, or individuals may be motivated to work harder in order to obtain the economic surplus. The mechanism by which these new wants are incorporated into all classes involves interclass competition, not only in consumption but in production: there must be sufficient mobility within the groups so that some individuals, at least, actually move from one group to another, while many more are actuated by a belief that they can do so.

The process is something like this. New articles are made available by commerce and taken up as a fashion by the wealthy and leisured members of society. The process may end there. If the various classes are not sufficiently closely related so that interclass competition in consumption is possible, if the general population have neither the desire nor the means to experiment with these new commodities, they will end as they began, articles of luxury for the rich. Commerce in the Middle Ages was largely in such luxuries; it was not until the seventeenth and eighteenth centuries that the ordinary individual would or could begin to include such goods in his own consumption. It

[1] See Hazel Kyrk, *Theory of Consumption*, for a statement of the existence of an economic surplus, and an available supply of varied economic goods as a stimulus to consumption change.

did not occur to the average villein or serf to desire spices or jewels or silken robes. He expected to live and die in his own stratum, content with a simple diet and coarse and unornamented clothing. Envy of the upper classes, closely followed by an attempt to imitate them, what Defoe called "apeing one's betters," is a comparatively modern phenomenon. The removal of political, legal, and economic restrictions upon the lower classes, the breakdown of feudal and manorial customs, were essential to its development.

As Tawney observes:

> The tendency and direction of the forces released by the Industrial Revolution, if that phrase is still to be retained, are not open to question. They were those described by Sir Henry Maine, when he wrote of "the beneficent private war which makes one man strive to climb on the shoulders of another and remain there." Compared with that of most earlier periods, the economic system which it created was fluid and elastic.[1]

The fluid and elastic system was not entirely created by the Industrial Revolution. It existed prior to the development of the Industrial Revolution — or such a great economic change could not have happened when and where it did — and was then enhanced in turn by the industrial development.

It is part of Tawney's criticism of the modern economic and social order to deplore "that beneficent struggle." He would substitute social and collective goals for those of individual gain in wealth and power. It is extremely dubious whether modern industrial society could have begun or could continue without the type of individualistic competition which he most decries. It may be limited and controlled, the rules of the game may be made more stringent and applicable to all, but it must be there. Ethically it

[1] R. H. Tawney, *Equality* (1930), p. 30.

may be undesirable; but economically it is essential to the development of modern industry.

Once society is sufficiently mobile, the luxury articles of the rich will seep down through the different social ranks, and perhaps end by becoming a necessity for all. By this time the upper classes will have taken up some other article of fashion. A contemporary described the process well:

> In England the several ranks of men slide into each other almost imperceptibly; and a spirit of equality runs through every part of the constitution. Hence arises a strong emulation in all the several stations and conditions to vie with each other; and a perpetual restless ambition in each of the inferior ranks to raise themselves to the level of those immediately above them. In such a state as this fashion must have an uncontrolled sway. And a fashionable luxury must spread through it like a contagion.[1]

Although this sort of thing occurred prior to the eighteenth century, it did not take place in a sufficiently general fashion to cause widespread comment. But at that time, eighteenth-century pamphleteers in England burst forth into a lamentation upon luxury in general and particularly the luxury of the lower classes. More will be said about this later.

Still another aspect of the problem exists which is not without interest. The qualitative and quantitative changes in demand noted above may serve as a stimulus to production in another way. So far we have only mentioned the fact that demand must increase and change in order to absorb the output of industry. It may also be true that changing consumption standards will act as an impetus to labor on the side of production. A transition has to be made from labor which is independent and which works in its own home, at its own time, to labor which works under strict discipline in a factory. Usually it is assumed that

---

[1] [T. Forster], *An Enquiry into the Causes of the Present High Price of Provisions* (London, 1767), p. 41.

labor was forced by circumstances to make this change. Certainly it is true that in England, at any rate, the acceleration of the enclosure movement, dispossessing agricultural labor in many districts, occurred conveniently about the time when masses of unskilled labor were needed in the new factories. It is true, as well, that the state disposed of paupers by transferring them by the cartload from parish workhouses to factories.[1] What could labor do but submit?

On the other hand, many laborers may have been motivated by the desire for increased consumption of material goods, whetted by the taste for luxury already acquired. They may have been willing to submit to the routine and dependent régime of the factory because wages there were higher and steadier. There is reason to think that this was true in the north of England, at least. Redford sees in this fact one explanation of the steady and wave-like migration of labor from the country-side to the town. He goes so far as to state that the difference in standard of living, which was in favor of the industrial town, was a motivating force in impelling labor to the industrial centers.[2]

Changes in demand or consumption, therefore, may be looked upon not only as necessary adjuncts to industrial change in the sense of providing a continually expanding and varying market, but as stimuli on the production side, too. As Malthus put it:

It is not the most pleasant employment to spend eight hours a day in a counting house. Nor will it be submitted to after the common necessaries and conveniences of life are obtained, unless adequate motives are presented to the mind of the man of business. Among these motives

[1] See Unwin, *Samuel Oldknow and the Arkwrights* (1924). Also cf. W. E. Rappard, *La Revolution industrielle . . . en Suisse* (1914), p. 231. The factory workers of the printed-cloth industry were recruited from the poorest elements in the population.

[2] A. Redford, *Labour Migration in England* (1924), p. 60.

is undoubtedly the desire of advancing his rank, and contending with the landlord in the enjoyment of leisure, as well as of foreign and domestic luxuries.[1]

Miss Kyrk stated the same idea more universally when she said, "For the sake of gains as consumers, individuals consent to more hazardous and less interesting work as workers."[2] In India the inverse has been found to be true; that is, when laborers have satisfied their fairly simple wants, which can be done in three or four days' work a week, they do not appear at the factory.[3] What is to make them continue labor which is disagreeable to them, if their material wants are satisfied? As may be imagined, the establishment of the factory system in India has been attended with many difficulties.

Of course, there have always been those who argued that necessity was the only spur to industry and efficiency. This view was particularly popular among the eighteenth-century English mercantilists whose aim was to keep labor cost, in the sense of wages, as low as possible in order that England might outsell competitors in world markets. Sir William Temple expressed their views perfectly when he said that "the only way to make them [the laborers] temperate and industrious, is to lay them under the necessity of labouring all the time they can spare from meals and sleep, in order to procure the necessaries of life."[4] Quotations of this sort could be multiplied without end. The question of necessity versus luxury as a motivating force to increase the efficiency of labor and the product of industry engendered a hot philosophical controversy between the mercantilists and their opponents. In more recent times the theory opposite to that of mercantilism has become

[1] *Principles of Political Economy* (2nd ed., 1835), p. 403.
[2] *Op. cit.*, p. 65.
[3] Pillai, *op. cit.*, chap. ix.
[4] *A Vindication of Commerce and the Arts* (London, 1786), p. 534.

more popular. The economy of high wages is a doctrine of which one hears a good deal.

Theoretically, then, it is possible to conclude that far-reaching and widespread industrial changes cannot occur except in a society in which demand and consumption standards are undergoing swift and radical readjustment. Such a society is characterized by mobility between classes, the introduction of new commodities leading to the development of new wants, and a rise in real income of the people as a whole. Let us examine briefly the origin of the Industrial Revolution in the light of these ideas.

III

The social and economic milieu of eighteenth-century England formed the background for the first appearance of the Industrial Revolution. From a country predominantly rural, with the greater part of industry carried on in the homes of the workers under various forms of the putting-out system, it was transformed by the end of the century into a country of growing industrialism with factories supplanting the home as the producing unit. It is unnecessary to describe the nature and process of this industrial change. It has been done by many economic historians and by no one more competently than by Mantoux. It may at least be hazarded, although the data are scarce and contradictory, that the standard of living of the general population was increasing at the same time.

The available wage data indicate that the wages of common day labor were certainly increasing in the districts most closely connected with economic expansion.[1] In

[1] E. W. Gilboy, "Wages in Eighteenth Century England," *Journal of Economic and Business History*, vol. ii, no. 4 (August, 1930), pp. 603-629. The statistical material for the analysis of wages and prices summarized above is given in more detail in this paper.

the north of England (the wage material is for the North and West Ridings of Yorkshire, and Lancashire) the money wages of unskilled labor had risen from a median of 9d. per day in 1700 to 1s. 9d. per day by 1790. During the same period the journeyman's daily wage had gone up from 1s. to 2s. 3d. The rise was especially rapid after 1760. Within ten years the laborer's rate went from 1s. to 1s. 6d., the journeyman's from 1s. 6d. to 2s.; whereas it had taken the first fifty years of the century for the rates to go from 9d. to 1s. and from 1s. to 1s. 6d., respectively. This upward swing of wages appeared as characteristically in the agricultural districts of the North Riding as in the industrial sections of Lancashire and the West Riding. Real wages, as measured in terms of the laborers' most important article of diet, oat bread, appear to have risen, too, by the end of the century. Other evidence as to the living conditions of the laboring classes gleaned from local records and descriptions of laboring life show a real improvement towards the end of the century, at least for the class of labor under discussion.[1] The balance of contemporary observation points in that direction.

A similar rise in real wages took place in London and the metropolitan district surrounding it. The rise is not as con-

---

[1] See A. P. Wadsworth and J. de L. Mann, *The Cotton Trade and Industrial Lancashire 1600–1780* (1931), bk. iv. Mr. Wadsworth's evidence as to the condition of the workers in the cotton industry, especially of the weavers, is conflicting. There are no comparable wage figures for various parts of the century. Arthur Young's figures for 1769 indicate that some of the wages were even lower than day-laboring rates, although the check weavers' were somewhat higher. The formation of the early weavers' societies, and their activities in trying to raise wages and improve working conditions, were the result of recurring periods of want due to bad harvests, wars, etc. Mr. Wadsworth's material leans towards the depressing side, although he cites some data as to the increase of luxury among the working population. He does not commit himself, however, on the course of the standard of living of the weavers during the century. Probably the question must be left open until wages are specifically investigated.

sistent nor as great as in the northern districts, but the median daily rate for the common laborer increased from 1s. 7d. in 1700 to 2s. in 1787. At the same period the wages of craftsmen went from 2s. 6d. to 3s. 2d. Most of this rise occurred before 1750. Wheat prices — again measuring by the chief food item of the laborers' budget — were falling slightly during the first part of the century, and rising during the second half. Subsidiary evidence as to the food, clothing, and general living conditions of the workers provide grounds for assuming a net gain in consumption by the end of the century. The same conclusion, it may be noted, was reached by Mrs. George, purely on the basis of pamphlet and general descriptive material.[1]

The data for the west of England are the least satisfactory of the sections investigated. There is no foundation, at any rate, for a conclusion as to rising consumption standards in this district. The median daily wage rate of common labor fluctuated in Gloucestershire around 1s. from 1736 to 1787, the only period for which figures were obtained. Craftsmen's wages were approximately 1s. 6d. per day for most of the period. Barley prices, representing the principal diet of the laborers, showed, if anything, a slight trend upwards, with extraordinarily high prices in the years of bad harvests, which appear to have afflicted the west with especial distress. Food riots were prevalent all over the country in the 'fifties and 'sixties, but struck the western counties with particular force.[2]

The apparent stability or, possibly, decline in the standard of living of the Gloucestershire laborer is of interest in connection with a suggestion noted in the previous section. The decay of the woolen industry of the west during the eighteenth century is well known. It was sup-

[1] M. D. George, *London Life in the Eighteenth Century* (1924).
[2] See Arthur Young, *Tour to the Southern Counties* (1772), p. 340.

planted by the rising textile industry of the north. The introduction of the factory system occasioned riots against machines wherever they were introduced. In the north these uprisings against the mechanism of modern industry eventually subsided. In the west, however, the workers refused to use the new machines and continued to oppose their introduction. Possibly there is a connection between the continued opposition of labor to machinery, the decline of the woolen industry of the west, and the low and unchanging standard of living characteristic of the working classes. It might be suggested that the impetus of a changing material standard was lacking, and consequently laboring-class opposition to mechanized labor in a factory could not be overcome. At least, it is plausible to suggest that this may have been a contributing factor to the decay of the industry, which depended, of course, on many other factors as well.

It is unwise to generalize about England as a whole. Distinct regional differences in the real and money wages of common labor in at least three sections of the country have been found. There may be other regional divergences; the study of wages in other trades may tell a different story. Contemporary literature, however, indicates that the situation of London and the north was more typical of the country than that of the west. Eighteenth-century social and political pamphlets are full of allusions to the growth of luxury among the lower classes. Some wrote to deplore it, others to praise it, but most writers noted its existence. Even those who stressed the darker side of working-class life were likely to let slip observations upon the inclusion of tea, wheat bread, sugar, and other luxuries of the day in the laborer's diet. On the basis of this pamphlet material alone, Lecky, an astute and eminent historian, concluded that the standard of living of the general population had risen during the century.[1] The amount of contemporary comment upon the growth of luxury is so great that it cannot be entirely ignored by the least optimistic of investigators. Some basis of fact must have existed.

It is clear that tea, sugar, and wheat bread became incorporated into the general working-class diet during the century. Meat was eaten more frequently. Cotton and silk clothes were worn by the poor as well as by the rich. More money was spent on recreation, in the form of frequenting fairs, interludes, etc.[2] Conditions in some of the new industrial towns offered better and more sanitary living conditions for the average worker than had been known before.[3] We may conclude tentatively that the consumption of the average laborer was more varied, and greater in amount by the end of the century than at the beginning.

The evidence on interclass mobility and competition is fully as difficult to evaluate. Instances occur in which laborers rose to become managers and even owners of factories. Redford quotes examples of apprentices rising to the position of manager of a mill, and the Reverend William MacRitchie, a contemporary observer, writing of opportunities for advancement in the Sheffield cutlery works, comments, doubtless with exaggeration, on "people rising every day from nothing to eminence, by dint of industry."[4] Wadsworth remarks of Lancashire: "In contrast with the regulated industry of France, or with the sixteenth century ideal of an ordered distributive state in which each

[1] *History of England in the Eighteenth Century* (1883), vol. vi, p. 186: "These complaints of growing extravagance in the industrial classes were too common in the latter half of the eighteenth century not to rest on some real foundation."

[2] Cf. George, Botsford, and many others. Evidence as to the popularity of amusements comes from Quarter Sessions Records, which record the efforts of the Justices of the Peace to decrease the number of these entertainments as injurious to the morals of the lower classes. Middlesex County Records are full of such indictments.

[3] Cf. the description of Mellor in Unwin, *op. cit.*; also Redford, *op. cit.*, p. 30.

[4] *Diary of a Tour through Great Britain in 1795* (1897), p. 67.

class performed its appropriate functions, this Manchester society possessed variety and spontaneity. But it appears almost rigid and bound by custom in comparison with working class life half a century later. . . ." [1] His own evidence throws little light on the rise of the weaver from a small master to a manufacturer. The later eighteenth century, however, appears to have been one of those periods in which the growth of new enterprise, taking place at an unusually rapid rate, so upset the customary equilibrium of social and economic arrangements that individuals were able to transcend class barriers.

Contemporaries expostulated upon competition in consumption between classes. It was complained that servants could not be told from their mistresses; that class distinction was disappearing from the country-side; and that the lower classes no longer knew their position in life. [2] For instance, Davis remarked that "a fondness for Dress may be said to be the folly of the age, and it is to be lamented, that it has nearly destroyed those becoming marks whereby the several classes of society were formerly distinguished." [3] The phenomenon was especially noticed in urban districts, in London more than anywhere else, where servants provided the link between the habits of consumption of the upper and lower classes. Down through each rank in the social scale conspicuous consumption of all kinds was imitated. Fielding describes the process as follows: "Thus while the Nobleman will emulate the Grandeur of a Prince the Gentleman will aspire to the proper state of the Nobleman, the Tradesman steps from behind his Counter into the vacant Place of the Gentleman. . . ." [4]

[1] *Op. cit.*, p. 325.
[2] For example, Defoe, *Giving Alms No Charity* (1704); the *Great Law of Subordination* (1724).
[3] *Friendly Advice to Industrious and Frugal Persons* (1817), p. 23.
[4] *Enquiry into . . . Increase of Robbers* (1753), p. 4.

It cannot be doubted in general that eighteenth-century England exhibited signs of social instability. How inclusive as to region and class of worker the increase of standard of living, how extensive the interclass competition in consumption and production, and how great the luxury of the laborers all remain to be investigated more thoroughly. The undoubted distress of certain periods, certain sections, and certain classes of workers cannot be disregarded. The fate of the hand-loom weavers, in both England and Switzerland, is a depressing tale. Nor can the evils of the early factories be overlooked. On the other hand, these unfavorable elements must not be overemphasized as they frequently have been in the past. For the present, it may be assumed that the balance was in favor of an increase of the standard of living.

The initiation of the Industrial Revolution in other countries appears to have been marked with some of the same characteristics. The Swiss weavers were very prosperous in the eighteenth century and formed the basis for the political agitation of the early 1800's. Rappard quotes a contemporary to the effect that "it was relatively easy to rise from the rank of manual worker to that of head of the industry."[1] In contrast, he is inclined to stress the misery of the early factories after the manner of the Hammonds. Children and beggars were the laboring force of many of the first factories, in degrading conditions. In this case, why did migration occur from the country to the cities, if the result were only misery? Figures are given to show that factories were supplied with very little labor from the home district. Visitors, too, commented favorably on the living conditions of the Swiss working classes, despite a lower level of wages than in other countries. Rappard attributes this to foreign optimism and appar-

[1] *Op. cit.*, p. 242.

ently disregards the fact that the standard of living may have risen. Still, he cites contemporaries on the instability and discontent of the early factor workers, their ambition for material well-being, and their going from factory to factory in search of better conditions. These conditions are not dissimilar to those which we have seen to characterize eighteenth-century England.

Pillai attributes the slow development of the factory system in India in large part to the low standard of living of the workers, and their strict caste organization which makes competition between classes unthinkable. He gives some evidence — not very complete — of a rise in wages of the lowest class of workers and of the breakdown of the caste system coincident with the growth of the factory system. The willingness of workers to labor more steadily, in the hope of acquiring the articles of comfort and luxury creeping in through the influence of foreigners, appears to be increasing.[1]

The United States imported the Industrial Revolution in a late stage and developed industrially in an exceptionally short period. It may be observed briefly that American society has been noted since its origin for its lack of class distinction, and for mobility between the indistinct class groups which did grow up; and for its general restlessness and striving for material comfort. America, in fact, exhibited in an intensified form the conditions out of which the Industrial Revolution grew in England.

In conclusion, we may say that demand is an important factor in facilitating the occurrence of industrial change, on the basis of a priori reasoning. The importance of stimulating demand is, indeed, extensively recognized by modern producers. Whereas in the early stages of the Indus-

[1] *Op. cit.*, p. 135.

trial Revolution demand was, if anything, in the van of production, today the reverse is true. Over-expanded industries resort to high-pressure salesmanship of the most far-fetched nature in order to increase a demand already existent, or to arouse it where there is none. The continued investigation of demand in relation to the Industrial Revolution is to be urged. Elaborate statistical researches cannot be expected. It would certainly be impossible to concoct even the most dubious "statistical" demand curve from eighteenth-century data. It is possible, however, to obtain data on wages and the prices of the main foodstuffs and to indicate crudely the course of real wages. Contemporary comment may be compared and sifted in order to obtain a net balance of opinion. The use of eighteenth-century English sources has led to the conclusion that changes in demand played an important part in the initiation of the Industrial Revolution. Changing consumption standards, the increase of population and shifting of individuals from class to class, and a rise in real income provided a stimulus to the expansion of industry which must not be underestimated. Although the mistake must not be made of exaggerating, in turn, the influence of demand, its significant relation to changes in production should be clearly recognized.

APPLIED ECONOMIC HISTORY: SOME RELATIONS BETWEEN ECONOMIC HISTORY AND MODERN BUSINESS MANAGEMENT

EDMOND E. LINCOLN

"Study the past if thou wouldst know the present and divine the future." — CONFUCIUS.

IT IS significant to find that one hundred years ago England, then the world's leading industrial country, was passing through a post-war depression in many respects very much like that now being experienced by the United States and other countries.[1]

[1] The English historian Trevelyan, in his review of this depression, makes the following statements:

"There were differences of opinion as to the economic cure for the distress of the time. Some . . . saw it in currency reform; more . . . in retrenchment; others in free trade; others in Factory Acts or in Socialism. . . . But all were agreed that reform of Parliament was the necessary first step before anything effective could be done." (*British History in the Nineteenth Century*, chap. xiv.)

In 1830, Macaulay, in his "Essay" on Southey's *Colloquies*, wrote as follows:

"The present moment is one of great distress. But how small will that distress appear when we think over the history of the last forty years; a war, compared with which all other wars sink into insignificance; taxation such as the most heavily taxed people of former times could not have conceived; a debt larger than all the public debts that ever existed in the world added together; the food of the people studiously rendered dear; the currency imprudently debased, and improvidently restored. Yet is the country poorer than in 1790? We firmly believe that, in spite of all the misgovernment of her rulers, she has been almost constantly becoming richer and richer. Now and then there has been a stoppage, now and then a short retrogression; but as to the general tendency there can be no doubt. A single breaker may recede, but the tide is evidently coming in.

"If we were to prophesy that in the year 1930 a population of fifty millions, better fed, clad, and lodged than the English of our time will cover these islands;

In 1837 the United States passed through a severe panic following a few years of unprecedented growth. Canals, highways, and railroads were being rapidly built. There had been great speculation in real estate. The federal government itself was so prosperous that it did not know what to do with its surplus cash. Finally much of the money was distributed to the various States, which in turn used it for building public works and more roads; and in at least one instance the federal grant was actually passed on to each citizen. There seemed to be no end to prosperity; but soon the break came, and land values dropped in many instances as much as 75 per cent or more. Banks failed; within a short time specie payments were suspended; and the blackest panic gripped the country. Thus, a hundred years ago our country experienced what may aptly be termed a "panic of plenty." Factories were closed, food riots were prevalent, unemployment was relatively the heaviest ever known, and the depression lasted for several years.

that Sussex and Huntingdonshire will be wealthier than the wealthiest parts of the West Riding of Yorkshire now are; that cultivation, rich as that of a flower garden, will be carried up to the very tops of Ben Nevis and Helvellyn; that machines constructed on principles yet undiscovered will be in every house; that there will be no highways but railroads, no travelling but by steam; that our debt, vast as it seems to us, will appear to our great-grandchildren a trifling encumbrance which might easily be paid off in a year or two — many people would think us insane. We prophesy nothing; but this we say: If any person had told the Parliament which met in perplexity and terror after the crash in 1720 that in 1830 the wealth of England would surpass all their wildest dreams; that the annual revenue would equal the principal of that debt which they considered as an intolerable burden; that for one man of ten thousand pounds then living there would be five men of fifty thousand pounds; that London would be twice as large and twice as populous, and that nevertheless the rate of mortality would have diminished to one-half of what it then was; that the post-office would bring more into the exchequer than the excise and customs had brought in together under Charles the Second; that stagecoaches would run from London to York in twenty-four hours; that men would be in the habit of sailing without wind, and would be beginning to ride without horses — our ancestors would have given as much credit to the predictions as they gave to Gulliver's Travels. Yet the prediction would have been true."

Again, in 1857 the United States passed through another serious panic, which according to the current accounts threatened the life of the republic. A far more serious situation faced the country after the break of 1873, which followed another "new era" of unprecedented expansion accompanied by extravagant railroad-building and the too rapid opening of up new lands on the western frontier. But within a few years specie payments were resumed in the United States, and by the early 'eighties we had once more entered upon a "new era" of prosperity, followed in due time by another depression in 1884–85.

Then came the world-wide panic of 1893, marked by appalling railroad receiverships, a new high record in business failures, long continued unemployment, the burning of corn for fuel, the feeding of wheat to live stock, excessive and unmarketable supplies of cotton, the bloody Homestead strike in the steel mills of western Pennsylvania, the even more serious Pullman strike and bloodshed in Chicago, the rise of the Socialist Party under Eugene V. Debs, serious discontent among the western farmers, the agitation for free silver by Bryan, and the threat that the United States Government would soon have to default on its debt payments and abandon the gold standard. There have been few gloomier periods in American industrial history than the long depression of the 'nineties, when farm produce was selling at unheard of low levels and ablebodied men in many parts of the country were glad to have an opportunity to work for from fifty cents to a dollar per day. Yet by 1900 we were again in a "new era" of prosperity.

But it seems unnecessary to multiply these historical examples. Every generation has its speculative craze, whether it be the "tulip mania" of 1630, or the "Mississippi Bubble" of a century later. Practically all the speculative orgies of John Law's brief but exciting career in France more than two hundred years ago were duplicated in the United States in the years 1928–29 — even to the phraseology appearing on some of the "investment" literature passed around to the gullible public. Each speculative boom is inevitably followed by a corroding and devastating depression, the severity of which is usually measured by the excesses of the preceding period. Thus it has been from the earliest days of recorded history, and thus it probably will be so long as mankind makes material progress.

We of the United States are fond of phrases and superlatives. Whenever the results of our own mistaken judgments become distressing, it is easy for us to say that "capitalism is on trial" and "civilization itself is at stake." In a similar manner not many years ago we talked about a "war to end war" and a "war to make the world safe for democracy." What of it? Civilization always has been and always will be at stake. Capitalism always has been and always will be on trial. The world never has been and never will be safe for democracy; nor has democracy ever been safe for the world.[1]

Curiously naïve solutions of our present difficult problems are suggested by newspapers, propagandists, so-called "economists," and even by business men who ought to know better. In September, 1930, we were told by a reputed "economist" that "if people during the next two weeks were to spend five dollars more on the average than they have been spending, the business depression would be

---

[1] As Irving Babbitt so well puts it:
"At the very moment when we were most vociferous about making the world safe for democracy the citizens of New York City refused to re-elect an honest man as their mayor and put in his place a tool of Tammany, an action followed in due course by a 'crime wave;' whereupon they returned the tool of Tammany by an increased majority." (*Democracy and Leadership*, p. 244.)

over." We were told further that an increase in advertising appropriations would inevitably expand sales and so bring back prosperity. One leading financial paper, at least a year and a half before the bottom of the present depression was being measurably reached, said that "if the corporations of this country would disgorge themselves of their surplus cash and pay it to its rightful owners — the stockholders — . . . frozen cash would be put to work for the alleviation of unemployment and the stimulation of business." Such notions when followed to the *reductio ad absurdum* would seem to be equivalent to saying that squandering makes prosperity, and that consuming more than we produce will create wealth. It is curious, although perhaps understandable, that so many optimistic Americans fail to realize that major economic difficulties almost always result from over-spending, unwise spending, mortgaging the future too far ahead, and capitalizing paper profits — and not from "over-saving." A knowledge of history and of human nature should show us that *saving* in the economic sense is absolutely essential to the creation of wealth, and is a very difficult process. Both individual self-interest and the well-known frailties of human nature effectively prevent any possibility of "over-saving;" the entire urge of existence is in the opposite direction. Perhaps if business men would devote to the study of economic principles, the development of economic thought, and economic history, a small part of the time which they now give to reading and listening to popular but superficial and misinformed discussions of economic policy, we would not have been plunged into so deep a depression, and we certainly would not have fumbled so miserably in trying to find the way out.

To the student of economic and political history it is one of the refreshing phases of human nature that each generation of business men endeavors to rediscover *for itself* those simple, fundamental truths which were ancient even in the days of Aristotle. Each generation sees a recurrence and a serious consideration of the self-same economic fallacies which have been exploded times without number during the past two or three thousand years. Whether the problem be that of bimetallism, "cheap" money, price maintenance, restriction of supply in order to secure higher prices — or any other of the multitudinous schemes for interfering with the so-called "laws of supply and demand," most every expedient has been tried over the centuries which have passed, with the same inevitable results. The multiplication table cannot be argued with, and the laws of economic gravity operate irrespective of the "wish-thoughts" of puny human beings.[1]

There has recently been much talk about the need for "leadership," in order to bring us out of our present economic difficulties. There has been a disposition always to assume that somebody other than ourselves should take the initiative. In surprisingly large number supposedly sound business men have looked to Washington and to the President of the United States for "leadership" — and they have vigorously criticised our national public officials

---

[1] To quote from a recent address made by Nicholas Murray Butler:

"As a matter of fact, it is extraordinary how little is said in the world that is new. The trouble is not to say what is new, but to get it done. If you will go back to Aristotle and then to the great philosophers of public life and policy in the Middle Ages and in the early modern time and to our own fathers of this nation, every question has been discussed, every principle stated, every ideal pictured and held up to view. The problem is not a problem primarily of knowledge; it is a problem of action. The task of the world is to get things done and to get them done in accordance with the wise plan and a high ideal. The high ideals and the wise plans have been before us for two thousand five hundred years. Those which immediately concern us were stated in classic form one hundred fifty and one hundred seventy-five years ago. There is no possible way of improving upon them. What Hamilton wrote, what Jefferson wrote, what Madison wrote — what is to be said not only that is better, but that is half so good?" (Lotos Club, New York, January 3, 1932.)

for not devising some scheme to bring us out of our economic *impasse*. Yet a reasonable knowledge of the industrial and political history of modern nations should be sufficient to indicate that under a *democracy* the only leader is the *average man*.

When each business man and each employee can recognize this simple fact, he is then in a position largely to work out his own salvation by greater industry and economy, so that individual budgets will be balanced and thereby the general business condition will be improved. It is simple to say, yet apparently difficult to realize, unless one's background has been enriched by a study of the past, that if each entity in our social system would follow that policy which from the long-run point of view is economically sound, there would then be no serious "collective" problem. In fact, it is probably safe to assert that many of our recent economic and social difficulties have resulted from our very zeal in attempting to save *humanity* while at the same time we have forgotten that our first job is to save our own economic souls. The only "superman" known to economic history is the humble individual who has learned always to keep his current income a little larger than his current outgo. He is the man whom nobody has known during the period of economic "jazz;" but he is mightier than kings and presidents, and without him our nation would again become a race of savages.

When times are booming and the future looks rosy, we stress "opportunity," and we glory in the freedom which the democratic organization of society supposedly confers upon the individual. When the clouds of depression hang heavy, we then desire "security," and "stabilization" becomes an economic shibboleth. Yet every "stabilization" plan suggested inevitably carries with it not only private sanction but federal legislation in order to insure enforcement. To adopt such plans would mean putting an ingloriously inefficient government into the management seat of American industry. Some of our business leaders have become so terrified by their own mistakes that they are ready to jump from the frying pan into the fire. Any plan which introduces further government interference inevitably decreases individual initiative and the stimulus to greater improvement and efficiency. If such be the case, most of those plans which may now be thought to have some merit, would if adopted tend to postpone the period of business recovery and to curtail still further business profits. The lessons of history should teach us that in economic affairs stability, even though theoretically attainable, would inevitably mean cessation of progress. However, human beings, once having reached a high plane of civilization, never stand still; and the cessation of progress must certainly mean retrogression. Complete "stabilization," therefore, economically speaking, is probably the equivalent of "stagnation."

It is no doubt true that the only way to prevent depressions is to prevent booms. Yet economic history teaches us that the severe taskmaster of depression and necessity has hitherto been required to guide us into economic and social reforms, better methods of conducting business, and sounder policies.

It is easy for those with insufficient background to be misled by figures and surface facts. Much attention has been given to the Five Year Plan in Russia. Because of many of the *apparent* achievements within recent years, it has frequently been assumed that the United States and other countries also need some kind of a "Supreme Economic Council," or a "planning" body.[1] Perhaps it is not

[1] With respect to the possibility of setting up an Economic Council which will be our industrial Moses, perhaps it is well to bear in mind the wise words of Adam Smith, written in 1776:

amiss first to point out that most people have no knowledge of economic conditions in Russia as they existed before the War. Recent measurements of progress are made from the "zero" point reached in 1921–22, when conditions were probably worse than they had ever been in modern history. Naturally even a mild *absolute* improvement from such low levels would seem *relatively* vast. However, it is not commonly appreciated that, if Russia had continued to progress up to the present time at the rate *actually* realized in the period 1900–15, her economic condition would now in most respects be quite superior to anything which has been realized under the Five Year Plan. Nor is it commonly known that an agricultural population of 80 per cent is now being sacrificed to an urban population of scarcely 20 per cent, and that recent industrial output has been far behind schedule.

It is a striking fact that during the past fifteen years the long-time debt of the United States has been increased perhaps $100,000,000,000. The national and local government debts have increased more than $25,000,000,000; real-estate loans and mortgages have expanded by at least this amount; the long-time borrowings of corporations have probably advanced by $25,000,000,000 or $30,000,000,000; and through government and private loans and direct investment our country has put more than $25,000,000,000 into foreign countries. All of this new debt, amounting to

(Note continued from previous page.)

"What is the species of domestic industry which his capital can employ, and of which the produce is likely to be of the greatest value, every individual, it is evident, can, in this local situation, judge much better than any statesman or law-giver can do for him. The statesman, who should attempt to direct private people in what manner they ought to employ their capitals, would not only load himself with a most unnecessary attention, but assume an authority which could safely be trusted, not only to no single person, but to no council or senate whatever, and which would nowhere be so dangerous as in the hands of a man who had folly and presumption enough to fancy himself fit to exercise it." (*Wealth of Nations*, bk. iv, chap. ii.)

perhaps one-third of the present wealth of the United States, was contracted on a *gold basis* during a period when the price level averaged almost 50 per cent higher than at present. In addition, many new and economically questionable forms of "consumer" credit were developed, and vast "pyramiding" loans on securities were made. It is probable that the aggregate long-term debts of the United States, plus the "frozen" short-time borrowings, now amount to at least 50 per cent of our entire estimated wealth measured in present prices — most of which obligations have been incurred during the past decade. It is also striking that the *known* shrinkage in security prices since the peak reached in 1929 has been at least $100,000,000,000 — or fully equivalent to the increase in our long-time debts since the War. Possibly this fact in itself indicates that our recent "new era" of prosperity was based not so much upon the creation of wealth as upon the creation of debt!

Almost all countries of the world formed the borrowing habit during the War, and when the War was over they continued to try to grow rich by going further into debt. As long as a false prosperity could be maintained on the basis of huge credit operations, it was easy to forget that capital and services equivalent to several hundreds of billions of dollars, or perhaps between one-third and one-fourth of the world's estimated wealth, were destroyed by the Great War. Our economic debts resulting therefrom were certainly not liquidated during the brief depression of 1921. It has been easy to forget that the actual *money* cost of the War to the United States alone, as estimated by the Secretary of the Treasury, was $39,000,000,000 up to June 30, 1931.

To those who have studied the records of the past it is clear that nations do not recover rapidly from the economic effects of major wars. Reference may be made to the devastating effects of the Thirty Years' War in Europe some three hundred years ago, as well as to the long years of hard times and misery which followed the Napoleonic Wars. Those familiar with the economic history of the United States know that it required at least a generation for our Southern States to recover from the destruction wrought by the Civil War.

Had such facts as the foregoing been carefully considered, our business men should have known that during the past decade our supposed "prosperity" was probably built on a foundation of sand. Our price level continued high as compared with pre-War, not because there was a fundamental economic justification therefor, but because of the vast amount of new short-time and long-time credit which was being created, no doubt quite unconsciously, in order to finance our post-War expansion. It is fortunately true that the United States owes nothing to other countries. Hence, no matter what happens, the same amount of *real* wealth will remain in the country after this period of liquidation is over.

However, our difficulty would seem to have been caused by the fact that a substantial proportion of our people and of our industries were discounting the future too heavily. Through easy credit operations, spurred on by security speculation and appreciation of "capital," many found it possible to spend next year's income; but in order to do this it was necessary by means of loans temporarily to secure possession of somebody else's "capital" which was created by past saving. As a result of these numerous credit operations, therefore, industry was expanded to a point where its productive capacity was considerably in excess of the power to consume through *current* income. Maladjustments between the factors of production inevitably developed, and now that we are in the depths of depression we find that our heavy burden of long-time debt is serving as a means of *redistributing the wealth* of the United States. Those who generously surrendered their claims on capital to those who were spending in excess of their income now find that they were making gifts in a disguised manner, whether to citizens of the United States or to numerous foreign countries. The process of such a liquidation is necessarily slow and exceedingly painful. No situation is more difficult to cope with than the readjustment of economic relationships.

Much grief might have been saved during recent years if business men could have realized, as did Adam Smith, that the *wealth* of a country consists not of its *money*, but of its farms and factories, its crops, cattle, buildings, equipment, stores of food, and the like. It is merely for convenience that these articles of wealth are measured in terms of money. Whether we rate the wealth of the United States at $400,000,000,000, or at half that amount, does not in the *long* run matter, provided we still have the same quantity of consumable and enjoyable goods. The immediate difficulty is that some of the necessities of life are not now equitably distributed because of our drastic economic readjustments. However, in due time proper relationships will be restored, with many properties changing hands in the process, and we shall then be ready to go ahead again for a new deal.

Likewise, *income* in the economic sense is measured by the quantity of commodities and services annually accruing to the individual — not by the pieces of money which he receives. It is almost beyond belief that in the year 1931 business men and government officials in the United States advocated the destruction of cotton, fruit, wheat, and a drastic curtailment of production in 1932 — all with a view to boosting prices for a few *producers*, to the great detriment of our own *consumers*, not to mention consumers throughout the world. We may be able to forgive Brazil for destroying millions of bags of coffee; but when half the world is hungry and naked it is difficult to forgive our own people in high places for fostering such outrageous fallacies. It would seem that a knowledge of the results of similar policies in the past might have saved us from these errors. While such measures were being advocated in public places, cities in the United States were floating "unemployment relief bonds." While government and state employees and our soldiery were whiling away their time at the taxpayers' expense, and with no reduction in compensation, enough food and fuel were wasting in our various states amply to supply the needs of all the unemployed. The tragedy is that many of the unemployed themselves were too lazy to pick up and carry away the food freely offered them, and the National Unemployment Relief organization, hampered by special interests and by politics, was unable to bring the vast army of needy people in touch with the excess supplies which Nature this year had so bountifully provided.

Had our business men applied the knowledge available, they should have known that the physical volume of output of the leading industries in the United States during the past ten or twelve years has not on the average increased much more than 3 per cent per annum. It might also have been noted that in many important industries the actual number of *units* produced increased very little between 1925 and 1929, at a time when prices of securities and the volume of loans were expanding with unprecedented rapidity. Our leaders might further have noted that population was increasing at the rate of about $1\frac{1}{2}$ per cent per annum during this period. Measured in current dollars, the average annual *increase* in production in the

United States could not possibly have amounted to more than $3,000,000,000, of which $1,500,000,000, would have been required merely to take care of the needs of an increasing population without any improvement in living standards.

Yet during this time it was customarily assumed that the American people, out of a total national income *averaging* less than $80,000,000,000, were probably "saving" up to $10,000,000,000 per year. If so, what was done with the savings? Some $12,000,000,000 to $15,000,000,000 went into foreign countries — from which the recoveries will probably be small. A considerably smaller amount went into non-productive public works and "improvements," and into certain pretentious but probably wasteful building operations. The balance must of course have gone back into the plant and equipment of the productive enterprises above mentioned. Through all of these channels it would be quite impossible to account, without duplication, for the amount of the annual increment to the national wealth which was commonly assumed. Yet, as previously indicated, while these operations were going on, the long-time debt of the United States, plus its equivalent in "frozen" short-time obligations, increased perhaps $100,000,000,-000. Consequently, although we have all been glad to believe that in the past ten or fifteen years we have gone farther on the road of progress than our hard-working and thrifty ancestors traveled in a century, yet it seems reasonably apparent that for the most part we were only marking time, and some of us, anticipating our future income, were using up part of the capital of the rest of us.

Because of the fact that we *feel* prosperous while prices are rising, it is easy for the average man to believe that the secret of prosperity lies through price maintenance or through artificial attempts to boost prices. It has been assumed that wholesale prices *should* hold at a level about 50 per cent above pre-War, just because they happened to settle at that figure for a few years, due to highly artificial conditions. It is easy to overlook the fact that prices rose about 50 per cent in the fifteen years preceding 1913; and then in scarcely two years they rose 50 per cent more to an index of 150. There was really no good reason why they should not have returned pretty rapidly to earlier levels when the War was over. The remarkable thing is that prices held at so high a level for so long a period. We have at last reached the pre-War level on the average, and have broken far below it in a number of important cases. This is quite consistent with improvements in production and more adequate supplies of goods. It is also a situation which ordinarily prevails after great wars. There is a good probability that after occasional moderate recoveries the long-time trend of prices may still be slowly downward, provided our currency is not tampered with. At any rate, business ought to be prepared for such an eventuality.

Although rapidly falling commodity prices accompany a business depression, all history shows that business can be fairly prosperous on a low price level or in a period of very slowly declining prices. Those who have not looked into the matter carefully may be surprised to know that during 75 of the past 118 years the general *trend* of prices in the United States has been downward. During all these years the only long period of generally rising prices in the United States not occasioned by war was the 16 years between 1897 and 1913. Few seem to realize that prices in the United States were gradually declining in the period 1926–29. Price rises do not as a rule precede a return to prosperity. On the contrary, the prices of fabricated goods in particular usually tend to decline for a time after the physical volume of business has increased. It is the continuing demand for goods which stimulates prices, rather than the reverse. Further, although the producers of raw materials may for a time lose as a result of lower prices, the producer of fabricated goods and the ultimate consumer may thereby gain. The key to a real recovery from our present deep depression, as in the past, will probably be found in the drastically lower costs and lower selling prices which will gradually develop and open up broader markets, so that heavier physical volume will again begin to pull up the net profits. These facts were well enough recognized by Adam Smith one hundred and sixty years ago when he said: "It is the natural effect of improvement, however, to diminish gradually the *real* price of almost all manufactures."

It is probably fallacious to try to "support" the price level in order, as is sometimes alleged, to make it easier for the debtor to pay his obligations. During the past decade a substantial proportion of the debts created has really been speculative or semi-speculative. There was in fact little possibility and perhaps little expectation of paying off at par all of the obligations incurred. In the wake of every great war, with far-reaching economic readjustments, many borrowers have *temporarily* grown rich on their debts. In general, it is the creditors and not the debtors who are to be pitied, and who usually suffer most in periods of violent economic collapse. Likewise, because of the inevitable lag in wages, a rapidly rising price level puts those who receive salaries and wages at a decided disadvantage. Their purchasing power does not keep pace with the increase in their cost of living.

In this connection the economic historian should pay his respects to the "price maintenance" fallacy. Over a period of two thousand years we have records of the inevitable failure of public attempts to "regulate" the price of commodities. Yet during the decade following the War, in order to maintain the "fiction" of prosperity and in order to "help" the debtor class, many governments, either consciously or unconsciously, attempted to "support" the price of their important raw materials — in due time incurring sufficiently disastrous results and building up still heavier public and private debt burdens. England tried rubber; Japan, silk; Cuba and others, sugar; Brazil, coffee; Canada, wheat; the United States, wheat and cotton — all with disastrous results. Probably this "racket" has been carried furthest in the United States under the most specious governmental and private reasoning. In the meantime, trade associations in this country were spending a good deal of their energy trying to maintain the price level, instead of trying to find ways of reducing costs and lowering prices in order to broaden the market. The case of copper is an outstanding example, supported for a year at 18 cents per pound until the spring of 1930, and now selling at an all-time low price of near 5 cents.

Again, many have mistakenly believed that our recent drastic decline in prices has been due to a "break-down of the gold standard," and have advocated some new standard of value, usually with a view to bringing about wild price "inflation." Some historical knowledge of the grief that has always come when the gold standard is abandoned and the printing presses begin to work overtime, should be sufficient to show the fallacy of this reasoning. Further, it is frequently suggested that we have not enough gold to maintain a reasonable price level, although as a matter of demonstrable fact the actual supply of monetary gold has been increasing in recent years more rapidly than the increase in the production of goods and trade; while the increased use of checks and bank credit has made it possible to carry on commercial transactions with a relatively smaller proportion of gold. *More gold than ever is being produced during this period of lower prices,* and vast supplies from the hoards of India have unexpectedly become available. *There is actually an adequate gold supply to maintain a price level far above that now prevailing.* Most countries of the world have in the past year or two been forced off the gold standard because of their heavy burden of debt payments, their political troubles which have destroyed confidence, and the legal interference with the normal movements of foreign trade.[1]

The experience of the industrial world since 1776 has thrown no new light on the phenomenon here described by Adam Smith. It seems to be an unchanging trait of human nature that when a business depression grows severe most people, including political and many so-called "business"

---

[1] Here we may again quote from the *Wealth of Nations*:

"No complaint, however, is more common than that of a scarcity of money. Money, like wine, must always be scarce with those who have neither wherewithal to buy it, nor credit to borrow it. Those who have either, will seldom be in want either of the money or of the wine which they have occasion for. This complaint, however, of the scarcity of money, is not always confined to improvident spendthrifts. It is sometimes general through a whole mercantile town, and the country in its neighbourhood. Over-trading is the common cause of it. Sober men, whose projects have been disproportioned to their capitals, are as likely to have neither wherewithal to buy money, nor credit to borrow it, as prodigals whose expense has been disproportioned to their revenue. Before their projects can be brought to bear, their stock is gone, and their credit with it. They run about everywhere to borrow money, and everybody tells them that they have none to lend. Even such general complaints of the scarcity of money do not always prove that the usual number of gold and silver pieces are not circulating in the country, but that many people want those pieces who have nothing to give for them. When the profits of trade happen to be greater than ordinary, over-trading becomes a general error both among great and small dealers. They do not always send more money abroad than usual, but they buy upon credit both at home and abroad, an unusual quantity of goods, which they send to some distant market, in hopes that the returns will come in before the demand for payment. The demand comes before the returns, and they have nothing at hand with which they can either purchase money or give solid security for borrowing. It is not any scarcity of gold and silver, but the difficulty which such people find in borrowing, and which their creditors find in getting payment, that occasions the general complaint of the scarcity of money." (Bk. iv, chap. i.)

leaders, believe that the situation can be cured by issuing more paper money, or its equivalent in bank credit not based on sound security. The most plausible although utterly fallacious reasonings are advanced in support of such policies; yet a slight acquaintance with economic history should be sufficient to demonstrate that this type of "medicine" does not cure the patient. The history of our own "continental" currency between 1780 and 1790, the experience of the French with the *assignats* a few years later, our "greenback issues" during the Civil War, and the experience of most of the belligerent European countries during and following the World War, should sufficiently indicate the dangers and the impossibilities of curing economic difficulties by "cheap" money or by unsound credit operations.

It is of course possible for countries to depreciate their currency and so scale down the burden of their foreign and domestic debts, as was done by Germany some ten years ago and as is now being done by England. However, it is easy to forget that in the process gold contracts are repudiated, increasing uncertainties are introduced into business and trade transactions, much income and many claims to wealth are confiscated, virtually all rights to property are redistributed — frequently accompanied by the destruction of important parts of the social order, as in the case of Germany. Any *apparent* prosperity at home is largely financed by the losses incurred by foreigners on their balances and in the bonded obligations which they hold. Virtually all of those countries which "restored prosperity" by debasing their currency or repudiating their debts in the period following the Great War have now again repudiated their obligations, and are once more tampering with their currency. Currency and credit are convenient tools with which to effect our economic transactions. The impairment of these tools inevitably disturbs our economic life and retards our economic progress.

There are probably few if any examples of "managed" currency which have resulted in anything but disaster; and the recently discovered "gold exchange standard" has been found to be a delusion and a snare. The facts of economic history continue to indicate that neither nations nor individuals can raise themselves by their boot-straps.

Along with other problems following the World War came an exaggerated feeling of nationalism resulting in increasingly higher tariffs against outsiders and heavier bounties to stimulate the production of goods at home. The channels of international trade, which were seriously interfered with during the War, have in the last few years of peace frequently been almost completely blocked. It is hard to believe that England, with her enormous burden of debt, would actually pay a heavy bounty in order to stimulate the production of beet sugar within her own borders, with climate and soil largely unsuitable — and this at a time when cane sugar throughout the world and even in British Colonies could be had for almost the cost of transportation! Yet such an action is typical of the policy which virtually all countries, including the United States, have been following during the past few years. This has resulted in raising the cost of living or holding it to a higher point than would otherwise have been necessary in most important countries of the world. Further, since virtually all international debts must in the last analysis be paid by goods or services, *these international tariff wars have made it practically impossible for nations to liquidate their foreign obligations*. Again, when the world is suffering from a surplus productive capacity, it should be apparent that an attempt to produce most of the major commodities within a country's own borders would lead to still further building of factory capacity and development of mines, with the inevitable result, sooner or later, that comparatively few in such industries would be able to make any profits whatever. The United States, after having built up a vast export trade during the War and in the years which followed, is now suffering rather acutely in spots as a result of the curtailment of exports, while our expensive, government-financed, and generally superfluous mercantile marine is largely idle.

Many people, carried away by the spirit of mercantilism so long ago discredited, have asserted that the United States would recover more promptly from her present difficulties if she would forget the rest of the world, impose still higher tariffs so as to prevent practically all importation, and try to maintain a higher wage scale. It has been assumed that such tactics as these, accompanied by a prohibition of immigration, would enable the United States to attain and hold a prosperity quite apart from that of other countries. No doubt our country because of its overwhelming importance must lead the way out of our present world difficulties. Yet history shows that economic progress has in general depended upon an interchange of goods between countries for the ultimate benefit of all. *Real* wages can be increased only through efficiency in production or freedom in trade. A policy of economic isolation has never been proved to be either practicable or profitable.[1]

At this point one might properly challenge the present immigration restrictions of the United States, in the light of our own historical development and the economic evolu-

---

[1] As Adam Smith has so well put it:

"Consumption is the sole end and purpose of all production; and the interest of the producer ought to be attended to, only so far as it may be necessary for promoting that of the consumer. . . . In the restraints upon the importation of all foreign commodities which can come into competition with those of our own growth or manufacture, the interest of the home-consumer is evidently sacrificed to that of the producer." (*Wealth of Nations*, bk. iv, chap. viii.)

tion of foreign countries. Since our natural resources are almost unlimited, would it not be the part of wisdom to encourage the movement of *desirable immigrants* to our shores, so that we could sell to them *directly* those goods which we now try to export at so great expense and difficulty because of the high tariff policies of foreign countries? Further, it would seem that annual armies of worthy immigrants such as those who built up the United States in past generations, would constantly call for more housing facilities and many other things which would keep the industries of our country almost continually expanding. Is it not probable that, notwithstanding opinion to the contrary, our present heavy unemployment may be partially the *result* of our decreased immigration; and would not England and Germany be far better off at the present time if their surplus population had, as in the years before the War, emigrated in substantial numbers to the newer countries?

Although our present unemployment and that in foreign countries is unprecedented and disturbing, this deplorable condition is primarily the *result* of serious economic maladjustments and not the *cause*. Most of the suggested "cures" for unemployment, when analyzed, are found to be of only temporary significance and of doubtful value. To cure the unemployment situation the causes must be removed. This requires time and patience. However, it is well to remember that much of our present unemployment is due to the too rapid shifting of population from farms to cities, the net movement in the period 1922–29 having been around 6,500,000, mostly adults, or about the same number as were out of work early in 1932. Further, the natural decline in the rate of population growth will over a period of time tend to exercise some automatic correction of the difficulty — as it has already seriously retarded the expansion of some of our basic industries.

From the long-run economic point of view, so-called "technological" unemployment is probably of relatively minor significance, and is by no means new. Lower costs resulting from mechanical improvements gradually lead to broader markets and the creation of new demands for both old and new industries, with a consequent increase in the number of jobs. It is striking that in the year 1929 there was virtually no unemployment in the United States, and relatively little in other countries. This fact alone should be sufficient to indicate that our present unemployment is not primarily due to the introduction of machinery and improved appliances and methods. More than forty-five years ago so well informed a man as Carroll D. Wright, first United States Commissioner of Labor, in his first annual report stated that due to the rapid development and adoption of machinery not only the United States but Western European countries were faced with over-production. He believed that most civilized countries of the world had all the railroads, harbors, ware houses, improved rivers, water supply systems, tramways, telegraph lines, and other facilities which they could possibly need. Although he admitted the *possibility* of new processes, he did not believe that there would be room for marked extension such as had been witnessed during the preceding fifty years, and stated that *the day of large profits was probably past.*

In the latter half of the eighteenth century Adam Smith, in his classical example of the gains resulting from the "division of labor," showed that ten people, each specializing in certain portions of the work, were able with only the crudest kind of machinery to make 48,000 pins in a day, whereas by the more primitive individual methods perhaps the output would have been less than 200. By a very simple division of labor and a little machinery, one person was enabled to do the work that would otherwise have required between 240 and 4,800 people to accomplish. About one hundred and twenty years later a survey was made by the United States Commissioner of Labor in which it was shown that further improvements in machinery and in the manufacture of common pins had resulted in *ninety times greater* efficiency than the *improved* methods just described by Adam Smith; and in the generation which has followed still further vast advances have been made.

From the short-time point of view it may seem unfortunate that almost every economic step forward must be based upon a readjustment of present social relationships and upon a departure from purely traditional thinking — all of which is painful. However, it still seems reasonable to believe that the average individual prefers the opportunities, conveniences, and luxuries of today to the drudgery, ignorance, servitude, and privations of yesterday. There was no problem of unemployment in primitive civilizations when everyone, including children and females, had to work long hours in order to wrest a minimum of subsistence from the soil; and financial panics were certainly rare before the manifold uses of "credit" were discovered!

The lessons of economic history are simple and free, but more necessary to forming sound judgments by the modern business manager than all the merely technical knowledge that can be bought at a price. Boosting prices artificially increases production, which ultimately breaks the market. Rising prices, instead of being a boon to the wage earner, are usually a disadvantage. Lower prices are necessary to broaden markets and to raise the world standard of living. A low price level rather than a high one is essential to *sound* expansion. After a severe decline an upturn in business usually and logically precedes rather than follows an upturn in the prices of finished goods. An upturn in the price of industrial stocks more often accompanies or even follows than anticipates an upturn in business activity. The value of common stocks in the last analysis is measured by demonstrated earning power; which because of the inevitable risks of ownership should be capitalized at a high rate. Money is not wealth, but merely a measure of value and a tool for facilitating the exchange of goods and services. "Cheap" money does not create but destroys prosperity. A "managed" currency is a misnomer — usually to camouflage debasement of the currency. Credit is merely a convenient tool to work with, and must be based on confidence and "capital," which in turn are the result of past industry and saving. Debt is not wealth, and neither nations nor individuals can ultimately grow rich by means of debt. The only way to recover from too much debt (the over-use of credit) is to stop borrowing — to liquidate. International debts can finally be paid only in goods and services. No modern nation can live unto itself alone, without thereby lowering the standard of living of its citizens. Real wealth and income are measured by the abundance and not by the scarcity of goods. Low interest rates do not make prosperity, but on the contrary interest rates tend to be low when business is least prosperous. Great size in business does not always mean strength or flexibility. Profitable mergers are usually made not in periods of prosperity but in periods of depression. Notwithstanding the growth of large organizations, there still seems to be ample opportunity for the small entrepreneur, and after each period of depression new and small but more efficient enterprises frequently arise to displace the old. Stock-market activities should be regarded as a residuum and a resultant, not as a cause or important part of business activity. Heavy expenditures by governments inevitably mean higher taxes and a lower standard of living for the citizens, with resultant repudiation, revolt, or even revolution, when the burden becomes too grievous. There are no statistical formulae or predetermined "plans" which will ever take the place of individual judgment. So far as industry and trade are concerned, it is not probable that the essential traits of human nature have changed to any appreciable degree over the past few generations or over the past few thousand years.

A careful study of economic history reveals surprisingly few *new* "problems." From the beginning of time the primary problem of the average man, consciously or unconsciously, has been to obtain the food and shelter necessary to his comfort. All our modern factory processes have been developed as a result of our attempts to find easier and more effective means of satisfying our most primitive wants, so that we can have more time for developing our higher wants and aesthetic tastes.

Practically every step in the march from savagery to twentieth-century civilization has been made possible by the application of *new ideas* — which usually result from an analysis of the experience of the past — to the age-old problem of "getting a living."

Our present high standards of living have arisen out of the struggles and disappointments of the past and the new ideas which have gradually resulted therefrom. Likewise, the fortunes of the future will be built upon the wastes and inefficiencies of the present. To be effective, however, ideas must be harnessed by *judgment*, based upon a recognition of certain fundamental economic principles which the history of human development has shown to be largely axiomatic. "Where there is no vision, the people perish: *but he that keepeth the law, happy is he*."

(Written in April, 1932.)

THE EFFECT OF SCIENTIFIC IN-VENTIONS UPON ECONOMIC TRENDS

RUDOLF A. CLEMEN

THE most important problem of the present, according to John Dewey, is what we are going to do with the new techniques which have come to us with the advent of the machine.[1] Certainly, our present age is what it is because of the new technology. On the one hand, the fact that contemporary thought is so preoccupied with the machine and its technology is striking evidence that we are far removed from any universally shared fear as to what we can do with them. At the same time, it is an indication that the force of nineteenth-century thought is still with us. Ruskin and Samuel Butler were not alone in indicating their dislike of the machine and its effects. Today, for many who dislike the machine age, it is the old story of Alice and the Red Queen rushing with all their bodily might to keep where they are — a Looking-Glass Land transferred to Twentieth-Century America. Some thinkers like Veblen [2] have taken a more or less impartial attitude about the place of Science and its effects in modern life, though they are not convinced that its dominance is altogether to be desired because of the loss of certain spiritual and intellectual factors. And other writers such as Spengler,[3] with his philosophy of decline and catastrophe, see the machine, the instrument of man's conquest of Nature, now

[1] *Saturday Review of Literature*, March 12, 1932.
[2] Thornstein Veblen, *The Place of Science in Modern Civilization* (1930).
[3] Oswald Spengler, *Man and Technics* (1932).

rising up against its creator. Going beyond these thinkers is Gandhi, who is engaged in an attempt to turn back a whole continent from the machine age to a simpler world.

Economic historians have, in the main, accepted the industrial revolution of the eighteenth and nineteenth centuries as the beginning of the modern world with its great material progress. For example, Professor Gay's lectures on the Industrial Revolution have had a remarkably stimulating effect upon many generations of students. It is only recently, however, that these historians have made careful, detailed studies of the development of mechanical inventions and their influence. And even now there is not much quantitative data on which to base judgment. In one such recent study Professor Usher goes so far as to declare that the true heroes of economic history are the scientists, the inventors, and the explorers.[1] To them is due the actual transformation of social life.

Dr. Willis R. Whitney, director of the Research Laboratory of the General Electric Company, states that there never was a time when technical and material progress was more constructively attempted and critically examined.[2] Those interested in technical progress look upon it as continuous, but do not necessarily overrate its importance. There must be a similar advance for the higher values in man. Our present inventions and discoveries are leading to new kinds of people with new kinds of minds.

This is the idea that underlies the concept of progress on which all our modern industrial development has been based. It is, declares Dr. Charles A. Beard, one of the most profound and germinal ideas at work in the modern age.[3] Blossoming as a definite philosophy in the eighteenth

---

[1] A. P. Usher, *A History of Mechanical Inventions* (1929), p. 5.

[2] Willis R. Whitney, "Technology and Material Progress," *Science*, May 8, 1931, p. 484.

[3] Charles A. Beard, ed., *A Century of Progress* (1932), p. 3.

century, it implied that mankind, by making use of science and invention, can progressively emancipate itself from plagues, famines, and social disasters and subjugate the materials and forces of the earth to the purposes of the good life — here and now.

When once the concept of progress had gripped men's minds there followed a great outburst of scientific invention, due to its general stimulus and the creation of a favorable creative atmosphere for exploring genius. As a consequence of 150 years of development we can say that our present generation is the heir of three industrial revolutions, the early industrial revolution itself, the electrical, and, finally, the chemical, whose influence has speeded up all of us.[1] It is the real significance of these revolutions and their influence on society that it is proposed to examine and evaluate in this essay. In doing so it will be necessary to concentrate on the broad outlines and to give, if possible, a fresh interpretation of some of the great events which have fashioned the industrial and social structure.

One fundamental change that has come over the face of the civilized world as a result of the revolutions mentioned is that with these inventions in science we have changed our plane of living from one of scarcity to one of plenty. Broadly speaking, this change has come about since that first revolution took place. In its essence this was a switch from farm products and agriculture and food, as the source of energy used in most of the world's work, to fossil coal and oil. As one writer has put it, "we are the spendthrift heirs of paleozoic ages."[2] To understand modern America

[1] R. A. Clemen, *The Possibilities of Developing New Industrial Markets for Farm Products*, University of Illinois College of Agriculture, Circular 330 (1928), p. 4.

[2] Harper Leech, *The Paradox of Plenty* (1932), chap. ii. The present writer is much indebted to Mr. Leech for many stimulating comments on the industrial revolutions.

it is desirable to dig below the superficial, commonplace statements of the economic and social effects which have followed the discovery and general use of coal, oil, and natural gas. The ultimate effects upon our ideas of value and wealth of tapping the vast reserves of potential energy buried in the earth have never been adequately examined, although a mass of statistics as to increased productivity of labor and the output of workers has been collected. Beneath such data is to be found the underlying reason why the general use of fossil fuel marks the most revolutionary change in human conditions and relations, except, perhaps, man's transition from hunting to agriculture.

Before man stumbled upon fossil fuel, the work that he could do was limited by the amount of energy he might convert from food into muscular work of man and beast, from firewood and other vegetation into heat, and from wind and water into power. The real significance of the industrial revolution of eighteenth-century England is that it was the point of leave-taking from the past in which human labor, or rather the energy of the food of man and beast, had been the source of all wealth. The result has been that with the change of energy sources we are now adapting our physical environment, our productive and distributive organizations, our modes of thought, folkways, and forms of human association to a way of life which is based upon fossil fuel rather than on the soil. Such a view of the roots of modern life differs somewhat in its emphasis from many of the usual textbook statements of the machine age, the industrial revolution, and the age of science. Yet it has a certain reasonableness on its side.

One aspect of this view is that it is by no means certain that the machine sprang like Athena from the brow of Zeus, i. e. the inventor and the scientist. It is quite as likely that we have been the beneficiaries of a great historical accident, rather than the active creators of a new economic world. A case can be made out for the contention that the kind and amount of machinery used in any age is determined by the kind and amount of energy available to drive the machines, and the modern machine age is a consequence of the opening up of new sources of energy. For illustration, the steam-power factory grew out of a mine pump. The sequence was this: the mine pump, which was transformed into a locomotive hauling the transformed mine car over the glorified mine tramway, became the railway, which made possible the concentration of population and the transport of food and raw materials necessary for the steam-power factory and the factory system. The inventors of the mine pump stumbled on their invention while trying to find a vacuum, not a new source of power. A vacuum would have been the only result of their labors had it not been for the flood waters in coal pits that were ruining vast properties. From such a conjunction of accidental discoveries and unrelated purposes the world of modern industry began.

This statement that the early inventions were accidental brings up the question as to whether industrial invention has been individual or systematic.[1] It would seem that many of the earlier inventions were finally developed in an accidental and unpremeditated fashion. One group of writers has held that there is usually one man connected with an invention who can be given all the credit. This is the heroic theory of invention. On the other hand, opposed to the heroic theory are the views of a number of historians, psychologists, and economists. They declare that a particular invention is merely the culmination of a

<hr />

[1] Ralph C. Epstein, "Industrial Invention: Heroic or Systematic?" *Quarterly Journal of Economics*, vol. xl (February, 1926), pp. 232–272.

train of efforts reaching back into the past. Invention is not a creation but a growth. An inventor owes a debt to society and the generation in which he is born as well as to preceding ones. This is the theory of small increments in invention. Ogburn and Thomas in holding to this view state that it would be an absurdity to conclude that, even if James Watt had died in infancy, the Industrial Revolution would not have occurred.[1]

But today the element of accident and unpremeditation is not so clear. Our increasingly great ability to invent is, in part, the result of the work of laboratory scientists and, in part, of practical men, many of them working under able administrative direction in the plants of great industries. We are different persons from the people of one hundred years ago, and this in large part explains the widespread exercise of inventive abilities and has encouraged research. Certainly this new method of invention is not heroic, but an orderly, evolutionary progress. But, as Professor Epstein points out, we need a great deal of factual data before a dogmatic and sound theory of inventions can become possible.

The question of the actual net social gains from the use of fossil fuel supplies, begun during the Industrial Revolution, has been strangely neglected by economists and statesmen. Yet, although it might be thought natural that there should result a marked betterment in living conditions immediately after the new power machinery began to be used, there was in reality no such sudden uplift. There was, on the contrary, greater misery and poverty. Two offsets to the new power machinery can be noted. One was the unprecedented increase in population, which doubled in

---

[1] William F. Ogburn and Dorothy Thomas, "Are Inventions Inevitable? A Note on Social Evolution," *Political Science Quarterly*, vol. xxxvii (March, 1922), p. 91.

one century. Yet, Malthus notwithstanding, this increase resulted not in famine, but in agricultural overproduction. The second offset is concentration, such as the creation of still more equipment to extract and utilize more and more of the energy stored in the earth. Increases in capital goods such as buildings, machinery, and railroads are not at once reflected in better living for the mass of people. With the new system, on the one hand workers were drawn inward from the country to factories, and, on the other hand, it was necessary to go farther and farther away to gather food for the fast growing industrial towns. This search leaped over political boundaries and oceans. Railroads and steamships aided in the concentration and expansion. The British Empire, the United States, and Argentina furnish illustrations on the world map of this industrial and commercial expansion which was first focussed in British coal pits.

The second and third revolutions — the electrical and the chemical — are going on together at the present time, although the second has been proceeding for a half century. This electrical, or second, industrial revolution is quite different from the first. Not at all a discovery of a natural resource resulting in the use of a new kind of energy supply, it is a revolutionary change in the methods of applying and distributing the energy of fossil fuel, with some supplementary energy from flowing water. Again, it differs from the first revolution in that it is not an historical accident, but really a conscious change in technology.[1] The first revolution applied concentrated power to industries and to the increased transportation made necessary by industrial concentration. On the other hand, the second revolution is a change in the location of power use.

The electrical revolution has hastened further the prog-

[1] Leech, *op. cit.*, pp. 68ff.

ress of mass production. But at the same time, with its novel motive forces, it began to rearrange the American social pattern that had apparently crystallized around steam economy. By the distributable energy of the modern power system sent over transmission lines to any place where work is to be done, and the portable energy of the internal-combustion engine in automobile and tractor, there has been a reversal of the economic trends set in motion by the first revolution. The first built up the size and importance of the transportation industries by making necessary the concentration of materials, while the second has minimized the need of transport because it moves power instead of materials to the work place.

The first revolution was emphasized by the growth of cities, but the second is setting in to redistribute industry throughout the country. In this second revolution it is seen that the barriers between town and country are being broken down. By carrying into the family circle labor-saving machines, "canned" information, and standardized mental excitements, the inventions of the electrical revolution have invaded every relation of life, and have spread urban standards, values, and types of conduct over the whole nation.[1]

To continue this thought of decentralization further, there are definite technical and economic forces bringing decentralization of American industry, which may correct most of the evils of centralization and congestion.[2] American industry can be expected to cease the complete manufacture and assembly of all the parts of a machine in one plant, using instead factories located at the source of the raw materials employed in their manufacture.

For a time, great industrial centers may persist as points at which the parts, manufactured elsewhere, are assembled

[1] Clemen, *loc. cit.*   [2] *Ibid.*

and from which they are shipped to local markets. Ultimately the great congested industrial centers will disappear even as points of assembly, for in the end parts will be shipped to the local markets for assembly. This revolutionary industrial change and the equally revolutionary social effects that will follow will come, not because of any Utopian reformer's crusade, but as the result of technical progress in the field of superpower.[1] Such also is the view recently stated by Dr. Glenn Frank, president of the University of Wisconsin.

Dr. Frank points out that heretofore we have had to build our factories at the sources of motive power. "The production of steel has stuck close by the coal mines of Pennsylvania. The production of flour has pitched its tent near the waterfalls of Minneapolis. And so on. Heretofore the flour industry has had to operate near the waterfalls, not near the wheat fields. Heretofore the iron industry has had to operate near the coal mines, not near the iron mines. All this will be changed as we perfect a nationwide interlocking power system."

The critics of our machine civilization have assumed that we could not have mass production without centralization, but now the probability is that we shall ultimately find it possible to carry on mass production more profitably in a decentralized than in a centralized industry. Indeed, in such a decentralized situation the national market for products of agriculture, as well as of industry, will be more easily and cheaply covered, and new products can become more widely and quickly known and used.

The third revolution is coming rapidly on the heels of the electrical. This is the chemical revolution, the earliest signs of which we have been seeing for the last few years.

---

[1] Middle West Utilities Company, *America's New Frontier*, chap. i and *passim*.

It is a revolution in materials and processes which was greatly accelerated by the World War. Out of the problems and experiences of that struggle there developed a number of chemical discoveries which, taken together, may be said to be the beginning of a new revolution in industry. We are so close to it that, unless we look carefully, we cannot see it. The future influence of the chemical laboratory on industry and agriculture can be appreciated by noting that chemistry deals primarily with raw materials and that the per capita consumption of raw materials in America has increased ninefold since 1800.

This chemical revolution is bringing forcibly before each business man a universal question, "Can I stay in business?" Every phase of modern life has been speeded up and changes are more rapid and unexpected than ever. The answer which the wise manufacturer makes to this question is, "I can, by the help of technical and economic research."

The foregoing survey of the industrial revolutions and their general influence is impressive, but not detailed as to the exact ways in which technology and science are revolutionizing modern life. The importance of this influence has been recognized, and the details are being worked out for the most remarkable presentation ever made of the more significant discoveries and inventions and their effect on industry and living conditions. This will be staged at the Century of Progress Exposition to be held in Chicago in 1933. The basic sciences, mathematics, physics, chemistry, biology, geology, and astronomy, together with the great biological science, medicine, are being given a popular treatment that will show by concrete, moving, dynamic exhibits how they have made their contributions to modern life. For example, in chemistry it is proposed to show in a clear, entertaining, and instructive manner that this is the fundamental science of the transformation of matter and is summarized in the laws formulating those transformations. The tools and methods of chemistry and how by means of them the chemist has developed natural resources and transformed them into the very necessities of our daily life will also be demonstrated.[1] In carrying out the first part of the program there will be presented a series of exhibits illustrating the various methods of producing changes in chemical composition, followed by an exhibit on atomic structure to show how the chemist interprets these changes in chemical composition in terms of his building stones — the chemical elements — and these again in terms of the electron and proton, of which all matter is made.

It is then proposed to show how the chemist has developed such materials as air, water, coal, cellulose, rubber, and oil. Here it is desired to contrast the uses of these materials before and after the advent of the chemist — changes that are truly representative of the century. It is also planned to demonstrate how the chemist has utilized his theoretical conceptions for the benefit of the human race. For example, it may be shown how by the application of the principle of catalysis he has produced ammonia and nitric and sulphuric acids, so necessary for the preparation of fertilizers, medicinals, explosives, etc.; how by the application of the principle of absorption he has purified sugar, oils, air, and water; how by his study of colloidal matter he has supplied us with mayonnaise dressing and paints; and how by means of electrical precipitation he is on the way to rid us of smoke and dust. The chemical applications of electricity will be amply demonstrated by showing the various phases of electro-chemistry and elec-

[1] "The Basic Sciences and Medicine, A Major Experiment in their Exposition," *A Century of Progress International Exposition*, February, 1932.

troplating. It is also proposed to exhibit biochemistry, and thereby to demonstrate the advances made in our knowledge of foods, the new work on vitamins, and the astounding researches in pharmaceuticals.

But exhibits in a great international exposition, though on a grand scale and under the authoritative advisory guidance of such a body as the National Research Council, can bring to the American public only a few of the more startling and relatively simple influences of science in changing social institutions. The need has long been felt for an adequate study of this whole field; not, as was the case with the sponsors of A Century of Progress Exposition, for popular education purposes, but for the more serious information of thinkers and leaders in American life as a basis for economic and social planning. With this thought in mind, several years ago a committee of scholars was appointed, known as the President's Committee on Social Trends, with the support of President Hoover, to carry on a thorough series of studies into significant social trends. Its purpose was similar to the work done previously by the Committee on Recent Economic Changes of the President's Conference on Unemployment, for which Professor Gay directed much of the research and contributed the illuminating introduction and summary in his incisive style.

One of the most interesting studies was one carried on personally by the director of the Committee himself, Professor William F. Ogburn of the University of Chicago. This dealt with "The Influence of Invention on Social Change." A great mass of data was accumulated by the director and his assistants — too much to be included in the printed report. To this careful study, with its penetrating conclusions, the present writer is deeply indebted. No one individual could hope to gather in a measurably short time such an array of data without the resources and work of a highly trained corps of investigators under skilled direction.

The influence of inventions spreads fanlike in a great many directions. An example is the talking picture, which competes with the theater, affects the export trade, aids in the teaching of languages, and expands the field for the acting profession but narrows it for musicians. Again, some inventions have a chainlike effect. For example, the automobile replaces the horse, with resulting abandonment of the stable, decrease in the number of flies, and, farther along in the chain of effects, reduction of the spread of infectious diseases. As Professor Ogburn has pointed out, "it is only by thinking of inventions as having very many effects that their true significance can be appreciated in causing many of the social changes of our time."[1] For illustration, the radio has a far greater influence than simply as a pleasure instrument for transmitting music or giving information in lectures. It affects the phonograph business, song-writing, air transportation, travel on the sea, lecture bureaus, political campaigning, styles of oratory, dance halls, and a vast variety of other matters. In all some 150 major changes are effected.

Finally, as a typical case of the various degrees and kinds of influences on society an invention can have, one may take the typewriter. Study of this invention indicates that the first effect of an invention is a change in the habits of the persons using it. When, as in this case, a numerous social class is affected, there grows up a new class of women typists and stenographers. This newly created group has a definite place in society and certain new relations to all other groups and classes. In this manner it makes for greater complexity in our social structure. Another effect of the typewriter is to change certain organizations which

[1] W. F. Ogburn, *The Influence of Invention on Social Changes*.

may have relied previously on other means, such as old-fashioned pen and ink. Business organizations are speeded up by the typewriter and made more efficient through better record keeping and accuracy, as well as greater dispatch in correspondence.

More indirect effects can be traced, as, for example, the manner in which the family is affected by the employment of the wives and daughters in offices. The typewriter has had, along with other mechanical devices now run by women, an important effect in changing the old precept that woman's place is in the home. The appearance of women on the streets and in places of business has affected manners and customs along ethical lines. And, finally, the typewriter has had a certain influence upon systems of thought and social philosophies. It is not too far-fetched to say that the typewriter, together with other inventions, may have been a very real element, by attracting women away from the home, in the development of a social philosophy of equality of men and women, feminism, and social justice.

By such effects as these, inventions and scientific discoveries give rise to social problems regarding which governments sooner or later find it necessary to form policies and to legislate in the public interest. The most important of these problems is, as was intimated in the first sentence of this essay, the general one of the adaptation of society to the machine age, as for example in such matters as strikes, industrial accidents, and the labor of children. "Science and the machine are running ahead of social organization, *and the problem is to speed up social invention.*" [1]

Such a vast number of revolutionary inventions have been developed,[2] in such a diversity of fields, with, as a

---

[1] *Ibid.*
[2] See Waldemar Kaempffert, *Modern Wonder Workers: A Popular History of American Invention* (1924).

result, an overwhelming array of possible influences and effects, that some simple method of surveying the phenomena must be followed. It is proposed to examine only three groups of inventions and those but briefly, *viz.* the inventions in electricity, chemistry, and transportation, and to note their influence on social institutions.

In discussing the influence of electrical inventions at a time so soon after the death of Edison, who so greatly contributed to inventions in this field, it is appropriate to use his work as an illustration. For he was an inventor of heroic mold, and his name has been a household word for nearly half a century. His claim to the title of the greatest American inventor grew out of his work and achievements in what is an important period from the economic historian's standpoint, *viz.* the decade between 1875 and 1885. And they constitute an astounding list of accomplishments. In the 'seventies Edison was in his prime, not only from the standpoint of physical being, but also from that of creative imagination. Fortunately for him, and for the world, the development of science and engineering had, during this era, reached just the point where men like Edison were required, and where they could find the fullest possible play for their particular genius.[1]

A great store of new facts in what is now called makroscopic physics had been assembled. To make these facts available for the everyday uses of society required just such an inventive genius and engineer as Edison proved himself to be. It was characteristic of him that he saw and seized the opportunity which was his, to his own and the world's advantage. In the years that followed Edison's contributions, vast and important but essentially different inventions from those of the earlier decade were made.

[1] Frank B. Jewett, "Edison's Contributions to Science and Industry,' *Science*, January, 1932, pp. 65, 66.

They were, in the main, contributions to the successful employment of his earlier work, and were devoid of the brilliance of imaginative insight of his prime. As science developed, the practical application of new knowledge came to require a type of training which Edison did not possess.

Edison's claim to greatness is based firmly on five achievements: first, his work in the field of telegraphy in the late 'sixties and early 'seventies; second, his production of the carbon telephone transmitter in 1876; third, his invention of the phonograph in 1877; fourth, his development of a practical incandescent lamp and of the system of electrical generation and distribution needed to employ it practically, in 1879 and the years following; and finally, his discovery of the plate current — the so-called "Edison effect" — in 1884. Of the five, the invention of the phonograph is his greatest achievement from the standpoint of daring imagination, while his development of a practical incandescent lamp and of all the adjuncts that were required to make it commercially available was his greatest engineering achievement.

No inventor ever touched the daily lives of so many people at so many points as did Edison. He probably contributed more than any other man to giving our modern world the equipment by which it is distinguished as modern. If we were to wake up in the morning and find that all the products of his inventiveness had disappeared in the night, there would not be an hour in the day when we should not from habit be making some familiar gesture only to find it end in futility. The lights would be out; the cooking appliances would be unresponsive; the phonograph would be silent; the movies would be closed; and the radio would be dead. And worse than that, a number of millions would find themselves out of work.[1]

[1] *The Christian Century*, October 28, 1931, p. 1336.

Some of the services of chemistry have been mentioned, and here it will be necessary only to list some of the other outstanding achievements in this field. For example, the development of many products from cellulose, including rayon, has been significant. This product, rayon, by its cheapness and widespread use, has lessened the distinctions between social classes, influenced dress styles and interior decorating, and encouraged the use of color, home laundering, soaking soaps, and dry cleaners. The amazing uses of plastics and varnishes is an illustration of the many influences of one invention. Nitrogen fixation has had great economic effects in freeing the United States from dependence upon foreign sources. In fertilizers it is increasing productivity per acre, and in explosives it is of service to mining and engineering. The coal-tar by-products are well known, and their influence is recognized. Much has been done with drugs, among others the pharmaceuticals, with resulting benefit to human sufferers.[1]

One of the fields where much can be done by chemistry and invention is agriculture. Here the utilization of farm by-products, as for example the use of corn stalks in the making of paper boards, insulation material, furfural, and many other non-food and industrial products, may do more to help solve the surplus farm crop problem than any other methods that have been tried. This is a field in which lies hope for the future.[2]

The social effects of the multitude of inventions in the transportation field have been overwhelming in their variety and importance. Of these there is space only to mention some of the effects of the automobile. In 1900 a new product was dropped into the midst of organized industry — a rock in a pool. And its influence has spread in ever-widening circles, touching the iron trade, changing

[1] Ogburn, *op. cit.*   [2] Clemen, *op. cit.*

the rubber-manufacturing business, and converting the petroleum industry's by-product into its backbone. Not satisfied with demanding huge quantities of materials and products, the new industry began to establish new industries itself.

The automobile is no mere substitute for the horse. It has greatly increased and dispersed transportation, cut down railroad traffic, lessened the isolation of the farmer, encouraged the consolidation of small schools and churches, aided in the decline of the small village, helped to disperse factories, and developed a new type of vacation. The automobile has also increased accidents, reduced the exercise of the lungs, affected manners and morals, aided criminals, increased the activities of the police and courts, and affected a great variety of businesses, including hotels and restaurants.

No other thing has affected so many people and so many industries. It has created new professions and enterprises all of which depend on it for their existence; it took basic materials and transformed them into a product that people regarded as useful to them. A new want was created, entirely different from a need. And it produced a mental reaction, stimulating people to want the automobile. The social effect is that when people begin to want things they become more alert mentally, more willing to work, more willing to do the unusual and to put their economic life on a higher plane. The automobile is an educational achievement, and is an illustration of the fact that inventions have aided materially in raising the thinking capacity of society.[1]

The influence of inventions can be brought home very clearly by examining various social institutions and by noting the inventions that have caused changes in them. Here it will be possible to consider only a few as examples.

[1] C. F. Kettering and Allen Orth, *A New Necessity* (1932).

The first institution that should be considered is government itself. The American Revolution and the French Revolution deliberately created certain societies with new characteristics. But in the main these characteristics were political, and their effects in other directions formed no part of the primary intentions of the revolutionaries. On the other hand, scientific invention and technique have so enormously increased the power of governments that it has become possible to produce far more profound and intimate changes in social structure than any that were contemplated by Jefferson or Robespierre.[1] Today the government of the United States, while unchanged in general form, presents some phases quite different from those in Andrew Jackson's time. For the social environment of the government itself has been revolutionized by steam, electricity, machinery, and science. New economic facts produce new political ideas and evolve novel concepts or applications of old ideas.[2] The industrial revolutions have emphasized as never before the rôle of government as a stabilizer of civilization. In our time this has been due largely to the influence of mass production, since business demands a stable government, lest it perish.[3]

The machine age has created a highly specialized and scientific society and new and bewildering forms of property. New instruments have been developed which facilitate the molding of public opinion, the climate in which governments make and execute policies. At the same time the burdens of government have been vastly multiplied. Unexpected conflicts are being continually introduced into society by inventions. For example, the number of radio

---

[1] Bertrand Russell, *The Scientific Outlook* (1931), p. 204.

[2] Charles A. and William Beard, *The American Leviathan: The Republic in the Machine Age* (1930), chap. i, "Government in a Technological Society."

[3] Edward A. Filene, *Successful Living in this Machine Age*, pp. 106ff.

stations which can operate is limited by nature and the government must regulate their use to prevent chaos. Again, new inventions bring new perils, as in the case of falling aircraft, the pollution of streams, and explosives. These new devices have enabled the violation of laws in novel ways. Finally, the beneficent arms of science have offered to government great opportunities to serve mankind. One instance is the science of bacteriology in fighting disease. If governments kept to the functions of the eighteenth century, modern society could hardly escape disaster. The government comes into daily contact with all industries and sciences as purchaser, regulator, promoter, and employer; and in so doing it has had to use the scientific method. But technology itself, as distinguished from pure science, has not made a single important contribution to the philosophy of government.[1]

One other social effect associated with government is liberty. Individual liberty has been diminishing during the past generation and is likely to continue, owing to two causes. One is that modern technique makes society more organic, and the other is that modern sociology makes men more and more aware of the laws whereby one man's acts are useful or harmful to another man.[2] In the scientific society of the future, individual liberty in any particular form will have to be that which is for the good of society as a whole.

Education is another great social institution that has been influenced by invention. In many cases the schools and colleges are changing their curricula to meet the effects of inventions such as cheap steel and electric power, which bring about changes in occupational classes and in the kind of training required. They are changing to adapt themselves to inventions promoting urbanism, and to such

---

[1] C. A. and W. Beard, *loc. cit.*   [2] Russell, *op. cit.*, p. 217.

various discoveries in science as, for example, those in heredity and environment, psychological tests, theory of formal discipline, health laboratories, radio, moving pictures, and scientific discoveries affecting religious doctrine. School attendance has been increased by machine inventions which lessen work at home, the employment of married women outside the home, and the freeing of children from factories. In rural regions especially, attendance has been aided by transportation inventions.

Countless inventions have affected the school buildings and equipment. Some of them are architectural and constructional inventions, adjustable desks, drinking fountains, school costumes, printing methods, photography, the card index, the phonograph, the player piano, the typewriter, the fountain pen, and maps and other presentation devices.[1]

However, there is a question raised by some writers as to whether our education is really grappling competently with the problem of developing mass education adapted to the machine age and mass production. Traditional education is not what people really need in this era, but training in how to think and thus to find out how to behave like human beings.[2]

One unfortunate result of technical invention is that our education has become too uniform. And in addition to formal education, three other educational agencies have become sources of uniformity, *viz.* the press, the movie, and the radio.[3] For example, largely as a result of technical and financial causes, the press has found that the larger the circulation of a paper, the higher its advertising rate and the lower the cost of printing. Big papers tend to

---

[1] Ogburn, *op. cit.*   [2] Filene, *op. cit.*, pp. 144ff.
[3] Russell, *op. cit.*, p. 191.

defeat small ones, for the majority of readers give their attention to a small number of papers or to a small number of syndicated papers. These influences have made newspapers a source of uniformity of opinion.

The institution of the family has been influenced by all inventions, of which only a few can be cited here. Packaging machinery and the electric coil centralize housework outside the home or alleviate it within, and tend to lessen the economic functions of the home. On the other hand, iceless refrigeration, the vacuum cleaner, and the radio have made work in the home more pleasant and have encouraged it. Naturally, these inventions have greater effects in towns and in apartments. The Pullman car and the development of suburbs tend to separate members of the family circle itself. The larger household is becoming reduced by labor-saving devices and competitive appeals for money. The size of the family itself has been affected by counter-influences the net result of which it is sometimes hard to estimate. For example, there are inventions leading to restriction of children which would reduce it, while on the other hand there is scientific lack of medical progress that tends to increase it. Most of these groups of inventions have some effect on divorce and separation, and upon such family functions as recreation.

How mass production will affect the organization of the family and its prestige is a matter for study. Since the head of the family is no longer in control of the economic process through which the family gets its living, he must be relieved of many of the responsibilities and also the prerogatives of the patriarch. For example, women can no longer be his subjects, and even children will discover that their economic well-being now comes not from the organization of the family but from the organization of industry. However, in one sense mass production does represent the historical triumph of the family — the triumph of the principle of common service.[1]

The last group of social institutions to consider includes those which fall under the head of public welfare. Though many of the results of inventions are indirect, yet they have been profound in affecting certain social problems, such as the adjustment between population, technological progress, and natural resources, with their resulting influence upon poverty and the standard of living. Among the more specific problems it is possible to mention only a few, as, for example, increasing old-age poverty, accidents and disabilities, the breakup of home life by separations, truancy, and unemployment. Naturally the successful tackling of these problems has been furthered by discoveries in medicine, psychiatry, nursing, child care, hospitalization, and rehabilitation of the physically defective. The administration of all welfare work is greatly aided by inventions in communication and transportation.

At all times inventions have presented certain problems of social policy. Some of them may be considered in concluding this essay. One perennial problem is the delay in the practical development of inventions, which is unfortunate. As to the most effective method of aiding in this matter there is difference of opinion. One suggestion is that organizations be formed which will promote inventions and turn back their profits into a development fund. Another problem is the high infant death rate in inventions, which occurs after their mechanical demonstration but before assurance of commercial success. This involves for its solution the encouragement of the inventor by some institutional expression other than the patent laws,[2] the only one we have at present.

But the fundamental problem of policy is the adaptation

---

[1] Filene, *op. cit.*, p. 96.   [2] Ogburn, *op. cit.*

of men and women to this new environment we have developed. It is quite different from that of primitive man and the lower animals. It is more complicated than appears at first sight because the environment is rapidly and constantly changing. Naturally there is a lag in any adjustment, for the habits of the individual man and those of society itself are more or less fixed by the limitations of human nature, and are slow to accommodate themselves to new material environment. An example cited by Professor Ogburn is child labor in industry, which arose from the slow adjustment of the family to the factory system. Industrial accidents in appalling numbers were due to delay in the perfecting of safety devices and workmen's compensation plans and laws. But it is not just to be too harsh in criticism of the lack of speedy adjustment, since there is a very great uncertainty and an absolutely unpredictable future in the matter of invention and its probable effects.

In summing up the effect of machines upon our civilization, Stuart Chase has set forth a balance sheet tabulating effects manifestly evil, effects manifestly good, and effects both good and evil. It is an impressive statement, though not, for lack of proper data, a statistical one.

The evils due to the manner in which the machine is at present operated, rather than those inherent in the machine itself, are given by Mr. Chase as follows: [1]

Too many machines; excess plant capacity; riotous waste of natural resources.
Too much labor in distribution and the overhead services.
Unemployment, cyclical and technological.
A badly balanced flood of goods, often useless, often adulterated.
Super-congestion in urban areas.
A devastating ugliness in many regions.
Smoke, noise and dust in needless volume.
Over-mechanized play.

[1] Stuart Chase, *Man and Machines* (1929), p. 334.

On the other hand, the effects manifestly good are given by Mr. Chase in this summary form:[1]

> The life-span of modern peoples has grown longer. The average expectancy of life has increased a third in the past two generations, due to medical and mechanical controls.
>
> Higher living standards have been secured for a larger percentage of the total population than has ever before been attained. . . .
>
> The shrinkage of space brought about by machinery is demonstrating more forcibly every day the essential social and economic unity of the world. It is inviting an era of international coöperation. While the logic is inevitable, the acceptance thereof is still reasonably remote.
>
> Class distinctions founded upon land ownership and patents of nobility are gradually disintegrating, while a leveling process in respect to prestige is going on between classes.
>
> Hours of labor have decreased in recent years. We still work harder and longer than have many former societies with a hundred holidays or so a year; but if the machine were permitted to function as a true labor saving device, we could undoubtedly do better in this respect than was ever done before. The curse of Adam has not been appreciably lifted, but it could be.
>
> Superstition is declining. . . . [Men] ask: "What makes this thing act the way it does?" . . .
>
> Certain machines, particularly the automobile, have tended to expand the ego, promote self-confidence and a sense of power in persons and classes who otherwise might go timidly to their graves. This virtue has its drawbacks, but on the whole, biologically and racially, it seems to register a gain.
>
> The mechanical operation of industry is beginning to introduce a "philosophy of fatigue," whereby elaborate tests determine just how long a given individual can work without fatigue poisons damaging his output. No other culture ever dreamed of such controls; controls which obviously make for better physical and mental health. . . .
>
> The necessities of industry have stimulated a great variety of researches into the fundamentals of physics and chemistry. . . .
>
> Cruelty as a social phenomenon has undoubtedly decreased during the last century . . . the radius of social sympathy has increased [e. g., the famine relief for China].

The conclusion drawn by Mr. Chase from his analysis is that the evils of the machine outweigh its benefits. He

[1] *Ibid.*, pp. 319–321.

asks the pertinent question, "Is the human brain capable of directing the billion horses of industry so that they shall not constantly break into wild stampedes?"[1] Fifteen years' experience of the present writer in some of the largest industries of this country leads to a serious doubt on his part as to the desirability of over-large organizations, and as to the ability of men to secure adequate managerial personnel for them.

Yet the machine age is here; it is not to be eliminated by academic theorizing; and it must be dealt with as best it may be by the men and women of our time. Like all things in life, it is not all evil nor all good. But it is futile to expect a world which is already aware of the advantages of material knowledge and mechanical substitutes for physical labor, and of the promise of freedom for better growth in the future, to reduce its efforts or change its present direction.

Man is essentially spiritual, but his tokens of values, his media of exchange, the expression of good-will to others, call for material and mechanical devices.[2] The Greek slave, the Egyptian fellah, and the man with the hoe have developed into the modern, less enslaved philosopher who sees that man is essentially spiritual. All material matters are to contribute to his higher nature. The great task is to endeavor to steer this modern, mechanical civilization so that people will be freed from slavery and find spiritual opportunity along their path.

---

[1] *Ibid.*, p. 336.　　　　　[2] Whitney, *op. cit.*, p. 486.

SOME HISTORICAL ASPECTS OF LABOR TURNOVER

ANNE BEZANSON

MUCH attention has centered recently upon the economic changes of the last two decades. One notable phase of this discussion is the study of the movement of labor. In the recent discussion of labor turnover, emphasis centered upon the movement away from industrial plants. Little was said about the significance of the movement of labor; much was said about its extent, its cost, and its wastefulness.

New statistical methods for measuring changes in personnel were devised; new departments for coping with problems of industrial relations were installed. Out of these came, first, an appreciation of the volume of labor changes and, second, an impetus for the reduction of labor turnover. The precision of measurement gave to the age-old problem of labor mobility the appearance of a new phenomenon, all the more impressive by reason of the inexactness of knowledge in the study of earlier epochs.

There is a note of concern in much of the recent discussion. There is an impression that labor turnover is chaotic and should be reduced in the interest of both the employer and the employee. There is an impression that, in active periods, the rate of turnover has reached enormous proportions.

All this is in striking contrast to the fervor and approval running through the descriptions of the movement of labor in earlier periods of American history. Here the attention is upon the opportunities of movement, the lure of new settlement, the chance for advancement. Even if one grant that in the past there has been a pardonable idealization in the account of labor movement to new settlements and distant frontiers, not all the divergence between present-day concern and the glamour of an early period can be tossed off as idealization. Many of the advantages of mobility are specifically cited by earlier writers.

In his treatise of 1870 on American political economy, Bowen wrote:

There are innumerable openings for private adventure, which require only an adventurous spirit and a very moderate amount of capital or credit. The step between the situations of a journeyman and a master-mechanic, a clerk and a small tradesman, a farm laborer and a small farmer, is a short one and very easily taken. If nothing better can be done, there is always the resource of removing to the West and becoming a pioneer in the settlement of government land, which is first obtained with a squatter's pre-emption right and paid for out of the proceeds of subsequent harvests or out of the enhanced value of the land when the neighborhood begins to be populated.[1]

Economists found in the opportunity for labor movement both an explanation of the existence of a high level of wages in this country and a means of lessening the impact of depressions. Bowen assures us that "the tide of emigration westward always becomes fuller and stronger in periods of commercial depression."[2] He reasons that "a check is thus immediately applied to the fall of Wages, which do not sink as low as might be expected from the general depreciation of property and diminution of the rate of profit."[3] Clark states the indirect effect of early migration upon the general level of wages more carefully:

It has been correctly said that, during the period when land seemed limitless in amount and labor and capital very scarce, the wages of any kind of labor were the amount that would induce men to work for others

[1] Francis Bowen, *American Political Economy* (New York, 1870), p. 178.
[2] *Ibid.*   [3] *Ibid.*

in lieu of becoming homestead farmers themselves. . . . Now the returns of a homestead settler consisted, as we have seen, mainly in the increased value of his farm. . . . It thus came to pass that in the village and city the artisan of every class received pay which, for a time, contained an element of land value. It was larger than it would otherwise have been by reason of the fact that so many workers were steadily drawn to the frontier farms by the prospect of independence which increased land value afforded. Those who remained behind demanded and received some offset for relinquishing those prospects.[1]

The same picture of a restless, migratory, advancing population might be cited from the writings of travelers, historians, and industrialists at all stages of early development. The direction differs; the inspiration remains. Whether the story of the conquest of the American continent be told in terms of the farmer, the trader, the pioneer, or the enterpriser, it is a story of the movement of labor.

We are not here concerned with questioning the fact of movement. The settlement of the West, the building of railways, and the growth of industries stand as lasting testimonials to the rapidity and extent of development. What we are concerned with is whether the statistical methods used at present in the study of labor turnover, if applied to past records, would throw some light upon the incidence and significance of the movement. Would a more detailed picture link present problems into some closer relationship with past experiences? It may be that we are witnessing a genuine transition in industrial affairs. It may be that the new emphasis indicates a new appreciation of the need of building more smoothly working organizations. Or, again, it may be that instability in modern industry is disproportionately emphasized, while the changes of earlier decades pass unexamined.

[1] J. B. Clark, *Documentary History of American Industrial Society*, pp. 48–49.

Many phases of the reasoning deserve review; some seem to lend themselves to statistical testing. If the early development provided an outlet for the experienced industrial worker, one would expect it to be accompanied by a high rate of exodus from individual plants. Yet it is in recent years that we find the major emphasis upon the labor losses of individual concerns. One struggles with the fact that the early period would seem to have given the greatest opportunity for choice between occupations; yet with the opportunity gone, the picture presented is one of still more instability. If the existence of unoccupied land "served as a constant force tending to keep up wages in the older regions"[1] we should expect little emphasis upon wage reduction in former depressions. Whatever the ultimate outcome, no previous depression furnishes so much discussion of the necessity of maintaining wage rates. If the chances for promotion and change of status by movement were real, one would expect length of service with any single concern to be short. Did labor turnover, as at present, ebb and flow with business activity, or did it follow some different pattern?

The writer has no conclusive answer to any of these puzzling questions. As an illustration of the way in which such answers might be found let us look at the labor turnover of an old plant on the eastern seaboard, in the middle of the nineteenth century, to see whether a series of such records would throw any light upon the periods to which they belong.[2] We show in chart form (see p. 696) the rate of monthly separations and entrances in a ship-building

---

[1] Richard T. Ely, *Studies in the Evolution of Industrial Society*, p. 59.

[2] I am indebted to Mr. Robert Gray for finding the original records and to other members of the Industrial Research Department for tabulating the data. The firm cited was well developed at the start of the period used in this article. It expanded during the Civil War, played a part in the World War, and is still in active operation.

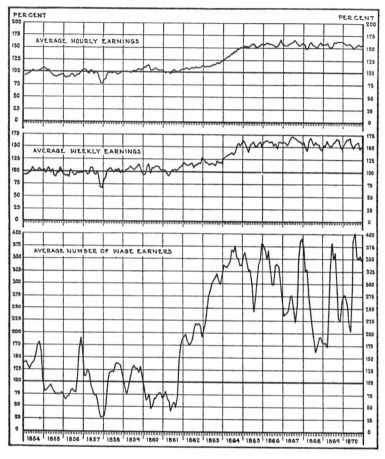

SEPARATION AND ENTRANCE RATES IN A SHIP-BUILDING
PLANT ON THE DELAWARE

(Monthly, 1854–70)

plant on the Delaware during the seventeen years 1854–70, the figures being based upon an actual count of the weekly pay-rolls. The record was clearly kept and well preserved, with the time and earnings of each employee indicated. In computing the turnover and hiring rates we have followed modern procedure as closely as possible.[1]

The seventeen years selected may be divided into three well-marked periods: (1) the pre-war years, 1854–60; (2) the war years, 1861–65; and (3) the post-war years, 1866–70. The pre-war period is characterized by extreme peaks in turnover; the war period by a rising level of turnover and the absence of lay-offs; and the post-war years by a declining turnover and a lower level of changes than obtained in pre-war years.

These seventeen years mark a dramatic period. The pre-war years are part of one of the golden ages of American business. Despite a wave of immigration, mining, farming, railroading, and manufacturing industries were competing with each other for employees.

During the decade that preceded 1860 the country had made the most remarkable progress in its history. Railways had extended until they began to form a truly national system of communication; settlement had spread rapidly through the prairie states and upon the Pacific coast; our foreign commerce was unprecedented; immigration was increasing; and new natural resources — not only the precious metals from the West, but copper and iron from Lake Superior — were developed. In spite of the financial crisis of 1857, the nation was prospering and growing as never before when the war broke out.[2]

Did our shipyard feel the stress of these changes? What is evident from the record is that the level of pre-war turn-

---

[1] In counting the separations any employee absent for four consecutive weeks was considered as turnover. This conforms closely to the modern procedure of clearing the rolls every three or four weeks. The period chosen is the same as that determined upon by the United States Coal Commission in studying the separations of miners.

[2] Victor S. Clark, *History of Manufactures in the United States*, vol. ii, p. 7.

over was extremely high. Compared with modern standards the plant had a serious problem. There is no year in this period with a turnover rate of less than 128; there are three years with rates above 200. The contour of the turnover curve in the crisis of 1857 has similarities to those in present cycles: rising during the boom, settling down to low levels as activity passes.

If we contrast the entrance and separation rates it is quite clear that there must have been a shortage of labor in 1856 and the first half of 1857. The firm was hiring employees steadily during all this period, but turnover rose so rapidly during 1856 that the loss of employees was greater than the additions to the roll.

From the depression of 1857 this particular plant recovered rapidly. Quite evidently it must have improved before other industries did, because the company was able to hire employees in 1858 while turnover was declining, showing that opportunities were greater than those afforded by other industries. The next year shows turnover and entrances quite evenly balanced; but by 1860 there is again evidence of labor shortage. The trend of entrances was steadily increasing, but it was overtopped by that of separations. From these facts it is fair to conclude that there must have been a shortage of ship-building employees at local rates in the year before the outbreak of war. This surmise is strengthened by the fact that months of high-turnover rates preceded the hiring of new employees. For instance, February of 1860 shows a turnover rate of 551 against an entrance rate of 154. That the firm aimed to expand its force in the spring is evident by entrance rates of 305 in March and 360 in April. The fact that its rolls show no total gain is explained by turnover rates of 420 in April and 439 in May.

In this record one does see a reflection of the feverish

pace of the decade of the 'fifties, a rapid and steady movement of labor. To be sure, no one can say where this movement was directed. We can, at this date, hope only to relate the movements of each decade to its happenings, to determine whether similar episodes brought similar changes. The workers of this shipyard may have been leaving to try their luck at other near-by yards; they may have been lured to other industries or have swelled the numbers of those engaged in railroad building.

We know little of where the workers were recruited for the railroad expansion which was halted by the depression of 1857. A historian of the State of Indiana tells us that "it is easy to trace the legal and documentary history of our early railroads, but to get beneath the veil and see the men at work is far more difficult." He continues: "Of the workers at work we have more detailed pictures of the Israelites working in Egypt than of our great-grandfathers building the railroads of Indiana."[1] The lack of information about the sources of supply of workers makes it all the more desirable to know something of the extent of changes which such periods of rapid expansion involved.

During the World War labor turnover emerged as a problem for particular emphasis. The disarrangement of business and the accompanying changes in employment created what was termed "an unprecedented instability of labor." At such times one sees the quickening of changes which would normally involve generations. That the abnormal stimulus of some industries and the curtailment of others will result in an extravagant and purposeless movement of labor is not unlikely.

Commenting upon the problem of the redistribution of labor in the United States during the World War, Professor Lippincott described the country as "unprepared for the

[1] Logan Esarey, *A History of Indiana to the Present*, p. 734.

greatest labor adjustment it has ever been called upon to make."[1] Have we not, at least in miniature, a similar problem in the disturbance of industrial pursuits during the Civil War? Would not a contrast of the experience of these two dramatic periods, when the spontaneous, gradual, and mild movements of labor which are continually at work reshaping industries were accelerated, show some parallels in the problems of labor distribution?

Let us look at the peace-time level of employment and wages in our shipyard and see how much expansion the Civil War entailed. In judging the extent of expansion the average yearly number employed during the seven pre-war years has been used as a base for the comparison with war years. The war activity may be readily judged by following the changes in the index of the number employed.[2]

During the pre-war years the trend of employment was downward from the level of 1854. When war opened the number on the pay-roll was less than two-thirds of the average pre-war period. In the first months after war was declared numbers increased quite slowly. Even by December, 1861, the rolls had not been built up to as high a point as was averaged in the high month of November, 1856. The next year, 1862, witnessed a striking increase. The average number employed in 1862 doubled, that of 1863 nearly trebled, the average of the pre-war years. Employment in 1864 climbed still higher.

The maximum number employed in August, 1864 was about 277 per cent above the average pre-war level. There was a drastic reduction in the summer of 1865, but the pay-roll was built up toward the end of the year to a higher

[1] Isaac Lippincott, *Problem of Reconstruction*, p. 106.
[2] The number employed is averaged from an actual count of all weekly pay-rolls. It is not taken from the mid-week.

point than it ever attained during the actual conflict, resembling in this respect the experience of industries after the World War. Disregarding monthly fluctuations, one may say that the rapid expansion of this plant began to-

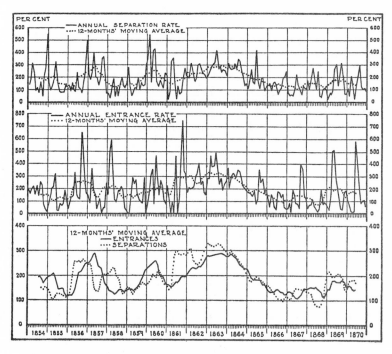

INDEX NUMBERS OF AVERAGE HOURLY AND WEEKLY EARNINGS AND OF EMPLOYMENT IN A SHIP-BUILDING PLANT ON THE DELAWARE

Base = Average 1854-60 (inclusive)

ward the close of 1861 and lasted till the middle of the third quarter of 1864.

For the post-war period the trend was downward from the beginning of 1866 to the end of the first quarter of 1869. This downward trend was interrupted by six months of expansion in the last quarter of 1867 and the beginning of 1868. Seasonal peaks in 1869 and 1870 brought the rolls back to as high figures as were reached in war years. Despite wide swings, at no time in the post-war years were numbers contracted to the level of pre-war years. The expansion of this plant may have been more or less than that of others. One will judge the process by which the number of employees was increased in a three-year period to three and a half times the pre-war level and to six times the number at work at the outset of war as difficult or easy according to his interpretation of the ease or scarcity of the Civil War labor market. From the literature of the Civil War period it is evident that the problem of an adequate supply of labor was uppermost in the minds of industrialists. Historians differ as to the extent of scarcity. Some point to the persistent efforts of employers to encourage immigration; others, like Fite, conclude "that the war-time scarcity of labor has surely been exaggerated." [1] He reasons that "manufacturing accomplishment was manifestly large, and on this fact is based the claim that the labor scarcity of the time has been exaggerated by succeeding generations. Industrial positions were readily vacated, but in a very large number of cases readily filled; comparatively few remained permanently unfilled." [2] To the writer this comment is far from being adequately supported by facts. It proves too much. To say that the needs of the country were shaped to its resources is to say nothing of the shortage of labor or the difficulties with which industry grappled. The whole progress of manufacture in the United States came about in the face of a shortage of both capital and labor. Is there any clearer indication of scarcity of labor than that positions are easily

---

[1] Emerson David Fite, *Social and Industrial Conditions in the North during the Civil War* (1930 ed.), pp. 198–199.

[2] *Ibid.*, p. 199.

vacated? In English industry during the World War, when the number leaving its armament plants was half the number taken on, the country felt it was faced with a new and staggering problem in labor adjustment. Is there any reason other than a condition of scarcity why employers will accept almost any applicant who offers himself for work? That a large number of positions were filled with inexperienced workers does not prove that labor conditions were not profoundly affected by the Civil War, nor that all positions were filled.

No one has dipped into the pay-roll records of the past with present statistical formulae for measuring changes in the movement of labor and brought factual data to bear on the problem. Without such an excursion one is forced to rely upon inference, occasional observation, incomplete press notes, and scattered comments difficult to reconcile. It is the thesis of the writer that an analysis of a series of pay-roll records would provide a more definite basis for the judging of Civil War industrial conditions than is now available. It is also believed that such study will throw some light on the more general problem of the effect of modern industrial organization upon the stability of labor.

If industries were crippled by labor shortage during the Civil War, stress should be evident in the recruiting and turnover of labor. Let us look again at the turnover and entrances of our shipyard during the period of war expansion.

The character of the war-time turnover differs much from earlier years. Instead of sharp peaks indicating lay-offs in pre-war years, there is a steady and gradual rise till the middle of 1864. The lowest turnover of the war years was 174 in 1861; the annual average of 1863 was as high as 282, with no month below 211. The tension of spring months is reflected in a turnover rate of 423 per cent in

1865. The entrances during the year 1861 show the sharpest increase in number of employees made in any part of the war. Throughout the war years the entrance rate exceeded the rate of separations in most months; but there was a period in 1862 when the margin was maintained with some difficulty. In all this time the firm was increasing its rolls against a continually mounting rate of turnover. The inability of the firm to continue hirings at the rapid rate of 1861 is shown by the trough in the entrance curve of 1862. Turnover continued upward and hiring slackened, heralding the need of wage adjustments. After wage increases, the firm went forward with its expansion until the end of the third quarter of 1864. Afterwards both the rate of hiring and the turnover rate moderated. In the years from 1861 to 1865 the twelve-months' moving average shows that the curve of turnover made almost a complete cycle, starting its swing at 150 in the spring of 1861, curving up to an average of 290 in September, 1863, and back to 153 by the end of 1865.

If one had to draw a conclusion from this single instance, he would infer that the demands of 1861 exhausted the possibilities of drawing labor easily from other sources without unusual inducements; that in the mid-period of the war industry was slowed down by the difficulty of recruiting employees; and that the labor of the last years of the war was obtained by wage increases to which employers of the period were little accustomed. In other words, one would see different labor problems in the various stages of war expansion.

At no time during the first years of war did the firm face the problem of wholesale adjustment of wages. It made slight modifications in the rates of individuals, and steadily increased the average hourly rates by scaling up the initial hiring rate when necessary. Adjustments were piecemeal.

There is no evidence of an abrupt wage increase forced by a complete review of wage necessities.

This policy is not surprising in terms of earlier practice. In the four years 1854–57 average hourly earned rates for all wage earners in the plant were a trifle over 10 cents. From March, 1858 to the end of 1861 the average was normally 11 cents per hour, reaching 12 cents only in rare instances. In other words, the average hourly rate rose very slightly in a period of about 8 years and in all gained less than 2 cents. The war-time increases must be judged against this background. By contrast with this gradual climb the movement of rates in 1864 was startling. Wage rates in the first quarter averaged about 14 cents per hour, in the second, 15, and in the last 6 months, 16 cents and over. An average of 17 cents was in effect by the beginning of 1865. Stated in terms of rate of increase the average rate of 1862 was about 9 per cent, that of 1863, 16 per cent, and that of 1864 slightly more than 40 per cent above the pre-war level. During 1865 and the following years rates ranged from 55 to 59 per cent above the average pre-war level.

The record of wages brought into relation with the high war-time turnover illustrates one contrast between present and former wage adjustments. Modern industry finds in labor turnover some guide to its wage policy. It is clear that the wages of the plant used for illustration were in no way tied up to its turnover experience. On the surface it appears that neither in the pre-war nor in the post-war years did turnover directly influence wage policy. In the pre-war years when turnover was high the customary rate of wages was retained for long periods. In the post-war period wages [1] were maintained though turnover and en-

---

[1] We are not stopping here to note the relation of wages to prices, nor the currency problems which affected the level of wages.

trances accompanied each other downward. The war level of rates not only continued, but rose even higher in 1867 than they had been during the conflict, a phenomenon not unlike that experienced at the close of the world struggle. Judged by modern standards even the post-war level of turnover, which at its lowest point barely touched 100 per cent, would be regarded as moderately high. Shipyards in this area after 1920 settled down to a turnover of less than 100 per cent and operated normally at ratios of change between 50 and 75.

The example cited may represent a movement of labor peculiar to a particular plant. It may have had more or less expansion than others. Its turnover may have been higher or lower than others. The turnover of the plant may represent the trend of others but differ from them in extent.

Had the recent studies of labor turnover ended with the finding that the ratio of changes in personnel gave a useful internal device to modern management for more effectively testing its own policies, the research would have had only indirect interest for the economic historian. The discussion went further: it was found that labor changes were, at most, only in part a measure of internal plant conditions. The rate of turnover not only varied within plants, but was affected by changes in outside business activity. The level of one firm might be higher or lower than others, but in general form the curves of one firm tended to follow the pattern of others in the same industry. In this is a hint of the possibilities in a study of representative material for a knowledge of other eras.

To take the view that changes in personnel are of interest only to the industrial plant is to take too narrow a view of the significance of the movement of labor. The total turnover is made up of the movement of workers from one occupation to another, from one district to another, from one plant to another, and from one status to another. It at least measures the extent of the process of redistribution of labor at the point at which the movement of adult industrial workers occurs.

Mobility as to both place and occupation has been considered as the most characteristic factor in American development. The changes observed in early years were synchronous with vast changes in the area of the country. We do not know to what extent trained workers contributed to this movement, how much it was primarily a movement of agriculturists, or to what extent workers were attracted to new lands or went to ply their own crafts in new surroundings. We are not even sure that new industries are not as great a lure to skilled workers as new lands.

The emphasis of early discussion was upon the vertical movement of labor. To throw light upon these changes would be to study by far the most significant of labor problems — that upon which our whole theory of wages rests, just as part of the explanation of differences in wages rests upon impediments to this movement. For such a study one must admit that the story of the past is irretrievably lost. We cannot determine from the amount of movement the channels into which the various streams of labor were directed.

The emphasis of the last two decades has been upon the horizontal movement of labor. It stresses only one aspect of the problem. Yet the horizontal movement of labor is the process by which vertical movement outside the individual plant is brought about. Involved in the changes are a medley of forces: movement from one plant to another may result in a change to a higher level of work in the same occupation, transfer to a new occupation, or the following of identical work in the same occupation. The process is wasteful or not according to whether employees are able to advance more rapidly by voluntarily entering a new concern than they would by remaining continually with one employer.

If in former periods different forces influenced the mobility, statistical measurement may be inadequate. For instance, if in early depressions there were considerable opportunities for the workman to "discharge the employer," one would find a completely different picture than modern records reveal. In the present period it is certain that an industrial depression eases the whole labor market and has a deterrent effect upon the movement of those who have opportunities for employment: employees seek new opportunities when business is active; all employers are able to reduce their turnover in times of inactivity.

All agree that labor shortage was the characteristic background out of which industry in the United States emerged. Scarcity continued in the period of small mills and centralized workshops. Labor turnover is one measure of the extent of this shortage. In the course of the development to large-scale mechanized plants the character of the changes in personnel, the causes which bring it about, or the extent of turnover may have changed. Study of early industrial records would show the extent to which artisans participated in the waves of migration. Analysis at various stages in the progress of industry should show the effect of the drift to larger organizations and more specialized methods of production. Analysis of active periods should show the amount of individual quitting which accompanied marked changes in wage levels. It may be that a comparison of labor stability in former periods will show that industrial promotion of the future must depend more upon the initiative, far-sightedness, and concern of business leaders.

TECHNOLOGICAL UNEMPLOYMENT

CHARLES E. PERSONS

THE newly coined phrase "technological unemployment" represents an attempt to express a newly apprehended accompaniment of modern industry rather than to name a new development. In the popular mind the phrase seems to stand for the fact that many workers are displaced from their accustomed niches in industry by the introduction of newly invented or improved machines. These machines are apt to be more effective, more completely automatic, or more remorseless in the resultant replacement of skilled workmen by unskilled laborers than were the cruder devices of earlier industry, which was less well equipped technically. In the conception of the well-informed industrialist or economist the phrase "technological unemployment" stands for a broader conception. These men of broader vision have in mind not only the effects of the increasing mechanization of industry on the displacement of laborers, but the broader development of technical changes. Their conception includes the labor-saving gains made through heightening the efficiency of management, the elimination of wastes, the merging of plants into more effective units, the greater productiveness of our increasingly scientific agriculture, and the changes resulting from the origination of new materials or the invention of new commodities. In the minds of these industrialists and economists, the workers affected when the motor vehicles displaced wagons, sleds, carriages, and bicycles were suffering from technological unemployment. The same statement applies to the laborers discharged when rayon and silk supplanted cottons and woolens in answer to changing style; to the actors and musicians who were adversely affected when the "talkies" ousted the silent screen from the moving-picture theaters; and to the employees in the phonograph industry whose occupation was invaded by the newest wonder of science — the radio. In this broader conception all technical changes may call for rearrangement of the labor force in the areas directly affected. They may produce unemployment as an immediate effect, and impose on wage-earners painful burdens of readjustment.

The present-day manifestations of these developments and popular appreciation of the problems involved have been repeatedly recorded in industrial history during and since the days of the Industrial Revolution. An article in the *American Daily Advertiser* of Philadelphia, June 8, 1821, on "Pauperism and its Causes" coupled the introduction of technical changes with unemployment in a manner needing only current phraseology to be entirely familiar a century later. "If all the works of labor that ought to be performed by man, are effected by machinery," asked the writer, "how and for what objects, can there be a demand for human labor?" And again, "Is not the positive, the direct object of Power Looms and Water Looms to dry up the employment of men? In what way then is the laboring class to obtain employment?" The moral is pointed by reference to the efforts of a committee in Rhode Island to cope with poverty. Employment had been one of their chief objects of inquiry.

But let these gentlemen [says our critic] look for a solution of their search, as to want of employment, in the existence of the numerous Cotton Mills in their own immediate vicinage. . . . On the whole can it be doubted that modern machinery is the chief cause of the Pauperism existing wherever it is found? As its direct tendency is to abridge the demand for men's labor, will it not be found one of the greatest evils that has ever fallen on the human race?

It would be possible to marshal a continuous series of quotations carrying the complaints against technological unemployment from 1820 to the present day. But we content ourselves with one additional bit of evidence from the senatorial investigation into labor problems in 1884. President John Jarrett, of the iron, steel, and tin workers, was testifying, and was asked: "What becomes of the skilled men when they lose their employment by the substitution of improved machinery?" His answer was highly suggestive: "So far there have been new mills building and the men have got work in these. In Chicago they have built new mills, which were put in operation last year and which give employment to some 800 men, and since they have got the whole concern in operation I suppose they must employ 2,000 men. Then there is another new mill at Scranton." This model answer, accurate and specific, epitomizes the process of labor adjustment to technical changes from 1820 almost to the present. Population moved westward. Workers displaced by technical changes found new employment on homesteads or in newly opened plants.

But the other avenue by which American workmen escaped the rigors of technological unemployment has been too little emphasized by our industrial historians. It is clearly suggested in Jarrett's answer. The westward movement, the growth of population, and the rapidly expanding demand for transportation and farm and factory equipment resulted in a constant expansion of our industries. Talent and skill remained scarce. Industrial promotion was constant and rapid. New plants or new industries bid promptly for capable workmen displaced by technical changes, and the hardships of technological unemployment in fortunate America were reduced to the minimum. While this is true of the past, the statement will arouse inevitable questionings. The westward movement is complete. Our older industries are no longer expanding, but contracting. The United States, more than other nations, needs to be on guard against unjustified diagnosis of the future in the light of past experiences. Many things are possible when a people is blessed with abundant lands and a wealth of natural resources which become impossible when the limits of lands and resources are touched. Problems easily resolved in our period of expansion will become of pressing import as our population grows beyond the possibility of proportionate expansion of resources. Skill and talent will not be scarce but plentiful. The road to industrial promotion will be progressively slower, the difficulties of employment readjustment constantly greater.

In other respects, also, our technological unemployment has new phases which make it in some sense a new problem. Technical changes today are widespread — almost world wide in some cases. They bring transformations of wholesale, not of retail, magnitude. The new mechanisms are of uncanny delicacy and efficacy. Their appearance portends the complete and immediate elimination of skill. And these changes come with a rapidity which, from the standpoint of the wage-earner, may fairly be termed terrifying. The power loom, patented in 1787, was a crude appliance fitted only to the weaving of the coarsest cloths. Its improvement and adaptation to finer cloths was a slow process. Scientific and technical aids to inventors were almost non-existent. Few factories existed to place wholesale orders for the newly invented machine. Mass production of looms was far in the future. Each loom was almost literally hand made, and those produced were sold and introduced to the trade against a barrier of sales resistance compounded of inertia and prejudice strong enough to cause the most brash of modern high-pressure salesmen to quail. After 25 years but 2,400 power looms were at work in the United Kingdom. As late as 1820 there were 240,000 hand looms and their numbers were still increasing.

Contrast this development of a century ago with the rapidity with which machines are introduced today. Professor Barnett supplies the data in his invaluable volume on labor and machinery. "The stone-planer was fully introduced in about seven years; the period of introduction of the linotype did not cover more than ten years; the number of narrow-mouth semi-automatic bottle machines did not increase much after six years; the 'flow and feed' devices for making bottles were fully introduced in five years."[1] This appalling rapidity of machine introduction and its wholesale character are due in part to the great advance in scientific and technical knowledge. The centuries' hoard of knowledge is marshalled to aid the inventor in solving his problem. Every device of technical progress is catalogued, pigeonholed, and ready to his hand. The world has been ransacked for materials, their possibilities tested and recorded, and full storehouses are available. Once the inventor has perfected his mechanisms, the factories and machine-shops stand ready to multiply the machines through the methods of mass production. The forces of sales distribution are always mobilized. The markets have been mapped and distribution highways laid down. Finally, the new machine may find its industry controlled by a few enormous concerns caught in the grip of destructive competition. Obstinate holding to old methods — even hesitation in taking on the new technique — spells the loss of markets and financial disaster.

The pace of industrial change is increasingly rapid. Its demands on labor's mobility are progressively strenuous. Skilled technicians and alert business men in well-accus-

[1] George E. Barnett, *Chapters on Machinery and Labor* (1926), p. 120.

tomed team work, caught in the current of modern competitive pressure, rapidly bring our new inventions to full fruition. Nor do modern machines allow any continuance of older methods; they are of devastating effectiveness. The earliest power looms were so crude and clumsy in operation that they could invade only the field of the coarsest hand weavers. Even then their superiority was so slight that by submitting to wage reductions the hand weavers could keep the field. By contrast, the stone-planer could do the work of eight stone-cutters. The linotype operator could set as much matter as four hand compositors. The semi-automatic bottle machine could produce as many bottles as four hand blowers with their corps of assistants, while the possibilities of the Owens bottle machine in its latest modification are almost unlimited. The machine with its tender represents forty hand shops in effectiveness. Each shop consisted of three blowers and four assistants. These are examples from industries which have found a faithful and painstaking historian. But they are fair examples. Nailing vanished as a trade when machines to cut nails were perfected. The makers of cigars by hand methods are facing complete defeat by the cigar-making machine. A long list of other trades and industries awaits the industrial historian who can rightly estimate the costs of progress as represented by technological unemployment. The fragmentary records available justify the conclusion that the potential displacement of labor and skill is multiplied by the perfection and efficiency of our modern machines.

Lack of complete historical data does not represent the only defects in our information. We are lamentably ill informed regarding present-day unemployment. There are no comprehensive and accurate unemployment statistics. If such existed, it would be all but impossible to

separate technological unemployment with certainty from
that due to cyclical or seasonal changes, or from the idleness arising from the maintenance of industrial reserves.
The bituminous-coal industry, for example, has wide seasonal fluctuation in employment. It is severely affected by
every swing downward of industrial activity in periods of
depression. The reserves of labor attached to every coal
field — one might almost say every mine — are extravagant. They represent wastes of competition, since every
operator attempts to have men enough at hand to produce
up to the peak of his possible markets. In addition to all
this, the industry is affected by many technical changes.
The development of oil burners and more efficient mechanical stokers has reduced the demand for coal. At the same
time machines for loading and mining coal have been introduced and forms perfected which are adapted to the varying natural conditions. Fully three-quarters of our bituminous coal is cut by machines today. Add to all this the inroads made in coal consumption by the advance in the
production and transmission of electrical power and the
increasing utilization of the gas engine, and the evidence
proves to a certainty that technological unemployment
exists. Still, to disentangle this brand of unemployment
from all the others chronically present in the coal industry
demands better information and probably more wit and
widsom than are available today.

It is probable that our incomplete information inclines
us to magnify unduly the volume of unemployment
chargeable to technical change. We know, for instance,
with almost complete exactness, how much employment on
the class I railroads has shrunk since the World War. But
we are not well informed in regard to the reciprocal development of the truck and bus industry, whose growth
accounts for much, if not the major part, of the railroads'

decline. It might prove that these technical changes have resulted in little change in the demand for labor. Again it may be accepted as a fact that our statistics of employment in manufacturing, as recorded by the United States Bureau of Labor Statistics, by the biennial Census of Manufactures, and by State bureaus of statistics, almost inevitably present a distorted picture in a country of rapid dynamic changes. We may allow that samples were taken from the industries in due proportion to their importance as employers of labor by the government statisticians building up employment indices. But samples and indices once established tend to become static. To introduce changes makes real difficulties for governmental statisticians and clerks and destroys the comparability of successive reports. But the relative importance of the established industries changes. New industries spring up. The loss in the established manufacturing industries may be balanced by the gains in employment opportunities offered by newly established plants. But of this the established indices tell us nothing until a new apportionment is made. Thus the federal Bureau of Labor Statistics only recently made provision for adequate reporting of the radio and the rayon industries. It still fails to secure reports from the construction industry; yet estimates of the recent expansion in this field run to 600,000 employees.

The biennial censuses of manufactures, likewise, give more satisfactory information regarding declining than they do of growing industries. The manufacture of cigars and cigarettes required nearly 139,000 employees in 1919, while 117,000 were sufficient in 1925, and 116,000 in 1927. Nearly 11,000 workers made motorcycles in 1919, but 3,900 were so employed in 1927. The phonograph industry furnished employment to nearly 29,000 wage-earners in 1919; this total fell sharply to 18,000 in 1921, and to

11,000 in 1925. In 1914, over 41,000 employees were engaged in producing carriages, wagons, sleighs, and sleds; the number fell abruptly to about 18,500 in 1919, and to 8,000 in 1923, while a figure of less than 3,500 was returned for the industry in 1927. This doleful information is fully chronicled. But new industries are late in finding a place on the census lists. Rayon was not separately reported until 1925; the number employed in that year rose steadily from 16,900 in January to 22,100 in December. Two years later the average number of employees was 26,300. The silk industry employed 108,000 annually in 1914 and 125,000 in 1923; the report for 1925 was 132,500. This number fell to 127,600 in 1927. The reports do not permit a comprehensive presentation. It is evident, however, that some of the deficiencies are highly important. The census, for example, still does not list the employees of the radio industry. The phenomenal growth of this product of technical changes is shown by the estimates of sets sold annually.

Year	Sets sold	Year	Sets sold
1922	100,000	1926	1,750,000
1923	250,000	1927	1,350,000
1924	1,500,000	1928	2,550,000
1925	2,000,000	1929	4,200,000

These estimates of annual sales seem justified by the census taken in April, 1930, which reported that of nearly thirty million families in the United States over twelve million possessed radio sets. This was over 40 per cent of the entire numbers of families. This eight years' development due to technical changes represents a notable increase in the volume of employment afforded. The production, sale, and servicing of these sets must have absorbed a considerable number of the workers displaced in industries adversely affected. These random examples will suggest that technical change is not a record of lost employment opportunity alone. It brings new demands for labor as well.

It is upon the ill-educated, the dull, and the old that the burdens of technological unemployment fall with crushing weight. It is at times when the declining industries are separated by wide divergence in the character of the labor demand from the growing industries that the volume of unemployment due to technical changes swells to alarming proportions. Carriage and wagon plants might be transformed into automobile factories and the bulk of the workers might be retained; but no similarly easy and painless transformation may be anticipated for the 30 per cent of our coal mines, measured by potential production, with which we might easily dispense, nor for 200,000 surplus coal miners whose presence in this "sick industry" reduces the average days of employment for coal miners to 200 annually.

Of the truth of the economist's conclusion, that in the long run technical changes bring beneficial results which are universally distributed, anyone can convince himself who will take the pains to become informed of the standards of living enjoyed by the generality of wage-earners before the Industrial Revolution. Textile machinery has provided better clothing for wage-earners and a more plentiful and certain supply. Technical improvements in agriculture and the new transportation agencies have not only removed the fear of famine, but given the laborer a more plentiful and varied food supply. His housing does not meet the exacting standard of five good rooms and a well-equipped bath room per family, but it is yet vastly better than the noisome tenements and barren hovels which housed mediaeval workers. This advance in standards of living has been achieved despite the great increase in population. Aided by machines, we are enabled to supply a population increased many fold with more and better goods, and richer and increasing opportunities. Our workmen live on a higher plane not only as regards creature comforts, but with respect to leisure, recreation, education, and opportunity. They enjoy more of the fruits of progress than did pre-Industrial Revolution workers. They see more, think more, live more, and know more than was conceivable for workers of the machineless ages. If they are not happier, should that be charged to the technique which makes their opportunities greater?

In the final adjustment society will enjoy more goods at the expense of less labor sacrifice. Labor will be fully employed, and will share in the benefits of cheapened production, enjoying more goods and more leisure. It is well to examine the steps in the process through which this happy outcome is to be accomplished. The new machine makes economies; it cheapens and hastens production; goods come to the consumers at a lower price. The users may, if they so choose, enjoy the old supply at lessened costs, or enlarge the supply while maintaining the accustomed expenditure; or it may happen that the lowered price will tap new layers of demand, greatly increase the consumption of the improved or novel article, and call for a great increase in production and an enlarged rather than a decreased labor force. The reaction of consumers to their new opportunities furnishes manifestations of what the economists term elasticity of demand.

The three possibilities may be aptly illustrated from material at hand. The stone-planer multiplied the efficiency of the worker eightfold. It materially decreased the cost of cut stone. But there was practically no increase in the demand. Production barely maintained the old levels.

The elasticity of demand was nil. The resultant pressure on the wage-earners made drastic readjustments necessary. Our historian says, "It may be roughly estimated that in 1900 there were between 20,000 and 25,000 stone cutters in the United States. By 1915 probably one-half of the stone cutters had been displaced from the trade " — a bare statement which covers a volume of unemployment, worry, defeated ambitions, and enforced reduction in standards of living for the stone-cutters and their families. This is most unfortunately not recorded by our industrial historians: unfortunately from the standpoint of the stimulus such a record would give to the solution of the problems of technological unemployment.

The glass industry showed greater elasticity of demand when its products were cheapened through the substitution of machine for hand methods; but the extraordinary efficiency of the Owens bottle machine outran all possible expansion of the demand, and imposed even more drastic penalties of readjustment on the bottle-blowers. There is dramatic material in the story of the transformation, within a decade, of an industry which had endured practically without change for thirty-five hundred years. In this survey, however, the facts must be baldly stated. In 1905, the production of 12,000,000 gross of bottles required the labor of 9,000 glass-blowers, 1,000 operators of semi-automatic machines, and 8,000 or more unskilled helpers, chiefly boys; in 1924, 18,000,000 gross of bottles were produced by 1,000 glass-blowers, 300 operators of semi-automatic machines, 1,500 attendants of automatic machines, and perhaps 1,000 unskilled helpers. The highly skilled workmen had been ruthlessly displaced from their traditional employment. We have no record of their passing, but presumably they were most frequently reduced to the status of unskilled workers; it is amazingly difficult to discover even a rumor regarding the direction of their movements or the privations of their journeys.

The introduction of the linotype in the printing industry furnishes a more cheerful illustration of the elasticity of demand. The machine, while efficient, was not overpoweringly so. Its ratio to hand work was as four to one, and the cheapened cost of composition stimulated the consumption of printing to an extraordinary degree. The popular magazines, the "best-seller" novels, and the penny newspapers owe their careers to this technical change. Here was elasticity of demand more than proportioned to the cheapened cost. Moreover, the compositors were exceptionally fortunate in another respect: the machine did not displace skill; rather it intensified the demand for skilled compositors. Knowledge of the technique of printing and make-up, ability to handle copy with understanding and dispatch, and capacity to keep the written text exactly in mind while setting type — all were needed by the linotype-operator as by the hand compositor. All that the hand worker had of skill and knowledge came into play at a more rapid rate when he became a machine operator. He had little beyond the fingering of the keyboard to acquire. For the printers, the fortunate juncture of these two factors, the great potential elasticity of demand and the intensified need for his skill, brought a happy outcome. Except for a slight lag in the early period of machine introduction, and putting aside the cases of the older men who could not, or would not, adapt themselves to the new methods of composition, there was no displacement of workers from the printing industry. Instead, the volume of employment has steadily increased and the wage rate has risen handsomely. In 1900, about 163,000 printers were reported to be earning $84,250,000, or about $500 per man. In 1925, 251,000 employees in the printing industry earned nearly $439,000,000, or about $1,750 per wage-earner. Even making allowances for the fact that the 1925 dollar in purchasing power was equal to but 53 per cent of that of 1900, this is a splendid rise in real income.

Nor does the cheer in this chapter of our industrial history exhaust itself with the rehearsal of the fortunate fate of the printers. Elasticity of demand for the printed page gave more, rather than less, employment. It spelled technological increase in employment rather than unemployment for the compositors. Moreover, its effects extended to the producers of raw materials; the papermakers and pulp-wood producers had reason to bless this technical change. The type founders, the manufacturers of printing presses, the producers of linotype machines, and those who furnished raw materials for their products, all shared in the prosperity induced by the fillip given to demand by the cheapening of the ultimate product. So powerful and pervasive may the result be when technical change makes fortunate conjunction with high elasticity of demand. Similarly fortunate results are shown by the radio industry, data concerning the growth of which were given above.

A most striking illustration of positive employment gain through technical change is furnished by the automobile industry. The manufacture of motor vehicles was too insignificant to warrant mention by the Census of 1900. Thirty years later it is stated that it employs directly 400,000 men. We have perhaps 26,000,000 motor vehicles in operation. The sale, service, and repair of this vast land fleet, together with the furnishing of raw materials and accessories for the cars annually produced, must furnish employment for many more workers than does the business of producing cars; here is a splendid credit item for technical change. The potential elasticity of demand for such vehicles was enormous. The old-style wagons, carriages, and sleighs could neither kindle the want nor release the funds which translate potential into effective demand. The development of automobile manufacture, with its subsidiary industries, in the short space of thirty years can only fitly be termed a splendid achievement of our technologists. It compels admiration. In the building of this new field of employment, the technological unemployment created has been overbalanced many fold.

These illustrations suggest that if the elasticity of demand for the new or cheapened product is sufficient to enlarge the demand for workers producing it, and for those engaged in producing raw materials and machinery, to the extent that it countervails the labor-saving efficiency of the technical change, no wage-earners will be displaced in the long run. There may be short-run lags in the process of readjustment; the immediate effect of the machine, may be to displace men or to render acquired skill valueless; but once the new demand becomes effective, these temporary displacements are covered. It may even happen, as in the case of the linotype and the automobile, that elasticity of demand — again in the long run — proves so great that the need for workmen increases rather than diminishes.

In the cases where, unfortunately, the elasticity of demand is not great, as illustrated in the case of the stone-planer, society contents itself with the old supply or a slightly increased volume of the goods. These commodities, however, are acquired at a lessened cost. There is, therefore, a surplus of buying power which the possessors will either spend or save. In the first alternative, we have increased demand for goods in fields near to or remote from the commodity affected by technical change. It may be difficult, even impossible, for the displaced workers to aid in fulfilling the enlarged demands for goods which the saving allows. But new demand exists, and in the long run the labor supply will be adjusted to the new opportunities. If the funds released be saved rather than spent, the reasoning is not materially affected. Funds saved are loaned, and spent by entrepreneurs equipping their plants for the production of goods. Cut stone and marble are cheaper since the advent of the stone-planer. Buildings cost less, and the funds released may be saved and invested in railroad bonds. The railway executives then put through the planned extension, and in so doing employ labor. The operation of the new mileage will mean continued employment and the stimulus of further productive enterprises. The magnitude of the labor displacement and of the savings in cost are thus functions of two variables: the elasticity of demand and the efficiency of the new invention. In the case of glass bottles demand increased greatly, but the efficiency of the Owens bottle machine nevertheless made devastating reductions in the number of wage-earners. Reports from the cigar industry regarding the effectiveness of the new machines suggest a similar result, aggravated by the probability that demand will show little elasticity.

All our variables fluctuate within limits not predictable in any given case, hence no rules of general application can be laid down. How heavy the burdens of technological unemployment are to be, how lengthy the process of adjustment, how severe the penalties imposed on the workmen displaced in loss of time, skill, or income, cannot be estimated in the individual cases or in the general result. But we may be sure of the final outcome: technical changes spell progress, and progress is widely shared; society gains. The disquieting factor is that the compensating burden of sacrifice falls on the skilled workers, whose skill is rendered less valuable, or of no value, because the machine now does the work that had previously called for highly trained muscles and nerves. The wage-earners and their dependents become a vicarious blood offering to the gods of industrial change. They suffer severe loss in the short run. It is these distressing short-run effects which arouse the current anxiety over technological unemployment. It may be that we have a million wage-earners temporarily unemployed as a result of recent technical changes in industry. Their readjustment in industry will be a matter of time. The "long run" of the philosophical economists has never been defined with exactitude. It is probably long enough to allow a generation of dislodged workers to starve to death in the absence of measures for relief. In the last ten years Great Britain has never had less than 1,000,000 of her 12,000,000 insured workers unemployed. In the long run they will all be reabsorbed in industry. We have seen that mobility of labor is a make-weight for the rapidity of industrial change; with increasing rapidity of progress, the demands on the laborers' mobility become sterner. The tendency of the economist or of the casual observer is undoubtedly to underestimate the difficulties facing workmen who must change their occupation. These are initial difficulties in the disorganized state of the labor market. Discharged men do not hear promptly of new posts which they might fill. They have no assurance that they will hear at all of the most eligible and accessible employment. When this opportunity is discovered, there are expenses for moving furniture and family distances which under modern conditions tend to be great. Home ownership may prove a very great handicap. Rather than sacrifice the painful savings of years, the displaced men will accept employment at greatly reduced wages. Worst of all and least considered of all the wage-earners' penalties is the ruthless breaking of all social connections. The children must be removed from their accustomed schools. All church, union, political, and social connections of the adults must be broken. Friendships are severed, relatives forsaken, and the associations of a lifetime abandoned.

A recently published study had to do with the fortunes of 370 cutters dislodged from the Chicago garment factories by a change to a cheaper quality of production and a consequent greater use of machine cutting of cloth. Most of these cutters were unusually fortunate in that they had received a "dismissal wage" of $500 — a payment unique in American industry. After two years 236 of the total were employed in trades or callings not at all similar to cutting; 42 were not employed. Six of the unemployed had never had a regular job since leaving the trade and several others had worked very little. It was estimated that 25 per cent of the men had better-paying employment than before the change, 40 per cent were in worse jobs, and 35 per cent had earnings approximately as good. A third of the men lost six months or more time. At least half of them changed trades at least once after getting a job. The evidence indicates that men from 35 to 39 years of age were most successful in making a favorable readjustment. Men younger as well as older experienced greater difficulties in getting re-established and suffered severe penalties in lost time and reduced income.

A second study covered 754 cases selected as representative on both an industrial and a geographical basis. The evidence is plain that displaced workers do not easily find new employment. Forty-five per cent, 344 workers, were still unemployed when interviewed. Of those employed only 11.5 per cent had been idle less than a month and more than half had been idle for more than 3 months. The

TECHNOLOGICAL UNEMPLOYMENT

experiences of those suffering longer periods of idleness are instructive: 45 per cent lost 4 months or more; 24 per cent 6 months or longer; 11 per cent 8 months or a longer period. Two-thirds of these workers went into entirely different industries. Almost one-half of them received lower wages at their new jobs than at the old. The older workers — those over 45 — were less frequently able to secure new employment. Their period of unemployment was longer than that of the younger workers.[1]

Until such time as society takes account of the hard position of these workers facing displacement and takes suitable measures to insure their readjustment in industry with the minimum of loss, it must expect their attitude toward newly invented machines to be something less than cordial. They have undergone a lengthy period of training in order to fit themselves to meet a recognized demand. Their acquired skill has served society acceptably until the advent of the machine. If there be any situation which justifies the application of the doctrine of vested interests, it is exemplified here. Since society is to benefit permanently from the change in methods, it can well afford to expend some part of its profits in softening the blow to the displaced workers.

A practical program is not lacking. There should be public employment agencies backed by an adequate research force and furnished with information allowing them to direct the workers affected by technical changes to their most eligible field of re-employment. There should be generous public aid in instruction and support so that the younger and more adaptable of these skilled workers may be retained and maintained in the status of skilled workers;

[1] An admirable collection of cases disclosing the actual effects of unemployment on the workers and their families has been recently published by the University of Pennsylvania Press (Marion Elderton, *Case Studies on Unemployment*, Philadelphia, 1931).

for the older men, in default of better provision, a secure fund for industrial pensions should be available. Furthermore, it is highly desirable that some agency should be found to divert the stream of apprentices from the trade or industry about to undergo the pains of reconstruction. It is manifestly absurd to repeat the mistake of the glass-bottle industry, where "an earlier reconstruction of an archaic apprenticeship rule would have kept a thousand or more men out of a dwindling handicraft."

Our pioneer experiment in setting up an unemployment insurance fund was established in the Chicago men's clothing market through collective bargaining between the Amalgamated Clothing Workers' Union and the Employers' Association. This experiment, which has been continued successfully since 1923, has furnished the model on which similar undertakings in other industries are based. Such experiments in private industry are admirable, but as a remedy for technological unemployment they have certain patent weaknesses. An industry may ease the transition for a small group adversely affected; but if the entire industry faces transformation, the magnitude of the problem exceeds the resources of the trade affected, while the emergency finds the industry wrestling with forces which tax to the limit its resources in capital and wisdom. These considerations cause thoughtful men to turn more and more to the remedy of nation-wide social insurance. Our full acceptance of the principles and practices of workmen's compensation, as well as the growing movement for social provision for the emergency of old-age dependency, inclines us to a sympathetic attitude towards such a remedy. Technological unemployment, at least, is an inevitable accompaniment of modern industry in just as true a sense and to as great a degree as are industrial accidents. The wage-earner is no more responsible for the one than the other, while the injustice of throwing the full burden of penalties on the workers should be as obvious in the case of such unemployment as it is in the realm of industrial accidents. By accepting social responsibility in the one case, we have set up an unanswerable precedent for like action in the other. Moreover, as in the case of workmen's compensation, the leading industrial countries of Europe have courageously and successfully accepted social responsibility for unemployment and are operating comprehensive systems of unemployment insurance. This, with us, is for the future. At best it represents a relief measure, not a cure. The adoption of unemployment insurance would undoubtedly support all other measures in the program for combating unemployment. It would bring with it exact and comprehensive statistics and thus remove the problem from the realm of controversy and uncertainty into the white light which plays on ascertained and indubitable evils. Furthermore, the system of unemployment insurance would establish costs rising with increasing unemployment. Thus we should have moving incentives for elimination of this most terrible and costly of all the industrial wastes. The industries and plants responsible would be clearly indicated and the extent of their participation defined. Programs for coping with the problem could then be definitely charted.

Our reliance in the future must be upon two developments which have made promising, albeit little noticed, beginnings. The first is the increasing sense of responsibility manifested by industrial leaders for the maintenance of stable employment conditions. The second is the spread of education and the strengthened capacity of our labor force to meet industrial changes. Bad as the present industrial depression has proved to be, its rigors have been greatly ameliorated by the practice of short time as an alternative to dismissal. To work the whole force fewer hours per day or fewer days per week, or to rotate the available employment so that every family dependent on the industry has at least the equivalent of the minimum of subsistence, is a procedure greatly to be desired. The certainty that the worthy worker will not be turned adrift and that his dependents have a sure defense against the worst evil of unemployment robs that grisly specter of more than half its terrors. The cost to the industry cannot be great; the gain to society at large, as well as to the workers, is tremendous. A compilation of the roll of honor of firms following this beneficent practice during the present depression, with the exact recital of their experience, the costs incurred, and the problems solved, would be extremely valuable as a stimulus to the extension of this plan for ameliorating the pangs of unemployment. Given this measure of security, the workers whose period of part-time employment proves lengthy would have a safe haven from which to seek new employment opportunities. Seeking a job with subsistence for himself and family assured is vastly different from pounding the pavements as an unattached, unwanted derelict who returns nightly to a family one day nearer the disaster of dire want.

Again, the wage-earners are better fitted to make necessary adjustments promptly and effectively. Our policy of rigid restriction of immigration is ridding us of the burden of non-English-speaking, unassimilated, and ignorant aliens who have hitherto swelled the ranks of the unemployed in every period of distress. The wage force contains a steadily increased proportion of individuals with high school and trade school training; it is of higher average intelligence. The new tasks are essayed by workers better fitted to perform them. Moreover the developments of our machine age, while they sometimes rob the worker of his skilled task and destroy the value of his trade training, have yet been potent educative influences in preparing the wage-earner to meet the new conditions. An efficient machine-tender can serve in most mechanized industries. He is more versatile than the stone-cutter, the glass-blower, or the hand compositor. His knowledge of technical equipment is adaptable to many fields. The all but universal distribution of such mechanical products as electric lights and other electrical household equipment, telephones, radios, and automobiles makes of the average householder an amateur machine-operator of sorts. He is well practiced in their operation. The machinery of the factory is not strange in his eyes. He understands machines. The old saying about the immigrant worker, "He can't run a wheelbarrow," is vanquished by the fact of common observation that almost every wage-earner can operate an intricate and delicate motor vehicle. The knowledge required for machine operation bids fair to become as universal as ability to read. This makes for great adaptability to the demands of a machine age and the emergencies of technological unemployment.

The argument then runs that the new phrase, "technological unemployment," expresses a century-old problem. It is neither a new nor a revived one, but a hardy perennial. It has, however, new aspects, since technical changes are more widespread, prompter, more destructive in the elimination of skilled workmen, and, above all, more rapid in introduction than has previously been the case. Our information is scanty and defective. It probably exaggerates the importance of technological unemployment, but it clearly indicates that the volume of such idleness is great. Technical changes may account for a million of our workless laborers. The argument of the economists as to the beneficial long-run effects of technical changes holds good.

The immediate effects, nevertheless, are often disastrous for the workers affected. They call for the prompt adoption of remedial action. This program will be based on acceptance of social responsibility for the evils of technological unemployment. The trend in that direction is unmistakable and the outcome cannot be doubted. The greatest present need is for more comprehensive, more accurate, and more vividly presented information.

THE SPECTER OF DEARTH OF FOOD: HISTORY'S ANSWER TO SIR WILLIAM CROOKES

JOSEPH S. DAVIS

THE question of food supply "is of urgent importance to-day, and it is a life and death question for generations to come. . . . England and all civilised nations stand in deadly peril of not having enough to eat." This was the keynote of a stirring presidential address by Sir William Crookes before the British Association for the Advancement of Science, on September 7, 1898.[1] For Europe and its offspring countries, wheat appeared the heart of the food supply; the crucial food problem was the wheat problem; and this, as he read "stubborn facts," was one of averting acute scarcity within a generation.

The details of the impending catastrophe no one can predict, but its general direction is obvious enough. Should all the wheat-growing countries add to their area to the utmost capacity, on the most careful

---

[1] The address as given appears in *Report of the Sixty-eighth Meeting of the British Association* . . . (London, 1899), pp. 2–38. Exclusive of portions unrelated to his main subject, and with some minor modifications, it was published in book form in London, 1899, with the title: *The Wheat Problem, Based on Remarks Made in the Presidential Address to the British Association at Bristol in 1898, Revised with an Answer to Various Critics, by Sir William Crookes, F. R. S., With Two Chapters on the Future Wheat Supply of the United States, by Mr C. Wood Davis, of Peotone, Kansas, and the Hon. John Hyde, Chief Statistician to the Department of Agriculture, Washington* [hereafter in this article referred to as *Crookes*]. Page references below are to this edition, except where otherwise indicated. In 1917 was published a *Third Edition with Preface and Additional Chapter Bringing the Statistical Information Up to Date, and a Chapter on Future Wheat Supplies by Sir R. Henry Rew, with an Introduction by Lord Rhondda*. From this edition the articles of Davis and Hyde were omitted.

calculation the yield would give us only an addition of some 100,000,000 acres, supplying at the average world-yield of 12.7 bushels to the acre, 1,270,000,000 bushels, just enough to supply the increase of population among the bread-eaters till the year 1931.[1]

Are we to go hungry, and to know the trial of scarcity? That is the poignant question. Thirty years is but a day in the life of a nation. Those present who may attend the meeting of the British Association thirty years hence will judge how far my forecasts are justified.[2]

These years have now elapsed. In striking contrast to Sir William's expectations, the wheat problem of 1931 was one of world surplus, not world shortage, actual or impending. The condition of surplus has persisted for four years; hopes of an early adjustment between supplies and requirements have been repeatedly disappointed, and readjustment is not yet (July, 1932) in sight.

"A permanently higher price for wheat is, I fear," said Crookes, "a calamity that ere long must be faced."[3] Actually, in the past year, wheat prices have fallen below the lowest that Sir William knew; in three of the past four years they have been, in relation to the general level of commodity prices, below the lowest level of the 1890's;[4] indeed, in most of the post-War period, wheat has been generally cheaper in terms of wages than ever before. The "calamity" feared today, by importing and exporting nations alike, is that of a permanently *lowered* price for wheat.

Sir William Crookes (1832–1919) was no irresponsible sensationalist. He was one of the most eminent scientists of his generation, who had done notable work in both physics and chemistry. Because of what he was, what he said commanded high respect. His discussion rested on considerable study and correspondence. He pondered the criticisms it evoked. Though his address was replete with

---

[1] *Crookes*, p. 33. [2] *Ibid.*, p. 34. [3] *Ibid.*, p. 7.
[4] *Wheat Studies of the Food Research Institute*, vol. viii (December, 1931), pp. 95–98. Crookes paid no attention to the general price level, or to the level of wages.

alarmist phrases, he disavowed any intent "to create a sensation, or to indulge in a 'cosmic scare.'" He sought "to treat the matter soberly and without exaggeration."

In the background of the address lay a real wheat stringency, which stood out in sharp contrast to the preceding abundance. In 1897, following reductions in wheat reserves, short crops of both wheat and rye were the rule in Europe and in most of the exporting countries as well. Wheat prices advanced materially, and the spectacular Leiter corner in the spring of 1898 drove them up sharply further, for a time. Widespread famine was reported in Russia and in parts of India. In Great Britain, the danger of food scarcity in the event of war had already evoked special concern, even in conservative grain and milling circles. Britain was importing some three-fourths of her wheat consumption requirements, and large quantities of other foodstuffs and feedstuffs as well. It is not surprising that Crookes could say, after a review of Britain's position: [1] "The burning question of today is, What can the United Kingdom do to be reasonably safe from starvation in presence of two successive failures of the world's wheat harvest, or against a hostile combination of European nations?" [2]

The second part of this question was answered, successfully, during the Great War. But no nation can today face the prospect of a great war, or even a general economic boycott, without the gravest concern, owing to customary or unavoidable dependence upon foreign countries for supplies of important foodstuffs, raw materials, and manufactures. To the first part of the "burning question" history since 1898 has given a reassuring answer. For various reasons, the maximum world wheat shortage that has occurred under modern peace-time conditions has not en-

[1] *Crookes*, pp. 3–7.   [2] *Ibid.*, pp. 7–8.

tailed a degree of food shortage involving undernutrition in any part of the world that was definitely part of the widening stream of national and international trade. Limits of space preclude elaboration of these topics.

Other questions remain. Why was the actual outcome, to 1931, the reverse of Sir William's dismal wheat forecasts? Was his hope justified that "before we are in the grip of actual dearth the Chemist will step in and postpone the day of famine to so distant a period that we, and our sons and grandsons, may legitimately live without undue solicitude for the future?"[1] Does mankind, as he confidently assumed, face the doom of dearth of food — a dearth which, later if not sooner, will cruelly fix limits to growth of population, demand painful contraction of human satisfactions, or do both?

The facts of economic history yield some answer. In retrospect, it is clear that he overrated the basic importance of wheat and underrated the potential expansion of its production, and that he did not see, or give due weight to, significant tendencies that time has revealed.

Like many who preceded and followed him, Crookes laid great stress on wheat as the foodstuff *par excellence*.

Wheat is the most sustaining food grain of the great Caucasian race which includes the peoples of Europe, United States, British America, the white inhabitants of South Africa, Australasia, parts of South America, and the white population of the European colonies.[2]

If bread fails — not only us, but all the bread-eaters of the world — what are we to do? We are born wheat-eaters. Other races, vastly superior to us in numbers, but differing widely in material and intellectual progress, are eaters of Indian corn, rice, millet, and other grains; but none of these grains have the food value, the concentrated, health-sustaining power of wheat, and it is on this account that the accumulated experience of civilised mankind has set wheat apart as the fit and proper food for the development of muscle and brains.[3]

[1] *Ibid.*, pp. 35–36.   [2] *Ibid.*, p. 8.   [3] *Ibid.*, p. 34.

Excellent foodstuff though it is, wheat merits no such encomium.[1] It has qualities that facilitate shipment, preservation, manufacture, and culinary use, and furnish special appeals to consumers; these, not its inherent superiority as food for man, are responsible for the displacement of other cereals by wheat as human food, though it remains the dearest of the cereals except rice.

In turn, however, the aristocrat of the grains itself is gradually taking a lesser position in the diet in countries in which it has long been the mainstay. In some countries, wheat consumption per capita has risen, but by less than that of other cereals (chiefly rye and corn) has declined. In many of the great wheat-consuming countries wheat consumption per capita has gone down, in some cases quite materially. The per capita food consumption of bread grains has declined in most of the bread-eating countries to which Sir William referred.

This tendency is due, not to dearth of wheat, but to lessening food requirements per capita, caused by many factors; to larger earning power per capita; and to competition of other foods, such as sugar, dairy products, and vegetables and fruits, which have become available in quantities and at prices that permit them to supply more of the food requirements of man.[2] "Bread is the staff of life" in most countries still, but man leans upon it far less than when this phrase was coined, and less even than thirty years ago. For many decades at least, apart from war, there has been a tendency toward broadening the base of the world's food supply, in respect of geography of

[1] See Alonzo E. Taylor, "The Place of Wheat in the Diet," *Wheat Studies of the Food Research Institute*, vol. v (February, 1929), pp. 147–174, and "Economic Nationalism in Europe as Applied to Wheat," *ibid.*, vol. viii (February, 1932), pp. 271–272.

[2] See Holbrook Working, "The Decline in Per Capita Consumption of Flour in the United States," *Wheat Studies of the Food Research Institute*, vol. ii (July, 1926), pp. 265–292.

production, improvement in transportation, and diversification of diet. Increasing actual use of wheat has accompanied decreasing essential dependence upon it or any other staple foodstuff.

The outstanding feature of Crookes' discussion was his emphasis on the "strictly limited" possibilities of expansion of wheat acreage. It seemed to him certain that, unless yields per acre could be radically improved, the era of wheat shortage would soon be at hand.

In discussing wheat potentialities, Crookes limited the "world" of his argument to what he called "contributory areas,"[1] and "the populations of European lineage inhabiting Asiatic Russia, the United States, Canada, Australasia, Chile, Uruguay, Brazil, South Africa, and Europe and its colonies."[2] To the wheat crops of these areas he added imports from "India, Persia, Syria, Anatolia, and North Africa," areas which he otherwise excluded from consideration. Below are given his data for 1871, 1881, and 1891 and his "prophetic figures" on wheat requirements for specific years by decades up to 1941.[3]

Year	Bread-eaters (in millions)	Bu. per capita for feed and seed[a]	Bushels (in millions)	Acres at 12.7 bu. per acre (in millions)
1871	371.0	4.15	1,540	121
1881	416.0	4.38	1,822	143
1891	472.6	4.50	2,127	167
1898	516.5	4.50	2,324	183
1901	536.1	4.50	2,412	190
1911	603.7	4.50	2,717	214
1921	674.0	4.50	3,033	239
1931	746.1	4.50	3,357	264
1941	819.2	4.50	3,686	290

[a] Seed requirement included at 0.6 bushels per capita. There is a strong probability that seed requirements per acre have decreased appreciably since 1898.

---

[1] *Crookes*, p. 10.   [2] *Ibid.*, p. 134.   [3] *Ibid.*, p. 13.

Apparently for the sake of conservatism, he used a constant per capita requirement despite a conviction that the upward trend shown for 1871 to 1891 would continue. He remarked [1] that there had been "a steady increase of unit wheat requirements by reason of the decrease of unit consumption of rye, maslin, spelt, and buckwheat." He pointed with alarm to the relatively slight increase in wheat and rye acreage as compared with population since 1871 and 1884, adding:

The area under *all* the bread-making grains is absolutely 2.2 per cent. less than thirteen years ago, notwithstanding an increase of one-fifth in requirements for bread.

It is clear we are confronted with a colossal problem that must tax the wits of the wisest.[2]

Crookes was surprisingly fortunate in his population forecast for 1931. No precise check-up of his population figures is possible, but an attempt in this direction yields figures for 1931, and the increase 1891–1931, close to those he gave. Clearly he did not overestimate the rate of population growth. He did not reckon upon a large increase of bread-eaters outside his "contributory areas." Shipments of wheat and flour to these outside areas have increased several-fold since the latter 'nineties, and markedly since the War, and some of these areas have increased their wheat production as well. This expansion, however, has come largely in response to cheap wheat; it would doubtless have been much less if Crookes' views as to wheat production had proved correct.

It is of interest to compare actual wheat figures for 1931 with the "prophetic figures." A provisional approximation for comparable areas is given on page 740, taking a conservative figure of 850 million bushels for Russia's crop, and ignoring the small exports from outside areas.

[1] *Ibid.*   [2] *Ibid.*, p. 15.

As it happens, 1931 was a year of moderate world production, chiefly because of low yields of spring wheat in North America and Soviet Russia. Even so, wheat production in 1931 exceeded Crookes' forecast of wheat requirements for the "contributory areas" by some 550 million bushels, or 16½ per cent — possibly more.

Sir William was not unaware of defects in the statistics he had to use,[1] but he concluded: "The maximum probable error would make no appreciable difference in my argument." Data even now available do not permit a close check of the acreage, yield, and production figures that he used for the 'nineties. It is probable that he underesti-

	Acreage (in millions)	Yield per acre (bu.)	Crop (million bu.)
Crookes' forecast of requirements	264	12.7	3,357
Actual	284.7	13.7	3,910
Difference	+7.8%	+7.9%	+16.5%

mated the true figures, and that the actual increase in the thirty-odd years has been less than the above comparison shows.[2] There is little question, however, that by 1931 the world's wheat acreage had expanded beyond the maximum that Crookes considered possible for all time. Expansion of wheat acreage has been the largest factor responsible for the contrast between Sir William's prophetic figures for 1931 and the actual outcome.

[1] Like his American authority, C. Wood Davis, on whose extended series of articles in the *Northwestern Miller* for 1897 Crookes evidently relied. The editorial note introducing this series stated (vol. xliii, p. 13): "Probably no man is in possession of as complete statistics on the world's wheat production as Mr. Davis, who has made it a subject of close study for years." Perusal of Davis' various writings suggests a bias toward underestimation.

[2] A recent examination of the data by D. M. K. Bennett of the Food Research Institute yields production figures for 1897 about 170 million bushels larger than Crookes gave.

Probably there has been, actually as in appearance, some improvement in world average yield per acre, in spite of the increased proportion of acreage in regions where average yields are and may be expected to remain relatively low. This improvement in yield has not been due, to any important extent, to increased applications of nitrogenous fertilizers, which Crookes thought the most hopeful source of gain. Artificial fixation of atmospheric nitrogen became feasible and is of great potential importance, but has not yet been of much significance in wheat growing.[1] Biological and agronomic science have contributed more than chemistry as such.[2]

Increased yields, expansion of the area actually sown to wheat, and further expansion of potential wheat acreage, are due to a multiplicity of factors which Crookes largely overlooked and in part failed to foresee. Before summarizing these factors, we may well review Sir William's forecasts for specific areas.

The United States he naturally discussed first, and with evident confidence. He said in part:

For the last thirty years the United States have been the dominant factor in the foreign supply of wheat, exporting no less than 145,000,000 bushels. This shows how the bread-eating world has depended, and still depends, on the United States for the means of subsistence. . . .

Almost yearly, since 1885, additions to the wheat-growing area have diminished, while the requirements of the increasing population of the States have advanced, so that the needed American supplies have been drawn from the acreage hitherto used for exportation. Practically there remains no uncultivated prairie land in the United States suitable for wheat-growing. The virgin land has been rapidly absorbed, until at present there is no land left for wheat without reducing the area for maize, hay, and other necessary crops. . . .

It is almost certain that within a generation the ever increasing popu-

[1] See R. E. Slade, in British Association . . . *Report of the Ninety-Eighth Meeting*, Bristol, 1930 (London, 1931), pp. 434–437.

[2] See President F. A. Bower's address, *ibid.*, pp. 12–13.

lation of the United States will consume all the wheat grown within its borders, and will be driven to import, and, like ourselves, will scramble for a lion's share of the wheat crop of the world. This being the outlook, exports of wheat from the United States are only of present interest, and will gradually diminish to a vanishing point. . . .[1]

Crookes' figure for the volume of United States exports, 145 million bushels, evidently applied to the decade ending with 1896–97. In the thirty years ending with 1897–98 net exports averaged 119 million bushels, but the average was held down by low exports prior to 1878–79. Contrary to an impression given in the quotation above, the trend of these exports was not generally downward from 1885 to 1898. There were downward drifts from peaks in the early 'eighties and the early 'nineties, but the record five-year average of 159 million bushels in the period ending with 1882–83 was exceeded in the five years ending with 1895–96 (172 million), closely approached in the five years ending with 1896–97, and again exceeded in the five years ending with 1897–98.[2]

For six years beginning with 1897–98, United States net exports averaged 218 million bushels a year, and only once fell as low as 191 million bushels. In the eleven years ending with 1913–14, however, net exports averaged only 112 million bushels a year, and only twice exceeded 124 million bushels. The trend in the fifteen years before the Great War broke out lent support to the view that before many years the United States would no longer be, on the average, a net exporter of wheat.

The actual position in 1931, however, was in striking contrast with Crookes' forecast, at almost every point. Under the stimulus of high prices and appeals to patriotism, wheat acreage expanded remarkably during the War.

[1] *Crookes*, pp. 16–18.
[2] U. S. Department of Agriculture, *Yearbook, 1931*, pp. 582–583.

While the peak of 1919 has not since been approached, subsequent expansion in semi-arid areas has offset much of the contraction in general-farming areas. Despite very low prices in 1922–24 and 1928–32, the level of wheat acreage remains much higher than Sir William anticipated, without pressing upon acreage of other grains. Moreover, there has been some improvement in average yields;[1] there has been a notable decrease in per capita food consumption of wheat, according to Holbrook Working, from about 5.4 bushels in the late 1890's to about 4.2 bushels in the 1920's;[2] and the rate of population growth continues to decline. The net result was that, in spite of huge additions to stocks, the average annual net exports in the five years ending with June, 1931 were 161 million bushels. The average annual surplus over domestic use for all purposes (including in one year very liberal amounts diverted to feed use because wheat was "dirt cheap" and corn was scarce) was 205 million bushels in this period. This is considerably larger than the largest five-year average up to the time that Sir William wrote.

Crookes' error in appraising the prospects as regards the United States probably rested, in part, on official underestimates of acreage in wheat and other crops in the 'nineties, consequent upon serious defects in the census of 1890. The true trend was greatly different from the trend that official estimates then current revealed.[3] In larger measure, however, the extreme failure of Crookes' forecast as to the United States was due to limits to his vision, in part quite pardonable ones. He did not foresee the great

---

[1] *Ibid.*, p. 560.

[2] "The Decline in Per Capita Consumption of Flour in the United States," *Wheat Studies of the Food Research Institute*, vol. ii (July, 1926), p. 273.

[3] See Holbrook Working, "Wheat Acreage and Production in the United States since 1866: A revision of Official Estimates," *Wheat Studies of the Food Research Institute*, vol. ii (June, 1926), pp. 237–264.

expansion of wheat acreage in the semi-arid regions of the Southwest and Northwest, made possible by new technique of dry farming and new developments in farm equipment; the rise of automotive machinery and improvements in feeding practice; increased yield per acre in grain and hay crops; and decreased per capita consumption of wheat for food. He probably overestimated the growth of population.

The annual average surplus over domestic use in the five years ending with June, 1931 (205 million bushels) — which, as in the 'nineties, somewhat understates the true surplus — would provide wheat food, at current rates of human consumption, for 49 million additional people. Population analysts now predict, on various assumptions that are subject to change as history unrolls its scroll, that the population of the United States is approaching a peak variously put at 145 to 175 million.[1] If the wheat acreage, average yield per acre, and per capita consumption for food should remain practically constant, the wheat requirements of the largest of these "maximum probable" populations could be met without appreciable resort to importation.

What the future holds in store, in these respects, one cannot safely predict. It is clear, however, that the potential wheat land of the United States is by no means all employed; that yields per acre are at least as likely to rise as to decline; and that per capita consumption, particularly in view of the changing age distribution of the population, is more likely to decline than to rise. If the United States ever becomes, on the average, a net importer of wheat, it is likely to be because the cultivation of wheat is not profitable enough to permit raising it on readily avail-

[1] The lower figure is a recent (1931) estimate of P. K. Whelpton, of the Scripps Foundation for Research in Population Problems.

able land, and not because we cannot raise enough wheat
to supply domestic requirements.

Considering Russia, the next largest exporter, Crookes
presented quite different arguments for not counting
heavily upon her in future. He asserted:

The yearly consumption of wheat per head during the last ten years
has declined 14 per cent., and the consumption of bread is quite 30 per
cent. less than is required to keep the population in health. The grain
reserved for seed has likewise decreased — the peasantry limiting their
sowing with the rise of taxation. The reduction of 14 per cent. in the
unit consumption of bread in Russia has added, during the last eighteen
years, 1,360,000,000 bushels to the general wheat supply. This facti-
tious excess temporarily staved off scarcity in Europe.

Although Russia at present exports so lavishly, this excess is merely
provisional and precarious. The Russian peasant population increases
more rapidly than any other in Europe. The yield per acre over European Russia is meagre.... The development of the fertile, though somewhat overrated "black earth" . . . progresses rapidly. But, as we have
indicated, the consumption of bread in Russia has been reduced to
danger point. The peasants starve, and fall victims to "hunger ty-
phus," whilst the wheat growers export grain that ought to be consumed at home.[1]

In a long footnote added later he quoted a report on famine
conditions in Russia in 1898–99. He stressed the climatic
limitations on wheat growing in Siberia, and quoted a recent statement by Prince Hilkoff, Russian minister of
Ways and Communications, that "Siberia never had
produced, and never would produce, wheat and rye enough
to feed the Siberian population."

There is good evidence that in a year or two following
short grain crops, such as those of 1891 and 1897, famine
stalked in large regions of Russia; but famine, though
recurring every few years, was not continuous. Local
shortages were of more frequent occurrence, owing to a
variety of factors. But a recent careful study calls in ques-

[1] *Crookes*, pp. 19–20.

tion the oft-expressed view that Russia's pre-War exports, broadly viewed, were made at the cost of keeping the Russian people hungry for bread.[1] At all events, rapid growth of population was accompanied, in the twenty-five years before the War, by more rapid expansion of grain area and production, so that Russia's contribution to international trade in grain rose, irregularly but surely, until in the five crop years before the War her wheat exports averaged 165 million bushels as compared with an average of 124 million bushels in the five calendar years 1893–97 and the 95-million figure that Crookes used.[2]

The War cut off Russia's exports. The subsequent revolution, with confiscatory policies that accompanied it, led to striking reductions in wheat acreage and production. These culminated, in a year of low yields, in widespread famine in 1921. Under the New Economic Policy agricultural recovery was rapid, and wheat exports were resumed on a modest scale in 1925–26 and 1926–27. After a check due to changes in Soviet policy and lower yields, the combination of fresh increases in acreage, bread rationing, and a bumper yield led in 1930–31 to the return of Russia to the ranks of major exporters, with wheat exports of 114 million bushels.

Russia is still, as in the 'nineties, much of an enigma. Probably expansion of wheat acreage and improvement in yield have gone further than Crookes expected, though not as far as comparisons of pre-War and post-War statistics would indicate.[3] Further gradual increases are not improb-

[1] V. P. Timoshenko, "Russia as a Producer and Exporter of Wheat," *Wheat Studies of the Food Research Institute*, vol. viii (March–April, 1931), p. 336.

[2] *Ibid.*, pp. 359–360, 375, and U. S. Department of Agriculture, *Yearbook, 1931*, p. 599.

[3] For comparison with current figures, the pre-War acreage and yield figures are officially considered substantially too low, but the adjustment made may be excessive. Timoshenko, *op. cit.*, pp. 304–306.

able. A continuance of Russian exports, varying greatly from year to year, is in prospect. But Timoshenko, on much the same grounds that Sir William stressed, now reckons improbable Russia's return to her pre-War level of wheat exports; and the tenor of his reasoning suggests that growth of population will tend materially to restrict Russia's contribution to the world wheat market.[1] In the world wheat situation as it is, however, this prospect causes no such concern to the rest of the world as Sir William expected.

Most of all, Crookes underestimated Canada's promise. Of her potentialities and prospective contributions to the export market he said:

> The most trustworthy estimates give Canada a wheat area of not more than 6,000,000 acres in the next twelve years, increasing to a maximum of 12,000,000 acres in twenty-five years. The development of this promising area necessarily must be slow, since prairie land cannot be laid under wheat in advance of a population sufficient to supply the needful labour at seed time and harvest. As population increases so do home demands for wheat.[2]

Canada's exports of wheat and flour had not much exceeded 10 million bushels in any year until 1897–98, when they reached nearly 25 million; and her wheat acreage had increased but slowly in the decade before 1898. Then began a strikingly rapid development which far outran Crookes' predictions. By 1910 the wheat area in the three prairie provinces had reached about 8 million acres. Under the stimulus of War prices, the suggested maximum of 12 million acres was passed in 1915. In 1921 the acreage exceeded 23 million acres; the figure for 1931 is 26 million, more than double the maximum Crookes postulated. While domestic requirements increased, production grew so much faster that in the twenty years from 1896–97 to

[1] *Ibid.*, pp. 363–369.   [2] *Crookes*, pp. 24–25.

1916–17 the upward trend of wheat and flour exports was at the (geometric) rate of 14.3 per cent a year. Although this rate was not maintained, in the five crop years ending with July, 1931 Canada's net exports averaged 295 million bushels a year, and her export surplus averaged at least 315 million bushels.[1] Such figures would have amazed Crookes, who mentioned none for comparison.

Canada's rise to the outstanding position in the world wheat trade was made possible by a combination of factors. Chief among these were the tide of immigration; the extension of railways; low railway rates and ocean freight rates; successful efforts in wheat breeding and selection to meet the climatic limitations affecting acreage and yield; and developments in agricultural machinery and technique.[2] Crookes did not foresee these developments, and consequently greatly underrated Canada's potentialities.

Undoubtedly there are limits to the expansion of Canada's wheat acreage and production. Now, as in 1898, there is need of discounting fantastic estimates of Canada's potential expansion. Yet "trustworthy estimates" of the present day indicate nearly as much room for increase above present levels as Sir William could see in 1898 from the levels of his day.[3] History's teaching is that all such predictions must be accepted with skepticism. Certainly, the principal factors now holding expansion in check are

[1] On this paragraph see C. P. Wright and J. S. Davis, "Canada as a Producer and Exporter of Wheat," *Wheat Studies of the Food Research Institute,* vol. i (July, 1925), pp. 217–286, esp. pp. 241–242, 261, 280, 284; vol. viii (December, 1931), pp. 174–176, 184, 190, 197.

[2] *Ibid.*

[3] Dr. D. A. McGibbon, of the Board of Grain Commissioners, recently reviewed the evidence and earlier estimates, and concluded that the maximum production of the Prairie Provinces would not exceed 670 to 700 million bushels, as compared with a peak to date of some 545 million in 1928. He expressed doubt as to whether Canada's net exports will ever substantially exceed the 1924–28 average of 262 million bushels. *Northwestern Miller,* February 17, 1932, p. 461.

depressed wheat prices, not Canada's inability to make heavier contributions to keep the world from starvation.

Australia Crookes passed by with a brief paragraph. "Climatic conditions," he said, "limit the Australian wheat area to a small portion of the southern littoral belt." [1] Strangely enough, he devoted more space to Queensland, which has never become an important wheat state, than to the four states which are now of roughly equal importance. He stressed the crop failures in Victoria and South Australia, and after citing an extremely low yield in the latter, concluded: "In most other districts the yield falls to such an extent as to cause Europeans to wonder why the pursuit of wheat-raising is continued." [2]

Yet Australia, which in Crookes' day was indeed a minor, erratic exporter of wheat, rose in the next thirty years to be a major exporter. In the five years ending with July, 1931 her net exports averaged about 100 million bushels a year. Wheat breeding and developments in machinery and technique permitted expansion of acreage and improvement in average yield — despite increasing resort to regions of low rainfall — and strikingly reduced the incidence of crop failure. Here too the present-day scientists foresee limits to Australia's wheat area, production, and exports,[3] but the prospects for further expansion from present levels are greater than they appeared to Sir William from the levels of his day; and the factors now chiefly responsible for retarded growth are depressed wheat prices.

For other export areas — notably Argentina, Austria-

---

[1] *Crookes*, p. 26.   [2] *Ibid.*

[3] A recent careful estimate of maximum level of acreage and crop is 20.4 million acres sown for grain, yielding an average crop of 284 million bushels. See A. H. E. McDonald, *The Future Development of the Wheat Growing Industry in Australia* (Institute of Pacific Relations, Honolulu, 1929). The exceptional peak in 1930–31 was 18.2 million acres, yielding 213 million bushels.

Hungary, Roumania, and India — Crookes was not seriously in error as to 1931. He gravely underestimated the expansion in the first fifteen years after 1898; but the War and post-War developments have in several cases helped his predictions to come true. In his 30-year forecast, Sir William went far astray, chiefly because he greatly underestimated the expansion of acreage in North America, Russia, and Australia. The reasons for this, and for the change in the outlook as well, may now be summarized.

The expansion of world wheat acreage in the thirty years after 1898 was greater than he thought possible to the end of time; and the limits of potential increase still appear wide. Average yields per acre increased moderately, without much aid from nitrogenous fertilizers. Wheat production by 1931 had materially exceeded his prophetic estimates. Wheat prices tended upward until 1914, but rose little more than prices in general. Destruction and disorganization during the Great War made wheat sharply dearer, for a few years. Subsequently, with peace and economic recovery, wheat prices declined to new low levels, in relation to prices in general. A far greater net increase in wheat output would have occurred under the stimulus of the "permanently higher prices" that Crookes feared. Thus far, at least, there has never been a safe basis for predicting that the world's need for wheat will overstrain the capacity of the world's wheat-producing soils.

The world's wheat-eating population grew faster than he expected, not in the areas he specially considered, but by extension in other areas because cheap wheat and flour were available. In most typical wheat-eating countries per capita consumption of bread grains has declined — and, in several, per capita consumption of wheat as well — not because less wheat was available but because of lessened food requirements and increased variety in the diet. The rate of population increase is declining, in most of the areas Crookes dealt with, not because of pressure on food supplies or because of higher death rates, but mainly because of the influence of higher standards of living in bringing about a great decline in the birth rate. Apparently the most rapid increase in population is occurring in Russia, where pressure on the means of subsistence is much greater than elsewhere in Europe or in America. Prosperity, and the opportunity to achieve higher planes of comfort, now appear to afford checks upon population growth more powerful than scarcity of food.

Wheat breeders have developed varieties with a shorter growing period, thus extending wheat-growing areas into colder regions with shorter summers. They have also developed varieties resistant to various diseases, lodging, and other handicaps that formerly made yields too unreliable in certain areas. Agronomists have learned the varieties adapted to conditions in different areas, large and small. They have discovered methods of selecting, treating, and testing seed, and the best time and method of seeding. They have developed cultivation practices suited to varied conditions, including rotations, the use of fallow, methods of preparation of the soil, the use of fertilizer (in Australia, phosphates), and economical methods of harvesting. Through development of the technique of dry farming, agronomic studies have paved the way for expansion of wheat culture into regions previously considered too arid for wheat.

The development of automotive machinery (notably the tractor) and supplementary equipment, facilitated by a vast increase in petroleum output, has helped in expansion onto drier lands, in application of improved methods of cultivation, and in overcoming the handicap of limited labor supply. Indirectly, through displacing horses and mules on farms and in cities, it has also released land formerly required for crops to feed work animals.

Progress has been made in bringing home to farmers information bearing upon all these matters, thus facilitating the application of knowledge. The lowering of costs of production, particularly in harvesting and handling operations, and the lowering of ocean freights, have aided in pushing back the "extensive margin" of wheat cultivation. Such developments as these have helped, indeed, to force out of wheat production large areas suitable for growing wheat, with yields well above the world average, but have permitted expansion of total wheat acreage and increase in average wheat yield. There is yet no indication that such developments in knowledge and practice are approaching their limits.

"As mouths multiply, food resources dwindle," Sir William wrote.[1] Actually, as mouths have multiplied, available supplies of food, for the world of commerce, have tended to increase so that per capita requirements are on the whole increasingly well satisfied, qualitatively and quantitatively. What Simon N. Patten wrote in 1885[2] is even truer today: "There never was a time in the world's history when the population was as well supplied with food and at so little outlay of labor as at the present time ... a smaller proportion of the population is engaged in agriculture than ever before; and this, not the price of food, is the true test."

Threat of coming dearth is not the central food problem. Demand, not resources, is the major factor limiting the food supply for the world of commerce. Nature's response

[1] *Crookes*, p. 3.
[2] *The Premises of Political Economy* (Philadelphia, 1885), p. 87.

to man's increasingly intelligent though still inefficient methods has been generous, not niggardly. An outstanding fact of economic history is that, with liberal opportunity for scientific investigation, the spread of communication and education, and broad scope for business enterprise, mankind has learned to multiply productive power faster than population increases. Political and social factors, not natural or economic limitations, are the principal obstacles to continuous advance in the plane of living.

What has been true in the past century may not, of course, be true indefinitely in centuries to come. Yet analysis of the factors responsible for these historic trends lends no support to the view that they will be reversed. Scientific discovery has proceeded at a quickening pace, not under the threat of general dearth but in the main under the stimulus of scientific curiosity, reinforced by the economic motives of reducing costs and increasing the number and appeal of marketable goods and services. With expansion of opportunities for the emergence and application of scientific talents, it is rash to predict a slackening of this pace. This same is true of specific applications of scientific knowledge to agriculture, manufacture, and transport. Business enterprise shows an increasing tendency not only to utilize scientific knowledge but to aid in expanding it. Governments are increasingly aiding both in widening its bounds and in developing means of bringing it home to individual producers.

There are no definable limits to these processes. The horizon recedes as we progress. Basic discoveries ever run in advance of their refinement, and refinement in advance of actual application. The presumption lies strongly against those who foresee an inevitably rising trend in the human cost of the food supply of nations, and with those who see ever-widening margins between the available means of sustaining life and the requirements therefor. Mankind may be able, indefinitely, to afford to spend a decreasing fraction of its available energy in getting a bare livelihood, and an increasing proportion in trying to make life more worth living.

Sir William Crookes himself said in 1917, in a passage out of harmony with the general tenor of his discussion: "'Starvation will be averted through the laboratory,' and the intelligent application of the results obtained by the work of the botanist and chemist will provide an assured future for the millions of bread-eaters in the world."[1] For the present at least, and probably for the indefinite future, the doom of general dearth appears neither inevitable nor even probable. The specter of coming dearth of food is a ghost that deserves to be laid.

[1] *Third Edition* ... p. 81.